Development of Modality in First Language Acquisition

Studies on Language Acquisition

Series Editors
Peter Jordens
Luke Plonsky
Martha Scholten

Responsible Editor
Peter Jordens

Volume 54

Development of Modality in First Language Acquisition

A Cross-Linguistic Perspective

Edited by
Ursula Stephany and Ayhan Aksu-Koç

DE GRUYTER
MOUTON

ISBN 978-1-5015-2071-6
e-ISBN (PDF) 978-1-5015-0445-7
e-ISBN (EPUB) 978-1-5015-0435-8

Library of Congress Control Number: 2020948123

Bibliographic information published by the Deutsche Nationalbibliothek
The Deutsche Nationalbibliothek lists this publication in the Deutsche Nationalbibliografie;
detailed bibliographic data are available on the Internet at http://dnb.dnb.de.

© 2022 Walter de Gruyter GmbH, Berlin/Boston
This volume is text- and page-identical with the hardback published in 2021.
Typesetting: Integra Software Services Pvt. Ltd.
Printing and binding: CPI books GmbH, Leck

www.degruyter.com

Contents

List of abbreviations used in the present volume —— VII

Ursula Stephany and Ayhan Aksu-Koç
Studying the acquisition of modality: An introduction —— 1

Katharina Korecky-Kröll
Requests in first language acquisition of German: Evidence from high and low SES families —— 25

Viktorija Kavaliauskaitė-Vilkinienė and Ineta Dabašinskienė
Gender differences in the acquisition of requests in Lithuanian —— 79

Maria D. Voeikova and Kira Bayda
Development of directive expressions in Russian adult-child communication —— 113

Gordana Hržica, Marijan Palmović and Melita Kovacevic
Acquisition of modality in Croatian —— 159

Marianne Kilani-Schoch
Competition of grammatical forms in the expression of directives in early French child speech and child-directed speech —— 191

Larisa Avram and Andreea Gaidargi
On the acquisition of dynamic, deontic and epistemic uses of modal verbs in Romanian —— 235

Ursula Stephany
Development of modality in early Greek language acquisition —— 255

Reili Argus
Acquisition of requests in Estonian —— 315

Klaus Laalo
Directives in Finnish language acquisition —— 347

Sigal Uziel-Karl
Modality in child Hebrew —— 379

Victoria V. Kazakovskaya
Epistemic modality in Russian child language —— 421

Treysi Terziyan and Ayhan Aksu-Koç
Epistemic and evidential modality in early Turkish child speech —— 453

Soonja Choi
The development of sentence-ending epistemic/evidential markers in young Korean children —— 491

Barbara Pfeiler and Alejandro Curiel
The acquisition of evidentiality in two Mayan languages, Yukatek and Tojolabal —— 525

Ayhan Aksu-Koç and Ursula Stephany
Conclusions —— 555

List of Contributors —— 575

Subject Index —— 577

List of abbreviations used in the present volume

1 Grammatical codes

1	1st person
2	2nd person
3	3rd person
ABS	absolutive
ACC	accusative
ADJ	adjective
ADV	adverb
ADVR	adverbializer
ANTIP	antipassive
AOR	aorist
ART	article
AUG	augment
AUX	auxiliary
BEN	benefactive
CAUS	causative
CL	clitic
CLF	classifier
CLIT	clitic
CNG	co-negative
COM	comitative
COMP	complement/complementizer
COMPL	completive
COND	conditional
CONJ	conjunction
CONN	connective
DAT	dative
DEF	definite
DEICT	deictic
DEM	demonstrative
DEO	deontic
DERIV	derivative
DET	determiner
DIM	diminutive
DIREC	directional
DISC	discontinuative
DIST	distal
DYN	dynamic
ELAT	elative
EM	epistemic marker
EMPH	emphatic
EPEN	epenthetic
ERG	ergative

EVID	evidential
EXCL	exclusive
EXIST	existential
F	feminine, female
FEM	feminine
FILL	filler
FOC	focus
FUT	future
FUT.IMP	future imperative
GEN	genitive
GM	generalizing modality marker
HON	honorific
HORT	hortative
ILL	illative
IMP	imperative
IMPRS	impersonal
INCOMPL	incompletive
IND	indicative
INDEF	indefinite
INDF	indefinite
INF	infinitive
INF1	1st infinitive
INF2	2nd infinitive
INF3	3rd infinitive
INFL	inflectional
INS	instrumental
INTENS	intensifier
INTERJ	interjection
INTR	intransitive
IPFV	imperfective
IRR	irrealis
LEX	lexical
LOC	locative
M	masculine, male
MASC	masculine
MDL	modal
MP	mediopassive
MV	modal verb
N	neuter
NEC	necessitative
NEG	negation/negative/negator
NEUT	neuter
NFIN	non-finite
NML	nominal
NMLZ	nominalizer
NOM	nominative
NONMDL	non-modal

NONPST	non-past
N.PROP	proper noun
OBJ	object
OBLIG	obligation
ONOM	onomatopoetic
OPT	optative
OSTEN	ostensive
PARTIT	partitive
PASS	passive
PFV	perfective
PL	plural
POL	polite
POSS	possessive
PP	past participle
PREF	prefix
PREP	preposition
PRO	pronoun
PROG	progressive
PRS	present
PSB	possibility
PST	past
PTCP	participle
PTL	particle
Q	question
QUOT	quotative
REFL	reflexive
REPORT	reportative
RI	root infinitive
SBJ	subject
SBJV	subjunctive
SE	sentence-ending
SG	singular
SOV	subject-object-verb
STAT	stative
SUBJ	subjunctive
SUP	supinum
TAM	tense-aspect-mood/modality
TOP	topic
TOPS	topic shift
TR	transitive
TRANSL	translative
V	verb
VOC	vocative

2 Other abbreviations

ADS	adult-directed speech
CDS	child-directed speech
CHAT	Codes for the Human Analysis of Transcripts
CHI	child, children
CHILDES	Child Language Data Exchange System
CLAN	Computerized Language Analysis
CS	child speech
DP	data point
FAT	father
HSES	high socio-economic status
ID	identifier
IQ	intelligence quotient
ISCED	International Standard Classification of Education
ISEI	International Socio-economic Index of Occupational Status
LSES	low socio-economic status
MLU	mean length of utterance
MOT	mother
MS	Microsoft
OECD	Organization for Economic Co-operation and Development
p	probability of rejecting the null hypothesis
PAR	parent(s)
RG	Russian Grammar
SAP	speech act participant
SE	standard error
SES	socio-economic status
TOK	tokens
TYP	types

3 Symbols

*0	missing inflection
[//]	retracing
=	clitic boundary
β	beta value, estimate of fixed effect

Ursula Stephany and Ayhan Aksu-Koç
Studying the acquisition of modality: An introduction

1 Aims of the volume

Providing statements, commanding actions, and posing questions are the essential communicative possibilities offered by any language.[1] According to Tomasello (2010: 84–86), the three basic motives for communication are requesting, i.e., "getting others to do what one wants them to", offering help "by informing others of things", and an "expressive or sharing motive".

Requests belong to one of the basic modal categories, namely deontic modality (see section 2). Although the semantic domain of modality has been "notoriously resistant to simple delimitation and definition" (Mithun 2016: 230; see also Nuyts 2006: 1), the traditional major types of deontic, dynamic, epistemic and, more recently, evidential modality have proved useful not only for the description of modality in the languages of the world (Coates 1995: 55; Nuyts 2016a: 4; Nuyts and van der Auwera 2016; Palmer 2001), but also for investigating the acquisition of modal systems (Stephany 1986; Choi 2006; Hickmann and Bassano 2016).

The basic communicative functions of requesting and informing manifest themselves in the split of verb forms into modal and non-modal ones early in ontogenesis (see Halliday 1975; Stephany 1983: 11, 1985 for Greek; Smoczyńska 1993 for Polish; Poupynin 1996 for Russian).

In this volume, the emergence and early development of modality in first-language acquisition is studied from a cross-linguistic and typological perspective with chapters focusing on agent-oriented (deontic and dynamic) or propositional (epistemic and evidential) modality (see section 2). Study of this domain of early acquisition does not only enhance the understanding of the way in which children construct their language, but can furthermore "give us important information about children's semantic development as well as about their social and cognitive development" (Choi 2006: 141).

The studies included in the present volume result from work of the Crosslinguistic Project of Pre- and Protomorphology in Language Acquisition

---

[1] See Dixon (2016: 48–73) on "what is necessary".

Ursula Stephany, University of Cologne
Ayhan Aksu-Koç, Boğaziçi University

https://doi.org/10.1515/9781501504457-001

(organized by Wolfgang U. Dressler on behalf of the Austrian Academy of Sciences). In this project the focus is on early longitudinal data (roughly 1;6 to 3;0 years) of mother–child interaction rather than cross-sectional material (but see the chapters by Korecky-Kröll and by Pfeiler and Curiel, this volume) taking not only child speech, but also child-directed speech and their interrelations into consideration. This is fundamental for tracing the developmental paths of early first language acquisition in languages of different types. The volume complements earlier ones on the acquisition of verbal inflection, nominal inflection, diminutives, adjectives, and nominal compounding (Bittner, Dressler, and Kilani-Schoch 2003; Stephany and Voeikova 2009; Savickienė and Dressler 2007; Tribushinina, Voeikova, and Noccetti 2015; Dressler, Ketrez, and Kilani-Schoch 2017).

In spite of the importance of modality relating to the communicative functions of language and consequently its ontogenesis, cross-linguistic investigations into its acquisition are few (Dittmar and Reich 1993; Ramat and Galèas 1995; Stephany 1986; Choi 2006; Hickmann and Bassano 2016). The original studies of fourteen typologically different languages of various genetic affiliations (see Table 1) included in the present volume are intended to increase our knowledge of the early development of modality. An important characteristic of the volume is the inclusion of some languages about whose acquisition little is known so far.

Table 1: Genetic affiliations of languages.

Language families	Branches	Languages
Indo-European	Germanic	German
	Baltic	Lithuanian
	Slavic	Russian
		Croatian
	Romance	French
		Romanian
	Greek	Greek
Finno-Ugric	Fennic	Estonian
		Finnish
Altaic	Turkic	Turkish
Semitic	North-West Semitic	Hebrew
Korean		Korean
American Indian	Mayan	Yukatek
		Tojolabal

In a cross-linguistic and typological study of the acquisition of modality, the respective development of the semantic domains of agent-oriented and propositional modality on the one hand and the acquisition of inflectional vs. lexical expressions of modal notions on the other are among the most promising topics of inquiry (see Hickmann and Bassano 2016 among others). Inflectional expressions of modality have been found to develop earlier than lexical ones in typologically and genetically different languages (e.g., the emergence of expressions of propositional modality in Turkish and Korean vs. Russian and Greek). The precocious development of these expressions in Turkish and Korean (see the chapters by Terziyan and Aksu-Koç and by Choi) as compared to their later development in Russian and Greek (see the chapters by Kazakovskaya and Stephany) can be explained by the fact that propositional modality is expressed by obligatory grammaticized means such as verbal inflections in Turkish or sentence-ending suffixes in Korean, but by optional lexical means (e.g., adverbs) in Russian and Greek. The productive use of grammaticized means of the expression of modal (as well as non-modal) notions marks an important achievement in terms of the development of language structure. In view of the early emergence of propositional modality in certain languages, it would be wrong to claim that this type of modality is beyond the cognitive capabilities of young children. Apart from a certain stage of cognitive development, the relevant factors of early acquisition are the structure of the native language and its usage as these are reflected in child-directed speech.

Due to the nature of the social relations in mother–child dyads, agent-oriented modality plays a central communicative role in mother–child interactions. It is for this reason that most language chapters of this volume are devoted to the study of directive speech acts.

As far as the developmental order of the expression of modal notions is concerned, it can be stated that the first distinction to emerge in the language of children acquiring different languages is that between verb forms marked for agent-oriented modality and non-modal ones (e.g., imperative vs. present/past tense). In languages in which propositional modality is expressed inflectionally on the verb as in Turkish or by obligatory sentence-suffixes as in Korean, the asynchrony between the emergence of agent-oriented and propositional modality is less marked.

After an overview of the semantic domains and expressions of modality in section 2, the pre- and protomorphological and the usage-based approaches to first language acquisition are considered in section 3. In section 4, summaries of the language chapters of the volume are presented.

2 Semantic domains and expressions of modality

2.1 Semantic domains of modality

A common classification of the different semantic domains of modality is that of agent-oriented modality referring to actions (Bybee and Fleischman 1995: 6) and propositional modality "concerned with the speaker's attitude to the truth-value or factual status of the proposition" (Palmer 2001: 8). While agent-oriented modality includes deontic and dynamic meanings (Palmer 2001; Choi 2006),[2] propositional modality refers to epistemic and evidential notions (Palmer 2001). Although there is no unanimity among scholars concerning the status of evidentiality, evidence from languages such as Turkish and Korean (see chapters by Terziyan and Aksu-Koç and by Choi, this volume) suggests that it should be included together with epistemic modality in the domain of propositional modality.[3] Certain authors consider epistemic modality to overlap with or even encompass evidentiality (Bybee and Fleischman 1995: 4; see also Choi 2006: 142). Aksu-Koç (2016: 143) reaches the conclusion that in Turkish evidentiality "is a modal category that is distinct from epistemic modality", but that, more generally, "the boundaries between the two categories are language specific" (2016: 144).

According to Bybee and Fleischman (1995: 6), agent-oriented modality "encompasses all modal meanings that predicate conditions on an agent with regard to the completion of an action referred to by the main predicate, e.g., obligation, desire, ability, permission and root possibility" (see also Bybee 1985: 166).[4] As pointed out by Lyons (1977: 826), "the origin of deontic modality [. . .] is to be sought in the desiderative and instrumental function of language: that is to say, in the use of language, on the one hand, to express or indicate wants and desires and, on the other, to get things done by imposing one's will on other agents. It is clear that these two functions are ontogenetically basic, in the sense that they are associated with language from the very

---

[2] Agent-oriented modality has also been called "root" modality (Coates 1983, 1995) and "event" modality (Jespersen 1924; Palmer 2001).
[3] While Bybee, Perkins, and Pagliuca (1994), van der Auwera and Plungian (1998) as well as Aikhenvald (2004) exclude evidentiality from the domain of modality, it is included by Bybee and Fleischman (1995), Palmer (2001), Nuyts (2006), Choi (2006) and Aksu-Koç (2016). Pfeiler and Curiel (this volume) take evidentiality as a semantically and lexically independent category rather than a modal one.
[4] "Root possibility predicates general enabling conditions (e.g., *it can take three hours to get there*). These include permission, which is a *social* enabling condition" (Bybee and Fleischman 1995: 5).

earliest stage of its development in the child." This claim is confirmed by the studies contained in the present volume.

Another basic insight is that "deontic modality is concerned with the necessity or possibility of acts performed by morally responsible agents" (Lyons 1977: 823) and is therefore "associated with the social functions of permission and obligation" (Bybee and Fleischman 1995: 4; see also von Wright 1951 and Palmer 1986: 96–97 among many others). In more general terms, Nuyts (2016b: 36) states that "deontic modality may be defined as an indication of the degree of moral desirability of the state of affairs expressed in the utterance, typically but not necessarily on behalf of the speaker" (see also Palmer 2001: 10). He argues that the concept of morality should be taken widely involving "'societal norms'" as well as "personal 'ethical' criteria of the person responsible for the deontic assessment" (Nuyts 2016b: 36). As mentioned above, agent-oriented modality includes dynamic meanings besides deontic ones (von Wright 1951: 1–2; Palmer 2001: 8–10). According to Nuyts (2016b: 34; see also Nuyts 2006: 2–3 and the references quoted there) "in the most narrow definition [. . .], dynamic modality is characterized as an ascription of the capacity or ability to the first-argument (or controlling) participant (usually the agent participant) of the verb to realize or effectuate the state of affairs expressed in the clause." This category "is not restricted to ability alone, but also covers the indication of a need or a necessity for the first-argument participant" (Nuyts 2006: 3).[5]

While the agent's volition and intention are both included in agent-oriented modality by Choi (2006: 142), volition is sometimes integrated in the category of deontic modality (Palmer 1986) and sometimes in dynamic modality (Palmer 2001). Since volition primarily refers to desires and "is less clearly related to action plans" than intention, Nuyts (2006: 9) wonders "whether that still counts as a modal notion". In this volume, we adhere to the more traditional view held by Palmer (1986, 2001) and Choi (2006) that volition belongs to agent-oriented modality.

While agent-oriented modality refers to the obligation and permission of "events not yet actualized", i.e., to "events that have not taken place but are merely potential", propositional modality (epistemic and evidential) is "concerned

---

5 Within dynamic modality, a distinction is drawn between participant-internal (participant-inherent) and participant-external (imposed) circumstances, e.g., physical or mental ability (e.g., *he can stand on his head without using his hands* (Nuyts 2016b: 34)) vs. some aspect of the situation (e.g., *the garage is free so you can park your car there* (Nuyts 2016b: 35)) (see also van der Auwera and Plungian 1998; Palmer 2001: 10; Nuyts 2006: 3; Mithun 2016: 230). Since this distinction does not seem to play a role in early first language acquisition, it will not be further pursued here.

with the speaker's attitude to the truth-value or factual status of the proposition" (Palmer 2001: 8). Concerning the two sub-domains of propositional modality, Palmer (2001: 8) states that "with epistemic modality speakers express their judgments about the factual status of the proposition" while "with evidential modality they indicate the evidence they have for its factual status" (for details see Palmer 2001: 8–9, 24–69). Epistemic modality thus indicates the speaker's "degree of confidence in a proposition" (Boye 2016: 117; see also Bybee, Perkins, and Pagliuca 1994: 179; Bybee and Fleischman 1995: 4) and therefore expresses the degree of probability of the state of affairs, typically (but not necessarily) according to the speaker's opinion (Nuyts 2006: 6; see also Nuyts 2016b: 38).

In a traditional view (see Kratzer 1978; van der Auwera and Plungian 1998), all modal categories can be characterized in terms of the notions of necessity and possibility (Nuyts 2006: 16, 2016b: 43; see also Stephany 1986: 376 and 1993: 134–135).[6] Since deontic modality originates in the desiderative and instrumental functions of language, it may be taken to be "necessity-based rather than possibility-based, with the converse being true for epistemic modality" (Stephany 1986: 376; see also Lyons 1977: 801–803).

Boye (2016: 117) points out that meanings of epistemic modality are "arranged along a scale which goes from high epistemic support of a proposition over neutral epistemic support to high epistemic support for the negative counterpart of a proposition" ("knowledge, certainty, epistemic necessity, probability, likelihood, uncertainty, epistemic possibility, doubt, unlikelihood, epistemic impossibility") (see also Bybee 1985: 165–166; Nuyts 2016b: 38). Epistemic modal expressions "typically take a whole clause as their explicit semantic scope" (Boye 2016: 135; see also Bybee 1985: 165; Bybee and Fleischman 1995: 6). This explains why they "readily occur in declaratives and interrogatives, but not in imperatives" (Boye 2016: 140).

The category of epistemic modality is of utmost communicative importance for sharing our degree of confidence in propositions. While it may therefore be hypothesized that all languages possess lexical epistemic modal expressions, these concepts also belong to the limited set of "grammaticizable notions" (Slobin 1997) and grammatical epistemic modal expressions are indeed found in many languages (Boye 2016: 118). Examples from the languages studied in this volume are Turkish, Korean, and Mayan (see the chapters by Terziyan and Aksu-Koç; Choi; Pfeiler and Curiel).

The category of evidentiality "refers to the 'evidence' that the speaker has for what (s)he says, or, in the traditional definition, it involves an indication of

---

[6] This view is not accepted by all researchers, however (Nuyts 2016b: 33).

the source of the information (Boas 1938: 133; Aikhenvald 2004)" (Squartini 2016: 58). Evidential and epistemic functions "intrinsically mark reduced reliability" (Squartini 2016: 62). Choi (2006: 142) thus includes evidentiality in epistemic modality "because by specifying, for example, the source of information (e.g., hearsay or direct evidence), the speaker conveys varying degrees of certainty of the proposition." According to Squartini (2016: 62), inferentials are the linking element between evidentiality and epistemic modality. Inferences can be considered as epistemic because they are "intrinsically less reliable than direct perceptions, and evidential since inferential reasoning is typically based on external indirect sources" (Squartini 2016: 62). It is worth noting that meanings which are classified as evidential in non-European languages "are traditionally classified as epistemic in the descriptive traditions of many European languages" (Squartini 2016: 62).

A summary of the characteristics and functions of the semantic domains of modality is presented in Table 2. Propositional modality is possibility-based rather than necessity-based, with epistemic modality concerning the speaker's judgment of the factuality or reliability of the proposition and evidentiality the directness or indirectness of the source of information (and implicitly also its reliability). While both deontic and dynamic modality are agent-oriented (concerning actions or events) and necessity-based (concerning obligation, permission, or commission on the one hand and ability or volition on the other), the source of modality is participant-external in the main functions of deontic modality, namely of obligation and permission (van der Auwera and Plungian 1998), but participant-internal in the main functions of dynamic modality, namely of ability and volition.

Table 2: Characteristics and functions of domains of modality.[7]

Epistemic	Evidential	Deontic	Dynamic
	propositional possibility-based	agent-oriented necessity-based	
speaker stance factuality, reliability	source of information direct: sensory evidence, indirect: inference, report	participant-external obligation, permission, commission	participant-internal ability, volition

---

[7] See Palmer (2001).

2.2 Formal means for expressing modal notions

Modality may be expressed inflectionally, syntactically, or lexically. The main inflectional device is mood (e.g., imperative, subjunctive, optative, evidential, conditional, indicative) and the main syntactic and lexical devices are modal verbs (e.g., *may, can, must*), verbs of desire and belief (*want, think, know*), adverbs (e.g., *probably, possibly, necessarily*), and adjectives (e.g., *certain, necessary*). Depending on the language, the burden of expression may be more on inflectional morphology or the lexicon. For example, while both agent-oriented and propositional modality are mainly expressed by modal verbs in German, Turkish predominantly uses inflectional morphology in both domains. While the optative and evidential are part of the inflectional paradigm of the Turkish verb, these notions are lexically expressed in German or Russian.

As far as language acquisition is concerned, the most important domains of agent-oriented modality are directives and volition/ability expressing deontic and dynamic meanings, respectively. Directives may be defined as speech acts that attempt "to get the hearer to perform some action" (Nikolaeva 2016: 73). The major types of directives are orders (commands) and requests. "While orders imply telling someone else what to do, requests involve asking someone to do something, with an option for the addressee not to comply" (Aikhenvald 2016: 147). Given the importance of requests for human social interaction, it is not surprising that "understanding and mastering directive speech acts [. . .] in a language is a key to successful communication" (Aikhenvald 2010: 331).

The main device for conveying requests is the canonical imperative "that typically expresses a command given to a second person" (van Olmen and van der Auwera 2016: 379; see also Aikhenvald 2010: 17). The imperative also serves other functions such as making recommendations, giving advice and permissions (Nikolaeva 2016: 75). In certain languages such as Finnish, there are also "non-canonical imperatives" conveying a request to a first or third person (van Olmen and van der Auwera 2016: 379; see also Aikhenvald 2010: 17). Non-canonical imperatives with inclusive first person plural reference are usually called hortatives (e.g., *let's go*) while those referring to the third person are most often described as jussives (e.g., *let him go*).[8]

Hortatives and jussives may be considered to be indirect requests. More generally, indirect requests include polite requests, suggestions, invitations, advice, offers, or proposals. Such functions may be expressed by a diversity of

---

[8] The term "hortative" is sometimes used in a broader sense in the literature. In some languages, such as Turkish, the optative may function as the hortative.

formal means like modal verbs (e.g., *you should take less salt*), several types of verb forms (e.g., subjunctive, indicative, infinitive) and sentence types (statements or questions; e.g., *smoking is prohibited in restaurants*; *could you pass the salt?*). Negative requests may function as prohibitions or warnings (e.g., *don't eat with your fingers! don't drop the plate!*).

As far as dynamic modality is concerned, the notions of volition and ability are especially important in early language acquisition.[9] Although ability is expressed by modal verbs in many languages (e.g., *I can swim*), it may also be conveyed by other lexical or by morphological means (e.g., Turkish *yüz-ebil-ir-im* (swim-PSB-AOR-1SG) 'I can swim'). In child-centered situations, negative forms expressing inability are more frequently encountered than affirmative ones. In contrast to ability, young children mostly express volition assertively with a verb for 'want' in the first person singular (see Pea and Mawby 1984, quoted by Choi 2006: 146) or some verb forms such as the optative (e.g., Turkish *ben oku-y(a)-(y)ım* (I read-OPT-1SG) 'let me read'). Expressions of volition may either function as indirect requests (e.g., *I want a cookie*; *I wanna play*) or denote intentions (e.g., *I won't go to bed*).

In most European languages (e.g., German, French, Greek), epistemic modality is expressed by modal or cognitive verbs (e.g., *he must be at home; she thinks he is at home*) while morphological means – suffixes and clitics or sentence-ending suffixes as in Korean and Japanese – are observed in many non-European ones (e.g., Turkish *ev-de ol-malı* (home-LOC be-NEC) '(he) must be at home', *ev-de ol-abil-ir* (home-LOC be-PSB-AOR) '(he) may be at home'). Just as modal verbs may express deontic or epistemic notions depending on context, morphological devices may also be multifunctional. Adverbs (e.g., *certainly, possibly*), adjectives (e.g., *certain, probable*) and nouns (e.g., *certainty, likelihood*), which have an inherent epistemic meaning, are other important markers of epistemic notions (Boye 2016: 118–119, 121) some of which may appear quite early in child speech.

Types of epistemic judgments commonly observed across languages are "speculative" (expressing "a possible conclusion"), "deductive" (indicating "the only possible conclusion"), and "assumptive" (expressing "a reasonable conclusion") (Palmer 2001: 6, 24–25). These categories may be marked with different forms as in the case of English modal verbs (with *may, must,* and *will,* respectively; Palmer 2001: 25–27) or with verbal affixes as in Turkish. In

---

9 Although Palmer (2001) includes volition within dynamic modality, Nuyts (2006) asks whether it counts as a modal notion.

English, speculative and deductive assertions contrast in terms of the "strength of the conclusion" (i.e., the degree of certainty/confidence), whereas deductive and assumptive assertions contrast in terms of the "type of inference" – the former are made from observed evidence and the latter from general knowledge (Palmer 2001: 25–31). Not all languages contain formal contrasts for distinguishing between strength of conclusion and type of inference, but contrast in terms of type of inference is mostly found in languages with evidential systems (Palmer 2001: 25), pointing to the close relationship between epistemic and evidential categories noted above (Squartini 2016: 62).

While all languages have certain means to express evidential notions, only about one fourth of the world's languages possess grammaticized evidential systems (Aikhenvald 2004: 1). The major types of information source that are typically marked in the latter concern direct evidence based on sensory information (vision or audition) and indirect evidence based on reported information (hearsay, folktales, and narratives) (Palmer 2001: 35). However, many formal systems also include distinctions for indirect evidence based on inferences from what has been observed or inferences from general knowledge (Aksu-Koç 2016: 143–144; Nuyts 2006: 10; Palmer 2001: 36; Plungian 2001: 351–353). As already noted, the last category overlaps with the deductive and assumptive judgments discussed above under epistemic modality. Whether such indirect inferences are part of epistemic or evidential systems depends on the language.

Languages differ in the subtleness of grammaticized evidential distinctions. Some formalize all three distinctions of direct evidence, evidence based on reported information, and evidence based on inference (and possibly more) with different markers,[10] many others observe a direct vs. indirect opposition, subsuming inference and report under a single indirect marker (e.g., Turkish) (Palmer 2001: 36; Plungian 2001). These distinctions are typically expressed by suffixes/clitics (e.g., Turkish: –mIş/-(y)mIş; see the chapter by Terziyan and Aksu-Koç), by sentence-ending suffixes (e.g., Korean: -tay, -ney, -kwuna; see the chapter by Choi), or by clitics and lexically (e.g., Yukatek Mayan, clitic for reportative: =b'in, verbal stem for quotative: k-; see the chapter by Pfeiler and Curiel). Languages where evidentiality is not grammaticized, such as European languages, use lexical means like certain adverbs (e.g., English *apparently, evidently, allegedly*) or verbs (e.g., English *it seems, I hear*) to modify a proposition for evidentiality.

---

10 For example, Tuyuca (Colombia) has five different markers; one for vision and another one for all the other senses, two separate markers for deductive and assumptive inferences, and a reportative marker (Barnes 1984: 260, quoted in Palmer 2001: 43).

Epistemically and evidentially modalized utterances play an important role in discourse as they enable participants to express their point of view and modulate meanings in terms of type of evidence and reliability (Palmer 2001: 58). In languages such as Japanese, Korean, and Turkish that use obligatory morphological means "to convey epistemic/evidential meanings with significant discourse functions embedded in them (e.g., taking the addressee's view into account), children acquire them from early on" (Choi 2006: 157–163).

An important result of naturalistic studies of the acquisition of modality noted in the literature[11] is a clear-cut "developmental asynchrony" of the production of agent-oriented and propositional modality, "particularly in languages that rely mostly on modal auxiliaries and mental verbs to express modality" (Hickmann and Bassano 2016: 431). Besides pragmatic and cognitive factors (Stephany 1993; Hickmann and Bassano 2016: 431–432), the grammaticized and thus obligatory character of the expression of propositional modality marked morphologically as in Turkish, Korean, and Japanese supports its more precocious emergence as compared to languages in which propositional modality is lexically expressed by modal verbs or adverbs such as English, German, Russian, Greek, and many others.[12]

3 Theoretical approaches to first language acquisition

Studies included in the present volume follow constructivist and non-nativist approaches to language acquisition, either the pre- and protomorphological model or usage-based frameworks.

3.1 The pre- and protomorphological approach

One of the main tenets of the constructivist and non-nativist pre- and protomorphological approach to language acquisition (Dressler and Karpf 1995; Dressler 1997: 5) is that inflection develops in three stages (also called 'phases'), namely

---
[11] See Stephany (1986, 1993) and Choi (2006) as well as studies on English, French, Greek, Polish, and Spanish quoted in Hickmann and Bassano (2016).
[12] But see Aksu-Koç and Stephany, this volume, and Stephany, this volume.

the premorphological stage, the protomorphological stage and the stage of "core morphology" or "morphology proper" (Dressler 1997: 6; Voeikova and Dressler 2002: 3–4; Dressler et al. 2017).

In the premorphological stage, children only produce isolated rote-learned word forms (Stephany and Voeikova 2009: 4; Dressler et al. 2017). If applied to the development of verbal inflection, the premorphological stage is characterized by the absence of oppositions within one and the same verbal lemma so that each verb occurs in a single form (Bittner, Dressler, and Kilani-Schoch 2003: xxi). In the course of language development, the number of grammatical forms will gradually exceed that of lemmas (Stephany and Voeikova 2009: 4). The protomorphological stage "manifests itself by the emergence of grammatical oppositions which develop into miniparadigms" defined as consisting of at least three different inflectional forms of a given lemma (Stephany and Voeikova 2009: 4). A weakened form of the criterion of miniparadigms has lately been extended to cover the acquisition of compounds (Dressler et al. 2017). The third stage of this developmental model is "core morphology", which initiates adult-like morphology (Dressler et al. 2017). Since most studies contained in the present volume are concerned with language development up to three years, later developments of inflection remain outside their scope.

The expression of modality in the premorphological stage may be characterized by the occurrence of rote-learned imperative forms and some verb forms conveying both modal and non-modal meanings (e.g., the German and Russian infinitive). There are also verbless requests. In the protomorphological stage, the inventory of inflectional forms will be enriched so that modal and non-modal meanings are formally distinguished. This may mean that old underdifferentiated forms specialize to a more restricted meaning (Stephany 1997: 323). At the same time, verb forms for expressing different modal functions (e.g., commands, indirect requests, hortatives, jussives) will develop.

It must be kept in mind that in order to get a full picture of inflectional development by studying the emergence of paradigms, non-modal as well as modal verb forms would have to be taken into consideration. Such a task is, however, beyond the scope of most studies contained in the present volume. Since the pre- and protomorphological model has been developed to account for the acquisition of morphology, it cannot be applied to the acquisition of lexical means for expressing modal notions (e.g., modal verbs or adverbs) although the emergence of the latter means may be mapped onto the stages of morphological development.

3.2 The usage-based approach

A fundamental claim of the constructivist, usage-based approach to language acquisition, grounded in cognitive linguistics, is "that language structure emerges from language use" (Tomasello 2003: 327). Grammatical knowledge is taken to emerge "from the categorization of experienced utterances" (Bybee 2010: 78). The course of acquisition thus consists in the children's "process of formulating partially schematic constructions on the basis of the specific utterances they have mastered and can use" (Bybee 2010: 78). An advantage of construction grammar and usage-based approaches for describing the development of modal notions and their expression is that "lexicon and grammar do not constitute distinct components but rather form a continuum from less to more abstract 'constructions'" (Boogaart and Fortuin 2016: 515). Furthermore, this approach stresses continuous grammatical development rather than distinct stages. Since modality and mood "crucially involve speaker attitude and perspective" these categories quite naturally lend themselves to a cognitive linguistic analysis emphasizing "the ways in which language users conceptualize the world from their own point of view ('construal')" (Boogaart and Fortuin 2016: 533).

While the pre- and protomorphological model stresses distinct developmental stages and the acquisition of abstract rules, the usage-based approach advocates a continuous development from item-based to more abstract schemas and constructions.

4 The development of modality in the different languages

The volume contains 14 language chapters, each of which is an original study of the acquisition of modality in a natural social setting by monolingual children acquiring genetically and typologically different languages.[13] Chapters are presented according to the genetic affiliation of languages and their concentration on agent-oriented or propositional modality. The chapters on German, Lithuanian, Russian (by Voeikova and Bayda), Croatian, French, Estonian, and Finnish address the development of deontic/dynamic modality and those on Romanian, Greek, and Hebrew cover both deontic/dynamic and epistemic/

---

[13] The children speaking the Mayan language Tojolabal are not strictly monolingual.

evidential modality while the chapters on Russian (by Kazakovskaya), Turkish, Korean, and Yukatek/Tojolabal are devoted to epistemic/evidential modality.

The study of *Requests in first language acquisition of German: Evidence from high and low SES families* by K. Korecky-Kröll deals with the interplay between social factors and the use of requests in spontaneous parent–child conversation, demonstrating that parenting style is closely linked to socioeconomic status (SES). A main difference between parents from high SES (HSES) and low SES (LSES) backgrounds are more conversation-eliciting strategies used by the former vs. a more behavior-directing style of the latter. Deontic modality serves as a testing ground for these differences and their impact on the children's development. Requests occurring in parental input and child output were investigated in four video recordings each of spontaneous interactions of 15 HSES and 14 LSES German-speaking children with their parents from age 2;11 to 4;11. The results of linear mixed-effects analyses of grammatical categories related to requests and speech acts in general confirm that LSES parents use more direct requests while questions for information prevail in the speech of HSES parents. However, differences between the children are smaller than hypothesized. LSES children ask similar amounts of questions for information as compared to HSES children and the number of requests used by both groups is also comparable. This suggests that the expression of children's basic needs, which seem to be similar in the two SES groups, is of more importance than input frequency.

The investigation of *Gender differences in the acquisition of requests in Lithuanian* by V. Kavaliauskaitė-Vilkienė and I. Dabašinskienė examines directive speech acts occurring in the speech of two Lithuanian children of different gender born in middle-class families, a girl aged 1;8–2;8 and a boy aged 1;6–2;7, and their input. The hypothesis is that, in Lithuanian culture, boys and girls are socialized differently, with boys being exposed to more direct requests but girls to more indirect ones. From early on, imperatives, which are formally simple and functionally typical for addressing requests to intimates in adult Lithuanian, are the most frequent expressions of direct requests found in child-directed speech as well as child speech. About 2;0, formally more elaborate indirect requests emerge. Surprisingly, both children use more indirect requests than their mothers, but these consist of simple constructions expressing wishes with 'want' or suggestions by hortatives. Contrary to the initial hypothesis, more direct requests were found in the girl's than the boy's input and, conversely, more indirect ones in the boy's. The authors explain this difference by different styles of the mothers in communicating with their children and suggest that gender differences may only begin to play a role in parenting styles with children beyond 3;0. Mothers at first consider it important to communicate effectively with their offspring, whereas familiarizing them with social norms ranks second.

The chapter *Development of directive expressions in Russian adult–child communication* by M. D. Voeikova and K. Bayda focuses on the expression of directives in early Russian language acquisition and is based on recordings of the speech of a boy (1;5–2;8) and a girl (2;0–3;7) in interaction with their caregivers. In the premorphological phase, direct requests are expressed by the imperative or the infinitive. Bare infinitives are probably elliptical renderings of modal expressions occurring in the input. In the course of development, the children's directive constructions become more complex and direct requests are distinguished from indirect ones. Imperatives do, however, predominate during the entire period of observation. The bare infinitive is abandoned by one of the children after 2;2 while the other develops a functional distinction between imperatives and infinitives, with imperatives expressing commands but infinitives suggestions and intentions. Hortatives and modal verb constructions emerge after 2;0 developing at a different pace in the speech of the two subjects. The authors attribute this to the mothers' parenting styles, one of them using hortatives from early on but the other preferring direct requests throughout the observation period. Contrary to other Russian children, the two subjects of the present study do not use nouns or adverbs in verbless requests in the early developmental phase but rather one-word utterances with *dat'* 'give'.

The investigation of the *Acquisition of modality in Croatian* by G. Hržica, M. Palmović, and M. Kovacevic is the first systematic attempt to trace the early development of agent-oriented modality in the speech of three monolingual Croatian children until the second part of their third year, taking CDS into consideration. The results are interpreted according to the developmental phases of the pre- and protomophology approach to first language acquisition. The distinction of non-modal and modal functions, i.e., between statements and requests, develops in the premorphological phase before the formation of miniparadigms when directives are inflectionally expressed by the imperative and the infinitive. While imperatives have a deontic function expressing commands, infinitives occurring in one-word utterances may have a dynamic meaning conveying volition so that there is a functional distinction between the two forms. In the subsequent protomorphological phase, the lexical devices of modal verbs and syntactic constructions are added to the children's repertoire so that more polite and indirect requests may be expressed besides direct ones. Modal verbs conveying the dynamic modal meanings of desire and ability emerge earlier than those expressing deontic modality, which are also less frequently used than the former. Child-directed speech provides the most important models for agent-oriented modal expressions, namely imperatives and modal verbs constructed with a main verb in the infinitive.

In her chapter *Competition of grammatical forms in the expression of directives in early French child speech and child-directed speech*, M. Kilani-Schoch investigates different devices for expressing directives used by two French-speaking toddlers aged 1;4–2;11 and 1;6–3;0 interacting with their parents. The focus is on obligation and prohibition conveyed by orders and indirect directives encoding strong directive illocutionary force. One of the main findings is that in child speech as well as child-directed speech second person singular present indicative forms (*tu* forms) compete with imperatives and deontically used root infinitives variably fulfilling this function in different developmental phases. Use of 2nd person singular present or future forms instead of the imperative is due to a certain development of spoken French. Variation sets (series of utterances with the same content repeated in varying form) occurring in child-directed speech but not in child speech, suggest that there is less competition between these forms in the latter than in the former. The chapter aims at accounting for the emergence and complementary or contrastive use of these three types of formal means (*tu* forms, imperatives, root infinitives) taking specific contexts, lexical content of verbs, and different degrees of illocutionary force into consideration. Emphasis is placed on the role of variation in child-directed speech fostering pragmatic flexibility of language use in the child.

In their chapter *On the acquisition of dynamic, deontic, and epistemic uses of modal verbs in Romanian*, L. Avram and A. Gaidargi inquire into the acquisition of the dynamic, deontic, and epistemic values of three principal modal verbs in Romanian. The central question is whether dynamic values emerge before deontic ones and whether there is a developmental gap between these agent-oriented meanings and epistemic ones in the speech of three children acquiring Romanian, observed within the 1;8–3;0 age range. The results indicate that dynamic modal values emerge before deontic ones whereas epistemic uses of verbs are not observed at all. Instead, epistemic notions are conveyed by epistemic adverbs, indicating that there is no 'epistemic gap' in the children's understanding of types of modality. The authors, who explore syntactic, semantic, and cognitive hypotheses for possible explanations, conclude that this developmental sequence is best explained by input, which shows striking similarities to child speech. In child-directed speech, dynamic uses of the modal verbs are found to be almost twice as frequent as deontic ones and epistemic modality is preferentially expressed by adverbs, resulting in lack of informative input for the epistemic use of modal verbs. The fact that epistemic adverbs have an inherent modal value and do not depend on contextual interpretation facilitates their acquisition and the expression of epistemic notions early on.

In her chapter on the *Development of modality in early Greek language acquisition*, U. Stephany explores the development of agent-oriented and propositional modality in the acquisition of Greek in a usage-based theoretical framework. The study is mainly based on the audio-taped longitudinal data from six monolingual children aged 1;8 to 3;0, interacting with their caretakers in natural speech situations. Main aspects of the analysis are the early split of modal–non-modal expressions, the emergence of dynamic compared to deontic expressions, and the developmental asynchrony of agent-oriented and propositional modality. The results show that the imperative and the subjunctive expressing deontic or dynamic meanings are distinguished from the present indicative conveying information by statements before 2;0. Inflectional expressions of deontic notions and lexical ones of dynamic notions emerge simultaneously before 2;0, but desire is more frequently expressed than ability. It is shown that the two domains of agent-oriented and propositional modality do not simply develop successively, but in a closely intertwined way since the non-factive future and epistemic adverbs may evolve before 2;0. However, the deontic or dynamic use of modal verbs clearly precedes their epistemic use. Greek children also express deontic and dynamic modality much more frequently than epistemic modality, since the latter is not grammaticized in their language. Since children construct their native language while using it and by using it, child-directed speech has a big impact on early language development.

In her chapter *Acquisition of requests in Estonian*, R. Argus deals with the developmental path of the linguistic means employed to express agent-oriented modality, more specifically requests, by two monolingual Estonian children between the ages 1;3 and 3;0, interacting with their caregivers. Analyses focusing on types of requests (e.g., commands, prohibitions, suggestions) and the formal means used in their expression (e.g., imperatives, modal verbs) reveals a continuous rather than a stagewise order of emergence of different linguistic means. Children's first direct requests are commands expressed by imperatives, the grammatically simplest verbal form in the language and the one most frequently used in child-directed speech. The first indirect requests are appeals for joint action expressed by hortatives and statements of the speaker's desired action expressed by the verb 'want', which are also the most frequent types of indirect requests occurring in child-directed speech. Cognitively and grammatically less complex requests, where the source of modality is within the speaker (e.g., commands), emerge first, whereas requests with a source of modality external to the speaker (e.g., appeals to social norms for desired action) are observed later. Argus argues that whether the requested act has to be performed only by the addressee, by the addressee and the speaker or by the addressee and a third party is a determining factor in the increasing complexity of directives and their order of acquisition.

In his contribution *Directives in Finnish language acquisition*, based on diary data as well as tape recordings, K. Laalo studies the development of directives in the spontaneous speech of two children aged 1;7–2;6 and their caregivers. The earliest contrast of verb forms is the one of modal and non-modal forms, namely between the 2nd person singular imperative and the 3rd person singular present indicative, conveying directives and statements, respectively. Such imperatives are formally simple and frequently modeled in child-directed speech. Other early directives are verbless utterances consisting of a noun in the partitive or illative, requesting food and places to go, respectively. A hortative emerging early is the inclusive imperative expressed by the passive, also frequently found in child-directed speech. Directives expressed by illative forms of the 3rd infinitive belong to daily routines of the caretakers. They are documented in the children's speech when playing parents with toys. Second person plural imperative forms, which are quite complex and rarely registered in child-directed speech, give rise to analogical formations demonstrating the child's active processing of the input. Finally, conditional forms used for suggestions and statements of desire are mitigating devices the children use for making indirect requests. There is evidence that the expression of directives in child speech is modeled by child-directed speech.

The chapter *Modality in child Hebrew* by S. Uziel-Karl presents a comprehensive description of the emergence and early development of agent-oriented (dynamic and deontic) and epistemic modality in child Hebrew from a usage-based perspective, comparing child speech with child-directed speech. The focus is on both inflectional and lexical forms. Naturalistic speech samples of two Hebrew-speaking girls, aged 1;5–3;0, and their primary caretakers are analyzed. The findings reveal a gradual developmental trajectory: Expressions of agent-oriented modality appear earlier than expressions of epistemic ones and use of modal verbal inflections such as the imperative precede the use of lexical devices, i.e., modal verbs, adjectives, and adverbs. Over time, the diversity of these means increases whereas the use of verbal inflections decreases and specific forms get to be functionally diversified. For example, the modal verb *yaxol* 'can, be able to' first expressing dynamic ability or deontic possibility is later used to convey epistemic probability. This is further illustrated by a detailed analysis of the inflected forms and functions of the verb *roce* 'want', which is most prominent in the early expression of dynamic modality. Developmental progression is found to be affected by patterns of use in child-directed speech, the pragmatics of mother–child communication as well as cognitive factors.

The study of *Epistemic modality in Russian child language* by V. V. Kazakovskaya discusses the acquisition of epistemic modality and the linguistic means of its expression (so-called 'parenthetical' modal words or epistemic markers) in the early stages of the acquisition of Russian. The data comprise naturalistic interactions of three typically developing children recorded from 1;5 to 4;0 years in interaction with their caregivers. The findings show that epistemic semantics and its basic means of expression start to develop in the third year of life, first with the marking of uncertainty ('probably'), then of certainty ('of course'). Of the three possible positions that an epistemic marker can occupy in a sentence, children prefer the sentence-internal position where it modifies the immediately adjacent constituent, following the most frequent pattern in child-directed speech. Over time, children's epistemic stance expands from a focus on objective situations in the here-and-now of the physical world to reflections on the mental world, first their own, then that of others. The analysis of child speech in relation to child-directed speech shows that the emergence and further development of epistemic markers is influenced not only by their diversity and frequency of occurrence in the input but also by the degree of certainty or uncertainty (modal strength) they express.

The chapter on *Epistemic and evidential modality in early Turkish child speech* by T. Terziyan and A. Aksu-Koç traces the emergence of morphological and lexical forms of expression of propositional modality in the speech of two girls aged 1;3–2;0 and 1;6–2;10 and their caregivers. The analysis focuses on the emergence and uses of the multifunctional tense-aspect-modality inflections for the expression of epistemic meanings of different strength and the use of the evidential inflection for its multiple functions. Findings indicate that the epistemic and evidential categories almost co-emerge. Adverbial expressions of epistemic modality appear along with inflectional ones whereas evidentiality is expressed inflectionally. Speculative utterances expressing possibility and deductive ones conveying near certainty, i.e., notions at the opposite poles of the epistemic scale, are observed first. New information and narrative production are the first functions to be expressed by the evidential form whereas the inferential and reportative functions that signal mode of information acquisition (source) are observed subsequently. Although the forms of high frequency in child-directed speech also occur frequently in child speech and emerge first, the match between the two registers in terms of frequency of functions is not so direct. The findings indicate that, in addition to input frequency, the cognitive accessibility and pragmatic character of the functions play a role in the development of propositional modality.

In *The development of sentence-ending epistemic/evidential markers in young Korean children*, S. Choi examines the acquisition of Korean sentence-ending suffixes that express different types of evidentiality and varying degrees of epistemicity as well as the speaker's assessment of the situation in relation to the listener's current state of knowledge. An in-depth discourse analysis is carried out on the data, which consist of longitudinal speech samples of five children between 1;8–4;0 in spontaneous interaction with their mothers. The findings show that children tune into the cognitive and interactional functions of the suffixes in discourse early on and by age 4 have acquired seven suffixes that mark distinctions relevant to new and old knowledge, degree of certainty based on shared information, source of information, and degree of (dis)agreement with the listener's assessment of the situation. This developmental sequence shows that children progress from an initial focus on their own experience to one that takes the listener's status of knowledge into account. The suffixes that are acquired earlier are the ones that have a higher degree of structural resonance (i.e., receive more partial or full repetition) in mothers' input than any other suffixes. Choi presents evidence for input frequency, discourse-pragmatic factors, cognitive factors, and degree of structural resonance as the mechanisms that may explain how children learn the intricate semantic and pragmatic functions of the Korean epistemic/evidential sentence-ending suffixes.

In their chapter *The acquisition of evidentiality in two Mayan languages, Yukatek and Tojolabal*, B. Pfeiler and A. Curiel investigate the development of the grammatical means for expressing quoted and reported information in Yukatek and Tojolabal, two Mayan languages with grammaticized evidentiality. The data consist of longitudinal recordings of spontaneous data of two Yukatek children between 1;1 and 3;3 interacting with their caregivers and cross-sectional data of six Tojolabal children between 2;0 and 3;7 as well as four schoolchildren between 5;6 and 11;1. The results demonstrate that reportatives and quotatives are rather scarce in child-directed and child speech. Caregivers use quotatives and reportatives not only for expressing source of information but also for metapragmatic purposes. Quotatives serve to prompt children´s utterances while reportatives are used to convey orders, wishes, or commitments presented from the perspective of another party. Children's speech shows that they learn to mark source of information from an early age on. Quotatives emerge first and reportatives are produced later in both languages, possibly due to the higher cognitive demands of conveying reported information not directly attested than expressing speech events that have just taken place in one's presence. The fact that evidentials are grammaticized in Mayan and are used as prompts by caretakers facilitate their acquisition. The analyses of Tojolobal children's narratives, where evidential use marks sophistication in this genre, indicate that development continues throughout childhood.

References

Aikhenvald, Alexandra Y. 2004. *Evidentiality*. Oxford: Oxford University Press.
Aikhenvald, Alexandra Y. 2010. *Imperatives and commands*. Oxford: Oxford University Press.
Aikhenvald, Alexandra Y. 2016. Sentence types. In Jan Nuyts & Johan van der Auwera (eds.), *The Oxford handbook of modality and mood*, 141–165. Oxford: Oxford University Press.
Aksu-Koç, Ayhan. 2016. The interface of evidential and epistemics in Turkish. In Mine Güven, Didar Akar, Balkız Öztürk & Meltem Kelepir (eds.), *Exploring the Turkish linguistic landscape: Essays in honor of Eser Erguvanlı-Taylan*, 143–156. Amsterdam: John Benjamins.
Barnes, Janet. 1984. Evidentials in the Tuyuca verb. *International Journal of American Linguistics* 50. 255–271.
Bittner, Dagmar, Wolfgang U. Dressler & Marianne Kilani-Schoch. 2003. Introduction. In Dagmar Bittner, Wolfgang U. Dressler & Marianne Kilani-Schoch (eds.), *Development of verb inflection in first language acquisition: A cross-linguistic perspective* (Studies on Language Acquisition 21), vii–xxxvii. Berlin & New York: Mouton de Gruyter.
Bittner, Dagmar, Wolfgang U. Dressler & Marianne Kilani-Schoch (eds.). 2003. *Development of verb inflection in first language acquisition: A cross-linguistic perspective*. (Studies on Language Acquisition 21). Berlin & New York: Mouton de Gruyter.
Boas, Franz. 1938. Language. In Franz Boas, *General Anthropology*, 124–145. Boston & New York: Heath.
Boogaart, Ronny & Egbert Fortuin. 2016. Modality and mood in cognitive linguistic and construction grammars. In Jan Nuyts & Johan van der Auwera (eds.), *The Oxford handbook of modality and mood*, 514–534. Oxford: Oxford University Press.
Boye, Kasper. 2016. The expression of epistemic modality. In Jan Nuyts & Johan van der Auwera (eds.), *The Oxford handbook of modality and mood*, 117–140. Oxford: Oxford University Press.
Bybee, Joan. 1985. *Morphology: A study of the relation between meaning and form* (Typological Studies in Language 9). Amsterdam: John Benjamins.
Bybee, Joan. 2010. *Language, usage and cognition*. Cambridge: Cambridge University Press.
Bybee, Joan & Suzanne Fleischman. 1995. Modality in grammar and discourse. In Joan Bybee & Suzanne Fleischmann (eds.), *Modality in grammar and discourse*, 1–14. Amsterdam: John Benjamins.
Bybee, Joan, Revere Perkins & William Pagliuca. 1994. *The evolution of grammar: Tense, aspect, and modality in the languages of the world*. Chicago: University of Chicago Press.
Choi, Soonja. 2006. Acquisition of modality. In William Frawley (ed.), *The expression of modality*, 141–171. Berlin: Walter de Gruyter.
Coates, Jennifer. 1983. *The semantics of the modal auxiliaries*. London: Routledge.
Coates, Jennifer. 1995. The expression of root and epistemic possibility in English. In Joan Bybee & Suzanne Fleischman (eds.), *Modality in grammar and discourse*, 55–66. Amsterdam: John Benjamins.
Dittmar, Norbert & Astrid Reich (eds.). 1993. *Modality in language acquisition/Modalité et acquisition des langues* (Soziolinguistik und Sprachkontakt/Sociolinguistics and Language Contact 6). Berlin & New York: Walter de Gruyter.
Dixon, Robert M. W. 2016. *Are some languages better than others?* Oxford: Oxford University Press.
Dressler, Wolfgang U. 1997: Introduction. In Wolfgang U. Dressler (ed.), *Studies in pre- and protomorphology*, 5–9. Wien: Verlag der Österreichischen Akademie der Wissenschaften.

Dressler, Wolfgang U. & Annemarie Karpf. 1995. The theoretical relevance of pre- and protomorphology in language acquisition. *Yearbook of Morphology 1994*, 99–122.

Dressler, Wolfgang U., F. Nihan Ketrez & Marianne Kilani-Schoch (eds.). 2017. *Nominal compound acquisition* (Language acquisition and language disorders 61). Amsterdam & Philadelphia: John Benjamins.

Dressler, Wolfgang U., F. Nihan Ketrez, Marianne Kilani-Schoch & Ursula Stephany. 2017. Introduction. In Wolfgang U. Dressler, F. Nihan Ketrez & Marianne Kilani-Schoch (eds.), *Nominal compound acquisition* (Language acquisition and language disorders 61), 1–18. Amsterdam & Philadelphia: John Benjamins.

Halliday, Michael A. K. 1975. *Learning how to mean: Exploration in the development of language*. London: Arnold.

Hickmann, Maya & Dominique Bassano. 2016. Modality and mood in first language acquisition. In Jan Nuyts & Johan van der Auwera (eds.), *The Oxford handbook of modality and mood*, 430–447. Oxford: Oxford University Press.

Jespersen, Otto. 1924. *The philosophy of grammar*. London: Allen and Unwin.

Kratzer, Angelika. 1978. *Semantik der Rede: Konttexttheorie, Modalwörter, Konditionalsätze*. Kronberg: Scriptor-Verlag.

Lyons, John. 1977. *Semantics*. 2 vols. Cambridge: Cambridge University Press.

Mithun, Marianne. 2016. Modality and mood in Iroquoian. In Jan Nuyts & Johan van der Auwera (eds.), *The Oxford handbook of modality and mood*, 223–257. Oxford: Oxford University Press.

Nikolaeva, Irina. 2016. Analyses of the semantics of mood. In Jan Nuyts & Johan van der Auwera (eds.), *The Oxford handbook of modality and mood*, 68–85. Oxford: Oxford University Press.

Nuyts, Jan. 2006. Modality: Overview and linguistic issues. In William Frawley (ed.), *The expression of modality*, 1–26. Berlin & New York: Mouton de Gruyter.

Nuyts, Jan. 2016a. Surveying modality and mood: An introduction. In Jan Nuyts & Johan van der Auwera (eds.), *The Oxford handbook of modality and mood*, 1–8. Oxford: Oxford University Press.

Nuyts, Jan. 2016b. Analyses of modal meanings. In Jan Nuyts & Johan van der Auwera (eds.), *The Oxford handbook of modality and mood*, 31–49. Oxford: Oxford University Press.

Nuyts, Jan & Johan van der Auwera (eds.). 2016. *The Oxford handbook of modality and mood*. Oxford: Oxford University Press.

Palmer, Frank R. 1986. *Mood and modality*. Cambridge: Cambridge University Press.

Palmer, Frank R. 2001. *Mood and modality*. 2nd ed. Cambridge: Cambridge University Press.

Pea, Roy D. & Ronald A. Mawby. 1984. The semantics of modal auxiliary use by preschoolers. In C. E. Johnson & C. L. Thew (eds.), *Proceedings of the Second International Congress for the Study of Child Language*, vol. 2, 204–219. Lanham, MD: University Press of America.

Plungian, Vladimir A. 2001. The place of evidentiality within the universal grammatical space. *Journal of Pragmatics* 33. 349–357.

Poupynin, Youri A. 1996. Usvoenie sistemy russkih glagol'nyh form rebenkom (rannie etapy) [Acquisition of the Russian verb system by children (early phases)]. *Voprosy jazykoznanija* 3. 84–95.

Ramat, Anna Giacalone & Grazia Crocco Galèas (eds.). 1995. *From pragmatics to syntax: Modality in second language acquisition*. Tübingen: Gunter Narr Verlag.

Savickienė, Ineta & Wolfgang U. Dressler (eds.). 2007. *The acquisition of diminutives: A cross-linguistic perspective*. Amsterdam: John Benjamins.

Slobin, Dan I. 1997. The origins of grammaticizable notions: Beyond the individual mind. In D. I. Slobin (ed.), *The crosslinguistic study of language acquisition*. Vol. 5: *Expanding the contexts*, 265–323. Mahwah, NJ & London: Lawrence Erlbaum.

Smoczyńska, Magdalena. 1993. The acquisition of Polish modal verbs. In Norbert Dittmar & Astrid Reich (eds.), *Modality in language acquisition/Modalité et acquisition des langues* (Soziolinguistik und Sprachkontakt/Sociolinguistics and Language Contact 6), 145–169. Berlin & New York: Walter de Gruyter.

Squartini, Mario. 2016. Interactions between modality and other semantic categories. In Jan Nuyts & Johan van der Auwera (eds.), *The Oxford handbook of modality and mood*, 50–67. Oxford: Oxford University Press.

Stephany, Ursula. 1983. *The development of modality in language acquisition*. Working Paper No. 43. Institute of Linguistics, University of Cologne.

Stephany, Ursula. 1985. *Aspekt, Tempus Modalität: Zur Entwicklung der Verbalgrammatik in der neugriechischen Kindersprache* (Language Universals Series 4). Tübingen: Gunter Narr Verlag.

Stephany, Ursula. 1986. Modality. In Paul Fletcher & Michael Garman (eds.), *Language acquisition: Studies in first language development*, 375–400. 2nd edn. Cambridge: Cambridge University Press.

Stephany, Ursula. 1993. Modality in first language acquisition: The state of the art. In Norbert Dittmar & Astrid Reich (eds.), *Modality in language acquisition/Modalité et acquisition des langues* (Soziolinguistik und Sprachkontakt/Sociolinguistics and Language Contact 6), 133–144. Berlin & New York: Walter de Gruyter.

Stephany, Ursula. 1997. The acquisition of Greek. In Dan I. Slobin (ed.), *The crosslinguistic study of language acquisition*, vol. 4, 183–333. Mahwah, NJ & London: Lawrence Erlbaum.

Stephany, Ursula & Maria D. Voeikova. 2009. Introduction. In Ursula Stephany & Maria D. Voeikova (eds.), *Development of nominal inflection in first language acquisition: A cross-linguistic perspective* (Studies on Language Acquisition 30), 1–14. Berlin & New York: Mouton de Gruyter.

Stephany, Ursula & Maria D. Voeikova (eds.). 2009. *Development of nominal inflection in first language acquisition: A cross-linguistic perspective*. (Studies on Language Acquisition 30). Berlin & New York: Mouton de Gruyter.

Tomasello, Michael. 2003. *Constructing a language: A usage-based theory of language acquisition*. Cambridge, MA & London: Harvard University Press.

Tomasello, Michael. 2010 [2008]. *Origins of human communication*. Paperback edn. Cambridge, MA & London: The MIT Press.

Tribushinina, Elena, Maria D. Voeikova & Sabrina Noccetti (eds.). 2015. *Semantics and morphology of early adjectives in first language acquisition*. Newcastle upon Tyne: Cambridge Scholars Publishing.

van der Auwera, Johan & Vladimir A. Plungian. 1998. Modality's semantic map. *Linguistic Typology* 2(1). 79–124.

van Olmen, Daniel & Johan van der Auwera. 2016. Modality and mood in Standard Average European. In Jan Nuyts & Johan van der Auwera (eds.), *The Oxford handbook of modality and mood*, 362–384. Oxford: Oxford University Press.

Voeikova, Maria D. & Wolfgang U. Dressler. 2002. Introduction. In Maria D. Voeikova & Wolfgang U. Dressler (eds.). *Pre- and protomorphology: Early phases of morphological development in nouns and verbs* (Lincom Studies in Theoretical Linguistics 29), 3–5. Munich: Lincom Europa.

von Wright, G. H. 1951. Deontic logic. *Mind* (New Series) 60(237). 1–15.

Katharina Korecky-Kröll
Requests in first language acquisition of German: Evidence from high and low SES families

Abstract: This chapter deals with the interplay between social factors and the use of requests in spontaneous parent-child conversation. Parenting style is closely linked to socioeconomic status (SES). Parents from high SES (HSES) backgrounds often follow conversation-eliciting parenting strategies, whereas parents from low SES (LSES) tend to use a more behavior-directing style. Many characteristics of parenting styles are related to the linguistic category of modality, and more precisely to the notion of requests. Different frequencies of requests as well as different ways of expressing them in HSES and LSES families thus provide a good testing ground for the interactional underpinnings of the acquisition of requests by young children as well as for SES differences. The use of requests in parental input and child output was investigated in video recordings of spontaneous interactions of 15 HSES and 14 LSES German-speaking children from age 2;11 to 4;11. Linear mixed-effects analyses of grammatical categories related to requests and to speech acts in general were conducted. Results confirm the expected differences of parenting style. While LSES parents use more requests (especially more direct requests), questions for information are more frequent in the speech of HSES parents. Corresponding to their input, LSES children use more direct requests (especially imperative infinitives) as compared to HSES children. Differences in conversational style of the two groups of parents were greater than those of the two groups of children.

1 Introduction

This chapter aims at linking two important topics of language acquisition research: On the one hand, it deals with the impact of socioeconomic status (SES) on parenting style and parental input – and as a consequence – also on children's linguistic development. On the other hand, it investigates the use of requests, i.e. ways of getting "others to do what one wants them to" (Tomasello 2010: 84), in parental input as well as in children's output. Not only frequencies of different grammatical categories involved in requests (such as imperatives or modal verbs), but also frequencies of direct and indirect directive speech acts are investigated

Katharina Korecky-Kröll, University of Vienna

https://doi.org/10.1515/9781501504457-002

within a broad quantitative analysis of 58 hours of spontaneous parent–child conversation. As four recordings were conducted within 1 ½ years for each family, changes in the use of requests over time have also been investigated.

From the literature, we know that the formal means used for requests may not only differ considerably across languages (Aikhenvald 2010), but also across different groups or individuals speaking the same language, and SES may be a relevant factor in this respect (Hart and Risley 1995).

In studies on language acquisition, SES is frequently assessed by the highest level of parental (most often: maternal) education: High SES (HSES) parents usually hold college or university degrees, low SES (LSES) parents often have only compulsory schooling (Ensminger and Fothergill 2003; Hoff 2006). Some studies also include family income (Rowe 2008), prestige of parental profession as opposed to unemployment (Hart and Risley 1995) or the entire family capital (consisting of financial, human, and social resources, cf. Chiu and McBride-Chang 2006).

SES has been shown to be a decisive factor for children's linguistic and cognitive development (Hart and Risley 1995) and also for their later school performance (Walker et al. 1994): Children from LSES families have smaller vocabularies (Hoff-Ginsberg 1998), show a slower phonological, morphological and syntactic development (Bowey 1995; Ravid 1995; Huttenlocher et al. 2010) and poorer performance not only in linguistic tests, but also in neurocognitive processing studies (Noble, Norman and Farah 2005). The most important mediating variable between SES and children's linguistic proficiencies is parental language input (Huttenlocher et al. 2010). In their groundbreaking study on the language experience of 42 American children aged 1–3, Hart and Risley (1995) demonstrate that by age 3, children from professional (or HSES) families have had 30 million words of cumulative experience more than children from welfare (LSES) families, an experience which is clearly reflected in the children's vocabularies and IQ scores at that age.

In addition, HSES parents' child-directed speech differs not only in quantity, but also in quality from that of LSES parents (Hoff 2003). According to various studies (Hart and Risley 1995; Hoff-Ginsberg 1991, 1998; Hoff, Laursen and Tardif 2002), parental conversation style is closely related to the SES of families (at least in Western cultures): Parents from HSES backgrounds, who mostly have broader knowledge about child development and child care issues (Rowe 2008), are more responsive to their children's verbalizations, initiate and sustain conversation with their children more frequently and encourage them more often to talk by asking them questions (Hoff 2003). HSES parents also tend to formulate requests in an indirect way, e.g., as questions, such as "Why don't you pick up the toys for me?" (Hart and Risley 1995: 57).

On the other hand, parents from LSES backgrounds, who often experience greater social stress and are thus more focused on goal-directed caretaking activities than play, use more behavior-directing speech acts (Hoff-Ginsberg 1991) such as direct commands and prohibitions ("Put it here!", "Don't touch it!"). Even when HSES and LSES parent-child dyads are investigated in different caretaking settings (e.g., book-reading, mealtime, dressing, toy play, cf. Hoff-Ginsberg 1991), SES differences in child-directed speech remain significant, although they may be slightly attenuated by the situational context: Book-reading situations motivate all mothers to use a larger vocabulary, longer utterances and more topic-continuing replies, while toy play tends to elicit more behavior-directing speech acts in all mothers. SES differences in parental input are most pronounced in mealtime and dressing situations.

The chapter is structured as follows: After an overview of the forms and functions of requests in German (section 2), the state of the art and the hypotheses concerning the acquisition of requests are addressed in section 3. The data and method are presented in section 4. The main part of the chapter (section 5) is devoted to the results of the study, the grammatical categories of requests (section 5.1) and their pragmatic functions (section 5.2). The results are discussed in section 6 and section 7 contains the conclusion.

2 Forms and functions of requests in German

2.1 Forms of requests

For reasons of feasibility,[1] the present grammatical analysis has been limited to verbs, especially to mood (e.g., imperative, subjunctive) and modal verbs.[2] In the following subsections, the grammatical categories of German imperatives, infinitives with imperative meaning, hortatives, modal verbs and the past subjunctive will be described. German examples have mainly been taken from the corpus investigated in the present study.

---

1 Modal adjectives (e.g., *möglich* 'possible'), adverbs (e.g., *vielleicht* 'perhaps') and especially modal particles (which are mostly untranslatable into English, e.g., *mal*, *doch*, cf. Thurmair 1989) are also frequent in German, but due to their highly context-dependent meanings (e.g., *mal* to make a command sound milder, as in *Gib mir mal eine Zigarette* 'give me [once] a cigarette', cf. Aikhenvald 2010: 98), they are not very promising for a broad quantitative investigation such as the present one which aims at discovering large overall tendencies.
2 This is in accordance with Stephany's (1983) study on the acquisition of modality, who also focused on these two categories because they have been "most systematically studied in linguistics" and also play an important role in early child language (Stephany 1983: 1).

2.1.1 Imperatives

In spoken German, the 2nd person singular imperative of all weak and many strong verbs is most frequently identical with the verb stem (*hör-en* listen-INF 'listen', example 1a). In certain phonological contexts as well as in written German, the singular imperative form has a schwa suffix (*-e*) (example 1b) (Duden 2016: §609).

(1) a. LSES father addressing a boy
    hör   auf mi&m   Beissen!
    break.IMP.2SG off with&DEF.ART.N.DAT.SG bite.INF
    'Stop biting!'
 b. HSES mother addressing a girl
    warte   bitte!
    wait.IMP.2SG please
    'Wait please!'

In strong verbs with a stem change from *e* to *i* in the present indicative, 2nd person singular imperatives are formed with the *i* stem vowel and without schwa suffix (example 2).

(2) LSES girl addressing her mother
    Mama hilf   mir!
    Mom help.IMP.2SG me
    'Mom, help me!'

Although the personal pronoun is usually dropped in 2nd person singular imperatives (example 3a), it may be overtly realized following the verb form, for the purpose of emphasis (example 3b).

(3) a. LSES mother addressing a girl
    tu   nicht so schmähtandeln!
    do.IMP.2SG not so humbug.INF
    'Don't humbug like that!'
 b. LSES mother addressing a girl
    und jetzt erzähl   du   was!
    and now tell.IMP.2SG you.2SG something
    'And now you tell something!'

The 2nd person plural imperative corresponds to the 2nd person plural present indicative with the pronoun dropped in unmarked contexts (example 4a). In emphasized contexts, the pronoun follows the imperative form (example 4b). As is common in other Bavarian varieties, the 2nd person plural imperative (like the 2nd person plural present indicative) is mostly realized with a *-ts* suffix in spoken Viennese German. This is an amalgam of the standard German 2nd person plural *-t* suffix (e.g., *ihr komm-t* 'you.PL come-PRS.2PL') and the old dual form *ös* 'you.DUAL' (example 4a) (see Glauninger 2010: 186–187, 193).

(4) a. HSES mother addressing a boy and a girl
    kommts   her   Schatzis!
    come.IMP.2PL here   treasure.DIM.PL
    'Come here, darlings!'
   b. LSES boy, 4;4, addressing his aunt, mother and brother
    baut   ihr   mal   was!
    build.IMP.2PL   you.2PL   once   something
    'You build something!'

Imperatives of the 3rd person plural polite form correspond to the 3rd person plural indicative (example 5a), but with the order of pronoun and verb reversed (example 5b).

(5) a. HSES mother addressing a girl
    junge   Dame, Sie   haben   noch   nicht   bezahlt.
    young.F   lady   they   have.PRS.3PL   still not   pay.PP
    'Young lady, you did not pay yet.'
   b. HSES girl, 4;9, addressing her mother
    nehmen   Sie   s(ie)   bitte   mit!
    take.PRS.3PL   they   her   please   with
    'Please take her with (you)!'

In our data, polite forms simulating adult-directed speech exclusively occur in three HSES mothers' role play with their daughters (e.g., customer and client in a shop). Two of the three HSES girls use polite imperatives in the last recording at mean age 4;8, whereas with the third one only polite indicative forms occur. Due to their scarcity and special contexts of use, polite imperatives will be excluded from the analysis (see 5.1).[3]

---

[3] 1st person plural imperatives were classified as hortatives (see 2.3).

2.1.2 Infinitives with imperative meaning

In certain contexts, short impersonal commands expressed by the infinitive may be perceived as less polite than imperative forms. In adult-directed speech, they are usually found in asymmetric public contexts (Duden 2016: §794; cf. also Aikhenvald 2010: 55), e.g., on prohibition signs, but they are also frequently found in doctors' or physical education teachers' instructions or in dangerous situations which require immediate reactions. Such warnings frequently occur in child-directed speech (example 6a), but parents also use them for harsh commands (maybe because the child has not reacted adequately to a previous request) (example 6b).

(6) a. LSES mother addressing a girl when cooking a hot soup
aufpassen!
watch.out.INF
'Watch out!'
b. LSES mother addressing a girl
MOT: *und dann ziehst bitte deine Patschen wieder an.*
and then put.2SG please your.PL slipper.PL again on
'And then you put your slippers on again please.'
CHI: *ha?*
huh
'Huh?'
MOT: *Patschen anziehen!*
slipper.PL put.on.INF
'Put on (the) slippers!'

Since root infinitives may serve different functions in the speech of young children, it may be difficult to distinguish between their dynamic and deontic meaning, i.e. between wishes (example 7a) and requests. The situation is clearer when the addressee is explicitly named and the context shows that the action is to be performed by the addressee rather than the speaker (example 7b). Many unclear cases do, however, remain (example 7c).[4] Children sometimes construct root infinitives with a 2nd person personal pronoun, which is ungrammatical (example 7d).

---

[4] In the present study, all cases where the context pointed to their functions as commands have been coded as requests, whereas clear cases of wishes were coded as assertive speech acts of volition.

(7) a. HSES girl, 3;1, addressing her mother
     schaukeln.
     swing.INF
     '(I want to) swing.'
  b. LSES boy, 3;0, addressing his mother
     hey Mama, nicht abnehmen!
     hey mom   not   take.off.INF
     'Hey mom, don't take (it) off!'
  c. HSES boy, 3;2, addressing his mother
     Zirkus spielen!
     circus play.INF
     '(I want to/let's) play circus.'
  d. LSES boy, 4;9, addressing his mother
     *aber *du   mitkommen!*
     you   *you.2SG come.with.INF
     'But you come with (me)!'

2.1.3 Hortatives

Hortatives are often regarded as 1st person plural imperatives (Eisenberg 2006: 203), but they are based on the present subjunctive paradigm (Duden 2016: §788).[5] As in other imperative-like constructions (see 2.1), the order of verb and pronoun is reversed (example 8a). In Viennese German, the pronoun *wir* 'we' is frequently realized as the clitic *ma* (example 8b).

(8) a. HSES boy, 3;0, addressing his mother
     rutschen   wir runter!
     slide.SBJV.PRS.1PL   we down
     'Let's slide down.'
  b. LSES boy, 3;1, addressing his father
     ta=ma   das!
     do.SBJV.PRS.1PL=we   this
     'Let's do this!'

---

[5] Nevertheless, the difference between indicative and subjunctive of the 1st and 3rd person plural is apparent only in the copula *sein* 'to be' (subjunctive/hortative: *seien* 'be.SBJV.1PL' vs. indicative *sind* 'be.IND.1PL'), therefore it is questionable whether the hortative of other verbs is really perceived as a present subjunctive form (Duden 2016: §788).

2.1.4 Modal verbs

The present singular indicative forms of German modal verbs (*dürfen* 'may', *können* 'can, may', *mögen* 'like', *müssen* 'must', *sollen* 'shall', *wollen* 'want') are characterized by ablaut[6] and preterite indicative endings of strong verbs (cf. Duden 2016: §644). Accordingly, the present indicative forms of modal verbs show zero marking in the 1st and 3rd person (e.g., *ich/er kann* 'I/he can'). Examples (9a, b, c) show typical requests containing modal verbs from our corpus.

(9) a. HSES mother addressing a boy
 N., kannst du den Apfel auch hergeben?
 N. can.PRS.2SG you.2SG DEF.ART.M.ACC.SG apple also give.here.INF
 'N., can you put the apple here, too?'
 b. LSES boy, 3;0, addressing his parents
 müss=ma tanken.
 must.PRS.1PL=we get gas
 'We must get gas.'
 c. HSES girl, 3;1, addressing her mother
 du sollst uns antauchen.
 you.2SG shall.PRS.2SG us push.INF
 'You shall push us (on the swing).'

2.1.5 Past subjunctives

The present subjunctive has almost disappeared from use in spoken German (apart from the hortative) and is limited to reported speech in the written language. The past subjunctive, however, does occur in spoken German, but it is infrequent. It is used in constructions expressing irrealis, conditionals and politeness (Duden 2016: §749–761), e.g., in polite requests. The 1st and 3rd person singular past subjunctive form *möchte* 'would like' (example 10a) from the infinitive *mögen* is highly grammaticized so that *möchten* is sometimes even regarded as a separate infinitive form (cf. Duden 2016: §824). Apart from the occasional use with other modal verbs (example 10b), auxiliaries or the copula, past subjunctive forms mostly occur in the periphrastic *würde* 'would' + infinitive construction (example 10c). They do not appear with lexical verbs in our corpus.

---

6 with the exception of *sollen*.

(10) a. HSES boy, 3;3, addressing his mother
   ich möchte was mit dir bauen!
   I like.PAST.SBJV.1S something with you.2SG build.INF
   'I would like to build something with you!'
   b. HSES mother addressing a girl
   du könntest mir ja auch was kochen.
   you.2SG can.PAST.SBJV.2S me indeed also something cook.INF
   'You could also cook something for me.'
   c. HSES mother addressing a girl
   oja, den Apfel, den
   oh yes DEF.ART.M.ACC.SG apple this.one.M.ACC.SG
   würde ich auch nehmen.
   will.PAST.SBJV.1S I also take.INF
   'Oh yes, the apple, I would also take this one.'

Although the grammatical categories discussed in this section all play an important part in the formation of requests, they are also found in other speech acts: For example, imperatives such as *entschuldige* 'excuse me' are more likely to be expressive speech acts (as defined by Searle and Vanderveken 1985) than pure requests. Likewise, modal verbs frequently express wishes or abilities, but not necessarily requests. Therefore, we have conducted two types of analyses, one investigating the frequencies of grammatical categories that are involved in requests (but are not necessarily used only in requests,[7] see 5.1) and another analysis limited to speech acts with the pragmatic function of requests (see 5.2).

2.2 Functions of requests

In order to identify constructions with imperatives, modal verbs or subjunctive forms functioning as requests, a detailed analysis of speech acts and coding of their pragmatic functions was conducted.

Speech acts to be found in child speech and child-directed speech are assertives (e.g., assertions, statements), directives (e.g., requests, questions), commissives (e.g., promises, offers, threats), and expressives (e.g., complaints, praises, greetings), see also Pagmar (2016: 8). Searle and Vanderveken (1985: 37–40)

---

[7] An exception are infinitives with imperative meaning: As infinitives are much more frequent in other contexts than the ones discussed above, the grammatical analysis has been limited to those with imperative meaning.

distinguish these speech acts according to the way they interfere with the addressee's world of action. While assertives (example 11a) say how things are (direction of fit: word to world), directive (example 11b) and commissive (example 11c) speech acts want to change the world (direction of fit: world to word) by getting the hearer (in directives) or the speaker (in commissives) to perform an action. Expressive speech acts (example 11d) show an empty direction of fit.[8]

(11) a. HSES mother addressing a boy
     ja,   das sind   die   amerikanischen Soldaten.
     yes this be.PRS.3PL DEF.ART.PL American.PL   soldier.PL
     'Yes, these are the American soldiers.'
   b. LSES mother addressing a boy
     geh   weg   vom   Fernseher!
     go.IMP.2S away from.DEF.ART.M.DAT.SG TV
     'Go away from the TV set!'
   c. HSES mother addressing a girl
     ich misch(e)   einmal die   Karten.
     I   riffle.PRS.1SG once   DEF.ART.PL card.PL
     'I will just riffle the cards.'
   d. HSES mother addressing a boy
     super gemacht!
     great make.PP
     'Very well done!'

The most prototypical directive speech acts are requests.[9] They have the goal of getting the addressee to perform an action that the speaker is interested in being done by the addressee. Due to the authority of parents or other caretakers, requests occur very frequently in child-directed speech. However, they are also frequent in child speech because children are in need of getting help and information from their caretakers.

---

[8] A fifth type of speech act, namely declaratives (e.g., speech acts for baptizing, firing from employment, declaring war, etc. cf. Huang 2014: 134), show a double direction of fit by changing the state of the world by words, but they do not occur in child speech and child-directed speech.

[9] We use the notion of requests both for commands, which are issued from a position of authority, and requests for which this is not the case (cf. Searle and Vanderveken 1985: 51). Thus we use the term requests as synonymous with Lyons' (1977) notion of mands, which comprise both requests and commands. Prohibitions are also analyzed as requests.

Requests are more characteristic of a behavior-directing than a conversation-eliciting parenting style. Since adults tend to direct children's behavior rather than that of other adults, requests very commonly occur in child-directed speech, but much less so in adult-directed speech (Newport, Gleitman and Gleitman 1977: 125). Examples for German requests are given below (examples 13–15).

Permissions (example 12a) are distinguished from requests in that the addressee's rather than the speaker's wish is fulfilled. A precondition for permissions is that "the speaker has the authority to permit or prohibit" (Aikhenvald 2010: 200).

Questions for information (example 12b) are also directive speech acts because the addressee is expected to give an answer (rather than to perform some action). Since questions are strongly conversation-eliciting, they will be treated separately from speech acts of requests.

Other directives comprise discourse markers (example 12c), solidarity markers (example 12d; cf. Aikhenvald 2008: 206 or Tomasello 2010: 86[10]), which are most often grammaticalized imperatives, or attention-directives (Hoff-Ginsberg 1991) such as *schau* 'look' (example 12e) or calling the addressee's name (example 12f). The latter will be distinguished from requests because directing a child's attention to an object of interest is different from directing the child's behavior by ordering the child to perform an action. Attention-directives serve the purpose of establishing joint attention and very frequently occur in child-directed speech because of the children's limited attention span. Children also use them often to get their parents' attention (example 12f).

(12) a. HSES mother addressing a boy
   ja, du darfst beginnen.
   yes you may.PRS.2SG start.INF
   'Yes, you may start.'
   b. HSES mother addressing a boy
   warum hat=s dir dort nicht gefallen?
   why have.PRS.3SG=it you.2SG there not please.PP
   'Why didn't you like it there?'

---

[10] Tomasello (2010: 86) stresses the importance of the third basic communicative motive of human cooperation, namely sharing emotions and attitudes. Thus, appealing to the child's solidarity may also be an effective way for a parent of getting a child to perform a task.

c. LSES mother addressing a girl
   na   wart   nur!
   well wait.IMP.2SG only
   'Just you wait!'
d. LSES father addressing a girl
   na   komm!
   well come.IMP.2SG
   'Come on!'
e. All parents addressing their children
   schau   mal!
   look.IMP.2SG once
   'Look!'
f. All children addressing their mothers
   Mama!
   Mom
   'Mom!'

Like other speech acts, requests may be direct or indirect (Searle and Vanderveken 1985: 10–11, Brown and Levinson 1987: 132–134): Direct requests are usually performed via imperatives, infinitives or hortatives (see examples 14 below), whereas indirect requests have the locutionary form of other speech acts, such as questions or statements (see examples 15 below). A category less frequently found in the data are elliptic requests[11] (example 13) which often lack the main verb and therefore cannot be classified as direct or indirect.

(13) HSES boy, 3;1, addressing his brother
     zurück an den   Start!
     back   to DEF.ART.M.ACC.SG start
     'Back to the start!'

The imperative[12] is regarded as the most prototypical and widespread grammatical category for expressing direct requests in the languages of the world (Aikhenvald 2010: 2; example 14a). Nevertheless, infinitives with an imperative

---

[11] cf. Stephany (1983: 8) and Aikhenvald (2010: 280–281).
[12] German imperatives usually occur in the 2nd person singular or plural (see also 2.2.1). The 3rd person plural polite imperatives occur very rarely in our data (see example 5b in 2.2.1: *Nehmen Sie s(ie) bitte mit!* 'Please take her with you!') and therefore have been excluded from the detailed analysis of imperatives, but they are still included in the general analysis of direct, indirect and elliptic speech acts.

meaning are also an important category for expressing direct requests in German (example 14b). Hortatives, which are often considered as 1st person plural imperative forms (see also 2.3), usually include the speaker and the addressee and are perceived as less direct and more polite than imperatives and infinitives with imperative meaning. Nevertheless, they are more direct than questions and statements and have therefore been classified as direct requests (example 14c).

(14) a. HSES mother addressing a girl
heb den Bären nachher wieder
pick.IMP.2SG DEF.ART.ACC.M.SG bear.ACC afterwards again
auf bitte!
up please
'Pick up the bear again afterwards please!'
b. HSES mother addressing a girl
langsamer reden Schatzilein!
slower talk.INF treasure.DIM.DIM.SG
'Speak more slowly, darling!'
c. LSES mother addressing a boy
spiel=ma ordentlich!
play.PRS.SBJV.1PL=we properly
'Let's play properly!'

Although questions and statements may both function as indirect requests for action and are thus usually considered as more polite than direct requests, this is more valid for questions (example 15a). Many requests in the form of statements (examples 15b and 15c) contain modal verbs, but there are others which do not (example 15d, which is a strong statement of social norms). Still, examples (15b) and (15c) show that requests in the form of statements containing modal verbs may be either more (15b) or less (15c) polite.

(15) a. LSES mother addressing a boy
bringst ma jetzt die Taschentücher her?
bring.PRS.2SG me now DEF.ART.PL tissue.PL here
'Do you bring me the tissues now?'
b. HSES mother addressing a girl in a game
darfst da ein Steinchen rausnehmen.
may.PRS.2SG you.2SG INDEF.ART.N.SG stone.DIM take.out.INF
'You may take out a tile.'

    c. LSES mother addressing a boy
       du   sollst   aufhören zum
       you.2SG shall.PRS.2SG   stop.INF to.DEF.ART.N.DAT.SG
       Hupfen im   Bett!
       hop.INF in.DEF.ART.N.DAT.SG bed
       'You shall stop jumping in bed!'
    d. LSES mother addressing a girl
       das sagt   man nicht!
       this say.PRS.3SG one   not
       'One doesn't say that!'

3 Acquisition of requests: State of the art and hypotheses

In three studies on the acquisition of modality in various languages, Stephany (1983, 1986, 1993) reports that categories of deontic modality such as requests or permissions are acquired before categories of epistemic modality (e.g., statements that are overtly marked for possibility, probability, certainty etc.). While both types of modality represent two basic acts that exist already at the prelinguistic stage, namely imperative acts for directing someone's behavior "with the purpose of obtaining objects or services" (Stephany 1983: 7) and declarative acts for establishing joint attention (Stephany 1993: 135), the former are much more important to fulfill the social needs of young children (see also Papafragou 1998).

    The first verbal categories of requests vary across languages. While in Bulgarian, Russian, Finnish, Turkish, and Hebrew imperatives appear first, the category of infinitives with modal meanings emerges earliest in English, German, Dutch, French, and Portuguese, and 3rd person singular present indicative forms with modal meanings are found in young Italian-speaking children (Stephany 1993: 135). In Greek, not only the imperative, but also the subjunctive are among the earliest verb forms to express modal meanings (Stephany 1985; Christofidou and Stephany 2003). Modal verbs with subject-internal sources of modality expressing dynamic meanings (e.g., *wollen* 'want', *können* 'can') are acquired earlier than those with subject-external sources which convey deontic meanings (e.g., *müssen* 'must', *sollen* 'shall', cf. Stephany 1993: 136).

    Kollndorfer (2009) investigates the acquisition of modality by the German-speaking HSES girl Lena (aged 1;7–4;3), who, like the participants of the present study, is growing up in Vienna, Austria. At age 1;9, Lena starts with the first attention-directing imperative *schau* 'look', which also very frequently occurs in her mother's speech. At 1;10 there seems to be a first contrast between the indicative form *ich habe* 'I have' and the infinitive *haben* '(to) have' with a modal meaning expressing a wish. However, such contrasts only become more systematic from 2;3 onwards. Infinitives expressing wishes decrease after 2;4 being replaced by constructions with modal verbs. Infinitives with a clear imperative meaning are used systematically from 3;8 onwards.

Although a first imitated modal verb (*mag* '(I) like') is found in Lena's speech at 1;7, a spontaneous example appears only at 2;0. Interestingly, this is *sollen* 'shall', which, in studies on other German-speaking children, is acquired later due to its subject-external source (Stephany 1993: 136). At 2;1, Lena uses spontaneous instances of *wollen* 'want' and *mögen* 'like' and at 2;2 of *können* 'can'. By age 2;6 all modal verbs have emerged. Their frequencies of use also increase from 2;3 onwards, and at age 4;0, Lena uses similar amounts of modal verb tokens as her mother. Past subjunctive forms are rare: The highly grammaticalized form *möchte* 'would like' (see also 2.5) appears from 2;3 onwards, and at 4;3, Lena also uses *könnte* 'could'. Overall, Lena predominantly expresses deontic and dynamic meanings by modal verbs and deontic meanings only rarely by imperatives whereas her mother uses similar amounts of modal verbs, modal particles (especially *mal* 'once') and verb forms marked for mood. Interestingly, there is no evidence for the use of modal verbs with a propositional (epistemic/evidential) meaning, neither in Lena's output nor in her mother's input until age 4;3.

Investigating the syntactic development of German-speaking HSES vs. LSES children aged 3–6 in two kindergartens in North Rhine-Westphalia, Germany, Hoffmann (1978) also reports some results on speech acts: While HSES children make more assertive speech acts and ask more questions in free play, LSES children do not yet use WH questions at age 3 and use more imperatives from age 4 onwards. Especially LSES boys have greater repertoires of commands, whereas girls, especially LSES girls, have developed greater resources for asking for things.

On the basis of the literature discussed above, the following hypotheses were formulated for the present study:

(1) Due to their predominantly behavior-directing parenting style, LSES parents will use more requests than HSES parents, especially more direct requests such as imperatives and infinitives with imperative meaning.
(2) In accordance with their input, LSES children will also use more requests than HSES children, especially more direct requests.
(3) HSES parents and children will use fewer requests in general and more indirect requests than their LSES peers in particular.

(4) Due to their predominantly conversation-eliciting parenting style, HSES parents will ask their children more non-modalized questions requiring an answer rather than an action compared to LSES parents.
(5) HSES children will also ask more questions because of the high frequency of questions modeled in their input.
(6) HSES parents will use more assertive speech acts providing their children with information on general topics of interest.
(7) No special hypotheses can be formulated concerning commissive and expressive speech acts since commissive speech acts not only include promises, possibly more frequent in HSES families, but also threats, which may be more typical of LSES families. Positive expressive speech acts that praise the child may prevail in HSES families while negative exclamations may dominate in LSES families. Since this chapter focuses on requests, the distinction between positive and negative expressive speech acts has not been studied here but has been investigated in a separate study (Korecky-Kröll 2017b).

4 Data and method

For the present study, 29 German-speaking parent–child dyads living in Vienna, Austria, have been investigated. The children had a mean age of 3;1 (age range: 2;11–3;3) at the beginning of the study which lasted over 1½ years and comprised four recordings per child. The groups were almost balanced for SES and gender (Table 1).

Like in most other studies on language acquisition (cf. Ensminger and Fothergill 2003), SES was primarily assessed by the main parental caretaker's[13] highest educational level (cf. OECD 1999[14]).

---

[13] The main caretaker was identified as the person that spent most time with the target child or the person that the child was most closely attached to. In our sample, these were 27 mothers and two fathers. Nevertheless, there were two special cases: One LSES mother was the main caretaker of two target children (namely of fraternal twins) and the last recording of one LSES girl was conducted with the mother (who had a higher educational level than the LSES father who had been the main caretaker in the first three recordings) because the father had left the family in the meantime.
[14] The LSES group included ISCED-97 levels 2a, 3b and 3c (i.e. from compulsory school to apprenticeship and vocational schools, but without high school diploma), whereas the HSES group had ISCED-97 levels 4 to 6 (i.e. from high school diploma of vocational colleges to Ph.D).

Table 1: Child participants.

SES	Gender	N of children	Subtotal SES
HSES	FEM	8	15 HSES
HSES	MALE	7	
LSES	FEM	6	14 LSES
LSES	MALE	8	
	Total	29	

The prestige of the parental profession was assessed according to the International Socioeconomic Index of Occupational Status (ISEI, cf. Ganzeboom and Treiman 1996). However, the assessment of the ISEI values affected the SES classification of only one child in the sample: One boy's mother held a significantly better job[15] than one would have expected from her formal educational level. Therefore, this boy was "upgraded" to the HSES group.

Four one-hour spontaneous speech video and supplementary audio recordings (Rowe 2012) were conducted in each of the children's homes at children's mean ages 3;1, 3;4, 4;4 and 4;8. Parents were asked to continue with their normal activities. Thus, situations showed considerable variation: Some parents asked their children to play a game, others decided to read storybooks, still others just engaged in spontaneous conversation. In a few cases, mealtime situations were also included in the recording (cf. Hoff-Ginsberg 1991). Sometimes, siblings or other adults (e.g., the other parent, a grandparent or a visitor) were also present, whereas in other cases, the conversations were restricted to the parent–child dyads.[16]

From each recording, 30 minutes with the richest verbal parent–child interaction were selected for transcription (most often two parts of different length, lasting 30 minutes in total).

All 30-minute samples were transcribed according to the CHAT conventions of the CHILDES Project (MacWhinney 2000) and tagged for parts of speech and morphology by using a lexicon-based approach (MacWhinney 2000): New lexical entries and morphological forms were identified, manually coded and added to a lexicon file. The MOR program of the CLAN program package was then used to automatically generate a morphological coding tier below each

---

[15] i.e. an ISEI value that exceeded the median of our sample by at least 10 points, cf. Czinglar et al. (2015: 214).
[16] The investigator maintained the role of an observer and had minimum interaction with the participants during the recordings.

speaker tier on the basis of the codings in the lexicon file. Ambiguous word forms were manually disambiguated (Korecky-Kröll 2017a: 98–99). Finally, the morphological coding tiers were used to calculate word form type and token frequencies of the grammatical categories described in 2.1.1–2.1.5 (i.e. imperatives, hortatives, modal verbs, past subjunctive).

To add the speech act codings according to the categories presented in 2.2 the morphologically coded files were imported into MS Excel (Korecky-Kröll 2017a: 111–112) by using the CLANTOCSV JavaScript program (Korecky 2015). Imperatives, infinitives with imperative meaning and hortatives were coded as direct requests, while modalized questions and statements were coded as indirect requests.

Spontaneous child speech as well as child-directed speech and citations (e.g., book reading, songs) were included in the analysis, while children's immediate imitations of utterances and parents' utterances directed to other adults or pets were excluded.

The lme4 package (Bates et al. 2015) of R (R Core Team 2015) was used to perform linear mixed effects analyses (cf. Winter 2013) of the relationship between frequencies of different categories of requests and socioeconomic status. In contrast to traditional by-subject and by-item analyses, linear mixed effects models "simultaneously treat subjects and items (or more generally, any categorical covariates) as random variables and allow for those random variables to be fully crossed with other random or fixed variables" (Libben, Westbury and Jarema 2012: 4). Therefore, these models are able to "adjust for multiple levels of multiple factors independently, and take into account how those factors interact" (Libben, Westbury and Jarema 2012: 4). Group variables, such as SES (two levels: HSES, LSES), and age-related variables, such as data point (DP: four levels: 1–4), were defined as fixed factors. Another fixed variable[17] was included in each model for the purpose of normalization, i.e. to take into account that LSES children and parents talk less than their HSES counterparts (see also Appendix for raw frequencies). Children's and parents' participant IDs were entered as random factors[18] in all models in order to account for individual variation. The dependent variable of each model was the log-normalized frequency of one category of requests or speech acts.

---

[17] e.g., log-normalized frequencies of all verb types/tokens for the grammatical categories and log-normalized frequencies of speech acts or requests for the speech acts.
[18] This procedure allowed us to also take into account the two special cases mentioned in fn. 13.

5 Results

In this section, the results of the grammatical categories of requests described in sections 2.1.1–2.1.5 will be reported first, followed by the results of the speech act analysis described in section 2.2. Tables containing percentages of the categories investigated (out of all verb types, verb tokens or speech acts) are always shown before the results of the statistical analyses are reported in the text.

5.1 Grammatical categories of requests

5.1.1 Overview

When considering all grammatical categories of requests (i.e. imperatives, hortatives, infinitives with imperative meaning, modal verbs, and past subjunctive forms), we find that they constitute around 25 % of all verb types (25.36 % in children and 25.22 % in parents) and between 26 and 27 % of all verb tokens (26.11 % in children and 26.7 % in parents, see the last column of Table 2). Proportions of grammatical categories of requests are always higher in the LSES group both for parents and children.

Table 2: Total grammatical categories of requests: % out of all verb types and tokens (raw frequencies).

	DP1	DP2	DP3	DP4	All DPs
Group					
HSES CHI TYP	25.02% (280)	25.48% (292)	23.32% (319)	21.04% (335)	23.46% (1226)
LSES CHI TYP	33.46% (266)	29.81% (279)	25.67% (250)	24.46% (281)	27.92% (1076)
Total CHI TYP	28.53% (546)	27.43% (571)	24.30% (569)	22.47% (616)	25.36% (2302)
HSES PAR TYP	24.90% (618)	24.52% (649)	22.85% (608)	22.39% (581)	23.65% (2456)
LSES PAR TYP	24.28% (463)	27.29% (539)	29.43% (510)	28.49% (584)	27.35% (2096)
Total PAR TYP	24.63% (1081)	25.70% (1188)	25.44% (1118)	25.08% (1165)	25.22% (4552)

Table 2 (continued)

Group	DP1	DP2	DP3	DP4	All DPs
HSES CHI TOK	26.18% (623)	25.85% (652)	24.24% (752)	21.27% (752)	24.08% (2779)
LSES CHI TOK	31.99% (565)	28.80% (675)	28.62% (638)	26.55% (703)	28.72% (2581)
Total CHI TOK	28.65% (1188)	27.27% (1327)	26.07% 1390	23.53% (1455)	26.11% (5360)
HSES PAR TOK	25.57% (1527)	27.33% (1780)	23.69% (1473)	24.55% (1452)	25.32% (6232)
LSES PAR TOK	27.12% (1139)	28.54% (1343)	29.79% (1145)	29.19% (1365)	28.65% (4992)
Total PAR TOK	26.21% (2666)	27.84% (3123)	26.02% (2618)	26.60% (2817)	26.70% (11224)

5.1.2 Imperatives

As shown in Table 3, LSES parents use considerably more imperative types as a proportion of all verb types at each of the four data points (10.49–14.25 %) than HSES parents (7.70–8.36 %), followed by LSES children (6.09–6.67 %) and finally HSES children (4.17–5.41 %).

Table 3: Imperatives of 2nd person singular and plural: % of all verb types and tokens at data points 1–4.

Data point	DP1	DP2	DP3	DP4
Group				
HSES CHI types	5.00%	5.41%	4.17%	4.21%
LSES CHI types	6.42%	6.09%	6.67%	6.44%
HSES PAR types	8.06%	8.24%	7.70%	8.36%
LSES PAR types	10.49%	11.65%	14.25%	12.93%
HSES CHI tokens	4.54%	5.27%	5.19%	4.84%
LSES CHI tokens	6.80%	5.72%	6.19%	6.76%
HSES PAR tokens	9.85%	11.53%	8.65%	11.14%
LSES PAR tokens	13.74%	14.28%	15.22%	14.26%

The same holds for imperative tokens as a proportion of all verb tokens: LSES parents use more (13.74–15.22 %) than HSES parents (8.65–11.53 %) and LSES children (5.72–6.80 %), whereas HSES children use the fewest (4.54–5.27 %).

The results of the linear mixed effects analysis demonstrate that SES differences are significant, especially in parents. LSES parents use significantly more imperative types (β = 0.131, SE = 0.044, p = 0.005) as well as imperative tokens (β = 0.141, SE = 0.057, p = 0.018) than HSES parents, whereas the SES effect is weaker in children and significant only in types (types: β = 0.091, SE = 0.038, p = 0.024, tokens: β = 0.085, SE = 0.051, p = 0.108). Frequent use of imperatives can thus be interpreted as an SES marker, especially in parents. As expected, LSES parents, who prefer a more behavior-directing parenting style, use more imperatives. While imperative use does not significantly change over time (as indicated by non-significant effects of data points), overall verb type and token frequencies, which were included as normalizing variables, show significant effects: Parents and children that use more verb types and tokens also use more imperatives (parents' types: β = 0.490, SE = 0.136, p < 0.001, parents' tokens: β = 0.853, SE = 0.130, p < 0.001, children's types: β = 0.444, SE = 0.082, p < 0.001, children's tokens: β = 0.620, SE = 0.094, p < 0.001).

5.1.3 Infinitives with imperative meaning

Although infinitives with imperative meaning are relatively low in overall type and token frequencies, they show considerable group differences (see Table 4): They have the highest frequencies in LSES children at the first data point (11.70 % of verb types and 6.80 % of verb tokens) and the lowest frequencies in HSES parents at the last data point (0.94 % of verb types and 0.47 % of verb tokens).

Infinitives with imperative meaning also yield significant SES effects in both children and parents: LSES parents and children use significantly more infinitives with imperative meaning than HSES parents and children, in types as well as in tokens (parents' types: β = 0.197, SE = 0.077, p = 0.015, parents' tokens: β = 0.283, SE = 0.087, p = 0.003, children's types: β = 0.245, SE = 0.071, p = 0.002, children's tokens: β = 0.262, SE = 0.081, p = 0.003). Thus, the SES effects on infinitives with imperative meaning are stronger for parents' tokens as well as for children's types and tokens, despite their lower overall frequencies in comparison to imperatives (see Table 4 vs. Table 3).

There are also significant effects of data points, especially in case of the children: At data points 3 and 4, when children have a mean age of 4;4 and 4;8, respectively, they use significantly fewer infinitives with imperative meaning (children's types at DP3: β = -0.158, SE = 0.070, p = 0.027, children's tokens at

Table 4: Infinitives with imperative meaning: % of all verb types and tokens at data points 1–4.

Data point Group	DP1	DP2	DP3	DP4
HSES CHI types	2.77%	3.32%	2.19%	1.07%
LSES CHI types	11.70%	8.65%	3.39%	2.35%
HSES PAR types	2.10%	1.96%	1.24%	0.96%
LSES PAR types	2.78%	3.59%	3.06%	3.22%
HSES CHI tokens	1.68%	2.30%	1.19%	0.54%
LSES CHI tokens	6.80%	5.25%	1.70%	1.40%
HSES PAR tokens	1.11%	0.94%	0.60%	0.47%
LSES PAR tokens	1.76%	2.42%	2.13%	1.99%

DP3: $\beta = -0.186$, SE = 0.082, p = 0.025, children's types at DP4: $\beta = -0.284$, SE = 0.073, p < 0.001, children's tokens at DP4: $\beta = -0.305$, SE = 0.084, p < 0.001). This can partially be attributed to the decrease of elliptic modal constructions reduced to infinitives (e.g., *du mitkommen!* 'you come.INF with (me)', see example 7d in 2.1.2), which are more frequent in younger children. But parents also use significantly fewer infinitives with imperative meaning when their children are older, although this significant effect is limited to the fourth data point and not as strong as in the children (parents' types at DP4: $\beta = -0.236$, SE = 0.067, p < 0.001, parents' tokens at DP4: $\beta = -0.257$, SE = 0.079, p = 0.002). Infinitives with imperative meaning may thus not only be regarded as SES markers, but also as age markers. Finally, the normalizing variables of overall verb type and token frequencies are also significant for frequencies of infinitives with imperative meaning: The more overall verb type and token frequencies children and adults produce, the more infinitives with imperative meaning they use (children's types: $\beta = 0.351$, SE = 0.132, p = 0.009, children's tokens: $\beta = 0.360$, SE = 0.128, p = 0.006, parents' types: $\beta = 0.547$, SE = 0.265, p = 0.042, parents' tokens: $\beta = 0.562$, SE = 0.253, p = 0.029).

5.1.4 Hortatives

Hortatives are very rare in general (from a minimum of 0.20 % of HSES children's verb tokens at DP4 to a maximum of 1.96 % of HSES parents' verb types at DP2, see Table 5).

Table 5: Hortatives: % of all verb types and tokens at data points 1–4.

Data point	DP1	DP2	DP3	DP4
Group				
HSES CHI types	0.80%	0.87%	1.17%	0.25%
LSES CHI types	1.51%	0.43%	0.62%	0.78%
HSES PAR types	1.73%	1.96%	1.24%	1.08%
LSES PAR types	1.84%	1.72%	1.50%	1.71%
HSES CHI tokens	0.42%	0.40%	0.61%	0.20%
LSES CHI tokens	0.96%	0.34%	0.27%	0.38%
HSES PAR tokens	0.92%	1.04%	0.71%	0.63%
LSES PAR tokens	1.00%	1.02%	0.88%	1.01%

There is no significant SES effect, neither in the parents nor in the children (parents' types: $\beta = 0.024$, SE = 0.063, p = 0.708, parents' tokens: $\beta = 0.031$, SE = 0.073, p = 0.664, children's types: $\beta = 0.008$, SE = 0.042, p = 0.854, children's tokens: $\beta = 0.009$, SE = 0.046, p = 0.847). Thus, hortatives cannot be regarded as SES markers.

There is a significant change over time in hortative use indicating that fewer hortatives are used at data point 4 in comparison to the three other data points, in both parents and children (parents' types: $\beta = -0.225$, SE = 0.067, p = 0.001, parents' tokens: $\beta = -0.219$, SE = 0.079, p = 0.007, children's types: $\beta = -0.112$, SE = 0.052, p = 0.035, children's tokens: $\beta = -0.126$, SE = 0.061, p = 0.042). Furthermore, the normalizing variables of verb type and token frequencies again yield significant effects in parents as well as children (parents' types: $\beta = 0.739$, SE = 0.239, p = 0.003, parents' tokens: $\beta = 0.698$, SE = 0.227, p = 0.003, children's types: $\beta = 0.200$, SE = 0.087, p = 0.024, children's tokens: $\beta = 0.204$, SE = 0.085, p = 0.012).

5.1.5 Modal verbs

In contrast to the frequent use of imperatives and infinitives with an imperative meaning typical of LSES, a large inventory of modal verbs is a marker of HSES. As shown in Table 6, LSES parents and children use fewer modal verb types and tokens than their HSES peers.

However, significant SES effects are only found for types (parents' types: $\beta = -0.056$, SE = 0.019, p = 0.006, parents' tokens: $\beta = -0.037$, SE = 0.029, p = 0.205, children's types: $\beta = -0.062$, SE = 0.024, p = 0.010, children's tokens: $\beta = -0.021$, SE = 0.045, p = 0.641). Modal verb use does not significantly

Table 6: Modal verbs: % of all verb types and tokens at data points 1–4.

Data point Group	DP1	DP2	DP3	DP4
HSES CHI types	15.37%	15.27%	14.55%	14.01%
LSES CHI types	13.33%	14.00%	13.86%	14.10%
HSES PAR types	11.00%	10.24%	10.56%	9.79%
LSES PAR types	8.81%	9.67%	9.52%	9.32%
HSES CHI tokens	18.91%	17.61%	16.54%	14.82%
LSES CHI tokens	17.16%	16.94%	19.29%	17.67%
HSES PAR tokens	12.29%	12.22%	12.40%	10.82%
LSES PAR tokens	10.33%	10.48%	10.80%	11.21%

change over time, but the normalizing variables of overall verb type and token frequencies again yield significant effects: Parents and children that use more verb types and tokens also use more modal verb types and tokens (parents' types: $\beta = 0.822$, SE = 0.071, $p < 0.001$, parents' tokens: $\beta = 0.995$, SE = 0.088, $p < 0.001$, children's types: $\beta = 0.686$, SE = 0.053, $p < 0.001$, children's tokens: $\beta = 0.790$, SE = 0.074, $p < 0.001$)

5.1.6 Past subjunctive

Another category that might be more typical for HSES is the past subjunctive. Indeed, slightly significant SES effects have been found for parents (types: $\beta = -0.157$, SE = 0.077, $p = 0.048$, tokens: $\beta = -0.235$, SE = 0.112, $p = 0.045$), but not for children (types: $\beta = -0.056$, SE = 0.046, $p = 0.234$, tokens: $\beta = -0.053$, SE = 0.055, $p = 0.341$). This may be due to the low frequencies of past subjunctive forms in the speech of all children, but parents' type and token frequencies are only marginally higher (see Table 7).

There is no significant change in the use of the past subjunctive over time, but significant effects are again found for the normalizing variables of verb type and token frequencies. The more overall verb type and token frequencies children and adults use, the more past subjunctive forms are to be found among them (parents' types: $\beta = 1.275$, SE = 0.236, $p < 0.001$, parents' tokens: $\beta = 0.929$, SE = 0.257, $p < 0.001$, children's types: $\beta = 0.292$, SE = 0.093, $p = 0.002$, children's tokens: $\beta = 0.236$, SE = 0.100, $p = 0.021$).

To summarize the analyses of grammatical categories, infinitives with imperative meaning turned out to be the clearest SES markers, followed by imperatives

Table 7: Past subjunctive: % of all verb types and tokens at data points 1–4.

Data point	DP1	DP2	DP3	DP4
Group				
HSES CHI types	1.07%	0.61%	1.24%	1.51%
LSES CHI types	0.50%	0.64%	1.13%	0.78%
HSES PAR types	2.01%	2.12%	2.10%	2.20%
LSES PAR types	0.37%	0.66%	1.10%	1.32%
HSES CHI tokens	0.63%	0.28%	0.71%	0.88%
LSES CHI tokens	0.28%	0.55%	1.17%	0.34%
HSES PAR tokens	1.41%	1.60%	1.34%	1.49%
LSES PAR tokens	0.29%	0.34%	0.75%	0.73%

of 2nd person singular and plural: LSES children and parents use significantly more of these two categories than their HSES peers. By contrast, modal verbs show only slight SES effects in favor of HSES children and parents, but they are limited to type frequencies. While hortatives do not show any significant SES effects and thus cannot be regarded as SES markers, past subjunctive forms do not show any SES effects in children either, but slight SES effects in favor of HSES parents.

5.2 Pragmatic functions of requests

5.2.1 Overview

To get a complete picture of the use of speech acts in our data, it is important to check whether there are any significant effects related to the general categories of assertive, directive, commissive and expressive speech acts before examining the category of directives in greater detail.

Table 8 shows the proportions of the different types of speech acts out of all speech acts as well as their raw frequencies. More than half of the children's speech acts belong to the assertive category (56.07 % for HSES children, 51.73 % for the LSES children). LSES children use slightly more directives (25.87 %) than HSES children (20.99 %), but expressive speech acts have exactly the same proportion (21.42 %) in both groups of children. Commissive speech acts are very rare (1.52 % in HSES, 0.97 % in LSES children).

Table 8: Children's speech acts: % (raw frequencies).

Group	Data point / Speech acts	DP1	DP2	DP3	DP4	All DPs
HSES	assertive	57.39% (2630)	55.77% (2522)	55.30% (2922)	55.97% (3147)	56.07% (11221)
HSES	directive	21.27% (975)	22.89% (1035)	20.50% (1083)	19.69% (1107)	20.99% (4200)
HSES	commissive	2.07% (95)	1.24% (56)	0.89% (47)	1.89% (106)	1.52% (304)
HSES	expressive	19.27% (883)	20.10% (909)	23.32% (1232)	22.46% (1263)	21.42% (4287)
Total HSES		100.00% (4583)	100.00% (4522)	100.00% (5284)	100.00% (5623)	100.00% (20012)
LSES	assertive	53.50% (2124)	49.03% (2189)	53.69% (2427)	50.88% (2293)	51.73% (9033)
LSES	directive	27.96% (1110)	25.98% (1160)	23.47% (1061)	26.34% (1187)	25.87% (4518)
LSES	commissive	0.68% (27)	1.01% (45)	0.80% (36)	1.38% (62)	0.97% (170)
LSES	expressive	17.86% (709)	23.99% (1071)	22.04% (996)	21.41% (965)	21.42% (3741)
Total LSES		100.00% (3970)	100.00% (4465)	100.00% (4520)	100.00% (4507)	100.00% (17462)

A significant SES effect is found only for assertive speech acts: LSES children use fewer assertive speech acts than their HSES peers (β = -0.490, SE = 0.022, p = 0.036). Otherwise we do not find any significant effects of data points, but only effects of the normalizing variable of overall speech acts: The more speech acts children use in total, the more assertive, directive and expressive speech acts they are found to use (assertive: β = 1.189, SE = 0.060, p < 0.001, directive: β = 1.122, SE = 0.106, p < 0.001, expressive: β = 0.917, SE = 0.127, p < 0.001). For commissive speech acts, which are quite rare, no significant effect of the normalizing variable was detected (β = 0.321, SE = 0.246, p = 0.196).

Within parental input (see Table 9), directive speech acts (42.35–51.59 % in HSES, 44.45–48.74 % in LSES) and assertive speech acts (34.75–43.92 % in HSES, 37.78–40.19 % in LSES) largely prevail over expressive speech acts (12.21–12.59 % in HSES, 10.95–14.63 % in LSES), and commissive speech acts are very rare (0.55–1.50 % in HSES, 1.62–2.13 % in LSES). Parents' speech acts show the usual significant effects of the normalizing variable of overall speech

Table 9: Parents' speech acts: % (raw frequencies).

Group	Data point Speech acts	DP1	DP2	DP3	DP4	All DPs
HSES	assertive	37.01% (2831)	34.75% (2766)	41.51% (3222)	43.92% (3339)	39.25% (12158)
HSES	directive	49.54% (3789)	51.59% (4106)	45.35% (3520)	42.35% (3220)	47.25% (14635)
HSES	commissive	1.24% (95)	1.26% (100)	0.55% (43)	1.50% (114)	1.14% (352)
HSES	expressive	12.21% (934)	12.40% (987)	12.59% (977)	12.23% (930)	12.36% (3828)
Total HSES		100.00% (7649)	100.00% (7959)	100.00% (7762)	100.00% (7603)	100.00% (30973)
LSES	assertive	38.62% (2032)	37.78% (2151)	40.19% (2160)	39.02% (2265)	38.89% (8608)
LSES	directive	48.74% (2564)	48.28% (2749)	44.45% (2389)	44.68% (2593)	46.51% (10295)
LSES	commissive	1.69% (89)	2.13% (121)	1.62% (87)	1.67% (97)	1.78% (394)
LSES	expressive	10.95% (576)	11.82% (673)	13.75% (739)	14.63% (849)	12.82% (2837)
Total LSES		100.00% (5261)	100.00% (5694)	100.00% (5375)	100.00% (5804)	100.00% (22134)

acts (assertive: $\beta = 1.221$, SE = 0.090, $p < 0.001$, directive: $\beta = 0.782$, SE = 0.060, $p < 0.001$, commissive: $\beta = 0.628$, SE = 0.242, $p = 0.011$, expressive: $\beta = 1.065$, SE = 0.160, $p < 0.001$), but no single SES effect. This is surprising, as we hypothesized that LSES parents would use more directives due to their more behavior-directing parenting style. Since this is not the case, we must take a closer look at the different categories of directive speech acts (see also 2.2, examples 12).

Some effects of data point can also be found in parental input: While assertive and expressive speech acts increase with children's age (assertive DP3: $\beta = 0.052$, SE = 0.022, $p = 0.021$, assertive DP4: $\beta = 0.062$, SE = 0.022, $p = 0.007$, expressive DP4: $\beta = 0.094$, SE = 0.042, $p = 0.026$), directive and commissive speech acts tend to decrease over time (directive DP3: $\beta = -0.036$, SE = 0.017, $p = 0.042$, directive DP4: $\beta = -0.058$, SE = 0.018, $p = 0.001$, commissive DP3: $\beta = -0.175$, SE = 0.072, $p = 0.017$).

5.2.2 Directive speech acts

As described in section 2.2, directive speech acts are a heterogeneous category comprising information questions, requests (including prohibitions), permissions as well as other directives.[19] Table 10 shows the proportions of these different subcategories of directive speech acts out of all speech acts in the children's data.

Table 10: Children's categories of directive speech acts: % of all speech acts at data points 1–4.

	Data point	DP1	DP2	DP3	DP4	All DPs
Group	**Speech acts**					
HSES	information questions	7.90%	8.93%	7.40%	8.70%	8.23%
HSES	requests	8.95%	9.64%	9.29%	7.63%	8.82%
HSES	permissions	0.11%	0.02%	0.06%	0.11%	0.07%
HSES	other directives	4.32%	4.29%	3.75%	3.25%	3.86%
Total HSES	directives of all speech acts	21.27%	22.89%	20.50%	19.69%	20.99%
LSES	information questions	10.43%	10.41%	9.93%	11.96%	10.69%
LSES	requests	11.54%	10.46%	8.98%	8.76%	9.88%
LSES	permissions	0.00%	0.00%	0.02%	0.02%	0.01%
LSES	other directives	5.99%	5.11%	4.54%	5.59%	5.29%
Total LSES	directives of all speech acts	27.96%	25.98%	23.47%	26.34%	25.87%

Whereas LSES children use fewer permissions (0.00–0.02 % of all speech acts as opposed to 0.02–0.11 % in HSES children), they use more other directives (4.54–5.99 %) than HSES children (3.25–4.32 %). Furthermore, we find slightly higher proportions of requests as well as information questions in LSES children (LSES: 8.76–11.54 % requests, 9.93–11.96 % information questions, HSES: 7.63–9.64 % requests, 7.40–8.93 % information questions). However, significant SES effects are only found for permissions (β = -0.060, SE = 0.023, p = 0.014) and other directives (β = 0.134, SE = 0.064, p = 0.046), but neither for requests nor for information questions. The lack of a significant effect of data point indicates that

---

[19] Other directives comprise discourse markers (example 12c in section 2.2), solidarity markers (example 12d; cf. Aikhenvald 2008: 206), which are most often grammaticalized imperatives such as *komm* 'come on', and attention-directives (Hoff-Ginsberg 1991) such as *schau* 'look' (example 12e), or calling the addressee's name (example 12f).

children's use of different categories of directives does not significantly change over time. Furthermore, higher-frequency categories of questions for information, requests and other directives show significant effects of total speech act frequencies (information questions: β = 0.968, SE = 0.153, p < 0.001, requests: β = 1.054, SE = 0.162, p < 0.001, other directives: β = 1.176, SE = 0.171, p < 0.001), whereas the rare permissions do not show any significant effect of the normalizing variable.

In contrast to children, parents' results (Table 11) show highly significant SES effects for questions for information (β = -0.220, SE = 0.050, p < 0.001) as well as for requests (β = 0.160, SE = 0.049, p = 0.003). Whereas LSES parents use significantly fewer questions for information (14.58–22.05 %) than HSES parents (20.28–29.26 %), they use significantly more requests (LSES: 19.37–25.36 %, HSES: 15.36–17.48 %). This main result is in accordance with the literature and with our initial hypotheses. There are no significant SES effects either for other directives or for the rare permissions that – in contrast to the three higher-frequency categories – even do not show an effect of total speech act frequency.

Table 11: Parents' categories of directive speech acts: % of all speech acts at data points 1–4.

Group	Data point / Speech acts	DP1	DP2	DP3	DP4	All DPs
HSES	information questions	29.26%	27.99%	25.30%	20.28%	25.74%
HSES	requests	15.36%	17.48%	15.50%	15.94%	16.08%
HSES	permissions	0.24%	0.06%	0.13%	0.11%	0.13%
HSES	other directives	4.68%	6.06%	4.42%	6.02%	5.30%
Total HSES	directives of all speech acts	49.54%	51.59%	45.35%	42.35%	47.25%
LSES	information questions	22.05%	15.56%	15.80%	14.58%	16.90%
LSES	requests	19.37%	25.36%	22.81%	24.86%	23.19%
LSES	permissions	0.10%	0.23%	0.06%	0.09%	0.12%
LSES	other directives	7.22%	7.13%	5.79%	5.15%	6.31%
Total LSES	directives of all speech acts	48.74%	48.28%	44.45%	44.68%	46.51%

Significant effects of data points are only found for frequencies of permissions (DP4: β = -0.098, SE = 0.048, p = 0.044) and questions for information (DP3: β = -0.100, SE = 0.033, p = 0.004, DP4: β = -0.153, SE = 0.033, p < 0.001), which both decrease in the parents' speech as children get older. This result on questions for information is also in accordance with previous studies (e.g., Newport, Gleitman and Gleitman 1977; Cameron-Faulkner, Lieven and Tomasello 2003; Bohnert-Kraus et al. 2016) showing that parents of younger children use particularly high numbers of questions to motivate their children to talk.

5.2.3 Requests

Turning to the investigation of different subcategories of requests, namely direct, indirect and elliptic requests, these may be related to one of two normalizing variables, either total speech act frequencies or total frequencies of requests. Analyses marked with (1) in Tables 12–17 represent the proportions of these categories in relation to the total number of speech acts, whereas analyses marked with (2) are limited to total frequencies of requests.

Table 12: Children's requests: % of all speech acts (1) and % of all requests (2) at data points 1–4.

Group	Data point Speech acts	DP1	DP2	DP3	DP4	All DPs
HSES	Direct (1)	2.25%	2.96%	2.27%	2.22%	2.41%
HSES	Direct (2)	25.12%	30.73%	24.44%	29.14%	27.29%
HSES	Indirect (1)	4.10%	4.02%	4.71%	3.75%	4.15%
HSES	Indirect (2)	45.85%	41.74%	50.71%	49.18%	47.00%
HSES	Elliptic (1)	2.60%	2.65%	2.31%	1.65%	2.27%
HSES	Elliptic (2)	29.02%	27.52%	24.85%	21.68%	25.71%
LSES	Direct (1)	4.96%	4.39%	2.90%	2.80%	3.72%
LSES	Direct (2)	43.01%	41.97%	32.27%	31.90%	37.66%
LSES	Indirect (1)	3.25%	3.40%	3.81%	4.02%	3.63%
LSES	Indirect (2)	28.17%	32.55%	42.36%	45.82%	36.73%
LSES	Elliptic (1)	3.32%	2.67%	2.28%	1.95%	2.53%
LSES	Elliptic (2)	28.82%	25.48%	25.37%	22.28%	25.61%

As indicated in Table (12), LSES children use more direct requests than their HSES peers in both analyses (i.e. no matter which normalizing variable is included). LSES children produce 2.80–4.96 % of all speech acts and 31.90–43.01 % of all requests as direct requests, whereas the HSES children's rate is 2.22–2.96 % (of all speech acts) and 24.44–30.73 % (of all requests). These SES effects for direct requests are significant (β = 0.170, SE = 0.065, p = 0.014 for the model including all speech acts, β = 0.114, SE = 0.041, p = 0.010 for the model including all requests). However, there are no significant SES effects for indirect and elliptic requests, except for indirect requests for model 2 where there is an SES trend close to significance (β = -0.111, SE = 0.055, p = 0.051) indicating that LSES children are slightly less likely to make indirect requests. The use of the three categories of requests does not change significantly over time, with the exception of model (2) of indirect requests, which shows a significant increase of indirect requests at the last data point (DP4: β = 0.122, SE = 0.059, p = 0.042). Otherwise we only find significant effects of the normalizing variable in all six models. Thus, if a child uses higher numbers of speech acts or requests, s/he will also use more direct, indirect and elliptic requests.

Parents' data (see Table 13) are more revealing with respect to SES effects: Like their children, LSES parents use higher proportions of direct requests than their HSES counterparts (LSES: 8.10–10.03 % of all speech acts and 39.40–41.81 % of all requests, HSES: 4.79–5.99 % of all speech acts and 30.92–35.06 % of all requests). Interestingly, this effect is particularly strong when the total of speech acts is included as a normalizing variable (β = 0.212, SE = 0.050, p < 0.001). As we have seen in Table 11, LSES parents strongly prefer requests among directive speech acts (as well as among all speech acts), and their preference for making direct requests is especially strong, whereas HSES parents, who in general prefer speech acts other than requests (e.g., questions for information), use particularly few direct requests. If we include total requests as a normalizing variable, the SES effect is still significant, but weaker (β = 0.081, SE = 0.031, p = 0.015).

Table 13: Parents' requests: % of all speech acts (1) and % of all requests (2) at data points 1–4.

Group	Data point Speech acts	DP1	DP2	DP3	DP4	All DPs
HSES	Direct (1)	5.39%	5.99%	4.79%	5.37%	5.39%
HSES	Direct (2)	35.06%	34.29%	30.92%	33.66%	33.51%
HSES	Indirect (1)	7.30%	8.90%	8.23%	7.71%	8.04%
HSES	Indirect (2)	47.49%	50.90%	53.12%	48.35%	50.01%
HSES	Elliptic (1)	2.68%	2.59%	2.47%	2.87%	2.65%
HSES	Elliptic (2)	17.45%	14.81%	15.96%	17.99%	16.48%
LSES	Direct (1)	8.10%	9.99%	9.38%	10.03%	9.40%
LSES	Direct (2)	41.81%	39.40%	41.11%	40.33%	40.55%
LSES	Indirect (1)	7.87%	10.12%	8.54%	11.10%	9.46%
LSES	Indirect (2)	40.63%	39.89%	37.44%	44.63%	40.78%
LSES	Elliptic (1)	3.40%	5.25%	4.89%	3.74%	4.33%
LSES	Elliptic (2)	17.57%	20.71%	21.45%	15.04%	18.67%

A similar effect is found for elliptic requests (see Table 13): Whereas SES is a significant factor in the model considering total speech acts ($\beta = 0.214$, SE = 0.085, p = 0.018), it is no longer significant in the model limited to total requests ($\beta = 0.034$, SE = 0.051, p = 0.511).

Particularly interesting results concerning the role of SES are obtained by the study of indirect requests. Table 13 shows that LSES parents use a proportion of 7.87–11.10 % indirect requests out of all speech acts and 37.44–44.63 % of all requests, whereas HSES parents' rate is 7.30–8.90 % of all speech acts and 47.49–53.12 % of all requests. Namely, there is no significant SES effect in the model including total speech acts as a normalizing variable ($\beta = 0.084$, SE = 0.062, p = 0.183). Thus, among all speech acts, both groups of parents show relatively similar preferences for indirect requests and the positive β value even indicates a very slight trend in favor of LSES parents: As LSES parents prefer requests among all speech acts in general, they also use slightly more indirect requests, but the difference between LSES and HSES parents is not significant. However, if total requests are included as a normalizing variable, we find a significant SES effect at the expense of LSES parents: Among all requests, LSES parents use significantly fewer indirect requests than HSES parents ($\beta = -0.084$, SE = 0.035, p = 0.023). This result is in accordance with our initial hypothesis that LSES parents prefer direct requests, whereas HSES parents favor indirect ones.

Finally, all normalizing variables show significant effects on parents' frequencies of direct, indirect, and elliptic requests, but there is no significant change over time in the use of these three categories of requests in parental input.

5.2.4 Direct requests

Turning to the three subcategories of direct requests, namely imperatives (IMP), infinitives with imperative meaning (INF), and hortatives (HORT), the only significant SES effects in children's data are found for infinitives with imperative meaning (Table 14).

Both models investigating infinitives with imperative meaning show significant SES effects (model 1: $\beta = 0.251$, SE = 0.078, p = 0.003, model 2: $\beta = 0.204$, SE = 0.072, p = 0.008), indicating that LSES children use significantly more infinitives with imperative meaning than HSES children, regardless of the normalizing variable that is included in the model (total speech acts (1) or total requests (2)).

Table 14: Children's direct requests: % of all speech acts (1) and % of all requests (2) at data points 1–4.

	Data point	DP1	DP2	DP3	DP4	All DPs
Group	Speech acts					
HSES	IMP (1)	1.16%	1.46%	1.21%	1.60%	1.36%
HSES	IMP (2)	12.93%	15.14%	13.03%	20.98%	15.46%
HSES	INF (1)	0.87%	1.28%	0.70%	0.34%	0.77%
HSES	INF (2)	9.76%	13.30%	7.54%	4.43%	8.72%
HSES	HORT (1)	0.22%	0.22%	0.36%	0.12%	0.23%
HSES	HORT (2)	2.44%	2.29%	3.87%	1.63%	2.60%
LSES	IMP (1)	1.56%	1.46%	1.88%	1.78%	1.67%
LSES	IMP (2)	13.54%	13.92%	20.94%	20.25%	16.92%
LSES	INF (1)	2.97%	2.75%	0.86%	0.82%	1.82%
LSES	INF (2)	25.76%	26.34%	9.61%	9.37%	18.37%
LSES	HORT (1)	0.43%	0.18%	0.15%	0.20%	0.23%
LSES	HORT (2)	3.71%	1.71%	1.72%	2.28%	2.38%

Although infinitives with imperative meaning are less frequent than imperatives, they show greater SES differences than imperatives: Whereas HSES children use 12.93–20.98 % of imperatives out of all requests, LSES children show a very similar rate of 13.54–20.94 % of imperatives. In contrast, HSES children use only 4.43–13.30 % infinitives with imperative meaning, whereas LSES children use approximately twice as many, namely 9.37–26.34 %. Finally, hortatives are equally rare in both groups of children (HSES: 1.63 % – 3.87 %, LSES: 1.71 % – 3.71 % out of all requests).

In addition, we find significant effects of data points that show a decrease of infinitives with imperative meaning as children grow older (model 1, DP3: $\beta = -0.174$, SE = 0.079, p = 0.031, DP4: $\beta = -0.281$, SE = 0.080, p < 0.001; model 2, DP3: $\beta = -0.157$, SE = 0.074, p = 0.037, DP4: $\beta = -0.240$, SE = 0.074, p = 0.002). These results are very similar to those of section 5.1.3, where types and tokens of infinitives with imperative meaning were investigated in relation to verb types and tokens.

Otherwise, we only find significant effects of the normalizing variables (in all models), but no SES effects for imperatives and hortatives and only one additional effect of data point for imperatives in model 2 indicating that children use more imperatives out of all requests at the fourth data point ($\beta = 0.149$, SE = 0.068, p = 0.031).

Table 15 shows the proportions of parents' subcategories of direct requests. LSES parents use 28.19–31.65 % of imperatives out of all requests, whereas

Table 15: Parents' direct requests: % of all speech acts (1) and % of all requests (2) at data points 1–4.

Group	Data point / Speech acts	DP1	DP2	DP3	DP4	All DPs
HSES	IMP (1)	3.82%	4.36%	3.75%	4.35%	4.07%
HSES	IMP (2)	24.85%	24.95%	24.19%	27.31%	25.32%
HSES	INF (1)	0.85%	0.77%	0.48%	0.37%	0.62%
HSES	INF (2)	5.53%	4.39%	3.08%	2.31%	3.83%
HSES	HORT (1)	0.72%	0.85%	0.57%	0.49%	0.66%
HSES	HORT (2)	4.68%	4.89%	3.66%	3.05%	4.10%
LSES	IMP (1)	5.87%	7.15%	7.22%	7.62%	6.98%
LSES	IMP (2)	30.32%	28.19%	31.65%	30.63%	30.12%
LSES	INF (1)	1.43%	2.00%	1.53%	1.60%	1.64%
LSES	INF (2)	7.36%	7.89%	6.69%	6.44%	7.09%
LSES	HORT (1)	0.80%	0.84%	0.63%	0.81%	0.77%
LSES	HORT (2)	4.12%	3.32%	2.77%	3.26%	3.33%

HSES parents use only 24.19–27.31 % of imperatives. For infinitives with imperative meaning, this difference is still greater: LSES parents' rate is 7.09 % across all data points, whereas HSES parents' rate is approximately half of it (3.83 % across all data points).

As mentioned above, there are more and partially stronger SES effects to be found in the parents' than in the children's data. While LSES parents use significantly more infinitives with imperative meaning (model 1: $\beta = 0.323$, SE = 0.081, $p < 0.001$, model 2: $\beta = 0.173$, SE = 0.072, $p = 0.023$) and also significantly more imperatives (model 1: $\beta = 0.202$, SE = 0.058, $p = 0.001$, model 2: $\beta = 0.088$, SE = 0.035, $p = 0.020$) than HSES parents, there is, however, no SES effect for hortatives.

These non-significant results concerning hortatives were to be expected. As hortatives occur with an almost equally low frequency in both groups of parents (HSES: 4.10 %, LSES: 3.33 % of all speech acts, see also section 5.1.4), they cannot be regarded as SES markers.

Whereas all normalizing variables show significant effects, effects of data points are only found for infinitives with imperative meaning (model 1, DP4: $\beta = -0.264$, SE = 0.077, $p < 0.001$, model 2, DP3: $\beta = -0.159$, SE = 0.072, $p = 0.030$, DP4: $\beta = -0.275$, SE = 0.072, $p < 0.001$) and for hortatives (model 1, DP4: $\beta = -0.221$, SE = 0.079, $p = 0.006$, model 2, DP4: $\beta = -0.228$, SE = 0.077, $p = 0.004$). As children get older, parents use significantly fewer of these categories (see also results in 5.1.3, Table 4).

5.2.5 Indirect requests

Investigating the two subcategories of indirect requests, namely questions and statements, in the children's data (see Table 16), we find that children clearly prefer statements over questions.

Table 16: Children's indirect requests: % of all speech acts (1) and % of all requests (2) at data points 1–4.

Group	Speech acts	DP1	DP2	DP3	DP4	All DPs
HSES	Questions (1)	0.96%	0.77%	0.64%	0.28%	0.64%
HSES	Questions (2)	10.73%	8.03%	6.92%	3.73%	7.30%
HSES	Statements (1)	3.14%	3.25%	4.07%	3.47%	3.50%
HSES	Statements (2)	35.12%	33.72%	43.79%	45.45%	39.69%
LSES	Questions (1)	0.58%	0.74%	0.33%	1.07%	0.68%
LSES	Questions (2)	5.02%	7.07%	3.69%	12.15%	6.89%
LSES	Statements (1)	2.67%	2.67%	3.47%	2.95%	2.95%
LSES	Statements (2)	23.14%	25.48%	38.67%	33.67%	29.84%

HSES children use 33.72–45.45 % of statements, whereas LSES children use fewer, but still 23.14–38.67 % of statements among all requests. In contrast, HSES children's questions range from only 3.74 to 10.73 %, which is quite similar to LSES children's questions which make up 3.69–12.15 % among all requests.

This is also reflected in the statistical results: We only find a significant SES effect for statements in model (2): Among all requests, LSES children use significantly fewer statements than HSES children (β = -0.126, SE = 0.058, p = 0.039). In addition, there is a significant effect of data point in this model: Children use significantly more statements expressing indirect requests at data point 4 than at the three earlier data points (β = 0.136, SE = 0.064, p = 0.036).

No significant SES effects are found for children's questions. Besides, effects of the normalizing variables are found in all models except for model (1) examining questions among all speech acts.

If children's statements with and without modal verbs are analyzed separately, significant SES effects in favor of HSES children for both models investigating statements with modal verbs are found (β = -0.156, SE = 0.074, p = 0.045 for model (1) investigating statements with modal verbs among all speech acts; β = -0.207, SE = 0.058, p = 0.001 for model (2) investigating statements with modal verbs among all requests), whereas there are no significant SES effects concerning statements without modal verbs.

Parents (see Table 17) also prefer statements over questions,[20] but the frequency differences between the two categories are less pronounced than in the children: Whereas HSES parents use 10.56–16.10 % of questions and 34.13–42.56 % of statements, LSES parents use only 6.10–11.68 % of questions and 28.85–38.53 % of statements out of all requests.

Table 17: Parents' indirect requests: % of all speech acts (1) and % of all requests (2) at data points 1–4.

Group	Data point / Speech acts	DP1	DP2	DP3	DP4	All DPs
HSES	Questions (1)	2.05%	2.81%	1.64%	1.70%	2.06%
HSES	Questions (2)	13.36%	16.10%	10.56%	10.64%	12.79%
HSES	Statements (1)	5.24%	6.08%	6.60%	6.01%	5.99%
HSES	Statements (2)	34.13%	34.80%	42.56%	37.71%	37.22%
LSES	Questions (1)	2.26%	2.25%	1.41%	1.52%	1.86%
LSES	Questions (2)	11.68%	8.86%	6.20%	6.10%	8.01%
LSES	Statements (1)	5.59%	7.87%	7.11%	9.58%	7.59%
LSES	Statements (2)	28.85%	31.02%	31.16%	38.53%	32.74%

Parents' data show one significant SES effect with respect to indirect requests expressed by questions: When questions are related to total requests (model 2), LSES parents use significantly lower frequencies of this type of indirect requests than their HSES counterparts (β = -0.164, SE = 0.077, p = 0.043). However, this effect does not show up when questions are related to total speech acts (model 1).

Furthermore, there are some significant effects of data points: Whereas parents make significantly fewer indirect requests in the form of questions at the fourth data point in both models (model 1: β = -0.168, SE = 0.070, p = 0.019, model 2: β = -0.173, SE = 0.069, p = 0.014), they use more requests in the form of statements at the third data point in model (2) (β = 0.071, SE = 0.034, p = 0.040). This last preference is also reflected in the children's results at the fourth data point (i.e. approximately three months later, see Table 16 above).

---

[20] Two examples of indirect requests by LSES parents were excluded from this analysis because they could neither be classified as questions nor as statements, but rather as "indirect imperatives" (i.e. as imperatives having the opposite intention, e.g., *tu mir jetzt noch einmal weh* 'hurt me once more (and the game will be over)!').

Otherwise, significant effects of the normalizing variables are found in three of the four models investigating parents' indirect requests and the fourth one (model 1 examining requests in the form of questions among all speech acts) shows a trend that is close to significance ($\beta = 0.432$, SE = 0.237, p = 0.072).

In contrast to the children, there is no significant SES effect if parents' statements with and without modal verbs are analyzed separately.

Summarizing the results of the detailed statistical analyses of speech acts, it may be held that our main hypothesis (1) has been confirmed: Comparing LSES parents to HSES ones, the former strongly prefer requests, especially direct requests. By contrast, the other hypotheses could only be partially confirmed. While both LSES and HSES children use similar amounts of requests overall, which refutes the first part of hypothesis 2, LSES children prefer direct requests, confirming the second part of hypothesis 2. The statistical results concerning indirect requests (hypothesis 3) are more complex and considerably depend on the normalizing variables included (see section 6). However, hypothesis 4 claiming that HSES parents ask more information questions has clearly been confirmed. By contrast, this does not hold for HSES children (which refutes hypothesis 5). Finally, hypothesis 6 claiming that HSES parents use more assertive speech acts than LSES parents could not be confirmed.

6 Discussion

The principal goal of the present chapter has been the investigation of large overall tendencies of conversation styles in families of different socioeconomic backgrounds: In accordance with previous studies and our main hypothesis (1) (see section 3), it was confirmed that LSES parents use a clearly more behavior-directing parenting style than HSES parents. This is reflected in the more frequent use of infinitives with imperative meaning and imperatives. These overall results proved to be highly robust across the different types of analyses.

While the overall speech act analysis yielded only one significant SES effect, namely fewer assertives in LSES children, the comparison of different directive speech acts showed clear SES differences mainly in parents. In spite of the fact that HSES parents asked many more questions for information than LSES parents and LSES parents uttered many more requests than HSES parents, both groups of children showed a surprisingly similar behavior with respect to these two main categories of directive speech acts, a result not hypothesized. Thus, LSES children asked similar amounts of questions for information as compared to HSES children, although they heard significantly fewer such questions from their parents. Also, HSES children produced similar amounts of requests as LSES children in spite of the fact that they heard requests much less often. What seems to be more important than input frequency is that the children's speech reflects their basic needs, which appear to be the same in both SES groups. Certainly, HSES children also want objects and services from their parents while LSES in turn need information, maybe even more, as their input may be less informative[21] and contingent on the child's focus of attention (Hoff 2006). However, as the development of the most important pragmatic categories takes at least up to age 11 (Cameron-Faulkner 2014), it seems plausible that SES differences in discourse will also emerge later than SES differences in vocabulary and grammar.

The results concerning different types of requests in both groups of parents were relatively complex and diverged according to the normalizing variables included in the statistical models. Thus, a preference for indirect requests among all requests could only be found in the speech of HSES parents if requests were included as a normalizing variable. However, once all speech acts were included in the analysis, the preference for indirect requests was no longer significant since HSES parents produced a greater number of speech acts other than requests. By contrast, the analysis of the speech of LSES parents, with their strong tendency to prefer requests among all speech acts, resulted in a significant preponderance of direct requests once all speech acts were included, but these parents also used a considerable number of indirect requests. It would therefore be misleading to simply claim that LSES parents prefer direct requests, whereas HSES parents prefer indirect ones. Rather, LSES parents prefer requests, especially direct ones, whereas HSES parents prefer other speech acts (e.g., questions for information and statements of fact), but when making requests, they tend to use more indirect requests (especially in the form of questions) than LSES parents.

Both groups of children also show considerable SES differences with respect to most categories of requests and other speech acts so that the overall tendencies to be found in their speech are similar to those of their parents. For example, the frequent use of infinitives with imperative meaning turned out to be a clear SES marker for the speech of both LSES parents as well as their children. However, SES differences in the parents' speech are usually larger. This means that the notion of SES is not just an abstract concept, but a reality in

---

[21] Although LSES parents showed amounts of (informative) assertive speech acts similar to those of HSES parents, their actual information content was possibly lower. But as this was not investigated in the present study, we do not know for sure.

children's everyday lives into which they will continuously be integrated while they grow and become older.

When comparing the results of the present study to those of Kollndorfer's (2009) case study on the Viennese HSES girl Lena, we find similar overall tendencies: While Lena's modal infinitives decrease after age 2;4, her modal verbs show an increase. The children of our study, who are considerably older, as they have a mean age of 3;1 at the beginning of the project, do no longer show an increase of modal verbs by age, but still a decrease of modal infinitives. However, our LSES children continue to show a high preference for infinitives, whereas our HSES children show a preference for modal verbs, which is also Lena's preferred way of expressing modality.

As reported by Stephany (1993), the earliest verbal categories of German-speaking children are infinitives with modal meanings. According to our results, infinitives with imperative meaning (which can be regarded as a subcategory of infinitives with modal meanings) remain typical for LSES children and their parents for quite a long time, although they show a significant decrease in all children and parents during children's fifth year of age.

The kindergarten study by Hoffmann (1978) revealed that HSES children used more assertive speech acts, a result that was replicated by the present study. However, in contrast to Hoffmann, we did not find more imperatives and fewer questions in LSES children, but only more infinitives with imperative meaning. In contrast to Hoffmann, who also found greater repertoires of commands in LSES boys and greater repertoires of means for asking for things in LSES girls, we did not find a significant gender difference within our overall quantitative analysis.

7 Conclusion

Although, from a scientific point of view, it is satisfying to obtain significant results, the outcome of the present study is also somewhat worrying. Having got to know the families investigated personally and the parents as being attentive to their children's needs and caring for their welfare, we would have hoped to find more even conversational patterns and less significant SES differences. But despite all political measures having been taken so far for attenuating SES effects on children's education, it seems that education unfortunately continues to be somehow 'inherited'. Of course, SES is much more than just the child's primary caregiver's level of education or prestige of profession: It comprises the entire home-learning environment including learning materials as well as literacy practices, the financial situation of the family, the neighborhood, the social network and many more factors. However, parental language input is a key variable mediating the effects of SES. Although there are several parents (from both HSES and LSES backgrounds) in our sample living in a tenuous financial situation, some of them manage to provide their children with rich and encouraging linguistic input, whereas others do not. This probably is a question of personal resilience, a variable which could not be investigated in the present study. In any case, it is up to politicians to further improve the situation of families with young children, so that all families, not only the most resilient ones, can provide their children with stimulating home environments. Austria, as many other European countries, is in need of increased financial and educational support for LSES families, special kindergarten and preschool programs for disadvantaged children and early compulsory kindergarten attendance for children quite generally.

Appendix

The tables in the Appendix show the raw type and token frequencies of the grammatical categories of requests analyzed in section 5.1 as well as the raw token frequencies of the speech acts analyzed in section 5.2, for each SES group separately. Types shared among participants have been counted once per participant and data point (rather than just once per SES group and data point).

Table 18: Children's grammatical categories: Types.

SES		DP	IMP	INF	HORT	MV	PAST SBJV	V	Total wordTYP
HSES	1	56	31	9	172	12		1119	3884
	2	62	38	10	175	7		1146	3996
	3	57	30	16	199	17		1368	4661
	4	67	17	4	223	24		1592	5332
Total HSES		242	116	39	769	60		5225	17873
LSES	1	51	93	12	106	4		795	2867
	2	57	81	4	131	6		936	3182
	3	65	33	6	135	11		974	3309
	4	74	27	9	162	9		1149	3827
Total LSES		247	234	31	534	30		3854	13185
Total		489	350	70	1303	90		9079	31058

Table 19: Parents' grammatical categories: Types.

SES	DP	IMP	INF	HORT	MV	PAST SBJV	V	Total wordTYP
HSES	1	200	52	43	273	50	2482	6973
	2	218	52	52	271	56	2647	7505
	3	205	33	33	281	56	2661	7588
	4	217	25	28	254	57	2595	7595
Total HSES		840	162	156	1079	219	10385	29661
LSES	1	200	53	35	168	7	1907	5143
	2	230	71	34	191	13	1975	5364
	3	247	53	26	165	19	1733	4891
	4	265	66	35	191	27	2050	5753
Total LSES		942	243	130	715	66	7665	21151
Total		1782	405	286	1794	285	18050	50812

Table 20: Children's grammatical categories: Tokens.

SES	DP	IMP	INF	HORT	MV	PAST SBJV	V	Total wordTOK
HSES	1	108	40	10	450	15	2380	12744
	2	133	58	10	444	7	2522	12794
	3	161	37	19	513	22	3102	15959
	4	171	19	7	524	31	3536	18116
Total HSES		573	154	46	1931	75	11540	59613
LSES	1	120	120	17	303	5	1766	9385
	2	134	123	8	397	13	2344	11584
	3	138	38	6	430	26	2229	11508
	4	179	37	10	468	9	2648	12726
Total LSES		571	318	41	1598	53	8987	45203
Total		1144	472	87	3529	128	20527	104816

Table 21: Parents' grammatical categories: Tokens.

SES	DP	IMP	INF	HORT	MV	PAST SBJV	V	Total wordTOK
HSES	1	588	66	55	734	84	5972	27221
	2	751	61	68	796	104	6513	29593
	3	538	37	44	771	83	6217	28935
	4	659	28	37	640	88	5914	27793
Total HSES		2536	192	204	2941	359	24616	113542
LSES	1	577	74	42	434	12	4200	18499
	2	672	114	48	493	16	4706	20237
	3	585	82	34	415	29	3843	17227
	4	667	93	47	524	34	4676	20607
Total LSES		2501	363	171	1866	91	17425	76570
Total		5037	555	375	4807	450	42041	190112

Table 22: Children's imperatives: Types and Tokens.

SES	DP	IMP.2SG TYP	IMP.2PL TYP	IMP.3PL TYP	IMP.2SG TOK	IMP.2PL TOK	IMP.3PL TOK
HSES	1	56	0	0	108	0	0
	2	61	1	0	131	2	0
	3	52	5	0	155	6	0
	4	65	2	7	168	3	8
Total HSES		234	8	7	562	11	8
LSES	1	50	1	0	117	3	0
	2	57	0	0	134	0	0
	3	63	2	0	134	4	0
	4	72	2	0	177	2	0
Total LSES		242	5	0	562	9	0
Total		476	13	7	1124	20	8

Table 23: Parents' imperatives: Types and Tokens.

SES	DP	IMP.2SG TYP	IMP.2PL TYP	IMP.3PL TYP	IMP.2SG TOK	IMP.2PL TOK	IMP.3PL TOK
HSES	1	196	4	0	583	5	0
	2	210	8	1	743	8	1
	3	200	5	0	532	6	0
	4	214	3	14	655	4	17
Total HSES		820	20	15	2513	23	18
LSES	1	195	5	0	572	5	0
	2	229	1	0	671	1	0
	3	246	1	0	584	1	0
	4	263	2	0	665	2	0
Total LSES		933	9	0	2492	9	0
Total		1753	29	15	5005	32	18

Table 24: Children's speech acts.

SES	DP	Assertive	Directive	Commissive	Expressive	Total speech acts
HSES	1	2630	975	95	883	4583
	2	2522	1035	56	909	4522
	3	2922	1083	47	1232	5284
	4	3147	1107	106	1263	5623
Total HSES		11221	4200	304	4287	20012
LSES	1	2124	1110	27	709	3970
	2	2189	1160	45	1071	4465
	3	2427	1061	36	996	4520
	4	2293	1187	62	965	4507
Total LSES		9033	4518	170	3741	17462
Total		20254	8718	474	8028	37474

Table 25: Parents' speech acts.

SES	DP	Assertive	Directive	Commissive	Expressive	Total speech acts
HSES	1	2831	3789	95	934	7649
	2	2766	4106	100	987	7959
	3	3222	3520	43	977	7762
	4	3339	3220	114	930	7603
Total HSES		12158	14635	352	3828	30973
LSES	1	2032	2564	89	576	5261
	2	2151	2749	121	673	5694
	3	2160	2389	87	739	5375
	4	2265	2593	97	849	5804
Total LSES		8608	10295	394	2837	22134
Total		20766	24930	746	6665	53107

Table 26: Children's directive speech acts.

SES	DP	Questions for information	Requests	Permissions	Other directives	Total directives
HSES	1	362	410	5	198	975
	2	404	436	1	194	1035
	3	391	491	3	198	1083
	4	489	429	6	183	1107
Total HSES		1646	1766	15	773	4200
LSES	1	414	458	0	238	1110
	2	465	467	0	228	1160
	3	449	406	1	205	1061
	4	539	395	1	252	1187
Total LSES		1867	1726	2	923	4518
Total		3513	3492	17	1696	8718

Table 27: Parents' directive speech acts.

SES	DP	Questions for information	Requests	Permissions	Other directives	Total directives
HSES	1	2238	1175	18	358	3789
	2	2228	1391	5	482	4106
	3	1964	1203	10	343	3520
	4	1542	1212	8	458	3220
Total HSES		7972	4981	41	1641	14635
LSES	1	1160	1019	5	380	2564
	2	886	1444	13	406	2749
	3	849	1226	3	311	2389
	4	846	1443	5	299	2593
Total LSES		3741	5132	26	1396	10295
Total		11713	10113	67	3037	24930

Table 28: Children's requests.

SES	DP	Direct	Indirect	Elliptic	Total requests
HSES	1	103	188	119	410
	2	134	182	120	436
	3	120	249	122	491
	4	125	211	93	429
Total HSES		482	830	454	1766
LSES	1	197	129	132	458
	2	196	152	119	467
	3	131	172	103	406
	4	126	181	88	395
Total LSES		650	634	442	1726
Total		1132	1464	896	3492

Table 29: Parents' requests.

SES	DP	Direct	Indirect	Elliptic	Total requests
HSES	1	412	558	205	1175
	2	477	708	206	1391
	3	372	639	192	1203
	4	408	586	218	1212
Total HSES		1669	2491	821	4981
LSES	1	426	414	179	1019
	2	569	576	299	1444
	3	504	459	263	1226
	4	582	644	217	1443
Total LSES		2081	2093	958	5132
Total		3750	4584	1779	10113

Table 30: Children's direct requests.

SES	DP	IMP.2SG/IMP.2PL	INF	HORT	Total direct requests (without IMP.3PL)
HSES	1	53	40	10	103
	2	66	58	10	134
	3	64	37	19	120
	4	90	19	7	116
Total HSES		273	154	46	473
LSES	1	62	118	17	197
	2	65	123	8	196
	3	85	39	7	131
	4	80	37	9	126
Total LSES		292	317	41	650
Total		565	471	87	1123

Table 31: Parents' direct requests.

SES	DP	IMP.2SG/IMP.2PL	INF	HORT	Total direct requests (without IMP.3PL)
HSES	1	292	65	55	412
	2	347	61	68	476
	3	291	37	44	372
	4	331	28	37	396
Total HSES		1261	191	204	1656
LSES	1	309	75	42	426
	2	407	114	48	569
	3	388	82	34	504
	4	442	93	47	582
Total LSES		1546	364	171	2081
Total		2807	555	375	3737

Table 32: Children's indirect requests.

SES	DP	Questions	Statements	Total indirect requests
HSES	1	44	144	188
	2	35	147	182
	3	34	215	249
	4	16	195	211
Total HSES		129	701	830
LSES	1	23	106	129
	2	33	119	152
	3	15	157	172
	4	48	133	181
Total LSES		119	515	634
Total		248	1216	1464

Table 33: Parents' indirect requests.

SES	DP	Questions	Statements	Total indirect requests
HSES	1	157	401	558
	2	224	484	708
	3	127	512	639
	4	129	457	586
Total HSES		637	1854	2491
LSES	1	119	294	413
	2	128	448	576
	3	76	382	458
	4	88	556	644
Total LSES		411	1680	2091
Total		1048	3534	4582

Sample of a coded CLAN transcript: HSES girl (CHI) and her mother (PAR)

*CHI:	oh oh [=! greift auf ein spielzeug zu] !
%mor:	INTERJ|oh INTERJ|oh !
%eng:	oh oh [=! reaching for a toy] !
*PAR:	das ghoert [: gehoert] nicht uns [=! zu CHI].
%mor:	PRO:dem|d-as V:01|gehoer-3S ADV|nicht PRO|wir-DAT.
%eng:	this does not belong to us [=! to CHI].
*CHI:	die &l +//.
%mor:	DET:art:def|d-ie +//.
%eng:	the &l +//.
*CHI:	ich hab(e) [*] versehn [: versehen] von da [: der] Lucy die blume mitgenomm(e)n und mit ihrer muschel [=! zu PAR]
%mor:	PRO|ich V:aux|hab-1S [*] N:05:n|versehen PREP|von DET:art:def|d-er n:prop|Lucy DET:art:def|d-ie N:02:f|blume mit#V:11|nehm-PP CONJ|und PREP|mit DET:pro:poss|ihr-er N:02:f|muschel.
%eng:	I have [*] accident taken the flower from Lucy and with her shell [=! to PAR].
*PAR:	na dann gibstas [: gibst es] ihr dann zurueck wenn sie kommt [=! zu CHI].
%mor:	CO|na ADV|dann zurueck#V:10|geb-2S PRO|es PRO|sie- DAT ADV|dann CONJ|wenn PRO|sie V:X|komm-3S.
%eng:	well then you give it back to her when she comes [=! to CHI].
*CHI:	ja.
%mor:	CO:ass|ja.
%eng:	yes.

*PAR:	das sind alles die barbiesachen [=! zu CHI] +//.
%mor:	PRO:dem|d-as V:S|sein-3P PRO:qn|all-es DET:art:def|d-ie N:02:f|barbie+sache-PL +//.
%eng:	these are all the barbie things [=! to CHI].
*PAR:	aua [=! an alle, schuettelt ihre hand] !
%mor:	INTERJ|aua !
%eng:	ouch [=! to all, shaking her hand] !
*PAR:	+, die koennen dann gleich da wieder ins barbiekoerbchen rein [=! zu CHI, stellt ihr ein koerbchen hin].
%mor:	PRO:dem|d-ie rein#V:mod|koenn-3P ADV|dann ADV|gleich ADV|da ADV|wieder PREP|in~DET:art:def|d-as N:05:n|barbie+korb&DIM3.
%eng:	they can go then right back into the barbie basket [=! to CHI, putting a little basket in front of CHI].
*CHI:	die muschel # kann ich jetz(t) behalten oder ?
%mor:	DET:art:def|d-ie N:02:f|muschel V:mod|koenn-1S PRO|ich ADV|jetzt V:07|behalt-INF CONJ|oder ?
%eng:	can I keep the shell, can't I ?
*PAR:	na@d [: nein] die gibst du ihr dann wieder zurueck wenn sie dann kommt [=! zu CHI].
%mor:	CO:neg|nein PRO:dem|d-ie zurueck#V:10|geb-2S PRO|du PRO|sie-DAT ADV|dann ADV|wieder CONJ|wenn PRO|sie ADV|dann V:X|komm-3S.
%com:	no you give it back to her when she comes [=! to CHI].
*CHI:	mh [=! bedauernd].
%mor:	CO|mh.
%eng:	mh [=! regretfully].
*PAR:	+< A [=! mahnend zu CHI, nennt den Namen des Kindes] !
%mor:	n:prop|A !
%eng:	n:prop|A [=! admonishingly to CHI, calling the child's name] !
*CHI:	wenn sie +//.
%mor:	CONJ|wenn PRO|sie +//.
%eng:	when she +//.
*CHI:	# wenn sie kommt dann geb(e) ich sie ihr +//.
%mor:	CONJ|wenn PRO|sie V:X|komm-3S ADV|dann V:10|geb-1S PRO|ich PRO|sie PRO|sie-DAT +//.
%eng:	when she comes then I give it to her +//.
*CHI:	aber trotzdem spieln [: spielen] wir dann mit ihr.
%mor:	CONJ|aber CONJ|trotzdem V:01|spiel-1P PRO|wir ADV|dann PREP|mit PRO|sie-DAT.
%eng:	but nevertheless we play with it.
*PAR:	ja jetz(t) ja [=! zu CHI].
%mor:	CO:ass|ja ADV|jetzt CO:ass|ja.
%eng:	yes now yes [=! to CHI].

Acknowledgements: Data collection and transcription were funded by the Wiener Wissenschafts-, Forschungs- and Technologiefonds (WWTF, SSH11-027) while the author held and is holding positions at the University of Vienna (2012–2015, since 2017) and the Austrian Academy of Sciences (2016). I am deeply indebted to Wolfgang U. Dressler, the principal investigator of the INPUT project, for his continuous support, fruitful discussions and his permission to use the project data for this chapter. I also thank my colleagues Christine Czinglar, Sabine Sommer-Lolei, Viktoria Templ, Kumru Uzunkaya-Sharma, and Maria Weichselbaum for their great cooperation in various steps of data collection, their coding and analysis, Basilio Calderone for statistical advice as well as numerous undergraduate students at the Department of Linguistics of the University of Vienna for their transcription work. Furthermore, I would like to express my thanks to the editors of this volume for their thorough work, their friendly support, and their patience. Last, but not least, I thank the children and parents for their participation.

References

Aikhenvald, Alexandra Y. 2008. Multilingual imperatives: the elaboration of a category in Northwest Amazonia. *International Journal of American Linguistics* 74(2). 189–225.

Aikhenvald, Alexandra Y. 2010. *Imperatives and commands*. Oxford: Oxford University Press.

Bates, Douglas, Martin Maechler, Ben Bolker & Steve Walker. 2015. Fitting linear mixed-effects models using lme4. *Journal of Statistical Software* 67(1). 1–48.

Bohnert-Kraus, Mirja, Katharina Korecky-Kröll, Andrea Haid, Christine Czinglar & Andrea Pamela Willi. 2016. Mediale Diglossie in Vorarlberg als Bereicherung oder als Hindernis für den monolingualen Spracherwerb? *SAL-Bulletin* Nr. 161 (September 2016), 5–29.

Bowey, Judith A. 1995. Socioeconomic status differences in preschool phonological sensitivity and first-grade reading achievement. *Journal of Educational Psychology* 87(3). 476–487.

Brown, Penelope & Stephen C. Levinson. 1987. *Politeness. Some universals in language use.* Cambridge: Cambridge University Press.

Cameron-Faulkner, Thea. 2014. The development of speech acts. In Danielle Matthews (ed.), *Pragmatic development in first language acquisition*, 37–52. Amsterdam: Benjamins.

Cameron-Faulkner, Thea, Elena Lieven & Michael Tomasello. 2003. A construction based analysis of child directed speech. *Cognitive Science* 27(6). 843–873.

Chiu, Ming Ming & Catherine McBride-Chang. 2006. Gender, context, and reading: a comparison of students in 43 countries. *Scientific Studies of Reading* 19. 331–362.

Christofidou, Anastasia & Ursula Stephany. 2003. Early phases in the development of Greek verb inflection. In Dagmar Bittner, Marianne Kilani-Schoch & Wolfgang U. Dressler (eds.), *Development of verb inflection in first language acquisition. A cross-linguistic perspective*, 89–129. Berlin: Mouton de Gruyter.

Czinglar, Christine, Katharina Korecky-Kröll, Kumru Uzunkaya-Sharma & Wolfgang U. Dressler. 2015. Wie beeinflusst der sozioökonomische Status den Erwerb der Erst- und Zweitsprache? Wortschatzerwerb und Geschwindigkeit im NP/DP-Erwerb bei Kindergartenkindern im türkisch-deutschen Kontrast. In Klaus-Michael Köpcke & Arne Ziegler (eds.), *Deutsche Grammatik in Kontakt. Deutsch als Zweitsprache in Schule und Unterricht*, 207–240. Berlin: Mouton de Gruyter.

Duden. 2016. *Die Grammatik*. 9th edn. Mannheim: Dudenverlag.

Eisenberg, Peter. 2006. *Grundriss der deutschen Grammatik. Band 1: Das Wort*. 3rd edn. Stuttgart: Metzler.

Ensminger, Margaret E. & Kate E. Fothergill. 2003. A decade of measuring SES: What it tells us and where to go from here. In Marc H. Bornstein & Robert H. Bradley (eds.), *Socioeconomic status, parenting and child development*, 13–27. Mahwah, NJ: Erlbaum.

Ganzeboom, Harry B.G. & Donald J. Treiman. 1996. Internationally comparable measures of occupational status for the 1988 International Standard Classification of Occupations. *Social Science Research* 25. 201–239.

Glauninger, Manfred M. 2010. Zwischen Hochdeutsch, Dialekt und Denglisch. „Innere Mehrsprachigkeit" und urbane Kommunikation am Beispiel der Jugendlichen im Ballungsraum Wien. In Stephan Gaisbauer & Klaus Petermayr (eds.), *Übergang. Kommunikation in der Stadt und an ihren Rändern*, 181–193. Linz: StifterHaus.

Hart, Betty & Todd R. Risley. 1995. *Meaningful differences in the everyday experience of young American children*. Baltimore: Brookes.

Hoff, Erika. 2003. Causes and consequences of SES-related differences in parent-to-child speech. In Marc H. Bornstein & Robert H. Bradley. (eds.), *Socioeconomic status, parenting, and child development*, 147–160. Mahwah, NJ: Erlbaum.

Hoff, Erika, Brett Laursen & Twila Tardif. 2002. Socio-economic status and parenting. In Marc H. Bornstein (ed.), *Handbook of parenting*, 231–252. 2nd edn. Mahwah, NJ: Erlbaum.

Hoff, Erika. 2006. How social contexts support and shape language development. *Developmental Review* 26. 55–88.

Hoff-Ginsberg, Erika. 1991. Mother-child conversation in different social classes and communicative settings. *Child Development* 62(4). 782–796.

Hoff-Ginsberg, Erika. 1998. The relation of birth order and socioeconomic status to children's language experience and language development. *Applied Psycholinguistics* 19(4). 603–629.

Hoffmann, Ludger. 1978. *Zur Sprache von Kindern im Vorschulalter. Eine Untersuchung in zwei Kindergärten aus dem niederdeutschen Sprachraum*. Köln & Wien: Böhlau.

Huang, Yan. 2014. *Pragmatics*. 2nd edn. Oxford: Oxford University Press.

Huttenlocher, Janellen, Heidi Waterfall, Marina Vasilyeva, Jack Vevea & Larry V. Hedges. 2010. Sources of variability in children's language growth. *Cognitive Psychology* 61. 343–365.

Kollndorfer, Kathrin. 2009. Entwicklung der Modalität im Erstspracherwerb des Deutschen. Vienna: University of Vienna MA thesis.

Korecky-Kröll, Katharina. 2017a. Kodierung und Analyse mit CHILDES: Erfahrungen mit kindersprachlichen Spontansprachkorpora und erste Arbeiten zu einem rein erwachsenensprachlichen Spontansprachkorpus. In: Claudia Resch & Wolfgang U. Dressler (eds.), *Digitale Methoden der Korpusforschung in Österreich*, 85–113. Wien: Verlag der Österreichischen Akademie der Wissenschaften.

Korecky-Kröll, Katharina. 2017b. Encouragements and discouragements in parental input: Evidence from high and low SES families. *Acta Linguistica Petropolitana* XIII/3, 576–589.

Korecky, Paul C. 2015. CLANTOCSV [Computer software].

Libben, Gary, Chris Westbury & Gonia Jarema. 2012. The challenge of embracing complexity. In Gary Libben, Gonia Jarema & Chris Westbury (eds.), *Methodological and analytic frontiers in lexical research*, 1–12. Amsterdam & Philadelphia: Benjamins.

Lyons, John. 1977. *Semantics*. 2 vols. Cambridge: Cambridge University Press.

MacWhinney, Brian. 2000. *The CHILDES Project: Tools for Analyzing Talk*. 3rd edn. Mahwah, NJ: Erlbaum.

Newport, Elissa L., Henry Gleitman & Lila R. Gleitman. 1977. Mother, I'd rather do it myself: some effects and non-effects of maternal speech style. In Catherine E. Snow & Charles A. Ferguson (eds.), *Talking to children: Language input and acquisition*, 109–149. Cambridge: Cambridge University Press.

Noble, Kimberly G., M. Frank Norman & Martha J. Farah. 2005. Neurocognitive correlates of socioeconomic status in kindergarten children. *Developmental Science* 8(1). 74–87.

OECD. 1999. *Classifying educational programmes. Manual for ISCED-97 Implementation in OECD countries*. OECD: 1999 Edition.

Pagmar, David. 2016. Illocutionary speech acts in Swedish parent-child interaction. Stockholm: University of Stockholm MA thesis.

Papafragou, Anna. 1998. The acquisition of modality: implications for theories of semantic representation. *Mind and Language* 13(3). 370–399.

R Core Team. 2015. R: A language and environment for statistical computing. R Foundation for Statistical Computing, Vienna, Austria. URL http://www.R-project.org/ (accessed 8 June 2017).

Ravid, Dorit. 1995. *Language change in child and adult Hebrew: a psycholinguistic perspective*. New York: Oxford University Press.

Rowe, Meredith. 2008. Child-directed speech: relation to socioeconomic status, knowledge of child development and child vocabulary skill. *Journal of Child Language* 35. 185–205.

Rowe, Meredith. 2012. Recording, transcribing, and coding interaction. In Erika Hoff (ed.), *Research methods in child language: a practical guide*, 193–207. Chichester: Wiley-Blackwell.

Searle, John R. & Daniel Vanderveken. 1985. *Foundations of illocutionary logic*. Cambridge: Cambridge University Press.

Stephany Ursula. 1983. *The development of modality in language acquisition* (Working Paper No. 43). University of Cologne: Institut für Sprachwissenschaft.

Stephany, Ursula. 1985. *Aspekt, Tempus und Modalität: Zur Entwicklung der Verbalgrammatik in der neugriechischen Kindersprache* (Language Universals Series, 4). Tübingen: Gunter Narr.

Stephany, Ursula. 1986. Modality. In Paul Fletcher & Michael Garman (eds.), *Language acquisition: studies in first language development*, 375–400. Cambridge: Cambridge University Press.

Stephany, Ursula. 1993. Modality in first language acquisition: The state of the art. In Norbert Dittmar & Astrid Reich (eds.), *Modality in language acquisition*, 133–144. Berlin & New York: Walter de Gruyter.

Thurmair, Maria. 1989. *Modalpartikeln und ihre Kombinationen*. Tübingen: Niemeyer.

Tomasello, Michael. 2010. *Origins of human communication*. Cambridge, MA: MIT Press.

Walker, Dale, Charles Greenwood, Betty Hart & Judith Carta. 1994. Prediction of school outcomes based on early language production and socioeconomic factors. *Child Development* 65(2). 606–621.

Winter, Bodo. 2013. Linear models and linear mixed effects models in R with linguistic applications. *arXiv* 1308.5499. http://arxiv.org/pdf/1308.5499.pdf (accessed 25 February 2017).

Viktorija Kavaliauskaitė-Vilkinienė and Ineta Dabašinskienė
Gender differences in the acquisition of requests in Lithuanian

Abstract: The present study investigates the early development of directive speech acts by two Lithuanian children of different gender, a girl aged 1;8–2;8 and a boy aged 1;6–2;7, and is based on longitudinal data of mother–child interactions. The results show that expressions of agent-oriented modality appeared at the very beginning of the observation period when both children produced direct and indirect requests. Direct requests were expressed by one-word utterances consisting of nouns, adverbs, infinitives, or imperatives and indirect requests contained statements of desire, need and hortatives. Toward the end of observation, the children acquired various other ways to express requests. The present study examines the working hypothesis that in Lithuanian culture boys and girls are socialized differently, namely that boys are exposed to more directives in the form of imperatives whereas girls are addressed by more indirect forms of requests. This hypothesis has not been confirmed by our results as more direct requests were found in the girl's CDS than the boy's. More research is needed in order to bring to light which other factors besides gender and age may play a role in developing the important communicative function of expressing requests. It might be expected that gender differences become more relevant for children beyond age three.

1 Introduction

Many popular and scientific publications hold the view that some miracles of nature conspire to make children acquire their complex language system so fast and easily. This phenomenon is discussed in different theoretical frameworks. In this study we follow the account of a usage-based approach to language acquisition developed by Tomasello (2003) and assume that children learn language in order to use it and by using it. This view of language acquisition is based on a functionalist model of language and relies on "the expression and comprehension of communicative intentions (intention-reading)" (Tomasello 2003: 325). Moreover, Tomasello emphasizes the importance of a construction-based approach to utterances rather than the position that constructions are mainly combinations of

---

Viktorija Kavaliauskaitė-Vilkinienė, Vytautas Magnus University
Ineta Dabašinskienė, Vytautas Magnus University

words and morphemes. Therefore, in his account "utterances are the primary reality of language from a communicative point of view because they are the most direct embodiment of a speaker's communicative intentions" (Tomasello 2003: 325–326).

The usage-based approach of language acquisition focuses on the availability of given structures in the input and tries to capture the very process of the child's development towards adult-like language competence. The input for a young child is specifically suited to the task of language learning because various speech adjustments provide multiple cues which can facilitate acquisition (Snow and Ferguson 1977; Kempe, Brooks, and Pirott 2001; Dabašinskienė 2009). Features of the macro-level, such as amount of speech, frequency of given structures, repetition and others, are important parameters of language acquisition. In spite of an extensive debate of the frequency effect, it is still unclear to what extent language acquisition is determined by distributional and frequency factors. In any event, frequency and distribution cannot be the main or only factors explaining language development because social, semantic and pragmatic factors as well as perceptual salience interact with the former (Behrens 2006). Since linguistic choices largely depend on social relations between interlocutors (Brown and Levinson 1987), language acquisition involves more than a mastery of grammatically correct linguistic expressions. Children have to learn to perform various speech acts as well as to acquire social conventions for appropriate and effective communication with specific addressees. Already at a very young age children must understand both the form and function of the speaker's utterance, learn to indicate their intents politely, and consider another person's point of view in order to discover and master Grice's (1975) conversational maxims for successful conversation (Ninio and Snow 1996; Karmiloff and Karmiloff-Smith 2002). As observed by Ninio and Snow (1996: 5), "children are involved into various politeness routines since the very young age, and the politeness rules form an integrated system with the societal regulation of interpersonal behavior in general."

Requests include all of the aspects mentioned above as they are determined by social context, culturally based conventions, and politeness rules. Depending on the situation they can be expressed in a direct or indirect way and form an important part of interpersonal interactions since "using a wrong way of requesting is a sure way towards a breakdown in communication" (Aikhenvald 2010: 331). Therefore, a significant developmental question arises as to when direct and indirect requests are acquired and how they are expressed in the course of children's development.

Researchers in the field suggest that the first expressions of requests used by children are pointing gestures, names of desired objects, words like *want*, *more*, and imperatives (Ervin-Tripp 1977: 178; Aikhenvald 2010: 326). Aikhenvald (2010: 325–326) emphasizes the early acquisition of imperatives and states that the high frequency of imperatives and other explicit directives in child speech (CS) mirrors the dominance of these forms in child-directed speech (CDS).

The structure and development of children's requests is discussed in detail by Gordon and Ervin-Tripp (1984), who emphasize that children differentiate their expressions of requests according to social and situational variables. As the authors observe, "by age 2;5 English-speaking children begin using auxiliaries and start to mark social contrasts with the use of imbedded [sic] requests" (Gordon and Ervin-Tripp 1984: 307). These findings suggest that already at a very young age children are able to understand the social dimensions of power and social distance and can conform to social rules in order to produce less direct forms of requests. It is observed that two-year-old children "are sensitive to power and familiarity [. . .]. They use significantly more imperatives to mothers than to fathers; siblings are given orders, but visitors receive polite requests" (Gordon and Ervin-Tripp 1984: 298). These results are consistent with Nakamura's (2001: 108) investigation of Japanese children, who used casual forms with peers and younger siblings but polite language with unfamiliar and older adults.

One of the social features claimed to determine expressions of requests is gender. It has become a truism that men and women differ in their linguistic behavior. In general, women's speech is claimed to be more polite than men's. Women are also said to be more supportive and to use more mitigations (see Lakoff 1973; Haas 1979; Tannen 1990; Holmes 1995). These differences have also been noticed in requests occurring in parent–child interactions. Bellinger and Gleason (1982) found that when speaking to their children, fathers used more imperatives, whereas mothers were inclined to use more indirect forms of request. Moreover, both fathers and mothers tend to use more imperatives and other forms of direct request when addressing their sons but not when speaking to their daughters (Gleason 1975; Cherry and Lewis 1976). The study by Ladegaard and Bleses (2003) also shows that caregivers address boys by using imperatives more often than girls and that such differences in received speech can cause gender differences in language use later on. Leaper, Anderson and Sanders' research (1998) also supports the gender effect of parental speech with sons in contrast to daughters. In their study, statistically significant results were observed in the amount of talking and use of supportive speech to which daughters as opposed to sons were exposed. However, in the same study only minimal evidence for differential use of directives was observed. Either no significant effect or only a small one when addressing boys versus girls was also found in some other studies (Lytton and Romney 1991; Ryckebusch and Marcos 2004; Endendijk et al. 2016).

Some studies, mainly on English, suggest that the gender parameter does indeed have an effect on children's linguistic behavior. The findings show that girls tend to be more cooperative and mitigate their language, whereas boys use a more controlling and assertive style of communication (Miller, Danaher and Forbes 1986; Sheldon 1990; Holmes 1997). However, there are also studies demonstrating the importance of age for gender-typical communication. Thus, Leaper (1991: 797) observed that "gender-typed communications were more likely at the middle childhood than the early childhood age level". Bellinger and Gleason (1982) found that by the age of four children's expressions of requests and their frequencies were similar to those of their parent of the same sex: it appears that boys produced more imperatives, whereas girls used more polite forms (expressed by questions). In contrast, other studies have revealed more similarities than differences. Thus, Leaper (1991) points out that communication patterns of boys and girls were more similar than different. Likewise, no significant difference in boys' and girls' use of mitigation in play situations was found by Ladegaard (2004).

Clark (2004: 576) points out that "in all cultures children have to learn how they are expected to speak as male or female participants in the society." As our data do not contain a sufficient amount of recorded father–child conversations, in most cases we can only take mothers' interactions with their children into consideration.

Given the divergent results concerning the production of requests by children and parents of different gender, gender-associated linguistic behavior continues to be an interesting area of investigation, so that a study of requests in Lithuanian language acquisition may yield worthwhile results.

Our expectations concerning the present study are that the boy will be exposed to more directives in the form of imperatives than the girl and that the girl for her part will encounter more indirect forms of requests than the boy.[1] The principal aims of this study are the following:

(1) The ability of two Lithuanian children of different gender to produce early directive speech acts will be analyzed and compared. More specifically, we will focus on the relative emergence and usage of different types of direct and indirect requests in the boy's and the girl's speech.

---

[1] This hypothesis is supported by a study on gender differences in Lithuanian diminutive production based on the data of the same children (Dabašinskienė 2012). This study has shown that the use of diminutives for the pragmatic function of endearment is more prominent when mothers are talking to girls. A higher number of diminutives in girls' CDS may therefore explain the greater frequency in their CS.

(2) The types and frequencies of requests occurring in CS and CDS will be determined and the relationship between the two registers in the acquisition of requests will be investigated.

The chapter is organized as follows: In section 2 the form and function of requests in Lithuanian is described. The data and method of investigation are presented in section 3. Section 4 is devoted to our results concerning the use of direct and indirect requests in Lithuanian CDS and their development in CS. The main findings are summarized in the conclusions.

2 Requests in Lithuanian

Lithuanian belongs to the conservative Baltic branch of the Indo-European language family. It is a fusional-inflecting language characterized by rich and complex inflectional morphology. The acquisition of Lithuanian verb morphology was studied by Wójcik (2000), where a brief introduction to the Lithuanian verb system is provided. The verb system is based on the tense (present, past, past frequentative, future), mood (indicative, conditional, imperative), and voice (active/passive) distinctions. Lithuanian verbs are inflected for three persons and two numbers (singular and plural).

The simplest verb form in Lithuanian is the imperative, which has a suffix -k- and is usually no longer than one or two syllables (e.g., *ei-k* 'go-IMP.2SG', *ei-k-ite* 'go-IMP-2PL'). The paradigm of Lithuanian imperatives is constituted by the second person singular and plural of the canonical imperative and the first person plural imperative expressing non-canonical imperatives. Second person plural imperative forms are used when addressing several addressees or one addressee when there is a social distance or an unequal social status between interlocutors. According to Lithuanian Grammar (1997: 244), "when referring to a future happening the 1st and 2nd person plural forms of the present tense acquire a meaning similar to that of the imperative mood, except that the order, instruction or advice to act is expressed in this case even more strongly than by the imperative form proper" (e.g., *ein-ate* 'go-PRS.2PL', *ein-ame* 'go-PRS.1PL'). Thus, although, the first and second person plural present indicative are excluded from the imperative paradigm, the modal meaning which they may convey nevertheless relates them to the other forms of this paradigm. The singular and plural second person forms of both imperative and present indicative express a more categorical command than the first person plural form which includes both the addressee(s) and the speaker (Lithuanian Grammar 1997: 708).

2.1 The state of the art

The literature on Lithuanian requests mainly takes a normative perspective of linguistic etiquette (Kučinskaitė 1990; Šukys 2003). A descriptive approach to requests is followed by Hilbig (2010), who focuses on a contrastive analysis of Lithuanian and English requests and shows that although both groups of Lithuanian and British English-speaking subjects mostly opted for a conventional indirect strategy, the Lithuanian data contained 20% less indirect requests than the British English data. While direct requests, whose canonical forms are constructions with imperatives, were mostly used to address intimates in Lithuanian, it seems that Lithuanian norms of politeness allow a more frequent and wider use of direct requests in a larger variety of contexts than British ones.

In a more recent comparative study on requesting in five languages (Lithuanian, Estonian, Finnish, French and Russian) it was found that, in all these languages, requests were typically expressed by interrogatives and conditionals (Pajusalu et al. 2017). As for requesting in Lithuanian, it was noted that a typical request form involved the particles *ar*[2] or *gal* with the modal verb *galėti* 'can, be able', as in the following examples: *ar gal-iu?* 'whether can-PRS.1SG?' or *gal gal-iu?* 'maybe can-PRS.1SG?', the latter being a more polite expression. The main mitigation strategies in Lithuanian requests appeared to be conditional and modal constructions (Pajusalu et al. 2017). The same mitigation strategies for indirect requests are mentioned by Hilbig (2010). It is worth mentioning that both of these studies rely on discourse completion tasks rather than natural conversations.

Very few studies have been concerned with the analysis of requests occurring in natural Lithuanian child language. Savickienė [Dabašinskienė] (1997) found that the first speech acts of a very young girl were direct requests. An analysis of the conversational structure of Lithuanian parent-child interaction with special attention to politeness phenomena shows that both direct and indirect requests occur from early on (Balčiūnienė 2009). The most extensive study of the acquisition of requests in Lithuanian was carried out by Kavaliauskaitė (2016). Although we shall include some of her results in our present study, the current

---

[2] Requests formulated in the form of a question with a modal construction function as mitigation devices. The conjunction *ar* has a number of meanings depending on its position and the sentence type; it can be translated as 'if, whether, or'. In questions, it has the function of a question particle. The modal particle *gal* 'maybe' can be used for marking a question, for expressing polite requests or doubt. Although it literally has an epistemic meaning it may also function as a mitigation device of requests by giving the addressee an option of refusal.

analysis takes a different perspective discussing acquisition of requests in the framework of gender effect.

2.2 Forms and functions of Lithuanian requests

Lithuanian possesses a wide range of expressions of direct and indirect requests (see Čepaitienė 2007; Hilbig 2010). Table 1 presents some of the main types distinguished in the CS and CDS data analyzed in the present study.

Table 1: Classification of Lithuanian requests.

Type	Subtype	Linguistic expression
Direct requests	Commands	Imperative (2nd person singular and plural)
		Verbless clauses
		Infinitive clauses
		Future tense clauses
	Prohibitions	Negative imperative
Indirect requests	Speaker's wish	Constructions with the verb *norėti* 'want'
		Constructions with the verb *reikėti* 'need'
	Polite requests	Expressions with the politeness marker verb *prašyti* 'please'
		Expressions with the politeness marker interjection *prašom* 'please'
	Hortatives (suggestions)	Constructions with the 1st person plural present tense
		Constructions with the 1st person plural imperative
	Questions	Speaker or hearer-oriented modal constructions asking for permission or a favor and questions about the addressee's future action
	Hints	Statements of speaker's likings and states
	Prohibitions	Constructions with the verb *negalima* 'not allowed'
	Warnings	Conditional clauses

Prototypically, direct requests (commands) are expressed by the second person singular or the second person plural imperative (examples 1 and 2).

(1) *duo-k*
    give-IMP.2SG
    'Give!'

(2) *duo-k-ite*
 give-IMP-2PL
 'Give!'

Other ways to express commands are verbless clauses (example 3), the infinitive (example 4), or future tense second person singular (example 5).

(3) *arbat-os*
 tea-GEN.SG
 'Tea!'

(4) *valgy-ti*
 eat-INF
 'Eat!'

(5) *duo-s-i*
 give-FUT-2SG
 'You will give (me).'

Verbless clauses consist of bare nouns or adverbs. Infinitives may function as strong demands in colloquial Lithuanian (Čepaitienė 2007: 166), but in CS they are rather elliptical constructions based on CDS questions to the child (e.g., *nor-i ger-ti?* (want-PRS.2SG drink-INF) 'do you want to drink?'). Future tense clauses pitched as declaratives function as strong commands, whereas an interrogative pitch mitigates the request turning it into an option to be complied with by the addressee or not depending on his/her possibility or willingness. Interrogative future tense clauses are thus to be classified as indirect requests so that in this case the only formal difference between direct and indirect requests is the intonation pattern.

Prohibitions are typically expressed by adding the negative prefix *ne-* to the imperative (example 6).

(6) *ne-duo-k*
 NEG-give-IMP.2SG
 'Don't give!'

One type of indirect requests are speakers' wishes expressed by verbs of desire (example 7) or verbs expressing a need (example 8). By such statements the addressee is indirectly asked to do something for the speaker.

(7) nor-iu   arbat-os
    want-PRS.1SG   tea-GEN.SG
    'I want some tea.'

(8) reik-ia   knyg-os
    need-PRS.3   book-GEN.SG
    'I need a book.'

In polite requests, two main politeness markers – the verb *prašyti* 'please' and the interjection *prašom* 'please' – can be added to the imperative, infinitive or a verbless expression (examples 9 and 10).

(9) ei-k   praš-au
    go-IMP.2SG   please-PRS.1SG
    'Go, please.'

(10) prašom   duo-ti
     please   give-INF
     'Give (me something), please.'

Other indirect forms of request include hortatives, which are the speaker's suggestions to perform some action together with the addressee. These have also been called non-canonical imperatives and are to be distinguished from canonical addressee-oriented ones (Aikhenvald 2010: 47). In Lithuanian, they can either be expressed by a verb in the first person plural present tense (example 11) or the first person plural imperative (example 12).

(11) ein-ame
     go-PRS.1PL
     'Let's go.'

(12) ei-k-ime
     go-IMP-1PL
     'Let's go.'

Hortatives may also be rendered by interrogatives, a mitigating device (e.g., *ein-ame?* (go-PRS.1PL) 'let's go'). Such hortatives are similar to other indirect requests conveyed by questions. These may either be speaker-oriented modal constructions asking for permission (example 13), hearer-oriented constructions asking for a favor (example 14), or questions about the addressee's future action, also serving as requests for a favor (example 15). They may contain one of the particles *gal* or *ar*.

(13) *(gal)   gal-iu   paragau-ti?*
    (maybe) can-PRS.1SG taste-INF
    'Can I taste (it)?'

(14) *(ar)   gal-i   paduo-ti   drusk-os?*
    (whether) can-PRS.2SG give-INF   salt-GEN.SG
    'Can you give me some salt?'

(15) *(ar)   duo-s-i?*
    whether give-FUT-2SG
    'Will you give me?'

Statements of speakers' likes and states of mind may also function as indirect requests. Thus, when a speaker mentions that he is cold this may indirectly ask the hearer to close the window.

Finally, caretakers may stop children's undesirable actions by using *negalima* 'not allowed' or warnings. Expressions with *negalima* function as statements of social rules (example 16). In our data, warnings are expressed by conditional clauses (example 17) and are similar to indirect prohibitions in so far as the speaker in both cases tries to prevent the addressee from carrying out some undesirable action.

(16) *ne-gali-m-a   taip dary-ti.*
    NEG-allow-PTCP-N   like do-INF
    'It is not allowed to act like this.'

(17) *jeigu taip   elg-s-iesi,   ne-duo-s-iu   saldain-io.*
    if   like.that act-FUT-2SG.REFL   NEG-give-FUT-1SG   candy-GEN.SG
    'If you act like this, I won't give you a candy.'

3 Data

The present investigation is based on the longitudinal data of two Lithuanian children, a girl Monika and a boy Elvijus, who were recorded in various everyday situations (e.g., playing, book reading, eating) interacting mostly with their mothers[3] at home. Both subjects are first-born children from middle-class families living in Lithuania. During the observation period, both the boy and the girl lived in Kaunas, the second largest city of Lithuania. The parents of both children hold university degrees and speak standard Lithuanian. Data collection for the girl started at age 1;8 and continued up to 2;8. The boy was observed from 1;6 through 2;7, except for a two-month break (from 2;5 to 2;6). Both children were recorded three or four times per week, each recording lasting about fifteen minutes. The corpus consists of about 20 hours of Elvijus' recordings and 27 hours of Monika's (see Tables 2 and 3 below). The data have been transcribed and coded using the CHAT conventions of CHILDES (MacWhinney 2000). The transcripts were coded for morphological analysis and double-checked. Adult utterances were transcribed orthographically. Contextual notes were inserted where necessary, every request was coded according to its linguistic properties and the context in which it occurs.

Table 2: Number of utterances and number and percentage of requests in Elvijus' CS and CDS.

Age	Elvijus			Elvijus' mother		
	No. of utterances	No. of requests	% of requests	No. of utterances	No. of requests	% of requests
1;6	1,073	97	9.04	1,288	235	18.25
1;7	1,247	106	8.50	1,650	244	14.79
1;8	1,589	109	6.86	1,231	209	16.98
1;9	2,089	108	5.17	1,383	162	11.71
1;10	2,010	115	5.72	1,410	172	12.20
1;11	1,370	124	9.05	1,374	156	11.35
2;0	1,726	119	6.89	1,331	169	12.70
2;1	1,138	128	11.25	895	98	10.95
2;2	912	103	11.29	867	98	11.30
2;3	1,403	102	7.27	831	86	10.35
2;4	1,000	91	9.10	856	94	10.98
2;7	782	72	9.21	458	37	8.08
Total	16,339	1,274	7.80	13,574	1,760	12.97

---

[3] Since the fathers appeared rarely in the recordings, most CDS data discussed in this paper only cover the mothers' speech.

Table 3: Number of utterances and number and percentage of requests in Monika's CS and CDS.

Age	Monika			Monika's mother		
	No. of utterances	No. of requests	% of requests	No. of utterances	No. of requests	% of requests
1;8	1,372	66	4.81	2,428	379	15.61
1;9	1,677	89	5.31	2,858	389	13.61
1;10	1,268	110	8.68	2,563	325	12.68
1;11	1,307	119	9.10	3,472	403	11.61
2;0	705	67	9.50	1,696	222	13.09
2;1	1,242	195	15.70	3,497	350	10.01
2;2	663	100	15.08	719	88	12.24
2;3	1,061	163	15.36	2,743	290	10.57
2;4	684	114	16.67	1,516	154	10.16
2;5	2,167	234	10.80	3,205	281	8.77
2;6	1,247	82	6.58	2,084	162	7.77
2;7	1,044	79	7.57	1,776	140	7.88
2;8	1,001	109	10.89	1,550	119	7.68
Total	15,438	1,527	9.89	30,107	3,302	10.97

4 The development of requests in Lithuanian

In this section the frequency and type of requests occurring in Lithuanian CS and CDS will be analyzed and compared to each other (see Tables 2 and 3).

A comparison of Tables 2 and 3 shows that the total percentage of requests used by both mothers is similar, although the boy's mother used them a little bit more frequently than the girl's (12.97% vs. 10.97%). There is no noteworthy difference of the total percentages of requests used by the two children either, since the amount of requests occurring in the boy's speech is only about 2.0% below that of the girl's (7.80% vs. 9.89%).

As is to be expected, the overall frequency of requests in CS differs more from CDS in the beginning of the observation period (until 2;1) than toward its end. The mothers' general tendency to use more requests in the early period than later on may be explained by the children's lack of an as yet adequate linguistic competence leading the mothers to frequently try to challenge them to perform some action or express themselves verbally.

From 2;1 onwards, i.e. during the last five months of recordings, the boy and his mother reveal a comparable frequency of the important functional category of requests, namely about 10%. The girl's path towards adult-like usage differs from the boy's as it incorporates a four-month period (2;1–2;4) marked by a higher frequency of requests in CS than CDS. In the last period (2;5–2;8), both corpora are again similar containing approximately 8% of requests.

4.1 Direct requests in CS and CDS

At the beginning of the recordings, the children's requests mostly consisted of one-word utterances containing a noun referring to the desired object, an adverb asking for more of some food or drink (examples 18 and 19) or other forms functioning as commands (imperatives, infinitive and future tense forms).

(18) Boy, 1;6
 da [= *dar*].[4]
 more
 '(Give me / I want) more.'

(19) Girl, 1;8
 kamboji [= *kamuol-ys*].
       ball-NOM.SG
 '(I want a) ball.'

Single nouns may be considered as elliptical requests with the verb omitted. At the beginning of the recordings, just a few nouns were used with this function, e.g., *lėlė*[5]'doll', *puš* (the child's invented word for a pen), *čičė* (the child's invented word for a baby's dummy), *arbata* 'tea', and *pasaka* 'fairy-tale'. While these nouns were mostly used in the nominative, they also sometimes occurred in the genitive or accusative. In standard Lithuanian, such constructions consist of a verb in the imperative and the object noun in the genitive or accusative.

In addition to verbless requests, both children used single verbs in the imperative without an argument in their first recordings (examples 20 and 21).

(20) Boy, 1;6
 guk [= *gul-k*].
     lie.down-IMP.2SG
 'Lie down.'

---

4 Standard forms indicated in square brackets.
5 A dot above a vowel marks length.

(21) Girl, 1;8
 ei-k.
 go-IMP.2SG
 'Go.'

The early acquisition of imperatives can on the one hand be explained by their simple form and important communicative function and on the other by the fact that they represent the most common form of requests in CDS (see below).

Another form of requests first found in the boy's speech at 1;6 and in the girl's at 1;9 are bare infinitives (examples 22 and 23). They serve as elliptical constructions with a verb of desire or noun omitted but predictable from the situational context.

(22) Boy, 1;6
 geti [= *ger-ti*].
   drink-INF
 'drink.'

(23) Girl, 1;9
 nelieši [= *ne-lies-ti*].
   NEG-touch-INF
 'Not to touch.'

Both children started to construct infinitives with an argument one month after their emergence (examples 24 and 25).

(24) Boy, 1;7
 deč [= *duo-ti*] *mašinis* [= *mašin-ą*].
   give-INF   car-ACC.SG
 'Give (me) a car.'

(25) Girl, 1;10
 mamu [= *mam-ą*]   *ei-ti.*
   mom-ACC.SG   go-INF
 'Go to mom.'

Although both children started to use the second person future tense for expressing direct requests already by 1;9, the girl made use of such forms more frequently than the boy (they constituted 0.3% vs. 3.1%, respectively) (examples 26 and 27). This may be explained by the frequency of second person singular future tense forms occurring in the children's CDS. The girl's mother used this form somewhat more frequently than the boy's (average frequency: 5% and 3% of all utterances, respectively). However, it mostly functioned as a question for information rather than a request.

(26) Girl, 1;9
 duoši [= *duo-s-i*]*!*
   give-FUT-2SG
 'You will give (me something)!'

(27) Boy, 1;9
 dosi [= *duo-s-i*].
   give-FUT-2SG
 'You will give (me something)!'

Besides positive requests for action, the children also employed negative requests expressing prohibitions. These were expressed by an imperative constructed with the negative prefix *ne-* (examples 28 and 29).

(28) Boy, 1;8
 neik [= *ne-ei-k*].
   NEG-go-IMP.2SG
 'Don't go.'

(29) Girl, 1;10
 ne-im-k.
   NEG-take-IMP.2SG
 'Don't take (it).'

The use of the linguistic expressions described so far underwent certain distributional changes in the course of the children's development. Until the end of the second year, nouns and infinitives were numerous in the boy's speech while future tense forms almost did not occur. During the same period, the girl's speech was marked by higher numbers of future tense forms and nouns, but not of infinitives. In the first half of the third year, all of these one-word requests decreased rather drastically in the speech of both children. This can be explained by the fact that the development of linguistic competence allows children to express more specific requests by verbalizing the extralinguistic situation to a greater extent. Thus, in the course of development, elliptical requests consisting of a noun denoting a desired object were replaced by a noun constructed with a verb.

As shown in Tables 4 and 5, the frequency of second person singular imperatives increased in both children's speech from 2;1 on, with one-word requests decreasing.

Table 4: The frequency distribution of linguistic expressions of commands in Elvijus' and his mother's speech.

Age	Commands									
	Imperative 2SG		Adverb		Noun		Infinitive		Future tense	
	Elv	Mot	Elv	Mot	Elv	Mot	Elv	Mot	Elv	Mot
1;6	19	167	5	0	45	0	18	0	0	0
1;7	12	189	17	0	58	0	11	0	0	0
1;8	18	159	4	0	53	0	24	0	0	0
1;9	26	125	5	6	18	0	41	0	2	0
1;10	24	151	4	3	10	0	39	0	0	0
1;11	11	122	0	4	9	0	15	0	0	0
2;0	25	127	0	3	13	0	3	0	0	0
2;1	63	73	1	4	6	0	10	0	2	0
2;2	51	85	0	0	5	0	0	0	0	0
2;3	85	74	0	0	1	0	0	0	0	0
2;4	52	78	0	0	5	0	1	0	0	0
2;7	58	35	0	0	0	0	0	0	0	0
Total	444	1,385	36	20	223	0	162	0	4	0

In the CDS of both children commands were mainly expressed by imperatives, a few adverbs and some occasional future tenses or infinitives (the latter only in the girl's CDS), while mere nouns were completely absent. In the CDS of both children second person singular imperatives dominated by far: In Elvijus' CDS they made up nearly 79% of all requests (N = 1,385; total 1,760) and in Monika's CDS they amounted to 84% (N = 2,777; total 3,302).

Although our analysis mainly focuses on mother–child interactions (the fathers' data comprise only 92 requests produced by Elvijus' father and 122 by Monika's), it is interesting to compare the types of requests made by each parent. The dominant pattern in both the fathers' and mothers' CDS is the use of second person singular imperatives. However, there is a greater difference between the two fathers than between the two mothers in this respect. While the boy's and the girl's mothers use 79% and 84% of imperatives in their CDS,

Table 5: The frequency distribution of linguistic expressions of commands in Monika's and her mother's speech.

Age	Imperative 2SG		Adverb		Noun		Infinitive		Future tense	
	Mo	Mot	Mo	Mot	Mo	Mot	Mo	Mot	Mo	Mot
1;8	25	320	8	3	33	3	0	1	0	0
1;9	43	335	5	5	23	0	4	0	13	1
1;10	37	281	6	3	12	0	3	0	13	0
1;11	26	330	2	1	15	0	3	1	15	0
2;0	13	180	0	1	2	0	3	0	3	0
2;1	124	297	0	4	3	0	13	1	1	0
2;2	75	78	0	0	0	0	0	0	0	0
2;3	121	238	1	1	19	0	0	0	0	1
2;4	89	129	0	0	0	0	0	0	0	0
2;5	185	240	0	0	4	0	0	0	2	0
2;6	61	133	0	5	0	0	0	0	1	1
2;7	68	112	0	1	0	0	0	0	0	0
2;8	64	104	0	1	0	0	0	0	0	0
Total	931	2,777	22	25	111	3	26	3	48	3

respectively, such forms of request amount to only 64% (N = 59; total 92) in the CDS of the boy's father but to 84% (N = 102; total 122) in that of the girl's. Compared to the boy's input, the girl's input by both parents contains more commands expressed by imperatives. It can be assumed that the more frequent usage of second person singular imperatives in the girl's speech than the boy's (61% and 35%, respectively) reflects the distribution in CDS. Consequently, our data do not lend support to the hypothesis defended by Gleason (1975) and others (Endendijk et al. 2016) that boys are exposed to more directives in the form of imperatives than girls. Since our analysis is based on the data from just two children, no far-reaching conclusions can, however, be drawn from our results. As shown above (section 1), there are findings from other languages that agree with ours. Possibly our findings can be linked to more general parenting styles prevailing in the two families, with the boy's family conceding more freedom to their child than the girl's.

To summarize, the development of the children's linguistic repertoire is characterized by the gradual change from a number of one-word utterances (nouns, adverbs, infinitives or future tense forms), which function as elliptical expressions of requests, to the dominant usage of mainly second person singular imperative forms sometimes constructed with nouns or adverbs. However, second person singular imperatives were observed from the beginning of the observation and altogether were the most frequent expressions of requests in the speech of both children. Since direct requests expressed by the imperative were also most frequent in CDS, the children's language slowly moved toward the adults' in this respect.

4.2 Indirect requests in CS and CDS

The subtypes of indirect requests can be characterized according to the complexity of their grammatical structure. While it is in principle possible to express a wish or need for a desired object or a suggestion for common action by one-word utterances, indirect requests containing modal markers or conditional clauses are grammatically more complex. The first example of an indirect request expressing a desire was observed very early in the boy's speech, at 1;6 (example 30).

(30) Boy, 1;6
    no [= *nor-iu*].
        want-PRS.1SG
    'I want (something).'

The girl started producing expressions of desire three months later than the boy. In the beginning, she used the verb *reikėti* 'need' (example 31) and one month later the verb *norėti* 'want' (example 32). While the girl constructed these verbs with an object noun from the very beginning, the boy used only one-word utterances up to 1;11 when 'want' statements increased and the construction was enriched by including a desired object or action.

(31) Girl, 1;9
    čič-ę   *jeika* [= *reik-ia*]. (*čičė* – the child's invented word)
    baby.dummy-ACC.SG   need-PRS.3
    'I need a baby dummy.'

(32) Girl, 1;10
    agienę [= *uogien-ę*] *noji* [= *nor-i*].
        jam-ACC.SG   want-PRS.2SG
    'I want the jam.'

Although both *want* and *need* serve to express the speaker's wishes, 'need' expressions occur much less frequently than 'want' expressions in the children's speech (see Table 6).[6] As far as 'want' statements are concerned, both children started to use them more frequently at 1;10–1;11. However, a rather stable tendency of using 'want' statements was only observed in the girl's speech while the boy produced noticeably fewer of them (19.6% vs. 6.4% of all requests, respectively).

Table 6: Frequency of wish statements expressed through the verbs *norėti* 'want' and *reikėti* 'need' in CS and CDS.[7]

Age	Speaker's wishes							
	norėti 'want'				*reikėti* 'need'			
	Elv	Mot	Mo	Mot	Elv	Mot	Mo	Mot
1;6	1	0	–	–	0	1	–	–
1;7	0	0	–	–	0	1	–	–
1;8	2	0	0	0	0	0	0	8
1;9	1	0	0	1	0	2	1	11
1;10	5	0	22	1	0	0	13	3
1;11	30	1	44	2	0	3	12	6
2;0	13	1	34	3	4	3	2	2
2;1	10	1	46	0	1	0	1	3
2;2	15	0	21	0	2	0	2	0
2;3	1	2	16	1	0	2	0	2
2;4	2	0	25	0	1	1	0	2
2;5	–	–	38	1	–	–	2	5
2;6	–	–	13	1	–	–	1	0
2;7	1	0	7	1	0	0	0	3
2;8	–	–	33	1	–	–	5	1
Total	81	5	299	12	8	13	39	46

In contrast to the children's speech, indirect requests expressed by wishes are not a typical feature of mothers' interactions with their children (see Table 6). However, mothers frequently use the verb *norėti* 'want' not in requests but in

---

[6] The numbers of the verb *norėti* 'want' in Table 6 differ from those provided in Table 7 since Table 6 only includes indirect requests while Table 7 displays all instances of the 1st and 2nd person singular.
[7] Cells with a hyphen indicate periods without recordings.

questions with a second person form enquiring about the addressee's needs or desires (example 33).

(33) Girl's mother, 1;8
   Monik-a,   nor-i   ger-ti?
   Monika-VOC.SG want-PRS.2SG drink-INF
   'Monika, do you want to drink?'

While acquiring expressions of desire, both children were exposed to different forms and functions (a request expressed with a first person form or a question about the child's needs expressed with a second person) of the verb *norėti* 'want' (see Table 7).

Table 7: The distribution of 1st and 2nd person singular forms of the verb *norėti* 'want' in CS and CDS.

Age	*norėti* 'want' PRS.2SG				*norėti* 'want' PRS.1SG			
	Elv	Mot	Mo	Mot	Elv	Mot	Mo	Mot
1;6	7	54	–	–	0	0	–	–
1;7	0	65	–	–	0	0	–	–
1;8	7	56	0	43	0	0	0	0
1;9	5	28	0	36	1	0	1	2
1;10	11	22	35	42	0	0	2	3
1;11	26	44	62	90	21	4	1	4
2;0	5	15	49	49	10	2	2	5
2;1	2	24	87	74	15	0	13	6
2;2	5	19	21	17	25	1	15	1
2;3	21	18	32	59	16	2	24	8
2;4	8	22	9	26	20	0	32	2
2;5	–	–	11	57	–	–	66	6
2;6	–	–	4	21	–	–	28	4
2;7	7	4	2	23	2	0	42	10
2;8	–	–	7	6	–	–	51	8
Total	104	371	319	543	110	9	277	59

When talking about their needs, both children used the first and the second person singular present forms rather frequently for expressing their desires while the second person singular was used more often than the first person by the mothers in addressing their children (see Table 7). With the second person singular form the children frequently referred not to their mothers, but to themselves. By stating their desires in such a way, they indirectly asked their mothers to do something for them. Additionally, the boy, but not the girl, sometimes expressed his desires in the subjunctive, a mitigating device marking a request as more polite (examples 34 and 35).

(34) Boy, 1;11
 nojėčiau [=norė-čia-u] ugienės [=uogien-ės].
     want-SBJV-1SG   jam-GEN.SG
 'I would like / want some jam.'

(35) Boy, 2;1
 nojėčiau [= norė-čia-u] taukinuko [= traukin-uk-o] as [= aš].
     want-SBJV-1SG   train-DIM-GEN.SG   I
 'I would like / want a train.'

In addition to expressions of desire, the children's speech also contained a number of other subtypes of indirect requests. The emergence and distribution of all indirect requests is presented in Tables 8 and 9.

Table 8: The distribution of indirect requests in the boy's speech.

Age	Indirect requests					
	Speaker's wishes	Polite requests	Hortatives	Questions	Hints	Prohibitions
1;6	1	0	9	0	0	0
1;7	0	0	7	0	0	0
1;8	2	0	8	0	0	0
1;9	1	0	11	0	1	0
1;10	5	1	20	0	0	0
1;11	30	0	49	2	0	0
2;0	17	0	45	0	5	0
2;1	11	0	17	4	0	0
2;2	17	0	23	2	0	1
2;3	1	1	8	2	1	0
2;4	3	1	20	2	0	0
2;7	1	0	8	2	1	0
Total	89	3	225	14	8	1

Table 9: The distribution of indirect requests in the girl's speech.

Age	Indirect requests					
	Speaker's wishes	Polite requests	Hortatives	Questions	Hints	Prohibitions
1;8	0	0	0	0	0	0
1;9	1	0	0	0	0	0
1;10	35	1	0	1	0	0
1;11	56	0	0	0	2	0
2;0	36	0	5	0	2	0
2;1	47	2	4	0	0	0
2;2	23	0	1	1	0	0
2;3	16	0	6	0	0	0
2;4	25	0	0	0	0	0
2;5	40	0	2	1	0	0
2;6	14	0	5	1	0	0
2;7	7	0	4	0	0	0
2;8	38	0	3	4	0	0
Total	338	3	30	8	4	0

Polite requests emerged at 1;10 in the speech of both children. The politeness formula *prašom* 'please' (example 36) emerged several months earlier than the verb *prašyti* 'please' (examples 37 and 38). Although both children always used the politeness formulas without being prompted to do so by their caretakers, it goes without saying that they were encouraged to add a politeness formula to their requests from early on. There are some examples in our data where the mothers ask the children to say 'please' or 'thank you', but the children do not always react positively to such prompts.

(36) Boy, 1;10
 p(r)ašom   sės-ti-s.
 please   sit-INF-REFL
 'Sit down, please.'

(37) Boy, 2;3
 im-k,   p(r)aš-au.
 take-IMP.2SG please-PRS.1SG
 'Take (it), please.'

(38) Girl, 2;1
 p(r)aš-au   palaiky-ti.
 please-PRS.1SG hold-INF
 'Hold (it), please.'

In spite of the formal simplicity of constructions containing a politeness marker they were rarely used not only in CS but also in CDS. This supports Hilbig's (2009: 207) findings that Lithuanians do not use formal politeness markers frequently in a familiar environment.

Indirect requests expressed by hortatives emerged earlier and were more frequent in the boy's speech than the girl's (examples 39 and 40, see Tables 8 and 9). In the first recordings of the boy, hortatives were observed alongside statements of desire, while the first indirect requests occurring in the girl's recordings were limited to statements of desire, with hortatives only emerging at 2;0.

(39) Boy, 1;6
 aname [= ein-ame].
    go-PRS.1PL
 'Let's go.'

(40) Girl, 2;0
 ei-k-ime   skin-ti.
 go-IMP-1PL   pick-INF
 'Let's go to pick up (something).'

While the boy preferred the first person plural present tense (examples 39 and 41), the girl used the first person plural imperative of hortatives (examples 40 and 42).[8] Whereas hortatives in the first person plural present tense constituted 95% of the 225 tokens of hortatives occurring in the boy's speech, 67% of the 30 tokens of hortatives found in the girl's data were in the first person plural imperative. The difference between the two children may be explained by the fact that the boy's mother favored hortatives in the first person plural present tense (88% of all hortatives, N = 251). In contrast to this, the girl's mother used fewer hortatives overall and both of their forms occurred with about the same frequency (first person plural imperative 53% and first person plural present forms 47%, N = 186). The greater number of hortatives occurring in the mother–boy

---

8 The difference between these forms is discussed in section 2.1.

than the mother–girl dyad may be taken to display a more cooperative style of communication in the former dyad as compared to the latter.

Hortatives do not only include declarative sentences, but also interrogative structures with the modal particle *gal* (examples 41 and 42).

(41) Boy, 2;4
    gal   į   muziej-ų   var-ome,   tėv-el-i?
    maybe to museum-ACC.SG go-PRS.1PL dad-DIM-VOC.SG
    'Maybe let's go to a museum, daddy?'

(42) Girl, 2;8
    gal   paukšč-iuk-us   dė-k-ime?
    maybe bird-DIM-ACC.PL put-IMP-1PL
    'Maybe let's put birds?' (talking about a puzzle)

Although the modal particle *gal* is often used in interrogative requests, it may serve as a mitigating device in declarative ones (examples 43 and 44). The cognitive verb *manyti* 'think' conveying epistemic meaning may be used for the same purpose (see example 43). Mitigation devices emerge at 1;11 and suggest that some progress has been made in formulating socially adequate requests.

(43) Boy, 2;4
    man-au,   gal   kel-iamės,   mam-a.
    think-PRS.1SG maybe get.up-PRS.1PL mom-VOC.SG
    'I think, maybe let's get up, mom.'

(44) Boy, 1;11
    gal   muzik-os   įjung-iame.
    maybe music-GEN.SG turn.on-PRS.1PL
    'Maybe, let's turn on music.'

Another type of indirect requests are questions asking the addressee for permission or a favor or inquiring about his future actions. Both children produced very few such questions (see Tables 8 and 9), the first of which concerned an addressee's future action. Some of them included question particles (example 45 vs. 46). The form without the modal particle *gal* 'maybe' is similar to commands expressed by future tense clauses (see examples 26 and 27 above).

(45) Boy, 1;11
    ga (l)   nulup-s-i?
    maybe peel-FUT-2SG
    'Maybe, you will peel (it)?'

(46) Girl, 1;10
    duo-s-i?
    give-FUT-2SG
    'Will you give me (something)?'

Indirect requests may also take the form of questions with the modal verb *galėti* 'can, could'. By using these questions, the children either asked for permission to carry out a certain action themselves (examples 47 and 48) or urged their mothers to do something for them (example 49). The requests expressed in the subjunctive (examples 48 and 49) demonstrate a higher degree of politeness.

(47) Boy, 2;1
    gal-iu   pajagauti [= paragau-ti]?
    can-PRS.1SG   taste-INF
    'Can I taste (it)?'

(48) Boy, 2;7
    gal   galėčiau [= galė-čia-u] nu-si-skin-ti?
    maybe   can-SBJV-1SG   PREF-REFL-pick-INF
    'Maybe I could pick (it)?'

(49) Girl 2;6
    galė-tum   atvež-ti šokolad-o?
    can-SBJV.2SG bring-INF chocolate-GEN.SG
    'Could you bring some chocolate?'

Another group of indirect requests serves to inquire about the addressee's willingness to comply with the request (examples 50 and 51).

(50) Girl, 2;2
    gal   noji [= nor-i]   čia   eit-i?
    maybe   want-PRS.2SG here go-INF
    'Would you like to come here?'

(51) Boy, 2;1
    gal   noji [= *nor-i*]   *palenktyniau-ti* *su* *man-imi?*
    maybe   want-PRS.2SG race-INF   with me-INS
    'Would you like to race around with me?'

A less frequently used subtype of indirect requests in CS are hints (see Tables 8 and 9), which can be defined as an indirect strategy "that realize the request by either partial reference to object [sic] or element needed for the implementation of the act [. . .], or by reliance on contextual clues" (Blum-Kulka and Olshtain 1984: 201). The children used hints to draw their caretaker's attention to an uncomfortable situation (examples 52 and 53).

(52) Boy, 1;9
    kak-uč-ių   *padajei* [= *padar-ei*].
    poop-DIM-GEN.PL   make-PST.2SG
    '(I) made a poop.' (wanting his mother to change the diaper)

(53) Girl, 1;11
    kak-ų   *tuli* [= *tur-i*].
    poop-GEN.PL   have-PRS.2SG
    '(I) have a poop.'

Almost all children's statements of this type covered situations related to diaper changing. In a few other situations the children stated their inability to perform some action or their discomfort indirectly asking the addressee for help (examples 54 and 55).

(54) Girl, 1;11
    ne-mok-u   *adajyti* [= *adajyti*].
    NEG-know-PRS.1SG   open-INF
    'I do not know how to open (it).'

(55) Boy, 2;0
    man *sata* [= *šalt-a*].
    I.DAT   cold-N
    'I am cold.' (wanting to get dressed)

A few hints were only found in the girl's CDS, asking the child to change her behavior (examples 56 and 57).

(56) Girl's mother, 1;8
 man ne-patink-a, kad tu čia laipioj-i.
 I.DAT NEG-like-PRS.3SG that you here climb-PRS.2SG
 'I don't like your climbing up here.'

(57) Girl's mother, 2;1
 Monik-a, šaltok-a, saky-č-iau.
 Monika-VOC.SG cold-N say-SBJV-1SG
 'Monika, I would say it is cold in here.' (asking the child to get dressed)

Indirect prohibitions stating social rules and containing the form *negalima* 'not allowed' were rare in the CDS of both children. The statement of social rules in order to prevent or stop children's undesirable actions can be taken as a way of familiarizing them with acceptable behavior (example 58).

(58) Boy's mother, 1;9
 ne-graž-u taip ne-gali-m-a.
 NEG-nice-N like NEG-allow-PTCP-N
 'It is not nice (to act like this), it is not allowed.'

Warnings which are used to stop children's misbehavior or inappropriate activities are another type of indirect requests, but unlike hints they are expressed by complex sentences containing a conditional clause (example 59). Warnings were rare in the CDS of both mothers and neither of the children used any of them. This is not only due to their complex construction but also to the fact that the social status of young children forbids them to give such advice to their mothers.

(59) Girl's mother, 2;7
 jeigu taip dary-s-i, paim-s-iu viską ir nebe-gau-s-i.
 if like do-FUT-2SG take-FUT-1SG all and NEG-get-FUT-2SG
 'If you act like this, I will take all of this and you won't get it.'

To sum up, children began to formulate indirect requests with simple one-word utterances expressing wishes or suggestions. About the age of 2;0 more elaborate indirect requests utilizing mitigating devices such as question intonation, modal particles and conditional mood were observed.

4.3 The acquisition of direct versus indirect requests

The majority of requests occurring in CS as well as CDS during the entire observation period were direct ones (see Tables 10 and 11).

Table 10: The distribution of direct and indirect requests in Elvijus' and his mother's speech.

Age	Elvijus		Elvijus' mother	
	Direct	Indirect	Direct	Indirect
1;6	87 (90%)	10 (10%)	167 (71%)	68 (29%)
1;7	99 (93%)	7 (7%)	189 (77%)	55 (23%)
1;8	99 (91%)	10 (9%)	159 (76%)	50 (24%)
1;9	95 (88%)	13 (12%)	131 (81%)	31 (19%)
1;10	89 (77%)	26 (23%)	154 (90%)	18 (10%)
1;11	43 (35%)	81 (65%)	126 (81%)	30 (19%)
2;0	52 (44%)	67 (56%)	130 (77%)	39 (23%)
2;1	96 (75%)	32 (25%)	77 (79%)	21 (21%)
2;2	60 (58%)	43 (42%)	85 (87%)	13 (13%)
2;3	89 (87%)	13 (13%)	74 (86%)	12 (14%)
2;4	65 (71%)	26 (29%)	78 (83%)	16 (17%)
2;7	60 (83%)	12 (17%)	35 (95%)	2 (5%)
Total	934 (73%)	340 (27%)	1,405 (80%)	355 (20%)
Total Requests	1,274 (100%)		1,760 (100%)	

Although the boy used both direct and indirect requests from the beginning of the observation, the number of indirect requests only increased considerably from 1;10 to 2;2. Indirect requests even outnumbered direct ones from 1;11 to 2;0 since wishes and suggestions in the hortative became frequent (see Tables 6 and 8). From age 1;10 until 2;7, these types of indirect requests dominated and the boy used even more indirect requests than his mother. Overall, the most frequent subtypes of requests occurring in Elvijus' speech were commands (73%), followed by hortatives (18%) and speaker's wishes (7%). Other subtypes (prohibitions, polite requests, questions, hints) were very scarce. The boy's mother mainly produced commands (80%) and hortatives (14%) so that direct requests were more numerous in her speech than the boy's. As opposed to this, the child formulated more statements of desire and hortatives than his mother.

Indirect requests emerged later than direct ones in the girl's speech, with a delay of four months as compared to the boy (at 1;10 in the girl but 1;6 in the boy). Starting from 1;10, the girl's speech was marked by a higher proportion of indirect requests than her mother's (with the exception of ages 2;3 and 2;7) (see

Table 11: The distribution of direct and indirect requests in Monika's and her mother's speech.

Age	Monika		Monika's mother	
	Direct	Indirect	Direct	Indirect
1;8	66 (100%)	0 (0%)	327 (86%)	52 (14%)
1;9	88 (99%)	1 (1%)	341 (88%)	48 (12%)
1;10	73 (66%)	37 (34%)	284 (87%)	41 (13%)
1;11	61 (51%)	58 (49%)	332 (82%)	71 (18%)
2;0	24 (36%)	43 (64%)	181 (82%)	41 (18%)
2;1	142 (73%)	53 (27%)	302 (86%)	48 (14%)
2;2	75 (75%)	25 (25%)	78 (89%)	10 (11%)
2;3	141 (87%)	22 (13%)	240 (83%)	50 (17%)
2;4	89 (78%)	25 (22%)	129 (84%)	25 (16%)
2;5	191 (82%)	43 (18%)	240 (85%)	41 (15%)
2;6	62 (76%)	20 (24%)	139 (86%)	23 (14%)
2;7	68 (86%)	11 (14%)	113 (81%)	27 (19%)
2;8	64 (59%)	45 (41%)	105 (88%)	14 (12%)
Total	1,144 (75%)	383 (25%)	2,811 (85%)	491 (15%)
Total Requests	1,527 (100%)		3,302 (100%)	

Table 11). This is due to the fact that the girl frequently expressed indirect requests by stating her desires.

The most common subtype of requests in the girl's speech were commands (75%) followed by wishes (22%). In contrast to this, her mother preferred commands (85%) and used only a small percentage of other subtypes (hortatives 5.6%, questions 4.1%, other subtypes < 2%).

A difference between parenting strategies in the two families concerns a considerable use of hortatives by the boy's mother in contrast to the girl's. This difference is reflected in the children's speech. There is no substantial difference in the use of direct and indirect requests in the two mother–boy and mother–girl dyads. While indirect requests amount to 27% and 25% in the boy's and the girl's speech, respectively, the values for their mothers are 20% vs. 15%.

Although it may seem surprising at first glance that both children used relatively more indirect requests than their mothers, this can be explained by the fact that most of these requests occurring in the children's speech were grammatically simple constructions expressing wishes with the verb for 'want' or suggestions with hortatives.

5 Conclusion

The principal aims of the present study have been to compare the early development of directive speech acts in two Lithuanian children of different gender and furthermore investigate the relationship between CS and CDS. The children started to formulate early direct requests as one-word utterances consisting of nouns, adverbs, infinitives or second person singular imperatives. Since in Lithuanian imperatives are the most typical expressions of requests used for addressing intimates (Čepaitienė 2007), they frequently occur in CDS. Given their functional importance and formal simplicity (Wójcik 2000), they are already found in the first recordings of the boy (1;6) as well as the girl (1;8). That imperatives are among the first verb forms to be acquired by young children has also been confirmed for Finnish (Laalo 2003), Spanish (Aguirre 2003), Croatian (Katičić 2003), Russian (Gagarina 2003), and Greek (Stephany 1985, 1997; Christofidou and Stephany 2003).

As far as our original hypothesis of gender-related differences in mothers' socializing patterns or parenting styles is concerned, this has not been substantiated by our results. Since a comparison of the mother–boy and the mother–girl dyad was the main focus of our study, we will nevertheless present a brief summary of the similarities and differences between the two dyads.

We have found that direct requests occur much more frequently than indirect ones in CS and CDS in both dyads (see Tables 10 and 11 in section 4.3). The most frequent form of direct requests in both dyads were commands, which, however, occurred three times more often in CDS than CS. In contrast to what had been expected, the girl's mother produced more direct requests than the boy's so that a higher number of indirect requests was found in the boy's CDS than in the girl's. Thus, the hypothesis that boys are exposed to more direct requests in the form of imperatives, whereas girls are addressed by more indirect forms, has not been confirmed. There is, however, another finding which is in line with the gender approach hypothesis, namely that diminutives are more dominant in the girl's and her mother's data than in the mother–boy dyad (Dabašinskienė 2012).

Although we found an interesting difference in the usage of indirect requests in the two mother–child dyads, this does not, however, seem to be related to gender but rather to a more cooperative style of communication to be observed in the mother–boy interactions than in the mother–girl dyad. Hortatives occur more frequently in the boy's CDS than in the girl's and so also in the boy's speech as compared to the girl's. In contrast to this, expressions of desire were found more often in the girl's and her mother's speech than in the mother–boy dyad. The girl's mother very frequently asked her daughter about her desires (in more than

500 instances; see Table 7) and the girl reacted by expressing them. The girl's mother thus used a strongly socially oriented style of communication towards her daughter. Other types of indirect requests besides hortatives and statements of desire were found less frequently in both dyads (Tables 8 and 9).

To conclude, we must admit that the available data do not provide evidence for a distinct socialization of boys and girls as far as the expression of requests is concerned, at least not at this early age. It can be assumed that integral parts of socialization such as communication style and attitudes to politeness are mechanisms by which boys as well as girls learn to make requests for action in socially acceptable ways. Possible gender differences concerning the expression of requests may well affect socialization beyond age three, i.e. after the period studied in the present paper. More polite formal means for indirect requests are generally more complex grammatically and are therefore acquired later by children of either gender. If parents fine-tune their speech to the children's linguistic competence, grammatically more complex indirect requests will appear in CDS when the child is older than three.

Our results suggest that the children's age plays a more important role in their socialization than gender. Mothers first try to communicate effectively with their offspring, whereas familiarizing them with social norms ranks second. Psychological research shows that children develop a clear sense of their own gender only around the age of three (Maccoby 1998) and that they develop separate social cultures and, consequently, different "verbal cultures" (Tannen 1999) due to their preference of same-sex groups, something which is often observed in institutional settings (kindergartens, schools, etc.). Future research on Lithuanian children older than three years of age is needed to clarify whether or when gender effects, including the use of different types of requests, come into play.

References

Aguirre, Carmen. 2003. Early verb development in one Spanish-speaking child. In Dagmar Bittner, Wolfgang U. Dressler & Marianne Kilani-Schoch (eds.), *Development of verb inflection in first language acquisition: A cross-linguistic perspective* (Studies on Language Acquisition 21), 1–25. Berlin & New York: Mouton de Gruyter.
Aikhenvald, Alexandra Y. 2010. *Imperatives and commands.* Oxford: Oxford University Press.
Balčiūnienė, Ingrida. 2009. *Pokalbio struktūros analizė kalbos įsisavinimo požiūriu* [Analysis of conversational structure from the perspective of language acquisition]. Kaunas, Lithuania: Vytautas Magnus University dissertation.
Behrens, Heike. 2006. The input–output relationship in first language acquisition. *Language and Cognitive Processes* 21 (1/2/3). 2–24.

Bellinger, David C. & Jean Berko Gleason. 1982. Sex differences in parental directives to young children. *Sex Roles* 8(11). 1123–1139.

Blum-Kulka, Shoshana & Elite Olshtain. 1984. Requests and apologies: A cross-cultural study of speech act realization patterns (CCSARP). *Applied Linguistics* 5(3). 196–213.

Brown, Penelope & Stephen C. Levinson. 1987. *Politeness: Some universals in language usage.* Cambridge: Cambridge University Press.

Cherry, Louise & Michael Lewis. 1976. Mothers and two-year-olds: A study of sex-differentiated aspects of verbal interaction. *Developmental Psychology* 12(4). 278–282.

Christofidou, Anastasia & Ursula Stephany. 2003. Early phases in the development of Greek verb inflection. In Dagmar Bittner, Wolfgang U. Dressler & Marianne Kilani-Schoch (eds.), *Development of verb inflection in first language acquisition: A cross-linguistic perspective* (Studies on Language Acquisition 21), 89–129. Berlin & New York: Mouton de Gruyter.

Clark, Eve V. 2004. Pragmatics and language acquisition. In Laurence R. Horn & Gregory Ward (eds.), *The handbook of pragmatics*, 562–577.Oxford: Blackwell Publishing.

Čepaitienė, Giedrė. 2007. *Lietuvių kalbos etiketas: semantika ir pragmatika* [The Lithuanian language etiquette: Semantics and pragmatics]. Šiauliai: Šiauliai University Press.

Dabašinskienė, Ineta. 2009. An easy way to language acquisition: Diminutives in Lithuanian child language. *Ad verba Liberorum: Linguistics & Pedagogy & Psychology* 1. 11–22.

Dabašinskienė, Ineta. 2012. Gender differences in language acquisition: A case study of Lithuanian diminutives. *Journal of Baltic Studies* 43(2). 177–196.

Endendijk, Joyce J., Marleen G. Groeneveld, Marian J. Bakermans-Kranenburg & Judi Mesman. 2016. Gender-differentiated parenting revisited: Meta-analysis reveals very few differences in parental control of boys and girls. *Plos One* 11(7). 1–33.

Ervin-Tripp, Susan M. 1977. Wait for me, roller-skate. In Susan M. Ervin-Tripp & Claudia Mitchell-Kernan (eds.), *Child discourse. Language, thought, and culture: Advances in the study of cognition*, 165–188. New York: Academic Press.

Gagarina, Natalia. 2003. The early development and demarcation of stages in three Russian-speaking children. In Dagmar Bittner, Wolfgang U. Dressler & Marianne Kilani-Schoch (eds.), *Development of verb inflection in first language acquisition: A cross-linguistic perspective* (Studies on Language Acquisition 21), 131–169. Berlin & New York: Mouton de Gruyter.

Gleason, Jean Berko. 1975. Fathers and other strangers: Men's speech to young children. In Daniel P. Dato (ed.), *Developmental psycholinguistics: Theory and applications*, 289–297. Washington: Georgetown University Press.

Gordon, David & Susan Ervin-Tripp. 1984. The structure of children's requests. In Richard L. Schiefelbusch & Joanne Pickar (eds.), *The acquisition of communicative competence*, 295–321. Baltimore & Maryland: University Park Press.

Grice, Herbert Paul. 1975. Logic and conversation. In Steven Davis (ed.), *Pragmatics: A reader*, 305–315. New York: Oxford University Press.

Haas, Adelaide. 1979. Male and female spoken language differences: Stereotypes and evidence. *Psychological Bulletin* 86(3). 616–626.

Hilbig, Inga. 2009. *Lietuvių ir anglų lingvistinis mandagumas: prašymai* [Lithuanian and English linguistic politeness: Requests]. Vilnius, Lithuania: Vilnius university dissertation.

Hilbig, Inga. 2010. *Lietuvių ir anglų lingvistinis mandagumas: prašymai* [Lithuanian and English linguistic politeness: Requests]. Vilnius: Vilnius University Press.

Holmes, Heather A. 1997. *Preschool children's collaborative problem-solving interactions: Influence of task, partner gender, and conversational style.* Poster presented at the Biennial Meeting of the Society for Research in Child Development, Washington, DC.

Holmes, Janet. 1995. *Women, men and politeness.* London: Longman.

Karmiloff, Kyra & Annette Karmiloff-Smith. 2002. *Pathways to language: From fetus to adolescent.* Cambridge, MA: Harvard University Press.

Katičić, Antigone. 2003. Early verb development in one Croatian-speaking child. In Dagmar Bittner, Wolfgang U. Dressler & Marianne Kilani-Schoch (eds.), *Development of verb inflection in first language acquisition: A cross-linguistic perspective* (Studies on Language Acquisition 21), 239–267. Berlin & New York: Mouton de Gruyter.

Kavaliauskaitė, Viktorija. 2016. Prašymų raiškos įsisavinimas lietuvių vaikų kalboje [The acquisition of requests in the speech of Lithuanian children]. *Taikomoji kalbotyra* 8. 160–187.

Kempe, Vera, Patricia J. Brooks & Laura Pirott. 2001. How can child-directed speech facilitate the acquisition of morphology? In Margareta Almgren, Andoni Barrena, Maria-Jose Ezeizabarrena, Itziar Idiazabal & Brian MacWhinney (eds.), *Research on child language acquisition: Proceedings of the 8th conference of the International Association for the Study of Child Language,* 1237–1247. Medford, MA: Cascadilla Press.

Kučinskaitė, Antanė. 1990. *Lietuvių kalbos etiketas* [The Lithuanian language etiquette]. Vilnius: Mokslas.

Laalo, Klaus. 2003. Early verb development in Finnish: A preliminary approach to miniparadigms. In Dagmar Bittner, Wolfgang U.Dressler & Marianne Kilani-Schoch (eds.), *Development of verb inflection in first language acquisition: A cross-linguistic perspective* (Studies on Language Acquisition 21), 323–350. Berlin & New York: Mouton de Gruyter.

Ladegaard, Hans J. 2004. Politeness in young children's speech: Context, peer group influence and pragmatic competence. *Journal of Pragmatics* 36. 2003–2022.

Ladegaard, Hans J. & Dorthe Bleses. 2003. Gender differences in young children's speech: The acquisition of sociolinguistic competence. *International Journal of Applied Linguistics* 13. 222–233.

Lakoff, Robin. 1973. Language and woman's place. *Language in Society* 2(1). 45–79.

Leaper, Campbell. 1991. Influence and involvement in children's discourse: Age, gender, and partner effects. *Child Development* 62. 797–811.

Leaper, Campbell, Kristin J. Anderson & Priscilla Sanders. 1998. Moderators of gender effects on parents' talk to their children: A meta-analysis. *Development Psychology* 34(1). 3–27.

Lithuanian Grammar. 1997. Vilnius: Baltos lankos.

Lytton, Hugh & David M. Romney. 1991. Parents' differential socialization of boys and girls: A meta-analysis. *Psychological Bulletin* 109(2). 267–296.

Maccoby, Eleonor E. 1998. *The two sexes: Growing up apart, coming together.* Cambridge, MA: Harvard University Press.

MacWhinney, Brian. 2000. *The CHILDES project. Tools for analyzing talk.* Mahwah, NJ: Lawrence Erlbaum Associates.

Miller, Patrice M., Dorothy L. Danaher & David Forbes. 1986. Sex-related strategies for coping with interpersonal conflict in children aged five and seven. *Developmental Psychology* 22 (4). 543–548.

Nakamura, Keiko. 2001. The acquisition of polite language by Japanese children. In Keith E. Nelson, Ayhan Aksu-Koç & Carolyn E. Johnson (eds.), *Children's language 10:*

Developing narrative and discourse competence, 93–112. Mahwah, NJ: Lawrence Erlbaum Associates.
Ninio, Anat & Catherine E. Snow. 1996. *Pragmatic development: Essays in developmental science*. Oxford: Westview Press.
Pajusalu, Renate, Maret Kaska, Birute Klaas-Lang, Karl Pajusalu, Anu Treikelder & Virve-Anneli Vihman. 2017. Characteristics of request formulation in Estonian, Finnish, French, Lithuanian and Russian. *Language Typology and Universals* 70(3). 455–488.
Ryckebusch, Céline & Haydée Marcos. 2004. Speech acts, social context and parent–toddler play between the ages of 1;5 and 2;3. *Journal of Pragmatics* 36. 883–897.
Savickienė [Dabašinskienė], Ineta. 1997. Komunikacija ir pokalbis ankstyvoje vaikystėje [Communication and conversation in early childhood]. *Darbai ir dienos* 5(14). 45–51.
Sheldon, Amy. 1990. Pickle fights: Gendered talk in preschool disputes. *Discourse Processes* 13. 5–31.
Snow, Catherine E. & Charles A. Ferguson (eds.). 1977. *Talking to children: Language input and acquisition*. Cambridge: Cambridge University Press.
Stephany, Ursula. 1985. *Aspekt, Tempus und Modalität: Zur Entwicklung der Verbalgrammatik in der neugriechischen Kindersprache* (Language Universals Series 4). Tübingen: Gunter Narr.
Stephany, Ursula. 1997. The acquisition of Greek. In Dan I. Slobin (ed.), *The crosslinguistic study of language acquisition*, vol. 4, 183–333. Mahwah, NJ: Lawrence Erlbaum.
Šukys, Jonas. 2003. *Kalbos kultūra visiems* [The language culture for all]. Kaunas: Šviesa.
Tannen, Deborah. 1990. *You just don't understand: Women and men in conversation*. New York: William Morrow.
Tannen, Deborah. 1999. *The argument culture: Stopping America's war of words*. New York: Ballantine Books.
Tomasello, Michael. 2003. *Constructing a language: A usage-based theory of language acquisition*. Cambridge, MA: Harvard University Press.
Wójcik, Paweł. 2000. *The acquisition of Lithuanian verb morphology: A case study*. Warsaw: Universitas.

Maria D. Voeikova and Kira Bayda
Development of directive expressions in Russian adult–child communication

Abstract: The paper focuses on the development of language tools used to express directive meanings in Russian L1 acquisition based on the recordings of the spontaneous speech of two Russian children, a boy (1;6–2;8 years) and a girl (1;6–3;7 years). The acquisition of directives in Russian begins with imperative or infinitive forms. Singular imperative forms (e.g. *Daj!* 'give.IMP.2SG') are dominant during the whole period of observation in both adults and children. From the beginning of the third year of life children start to use the hortative and its frequency steadily increases both in child-directed speech and child speech. Periphrastic constructions with the imperative particle *davaj* (*Davaj spojom!* 'Let's sing!'), modal adverbs (*Nado poigrat'!* 'It is necessary to play') and elliptic constructions occur later in Russian child speech. Indirect requests expressed by hortatives and constructions with modal verbs and particles are deeply influenced by child-directed speech and therefore develop at a different pace in the speech of the two subjects. However, as far as the repertoire of verb forms used in directive utterances is concerned, children are selective in the choice of imperative lemmas and do not simply repeat the forms used by their parents.

1 Introduction

Requesting and informing are basic communicative motives (Tomasello 2008: 84–86) and manifest themselves in the early development of a distinction between modal and non-modal verb forms (Halliday 1975; Stephany 1986; for Russian see Poupynin 1996). According to Halliday such utterances found in young children's speech represent "the use of language to control the behaviour of others, to manipulate the persons in the environment – the 'do as I tell you' function" (Halliday [1973] 2003: 306). Children express requests as well as statements as soon as they start to utter verbs. However, there are individual differences in the choice of grammatical forms of early requests.

Maria D. Voeikova, Russian Academy of Sciences and Saint Petersburg State University
Kira Bayda, Russian Academy of Sciences at Saint Petersburg

In the beginning, the distinction between modalized and non-modalized utterances is not always clear and according to Cameron-Faulkner (2014: 43–44) the function of about 60% of children's early utterances is not easily interpretable (see also Stephany 1993: 136). They may either be mere indications of objects or actions of interest or else requests for desired objects or parental care. By directives the speaker attempts "to get the hearer to perform some action" (Nikolaeva 2016: 73).

The most frequent type of directives, namely requests, are "defined linguistically as a class of grammatical constructions, including imperative, interrogative and declarative request forms" (Drew and Couper-Kuhlen 2014: 8). "While orders imply telling someone else what to do, requests involve asking someone to do something, with an option for the addressee not to comply (though the assumption often is that they will)" (Aikhenvald 2016: 147). Requests for objects or actions are basic in the communication of both apes and human beings (Tomasello 2003: 11, 37, 2008: 84–87) and appear early in the acquisition of any language (Aikhenvald 2010: 326–330; Bates 1976; Bruner 1975; Ervin-Tripp 1976, 1977; Ivanova and Voeikova 2014; Stephany and Voeikova 2015). In Russian, as in many languages, the most common way of expressing requests is the imperative. Indirect forms of directives are hortatives and jussives as well as questions, constructions with modal verbs, modal adverbs, and adjectives (see Section 2).

The literature on the acquisition of directives in Russian is not very extensive. It was initiated by Gvozdev's famous study ([1949] 2007) on the language development of his son Ženja based on his commented diary notes "From the first words to the first grade" (Gvozdev 1981).[1] The original study by Gvozdev (1949) describes important milestones in the acquisition of the Russian lexical and grammatical system from one-word to multiword utterances. In Ženja's speech early requests expressed by the imperative or the infinitive *dat'* 'give. INF' emerged prior to declarative utterances (Gvozdev 1990: 24). Besides verbal forms Ženja also used nouns in the nominative, partitive genitive or accusative to get objects he wanted (e.g. *saxar* 'sugar.NOM/ACC', *blin-a* 'pancake-GEN').

Several researchers point out that young children frequently use verbless utterances consisting of a noun for requesting. Smiley and Huttenlocher ([1995] 2014: 42) found that persons' names in child speech (CS) perform this function even more frequently than object or event words: "When object and event words are used, the object or event is requested; when a person's name is used, the request is for an object or action, to summon the named person, or to make a non-specific request (i.e., to complain)."

---

[1] This is an edition of Gvozdev's diary notes provided by his niece Prof. Dr. E. S. Skoblikova.

Unlike Ženja Gvozdev, Luria's daughter "never uttered the name of the object she wanted" but simply said *dat'* 'give.INF' (Luria 1992: 14; as quoted in Ceitlin 2008: 328). She exclusively used nouns to name things whereas verbs were predominantly uttered to express her desires. These observations demonstrate individual variation in the earliest request forms.

Ceitlin (2008), based on her numerous investigations of child Russian (summarized in Ceitlin 2009), points out that both primary speech functions of requests for objects and naming develop in parallel from early on. As found for two monolingual Russian children by Gagarina (2003: 146–147, Table 6), modal and non-modal verb forms emerge almost simultaneously around the turn to the third year. One of the earliest verb forms used by Russian children is the infinitive, which serves a variety of functions. While some infinitives may denote on-going processes or even past events, their majority has a modal function (Gagarina 2002: 9–10).[2] This agrees with Poupynin's (1996: 89) suggestion that infinitives in CS serve as intermediary forms with a broad set of functions including modal meaning. However, already before 2;0, modal infinitives are often replaced by imperatives so that the remaining infinitives mostly express non-modal meanings substituting for a number of not yet acquired finite verb forms.[3] In her study of Russian language acquisition Ceitlin (2008) stresses the role of situations in which things are exchanged between a child and her caretaker concentrating on requests for giving and taking. This agrees with Gagarina's (2008: 111–114) finding that *dat'* 'to give' is among the first verbs occurring in the early utterances of a number of Russian children.

Focusing on the semantic subclasses of verbs used in the imperative Ivanova and Voeikova (2014) found that young Russian children not only use verbs of giving and taking in the imperative but also prototypical manipulative verbs more generally, such as verbs of constructing and destroying, moving and putting. In contrast to this, their parents frequently use forms for manipulating children's behavior and getting their attention, like *smotri* 'look', *davaj* 'come on'. Such forms do not occur in CS in the earliest phases.

The present paper analyzes the various forms of directives occurring in the speech of two monolingual Russian children (a boy and a girl) until the last part of their third and fourth year, respectively, as well as the child-directed speech (CDS) of their caregivers. The analysis will not be limited to imperatives and infinitives but will include all members of the enlarged imperative paradigm as

---

[2] It should be noted that infinitives referring to ongoing processes or past events are ungrammatical and do not occur in adult speech while the modal meaning is rare.
[3] Infinitives functioning as intermediary forms are called "optional infinitives" by Wexler (1994).

well as indirect requests expressed by constructions with modal adjectives or adverbs among others (see section 2). Special attention will be given to the order of emergence as well as the different functions of these expressions.

Our investigation is carried out in the functionalist framework of the Project of Pre- and Protomorphology in language acquisition (Dressler and Karpf 1995) based on the principles of Natural Morphology (e.g. Dressler et al. 1987; Kilani-Schoch and Dressler 2005: 24). According to the pre- and protomorphology model, the premorphological phase of language acquisition is characterized by the absence of inflectional oppositions while in the protomorphological phase children contrast different inflectional forms of given lemmas so that the number of forms exceeds the one of lemmas (Bittner, Dressler, and Kilani-Schoch 2003: xxxix; Stephany and Voeikova 2009: 4–5; Xanthos et al. 2011). Both of our subjects demonstrate that they are still in the premorphological phase from the beginning of the observation up to 1;7 or 1;8, when the protomophological phase starts. Since the girl was observed beyond three years and data collection for the boy ended at 2;8, a comparison of their development was possible including the protomorphological phase.

The paper is structured as follows: The means of expression of directives in modern spoken Russian are described in section 2. The data and method of analysis are presented in section 3. In the main part of the chapter (section 4) the different types of requests occurring in the speech of both children and their child-directed speech are analyzed. Section 5 contains the conclusions including a comparison of the two subjects.

2 Directives in Russian

Directives constitute a subcategory of deontic modality based on the notion of necessity and express an attempt of the speaker to cause a specific action by the performer, who usually coincides with the addressee (Xrakovskij and Volodin [1986] 2001: 13–18).

As in many other languages, prototypical Russian directives contain a verb in the 2nd person singular or plural imperative.[4] Second person singular

---

[4] The Russian verbal categories include three tenses (past, present and future), two verbal aspects (perfective and imperfective), three moods (indicative, imperative and subjunctive), two voices (active and passive), three persons (first, second and third), two grammatical numbers (singular and plural) and three genders (masculine, feminine and neuter) distinguished in the past tense.

imperatives differ from present or future indicative forms in that they either coincide with the bare stem or carry the suffix –*i*.[5]

According to some typologists the imperative in certain languages forms a paradigm including the first and third person besides the second (Birjulin and Xrakovskij 2001: 18–20, 24–28; Xrakovskij and Volodin 2001: 27–35, 108–131; Gusev 2013: 223–244; Aikhenvald 2010: 49–55).[6] While second person imperatives express direct requests, first person plural imperatives convey hortative meanings and the third person singular and plural expresses jussives. Aikhenvald (2010: 18–65) distinguishes between canonical imperatives of the second person and non-canonical imperatives, counting hortatives and jussives among the latter. The formal reason for attributing an enlarged imperative paradigm to the Russian language is the possibility of combining canonical as well as non-canonical imperatives with the mitigating particle -*ka* (e.g. *polej-ka cvety* (water.IMP.2SG-PTL flowers) 'just water the flowers/do water the flowers'[7]).

The most common type of non-canonical imperatives are hortatives, whose form depends on verbal aspect. First person plural future forms of perfective verbs may express a hortative meaning if used without a subject pronoun (e.g. *spoj-om* (sing-FUT.1PL) 'let's sing'). This form refers to the speaker and one or several addressees. Perfective hortatives consist of the 1st person plural future and are optionally accompanied by the particle *davaj* 'let's' (e.g. *davaj spoj-om* (PTL sing-FUT.1PL) 'let's sing'). Imperfective hortatives are obligatorily formed periphrastically with the particle *davaj* 'let's' followed by the infinitive (*davaj pet'* 'let's sing.IPFV. INF'). This particle can also be marked for plural by the –*te* suffix.[8] All first and second person plural imperative forms carrying the suffix –*te* (including canonical imperatives) are addressed to several recipients (and also function as polite forms) (e.g. 'let's sing': *spoj-om-te* (sing-FUT.1PL-PL), *davaj-te pet'* (let.us-PL

---

5 This depends on whether the finite forms bear stress on the stem or on the ending: Only verbs with final stress in the present or future take an ending in the imperative singular (e.g. /big-í/ 'run-IMP.2SG' vs. /big-ú/ 'run-PRS.1SG', but /s'at'/ 'sit.down.IMP.2SG' vs. /s'ád-u/ 'sit.down-FUT.1SG'). All second person plural imperatives add the suffix -*te* /-ti/ to the singular imperative form (e.g. / s'at'-ti/ 'sit.down-IMP.2PL' and /big-íti/ 'run-IMP.2PL').
6 It is debatable whether first person singular forms expressing intentions and wishes and third person jussives should be considered as parts of the imperative paradigm. While Bondarko and Bulanin (1967) exclude such forms, Birjulin and Xrakovskij (2001:18–20, 24–28) include them for the formal reason that they may be used with the particle -*ka* (which is typical for all imperatives).
7 The meaning of Russian -*ka* is closest to the German particle *mal* 'just'.
8 This particle may be inflected because it is a grammaticalized imperative form.

sing.IPFV.INF)).⁹ The modal particle *davaj* is a grammaticalized imperative form of the imperfective verb *davat'* 'give.INF' serving as a "multifunctional cooperative marker which signals not only proposals for common action [. . .] but also negotiations of planned actions" (Stephany and Voeikova 2015: 6).

The third person directive, the jussive, is formed periphrastically by the modal particle *pust'* or its colloquial form *puskaj* 'let' and the third person present or future indicative (e.g. *pust' on spoj-ot* (let he sing-FUT.3SG) 'let him sing') (Švedova 1980: 622). Similar to other modal particles, *pust'* originates from the imperative of the verb *pustit'* 'to let'. In all periphrastic requests, i.e. jussives and hortatives, the mitigating particle *–ka* is added to the modal particle rather than to the verb (e.g. *pust'-ka on spo-et* (let-PTL he sing-FUT.3SG) 'just let him sing').

In Russian, all directive forms may be negated.¹⁰ While negated imperfective imperatives function as prohibitions concerning controlled actions (example 1a), negated perfective ones are preventives warning a person against performing an undesirable and uncontrollable action (example 1b) (Xrakovskij 1990; Birjulin 2012; Zorikhina-Nilsson 2013).

(1) a. *Ne šum'-i!*
    not make.noise.IPFV-IMP.2SG
    'Don't make noise!'
  b. *Ne upad'-i!*
    not fall.down.PFV-IMP.2SG
    'Mind your step!'

Rathmayr (1994) and Larina (2005: 30–34), basing themselves on the analysis of spontaneous dialogues, found that a majority of Russian requests are expressed in the imperative, which is, however, not impolite due to subtle aspectual and contextual distinctions (Benacchio 2010: 51–54; see also Stephany and Voeikova 2015). A discourse-completion experiment performed with adult subjects has shown that requests of this kind constitute up to 35% of all directive utterances (Ogiermann 2009: 198).

In addition to the enlarged imperative paradigm there are other forms for expressing directives in Russian. The most important of these are lexical means, namely modal verbs, adverbs, and adjectives. Besides, indicative tense forms (present, perfective and imperfective future, perfective past), the subjunctive, and

---

9 Plural hortatives ending in *–te* do not occur in our data because the tape-recorded situations mostly involve only the speaker and one addressee.
10 On the scope of negation in Russian imperatives see Gusev (2003).

the infinitive may carry modal meanings. Modal adverbs and adjectives as well as directive infinitives are of utmost importance in CS and CDS.

Deontic modal meanings are mostly expressed by modal adverbs such as *nado* 'necessarily' (example 2) or adjectives such as *dolžen* 'obliged' (example 3) rather than by modal auxiliaries, which are not numerous in Russian compared to Germanic languages (Kholodilova 2015: 369–370).

(2) *Nado   popit.*
    necessarily drink.INF
    'One should/has to drink.'

(3) *Ty   dolžen pomyt'   ruk-i.*
    you obliged wash.INF hand-ACC.PL
    'You must wash your hands.'

The modal verb *xotet'* 'want' may also be used for indirect requests (example 4).

(4) *Ja xoč-u   popi-t'.*
    I   want-PRS.1SG drink-INF
    'I want to drink.'

Future (or present) tense forms may put strong pressure on the addressee without a possibility of not complying with the request (Švedova 1980: 619–620; Xrakovskij and Volodin 2001: 202–204). In such constructions, the subject pronoun is normally dropped as in example (5),[11] but it is not ungrammatical to keep it.

(5) Filipp, CDS, 1;6
    Deduška-u   potom   popros-iš.
    grandpa-ACC afterwards ask.PFV-FUT.2SG
    '(You) will ask grandfather afterwards (preventing the child from doing this presently).'

In contrast to the constructions just mentioned, interrogative indicative forms, which are mostly in the future perfective and function as indirect requests, do not put pressure on the addressee and are rather frequent in CDS (Xrakovskij and Volodin 2001: 207–210), see example (6).

---

[11] Russian is not strictly a pro-drop language since the subject pronoun is kept in many instances. It is arguable whether its omission has extra semantic or pragmatic value (Nikolaeva 2015).

(6) Filipp, CDS, 2;6
    A   daš   mne   nemnožko kaš-i?
    but give.PFV.FUT.2SG me   some   porridge-GEN
    'And will you give me some porridge?'

Urgent commands may typically be expressed by perfective past tense forms of motion or phasal verbs (e.g. *poš-l-i* (go.PFV-PST-PL) 'we/you/they must go'; *konči-l-i razgovory* (finish.PFV-PST-PL conversations) 'stop talking'). They do not admit any kind of objection. The required action is presented as if it had already started or even been completed. This is why such forms cannot be negated. The pragmatic value of such commands varies from a very insistent and direct style in the speech of a military officer to a rather friendly but highly controlling one in the speech of a teacher.

Commands expressed by the infinitive are mostly limited to special contexts such as the army (e.g. *vsta-t'!* (stand.up-INF) 'stand up!'), the court, manuals and communication with animals. In colloquial Russian they are considered as impolite and are therefore rarely used. They occasionally occur in CDS or in teacher language when several people are addressed.

3 Data and method

The data studied in this paper involve the spontaneous speech of two Russian children growing up in educated middle-class families, a boy Filipp recorded from 1;6 to 2;8 and a girl Liza recorded from 1;6 to 3;7.[12] Since Filipp was only recorded up to 2;8, comparable data of the two children end before 3;0. The recordings were made once or twice a month during typical daily activities and transcribed following the CHAT conventions (MacWhinney 2000). They were morphologically coded by the MORCOMM program (Gagarina, Voeikova, and Gruzintsev 2003) and analyzed using the CLAN programs (MacWhinney 2000).

For the present study, only directive utterances occurring in the speech of the two children and their caretakers were analyzed, with exact repetitions and quoted texts (poems and songs) excluded. These utterances were classified according to their form (imperative, hortative, jussive or constructions with modal verbs, adverbs and adjectives, as well as indirect requests conveyed by future or past tense forms).[13] Pragmatic nuances expressed by politeness particles, formulas

---

12 Liza's language development is described in detail by her mother (Eliseeva 2015).
13 Present tense forms with a modal function do not occur in our data.

occurring in prohibitions, warnings of undesired actions, suggestions or statements of necessary actions have also been taken into account. Tables 1 and 2 show the number and percentage of directive utterances occurring in the speech of the children and their caregivers by monthly intervals.

Table 1: Frequency and percentage of directive utterances in Filipp's CS and CDS.

Age	CS		CDS	
	directives	all utterances	directives	all utterances
1;6	66 (7.9%)	836	274 (19.8%)	1384
1;7	54 (13.6%)	398	326 (35.9%)	909
1;8	81 (8.3%)	977	117 (9%)	1304
1;9	50 (5.6%)	895	98 (8%)	1227
1;10	8 (3.8%)	213	3 (1.1%)	272
1;11	32 (13%)	246	84 (22.4%)	375
2;0	14 (4.1%)	341	25 (5.6%)	448
2;1	15 (2.1%)	728	58 (5.9%)	989
2;2	20 (2.8%)	704	97 (10.9%)	890
2;3	15 (2.6%)	577	22 (2.8%)	787
2;4	23 (3.4%)	673	48 (5.3%)	906
2;5	18 (2.8%)	642	36 (4.6%)	789
2;6	5 (1.5%)	338	76 (14.9%)	510
2;7	24 (4.4%)	547	48 (5.9%)	820
2;8	18 (3%)	601	27 (4.4%)	614

Table 2: Frequency and percentage of directive utterances in Liza's CS and CDS.

Age	CS		CDS	
	Directives	all utterances	directives	all utterances
1;6	13 (8.7%)	149	58 (10.9%)	532
1;7	3 (0.7%)	443	317 (14.6%)	2176
1;8	6 (3.3%)	181	47 (12.5%)	375
1;9	8 (0.6%)	1309	66 (2%)	3337
1;10	16 (3.4%)	476	130 (14.4%)	902
1;11	6 (1.6%)	375	31 (5.5%)	559
2;0	17 (4.5%)	378	55 (10.3%)	535
2;1	10 (3.3%)	299	28 (7.2%)	391
2;2	12 (3.4%)	357	33 (8.5%)	386
2;3	5 (3.8%)	133	16 (9%)	177
2;4	33 (10.3%)	320	76 (14.2%)	535
2;5	17 (5.2%)	329	85 (14%)	608

Table 2 (continued)

Age	CS		CDS	
	Directives	all utterances	directives	all utterances
2;6	33 (11%)	301	151 (17%)	886
2;7	17 (16.2%)	105	28 (16.9%)	166
2;8	17 (8.5%)	199	61 (14.5%)	422
2;9	72 (10.3%)	698	277 (16.2%)	1713
2;10	55 (9%)	613	102 (11.3%)	900
2;11	46 (9.4%)	487	122 (18.7%)	654
3;0	30 (5.1%)	588	107 (12.7%)	844
3;5	2 (1.3%)	149	30 (16.3%)	184
3;7	7 (2.2%)	318	58 (13.2%)	440

Although children started with different percentages of directives in relation to all utterances and to a certain extent followed different developmental paths, the mean rate of directives occurring in their speech is nearly identical, namely 5.3% in Filipp's speech and 5.8% in Liza's. The corresponding rate in their mothers' speech is twice as high, namely 10.4% and 12.4%, respectively. There are peaks of the numbers of directives occurring in the children's speech at different points in time: While Filipp utters a lot of requests in the earliest recordings (from 1;6 to 1;9 and at 1;11), Liza uses most directives in the period from 2;4 to 3;0. With Filipp, the peaks of the number of directives mostly correspond to those of his mother, while with Liza the percentage of directives is relatively small in the first months in spite of the fact that in her CDS the share of directives exceeds 10% from the very beginning. A reason for the rarity of early directives in the girl's speech may be found in the high responsiveness of Liza's mother, who used to ask her daughter about her desires before the child had a chance to make a request. The details of the interaction in the two mother–child dyads with respect to the expression and function of directives will be described in Section 4.

4 Directives in Russian CS and CDS

4.1 Types of directives

In the present section, the types of directives occurring in CS will be compared to those used by the caregivers. Both caregivers make use of a broad set of linguistic means of requesting from the very beginning (Figure 1a–b).

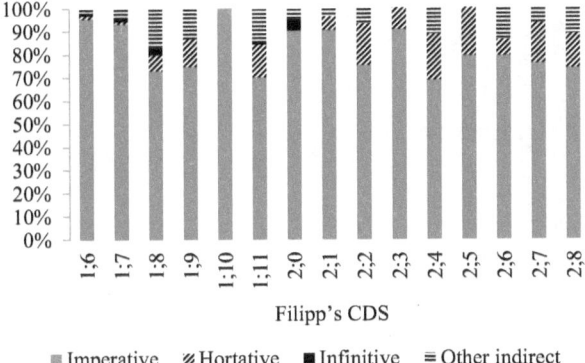

Figure 1a: Percentages of different types of directives relative to the number of all directives in Filipp's CDS.

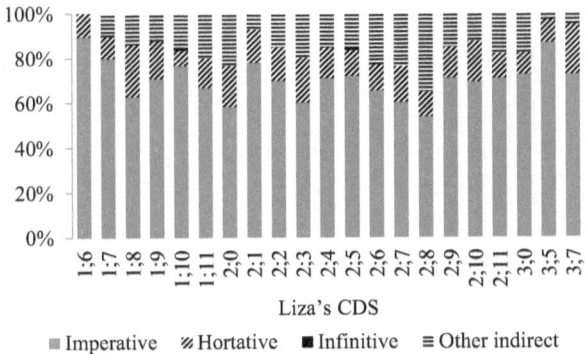

Figure 1b: Percentages of different types of directives relative to the number of all directives in Liza's CDS.

Throughout the observation period more than 50% of requests occurring in CDS are expressed by the imperative. This is especially characteristic of Filipp's mother, whose share of imperatives exceeds 90% in three recordings up to the child's age of 2;3. Liza's mother, whose speech is rich in hortatives besides imperatives from early on, reaches this maximum of imperatives only twice (at 1;6 and 3;5). As compared to imperatives, bare infinitives, which mainly express proposals concerning the child's actions or common actions of mother and child, are extremely rare in Filipp's CDS and there is only a single such token to be found in Liza's input. Both caregivers couch prohibitions in negated imperatives or negative modal adverbs (or adjectives). While Filipp's mother expresses prohibitions quite frequently from early on, Liza's mother does so mostly in

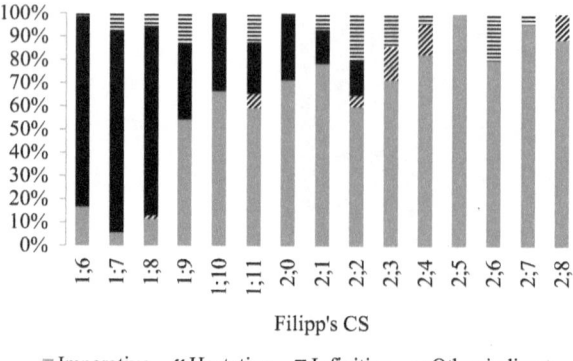

Filipp's CS

■ Imperative　░ Hortative　■ Infinitive　≡ Other indirect

Figure 2a: Percentages of different types of directives in relation to the number of all directives in Filipp's CS.

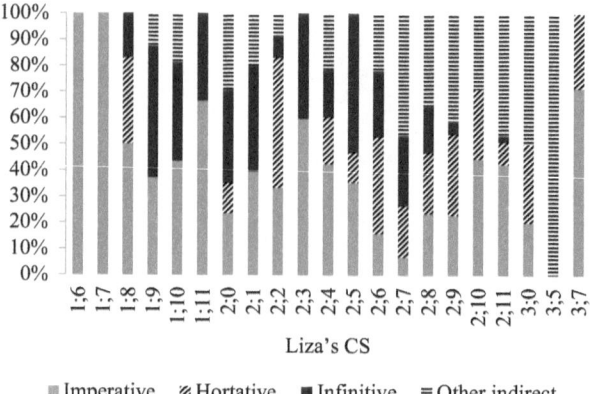

Liza's CS

■ Imperative　░ Hortative　■ Infinitive　≡ Other indirect

Figure 2b: Percentages of different types of directives in relation to the number of all directives in Liza's CS.

later periods. The share of indirect requests expressed by hortatives and modal predicates followed by infinitives is less than 10% in Filipp's mother's CDS, but amounts to 25% in some sessions of Liza's input.

Request types found in CS are presented in Figure 2a–b. The most important difference between the children is that, in the early recordings, Liza starts with 100% of imperatives,[14] whereas Filipp uses up to 80% of infinitives. Another

---

[14] Early infinitives were also registered in the diary notes of Liza's mother (Eliseeva 2015: 131–132). However, these earliest forms were truncated and may therefore be ambiguous. Ceitlin (2008: 323) points out that early directive infinitives are typical for most Russian children.

difference is that although both Liza and Filipp begin to formulate indirect requests at 2;2, their frequency increases during Liza's further development, whereas they almost disappear in Filipp's speech recorded up to 2;8 (for an explanation see section 4.5).

The following subsections are devoted to the description of the different types of directives occurring in CDS and their development in the children's language.

4.2 First modal expressions

First directives already occur during the holophrastic phase when the children's MLU does not yet reach two words per utterance. This period lasts up to 1;8 for Filipp and 1;9 for Liza. During this period, it is not always possible even for mothers to distinguish the children's modal from non-modal utterances, i.e. requesting an object from simply naming it.

In the earliest phase, both children prefer a single verb form, either the imperative or the infinitive, to convey requests and only use one or a small number of verbs for this function. Thus, 95% of Filipp's early requests are infinitives of the verb *dat'* 'give.INF', whereas Liza starts with 100% imperatives of three different verbs: *daj* 'give.IMP.2SG', *otdaj* 'give.back.IMP.2SG' and *sjad* 'sit.down.IMP.2SG'. While, at 1;5, Filipp's first *dat'* instances must rather be attributed to babbling, in the next month his mother reacts to them as if the boy had asked for something (example 7).

(7) Filipp, 1;6
    FIL: *Dat'*   *Malja.*
            give.INF   Malja.NOM
            'Give (me) Malja (the name of the cat).'
    MOT: *Malju*   *dat'?*
            Malja.ACC   give.INF
            'Should I give you Malja?'

Such reactions by his mother will help Filipp to understand that the infinitive *dat'* functions as a request causing some action by the addressee. An example of Liza's early requests expressed by the imperative is given in (8).

(8) Liza, 1;6
    LIZ: *Otdaj!*
            give.back.IMP.2SG
            'Give back!' (looking at the toys on the floor).

MOT: A   kogo   otdat'-to?   Medvežonk-a?
     but who.ACC   give.back.INF-PTL   teddy.bear-ACC
     'And what do you want me to give you back? The teddy bear?'

The first period of observation corresponds to the premorphological phase as also described for Liza by Gagarina (2003: 138). In this phase, children either do not produce morphologically contrasted forms of a given lemma or do not use different forms of a lemma with clearly distinguished functions. This can be seen in the frequency list of verb forms produced by Filipp at 1;7 in (9).

(9) Verb forms produced by Filipp at 1;7
     1   ber-et   take.IPFV-PRS.3SG,
     1   da-m   give.PFV-FUT.1SG,
     1   daj   give.PFV.IMP.2SG,
     47 da-t'   give.PFV-INF,
     3   ode-l   put.on.PFV-PST.MASC.SG

The verb *dat'* 'give' is the only one being used in three different forms. However, the imperative and the future occur only once while the infinitive is the predominant form for making requests. The function of the future form is unclear.

Liza's frequency list of verb forms at 1;8, the last month of the premorphological period, shows that she only uses one form per verb (examples 10[15]).

(10) Verb forms produced by Liza at 1;8
     1   by-l   be.IPFV-PST.MASC.SG,
     1   chisti-t'   clean.IPFV-INF,
     2   kopa-et   dig.IPFV-PRS.3SG,
     1   my-t'   wash.IPFV-INF,
     3   sjad'   sit.down.PFV.IMP.2SG,
     1   slez-t'   get.off.PFV-INF,
     1   sobira-t'   collect.IPFV-INF,
     1   sp-it   sleep.IPFV-PRS.3SG,
     1   upa-li   fall.down.PFV-PST.PL,
     1   zalez-la   climb.up.PFV-PST.FEM.SG

---

[15] The imperative forms of the verbs *dat'* 'give' and *otdat'* 'give back' mentioned above emerge earlier, at 1;6.

Although our subjects never used verbless requests consisting of a noun during the recordings, such utterances were observed by Gvozdev (2007: 162). Examples he quotes are *ešče mak-a* 'more milk-GEN' (Ženja, 1;9), *blin-a* 'pancake-GEN' (Ženja, 1;10). This way of requesting does not directly originate from the input because adults use holophrastic requests consisting of nouns only in special contexts such as the speech of surgeons (e.g. *scalpel, tampon*).

The diversity of verb forms starts to increase at 1;8 in Filipp's speech and at 1;9 in Liza's. Filipp uses 29 verb lemmas in 40 different forms between 1;8 to 1;9 and Liza uses 50 verb lemmas in 102 forms between 1;9 and 1;10. While most of them still occur in a single form, Filipp contrasts different inflected forms of three verbs and Liza of nine of them. This may be considered as the beginning of the protomorphological phase in the children's development of verb morphology. The impact of this development on directives is that they are now expressed not only by either imperatives or infinitives but by both of these categories as well as a new form, namely hortatives.

4.3 Direct requests

4.3.1 Infinitives

As stated in section 4.1, the infinitive is one of the first forms of direct requests used by many Russian children. Bare infinitives are very rarely found in CDS and express elliptical indirect rather than direct requests so that CS is only indirectly influenced by CDS in this respect. Liza's mother uses one directive expressed by the bare infinitive (example 11) and in Filipp's mother's CDS 14 such expressions occur during the entire observation period.

(11) Liza, CDS, 2;5
      Podnja-t'   etogo   lošarik-a.
      pick.up-INF this.ACC ball.horse-ACC
      'Pick up this ball horse (a little horse made of balls).'

Direct orders expressed by infinitives sound very rude in Russian so that parents avoid them and use standard elliptical infinitive constructions. Children pick up their first infinitives from a number of constructions containing an infinitive, namely modal expressions (*nado spat'* 'necessarily sleep.INF), analytical tense forms (*budu spat'* 'shall.FUT.1SG sleep.INF') and elliptical questions such as example (12). In the first months of observation, Liza's mother also uses bare infinitives in questions without a modal verb, adverb or adjective to ask her daughter about her desires. Such sentences are grammatically correct and may also be addressed to adult persons. However, in the first months of observation when children start to use directive infinitives, their share in CDS does not exceed 10%.

(12) Liza, CDS, 1;6
(The mother tries to calm Liza, who is pointing to the table and whining.)
Da-t' tebe popi-t'? Nali-t' popi-t'?
give-INF you.DAT drink-INF pour-INF drink-INF
'Should I give you (something) to drink? Should I pour you (something) to drink?'

Children can sometimes correctly answer such questions as (12) by using the bare infinitive in their response. Such repetitions occur once in Liza's CS and eighteen times in Filipp's. Half of such answers are registered in the premorphological period and are very close to babbling. This may have influenced the choice of the infinitive for expressing directives at this time in Filipp's CS.

Another source of infinitives are modal constructions where the infinitive is preceded by a modal adverb or adjective (example 13).

(13) Filipp, CDS, 1;6
Štany-to nado ode-t'.
pants.ACC-PTL necessarily put.on-INF
'It is necessary to put on the pants.'

Table 3 shows the percentages of different types of infinitive constructions occurring in CDS. Their use remains stable during the entire period of observation. They are most often constructed with verbs of desire such as *xotet'* 'want'

Table 3: The use of infinitives in CDS (percentage relative to all infinitives).

Type of infinitive construction	Liza's CDS	Filipp's CDS
Verbs + INF	431 (41.1%)	253 (38.5%)
Modal adverbs or adjectives + INF	360 (34.3%)	179 (27.3%)
Imperfective future tense: AUX + INF	195 (18.6%)	131 (20%)
Elliptical questions with bare infinitives	62 (5.9%)	79 (12%)
Directive infinitives	1 (0.1%)	14 (2.2%)
Total	1049 (100%)	656 (100%)

or verbs of motion (about 40% in the speech of both mothers). The share of infinitive constructions containing a modal adverb or adjective is close to 30% for both caregivers. Together with the periphrastic imperfective future tense, which amounts to about 20% of directives in the CDS of both mothers, such constructions are the most likely source of directive infinitives in the children's early speech.

As discussed in section 4.2, the infinitive is Filipp's dominant way of expressing directive meaning during the premorphological phase (1;6–1;8), see example (14).

(14) Filipp, 1;6
Dat' tigr-a.
give.PFV.INF tiger-ACC
'Give tiger (asking for a toy).'

In the first month of recordings (1;6) infinitive utterances constitute almost 82% of the boy's requests (mostly formed with the verb *dat'* 'give.INF') while imperatives only amount to about 17% (mostly *daj* 'give.IMP.2SG') (Table 4). From 1;8 to 2;0, the number of verbs used in directive infinitives gradually increases whereas the number of infinitive tokens of each verb declines. However, after the age of 2;2, infinitives disappear in this function and are replaced by standard forms, namely imperatives. Since Filipp replaces infinitives by imperatives quite early, no functional distinction between the two forms can be detected as long as he uses both of them.

In contrast to Filipp, Liza exclusively expresses direct requests by two frozen imperatives (*otdaj* 'give.back.IMP' and *sjad'* 'sit.down.IMP') in the first two months of observation (1;6–1;7) (Table 5). But much as with Filipp, infinitives occur in directives in addition to imperatives during a long period (from 1;8 to 2;11). However, after 1;11, infinitives in her speech start to express indirect requests, namely intentions and suggestions (example 15), so that they are functionally distinguished from imperatives. After 2;9, infinitives with a directive function almost totally disappear from Liza's speech. From 2;4 on indirect requests are expressed by hortatives among other constructions (see sections 4.4 and 4.5).

Infinitive constructions without a modal or future auxiliary such as (15) may be interpreted as elliptical constructions expressing the child's intentions, but they may also express requests. Since the modal component is omitted, such utterances can express a wide range of directives from commands to mere suggestions.

Table 4: Frequency (and percentage) of imperatives and directive bare infinitives relative to all directives in Filipp's CDS and CS.[16]

Age	CDS		CS	
	Imperative	Infinitive	Imperative	Infinitive
1;6	245 (89.4%)	3 (1.1%)	11 (16.7%)	54 (81.8%)
1;7	295 (90.5%)	5 (1.5%)	3 (5.6%)	47 (87%)
1;8	73 (62.4%)	3 (2.6%)	8 (9.9%)	57 (70.4%)
1;9	62 (63.3%)	0	25 (50%)	15 (30%)
1;10	3 (100%)	0	4 (50%)	2 (25%)
1;11	54 (63.3%)	1 (1.2%)	19 (59.4%)	7 (21.9%)
2;0	19 (76%)	1 (4%)	10 (71.4%)	4 (28.6%)
2;1	48 (82.8%)	0	11 (73.3%)	2 (13.3%)
2;2	67 (69.1%)	0	12 (60%)	3 (15%)
2;3	20 (90.9%)	0	10 (66.7%)	0
2;4	31 (64.6%)	0	19 (82.6%)	0
2;5	27 (75%)	0	17 (94.4%)	0
2;6	58 (76.3%)	0	4 (80%)	0
2;7	35 (72.9%)	0	23 (95.8%)	0
2;8	20 (74.1%)	0	16 (88.9%)	0

(15) Liza, 2;0
 (Liza intends to look for a toy herself)
 Iskat' *čerepašonk-a.*
 look.for.INF baby.turtle-ACC
 'Look for a baby turtle.'

Ceitlin (2008: 322) points out that 90% of all early infinitives in CS are suggestions for future joint actions and the remaining 10% express children's own intentions. This also seems to apply to Liza, although we did not check it in detail.

The question is why Russian children, in contrast to their caregivers, use infinitives with modal functions so frequently (see Tables 4 and 5). According to Gagarina (2002: 12–19), one reason may be their placement in a salient final position in CDS,[17] as in examples (12–13). In Liza's CDS, the infinitive is placed in final position in 64% of utterances and in Filipp's CDS this is the case in 56%

---

16 Interrogative infinitives occurring in yes/no questions and asking for information rather than action as in example (12) have been excluded in Tables 4 and 5.
17 Gagarina (2002: 17–18) also holds that the infinitive suffix as such is salient.

Table 5: Frequency (and percentage) of imperatives and directive bare infinitives relative to all directives in Liza's CDS and CS.

Age	CDS		CS	
	Imperative	Infinitive	Imperative	Infinitive
1;6	52 (89.7%)	0	13 (100%)	0
1;7	250 (78.9%)	0	3 (100%)	0
1;8	27 (57.4%)	0	3 (50%)	1 (16.7%)
1;9	46 (67.6%)	0	3 (37.5%)	4 (50%)
1;10	98 (74.8%)	0	7 (43.8%)	6 (37.5%)
1;11	20 (62.5%)	0	4 (66.7%)	2 (33.3%)
2;0	32 (58.2%)	0	4 (23.5%)	6 (35.3%)
2;1	21 (75%)	0	4 (40%)	4 (40%)
2;2	23 (69.7%)	0	4 (33.3%)	1 (8.3%)
2;3	9 (56.3%)	0	3 (60%)	2 (40%)
2;4	51 (66.2%)	0	14 (42.4%)	6 (18.2%)
2;5	61 (71.8%)	1 (1.2%)	6 (35.3%)	9 (52.9%)
2;6	96 (63.6%)	0	5 (15.2%)	8 (24.2%)
2;7	15 (53.6%)	0	1 (5.9%)	4 (23.5%)
2;8	29 (48.3%)	0	4 (23.5%)	3 (17.6%)
2;9	182 (63.4%)	0	14 (18.4%)	3 (4%)
2;10	65 (61.9%)	0	20 (35%)	0
2;11	77 (60.6%)	0	19 (40.4%)	1 (2.1%)
3;0	76 (69.1%)	0	6 (20%)	0
3;5	26 (86.7%)	0	0	0
3;7	42 (72.4%)	0	5 (71.4%)	0

of such utterances. In utterances with *dat'* 'give.INF' this percentage even rises to 64% (49 of 76 instances). The importance of these numbers becomes clear when they are compared to imperative forms occurring in sentence-final position, which merely amount to 3% and 12% of all multiword utterances occurring in Liza's and Filipp's CDS, respectively. Imperatives are in most cases followed by direct objects, other NPs or adverbials that make them less salient for perception as compared to infinitives.

As pointed out above, Liza does not start with infinitives in the earliest phase of development in spite of the fact that her mother frequently asks questions with the verb in the infinitive as in example (12). The reason may be that Liza does not, in general, repeat much after her mother, whereas Filipp demonstrates a more repetitive strategy. According to an analysis with the help of the CHIP program (MacWhinney 2000) Liza only repeats about 7% of her mother's utterances on average completely or in parts, whereas the corresponding value for Filipp is 28% (for details see Voeikova 2015a: 55–57), see (16).

(16) Filipp, 1;11
   MOT: *Razobrat'*   *ix*   *xoč-eš,*   *da?*
         disassemble.INF them want.IPFV-PRS.2SG yes
         'You want to disassemble them, right?'
   CHI: *Razobrat'.*
         disassemble.INF
         'Disassemble.'

As shown above (see examples 7 and 14–16), child-specific requests expressed by the infinitive do not necessarily refer to the addressee as the performer of the desired action. As opposed to this, imperative forms, to which we will turn next, request an action from the addressee.

4.3.2 Imperatives

The imperative constitutes the basic means for expressing the directive function in Russian (see section 2). As shown in Tables 4 and 5, it is the most frequent directive form used in CDS during the whole period of observation, found in 50% and at times even 100% of all caregivers' directives (examples 17 and 18). In example (19) the imperative is mitigated by the particle *–ka*.

(17) Liza, CDS, 2;6
   Liz-ka   *zalez'*   *na*   *brat-a!*
   Liza-DIM climb.IMP.2SG onto brother-ACC
   'Liza, climb onto (your) brother!'

(18) Filipp, CDS, 2;6
   Rasskaž-i,   *čto*   *sluči-l-os'*   *s*
   tell-IMP.2SG what happen-PST-NEUT.SG with
   želt-oj   *šapočk-oj.*
   yellow-FEM.INS cap.DIM-INS
   'Tell what has happened to the little yellow cap.'

(19) Liza, CDS, 1;10
   Liza, *a*   *rasskaž-i-ka*   *čto*   *ja* *dela-ju?*
   Liza and tell-IMP.2SG-PTL what I   do-PRS.1SG
   'Liza, now would you tell me what I am doing?'

Although the imperative is by far the most frequent request form in CDS and also the most frequent form in CS overall, there are certain verbs preferably used in the imperative by the caretakers and others by the children. Imperative forms of verbs such as *skaž-i* 'say-IMP.2SG' or *rasskaž-i* 'tell-IMP.2SG' used by the caretakers aim at stimulating the children's speech production (examples 18–20). In spite of their high frequency in the input, children do not use them but prefer verbs of giving and taking, asking for actions rather than speech.

(20) Filipp, CDS, 1;6
 Skaž-i tigr!
 say-IMP.2SG tiger
 'Say tiger!'

In the children's speech, the use of *daj* 'give.PFV.IMP' and its perfective and imperfective derivatives *otdaj* 'give.back.PFV.IMP.2SG' and *davaj* 'give.IPFV.IMP' for expressing direct requests is most remarkable. As pointed out by Poupynin (1996: 88) and Ceitlin (2008), the verb *dat'* 'give' occurs earlier and more frequently than any other verb in the speech of many Russian children. This can be explained by the fact that many mothers try to involve their children in verbal communication by taking and giving different objects and commenting on this activity. Exchanging things seems to constitute an important early form of communication between adult and child. 'Give'-forms also constitute a large share of Filipp's and Liza's utterances during the first two months of observation (92% of Filipp's and 100% of Liza's verb tokens). In the first month, Liza only uses the frozen imperative form *otdaj!* 'give.back.PFV.IMP.2SG' to express 'give' rather than 'give back' and in the second month both *daj!* 'give!' and *otdaj!* 'give'. Filipp starts with the infinitive *dat'* (give.PFV.INF) 'give!'

Due to the high frequency of the verb *dat'* 'to give', some of its forms (*dat'* INF and *daj* IMP.2SG) assume a particle-like causative function as in example (21), though this is ungrammatical in adult speech (see also Ceitlin 2009: 230).

(21) Filipp, 1;6
 Da-t' otdaj.
 give.PFV-INF give.back.IMP.2SG
 'Make giving back!'

After the decrease of *dat'* 'give' infinitives at 1;9, Filipp starts to use the imperative *daj* 'give.IMP.2SG' (example 22), which remains extremely frequent until the end of the observation period.

(22) Filipp, 1;9
    Mašin-a,   mašin-y   daj.
    car-NOM.SG car-ACC.PL give.IMP.2SG
    'Give (me) the car, cars.'

Other verbs frequently occurring in the imperative in our child data are intransitive verbs of movement or posture like the perfective verbs *pusti* 'let.go.IMP.2SG', *sjad'* 'sit.down.IMP.2SG', *idi* 'go.IMP.2SG', *ložis'* 'lie.down.IMP.2SG' and *vstavaj* 'stand.up/get.up.IMP.2SG' appearing before 2;0. After 2;0 transitive verbs of object manipulation such as *počinit'* 'repair', *vključit'* 'switch on', *položit'* 'put down' are often accompanied by a direct object (example 23).

(23) Filipp, 2;1
    Na,   počin-i   sobak-u.
    take.PTL repair.PFV-IMP.2SG dog-ACC
    'Take and repair the dog.'

The lexical inventories of the two children differ. In Filipp's smaller lexical inventory of the early period from 1;6 to 2;4, verbs of exchange play a greater role than in Liza's more extensive lexicon. In contrast to Filipp, the prototypical imperative *daj* 'give!' that is first registered at 1;7 in Liza's CS is only found next at 2;4. A month later it is followed by its imperfective counterpart *davaj* 'to give' used as an imperative as well as a modal particle in hortatives (see section 4.4). The prefixed verb *otdaj* 'give back' is overused until 1;11 for simply requesting objects rather than reclaiming them. From 2;1 on Liza likes to initiate intellectual activities like reading, telling or playing by *čitaj* 'read.IPFV.IMP.2SG', *rasskaž-i* 'tell.PFV-IMP.2SG' or *igraj* 'play.IPFV.IMP.2SG' (example 24).

(24) Liza, 2;1
    Rasskaž-i-ka   pro   obezjan.
    tell.PFV-IMP.2SG-PTL about monkey.ACC.PL
    'Now tell about monkeys.'

Lexical preferences of the two children for expressing directives are determined by their favorite occupations during the recording sessions and are served by a restricted set of verb forms. Individually preferred frozen initial directive forms (the infinitive for Filipp and the imperative for Liza) later on start to compete with specialized forms for expressing indirect directives, the most frequent of which is the hortative. It is noticeable that neither Liza nor Filipp make mistakes concerning the form of imperatives or infinitives.[18]

4.4 Indirect requests

4.4.1 Hortatives and other constructions with the particle *davaj*

As mentioned in Section 2, the hortative is considered a "non-canonical imperative" addressed to both the addressee and the speaker (Aikhenvald 2010: 47). In child-centered situations, this form of request plays an even greater role than in adult-directed speech, since there are many actions which children cannot perform without an adult's help. Hortatives constitute the second most frequent form of requests after imperatives in our CDS data. They occur from the very beginning either introducing the speaker's own actions (example 25) or trying to initiate joint activities (example 26).

(25) Filipp, CDS, 1;7
 Davaj poprobuem ešče sumočk-e ruck-u pridela-em.
 let try.PFV.FUT.1PL again bag-DAT handle-ACC attach.PFV-1PL
 'Let's try again to attach the handle to your bag.'

(26) Liza, CDS, 1;7
 Tak, davaj lošad-k-u iskat'.
 Well let horse-DIM-ACC look.for.IPFV.INF
 'Well, let's look for the horsey.'

Ninety-five percent of hortative tokens occurring in CDS contain the salient sentence-initial, unchangeable particle *davaj* 'let'. Most of the first hortatives occurring in CDS signal the starting point of a joint activity and do not necessarily require any action by the children, as for instance in situations in which the mother reads to the child from a book. Such hortatives also often introduce routine games. Later on (beginning at 1;9 for both Liza and Filipp), children are expected to react to their mothers' suggestions by starting some routine activity. Although in example (27) Liza's mother is obviously not going to spill water over herself she uses the inclusive hortative not only because the girl is unable to wash herself but to signal that this is a common activity. This routine consists of

---

[18] Some Russian children do make such errors, however (see Ceitlin 2009: 232–244).

a sequence of actions, namely Liza going to the bathroom, taking off her clothes and letting her mother wash her.

(27) Liza, CDS, 2;2
 Liza, davaj oblivat'sja i sobirat' igruški.
 Lisa let spill.over.ourselves.IPFV.INF and collect.IPFV.INF toys
 'Liza, let's spill water over ourselves and collect the toys.'

Due to a special cooperative style of her mother, hortatives are especially frequent in Liza's CDS from early on (Table 6). This may have an impact on the girl's behavior insofar as the first instances of hortative constructions are registered in her speech already at 1;8 and their constant use is observed from 2;2 on. In contrast to Liza, hortatives occur very rarely in Filipp's speech throughout the entire observation period. This may possibly be attributed to the fact that his

Table 6: Frequency (and percentage) of hortatives relative to all directives in Liza's and Filipp's CDS and CS.

Age	Liza		Filipp	
	CDS	CS	CDS	CS
1;6	6 (10.3%)	0	4 (1.5%)	0
1;7	31 (9.8%)	0	3 (0.9%)	0
1;8	10 (21.3%)	2 (33.3%)	7 (6%)	1 (1.2%)
1;9	11 (16.7%)	0	10 (10.2%)	0
1;10	9 (6.9%)	0	0	0
1;11	4 (12.9%)	0	11 (13.1%)	2 (6.3%)
2;0	10 (18.2%)	2 (11.8%)	0	0
2;1	4 (14.3%)	0	3 (5.2%)	0
2;2	5 (15.2%)	6 (50%)	16 (16.5%)	1 (5%)
2;3	3 (18.8%)	0	2 (9.1%)	2 (13.3%)
2;4	10 (13.2%)	6 (18.2%)	9 (18.8%)	3 (13%)
2;5	10 (11.8%)	2 (11.8%)	7 (19.4%)	0
2;6	17 (11.3%)	12 (36.4%)	5 (6.6%)	0
2;7	4 (14.3%)	3 (17.6%)	8 (16.7%)	0
2;8	6 (9.8%)	4 (23.5%)	4 (14.8%)	2 (11.1%)
2;9	36 (12.5%)	19 (25%)		
2;10	17 (9.2%)	12 (22%)		
2;11	12 (16.5%)	4 (8.5%)		
3;0	10 (9.3%)	9 (30%)		
3;5	3 (10%)	0		
3;7	13 (22.4%)	2 (28.6%)		

mother uses hortatives less consistently than Liza's in the first months of observation. They are completely absent in some recordings (e.g. at 1;10 and 2;0), whereas in Liza's CDS their share is about 10% throughout the observation period. Thus, the effect of CDS on the use of hortatives, at least in Liza's case, is clear.

In Filipp's speech hortative constructions such as example (28) only scarcely occur before 2;2. Between 2;2 and 2;8 the boy uses hortatives more rarely than Liza (Table 6).

(28) Filipp, 1;8
Pojd-em   spat'.
go.PFV-FUT.1PL sleep.IPFV.INF
'Let's go to sleep.'

First person perfective future forms, which occur from early on in both children's speech, may either have a modal or a non-modal function. As soon as the children introduce such utterances by the particle *davaj* 'let (lit. give)' they unambiguously assume a hortative meaning. Liza uses such hortatives from 2;2 on and Filipp from 2;4 on (example 29).

(29) Liza, 2;2
Davaj poigraj-em   kresl-o.
Let   play-IMP.1PL armchair-ACC
'Let's play (in/with) an armchair.'

Later on, the children use *davaj* in constructions with the verb in the 1st or 3rd person singular future in order to propose an action to be performed by the child himself or a third person (examples 30 and 31).

(30) Filipp, 2;8
Gav, davaj ja   tebja   zaber-u.
Woof let.PTL I.NOM you.ACC take.PFV-FUT.1SG
'Dog, let me take you.'

(31) Liza, 3;0
Pif   davaj ešče bud-et   skakat'.
Pif.NOM let.PTL again be-FUT.3SG jump.INF
'Let Pif (a dog) jump again.'

Such constructions[19] often occur when the interlocutors plan a game and negotiate the roles of participants in such a scenario with each other. In example (32), Liza wants to take the car from the boy Vanja. When asked by her mother what she wants to do, Liza pretends to be planning to build a house hoping that Vanja will accept and give her the car.

(32) Liza, 2;8
 (looking at Vanja, who is putting sand into his toy car)
 LIZ: *Davaj ja.*
 let.PTL I
 'Let me (do this).'
 MOT: *A čto ty xočeš, Liza?*
 'And what do you want, Liza?'
 LIZ: *Davaj ja postroj-u dom.*
 let.PTL I build.PFV-FUT.1SG house
 'Let me build a house.'

In the course of development, the frequency of the particle *davaj* increases because it can also serve as a positive answer to a proposal. If the addressee agrees with the suggestion (or proposal) he or she may repeat the entire suggestion or just say *davaj* as in (33).

(33) Liza, 2;7
 LIZ: *Davaj na skameečku my sjadem.*
 let.PTL on bench.DIM.ACC we sit.down.PFV.FUT.1PL
 'Let us sit down on the bench.'
 MOT: *Nu davaj.*
 well let.PTL
 'Well, let's (do it).'

Another type of constructions with the particle *davaj* either preceding or following the verb are (mostly imperfective) imperatives that harshly urge the addressee to comply with the request (example 34).

---

[19] Non-hortative use of *davaj* makes up about 8% of all utterances with *davaj* in both adult data sets, whereas the children's data differ in this respect: In Filipp's speech non-hortative *davaj* amounts to 2.8% as compared to 13.3% in Liza's.

(34) Filipp, CDS, 1;8
 Davaj sobirajsja spat'.
 let.PTL prepare.IPFV.IMP.2SG sleep.INF
 'Now prepare yourself for sleep (without delay).'

This function is normally expressed by most demanding imperative forms of the imperfective rather than the perfective aspect (see Padučeva 1996; Benacchio 2010; Stephany and Voeikova 2015: 83; Voeikova 2015b). And indeed, in our data, imperfective imperatives occur in 87% of imperative constructions with *davaj*.

Furthermore, the particle *davaj* is found in elliptical directive constructions with the verb omitted. These are used in everyday activities such as playing games, reading books or daily routines so that the repeated actions do not need to be specified (examples 35 and 36).

(35) Liza, CDS, 2;0
 Davaj pro gus-ja togda.
 let.PTL about goose-ACC then
 'Let's (read) about the goose then.'

(36) Filipp, CDS, 2;6
 Davaj na motocikl.
 let.PTL on motorcycle.ACC
 'Let's (sit down) on the motorcycle.'

Such utterances are not only characteristic of CDS but of spoken Russian more generally. They first appear in Liza's speech at the age of two, simultaneously with non-elliptical hortatives. Thus, at this point she has extended the repertoire of directive constructions to four different types (imperatives, infinitives, hortatives and elliptic utterances with *davaj*). While Liza starts using directive utterances with an omitted verb form quite early, only a single example occurs late in Filipp's speech. One possible reason for this difference is the correspondence between the input and the speech production of children. While almost one third of all utterances with *davaj* used by Liza's mother are verbless (108 of 371), Filipp's mother tends to keep the verb after *davaj* in most cases (156 from 171).

4.4.2 The modal predicate *nado* 'necessarily'

Constructions with the adverb *nado* 'necessarily' and the verb in the infinitive differ from other directives by drawing on an external source of modality. They are used very often by both caregivers from the beginning of observation (examples 37 and 38).

(37) Filipp, CDS, 2;8
   Nado   tut   položit'   pugovic-u.
   necessarily here put.INF button-ACC.SG
   'It's necessary to put the button here.'

(38) Liza, CDS, 3;0
   Vot   eto   nado   rasskazat mam-e.
   here.PTL this necessarily tell.INF   mother-DAT.SG
   'It is necessary to tell mommy this.'

In such directives, speakers refer to habitual practice or social rules, thus distancing themselves from any personal preferences. The frequency of constructions with *nado* 'necessarily' occurring in CDS and CS is presented in Table 7.

Table 7: Frequency (and percentage) of constructions with *nado* 'necessarily' relative to all directives in Liza's and Filipp's CDS and CS.

Age	Liza		Filipp	
	CDS	CS	CDS	CS
1;6	0	0	16 (5.8%)	0
1;7	6 (1.9%)	0	9 (2.8%)	1 (1.9%)
1;8	4 (8.5%)	0	17 (14.5%)	8 (9.9%)
1;9	5 (7.4%)	0	14 (14.3%)	3 (6%)
1;10	6 (4.6%)	0	0	2 (25%)
1;11	2 (6.3%)	0	8 (9.5%)	0
2;0	3 (5.5%)	0	5 (20%)	0
2;1	0	0	5 (8.6%)	1 (6.7%)
2;2	0	0	5 (5.2%)	2 (10%)
2;3	2 (12.5%)	0	0	1 (6.7%)
2;4	4 (5.2%)	4 (12.1%)	3 (6.3%)	0
2;5	4 (4.7%)	0	1 (2.8%)	1 (5.6%)
2;6	7 (4.6%)	5 (15.2%)	4 (5.3%)	1 (20%)
2;7	3 (10.7%)	4 (23.5%)	2 (4.2%)	0
2;8	9 (15%)	0	1 (3.7%)	0
2;9	11 (3.8%)	13 (17.1%)		
2;10	2 (2.4%)	7 (12.3%)		

Table 7 (continued)

Age	Liza		Filipp	
	CDS	CS	CDS	CS
2;11	3 (1.9%)	12 (25.5%)		
3;0	4 (3.6%)	10 (33.3%)		
3;5	0	2 (100%)		
3;7	0	0		

In Liza's speech, constructions with *nado* constitute 11.4% of all directives but only 4.7% in her CDS. While in parental speech this construction mostly refers to an action to be performed by the addressee, Liza often uses it to regulate her own actions, as in example (39).

(39) Liza, 2;6
Telefon   nado   položit'.
phone.ACC   necessarily   put.INF
'It is necessary to put down the phone.'

While utterances with *nado* emerge in Liza's speech only by 2;4, they are found in Filipp's speech already at 1;7 (Table 7). However, the boy prefers to use the negated modal predicate *ne nado* 'not necessarily' for protesting against his mother's commands or actions (example 40).

(40) Filipp, 1;8
MOT: *Kušat'-to   nado,   pokušaeš   i   budeš   igrat.*
       eat.IPFV.INF-PTL   necessarily   eat.PFV.FUT.2SG and   will.FUT.2SG   play
       'But it is necessary to eat and (then) you will play.'
FIL: *Ne   nado!*
       not   necessarily
       'It is not necessary!'

The share of negative vs. affirmative constructions with the modal predicate *nado* differs greatly in the two adult–child dyads (Table 8).

As shown in Table 8, the children tend to copy their parents' strategies. Thus, in Filipp's and his mother's speech *nado* is most often used in negative contexts, expressing prohibitions (almost one third of all directives at 1;6 and 1;8). While Filipp's mother usually indicates which action is necessary or unnecessary, Filipp uses the formula *ne nado* 'not necessarily' without a following infinitive in order to

Table 8: Percentage of negative (prohibitive) and affirmative constructions with the modal predicate *nado* 'necessarily' in Liza's and Filipp's CS and CDS.

Subject	Negative	Affirmative	Total
Liza	19%	81%	68
Liza's MOT	31%	69%	85
Filipp	70%	30%	20
Filipp's MOT	82%	18%	90

avoid an action pressed for by his mother which he does not want to perform (see example 40 above).

In contrast to the dyad of Filipp and his mother, Liza's mother typically uses affirmative constructions with *nado* and so does Liza (see example 39 above). In Liza's CDS, prohibitions reach 12% only at 2;8, but in most recordings their share is less than 4%. Thus, it is not accidental that Liza starts to use negative constructions with *ne nado* only at 2;6. But even at that point they are only rarely found in her conversations with toys. The use of affirmative and negative directives with *nado* 'necessarily' demonstrates different parenting styles of the two caregivers. While Liza's mother exhibits "high guidance" discussing and explaining things to her daughter, Filipp's mother tends to adopt a "high control strategy" using many directives and prohibitions (Taylor, Donovan, Miles, and Leavitt 2009). This shows that parents belonging to the same higher SES may nevertheless use different parenting styles. Liza uses constructions with *ne nado* mostly to regulate the actions of her toys in situations of role play and sometimes to comment on her own actions, recollecting utterances earlier used by her caregivers.

4.4.3 The verb *xotet'* 'want'

The verb of desire *xotet'* 'want' not only expresses desires but may also convey indirect requests (see section 2). It was observed in Liza's data only at 2;11 and rather frequently again at 3;7 (11 instances) when many of the examples appeared in the context of a story in which the girl talked about the desires of different protagonists (example 41).

(41) Liza, 3;7
 Potom miška tože govor-it   im:
 then   bear   also say-PRS.3SG they.DAT
 "Xoč-u   v   mašink-u!"
 want-PRS.1SG into car-ACC
 'Then the bear also tells them: "I want (to get) into the car!"'

While Liza refers to the wishes of other protagonists with this verb, Filipp rather uses *xotet'* 'want' to express his own desires or his unwillingness to do something. Already by 1;11 he declares that he does not want something two to twelve times per recording. Almost half of the forms of *xotet'* are negated and serve to reject some action, as in example (42).

(42) Filipp, 2;4
 Ne xoč-u   ja prygat'   ja
 not want-PRS.1SG I jump.INF I
 xoč-u   ezdit'.
 want-PRS.1SG ride.INF
 'I don't want to jump, I want to go (by vehicle).'

Both children's parents use *xotet'* 'want' frequently in the second person in interrogative sentences inquiring about their children's wishes. Liza's mother also comments on her daughter's or her elder son's desires. Filipp's mother furthermore uses *xotet'* in the affirmative or the negative in a game speaking on behalf of toys as in example (43). The tone in which she utters the example shows that this is an instance of naughty behavior that should not be copied.

(43) Filipp, CDS, 2;4
 Ne xoč-u   bol'she exa-t' na poezd-e,
 not want-PRS.1SG more   go-INF by train-LOC
 xoč-u   na mašin-e!
 want-PRS.1SG by car-LOC
 'I don't want to go by train, I want to go by car!' (speaking in place of a monkey in a whiny tone).

This recording is the only one in Filipp's data in which his mother repeats *xoč-u* 'want-PRS.1SG' 14 times in a game. Otherwise, both children most often hear this verb in the second person singular in questions. Although this is common in the speech of young children generally, in our data the children only rarely use the verb *xotet'* 'want' in affirmative sentences referring to themselves.

4.4.4 Jussives, future forms and questions

Jussives, future forms and questions expressing indirect requests occur even more rarely in our data than constructions with *nado* 'necessarily' or *xotet'* 'want'. The rare use of jussives (see Table 9) can be explained by the fact that they refer to a third participant who is absent in most of the available recording sessions.

Table 9: Frequency (and percentage) of jussives relative to all directives in Liza's and Filipp's CDS and CS.

Age	Liza		Filipp	
	CDS	CS	CDS	CS
1;6	0	0	0	0
1;7	2 (0.6%)	0	0	0
1;8	1 (2.1%)	0	0	0
1;9	3 (4.4%)	0	1 (2%)	0
1;10	1 (0.8%)	0	0	0
1;11	1 (3.1%)	0	0	0
2;0	0	0	0	0
2;1	0	1 (3.6%)	0	0
2;2, 2;3	0	0	0	0
2;4	4 (5.2%)	2 (2.6%)	0	1 (4.3%)
2;5	0	0	0	0
2;6	2 (1.3%)	0	0	0
2;7	0	0	0	0
2;8	2 (3.3%)	1 (1.7%)	0	0
2;9	7 (2.4%)	9 (11.8%)		
2;10	1 (0.9%)	0		
2;11	3 (2.4%)	2 (4.3%)		
3;0	5 (4.5%)	0		
3;5, 3;7	0	0		

In the speech of Liza's mother, there are 32 instances of jussive constructions expressed by the particle *pust'* 'let'. They either urge the addressee to allow a third person to do something (example 44) or let an inanimate object be in some position (example 45).

(44) Liza, CDS, 2;8
    A   pust Van-ja   pomož-et,   Liza.
    but let   Vanja-NOM help-FUT.2SG Liza
    'Liza, let Vanja help (you).'

(45) Liza, CDS, 2;6
    Pust lež-it vot tak.
    let lie-PRS.3SG here this.way
    'Let it lie here this way.'

Liza uses jussives rarely, mostly speaking about inanimate objects, as in example (46).

(46) Liza, 2;8
    Pust' mokr-oe bud-et.
    Let wet-NEUT be-FUT.3SG
    'Let it be wet.'

Filipp and his mother only use one jussive construction each (example 47).

(47) Filipp, 2;4
    Pust' ona sid-it.
    let she.NOM sit-PRS.3SG
    'Let her sit.'

While jussives introduced by the particle *pust'* are concerned with a third person, future forms of the 2nd person singular, which must be distinguished from future forms of the 1st person plural expressing hortatives, occur only very rarely in CDS as well as CS (see Table 10). They may function as proposals (example 48) although in Standard Russian they may also express strong direct requests (e.g., *Ty sejčas že pojdeš spat'* (you.SG immediately PTL go.FUT.2SG sleep.INF) 'you will go to bed immediately'). Proposals expressed by 2nd person singular future forms are registered in Filipp's and Liza's speech only by 2;3 and 2;6, respectively.

(48) Filipp, CDS, 1;8
    Sejčas sup podogre-ju,
    now soup.ACC heat-FUT.1SG
    bud-eš est'.
    be-FUT.2SG eat.INF
    'Now I'll heat the soup and you will eat it.'

Table 10: Frequency (and percentage) of modalized 2nd person future forms relative to all directives in CDS and CS.

Age	Liza		Filipp	
	CDS	CS	CDS	CS
1;6	0	0	1 (1.5%)	0
1;7	5 (1.6%)	0	2 (3.7%)	0
1;8	0	0	4 (4.9%)	0
1;9	1 (1.5%)	0	4 (8%)	0
1;10	7 (5.3%)	0	0	0
1;11	0	0	3 (9.4%)	0
2;0	0	0	0	0
2;1	1 (3.6%)	0	0	0
2;2	1 (3%)	0	1 (5%)	0
2;3	1 (6.3%)	0	0	1 (6.7%)
2;4	0	0	0	0
2;5	2 (2.4%)	0	0	0
2;6	3 (2%)	1 (0.7%)	2 (40%)	0
2;7	0	0	3 (12.5%)	1 (4.2%)
2;8	1 (1.7%)	2 (3.3%)	1 (5.6%)	0
2;9	3 (1%)	0		
2;10	2 (1.9%)	0		
2;11	1 (0.8%)0	0		
3;0	3 (2.7%)	1 (0.9%)		
3;5, 3;7	0	0		

Indirect requests expressed by questions are also rare and occur only in CDS (example 49).

(49) Liza, CDS, 1;7

Lizka,   a   spa-t'   pojd-jom?
Liza.DIM and sleep-INF go-FUT.1PL
'Liza, and now shall we go to sleep?'

Liza's reactions show that she can understand the directive meaning of such interrogatives already at the age of 1;6 (example 50). However, Liza has not started to use such constructions herself by the end of the observation period.

(50) Liza, CDS, 1;6

(Liza's mother has asked Liza to point at a ship in a picture book. Liza says 'ship', but does not show it. After her mother's question she points to it.)

MOT: *a   čto,   palčik-om   ne   mož-eš?*
       but   what   finger-INS   not   can-PRS.2SG
       'Can't you do that with your finger?'

4.5 The role of aspect in positive and negative directives

4.5.1 Politeness

In situations where hierarchical relations between interlocutors are already established (such as between child and parent) direct expression of politeness is less important (Ervin-Tripp 1976: 59–64; Zorikhina-Nilsson 2012: 202). Therefore, it is not to be expected that politeness formulae will be frequent in child–adult communication. Depending on the language and its means for expressing direct and indirect requests, politeness may still begin to play a role quite early in language acquisition. Stephany (1986: 382–383) found that some young Greek children distinguish between direct requests expressed by the imperative and more polite indirect ones expressed by the subjunctive. Thus, a boy of 1;9 used the imperative to address a person considered to be of lower social rank (the interviewer) but the polite subjunctive to address his mother. Although we know of examples of polite indirect requests from child Russian, they do not occur in our recorded material.

Several authors postulate that in Russian affirmative sentences the perfective imperative is more formal and polite than the corresponding imperfective one, whereas in informal situations both aspectual forms are acceptable (see Benacchio 2010; Padučeva 1996; Zorikhina-Nilsson 2012). In our data from very young children interacting with their caregivers at home, both perfective and imperfective imperatives occur in CDS and CS and in most cases they do not differ pragmatically (Voeikova 2015b). Thus, Filipp and his mother use perfective and imperfective verbs in the imperative from the very beginning and in many cases they are used in contrast (Stephany and Voeikova 2015: 79). Unlike Filipp, Liza only utilizes perfective imperative forms during the premorphological phase (from 1;6 to 1;8) and starts to use imperfective verbs in the imperative during the protomorphological phase (starting from 1;9). Liza's mother prefers perfective forms (51a), whereas her grandmother often uses imperfective ones (51b), maybe due to the more old-fashionned demanding style of speaking to children.

(51) Liza, CDS, 2;1
   (a) MOT: *sjad'*   *na divan i*   *rasskaži*
               sit.PFV.IMP.2SG on sofa and tell.PFV.IMP.2SG
               pro   *sorok-u.*
               about   magpie-ACC
               'Sit down on the sofa and tell about the magpie.'
   (b) GRM: *a*   *teper' sadis'*   *i*   *čitaj*
               and   now   sit.IPFV.IMP.2SG and read.IPFV.IMP.2SG
               zajčik-u knižk-u.
               hare-DAT book-ACC
               'And now sit down and read a book to the hare.'

Example (51a) uttered by Liza's mother contains two perfective imperatives and sounds as a first proposal that can be easily declined. In example (51b) Liza's grandmother uses two imperfective imperatives. They sound more demanding, as if both activities had already been discussed earlier and it now was time to start them. In this case there is less opportunity to object. There are only two instances where Liza's mother uses the imperfective imperative in contrast to the perfective one for strengthening a request. The fact that neither of the children's mothers continuously contrasts perfective and imperfective imperatives does not, however, mean that they neglect politeness. Both caregivers constantly admonish their children to use polite formulae, the most important of which is *požalujsta* 'please' (example 52).

(52) Filipp, CDS, 1;6
     A   *gde*   *volšebnoe slovo "požalujsta"?*
     but   where   magic   word   please
     'And where is the magic word "please"?'

Filipp's mother uses polite formulae almost in every recording with an average of 2.5 instances. Before 1;11 she does so mostly for educational purposes, but later on she starts to include *požalujsta* 'please' spontaneously in her directives addressed to Filipp. The boy does not use *požalujsta* 'please' in directive utterances, but only utters this formula in response to his mother's *spasibo* 'thank you'. Liza's mother strives to teach her daughter to express herself politely by using *požalujsta* 'please' in her own directives or by asking the child to use this formula, especially in the first months of observation. In spite of this, Liza only begins to adopt it at 2;0 but usually as a result of some "politeness drill".

    Polite formulae for requests or thanking as well as greetings seem to play a lesser role for Russian adult–child interaction in comparison to English (for English see Lieven, Pine and Dressner-Barnes 1992; for Russian see Voeikova and Čistovič 1994).

4.5.2 Prohibitions and warnings

Prohibitions and warnings are expressed by negated imperatives. The choice between perfective and imperfective verbs under negation is quite different from the affirmative imperatives: While prohibitions (example 53) are formed from imperfective verbs (Birjulin 1994, 2012), perfective verbs are used in warnings (example 54) for preventing undesirable uncontrolled actions (Bogusławsky 1985).

(53) Filipp, CDS, 1;6
 Ne krič-i.
 not shout.IPFV-IMP.2SG
 'Don't shout.'

(54) Liza, CDS, 2;8
 Ne uron-i Vanj-u Liza.
 not drop.PFV-IMP.2SG Vanja-ACC Liza
 'Don't drop Vanja, Liza.'

This pragmatic difference is the same in all Slavic languages (for details see Zorikhina-Nilsson 2013). While warnings such as example (54) are extremely rare in parental speech in CDS, prohibitions are frequent. They may not only be expressed by negated imperfective imperatives but also by constructions with the negated modal predicate *ne nado* 'not necessarily', by *nelzja* 'prohibited' or *xvatit* 'enough' followed by an infinitive. Examples such as (55) are indirect requests often drawing on social rules.

(55) Filipp, CDS, 2;0
 Ne nado obižat' sobačk-u.
 not necessarily offend.IPFV.INF dog.DIM-ACC
 'One shouldn't offend the dog.'

Prohibitions may also be indirectly expressed by asking the child a question in order to restrain him or her from performing some undesirable action (example 56). Such discouraging questions are rather marginal.

(56) Filipp, CDS, 2;2
 Začem ty eto delaj-eš?
 why you this.ACC do.IPFV-PRS.2SG
 'Why are you doing this?'

Prohibitions expressed by negated imperfective imperatives are rare in CS and first occur at 1;11 in Filipp's speech and only at 3;0 in Liza's. An example of the negated perfective imperative (a warning) only appears in one of Liza's recordings as a reaction to her mother's remark.

Figure 3 demonstrates the number of different prohibitions occurring in CS and CDS. In the first months of observation, parents do not ask questions to prevent the children from performing undesired actions but either use direct negated imperfective imperatives or constructions with *nel'zja* 'not allowed' and *ne nado* 'not necessarily'.

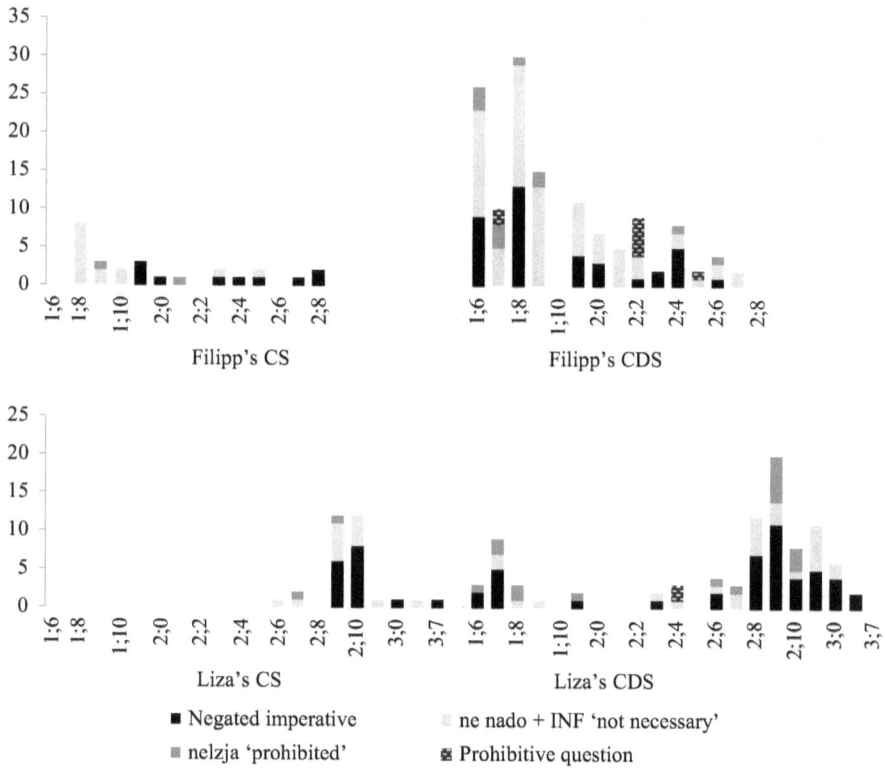

Figure 3: Number of prohibitions in CS and CDS (tokens).

Liza's mother normally uses a very small number (at most five) of prohibitives per recording throughout the observation period. But there is one peak very early (1;6 to 1;8) and another one much later (2;8 to 2;11). Liza does not express any prohibitives until 2;6, although she regularly uses one or two different prohibitive constructions later on. With Filipp's mother, the number of prohibitions decreases from thirty at 1;8 to two at 2;7 and they have even disappeared during the last recording. Filipp starts to use prohibitive constructions at 1;8 with the isolated expression *ne nado* 'not necessarily' used to protest against his mother's actions (like washing and feeding him or changing his clothes) (see section 4.4.2). The use of *ne nado* declines after 1;10 giving place to negated imperatives used to regulate his mother's and his toys' actions (example 57).

(57) Filipp, CS, 2;0
   Ne   trogaj   sobačk-u!
   not   touch.IPFV.IMP.2SG   doggy-ACC
   'Don't touch the doggy!'

Both children avoid warnings and only use prohibitions expressed by negated imperfective imperatives to regulate their parent's actions and protest against any undesired activities. In general, all types of negated imperatives are extremely rare in children's speech and mirror the input frequency: Filipp's CDS contains most negative directives before 1;9 and the peak of negative requests in the boy's speech is located at 1;8. Prohibitions continue to be moderately frequent in Filipp's CS and CDS until 2;4. In Liza's CS prohibitions only emerge at 2;6 and reach their peak at 2;9 after the peak in CDS at 2;8.

5 Conclusions

The objective of this chapter has been to study the development of early directives in the speech of two Russian children comparing their speech to the child-directed speech of their caregivers.

During the first months, both children use elementary forms of requests expressed by either infinitives or imperatives without, however, contrasting these forms functionally and without using them with one and the same verb. This phase in the children's development coincides with the period of premorphology during which contrasting inflectional forms of neither verbs nor nouns are produced (Gagarina and Voeikova 2009; Gagarina 2003, 2008). Each child has a preference for one of two directive forms, the infinitive in Filipp's case and the imperative in Liza's. In the beginning both children use requests with verbs of exchange, in particular *dat'* 'give' and its derivatives. Later on, they differ in the preferred topics of their requests. While Filipp asks to handle objects or requests his mother to stay nearby, Liza likes to ask her mother for mental activities like reading or telling stories. In contrast to the children, the mothers often request their children to speak or look at pictures by using imperative forms such as *skaži* 'say!' or *smotri* 'look!'. There is thus no immediate impact of CDS on CS concerning request forms of specific verbs.

The unusual way of using the bare infinitive rather than the imperative for requests disappears in Filipp's speech after 2;2. Although Liza continues to use infinitives through 2;9, she starts to distinguish their functions from those of imperatives after 1;11. While imperatives express commands, she may use bare infinitives to convey suggestions and intentions.

Canonical imperatives, i.e. imperatives of the 2nd person (mostly singular), prevail in both CDS and CS. More than 50% of directives in the speech of both mothers are expressed by imperatives during the entire period of observation. In some recordings of the boy's speech, they may even reach 90%. Bare infinitives are avoided in this function by both caregivers. Therefore, the modally used bare infinitives found in CS most likely have the elliptical renderings of affirmative or interrogative modal expressions occurring in CDS as their source.

While direct requests are most often expressed by imperatives, the mothers use a number of different constructions for indirect ones. The most important of these are hortative constructions, which typically consist of the particle *davaj* 'let' and a verb in the infinitive of imperfective verbs or the 1st person plural future of perfective ones. While Filipp's mother prefers direct requests throughout the observation period, Liza's mother uses hortatives besides other constructions conveying indirect requests from early on. Although hortatives function as suggestions in her mother's speech, Liza also uses them to express her intentions. While hortatives increase in the course of Liza's development, they only play a minor role in Filipp's. This difference between the two children reflects the differences in their input.

Besides hortatives, other indirect requests are expressed with the help of the adverb *nado* 'necessarily' followed by the infinitive. Liza uses such constructions in the affirmative to regulate her own activities or those of others, whereas Filipp prefers negated *ne nado* 'not necessarily' constructions to protest against his mother's commands or actions.

Contrary to what has been found in other studies of Russian language acquisition (see section 1) and that of many other languages, our subjects did not use verbless utterances consisting of nouns to express requests. In the early period, both Filipp and Liza ask for objects by simply uttering the infinitive or imperative of the verb *dat'* 'give' without an object noun. By 2;11, Liza expresses desires, mostly of other persons, by the affirmative form of *xotet'* 'want' while, by 1;11, Filipp mostly uses the negative form of this verb for refusals.

The children demonstrate similarities as well as differences in their development of requests. As compared to Liza, Filipp is more repetitive, relying more heavily on the input than the girl.

Filipp replaces infinitives by more appropriate imperatives in the course of development, while Liza first develops a functional difference between the imperative and the infinitive using imperatives for direct requests and infinitives for indirect ones. Later on, she replaces the inappropriate infinitives by hortatives or other constructions.

Our study shows that directive expressions develop in two phases in early Russian child language. In a first phase, direct requests are expressed by short verb forms of a single or a few verbs, either the imperative or the infinitive. In the course of development, directive constructions become more complex and the inventory of verb forms expressing requests is enriched. Furthermore, direct requests are formally as well as functionally distinguished from indirect ones.

Acknowledgements: We express our deep gratitude to Ursula Stephany and Ayhan Aksu-Koç for their numerous comments on previous versions of our chapter and suggestions for improvement. All remaining errors are our own. We gratefully acknowledge the financial support of the Russian Scientific Foundation, grant 14-18-03668.

References

Aikhenvald, Alexandra. 2010. *Imperatives and commands* (Oxford Studies in Typology and Linguistic Theory). Oxford: Oxford University Press.

Aikhenvald, Alexandra. 2016. Sentence types. In Jan Nuyts & Johan van der Auwera (eds.), *The Oxford handbook of modality and mood*, 141–165. Oxford: Oxford University Press.

Bates, Elizabeth. 1976. *Language and context: The acquisition of pragmatics*. New York: Academic Press.

Benacchio, Rosanna. 2010. *Vid i kategorija vežlivosti v slavjanskom imperative* [Aspect and the category of politeness in the Slavic imperative] (Slawistische Beiträge 472). Munich & Berlin: Otto Sagner.

Birjulin, Leonid. 1994. *Semantika i pragmatika russkogo imperativa* [Semantics and pragmatics of the Russian imperative] (Slavica Helsingiensia 13). Helsinki: Helsinki University Press.

Birjulin, Leonid. 2012. Morfologija imperativa v slavjanskih jazykah [Morphology of the imperative in Slavic languages]. In Maria D. Voeikova (ed.), *Ot formy k značeniju, ot značenija k forme: sbornik statej v čest' 80-letija Aleksandra V. Bondarko* [From form to meaning, from meaning to form: Selection of papers for the 80th anniversary of Alexandr V. Bondarko], 52–72. Moscow: Jazyki slavjanskih kul'tur.

Birjulin, Leonid A. & Viktor S. Xrakovskij. 2001. Imperative sentences: Theoretical problems. In Victor S. Xrakovskij (ed.). *Typology of imperative constructions* (LINCOM Studies in Theoretical Linguistics 9), 3–50. Munich: LINCOM Europa.

Bittner, Dagmar, Wolfgang U. Dressler & Marianne Kilani-Schoch. 2003. Introduction. In Dagmar Bittner, Wolfgang U. Dressler & Marianne Kilani-Schoch (eds.), *Development of verb inflection in first language acquisition: A cross-linguistic perspective* (Studies on Language Acquisition 21), vii–xxxix. Berlin: Mouton de Gruyter.

Bogusławski, Andrzej. 1985. The problem of the negated imperative in perfective verbs revisited. *Russian Linguistics* 9(2/3). 225–239.

Bondarko, Aleksandr V. & Lev L. Bulanin. 1967. *Russkij glagol* [The Russian verb]. Leningrad: Prosveščenie.

Bruner, Jerome. 1975. The ontogenesis of speech acts. *Journal of Child Language* 2. 1–19.

Cameron-Faulkner, Thea. 2014. The development of speech acts. In Danielle Mathews (ed.) *Pragmatic development in first language acquisition*, 37–52. Amsterdam: John Benjamins.

Ceitlin, Stella N. 2008. Vyraženie pobuždenija v detskoj reči [Expression of requests in child language]. In Alexandr V. Bondarko & Sadje A. Shubik (eds.), *Problemy funkcionalnoj grammatiki: kategorizacija semantiki* [Problems of functional grammar: categorization of semantics], 309–330. Saint Petersburg: Nauka.

Ceitlin, Stella N. 2009. *Očerki po slovoobrazovaniju i formoobrazovaniju v detskoj reči* [Essays on word- and form-building in child language]. Moscow: Znak.

Dressler, Wolfgang U. & Annemarie Karpf. 1995. The theoretical relevance of pre- and protomorphology in language acquisition. *Yearbook of Morphology 1994*. 99–124.

Dressler, Wolfgang U., Willi Mayertaler, Oswald Panagl & Wolfgang Ullrich Wurzel. 1987. *Leitmotifs in natural morphology*. Amsterdam: John Benjamins.

Drew, Paul & Elizabeth Couper-Kuhlen. 2014. Requesting: From speech act to recruitment. In Paul Drew & Elizabeth Couper-Kuhlen (eds.), *Requesting in social interaction* (Studies in Language and Social Interaction 26), 1–34. Amsterdam: John Benjamins.

Eliseeva, Marina B. 2015. *Stanovlenie individual'noj jazykovoj sistemy rebjonka: rannie etapy* [Establishment of the individual language system of a child: The early phases]. Moscow: Jazyki slavjanskix kul'tur.

Ervin-Tripp, Susan. 1976. Is Sybil there? The structure of some American-English directives. *Language and Society* 5. 25–66.

Ervin-Tripp, Susan. 1977. "Wait for me, Roller Skate!" In Susan Ervin-Tripp & Claudia Mitchell-Kernan (eds.), *Child discourse*, 165–188. New York: Academic Press.

Gagarina, Natalia. 2002. Thoughts on optional infinitives in Russian. In Daniel Hole, Paul Law & Niina Ning Zhang (eds.), *Linguistics by heart* (Webfest for Horst-Dieter Gasde), 1–23. Berlin: Zentrum für Allgemeine Sprachwissenschaft.

Gagarina, Natalia. 2003. The early verb development and demarcation of stages in three Russian-speaking children. In Dagmar Bittner, Wolfgang U. Dressler & Marianne Kilani-Schoch (eds.), *Development of verb inflection in first language acquisition: A cross-linguistic perspective* (Studies on Language Acquisition 21), 131–169. Berlin: Mouton de Gruyter.

Gagarina, Natalia. 2008. *Stanovlenie grammatičeskih kategorij russkogo glagola v detskoj reči* [Construction of grammatical categories of the Russian verb in child speech]. Saint Petersburg: Nauka.

Gagarina, Natalia & Maria Voeikova. 2009. Acquisition of case and number in Russian. In Ursula Stephany & Maria D. Voeikova (eds.), *Development of nominal inflection in first language acquisition: A cross-linguistic perspective* (Studies on Language Acquisition 30), 179–216. Berlin: Walter de Gruyter.

Gagarina, Natalia, Maria D. Voeikova & Sergey Gruzincev. 2003. New version of morphological coding for speech production of Russian children (in the framework of CHILDES). In Peter Kosta, Joanna Blaszczak, Jens Frasek & Ljudmila Geist (eds.), *Investigations into formal Slavic linguistics*, 243–258. Frankfurt a.M.: Peter Lang.

Gusev, Valentin Yu. 2003. Imperativ i inye značenija: Slučai netrivialnogo vzaimodejstvija [The imperative and other meanings: Cases of non-trivial interaction] In *Grammatičeskije kategorii: ierarxii, svjazi, vzaimodejstvija* [Grammatical categories: hierarchies, connections and interactions]. *Materialy meždunarodnoj naučnoj konferencii* [Materials of an international scientific conference], 46–51. St. Petersburg: Institute for Linguistic Studies, Russian Academy of Sciences. http://iling.spb.ru/typo/grammcat2003.html (accessed 1 November 2016).

Gusev, Valentin Yu. 2013. *Tipologija imperativa* [The typology of the imperative]. Moscow: Jazyki slavjanskix kul'tur.

Gvozdev, Aleksandr N. 1981. *Ot pervyx slov do pervogo klassa: Dnevnik naučnyx nabljudenij* [From the first words to the first grade: A scientific diary]. Saratov: Saratov University Press.

Gvozdev, Aleksandr N. 1990. *Razvitie slovarnogo zapasa v pervye gody žizni rebjonka* [Development of the lexicon in the first years of the child's life]. Saratov: Saratov University Press.

Gvozdev, Aleksandr N. 2007 [1949]. *Voprosy izučenija detskoj reči* [Issues of the investigation of children's speech]. Moscow: Tvorčeskij centr Sfera.

Halliday, Michael A. K. 1975. *Learning how to mean: Explorations in the development of language*. London: E. Arnold.

Halliday, Michael A. K. 2003 [1973]. The functional basis of language. In Jonathan Webster (ed.) 2003. *Collected works of M.A.K. Halliday. On language and linguistics*. Vol. 3, 298–322. London & New York: Continuum.

Ivanova, Kira & Maria D. Voeikova. 2014. Imperativy nesoveršennogo vida na rannix etapax usvojenija det'mi russkogo jazyka [Imperfective imperatives in early child Russian]. *Scando-Slavica* 60(2). 212–230.

Kholodilova, Maria. 2015. Grammatikalizacyja russkix modalnyx glagolov [Grammaticalization of Russian modal verbs]. *Acta Linguistica Petropolitana* 11(1). 369–400.

Kilani-Schoch, Marianne & Wolfgang U. Dressler. 2005. *Morphologie naturelle et flexion du verbe français*. Tübingen: Gunter Narr Verlag.

Larina, Tatiana. 2005. Cultural values and negative politeness in English and Russian. *Respectus Philologicus* 8(13). 25–39.

Lieven, Elena, Julian Pine & Helen Dresner-Barnes. 1992. Individual differences in early vocabulary development. *Journal of Child Language* 19. 287–310.

Luria, Aleksandr R. 1992. Iz dnevnika za 1938–1941 gody: Nabljudenija za razvitiem dočeri [From the diary on the years 1938–1941: Observations on my daughter's development]. *Vestnik MGU* [Proceedings of Moscow State University], Series 14. Psychology 2. 12–16.

MacWhinney, Brian. 2000. *The CHILDES Project: Tools for analyzing talk*. Mahwah, NJ: Lawrence Erlbaum Associates.

Nikolaeva, Irina. 2016. Analyses of the semantics of mood. In Jan Nuyts & Johan van der Auwera (eds.), *The Oxford handbook of modality and mood*, 68–85. Oxford: Oxford University Press.

Nikolaeva, Tatiana M. 2015. Predložnyj variant/variant bespredložnyj [Variants with or without preposition]. *Acta Linguistica Petropolitana* 11(1). 233–248.

Ogiermann, Eva. 2009. Politeness and indirectness across cultures: A comparison of English, German, Polish and Russian requests. *Journal of Politeness Research* 5(2). 198–216.

Padučeva, Elena V. 1996. Semantika i pragmatika nesoveršennogo vida imperativa [Semantics and pragmatics of the imperfective imperative]. In Elena V. Padučeva, *Semantičeskie issledovanija* [Studies in semantics], 66–83. Moscow: Jazyki russkoj kul'tury.

Poupynin, Yuri. 1996. Usvoenie sistemy russkix glagol'nyx form rebenkom (rannie etapy) [Acquisition of the system of Russian verb forms by a child (the early stages)]. *Voprosy jazykoznanija* 3. 84–95.

Rathmayr, Renate. 1994. Pragmatische und sprachlich konzeptualisierte Charakteristika russischer direktiver Sprechakte. In Hans R. Mehlig (ed.), *Slavistische Linguistik*, 251–277. Munich: Otto Sagner.

Smiley, Patricia & Janelien Huttenlocher. 2014 [1995]. Conceptual development and the child's early words for events, objects and persons. In Michael Tomasello & William E. Merriman (eds.), *Beyond names for things*, 21–61. Hillsdale, NJ & London: Lawrence Erlbaum Associates, 1995, and New York & London: Psychology Press, 2014.

Stephany, Ursula. 1986. Modality. In Paul Fletcher & Michael Garman (eds.), *Language acquisition: Studies in first language development*, 375–400. 2nd edn. Cambridge: Cambridge University Press.

Stephany, Ursula. 1993. Modality in first language acquisition: The state of the art. In Norbert Dittmar & Astrid Reich (eds.), *Modality in language acquisition/Modalité et acquisition des langues*, 133–144. Berlin & New York: Walter de Gruyter.

Stephany, Ursula & Maria D. Voeikova. 2009. Introduction. In Ursula Stephany & Maria D. Voeikova (eds.), *Development of nominal inflection in first language acquisition: A cross-linguistic perspective* (Studies on Language Acquisition 30), 1–14. Berlin: Walter de Gruyter.

Stephany, Ursula & Maria D. Voeikova. 2015. Requests, their meanings and aspectual forms in early Greek and Russian child language. *Journal of Greek Linguistics* 15(1). 66–90.

Švedova, Natalia Yu. (ed.). 1980. Russkaja grammatika-80 [Russian grammar-80]. Moscow: Nauka, AN SSSR.

Taylor, Nicole, Wilberta Donovan, Sally Milles & Lewis Leavitt. 2009. Maternal control strategies, maternal language usage and children's language usage at two years. *Journal of Child Language* 36(2). 381–404.

Tomasello, Michael. 2003. *Constructing a language. A usage-based theory of language acquisition*. Cambridge, MA & London, England: Harvard University Press.

Tomasello, Michael. 2008. *Origins of human communication*. Cambridge, MA: MIT Press.

Voeikova, Maria D. 2015a. *Stanovlenie imeni* [Establishment of the noun]. Moscow: Jazyki slavjanskix kul'tur.

Voeikova, Maria D. 2015b. Varjirovanie form SV/NSV v imperative: analiz faktorov [The variation of PFV/IPFV forms in the imperative: an analysis of factors]. In *Acta Linguistica Petropolitana* XI(1). 551–571.

Voeikova, Maria D. & Inna A. Čistovič. 1994. Pervye slova russkogo rebenka [First words of a Russian child]. In *Bulleten fonetičeskogo fonda russkogo jazyka* 5. 94–112.

Wexler, Kenneth. 1994. Optional infinitives, head movement and the economy of derivation. In David Lightfoot & Norbert Hornstein (eds.), *Verb movement*, 305–350. Cambridge & New York: Cambridge University Press.

Xanthos Aris, Sabine Laaha, Steven Gillis, Ursula Stephany, Ayhan Aksu-Koç, Anastasia Christofidou, Natalia Gagarina, Gordana Hrzica, Nihan F. Ketrez, Marianne Kilani-Schoch, Katharina Korecky-Kröll, Melita Kovačević, Klaus Laalo, Marijan Palmović, Barbara Pfeiler, Maria D. Voeikova & Wolfgang U. Dressler. 2011. On the role of morphological richness in the early development of noun and verb inflection. *First Language* 31(4). 461–479.

Xrakovskij, Viktor S. 1990. Povelitelnost' [Imperativeness]. In Aleksandr V. Bondarko (ed.), *Teorija funkcional'noj grammatiki. Temporal'nost'. Modal'nost'* [Theory of functional grammar. Temporality. Modality], 185–237. Leningrad: Nauka.

Xrakovskij, Viktor S. & Aleksandr P. Volodin. 2001 [1986]. *Semantika i tipologija imperativa. Russkij imperativ.* [Semantics and typology of the imperative: The Russian imperative]. Leningrad: Nauka.

Zorikhina-Nilsson, Nadežda V. 2012. Intentional'nost' grammatičeskogo značenija vidovyx form glagola v imperative: teorija rečevyx aktov i vežlivost' [Intentionality of grammatical meaning of aspectual forms in the imperative: Speech-act theory and politeness]. In Maria D. Voeikova (ed.), *Ot formy k značeniju, ot značenija k forme: sbornik statej v čest' 80-letija Alexandra V. Bondarko* [From form to meaning, from meaning to form: Selection of papers for the 80th anniversary of Alexandr V. Bondarko], 190–207. Moscow: Jazyki slavjanskix kultur.

Zorikhina-Nilsson, Nadežda V. 2013. The negated imperative in Russian and other Slavic languages: Aspectual and modal meanings. In Folke Josephson & Ingmar Söhrman (eds.), *Diachronic and typological perspectives on verbs*, 79–105. Amsterdam/Philadelphia: John Benjamins.

Gordana Hržica, Marijan Palmović and Melita Kovacevic
Acquisition of modality in Croatian

Abstract: In this paper, the development of modal expressions in the acquisition of Croatian is analyzed using data from three monolingual children aged 1;0 to 3;0 while taking child-directed speech into consideration. In the premorphological phase of language acquisition, a high percentage of imperatives expressing modality was observed. The imperative is the morphologically simplest form conveying deontic modality. In the subsequent protomorphological phase, more complex forms appeared, such as constructions with modal verbs, and more diverse modal meanings were expressed, including indirect or polite requests as well as wishes, promises and possibilities.

1 Introduction

The acquisition of expressions of modality may be considered an important step in language and cognitive development. When speakers use modal expressions, they add their own or others' attitude or involvement to the content they are communicating, whether it be a wish, command, promise, doubt, or expression of certainty or uncertainty about a state of affairs. Modal expressions can express agent-oriented or epistemic modality (Choi 2006; Hickmann and Bassano 2016). Agent-oriented modality is further divided into dynamic modality (conveying desire, intention, ability and volition) and deontic modality (obligation, command, permission and prohibition) (e.g. Nuyts 2005; Nuyts 2006; Nuyts, Byloo and Diepeveen 2010). There is general agreement in the literature that children acquire agent-oriented modality before epistemic modality (Choi 2006; Hickmann and Bassano 2016; Stephany 1986; see also Bybee and Fleischman 1995). In the present study we will deal only with the early stages of the development of agent-oriented modality.

Our analysis is based on the model of morphological development proposed by Dressler and colleagues (Dressler and Karpf 1995; Dressler, Kilani-Schoch and Klampfer 2003). This model includes an initial premorphological phase characterized by a limited number of lexically stored word forms that the children have not yet analyzed morphologically. In the subsequent protomorphological phase, children begin to generalize and creatively manipulate morphology (Dressler,

Gordana Hržica, University of Zagreb
Marijan Palmović, University of Zagreb
Melita Kovacevic, University of Zagreb

https://doi.org/10.1515/9781501504457-005

Kilani-Schoch and Klampfer 2003: 392). This is evidenced by the emergence of mini-paradigms, which are "incomplete paradigm[s] corresponding to a non-isolated set of minimally three phonologically unambiguous and distinct inflectional forms of the same word type produced spontaneously in contrasting syntactic or situative contexts in the same month of recordings" (Dressler, Kilani-Schoch and Klampfer 2003: 396). While two or three morphologically different forms of the same lemma may at first be stored as unanalyzed units, a larger number of mini-paradigms will lead to inflectional generalizations across lemmas. The notion of mini-paradigm is suitable to expand our understanding of the development of inflectional forms in the verbal and nominal domains.

The chapter is structured as follows: After a review of previous research on the acquisition of modality in Croatian in Section 2, the expressions of agent-oriented modality in standard Croatian are described in Section 3. Section 4 presents the aims, data and method of the study. An overview of the development of morphology and syntax in Croatian language acquisition is followed by an analysis of the inflectional, lexical and syntactic expressions of modality in Croatian child speech in Section 5 and agent-oriented modality in child speech is compared to the input. Section 6 contains a discussion of the results and some general conclusions.

2 Previous research on the acquisition of modality in Croatian

We are unaware of studies focused specifically on the acquisition of modal expressions in Croatian. Nevertheless, some studies on Croatian children have examined expressions carrying modal meanings. For example, researchers have noted that Croatian children frequently use imperatives and have attributed this to the fact that imperatives are simple, yet informative, even in the one-word phase (Anđel et al. 2000). Hržica and Ordulj (2013) analyzed Croatian constructions containing a modal verb and an infinitive as "pivot schemes", i.e. as combinations of a permanent element with different main verbs filling the slot after the modal verb. Similarly, Karabalić (2011) discussed such pivot constructions from the perspective of dependency grammar as valency complements of the modal verbs.

Regardless of language, children begin very early in their development to express requests (deontic modality), e.g. by "request gestures" (Cochet and Vauclair 2010) or single-word utterances consisting of a noun (e.g. *sok-a!* (juice-GEN.SG) 'juice!'). In Croatian, early forms of requests also include imperatives (Anđel 2000). Acquisition of the full repertoire of modal forms and their functions in Croatian continues for many years.

3 Expressions and functions of agent-oriented modality in Croatian

In Croatian, as in many other languages, modal meanings may be expressed using various formal devices based on morphology, syntax or the lexicon. The main inflectional devices are the imperative and conditional, although the present indicative may also be used, usually with perfective verbs occurring in complex sentences. Modal verbs are the main lexical device for expressing modality in Croatian. These verbs may express either agent-oriented or propositional modality. Modal adverbs typically convey propositional meanings such as possibility or certainty.

In child speech (CS) and child-directed speech (CDS), most requests are expressed using the 2nd singular form of the imperative of full verbs. Verbs with the present stem ending in a consonant (except *j*) add the suffix *–i* in the imperative singular. Verbs with a present stem ending in *j* do not take a suffix. Hortatives are expressed by the 1st person plural of the imperative of *ići* 'to go' and the infinitive of the main verb (example 1). Infinitives are marked inflectionally with the suffix *-ti* (rarely *-ći*, as a result of phonological change) added to the stem. In Croatian, imperatives rather than infinitives are the morphologically simplest forms of verbs.

(1) *Ide-mo   gleda-ti.*
    go-IMP.1PL watch-INF
    'Let's go watching.'

The negative particles *nemoj* (singular) and *nemojte* (plural) 'don't' express prohibitions and may occur alone or in constructions with the infinitive of a main verb. Negative commands can also be expressed using the negative particle *ne* 'not' and the infinitive of the main verb. Both constructions are found in the Croatian child language corpus in the CHILDES database (Kovacevic 2002), as shown in examples (2) from Antonija's corpus at 2;8.

(2) CDS, Antonija, 2;8 (Kovacevic 2002)
    a. MOT: *Nemoj to   sad u   usta!*
            don't this now in mouth
            'Don't (put) this into your mouth!'
    b. MOT: *Ne to   u   usta   stavlja-ti!*
            no this in mouth   put-INF
            'Don't put this into your mouth!'

The conditional may express agent-oriented dynamic meanings such as wishes or propositional meanings such as possibility. There are two conditional forms in Croatian, present and counterfactual (or past). They are formed using different tense forms of the auxiliary *biti* 'to be' and the active participle. The present conditional is formed by the aorist of the auxiliary and the active participle and can be found in CDS (example 3a) and very rarely in CS (example 3b). Young children omit the participle of the main verb, retaining only the auxiliary and the noun in the genitive or accusative. In this case the auxiliary conveys the modal meaning, the main verb is inferred and the most informative part, the object of desire, is overtly expressed (example 3b).

(3) Vjeran, 2;5 (Kovacevic 2002)
    a. MOT: *Ako vam se ne*
             if you.DAT.PL REFL no
             dolaz-i gore, ja bi-h iš-la.
             come-PRS.3SG upstairs I be-AOR.1SG go-PTCP.F.SG
             'If you don't (want to) come upstairs, I will leave.'
    b. CHI: *Ja bi-h bager-Ø.*
             I be-AOR.1SG excavator-ACC.SG
             'I would (like to have) excavator.'

As in other Slavic languages, Croatian verbs come in perfective-imperfective pairs. The present indicative can only be expressed using imperfective verbs. Although present indicative forms usually convey non-modal statements of fact, they can also function as requests, e.g. by stating social rules, usually in an impersonal (reflexive) construction (similar to e.g. Russian, cf. Stephany and Voeikova 2015) as in example (4). The present form of perfective verbs conveys a conditional meaning (Geld and Zovko Drinković 2007), as in example (5).

(4) CDS, Antonija, 2;3 (Kovacevic 2002)
    MOT: *To se stav-i unutra.*
          this REFL put.IPFV-PRS.3SG inside
          'This is to be inserted.'

(5) CDS, Vjeran, 3;2 (Kovacevic 2002)
    MOT: *Možda stav-i u džepić da*
          maybe put.PFV-PRS.3SG in pocket.ACC.SG so
          ne nađ-emo.
          not find.PFV-PRS.1PL
          'Maybe he puts (it) in a pocket so that we don't find it.'

Imperatives of perfective verbs can be combined only with the infinitive of imperfective verbs (example 6).

(6) *Prestani   plakati!*
     stop.PFV.IMP.2SG cry.IPFV.INF
     'Stop crying!'

The primary lexical means for expressing modality in standard Croatian are the modal verbs *htjeti* 'want', *moći* 'can', *morati* 'must', *trebati* 'need' and *smjeti* 'may'. While *htjeti* 'want' expresses only dynamic modality, the other modals may convey deontic/dynamic or epistemic meanings. However, epistemically used modals are found in neither CS nor CDS of our corpus. Croatian modal verbs function as auxiliaries in constructions with a main verb in the infinitive, namely as "verbs that serve for the modification of some other action in terms of necessity, possibility or probability" (Silić and Pranjković 2007: 185). Modal verbs plus infinitive are typically used for expressing dynamic (agent-oriented) modality (example 7).

(7) *On hoće   čitati.*
     he want.PRS.3SG read.INF
     'He wants to read.'

In CS and CDS, the modal verb *htjeti* 'want' often functions as a main verb and is constructed with a noun in the genitive or accusative; e.g. *hoću kolača* (want.PRS.1SG cake.ACC.SG) 'I want some cake'.

4 Aims, data and method

The present study focuses on the development of linguistic devices expressing dynamic and deontic functions of agent-oriented modality in early Croatian child language. It is based on the corpora of three children, Antonija, Marina and Vjeran, which were fully transcribed and morphologically coded. The Croatian Corpus of Child Language consists of longitudinally collected speech samples of three monolingual children acquiring Croatian from the onset of speech to approximately three years of age and is available in the CHILDES database (MacWhinney 2000; Kovacevic 2002).

Antonija was recorded about three times per month between the ages of 1;3 and 2;8 (10 hours of audio recordings in total). The recordings took place at home during spontaneous interactions with family members. Marina was also recorded at home two to three times per month between the ages of 1;5 and 2;11 (21 hours of audio recordings in total). Vjeran was sometimes recorded at home and sometimes in the playground. He was recorded three times a month on average between the ages of 0;10 to 3;2 (35 hours of audio recordings in total). Further information about the corpus is presented in Table 1.

Table 1: The Croatian Corpus of Child Language (CHILDES database).

	Child		
	Antonija	Marina	Vjeran
Age	1;3–2;8	1;5–2;11	0;10–3;2
Hours of recordings	10	21	35
Number of lemmas in CS	1,322	1,745	3,632
Number of lemmas in CDS	2,865	2,538	10,738
Number of tokens in CS	15,019	25,302	49,481
Number of tokens in CDS	35,899	37,984	133,533

Recordings from the onset of speech to 2;8 were selected for the present study. The morphological lexicon for Croatian was used for automatic morphological coding of the transcripts. The morphologically coded corpus was then further analyzed using other CLAN programs (MacWhinney 2000).

Since our goals were to examine utterances in which agent-oriented modality was expressed inflectionally or lexically, we compiled all instances of utterances containing verbs in the imperative mood, infinitives with modal meaning, hortatives (*idemo, ajmo, hajmo, hajdemo*, all roughly meaning 'let's'), jussives (*neka*, roughly meaning 'let (her/him/them)') and modal verbs. Finally, transcripts were checked for other examples of modality (e.g. polite requests, suggestions, invitations, offers, proposals).

The numbers of lemmas, inflectional types and tokens were computed for each of the three children on a monthly basis. Mean length of utterance (MLU) was calculated in terms of words in order to analyze the development of syntax in the early months of language acquisition.

5 Results

5.1 General development of morphology and syntax in Croatian child language

Morphological development can be measured by an increase in the ratio of inflectional types of lemmas and the emergence of mini-paradigms. As mentioned above, a mini-paradigm is defined as the occurrence of at least three grammatical forms of a verbal or nominal lemma in one month of recording (Dressler, Kilani-Schoch and Klampfer 2003: 396). The emergence of mini-paradigms signals the beginning of the protomorphological phase in child language development.

In previous work, the onset of protomorphology was established for Antonija at 1;7, when she first used a nominal mini-paradigm (Kovacevic et al. 2009). Based on the same criterion, we determined the beginning of protomorphology to be 1;6 for Marina and 1;7 for Vjeran.

Since modal meanings are most often expressed by verbal inflection, mini-paradigms in verbs are a crucial indicator of the development of modality. For Marina and Antonija, both verbal and nominal mini-paradigms appear within the same month, while in Vjeran's data the first verbal paradigm occurs one month later. First verbal mini-paradigms comprise present, imperative and infinitive forms (Table 2).

Table 2: First mini-paradigms of main verbs in the protomorphological phase in three Croatian children.

Mini-paradigm	Child		
	Antonija	Marina	Vjeran
Age	1;7	1;6	1;8
baciti	IMP.2SG		
'to throw'	PRS.1SG		
	PRS.1PL		
ići		IMP.2SG	
'to go'		INF	INF
		PRS.1SG	PRS.3SG
		PRS.3SG	PRS.3PL
		PRS.1PL	
raditi		IMP.2SG	
'to work'		INF	
		PRS.3SG	

Table 2 (continued)

Mini-paradigm	Child		
	Antonija	Marina	Vjeran
gledati 'to look'		IMP.2SG INF PRS.3SG	
složiti 'to put together'			INF PTCP.FEM.SG PRS.3SG

Modal meanings may be expressed syntactically as well as morphologically, so syntactic development also plays a role in the acquisition of modality. A number of studies have shown the validity of MLU for capturing the syntactic complexity of early child language (e.g. Rice et al. 2010). In the present study, MLU has been calculated in terms of words (MLUw) rather than morphemes, because the two measures show a correlation above 0.95 in several languages including Croatian (Kuvač Kraljević and Palmović 2007) and because the original form of our transcripts would not support an automatic calculation of MLU in morphemes.[1] The children occasionally start to produce multi-word utterances as early as 1;4, and MLUw exceeds 2.0 around 1;10 (Table 3). It is therefore quite likely that syntactic constructions expressing modal meanings emerged in the last third of the second year (for a detailed overview see section 5.4.).

Table 3: Milestones in the development of morphology and syntax in three Croatian children.

	Antonija	Marina	Vjeran
First mini-paradigms:			
Nouns	1;7	1;6	1;7
Verbs	1;7	1;6	1;8
MLUw > 2	1;9	1;11	1;9

Tables 2 and 3 show that in the two girls' speech, the first verbal mini-paradigms containing imperatives or infinitives appear at the same time as those of nouns. In Vjeran's speech, mini-paradigms containing imperatives or

---

[1] For a more recent view on MLU calculated in morphemes or words see MacWhinney (2018).

infinitives emerge one month later than nominal ones. In all children, mini-paradigms containing imperatives or infinitives develop even before MLUw exceeds 2.0. This shows that among the three children studied, the development of noun and verb inflection sets in about the same time.

5.2 Expressing modality inflectionally in Croatian child language

In this section, the emergence of inflectional devices for expressing modality in Croatian child language in the pre- and protomorphological phases will be studied.

5.2.1 The imperative

In all three children, one of the earliest verb forms used to express direct requests (commands) is the imperative (examples 8). It is first observed at 1;5 and every month thereafter throughout the recording period.

(8) a. Antonija, 1;5
   (while her mother is putting toys away)
   Čekaj!
   wait.IMP.2SG
   'Wait!'
b. Marina, 1;5
   (while her mother is taking a ball)
   Daj (repeats three times).
   give.IMP.2SG
   'Give (it to me)!'
c. Vjeran, 1;5
   Daj   mi.
   give.IMP.2SG me
   'Give (it to) me!'

In the premorphological phase, more than 25% of both verbal lemmas and tokens occur in the imperative (Table 4). Initially, the inventory of lemmas used in the imperative is limited and the verbs most frequently occurring in this form differ among the three children. While Antonija and Marina predominantly stick to a single verb, Vjeran uses two verbs quite frequently in the imperative

Table 4: Verbs used in the imperative in the premorphological phase (lemmas and tokens).

Subject	Antonija	Marina	Vjeran
Age	1;5–1;6	1;5	1;5–1;6
Verbal lemmas	10	24	24
Verbs in IMP	4	7	7
% of IMP lemmas	40%	29%	29%
Verb forms (tokens)	50	62	91
IMP (tokens)	13	19	24
% of IMP (tokens)	26%	31%	26%

(Table 5). The most frequently used verbs account for 60% of imperative tokens in the three children's speech.

Table 5: Percentages of the most frequent verbs occurring in the imperative during the premorphological phase (tokens).

Age	Antonija	Marina	Vjeran
	1;5–1;6	1;5	1;5–1;6
Total of IMP tokens	13	19	24
% of imperative tokens constituted by the most frequently used lemmas by each child			
čekati 'wait'	9 (69%)	–	–
čičiti 'sit down'	–	12 (63%)	–
baciti 'throw'	–	–	9 (38%)
dati 'to give'	–	–	6 (25%)
Total	69%	63%	63%

Dati 'give', one of the two quite frequently occurring verbs in Vjeran's data, is known as a light verb (Hržica 2011) that can express requests in general. Antonija frequently uses *čekati* 'wait' in the imperative to stop certain actions (example 9).

(9)   Antonija, 1;6
      (Antonija has found another pen and wants to take it.)
      Čekaj [/] čekaj   d(r)ugu.
      wait.IMP.2SG   other
      'Wait, (I want) the other (one).'

The children also employ semantically more specific verbs such as *baciti* 'throw' (example 10) or *čičiti* 'sit' in requests or warnings.

(10) Vjeran, 1;6
 (Vjeran and his caretaker are playing with a ball)
 Baci   ga.
 throw.IMP.2SG it
 'Throw it!'

During the premorphological phase, imperative forms express requests for attention, objects or actions, typically as part of a game (Table 6). The three children use different verbal lemmas to formulate these requests.

Table 6: Use of imperatives during the premorphological phase.

Function	Form	
Request for object	*daj!* 'give!'	VJE
Request for action	*baci!* 'throw!'	ANT, VJE
	čekaj! 'wait!'	ANT
	otvori! 'open!'	MAR
	nacrtaj! 'draw!'	MAR
	kupi! 'buy!'	MAR
	nosi! 'carry!'	VJE

Although the number of verbal lemmas used in the imperative and that of imperative tokens rises considerably in the protomorphological phase, the fact that the percentages of both categories remain nearly constant, reveals the functional importance of this grammatical category for expressing requests in early Croatian child speech throughout the observation period (compare Tables 4 and 7).

In the protomorphological phase, the children continue to use the familiar imperative forms while adding imperatives of new verbs to their repertoire. However, up to 87% of imperatives come from only four verbs. By now, the imperative of *dati* 'give' most frequently occurs in the speech of two of the

Table 7: Frequency of lemmas and tokens in the imperative in the protomorphological phase.

	Antonija	Marina	Vjeran
	1;7–2;8	1;6–2;8	1;7–2;8
Verbal lemmas	230	235	252
Verbs in the IMP	77	68	60
% of IMP lemmas	33%	29%	24%
Verb forms (tokens)	2,343	3,764	2,384
IMP (tokens)	685	1,211	508
% of IMP (tokens)	29%	32%	21%

children (ranging second in the boy's speech) and the inventories of verbs most frequently used in the imperative coincide (Table 8).

Table 8: Verbs most frequently used in the imperative in the protomorphological phase.

	Antonija	Marina	Vjeran
Total of IMP tokens	685	1,211	508
dati 'give'	259 (38%)	371 (31%)	146 (29%)
gledati/vidjeti 'look'	73 (11%)	340 (28%)	178 (35%)
hajde 'come.on'	73 (11%)	256 (21%)	86 (17%)
nemoj 'don't'	23 (3%)	13 (1%)	29 (6%)
Total	63%	81%	87%

In the protomorphological phase, the imperative of the defective verb *hajde* 'come.on' is often used as an interjection (example 11).

(11) Antonija, 2;2
 Ajde [: *hajde*]   *idemo*   *van.*
 come.on.IMP.2SG go.PRS.1PL out
 'Come on, let's go out.'

In Croatian CS, as well as in the standard language, the imperative form *hajde!* 'come on!' serves to intensify a request containing another verb in the imperative (examples 12). In CS, the form also occurs as a kind of directive particle in incomplete ungrammatical constructions (examples 13).

(12) a. Marina, 2;5
     Ajde [: *hajde*]   *uzmi.*
     come.on.IMP.2SG take.IMP.2SG
     'Come on, take it.'
  b. Antonija, 2;8
     Ajde [: *hajde*]   *papaj.*
     come.on.IMP.2SG eat.IMP.2SG
     'Come on, eat.'

(13) a. Marina, 2;1
     Ajde [: *hajde*]   *avteka* [: *auteka*].
     come.on.IMP.2SG car.ACC.SG
     'Come on, (give me) the car.'
  b. Vjeran, 2;6
     Ajde [: *hajde*]   *još*   *jednom.*
     come.on.IMP.2SG more once
     'Come on, once more.'

The defective verb *nemoj* 'don't' serves to construct a periphrastic negative imperative form, combined with the infinitive of a main verb (examples 14).

(14) a. Antonija, 2;6
     Nemoj   *se*   *(s)mijati!*
     don't.IMP.2SG REFL   laugh.INF
     'Don't laugh.'
  b. Marina, 2;6
     Nemoj   *stavit* *nemoj.*
     don't.IMP.2SG put.INF   don't.IMP.2SG
     'Don't put (it there).'
  c. Vjeran, 2;5
     Nemoj   *pličat* [: *pričat*].
     don't.IMP.2SG talk.INF
     'Don't talk.'

The defective verb *hajde* 'come on' with its hortative tone allows the imperative to be used for less direct requests while the defective verb *nemoj* 'don't' does the same for prohibitions.

5.2.2 The infinitive

As is the case in many languages (Hickmann and Bassano 2016), the children in our study start quite early to use the infinitive in one-word utterances for expressing mostly modal (but also sometimes non-modal) meanings. Although the infinitive is constructed with modal verbs in standard Croatian (and in CDS), the modal verb is missing in the early CS of our sample. Since infinitives may convey both modal and non-modal meanings (Stephany 1986: 385–386), their modal functions, like the expression of desire, intention, suggestions or requests, have to be inferred from the context, such as the caregivers' reactions (examples 15).

(15) a. Vjeran, 1;5
    CHI: *Hodati.*
             walk.INF
             'walk'
    MOT: *Hoćeš   hodati?*
             want.PRS.2SG   walk.INF
             'Do you want to walk?'
   b. Antonija, 1;7
    CHI: *Doći.*
             come.INF
             'Come.'
    MOT: *Doći-će   Zvonimir.*
             come-FUT.3SG   Zvonimir
             'Zvonimir will come.'
   c. Marina, 1;5
    CHI: *Čičiti.*
             sit.INF
             'Sit.'
    MOT: *Čičiti   gore   oćeš* [: *hoćeš*]?
             sit.INF   up   want.PRS.2SG
             'Do you want to sit up here?'

Already in premorphology, the children begin to use bare infinitives carrying modal meanings in one-word utterances (Table 9). In Anonija's speech, they are found slightly later (at 1;7) and occur much less frequently than with the other two children.

Table 9: Modal use of the infinitive in the premorphological phase.

	Antonija 1;5–1;6	Marina 1;5	Vjeran 1;5–1;6
Verbal lemmas	10	24	24
Verbs in INF	–	8	5
% of INF lemmas	–	33%	21%
Verb forms (tokens)	50	62	91
INF (tokens)	–	12	16
% of INF (tokens)	–	19%	18%

Since Croatian children start to correctly construct the infinitive with modal verbs quite early in protomorphology (Marina and Vjeran at 1;7 and Antonija at 1;9), one-word utterances consisting of the bare infinitive only occur during a limited period of time.

To summarize, the two verb forms used in parallel by the three Croatian children for expressing agent-oriented modality in the premorphological phase are the imperative and the infinitive occurring in one-word utterances. While the imperative expresses deontic modal notions, namely requests and prohibitions, the infinitive may also convey dynamic modal notions, such as volition and intention. Since infinitives used in one-word utterances expressing such functions do not occur in either standard Croatian or CDS, the children's source of these forms are modal verb constructions or periphrastic future tense forms, the latter of which also often signal dynamic modal meanings (volition or intention).

5.3 Expressing modality lexically and syntactically in Croatian child language

5.3.1 Modal verb constructions

All five Croatian modal verbs described by Silić and Pranjković (2007) are observed in the speech of the three children during the period of observation: *htjeti* 'want', *moći* 'can', *morati* 'must', *trebati* 'need' and *smjeti* 'may', but only *htjeti* 'want' and *moći* 'can', expressing the dynamic notions of wishes and ability, appear at the beginning of the protomorphological phase (Table 10). Wishes are much more frequently voiced than ability.

In the beginning of the protomorphological phase, mini-paradigms of modal verbs have not yet developed, but later on several person–number forms of these

Table 10: Frequency of modal verbs at the beginning of the protomorphological phase (tokens).

	Antonija 1;7–1;10	Marina 1;6–2;0	Vjeran1; 7–1;9
Verbs (tokens)	142	696	249
Modal verbs (tokens)	11 (8%)	33 (5%)	48 (19%)
htjeti 'want'	10 (91%)	26 (79%)	46 (96%)
moći 'can'	1 (9%)	7 (21%)	2 (4%)

verbs are to be observed (Table 11). They appear two to six months later than those of full verbs (see Table 2), namely at 1;10 in Vjeran's speech, at 1;11 in Antonija's and at 2;1 in Marina's.

Table 11: Frequency of modal verbs in the second part of the protomorphological phase (tokens).

	Antonija 1;11–2;8	Marina 2;1–2;8	Vjeran 1;10–2;8
Verbs (tokens)	2,201	3,068	2,135
Modal verbs (tokens)	417 (19%)	324 (11%)	459 (21%)
htjeti 'want'	178 (43%)	144 (44%)	336 (73%)
moći 'can'	155 (37%)	122 (38%)	65 (14%)
morati 'must'	80 (19%)	41 (13%)	46 (10%)
trebati 'need'	2 (<1%)	15 (5%)	6 (1%)
smjeti 'may'	2 (<1%)	2 (<1%)	6 (1%)

Examples of the earliest modal verbs *htjeti* 'want' and *moći* 'can' are presented in (16) and (17). Desire is expressed much more often by the boy than the girls. Both verbs are sometimes negated.

(16) a. Antonija, 1;9
   Oćem [: *hoću*] *još.*
   want.PRS.1SG   more
   'I want more.'
   b. Marina, 1;10
   Hoćeš   *gledati*   *ovo?*
   want.PRS.3SG   watch.INF   this
   'Do you want to watch this?'

    c. Vjeran, 1;8
      Oće [: *hoću*]   *još*.
      want.PRS.3SG more
      '(He) wants more.' (referring to himself)

(17) Antonija, 1;9
    Ja ne mogu   tamo.
    I   not can.PRS.1SG there
    'I cannot (go) there.'

Three to seven months after the emergence of the first modal verbs, their inventory is enlarged and they develop mini-paradigms. Frequency of use of modal verbs increases, albeit at different rates, and their constructions become more complex. Nevertheless, modal verbs continue to be limited to deontic or dynamic meanings and are not used epistemically until the end of observation at 2;8.

Since the modal verb *htjeti* 'want' appears early and is used more frequently than any of the other modals, its forms have been traced in order to study the development of shifters and of productivity. As is common in child speech, the first form to emerge is the 3rd person singular present, which is initially overgeneralized by referring to the speaker or addressee (examples 18).

(18) a. Antonija, 1;6
      Oće [: *hoću*]   *to.*
      want.PRS.3SG that
      'Wants that.' (referring to the speaker)
    b. Marina, 1;6
      Neće [: *neću*]   *papati.*
      not.want.PRS.3SG eat.INF
      'Does not want to eat.' (referring to the speaker)
    c. Vjeran, 1;8
      Oće [: *hoću*]   *žuti*   *auto.*
      want.PRS.3SG yellow car
      'Wants a yellow car.' (referring to the speaker)
    d. Vjeran, 1;7
      Ti   *oće* [: *hoćeš*]   *žutu?*
      you.2SG want.PRS.3SG yellow
      'You want a yellow one?' (referring to the listener)

The children's overgeneralization of the regular ending –*m* of the 1st person singular present (e.g. *ide-m* 'go-PRS.1SG') to *htjeti* 'want' (*oćem* instead of standard *hoć-u* 'want-PRS.1SG')[2] demonstrates morphological productivity (examples 19).

(19) a. Antonija, 1;9
　　　Oćem [: *hoću*] *još*.
　　　want.PRS.1SG　more
　　　'I want more.'
　　b. Marina, 2;2
　　　Obuć(i)　　　*se*　　*oćem* [: *hoću*].
　　　get.dressed.INF　myself　want. PRS.1SG
　　　'I want to dress myself.'
　　c. Vjeran, 2;8
　　　Nećem [: *neću*] *čaja*.
　　　not.want.PRS.1SG　tea
　　　'I don't want tea.'

As is to be expected, once the 1st and 2nd person singular of the verb *htjeti* 'want' have been acquired, the 3rd person is correctly restricted to referents other than the interlocutors so that its overgeneralized use slowly disappears.

After being used in one-word utterances, modal verbs are constructed with an object noun or pronoun, a main verb in the infinitive, or both (examples 20). All three children begin constructing modal verbs with a main verb in the infinitive at 1;11 and do so more frequently as they get older (Table 12).

(20) a. Marina, 1;11
　　　Ne　*možeš*　　　*strgati*.
　　　not　can.PRS.2SG　break.INF
　　　'You cannot break.'
　　b. Vjeran, 2;3
　　　Moram　　　　*to*　　*dirati*.
　　　must.PRS.1SG　that　touch.INF
　　　'I must touch that.'
　　c. Antonija, 2;4
　　　Sad　*moram*　　　　*to*　　*op(r)ati*.
　　　now　must.PRS.1SG　that　wash.INF
　　　'Now I must wash that.'

---

[2] *Hoć-u* 'want-PRS.1SG' follows a historical non-productive conjugation.

Table 12: Frequency of constructions comprising a modal verb and a main verb in the infinitive (tokens).

	Antonija	Marina	Vjeran
1;11	23% (3/13)	17% (2/12)	8% (4/48)
2;0	22% (4/18)	17% (4/24)	10% (5/51)
2;1	35% (17/49)	36% (4/11)	6% (4/61)
2;2	34% (19/55)	32% (6/19)	11% (5/46)
2;3	33% (18/55)	20% (5/25)	20% (11/54)
2;4	38% (10/26)	–	34% (34/101)
2;5	36% (29/80)	38% (22/58)	26% (14/54)
2;6	35% (11/31)	41% (28/69)	36% (19/52)
2;7	53% (26/49)	49% (38/78)	42% (5/12)
2;8	54% (28/52)	41% (25/61)	39% (11/28)
Total	38% (165/428)	37% (134/357)	22% (112/507)

5.3.2 Hortative constructions

Indirect requests expressed by non-canonical imperatives such as hortatives emerge only towards the end of the children's second year but remain rare. They typically function as suggestions encouraging the addressee to participate in some activity together with the child. In Croatian child language, hortative constructions may either be expressed by the 1st person plural present of the verb *ići* 'to go' (*idemo* go.PRS.1PL) or the form *hajdemo* (let's.go.PRS.1PL). Both may be followed by a main verb in the infinitive (example 21).

(21) Vjeran, 2;8
 Tata   ajmo [: hajdemo]   se.igrati.
 daddy let's.PRS.1PL   play.INF
 'Daddy, let's play.'

5.3.3 Polite requests

In Croatian, polite requests are often constructed with the 1st person singular present of the verb *moliti* 'to ask for, please'. A few instances of this formulaic device are found quite early in the speech of the three children (examples 22).

(22) a. Vjeran, 1;8
   Molim čokolade.
   please.PRS.1SG chocolate
   'Please (give me) some chocolate.'
   b. Antonija, 2;4
   Daj mi lijepo
   give.IMP.2SG me nicely
   te molim.
   you.ACC.SG ask.PRS.1SG
   'I'm asking you nicely to give it to me.'

5.4 Summary of the development of agent-oriented modality in Croatian child language

The order of emergence of verbal devices expressing modality is similar across the three children (Table 13). Inflectional expressions appear first. In Marina's and Vjeran's speech, imperatives and modally used infinitives emerge at the same time, while in Antonija's speech imperatives slightly precede infinitives. This confirms previous results reported for Antonija (Anđel et al. 2000). Although imperatives appear early and are used frequently by the three children, they are initially limited to a few verbs, a phenomenon also found in other languages (e.g. Stephany 1986).

Table 13: Age of emergence of modal devices in the speech of three Croatian children.

	Inflectional			Lexical		Syntactic	
	IMP	INF	HORT	MV	Pol. requests	MV +INF	HORT
ANT	1;5	1;7	1;11	1;9	1;10	1;11	1;11
MAR	1;5	1;5	1;11	1;9	2;5	1;11	1;11
VJE	1;5	1;5	1;11	1;7	1;8	1;11	1;11

Table 13 shows that lexical devices, namely modal verbs and a politeness formula, emerge after inflectional devices (with the exception of hortative forms). Syntactic constructions such as modal verbs constructed with infinitives or hortative constructions appear last in all children. Considering the development of Croatian modal meanings expressed by verbs in the theoretical framework of the pre- and protomorphology model of language acquisition, premorphology is characterized by the limitation of the children's speech to at most two inflectional verb forms. In the next developmental phase of protomorphology, the lexical inventory widens and these forms enter into verbal paradigms together with non-modal verb forms and syntactic constructions are added to morphological ones.

The frequencies of different devices used to express agent-oriented modality in Croatian CS throughout the period of observation are presented in Figure 1. The following ranking by frequency has been observed: imperative > modal verbs > modal verb constructions. Infinitives in one-word utterances expressing modal meanings are rare overall since they are restricted to the early months of

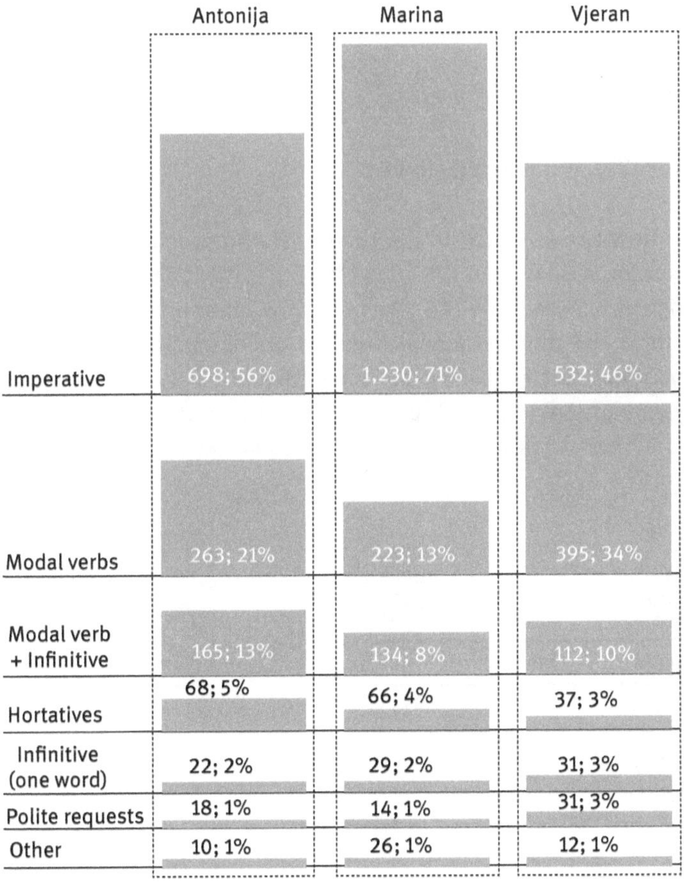

	Antonija	Marina	Vjeran
Imperative	698; 56%	1,230; 71%	532; 46%
Modal verbs	263; 21%	223; 13%	395; 34%
Modal verb + Infinitive	165; 13%	134; 8%	112; 10%
Hortatives	68; 5%	66; 4%	37; 3%
Infinitive (one word)	22; 2%	29; 2%	31; 3%
Polite requests	18; 1%	14; 1%	31; 3%
Other	10; 1%	26; 1%	12; 1%

Figure 1: Frequency of devices for expressing modal meanings in the speech of three Croatian children (tokens).

language development. Hortatives and some kinds of polite requests also occur infrequently.

Figure 1 shows that during language acquisition up to three years, the three Croatian children use a large repertoire of formal devices to express modality. The two types of agent-oriented modality, deontic and dynamic, appear almost simultaneously. Children also progress to indirect requests and broaden their repertoire of forms encouraging the hearer to join them in performing certain actions.

5.5 Comparison of agent-oriented modality in CDS and CS

CDS contains a more diverse set of devices for expressing modality than CS, although the most frequent devices in CDS are also present in CS.

5.5.1 Expressing modality inflectionally in CDS

In order to examine how CDS is tuned to CS, the forms and functions of inflectional devices expressing modality in CDS have been analyzed during the pre- and protomorphological phases (Table 14). As in CS, the imperative is the main inflectional device for conveying the modal function of commands throughout the period of observation. Nevertheless, the imperative is not as prevalent in CDS as it is in CS (compare Table 14 to Tables 4 and 7). In contrast to CS, infinitives in CDS are constructed mainly with modal verbs so that bare infinitives do not occur.

Table 14: Frequency of verb and imperative tokens in CDS in the pre- and protomorphological phases.

	Antonija	Marina	Vjeran
Age	1;5–1;6	1;5	1;5–1;6
Verbs	265	446	416
Imperatives	46 (17%)	102 (23%)	156 (37%)
Age	1;7–2;8	1;6–2;8	1;7–2;8
Verbs	10,057	6,651	17,046
Imperatives	1,478 (15%)	1,408 (21%)	4,128 (24%)

It is interesting to note that about one third to half of imperative tokens occurring in CDS in both phases come from only four verbs: *dati* 'give', *vidjeti* 'look at', *hajde* 'come on, let's' and *nemoj* 'don't' (Table 15). While *vidjeti* 'look at' and *hajde* 'come on' express requests for the benefit of the addressee or suggestions, *dati* 'give' and *nemoj* 'don't' convey commands or prohibitions. The two defective verbs *hajde/hajdemo* 'let's go' and *nemoj* 'don't', which are limited to the imperative, emerge later in CS than being used in CDS. Besides *nemoj* 'don't', caretakers also use the verbs *čekati* 'wait' and *paziti* 'watch out' to stop the children from performing undesirable actions.

Table 15: Principal verbs used in the imperative in CDS in the pre- and protomorphological phases (tokens and percentages).

	Antonija	Marina	Vjeran
Age	1;5–1;6	1;5	1;5–1;6
Total of imperative tokens	46	102	156
	Imperative tokens per verb (%)		
dati 'give'	3 (6%)	5 (5%)	11 (7%)
gledati/vidjeti 'look'	1 (2%)	27 (26%)	9 (6%)
hajde/hajdemo 'let's go'	7 (15%)	14 (14%)	38 (24%)
nemoj 'don't'	5 (11%)	4 (4%)	13 (8%)
Total	34%	49%	45%
Age	1;8–2;8	1;7–2;8	1;7–2;8
Total of imperative tokens	1,478	1,408	4,128
	Imperative tokens per verb (%)		
dati 'give'	159 (11%)	87 (6%)	265 (6%)
gledati/vidjeti 'look'	115 (8%)	237 (17%)	705 (17%)
hajde/hajdemo 'let's go'	206 (14%)	242 (17%)	915 (22%)
nemoj 'don't'	122 (8%)	174 (12%)	200 (5%)
Total of imperative tokens	41%	52%	50%

One of the main functions of imperatives in CDS is to request action (examples 23).

(23) a. Marina, 2;5, CDS
    Ti   skupa   sa   mnom   pjevaj.
    you   together with me   sing.IMP.2SG
    'Sing together with me.'

b. Vjeran, 2;6, CDS
Izvadi tog miša iz usta.
take.out.IMP.2SG that mouse from mouth
'Take that mouse out of your mouth.'

The frequently found imperative *dati* 'give' often serves merely as an intensifier in directive constructions with another verb in the imperative (examples 24). Interestingly, up to four imperative forms may co-occur within one utterance (example 25). In such cases, the first two are intensifiers, the third functions as a kind of aspectual verb and only the fourth carries lexical meaning.

(24) a. Marina, 2;7, CDS
Daj ugasi ovaj kazić.
come.on.IMP.2SG turn.off.IMP.2SG that cassette.player
'Come on, turn off that cassette player.'
b. Vjeran, 1;10, CDS
Daj mi pokaži.
come.on.IMP.2SG me show.IMP.2SG
'Come on, show me.'

(25) Marina, 2;7, CDS
Ajde daj odi.
come.on.IMP.2SG come.on.IMP.2SG go.IMP.2SG
gaće obuci.
panties put.on.IMP.2SG
'Come on, come on, go (and) put your panties on.'

5.5.2 Expressing modality syntactically and lexically in CDS

Unlike CS, all five modal verbs of standard Croatian already occur in CDS in the premorphological phase and continue to be used throughout the protomorphological phase (Tables 16 and 17). Their percentage remains similar in the protomorphological phase when compared to the premorphological phase, although there is a slight increase in the data of all three children.

The overall frequency of modal verbs is lower in CDS than in CS, reflecting the more frequent use of other forms for expressing modality in CDS. Adults use complex constructions for expressing modality more often than children, namely, indirect and polite requests or conditionals (see Figure 2).

Table 16: Frequency of modal verbs in CDS in the premorphological phase (tokens).

	Antonija	Marina	Vjeran
Age	1;5–1;6	1;5	1;5–1;6
Verbs	265	446	416
Modal verbs	16 (6%)	26 (6%)	42 (10%)
htjeti 'want'	7 (44%)	8 (31%)	20 (48%)
moći 'can, may'	3 (19%)	14 (54%)	15 (36%)
morati 'must'	2 (12%)	2 (8%)	1 (2%)
trebati 'need'	1 (6%)	1 (4%)	2 (5%)
smjeti 'may'	3 (19%)	1 (4%)	4 (9%)

Table 17: Frequency of modal verbs in CDS in the protomorphological phase (tokens).

	Antonija	Marina	Vjeran
Age	1;7–2;8	1;6–2;8	1;7–2;8
Verbs	10,057	6,651	17,046
Modal verbs	699 (7%)	619 (9%)	2,307 (13%)
htjeti 'want'	414 (59%)	233 (38%)	1,287 (56%)
moći 'can, may'	109 (16%)	243 (39%)	599 (26%)
morati 'must'	103 (15%)	83 (13%)	283 (12%)
trebati 'need'	56 (8%)	25 (4%)	64 (3%)
smjeti 'may'	17 (2%)	35 (6%)	74 (3%)

In the premorphological as well as the protomorphological phase, the most frequent modal verbs in CDS are *htjeti* 'want' and *moći* 'can, may'. While in Antonija's and Vjeran's CDS, *htjeti* 'want' is more commonly used, in Marina's the most frequent modal verb is *moći* 'can, may'. Both the children and their caretakers most often use the verbs *htjeti* 'want' and *moći* 'can' to express dynamic modality. Differences in the frequencies of modal verbs between CS and CDS may be motivated by different communication needs. While the children use the modal verbs *htjeti* 'want' and *moći* 'can' to express their wishes and ability (or inability), the caretakers more commonly give commands using the imperative of full verbs. Adults use the modal verb *htjeti* 'want' mostly in the second person singular asking children for their desires or trying to clarify their needs. A typical use of the verb *htjeti* 'want' in CS versus CDS is shown in example (26). While *moći* 'can, may' is used dynamically in CS expressing desire or ability, its function in CDS is more commonly deontic, granting permission or forbidding some action

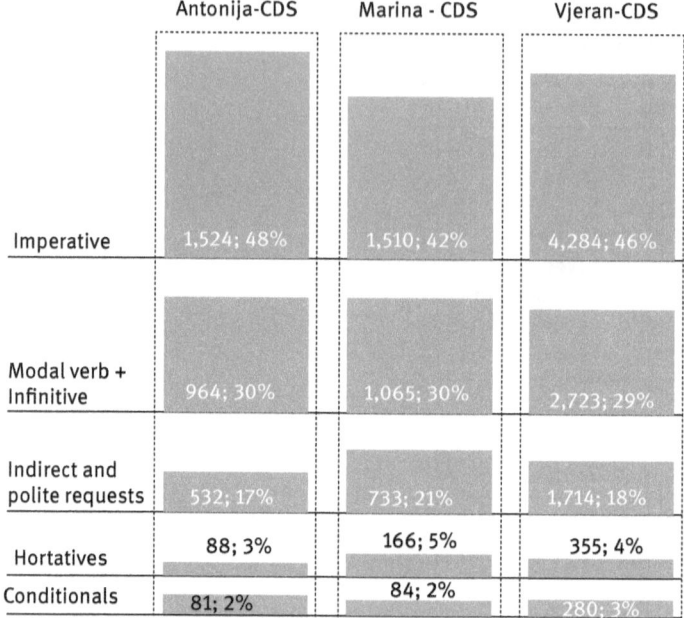

Figure 2: Frequency of devices for expressing modal meanings in Croatian CDS.

(examples 27). Marina's mother often uses *moći* 'can, may' in questions asking the child to perform certain actions, which explains her frequent usage of this verb. The caretakers also sometimes use *smjeti* 'may' for granting permission.

(26) a. Antonija, 1;9, CS and CDS
 Oćem [: *hoću*] *još!* (CS)
 want.PRS.1SG more
 'I want more!'
 Što hoćeš još? (CDS)
 what want.PRS.2SG more
 'More of what do you want?'

(27) a. Antonija, 2;6, CDS
 Ne možeš ići.
 not may.PRS.2SG go.INF
 'You may not go.'

b. Vjeran, 2;4, CDS
Kad obučemo šlapice onda možeš
when put.on.PRS.1PL slippers then may.PRS.2SG
ić(i) dolje.
go.INF down
'You may go down when we have put the slippers on.'

The verb *moći* 'can' is also used for seeking consent from the addressee (example 28). The function of this verb as an interjection contributes to its extensive usage in CDS.

(28) Antonija, 2;3, CDS
Smeđu ćemo-napraviti, može?
brown.ACC.SG FUT.1PL-make can.PRS.3SG
'We will make a brown one, alright?'

Other modal expressions occurring in CDS are hortatives and conditionals. These forms are used less often than imperatives and modal verb constructions, but more frequently than in CS (compare Figures 1 and 2). The main function of hortatives is to encourage the addressee to engage in joint actions with the speaker. Other indirect requests expressed by using the conditional or questions are also rare (examples 29). Polite requests containing the verb *moliti* 'please' commonly occur in the input of all three children.

(29) a. Antonija, 2;8, CDS
To bi ti miješala?
that be.AOR.2SG you stir.PTCP.F.SG
'Would you like to stir this?'
b. Marina, 2;8, CDS
Zašto radiš gluposti?
why do.PRS.2SG stupid.thing
'Why are you doing stupid things?'

5.5.3 Comparison of agent-oriented modality in CDS and CS

The caretakers of the three children use a similar range of devices for expressing modal meanings as the children (compare Figures 1 and 2). Imperatives are most frequent, followed by modal verbs almost exclusively constructed with infinitives. The large percentage of imperatives is partially due to the fact that the defective verbs *hajde* 'come on' and *nemoj* 'don't' encouraging the children to engage in some action or expressing prohibitions play a predominant role in CDS.

While children produce most modal verbs in isolation, their caretakers construct them almost exclusively with a main verb in the infinitive or rely on an infinitive in the preceding utterance. As is to be expected, ungrammatical requests consisting of a bare infinitive only occur in children's early development and are not found in CDS. The children's utterances with bare infinitives are probably modeled by modal verb constructions of CDS. Indirect and polite requests are much more common in CDS than CS. They consist of requests containing the verb *moliti* 'please', questions in the present tense and statements in the future tense.

Taken together, hortatives, conditionals and forms expressing indirect and polite requests account for up to 27% of modal expressions in CDS but only 6% in CS.

6 Discussion and conclusions

Croatian is a morphologically rich, inflecting-fusional language with morphosyntactic devices for expressing modality. The development of modality is therefore interlinked with the acquisition of inflectional morphology, in particular with the imperative as opposed to the present indicative. The most important distinction developing in early Croatian verbal morphology is that between indicative and imperative forms, i.e. between non-modal functions of statements and modal functions of requests. This finding is in accordance with studies of other languages (see Stephany 1985 for Greek and a review of the literature; for a more recent review see Hickmann and Bassano 2016).

Young children use all three of the main devices for expressing agent-oriented modality: inflectional, lexical and syntactic. While inflected forms (imperative, infinitive) emerge earliest, syntactic constructions (modal verb constructions) appear last. From early on, children express both dynamic and deontic modal meanings. In many cases, a functional distinction between the use of imperatives and infinitives can be observed. While imperatives express deontic modality (commands), infinitives occurring in one-word utterances may have a dynamic meaning conveying volition. Modal verbs expressing dynamic modality (*htjeti* 'want' and *moći* 'can') emerge earlier than modal verbs expressing deontic modality (*morati* 'must', *smjeti* 'may'), which are less frequently used than the former. Although the same frequency relations of these modal verbs hold in CDS, their functions differ from those in CS. While *moći* 'can' expresses the dynamic notion of ability in CS, it is more often used deontically for permission or prohibition in CDS. While children use *htjeti* 'want' to express their desires, adults use this verb most often in the second person singular to ask for children's wishes. In the course of development, children begin to apply more complex modal verb constructions as well as other devices conveying indirect requests.

Many studies have shown that CDS is a rich source of information tuned to children's gradual acquisition of their native language. Although it provides a relatively simplified register, it still displays the variability and complexity of the structure of the language being acquired (see e.g. Stephany 1985 for Greek and Aksu-Koç, Terziyan and Taylan 2014 for Turkish).

Several aspects of Croatian CDS point to its possible contribution to the development of agent-oriented modality in child language: (1) The principal devices for expressing modality in CDS, imperatives and modal verb constructions, also predominate in child language. However, the first emerge much earlier than the latter. (2) A steady use of formal devices for expressing modality in CDS contributes to the gradual acquisition of standard and more complex forms in child language, such as progression from infinitives in one-word utterances to constructions of a modal verb with an infinitive.

The first expressions of dynamic and deontic modality appear in the earliest phase of language development, i.e. premorphology, which lasts from age 1;5 to the formation of the first mini-paradigms. During the subsequent protomorphological phase, lasting until the end of observation at 2;8, the children expand their repertoire of verb forms used for expressing modal notions, adding more lexical devices and using syntactic constructions with modal verbs. By the end of the protomorphological phase, children have started to make indirect requests.

The present study is the first systematic attempt to trace the early development of agent-oriented modality in the speech of Croatian children until the second part of their third year taking CDS into consideration. Future studies of the acquisition of modality in Croatian should examine a larger sample and extend the age range of subjects since, by the end of the third year, agent-oriented modality has not been fully mastered nor has expression of epistemic modal notions emerged.

Acknowledgements: We are very grateful to the editors of the volume, who made substantial contributions to the conceptual and theoretical background of the chapter and critically revised the text. We would like to thank them for their patience, time and effort in editing this chapter.

References

Aksu-Koç, Ayhan, Treysi Terziyan & Eser Erguvanlı Taylan. 2014. Input offers and child uptakes: Acquiring mood and modal morphology in Turkish. *Language, interaction and acquisition* 5(1). 62–81.
Anđel, Maja, Sabine Klampfer, Marianne Kilani-Schoch, Wolfgang U. Dressler & Melita Kovacevic. 2000. Acquisition of verbs in Croatian, French and Austrian German – an outline of a comparative analysis. *Suvremena lingvistika* 49–50(1). 5–25.
Barić, Eugenija, Mijo Lončarić, Dragica Malić, Slavko Pavečić, Mirko Peti, Vesna Zečević & Marija Zinka, 1997. *Hrvatska gramatika* [Croatian grammar]. Zagreb: Školska knjiga.
Bybee, Joan L. & Suzanne Fleischman (eds.). 1995. *Modality in grammar and discourse.* Amsterdam & Philadelphia: John Benjamins.
Choi, Soonja. 2006. Acquisition of modality. In William Frawley (ed.), *The expression of modality*, 141–171. Berlin: Mouton de Gruyter.
Cochet, Hélène & Jacques Vauclair. 2010. Pointing gestures produced by toddlers from 15 to 30 months: Different functions, hand shapes and laterality patterns. *Infant Behavior and Development* 33. 432–442.
Dressler, Wolfgang U. & Annemarie Karpf. 1995. The theoretical relevance of pre- and protomorphology in language acquisition. In Geert Booij & Jaap van Marle (eds.), *Yearbook of morphology 1994*, 99–122. Dordrecht: Kluwer.
Dressler, Wolfgang U., Marianne Kilani-Schoch & Sabine Klampfer. 2003. How does a child detect morphology? Evidence from production. In Harald R. Baayen & Robert Schreuder (eds.), *Morphologial structure in language processing*, 391–425. Berlin: Mouton de Gruyter.
Geld, Renata & Irena Zovko Divković. 2007. Perfectives, imperfectives and the Croatian present tense. In Dagmar Divjak & Agata Kochanska (eds.), *Cognitive paths into the Slavic domain*, 111–148. Berlin: Mouton de Gruyter.
Hickmann, Maya & Dominiqe Bassano. 2016. Modality and mood in first language acquisition. In Jan Nuyts & Johan van der Auwera (eds.), *The Oxford handbook of modality and mood*, 430–447. Oxford: Oxford University Press.
Hržica, Gordana. 2011. *Glagolske kategorije aspekta, vremena i akcionalnosti u usvajanju hrvatskoga jezika* [Aspect, tense and actionality in acquiring Croatian as a first language]. Zagreb: University of Zagreb dissertation.
Hržica, Gordana & Anatonia Ordulj. 2013. Dvočlane glagolske konstrukcije u usvajanju hrvatskoga jezika [Two-word utterances with verbs in the acquisition of the Croatian language]. *Rasprave Instituta za hrvatski jezik i jezikoslovlje* 39(2). 433–456.
Karabalić, Vladimir. 2011. Sintaksa glagola nepotpunog značenja u hrvatskom i njemačkom jeziku na primjeru modalnih glagola [Syntax of Croatian and German verbs of incomplete meaning exemplified by modal verbs]. *Suvremena lingvistika* 37(72). 171–185.
Katičić, Radoslav. 2002. *Sintaksa hrvatskoga književnog jezika* [Syntax of the Croatian language]. Zagreb: HAZU-Globus.
Kovacevic, Melita. 2002. *Croatian corpus of child language.* CHILDES. https://childes.talkbank.org/access/Slavic/Croatian/Kovacevic.html (accessed September 15, 2018).
Kovacevic, Melita, Marijan Palmović & Gordana Hržica. 2009. The acquisition of case, number and gender in Croatian. In Ursula Stephany & Maria Voeikova (eds.), *Development of*

nominal inflection in first language acquisition: A cross-linguistic perspective (Studies on Language Acquisition 30), 153–177. Berlin & New York: Mouton de Gruyter.

Kuvač Kraljević, Jelena & Marijan Palmović. 2007. *Metodologija istraživanja dječjeg jezika* [Methodology in child language research]. Zagreb: Naklada Slap.

MacWhinney, Brian. 2000. *The CHILDES Project: Tools for analyzing talk.* Mahwah, NJ: Lawrence Erlbaum Associates.

MacWhinney, Brian. 2018. *Tools for analyzing talk.* Part 2: *The CLAN program.* https://doi.org/10.21415/T5G10R

Nuyts, Jan. 2005. The modal confusion: On terminology and the concepts behind it. In Alex Klinge & Henrik Hegel Müller (eds.), *Modality: Studies in form and function*, 5–38. London: Equinox.

Nuyts, Jan. 2006. Modality: Overview and linguistic issues. In William Frawley (ed.), *The expression of modality*, 1–26. Berlin: Mouton de Gruyter.

Nuyts, Jan, Pieter Byloo & Janneke Diepeveen. 2010. On deontic modality, directivity, and mood: The case of Dutch *mogen* and *moeten*. *Journal of Pragmatics* 42(1). 16–34.

Rice, Mabel L., Filip Smolik, Denise Perpich, Travis Thompson, Nathan Rytting & Megan Blossom. 2010. Mean length of utterance levels in 6-month intervals for children 3 to 9 years with and without language impairments. *Journal of Speech, Language, and Hearing Research* 53(2). 333–349.

Silić, Josip & Ivo Pranjković. 2007. *Gramatika hrvatskoga jezika za gimnazije i visoka učilišta* [Croatian grammar for high schools and universities]. Zagreb: Školska knjiga.

Stephany, Ursula. 1985. *Aspekt, Tempus und Modalität: Zur Entwicklung der Verbalgrammatik in der neugriechischen Kindersprache.* (Language Universals Series 4). Tübingen: Gunter Narr.

Stephany, Ursula. 1986. Modality. In Paul Fletcher & Michael Garman (eds.), *Language acquisition*, 375–400. 2nd edn. Cambridge: Cambridge University Press.

Stephany, Ursula & Maria Voeikova. 2015. Requests, their meanings and aspectual forms in early Greek and Russian child language. *Journal of Greek Linguistics* 15. 66–90.

Marianne Kilani-Schoch
Competition of grammatical forms in the expression of directives in early French child speech and child-directed speech

Abstract: This chapter investigates the early expression of directives in the interaction of two French-speaking toddlers (aged 1;4/1;6–2;11/3;0) with their parents. More specifically it deals with deontic modality and focuses on obligation and prohibition as expressed by orders and indirect directives not giving the addressee the option of non-compliance. One of the main findings is that in child speech as well as child-directed speech second person present indicative forms are used in lieu of imperatives. Moreover, alongside other meanings, root infinitives occur in child speech with a deontic meaning. Hence, root infinitives, present indicative forms and imperative forms appear as potential rival means of encoding a strong directive illocutionary force. The chapter aims at accounting for the emergence and complementary or contrastive functional use of these three types of formal means and at determining the factors which may explain their distribution. The discussion centers on the extent to which the different forms are specialized for specific contexts of use, the lexical content of the verbs occurring in such utterances and the different degrees of illocutionary force of the latter, both in child speech and child-directed speech.

1 Introduction

While several language acquisition studies on both direct and indirect requests have been published over the last decades (for an overview see, e.g., Cameron-Faulkner 2014; Zufferey 2015), research bearing more specifically on orders is less widespread (see e.g., Bates 1976; Mueller Gathercole, Sebastián, and Soto 2002; Grosse et al. 2010).

The present chapter studies deontic modality. This is one subdomain of agent-oriented modality,[1] the other one being dynamic modality (see Choi 2006; Hickmann and Bassano 2016: 431). "Dynamic modality [. . .] refers to

---
[1] This category was introduced by Bybee (1985: 166) and was first adopted for the study of language acquisition by Gerhardt (1991) and Choi (2006).

Marianne Kilani-Schoch, University of Lausanne

https://doi.org/10.1515/9781501504457-006

how children express agents' desire, ability, and capacity toward an action, including also volition and intention, while deontic modality refers to how they express obligation, permission, and interdiction" (Hickmann and Bassano 2016: 431; see this volume, Introduction). Within deontic modality, the present chapter focuses on obligation and prohibition as expressed by orders and indirect directives in the interaction of two French-speaking toddlers with their parents (1;4/1;6–2;11/3;0). The starting point of the study is the function of orders, i.e. telling an addressee what to do (Aikhenvald 2010: 128).[2] We thus do not only take forms and their meanings into consideration, but also their pragmatic functions.

Directive speech acts are commonly defined as "attempts (of varying degrees [. . .]) by the speaker to get the hearer to do something" (Searle 1976: 11; see also Stephany 2013). "A directive subsumes orders, requests, instructions, and also advice and permission, all of these reflecting different degrees of control and attitude on behalf of the 'commander'" (Aikhenvald 2010: 198). Searle (1977: 28) conceptualizes these differences in terms of illocutionary force: "The illocutionary point of request is the same as that of order: both are attempts to get hearers to do something. But the illocutionary forces are clearly different." Lyons (1977: 749) suggests that commands differ from requests in that they do not give the addressee the option of not complying with the mand, i.e. of not performing the action. As formulated by Aikhenvald (2016: 147): "While orders imply telling someone else what to do, requests involve asking someone to do something, with an option for the addressee not to comply (though the assumption often is that they will)." However, Leech (2014: 62) underlines that the judgment on the option of compliance or noncompliance "is scalar rather than absolute" so that the distinction between direct directives, i.e. orders, and indirect directives, at least those with a relatively strong illocutionary force, is not straightforward. Aikhenvald (2010: 199) notes that "numerous examples can occupy the middle ground between 'telling' and 'asking'." Moreover, although "imperatives – or imperative mood – are the dedicated grammatical device whose core meaning is that of a directive speech act, a command" (Aikhenvald 2010: 395),[3] directive speech acts "can be expressed through a variety of means" and "one can command without using an imperative" (Aikhenvald 2010: 2, see also Lyons 1977: 747 on the possibility of transmitting a command or request indirectly).

---

[2] Here, "order" will be understood as a synonym of "command" and no distinction will be made between them.
[3] On the other hand, imperatives are polysemous and may convey a wide range of speech acts associated with different degrees of illocutionary force (see e.g., Aikhenvald 2010: 198; Leech 2014: 61).

Taking this perspective, the present chapter is centered on orders as well as indirect directives or requests in child speech (henceforth CS) that tell rather than ask the addressee to do something and do not give him the option of non-compliance. In other words, besides direct directives which are prototypically encoded by imperatives, the chapter embraces indirect directives, e.g., statements of an addressee's future action, which have an illocutionary force close to direct orders.

We base our distinction between 'telling' or 'ordering' and 'asking' on the following suggestion of Aikhenvald's (2016: 147): "The 'asking' rather than 'telling' or 'ordering' overtone is commonly signaled by additional means: *please*, *kindly*, an interrogative tag, or a performative parenthetical such as *I beg you*" (see Section 3.2).

The theoretical distinction between direct and indirect directives adopted here is the one made by Lyons (1977: 785), who refers to the pairing of form and function. An utterance conveying a single illocutionary force is a direct speech act, whereas it is an indirect one if it may have two illocutionary forces, i.e. it does not convey the illocutionary force associated with its sentence form. Accordingly, an imperative sentence with the contextually defined function of order is a direct directive, while statements or interrogative types of sentences expressing an order are indirect.

The motivation for studying the specific subset of direct and indirect directives with a strong illocutionary force first comes from the observation that, in some varieties of French, the imperative may be supplemented or even substituted by forms such as the 2nd person singular present indicative for the expression of an order, e.g., *tu viens* 'you come' for *viens* 'come'. Second, the high frequency of directives in child speech, in particular imperatives, has often been pointed out in the literature (Aikhenvald 2010: 326; see also Bates 1976 among many others). But indicative forms expressing directives are not often mentioned (e.g., Mueller Gathercole, Sebastián, and Soto 2002: 396; Rojas Nieto 2011: 48; Avram and Coene 2007: 236; Stephany and Voeikova 2015: 73). Third, it is well-known from research on the so-called optional infinitive stage in the acquisition of a number of languages that root infinitives are used with directive meaning (e.g., Lasser 2002; Kilani-Schoch and Dressler 2002; Avram and Coene 2007).

Given the extent of the field covered by directive strategies, the present study is limited to the imperative mood and its principal rivals, namely root infinitives and the 2nd person singular present indicative. The third person singular present indicative with *on* and the emergence of deontic modal verb forms will only be briefly mentioned.

The aim of the chapter is to account for the emergence and use of the three major types of grammatical forms with which the strongest illocutionary force of directives is expressed and to examine to what extent these forms are complementary or rival in function in a given developmental phase. The question of whether they are pragmatically specialized and thus limited to specific contexts of use and whether this has consequences for the pace of development of directives in child speech and child-directed speech (henceforth CDS), is also explored.

The structure of the chapter is the following: After a short description of the grammatical forms expressing directives in the target language in Section 2, the data and methodology are presented in Section 3. Section 4 contains the results of the analysis on the use and meaning of imperatives as compared to root infinitives and the 2nd person singular present indicative forms expressing directives in both CS and CDS. Section 5 presents the development of compound future and modal verb constructions. We conclude with a discussion of the increasing variability of the pragmatic meanings of these forms in CS in relation to their even greater variability in CDS.

2 Imperatives and other directive forms expressing obligation and prohibition in French

In this section, the forms of the French target system expressing obligation and prohibition studied in the present chapter will be described; namely 2nd person imperatives, 2nd person singular present indicatives, third person singular present indicatives with the subject pronoun *on*, root infinitives, as well as modal verbs related to the latter. Compound futures alluded to throughout the chapter will also be shortly presented. An overview of French expressions of deontic modality is displayed in Table 1.

2.1 Imperatives

In French, as in a number of other languages, the 2nd person singular of the imperative is generally identical to the unmarked present singular indicative form or stem[4] ((*tu*) *parles* 'you speak'- *parle* 'speak', (*tu*) *finis* '(you) finish'- *finis* 'finish', etc.). A small number of suppletive verbs (e.g., *être* 'be', *avoir* 'have') lack an imperative form and take the present subjunctive form instead (*es* be.PRS.2SG – *sois* be.SUBJ.2SG 'be', *as* have.PRS.2SG – *aies* have.SUBJ.2SG 'have' > IMP.2SG *aie*).

---

4 The three persons of the present singular are generally homophonous.

Table 1: Main forms expressing deontic modality in French.

Linguistic means	Verb form*	Prototypical function	Gloss
		Direct directives	
Imperative 2SG	viens, ne viens pas	order, prohibition	'come', 'don't come'
Imperative 2PL	venez, ne venez pas	order, prohibition	'come', 'don't come'
Root infinitive	prendre deux gouttes	prescription	'take two drops'
	ne pas pleurer		'(do) not cry'
		Indirect directives	
Imperative 1PL	allons-y	hortative	'let's go'
PRO *on* + PRES.3SG	on y va	hortative	'let's go'
	on ne touche pas	statement of social rules (speaker-external source)	'one does not touch'
PRO *tu* + present/ compound future 2SG	tu viens tu vas venir	statement of an addressee's immediate action or one in the near future	'you come' 'you will come'
modal verb	tu dois venir	statement of an addressee's obligation (speaker-internal source)	'you must come'
	tu peux venir	statement of a speaker's attitude towards a potential future event (permission)	'you may come'
impersonal modal verb	il faut venir	statement of an addressee's obligation (speaker-external source)	'one must come'

*All positive forms listed below can be cast in the negative form as in the examples of *ne viens pas, ne venez pas* 'don't come' to express prohibition. They are not repeated in the table.

The difference between 2nd person singular imperative and present singular indicative forms is the co-occurrence of a subject clitic pronoun (or a subject noun) in case of the latter as in all other finite forms. Moreover object pronouns used with the imperative or the indicative present forms contrast in their place before or after the verb, and sometimes in form. With positive imperatives, object pronouns are placed after the verb: *donne-le* 'give it', whereas they are preposed in structures containing an explicit subject: *tu le donnes* 'you give it'. By contrast, the negative imperatives require proclitics: compare *ne le donne pas* 'don't give it' and *tu ne le donnes pas* 'you don't give it'. The alternating position of object pronouns is probably one of the reasons why the use of the 2nd person singular imperative in directives may correspond to a difference of register and represent a more formal device than the 2nd person singular present indicative forms (see Section 2.2), unless the imperative is a highly frequent form of the verb (e.g., *viens* 'come', *donne* 'give').

Even though the 2nd person singular imperative can convey direct directives with different degrees of illocutionary force depending on the context (cf. *sors!* get.out.IMP.2SG 'get out' suggested to a cat in opening the door of a balcony vs. addressed to people in a house in case of fire), utterances in the imperative are usually stronger than indirect directives expressed by other modal constructions (Aikhenvald 2010: 198–200). Indeed, imperatives as the shortest verb forms often express abrupt orders with overtones of urgency and immediacy, whereas directives with lower illocutionary strength correspond to more complex formal means (Aikhenvald 2010: 46) (but see Section 2.2). Urgency is thus a feature often linked to the strength of orders and thus more often conveyed by imperative than by 2nd person singular present indicative forms with *tu*.

Several frequently used imperative forms have desemanticized to merely pragmatic uses whereby they tend to become discourse markers or interjections: *tiens* (hold.IMP.2SG) 'really', *dis* (say.IMP.2SG) 'say', *attends* (wait.IMP.2SG) 'wait'. This also holds for the 1st and 2nd plural imperative *allons* (go.IMP.1PL) 'come on' and *allez* (go.IMP.2PL) 'go, come on'.

2.2 Second person singular present indicative forms

Although, according to the definition presented in Section 1, second person singular present indicative forms (henceforth *tu*-forms) serve the category of indirect speech acts, a *tu*-form may reinforce a direct speech act, e.g., when it is used immediately after the imperative form of the same verb (e.g., *laisse, tu laisses* 'don't, you don't'). In contrast, a face-threatening act expressed with a *tu*-form conveys a relatively weaker illocutionary force than the same speech act in the imperative (e.g., *tu me laisses tranquille* 'you leave me alone (lit. quiet)' for *laisse-moi tranquille* 'leave me alone (lit. quiet)') (see Sections 4.4, 4.5). Notice that it is not entirely clear to what extent the mitigating effect may also be due to a register difference.

2.3 Third person singular present indicative forms with the subject pronoun *on*

A prototypical order expressed in the imperative implies the speaker's control over the activity to be performed by the addressee. The speech act is more indirect if control is presented as shared by the speaker with the addressee. This is the case with the use of the 3rd person singular subject pronoun *on* either referring to the 1st person plural or the 2nd person singular. In such cases the performer of the action expressed by the *on* construction is the addressee, but the speaker pretends to express a suggestion concerning both speaker and hearer in order to mitigate the request, e.g. *on va au lit* 'we go to bed' uttered at the child's bedtime. Since the directive is cast in a statement of fact of the desired action, it still keeps a strong illocutionary force: the utterance does not leave the addressee the option of not complying with the directive. The *on*-form is a hortative, i.e. a directive addressed to the speaker and the addressee (Aikhenvald 2010: 48).

2.4 Compound future forms

Compound verb forms correspond to constructions with the semi-auxiliary *aller* 'go' + INF expressing the immediate future. *Tu*-forms and *on*-forms combined with the compound future may function as directives depending on who utters them addressing whom in which circumstances. A statement of an immediate future action which is a speaker's wish but which the addressee is reluctant to perform has a strong illocutionary force if made by an authority such as the child's mother. Such directives may be slightly mitigated by use of the pronoun *on* (see Section 2.3) rather than *tu* (e.g. *après tu vas te coucher* 'afterwards you go to bed' or *après on va se coucher* 'afterwards we will go to bed' in cases where only the child will go to bed). Since directives cast in the compound future are presented as less urgent than orders expressed with the imperative and call for less immediate action than orders in the second person singular present indicative, they have a polite or mild overtone.

2.5 Modal verbs

The French verbs *devoir* 'must' and *pouvoir* 'can, may', which both have an epistemic and deontic meaning, are not as specific syntactically and morphologically as in languages such as German or English so that their status as modal verbs is disputed (see e.g., Champaud, Bassano, and Hickmann 1993: 189; Hickmann and Bassano 2016).

Modal verb forms differ with regard to their face-threatening potential: *tu dois* 'you must', is closer to an order cast in the imperative than the impersonal *il faut* 'it must'. What seems to be at stake here is the speaker-internal (*tu dois*) vs. speaker-external source of modality (*il faut*). The stronger illocutionary force conveyed by an utterance containing *tu dois* relates to the position of authority that it presupposes for the speaker.

2.6 Root infinitives

Root infinitives are structurally independent infinitival forms occurring autonomously in an utterance, i.e. without any finite verb form (see, e.g., Phillips 1995). It has been argued that infinitival main clauses have a wide range of uses in languages such as French and German (Lasser 2002: 778; Laaha and Bassano 2013), e.g., expression of desire, surprise, elliptical answers, rhetorical questions, instructions. In many languages, a major function of root infinitives is the expression of positive or negative orders, e.g., German *aufhören* 'stop', French *prendre deux gouttes* 'take two drops', *pas pleurer* '(do) not cry' (Lasser 2002: 774; Aikhenvald 2010: 281).

Deontically used root infinitives as opposed to dynamically used ones are distinguished on the basis of agency: Root infinitives expressing orders are oriented towards an addressee who has to comply, whereas dynamic volitive root infinitives rather express a speaker's desire (see Section 4.3).

3 Data and methodology

3.1 The data

This study is based on the corpora of two children from Lausanne, a city in French-speaking Switzerland: Sophie (SOP) and Emma (EMM), interacting with their parents. Sophie was recorded from 1;6 to 3;0 every 10 days for about half an hour each time and Emma from 1;4 to 2;11 (Table 2). Emma's data are more limited than Sophie's since she was generally recorded only twice a month and some of her recordings are very short (especially those at 1;6, 1;7, 2;0; the recordings at 1;7 are complemented by diary notes).

Both children grew up in upper-middle class families. Recording situations of the children vary between playing and everyday situations (e.g., eating, washing, book reading, and having a bath). Transcription and coding have been done according to the CHAT conventions of CHILDES (MacWhinney 2000).

Table 2: CS and CDS data.

Corpus	Age	Utterances		Recordings	Hours
		CS	CDS		
Sophie	1;6–3;0	15,763	12,478	46	29
Emma	1;4–2;11	7,335	6,639	40	18

3.2 Methodology: Identifying directives expressing obligation and prohibition

In order to gather all root infinitives, *tu*-forms and other rival forms of the imperative with the meaning of strong directives in the two corpora, a qualitative follow-up of the variants displayed by the lexemes occurring in directives in CDS and CS has been carried out. Each form potentially expressing obligation or prohibition has been manually analyzed in its sequential environment, which means that not only the preceding turns of caretaker and child were scrutinized, but also the following ones. The implications of the potentially strong directive as well as the caretaker's interpretation of the child's utterance[5] were taken into consideration. Nevertheless, the identification of the illocutionary status and force conveyed by the forms remains a tricky task. For instance, the child's reply to the directive does not necessarily allow the assessment of differences in illocutionary force on the basis of (non)compliance as the reply may be the same whether expressed by an imperative or a *tu*-form (example 1).

(1) a. Sophie, 1;9 (the child has put a marble in her mouth)
    MOT: *Coquine   crache!*
         mischievous spit.IMP.2SG
         'Mischievous one, spit!'
    SOP: *Non   pas kak [: crache].*
         no   NEG spit
    for: *non   je   ne   crache   pas*
         no   I   not   spit.PRS.SG not
         'No, I don't spit.'

---

[5] To be sure, a caretaker's interpretation is not always accurate as evidenced by the early ability of children to repair misunderstandings (Filipi 2014: 73–74).

b. Sophie, 2;9
   MOT: *Tu ouvres maintenant.*
         you open.PRS.2SG now
         'You open now.'
   SOP: *Non.*
         'No.'

Within the set of forms expressing agent-oriented deontic or dynamic modality, the following contextual cues have been taken into account in order to identify forms conveying obligation and prohibition and distinguish them from requests leaving an option of noncompliance on the one hand, and to differentiate between agent-oriented deontic modality and dynamic modality expressing desires or wishes, on the other:[6]

a. prosody and syntax: children's interrogative utterances, which do not strictly impose compliance on the addressee, were excluded from requests in the strict sense. Examples of directives cast in the interrogative form not leaving the option of noncompliance have nevertheless been found in CDS, e.g., *on va bientôt aller au lit?* 'does one go to bed soon?' has clearly the function of an order rather than a request;

b. politeness: utterances containing a politeness marker such as *s'il te plaît* 'please' were also excluded as not belonging to the category of strong directives (see example 3);

c. the addressee's reply (e.g., *d'accord* 'okay' instead of *oui* 'yes') has been deemed as generally following a wish rather than an order (but see, e.g., Sections 4.3 and 4.5, examples 10a, b, 27);

d. the co-occurrence of temporal adverbials indicating the ordering of actions to be performed (e.g., *tu laves le visage d'abord* 'you wash the face first', *après* 'next') was taken as a hint that the sentence was a directive without an option of refusal;

e. auto-reformulations by the speaker, e.g., replacing a main verb construction by one with a modal verb, have been interpreted as making the force of the directive explicit, e.g., a prohibition as in example (2).

---

[6] Gestures could not be analyzed since the children were audiotaped rather than videotaped.

(2) Sophie, 2;10
    Le   poulet   tu   prends   pas,
    the   chicken   you   take.PRS.2SG not
    (tu)   peux   pas   prendre   (le)   poulet.
    (you) can.PRS.2SG not   take.INF   (the) chicken
    'You don't take the chicken, (you) can't take (the) chicken.'

f. hetero-reformulations and questions of information by the addressee are other relevant cues. Thus, requests for the use of a politeness marker suggest that the child's utterance has been interpreted as an order by the adult (example 3).

(3) Sophie and Mother, 3;0
    SOP: *Tu   poses   ça   ici.*
           you.2SG put.PRS.2SG this here
           'You put this here.'
    MOT: *Ah ah!*
    SOP: *S'il te plaît.*
           'Please.'
    MOT: *D'accord alors.*
           'Okay then.'

Among root infinitives, those containing cues for the speaker's will of having the addressee carry out an action were considered as orders. In example (4a), the cue is provided by the occurrence of the address form *Maman* 'Mommy' before the root infinitive, which designates the mother as the performer of the desired action. Since only the mother can fill the bottle with limonade, *mettre* in example (4b) must be interpreted as expressing an order.

(4) Sophie, 2;2
    a. MOT: *Vas-y,   appuie   fort!*
               go.IMP.2SG-there press.IMP.2SG hard
               'Go, press hard!'
       SOP: *Non   a   dur.*
               no   FILL   hard
               Maman a   faire.
               Mommy FILL   do.INF
               'No (it's) hard, Mommy (must) do (so).'

b. *Encore   mettre   Doranna.*
   once.more put.INF   Orangina
   'Add Orangina [name of a limonade] another time.'

By contrast, in example (5), the mother's question shows that the child is the implicit subject so that the infinitive should not be analyzed as a prohibition. Rather the child's utterance has a dynamic meaning expressing inability.

(5) Sophie, 2;6
    SOP: *Pas   d'   éteindre.*
          not   PREP   turn.off.INF
    for: *pas   éteindre*
          not   turn.off.INF
          '(I cannot) turn (it) off.'
    MOT: *T(u) arrives pas?*
          'You cannot?'

The child's reformulation of her own utterance may also serve as a cue for interpreting it. Since the imperative is reformulated as a root infinitive in example (6), the latter may be taken as expressing an order (see Section 4.3).

(6) Sophie, 2;0
    Maman essaie   Maman, Maman essayer Maman.
    Mommy try.IMP.2SG   Mommy Mommy try.INF Mommy
    'Try, Mommy.'

Ambiguous root infinitives which may be interpreted as either conveying a wish or an order are frequently found in the data.

4 Imperatives, root infinitives and *tu*-forms in CS

4.1 Overview

The number of lexical types (lemmas) and tokens of imperatives,[7] root infinitives, and *tu*-forms occurring with a directive meaning in the CS or CDS of the

---

[7] The occurrence of exclamative *dis* (lit. say.IMP.2SG) 'really!' in CDS (Sophie's and Emma's CDS 10 tokens each) have been excluded from the counts.

two children are presented in Table 3. The table indicates the number of forms in each category as well as the respective percentage of tokens in relation to the total of verb tokens.

The average frequencies of imperatives in CS and CDS are quite close to each other, although they are slightly higher in CS than CDS. While both children use imperatives more often than root infinitives or *tu*-forms in their directives, Sophie prefers root infinitives to *tu*-forms, but with Emma it is the other way around.

In the CDS of both children, directives are also most often expressed by imperative forms. Just as in Emma's speech, *tu*-forms are more frequently found in her CDS than in Sophie's. This feature is an example of the more informal and regionally marked style of the speech of Emma's father (see also Section 5).

Table 3: Frequency (types/tokens) and percentage (tokens) of imperatives, root infinitives and *tu*-forms with directive meaning.

	Total verb tokens	IMP	%	Root INF	%	Tu-forms	%
SOP	5,628	33/556	9.9	22/70	1.2	18/43	0.8
		32/345[a]	6.1				
EMM	4,038	45/395	9.8	18/29	0.7	30/72	1.8
		44/256[b]	6.3				
SOP CDS	11,771	64/848	7.0	1/3	0.02	17/47	0.4
EMM CDS	6,954	50/606	8.7	2/4	0.06	43/111	1.6

[a]Without *attends* 'wait' (211 tokens).
[b]Without *regarde* 'look' (124 tokens).

Imperatives and root infinitives emerge early in both children's speech (Emma 1;4, Sophie 1;8), several months before *tu*-forms, which require mastery of the shifting 2nd person pronoun. According to the regional preference noted above, Emma starts to use *tu*-forms earlier than Sophie (EMM 1;10, SOP 2;7).

4.2 Imperatives

The imperative remains the most frequent means for expressing orders in both children's speech throughout the observational period. In Emma's speech, imperatives occur already at 1;4, almost simultaneously with root infinitives, with which they often alternate in the same recording or in successive ones (Emma 1;4 *donne* give.IMP.2SG 'give', 1;5 *donner* give.INF 'give', 1;6 *regarder* look.INF, 1;7 *regarde* 'look. IMP.2SG').

In Sophie's speech, imperative forms emerge at 1;8, two months after the first unambiguous 3rd or 1st person singular present indicative forms (e.g., 1;6 *p(l)eut* 'rains' 1;7 *aime* '(I) like'). From the beginning, a greater proportion of imperatives alternate with root infinitives of the same lexemes in Sophie's speech than in Emma's (see Section 4.3).

Imperative forms which do not contrast with another inflectional form of a given lemma are scarce: 2 lemmas in Sophie's speech (2;7 *file* 'clear out', 2;8 *plains-toi* 'complain') and 3 lemmas in Emma's (1;11 *sonnez* 'ring.IMP.2PL', 2;3 *avale* 'swallow', 2;11 *entre* 'come in').[8]

The token frequencies of imperative forms are variable throughout the corpus so that the overall development is quite difficult to characterize. What appears more clearly, however, is the frequent use of the imperative form *attends* 'wait' in Sophie's third year. This form is partly pragmaticalized, i.e. it has acquired an interactional function.

The cumulative development of lemmas gives a clue on how they diversify (see Table 4). New lemmas occur almost in each recording session. More revealing about the development, however, is the comparison of lemmas in CS and CDS. Sophie's CDS shows twice as many lemmas used in the imperative (64 lemmas used in 1 inflectional type each)[9] as her own speech (32 lemmas used in 1 inflectional type each). Almost all imperative lemmas in Sophie's production also occur in CDS. Only three of them are not found in CDS (*accroche* 'attach', *mange* 'eat', *pars* 'go away'). The only example which is probably not missing from CDS due to corpus size is *pars* 'go away', because it is likely to be considered too rude to be used by the mother.

Unlike Sophie, the high number of imperative lemmas in Emma's speech (45 lemmas) is close to their number in CDS (50 lemmas). In addition, the types are more diverse: Emma uses several forms of plural imperatives (4 lemmas occur in both 2nd person singular and 2nd person plural; another lemma is used only in 2nd person plural) and even one subjunctive form filling the cell in the suppletive paradigm of *être* (*sois* 'be'). By contrast, Sophie uses a single plural imperative: *allez* (go.2PL) 'go' (see Table 4).

These differences between the two children may be accounted for by a more general feature: Emma is an early talker, which is partly due to her position as

---

8 Besides infinitive forms, imperative forms mainly contrast with indicative present singular forms, past participle forms, and later on, for some lexemes, with imperfect (Sophie and Emma) and conditional forms (Sophie).

9 1 lemma is used in 2 inflectional types and another one in 3 inflectional types.

an only child in the family. In contrast, Sophie is a third child. The different family circumstances of the two girls are illustrated, among other things, by the higher total number of verb lemmas in Emma's corpus (205) than in Sophie's (189), despite the smaller size of the former.

Table 4: Imperatives: Cumulative development of lemmas and inflectional types in Sophie's and Emma's speech.[a]

	Sophie			Emma	
Age	Imperatives	Gloss	Age	Imperatives	Gloss
			1;4	donne	give
			1;5	attends, raconte, tiens	wait, narrate, hold
			1;7	appuie, regarde	press, look
1;8	tiens	hold	1;8	attendez, laisse, pars, partez	wait.2PL, leave, go.away, go.away.2PL
1;9	donne, essaie, va, viens	give, try, go, come		–	–
1;10	assieds(-toi), attrape	sit down, catch		allez, arrête, dis, mets, rince	go.2PL, stop, say, put, rinse
1;11	attends	wait		sonnez,[b] souffle, tourne, viens	ring.2PL, blow, turn, come
2;0	regarde	look		mélange	mix
2;1	cherche, passe, souffle	look for, pass, blow		bois, dépêche-toi	drink, hurry up
2;2	appuie, mets, montre	press, put, show		regardez, dessine, bouge	look.2PL, draw, move
2;3	–	–		fais voir, avale	show, swallow
2;4	ferme, joue, mange, ouvre	close, play, eat, open		cherche, tenez	look for, hold.2PL
2;5	–	–		sois	be
2;6	dis, fais, finis	say, do, finish		prends, sors	take, go out

Table 4 (continued)

	Sophie			Emma	
Age	Imperatives	Gloss	Age	Imperatives	Gloss
2;7	allez, arrête, file	go.2PL, stop, clear out	–	–	–
2;8	plains-toi,[b] prends	complain, take		attrape, dors	catch, sleep
2;9	accroche, laisse, range, touche	hang, leave, tidy touch		enlève, lave, pose, va	remove, wash, place on, go
2;10	pars, tourne-toi	go out, turn		compte, ferme, ouvre, flotte	count, close, open, float
2;11	–	–		entre, tire	come in, pull
3;0	–	–		(no recording)	

[a]Only plural forms have been marked by 2PL. The single 1PL of the data (Emma 1;10 *allons*) has not been included in the table since its use is unclear.
[b]Occurring in a song.

The first lemmas used in the imperative mostly belong to a class of dynamic verbs concerning basic interactions between child and caretaker (e.g., Sophie 1;8, Emma 1;5 *tiens* 'hold', Sophie 1;9, Emma 1;4 *donne* 'give', Sophie 1;9, Emma 1;11 *viens* 'come', Sophie 2;0, Emma 1;7 *regarde* 'look'). That is, they are either deictics linked to the speech situation (*viens*), visual attention getters (*regarde*) or imperatives denoting general actions, e.g., motion verbs (Sophie 1;9 *va* 'go', Emma 1;8 *pars* 'go away') (cf. Bassano 2010). These imperatives may be taken to be contextual, the full meaning of which is recoverable from the speech situation. Verbs associated with game activities are also used before the turn to the third year (Sophie 1;9 *essaie* 'try', 1;10 *attrape* 'catch', Emma 1;7, 1;10 *appuie* 'press', *mets* 'put'). Progressively imperatives diversify in terms of actions or behaviors to be carried out by the addressee, including change of state verbs (Sophie 2;4, Emma 2;10 *ouvre* 'open', *ferme* 'close') and more abstract verbs (e.g., Sophie 2;6, Emma 1;10 *dis* 'say', Emma 2;1 *dépêche-toi* 'hurry up', 2;10 *compte* 'count'). Eventually, more specific actions and manipulations of objects are denoted by imperative forms: Emma 2;3 *avale* 'swallow' (this is more specific than the hyperonym *mange* 'eat'), 2;9 *enlève* 'remove', *pose* 'put down', 2;11 *tire* 'pull' (all denoting actions relating two entities with a variable spatial positioning and following a specific directionality).

The relation between the speech situation and the use of the imperative can be illustrated in Sophie's speech by the examples of playing dinner party, where the adult's and child's roles are reversed, and of talking to the family dog. In these cases, the imperative forms seem to be imitations of routinized forms addressed by caretakers to children or dogs in similar situations, as shown by the effortful realization of the imperative construction in example (7).

(7) Sophie 2;7 (referring to the family dog)
    e   *mord*   *Goutte,*
    FILLER   bite.PRS.3SG   drop.N.PROP
    for: *il*   *mord*   *Goutte*
        he   bite.PRS.3SG   drop.N.PROP
    'Drop is biting.'
    e   *mord*   *mon pantalon*   *zut!*
    FILL   bite.PRS.3SG   my   pants   INTERJ
    for: *il*   *mord*   *mon pantalon*   *zut*
        he   bite.PRS.3SG   my   pants   gee
    'He is biting my pants, gee.'
    File   *de là/*   *file*   *le [: de] là!*
    clear.out.IMP.2SG   from there   clear.out.IMP.2SG   from   there
    'Clear out from there, clear out from there!'

The most pragmaticalized imperative forms such as *tiens* 'really' or *dis donc* 'really' which have entirely lost their literal meaning ('hold' and 'do say') and have become interjections expressing surprise typically occur only in CDS and are acquired later as are other opaque discourse markers. Although the imperatives produced by the two girls mainly have a literal meaning, partly pragmaticalized imperative forms begin to occur already in the third year (Sophie 2;7 *allez* go.IMP.2PL 'go', 1;11/2;1 *attends* wait.IMP.2SG 'wait'; Emma 1;10 *allez* go. IMP.2PL 'go'), as mentioned above. From 2;1 onwards, this function seems to have been taken up by Sophie, who overuses *attends* (e.g., more than 60 tokens at 2;5 and 2;6) as a way of structuring the interaction rather than denoting content (Kerbrat-Orecchioni 2005: 50). *Attends* is repeatedly produced in order to block the addressee's next verbal or non-verbal actions. This suggests that the child is exploiting a new conversational means that allows holding the floor and keeping control over the course of interaction.

To summarize, the development of lemmas used in the imperative for expressing orders before the age of 3;0 shows a semantic as well as a pragmatic diversification of meaning and an increase in conceptual complexity. The semantic meanings of the imperative developing in the third year correspond to more subtle cognitive differentiations, while most (partly) pragmaticalized meanings bear on the organization of interaction. A progression towards more abstract semantic and pragmatic meanings can thus be observed.

4.3 Root infinitives

In the early period of CS, the main means for expressing orders verbally are imperatives and root infinitives. This section examines root infinitives and compares them with imperatives in order to find out whether these linguistic forms are functionally in competition. We first focus on the relation between lemmas expressing orders in the imperative and those rendering them by root infinitives during the period where root infinitives are the most numerous (until 1;10 in Emma's speech and 2;4 in Sophie's speech).

The functions of root infinitives occurring in early French CS vary between (non-modal) statements (example 8a), agent-oriented dynamic modal meanings (example 8b) and deontic modality (example 8c).

(8) a. Sophie, 2;4 (describing a game)
      e   mettre de   l'   eau
      FILLER put.INF of   the water
      for: je   mets   de l'   eau
            I   put.PRS.1SG of the water
     '(I) am putting some water.'
   b. Sophie, 2;3
      Encore   *faire.*
      again   do.INF
     '(I want to) do again.'
   c. Sophie 2;2
     MOT: *Moi*   *je*   *n'*   *ai*   *pas*
             me   I   NEG   have.1SG NEG
             de   *bonbon.*
             of   candy
        'I don't have any candy.'
     SOP: *é*   *che(r)cher.*
             FILLER search.INF
        'Search (for it).'

MOT:	*Où*	*je*	*dois*	*aller*	*en*
	where	I	must	go	INDF.PRO
	chercher?				
	search.INF				

'Where shall I search for it?'

As can be seen in Table 3 (Section 4.1 above), root infinitives are more numerous in Sophie's CS (1.2% of verb forms) than in Emma's (0.7%). In the present study only root infinitives expressing deontic meaning are counted but the overall number of root infinitives in Sophie's data is much higher since they are also used for rendering non-modal meanings (Kilani-Schoch and Dressler 2002).

It is interesting to note that most root infinitives are accompanied by imperative forms of the same lemma which are used for the same function in the children's data. Prohibitions are preferably conveyed by the negator *pas* preposed to a root infinitive (e.g., Sophie 2;6 *pas crier* '(do) not scream'; Emma 1;9 *pas tirer* '(do) not pull') rather than by an imperative (*ne crie pas* 'don't cry'), the negation of which is syntactically more complex.

The fact that prohibitions are preferably encoded by root infinitives with a preposed negative particle in French child language more generally (cf. Mueller Gathercole, Sebastián and Soto 2002) is clearly demonstrated by Sophie's speech since more than half of the total number of negative verb forms expressing prohibitions (modal forms including *on*-forms) are root infinitives with a preposed negator.[10] Although, in Emma's speech, negative root infinitives and imperatives are more balanced,[11] negative root infinitive tokens also exceed negative imperatives (see Table 6 in Section 4.5).

Verbal lemmas used for expressing orders in the imperative or by root infinitives develop differently in the speech of the two children: Sophie uses more root infinitives for a much longer period than Emma.

During the root infinitive period (Sophie 1;6–2;4, Emma 1;4–1;10), Sophie produces almost the same number of lemmas used in root infinitives as in imperatives (17 RI – 19 IMP) whereas Emma uses less root infinitives (9 RI vs. 16 IMP). Most of the lemmas found in Sophie's speech as deontic root infinitives also occur in the imperative (12 out of 17 lemmas), while, in Emma's speech, only 5 of 9 lemmas found as root infinitives are also used as imperatives.

---

10 We leave the discussion of the frequency of negative orders in child language for another study (cf. Mueller Gathercole, Sebastián, and Soto 2002).

11 A striking finding in Emma's CS is the occurrence of the formal negator *ne* together with *pas* 'not': 2;2 *ne bouge pas* 'don't move', 2;8 *ne mélange pas* 'don't mix'. Indeed this construction is not observed in Emma's CDS at all.

The question is to what extent these figures hint at a competing use of the two forms.

This issue will be examined by turning to a qualitative perspective studying alternations between imperatives and root infinitives of the same lexemes in order to find out whether some pragmatic features characterize the use of either form in terms of function or illocutionary force.

One of the main questions raised by this kind of analysis is the relation between root infinitives and compound verb forms[12] (see e.g., Wijnen, Kempe, and Gillis 2001; Ambridge and Lieven 2011: 152–159 for an overview; Laaha and Bassano 2013).[13] In other words, do root infinitives used by the children stand for deontic constructions such as *tu dois* + INF 'you must INF', *tu vas/va* + INF 'you are going to/go' or *il faut* + INF 'it must INF', i.e. are they elliptic forms of such adult constructions?

A first category of examples (9 and 10) suggests that imperatives and root infinitives may be functionally rather similar. The root infinitive *donner* 'give' in (9b) expresses the same kind of directive as the imperative in (9a). The context does not provide cues for interpreting the root infinitive as a truncated deontic construction such as (*tu dois*) *donner* 'you must give' but rather hints at a "genuine" root infinitive: the child's root infinitive is a reply to the mother's root infinitive *pas toucher* 'don't touch', which is a probable trigger of the form. Furthermore, deontic uses of *devoir*, specifically *tu dois* 'you must', emerge much later in the speech of Sophie, namely at 2;11 (see Table 7 in Section 5). The same alternation of the imperative and root infinitive of *donner* 'give' is found in Emma's early productions (1;5).

(9) a. Sophie, 1;9
    MOT: *Lequel   t'   aimerais   alors?*
         which.one   you   like.COND.2SG then
         'Which one would you like?'
    SOP: (unintelligible)
    MOT: *Celui-là?*
         'That one?'
    SOP: *Donne   Dé [: Dzé]*   (cuddly toy)
         give.IMP.2SG   N.PROP

---

[12] Compound verb forms correspond to constructions with the semi-auxiliary *aller* 'go' + INF expressing the immediate future or with a modal verb such as *devoir* 'must', *pouvoir* 'can' + INF.

[13] The frequency of these structures in CDS and the lexical relation between compound verb forms in CDS and root infinitives in CS will be analyzed in a further study.

MOT: *Oui   prends   Dzé!*
      yes   take.IMP.2SG Dzé
      'Yes, take Dzé.'
b. MOT: *Qu'est-ce que tu entends?*
      'What do you hear?'
MOT: *Ça, la cassette.*
      'This, the tape.'
MOT: *Pas   toucher!*
      not   touch.INF
      'Don't touch.'
SOP: *a   néné [: donner].*
      FILL   give.INF
MOT: *Tu veux que je te donne?*
      'You want that I give (it) to you?'

In example (10a), the root infinitive *mettre* 'put' is a likely substitute of the imperative plus the 2nd person singular reflexive pronoun (*mets-toi là* (lit. put.IMP.2SG-you (rself) there) 'sit there') rather than of a modal construction such as *tu dois te mettre* (lit. you must you.ACC put.INF) or *(il) faut te mettre* (lit. (it) must you.ACC put.INF) 'you must sit'. There are two facts which support this analysis. First, an attempt at the reflexive imperative structure only occurs two months later in the same context (10b). Second, this construction is quite complex: not only does the position of the reflexive pronoun alternate in the indicative full form and the imperative (see Section 2.1), but also its form differs (*te – toi*). This complexity is illustrated by the fact that the correct use of the 2nd person singular reflexive imperative only appears at 2;10 in Sophie's speech: *tourne-toi* 'turn around'.[14] It must be added that the face-threatening act proper to the imperative or root infinitive is somehow softened by the address form *Maman* 'Mommy' in example (10a). In example (10b) the context of a game explains that the mother accepts to comply without protest. So the caretaker's reaction does not contradict the interpretation of the root infinitive as conveying the same function and illocutionary force as the imperative.

(10) a. Sophie 2;1 (Sophie would like to go outside)
    MOT: *Viens alors.*
           'Come then.'
    SOP: *Là   Maman.*
           'There Mommy.'

---

14 See example (10b) for an erroneous placement of the pronoun.

SOP: *Maman mettre là Maman.*
　　　Mommy put.INF there Mommy
for:　*mets- toi là.*
　　　put.IMP.2SG you there
　　'Mommy, sit down there.'
MOT: *Alors, qu'est-ce qu'on fait?*
　　'So then, what do we do?'

b. Sophie 2;3
SOP: *Mets ici toi.*
　　　put.IMP.2SG here you.REFL.2SG
for:　*Mets toi ici*
　　　put you.REFL.2SG here
　　'Sit here.'
MOT: *Ici moi oui.*
　　'Here me, yes.'

In other contexts, a functional difference between an order expressed by the imperative (11a) and an indirect directive with a weaker force expressed by a modal verb construction reduced to a root infinitive may be assumed (11b), as suggested by the mother's response. This interpretation also hinges on the fact that at 2;3 Sophie just started to produce a couple of modal constructions with *vouloir* (2;2 *veux voir* (lit. want.PRS.1SG see.INF) 'want to see') and *pouvoir* (e.g., the first (conventional) polite indirect request *peux chercher bonbons?* 'could (you) look for candies?' at 2;2) (see Table 7 in Section 5). It is thus plausible that in example (11b) the root infinitive functions as an elliptic modal verb construction, much as in the preceding period.

(11) a. Sophie, 2;1
　　FAT: *Il va ton bobo?*
　　　　'Is your pain gone?'
　　SOP: *Oui.*
　　　　'Yes.'
　　SOP: *Foufe [: souffle] Papa.*
　　　　blow.IMP.2SG Daddy
　　　　'Blow, Daddy!'
　　MOT: *Souffle!*
　　　　'Blow!'

b. Sophie, 2;3 (looking at a picture book)
MOT: *Et ça qu'est-ce que c'est?*
'And what is this?'
SOP: *è   bigies [: bougies].*
FILL   candles
'(Some) candles.'
MOT: *Des bougies.*
'Some candles.'
SOP: *a   fafer [: souffler].*
FILL   blow.INF
'(Must) blow.'
SOP: *Maman   a   tafer [: souffler].*
Mommy   FILL   blow.INF
MOT: *Maman elle doit souffler?*
Mommy she must blow?
'Mommy must blow?'
SOP: *Oui.*
'Yes.'

Hence, in the early root infinitive period, a pragmatic distinction in illocutionary force between root infinitives and imperatives is found alongside functionally undifferentiated uses. We must therefore try to find further evidence of a possible competition between the two forms expressing deontic meaning during this period.

Let us consider utterances with self-corrections or reformulations involving imperatives and root infinitives, as exemplified in Section 3.2 above. In Sophie's data, there are 4 instances of an imperative reformulated as a root infinitive (see example 6 repeated here as 12a and example 12b).

(12) a. Sophie, 2;0
Maman   essaie   Maman,
Mommy   try.IMP.2SG   Mommy
'Try, Mommy.'
Maman   essayer   Maman.
Mommy   try.INF   Mommy
'Try, Mommy.'

b. Sophie, 2;4
Regarde   la   poupée,   regarder   Maman.
look.IMP.2SG the   doll   look.INF   Mommy
'Look at the doll, look Mommy.'

In Emma's speech, a single example of this kind occurs (example 13).

(13) Emma, 1;7
      EMM: *Veux   encore.*
            want.PRS.1SG   still
            '(I) still want.'
      FAT: *Quoi, le dentifrice?*
            'What, the toothpaste?'
      EMM: *Appuie,   appuyer.*
            press.IMP.2SG   press.INF
            'Press, press.'

The sequence of forms, i.e. the reformulation of a shorter imperative by a longer root infinitive may be interpreted as increasing the force of the order iconically, provided there is no contextual indication for an interpretation in terms of a reduced modal construction such as *tu dois appuyer* 'you must press' or *il faut appuyer* 'one must press'. Note that, in our data, root infinitives are generally not related to the occurrence of such constructions in the caretaker's preceding turns: their use in the conversational exchanges is independent or occasionally follows a caretaker's root infinitive, as shown by example (9) above.

In addition, Emma does not use the modal *devoir* 'must' (with deontic meaning) before 2;6 and *(il) faut* 'one must' appears even later (at 2;8) (see Table 7 in Section 5).

Since no link between root infinitives and modal constructions can be established, we conclude that (12) and (13) are indeed further examples of orders expressed by root infinitives. The fact that in these utterance sequences of CS root infinitives always follow the imperatives rather than vice versa corroborates the hypothesis of a contextual strengthening in illocutionary force of the first (but see Section 4.5) so that no real competition between the two constructions takes place.

Considering that most of the instances of the imperative and root infinitive of one and the same verb are produced at different points in time (Sophie 1;10 *ouvrir* 'open.INF', 2;4 *ouvre* 'open.IMP.2SG'; 1;9 *va* 'go.IMP.2SG', 2;2 *aller* 'go.INF'; 2;2 *faire* 'do.INF', 2;6 *fais* 'do.IMP.2SG'; Emma 1;9 *chercher* 'search.for.INF', 2;4 *cherche* 'search.for.IMP.2SG'; 1;9 *tirer* 'pull.INF', 2;11 *tire* 'pull.IMP.2SG'), we must conclude that the competition between the two types of forms is limited to a few examples in the very early production of the children before the third year. From 2;5 on in Sophie's speech and 1;11 in Emma's, root infinitives progressively disappear being replaced by imperatives as well as modal verb constructions.[15]

To summarize, what we have seen so far on the uses of root infinitives and imperatives in the early period of both children's speech is that some instances of alternation between both forms suggest that they are in competition for expressing strong directives. However, in other alternations and reformulations differences of illocutionary force may be assumed to exist.

4.4 *Tu*-forms

As shown above (Section 4.1, Table 3), an important difference between the two corpora of CS resides in the use of *tu*-forms with deontic meaning. This provides evidence for the children's similarities and dissimilarities concerning their choice of linguistic means for expressing requests.

In both Sophie's and Emma's speech, the majority of *tu*-forms have an imperative correspondent. The question is which pragmatic functions the *tu*-forms fulfill in contrast to the imperative.

Imperatives and *tu*-forms are not always used interchangeably in the children's speech. To account for their pragmatic distribution, two main factors, i.e. discourse type (instructions vs. other discourse types, modal types included) and discourse contrast (i.e. emphasis on the differentiation between two referents, see Allen, Skarabela and Hugues 2008: 113),[16] have proved to be relevant (see Table 5 and Section 4.5).

One discourse type consists in instructions, i.e. directives that describe the addressee's actions which are required for achieving a specific goal (e.g., recipes).

In the speech of both children, instructions are expressed by indicative constructions often containing a temporal adverbial *après* 'after' or *puis (après)* 'then (after)' (examples 14a and b) or a comparative adjunct (*comme ça* 'like that') (examples 14 and 15).

---

[15] Note however that some root infinitives occur much later than the imperative of the same verb, e.g., Sophie *aller* 'go' IMP 1;9, RI 2;2, *souffler* 'blow' IMP 2;1, RI 2;2 Emma *raconter* 'narrate' IMP 1;5, RI 2;3.

[16] Allen (2000: 488) describes typical situations of explicit contrast as follows: a child "wanting to prohibit others from doing something he or she is doing, or when a child wants to do something someone else is doing".

Table 5: Frequency (types/tokens) and percentage of *tu*-forms in CS by pragmatic factors*.

	Total of *tu*-forms	Discourse type	%	Discourse contrast	%
SOP	18/43	4/8	19	9/9	21
EMM	30/72	7/18	25	14/18	25

*Percentages in relation to the total of *tu*-forms (tokens)

(14) a. Sophie, 2;9
   T(u)   appuies,   puis   après   tu
   you.2SG   press.PRS.2SG then   after   you.2SG
   fais   comme ça,
   do.PRS.2SG like   that
   après   tu   fais   comme ça.
   after   you.2SG do.PRS.2SG like   that
   'You press and then you do like that, then you do like that.'
   b. Emma, 2;9
   Tu   mets   dans le nez
   you.2SG put.PRS.2SG into the nose
   après,   comme ça.
   afterwards like that
   'Then you put into the nose, like that.'
   Je vais   essayer   ça,   c'est
   I   go.PRS.1SG try.INF   that this.is
   un jeu.
   a   game
   'I will try that, it's a game.'

Instructions may also be constructed as coordinate clauses reflecting the order of successive actions (example 15).

(15) Emma, 2;9
   Tu   poses   la   canne à   pêche
   you.2SG put.PRS.2SG the   rod   for   fishing
   comme ça   et   tu   la   mets   là.
   like that and   you.2SG it   put.PRS.2SG there
   'You put the fishing rod like that and you put it there.'

As long as the child describes a procedure to follow, as in situations of play, and does not state the immediate actions to be taken by the addressee, the illocutionary force of *tu*-forms is less strong than the one of orders. It may, however, be difficult to draw a distinction between the two, as in example (15), *tu la mets là* 'you put it there' which, given the content of the action, resembles an order. The father's lack of reaction contributes to this intricacy.

Once children's morphosyntactic knowledge has sufficiently developed, *tu*-forms also occur in coordinated constructions or run-on clauses containing both a contrastive non-clitic subject pronoun (*moi*, 'me' Emma 1;10, Sophie 2;2, *toi* 'you.SG') and a grammatically required clitic subject pronoun (*je* 'I', *tu* 'you.SG') (examples 16) (cf. Caët and Morgenstern 2015) which typically emphasize the differentiation between speaker and addressee.[17] These examples are to be interpreted as directives cast in the shape of non-modalized statements of fact concerning the present or the immediate future. More indirect directives conveying a weaker illocutionary force would contain a modal verb with a deontic meaning of permission *tu peux* + INF 'you may', as in the following example from Emma at 2;7, *tu peux la prendre la canne à pêche* (lit. you may it take the fishing rod) 'you may take the fishing rod', which alternates with the non-modalized construction *tu la prends*. Since the children already use modal verb constructions with *peux* 'you can, may' at this age (Sophie from 2;9 on, Emma from 2;4 on, see Table 7 in Section 5), the non-modalized directives of these examples can be understood as telling the addressee what to do. Thus, in this particular context, *tu*-forms have a strong directive meaning conveying obligation.

(16) a. Sophie 2;10
    Moi   *je*   *lis,*
    me   I   read.PRS.1SG
    toi   *tu*   *regardes*   *les*   *images.*
    you.SG   you.SG   look.at.PRS.2SG   the   pictures
    'I read and you look at the pictures.'

---

17 Strong non-clitic subject pronouns, such as *moi* 'me', *toi* 'you.SG', as opposed to weak clitic ones (*je* 'I', *tu* 'you.SG') fulfill several pragmatic functions such as emphasis, topicalization and contrast. The non-clitic 1st person singular subject pronoun *moi* 'me' emerged in Emma's and Sophie's speech at 1;10 and 2;2 respectively (subject clitics at 1;8 and 2;4) and the corresponding 2nd person singular pronoun *toi* 'you.SG' at 1;9 and 2;4 (subject clitics at 1;7 and 1;9).

b. Emma 2;8
Moi   je   dors   aussi   et
me   I   sleep.PRS.1SG   also   and
toi   tu   dors   aussi.
you.SG   you.SG sleep.PRS.2SG   also
'I sleep and you sleep as well.'

In contrast to some of the examples of an alternation between root infinitives and imperatives presented in Section 4.3, those between the imperative and *tu*-forms of the same lemmas suggest that the two categories do not always fulfill the same function and are more clearly distinguished pragmatically in the children's speech.

4.5 Comparison of the functions of imperatives, root infinitives and *tu*-forms in CS and CDS

In this section we first examine the functions which imperatives, root infinitives and *tu*-forms have in CDS in relation to the functions in CS presented in Sections 4.2 to 4.4. Second, the functions of the highly frequent verb *mettre* 'to put' occurring in root infinitives (CS), the imperative (CS and CDS) and the *tu*-form (CS and CDS) are analyzed. Examples of alternations between the imperative and *tu*-forms of *attendre* 'to wait' are added.

One of the main functions of the imperative in CDS throughout the whole period investigated is to support and encourage the child in her ongoing activities, e.g., *essaie* 'try', *tire* 'pull', *appuie* 'press', *dessine* 'draw', *bois* 'drink', *fais toute seule* 'do by yourself', *compte* 'count', *raconte* 'relate', *lis* 'read', *chante* 'sing'. The 2nd person singular and plural imperative forms of *aller* 'go', *vas-y* 'go' and *allez* 'go', are typically used to support a subsequent imperative: *allez viens!* 'come on, come!'.

In addition, imperatives often serve as attempts to control the child's behavior, e.g., *viens* 'come', *mets-toi debout* 'get up', *assieds-toi* 'sit down', *dépêche-toi* 'hurry up', *attends* 'wait', and to point to urgent actions: e.g., *crache* 'spit', *souffle* 'blow', *ferme les yeux* 'close your eyes'. Finally, as is to be expected, the imperative is used in prohibitions: *arrête* 'stop', *gicle pas* 'don't splash'.

A specific function of the imperative in CDS is also linked to a particular exchange in the interaction: for instance, Sophie's mother uses *regarde* 'look' not only as an attention-getter but also to ground her objection in what the child just said and mitigate it (example 17).

(17) Sophie, 1;7
    SOP: *Dort.*
           sleep.PRS.3SG
           '(He) is sleeping.'
    MOT: *Il dort?*
           'Is he sleeping?'
    MOT: *Non,   regarde.*
           no   look.IMP.2SG
           'No, look.'
    MOT: *Celui-là il ne dort pas.*
           'This one is not sleeping.'

The children's preference for encoding prohibitions by root infinitives (see Section 4.3), more clearly found in Sophie's speech, can be related to their use in CDS: besides repetitions of root infinitives produced by the children (Kilani-Schoch et al. 2009), the few other examples which do occur are mostly negative constructions expressing prohibitions (e.g., Sophie's CDS: 1;9 *pas toucher* '(do) not touch'; Emma's CDS, e.g., 1;8 *pas décoller* '(do) not remove', 2;0 *pas rincer* '(do) not rinse'). The spontaneous uses of root infinitives in the parents' speech are concentrated at the early age, which suggests fine-tuning.

Tu-forms are also often used to express prohibitions, more so in both children's CDS than in their own speech (see Table 6).

Table 6: Proportion of negative imperatives, root infinitives and *tu*-forms with respect to the total of negative forms expressing prohibitions (tokens and percentages).

	Total NEG forms*	NEG IMP	%	NEG root INF	%	NEG *tu*–forms	%
SOP	33	4	12.1	18	54.5	4	12.1
SOP CDS	46	10	21.7	2	4.3	13	28.3
EMM	27	6	22.2	7	25.9	4	14.8
EMM CDS	86	33	38.4	4	4.7	30	34.9

*This total includes other negative forms such as modal forms, compound future forms and *on*–forms.

Nevertheless some verbs show an alternating use of negative imperative forms and negative *tu*-forms for the same function in CDS (Sophie's CDS, *toucher* 'touch', *faire* 'do', *renverser* 'knock over'; Emma's CDS, *mettre* 'put', *gicler* 'splash', *crier* 'scream', *faire* 'do'). A difference in the illocutionary force conveyed by the two forms is hard to assess as contextual variation prevails.

Depending on the child's age, root infinitives may alternate with *on*-forms in the speech of Sophie's mother, with the imperative appearing last (examples 18).

(18) a. SOP's CDS, 1;8

Oui   on   enregistre,   mais   on
yes   one   record.PRS.3SG   but   one
touche   pas.
touch.PRS.3SG   not
'Yes, we are (lit. one is) recording but one does not touch.'

b. 1;9

La   cassette pas toucher!
the cassette not touch.INF
'Don't touch the cassette.'

c. 1;10

Tu   touches   pas le   micro, tu
you.SG   touch.PRS.2SG   not the mike   you.SG
renverses   pas.
knock.over.PRS.2SG   not
'You don't touch the mike, you don't knock over.'

d. 2;2

Non, touche   pas [/] touche
no   touch.IMP.2SG   not   touch.IMP.2SG
pas.
not
'No, don't touch, don't touch.'

It is noticeable that negative imperatives do not occur in CDS in the early period (before 1;9 in Sophie's CDS and 1;10 in Emma's CDS), suggesting that strong directive speech acts are being avoided with toddlers and *tu*-forms, *on*-forms and constructions with modal verbs are used instead. Later on, however, the chronological distribution of the forms expressing prohibitions becomes less straightforward so that they constitute potential rivals.

Turning to the use of imperatives and *tu*-forms in CDS, what is most striking is that they follow each other in the same sentence: Some examples (13 in Sophie's CDS, 6 in Emma's CDS) which display the rephrasing of an imperative or conversely that of an indicative form are variation sets defined by Küntay and Slobin (1996: 267) as a series of utterances in which the same content or communicative intent is repeated in varying form (example 19; see also Arnon and Clark 2011: 4).[18]

(19) Sophie's CDS, 2;6
Dis   au.revoir   à   M,
say.IMP.2SG good.bye   to   M
tu   dis   au.revoir à M.
you.2SG   say.PRS.2SG good.bye to M
'Say good bye to M, you say good bye to M.'

In these variation sets no clear pragmatic difference between the two forms in terms of the strengthening of illocutionary force or a greater degree of politeness can be found. Variation sets recur throughout the data with a varying order of the imperative and the *tu*-form as shown by example (20). There is no indication that these sets are motivated by the child's reaction.

(20) Emma's CDS, 2;0 (referring to a ball)
Tu   la caches,   cache   la.
you   it hide.PRS.2SG hide.IMP.2SG it
'You hide it, hide it.'

Variation sets are also found in instructions, as in example (21), where the mother explains to the child how to proceed for complying with her order of storing away the book. For this purpose, the mother uses a *tu*-form.

(21) Sophie's CDS, 2;6 (referring to a book)
MOT: *Range-le,   t(u)   arrives?*
     store.away.IMP.2SG-it   you.2SG   succeed.PRS.2SG
     'Store it away, do you succeed?'
SOP: *Non.*
     'No'.

---

18 The rephrasing of imperatives and *tu*-forms in successive utterances is an extreme case of variation set as defined by Küntay and Slobin (1996: 267) in that the verb forms serve identical functions and neither lexical substitution nor a change of reference takes place.

MOT: *Tu   le   poses*
     you   it   put.PRS.2SG
     par.dessus   simplement.
     on.top   simply
     'You simply put it on top.'

Whereas examples of instructions are easy to document in CDS, examples of contrast between 1st and 2nd person singular non-clitic pronouns (*moi, toi*) in directive speech acts such as the ones examined in CS (see examples 16a and b above) are scarce. In CDS, competition between the imperative and *tu*-forms prevails.

Next, verbs occurring in the three forms of the imperative, root infinitive and *tu*-form in CS will be compared to their use in CDS. For lack of space we limit ourselves to a few lemmas, beginning with the most frequent verb *mettre* 'to put'.

In Sophie's speech, the imperative seems to be used mainly in the context of games or other activities in which the mother is taking part, e.g., at 2;2, *mets ça là-haut* 'put this up there'. Or it expresses urgency, for example in setting the conditions of the interaction with the mother (see Section 4.3, example 10b, *mets ici toi*, for *mets-toi ici* 'sit here'). As we have seen, two months before, the same order is conveyed by the root infinitive of the verb (example 10a, *Maman mettre là Maman* 'Mommy sit.INF there Mommy'). Finally, some isolated *tu*-forms of *mettre* are found in the girl's speech, as in the following example of an instruction given in response to her mother's question (example 22).

(22) Sophie, 2;8 (playing store)
    MOT: *Alors   qu'est.ce.que   je   fais*
         then   what   I   do.PRS.1SG
         maintenant   avec   ces   sous?
         now   with   these   cents
         'Then what shall I do now with these cents?'
    SOP: *Ben   tu   mets   comme   ça.*
         INTERJ   you.2SG   put.PRS.2SG   like   this
         'Well, you put like this.'

The distribution of the pragmatic functions of the three forms of *mettre* in CS matches their distribution in CDS. However, variation sets of *tu*-forms and imperatives only occur in CDS (example 23).

(23) Sophie's CDS, 2;3
   Maintenant   tu   mets   le   bouchon,
   now   you.2SG   put.2SG   the   cork
   mets   le   bouchon.
   put.IMP.2SG the   cork
   'Now you put the cork, put the cork.'

A comparable parallelism between CS and CDS is also found in Emma's data. Reflecting the father's frequent use of *tu*-forms more generally, Emma produces many *tu*-forms with a strong directive meaning (e.g., 1;10, *tu mets ça* 'you put this'), but alternatively uses imperatives (e.g., 2;6, *mets le doigt là* 'put the finger there') without a clear difference in meaning. However, it is noticeable that the few examples of the politeness marker *s'il te plaît* 'please' are preferably combined with *tu*-forms (e.g., 2;9 *tu le mets au bord s'il te plaît* 'you put it aside, please'), as in her father's speech, suggesting some difference in illocutionary force between the two forms.

The examination of the functions of imperative and *tu*-forms in CS suggests that their distribution is often pragmatically controlled. There are, however, other cases where their functions seem to be truly identical. As is to be expected, such examples are more likely to occur with highly frequent verb lemmas such as *attendre* 'to wait'.

As mentioned in Section 4.2, the imperative of *attendre* is partially pragmaticalized and has an interactional function. The question is whether the imperative *attends!* 'wait!' still occurs with the full semantic meaning of the lexeme or whether *tu*-forms (*tu attends* 'you wait') have taken over this function. In the latter case, we would hypothesize that the illocutionary force conveyed by *tu*-forms is as strong as that of an order.

The partially pragmaticalized imperative *attends* is most often used for initiating a statement of a speaker's immediate future action (example 24a) or an order (example 24b).

(24) a.   Sophie, 2;4
          Attends,   va   faire   un
          wait.IMP.2SG   go.PRS.3SG   make.INF   a
          petit   café,   moi.
          small   coffee   me
     for: attends,   je   vais   faire
          wait.IMP.2SG   I   go.PRS.1SG   make
          un   petit   café,   moi.
          a   small   coffee   me
          'Wait, (I) am going to make a small coffee.'

b. 2;6
Attends, viens là.
wait.IMP.2SG come.IMP.2SG there
'Wait, come here.'

The imperative *attends* is never constructed with a syntactic complement in the children's speech. By contrast, the semantic *tu*-forms may appear with object pronouns in their later development (examples 25).

(25) a. Sophie, 3:0
Et moi tu m' attends.
and me you.2SG me wait.PRS.2SG
'And you wait for me.'
b. Emma, 2;7
Tu m' attends moi.
you.2SG me wait.PRS.2SG me
'You wait for me.'

In CDS, the imperative happens to be constructed with a quantifier (*un petit peu* 'a little bit') or a temporal complement (*une minute/seconde* 'one minute/ second') only. These elements also activate the full semantic meaning of *attendre* 'to wait'. The single example of a construction of this verb with a subordinate complement, however, shows up with a *tu*-form (example 26).

(26) Emma's CDS, 2;8
T' attends qu' on vienne te
you.2SG wait.PRS.2SG that one comes you.2SG
chercher.
pick.up.INF
'You wait until we come to pick you up.'

In spite of the syntactic restrictions just described, the full semantic meaning of *attendre* is not limited to the use of finite forms such as the present indicative. Consider the following alternations between the imperative and the *tu*-form in Sophie's CS and Emma's CDS (examples 27a, b and 28a, b), occurring in similar contexts. Both constructions of each example indeed instantiate the full semantic meaning of the imperative *attends*. These examples also demonstrate that *tu*-form and imperative may both be used to express orders. In other words, examples (27 a) and (b) show that also in CS the pragmatic distinction between imperative and *tu*-form may be neutralized so that the two forms are interchangeable.

(27) a. Sophie, 3;0
    MOT: *Comment on fait pour voir si t'es prête?*
          'How does one do to see whether you are ready?'
    MOT: *Voilà.*
          'Here you are.'
    SOP: *Non,   t(u)   attends.*
          no   you.2SG   wait.PRS.2SG
          'No, you wait.'
    MOT: *Oui, j'attends, j'attends.*
          'Yes, I'm waiting, I'm waiting.'
    MOT: *Mais   dépêche-toi   un   peu.*
          but   hurry.up.IMP.2SG-yourself a   bit
          'However, hurry up a little bit.'
b. Sophie, 2;5
    MOT: *Tu   viens   après?*
          you   come   afterwards
          '(Do) you come afterwards?'
    SOP: *Oui,   attends.*
          yes   wait.IMP.2SG
          'Yes, wait.'
    MOT: *D'accord, j'attends.*
          'Ok, I'm waiting.'

(28) a. Emma's CDS, 2;7
    Je   peux   pas   m'   occuper
    I   can.PRS.2SG   not   me   take.care.INF
    de   toi   maintenant, tu   attends
    of   you.2SG   now   you   wait.PRS.2SG
    un   petit   peu.
    a   little   bit
    'I cannot take care of you now, you wait a little bit.'
b. Emma's CDS, 2;8
    Tu   veux   te   brosser
    you   want.PRS.2SG yourself   brush.INF
    les   dents?   Alors   attends   un   petit
    the   teeth?   Then   wait.IMP.2SG   a   little
    peu.
    bit
    '(Do) you want to brush your teeth? Then wait a little bit.'

In sum, the picture of the pragmatic functions of imperative and *tu*-forms in the children's speech is mixed. On the one hand, *tu*-forms and imperatives have a tendency to perform specialized functions such as prohibition, instruction and discourse contrast and vary in the strength of illocutionary force conveyed more so than in CDS. On the other hand, they serve the same functions and are thus in competition as in the caretakers' speech.

5 Development of the compound future and modal verb constructions expressing obligation and prohibition

The emergence of first verb constructions expressing obligation and prohibition does not follow exactly the same chronological order in the two children, as is apparent from Table 7.

Table 7: Emergence of the compound future and modal verb constructions in CS.

SOP Age	Verb forms	Linguistic means	Speech acts	Glosses	EMM Age
2;1	on va chercher PRO go.PRS.3SG look.for.INF	hortative, compound future	indirect directive (statement of speaker and addressee's future action)	'one/we will look for it'	2;0
2;2	peux chercher? can.2SG search.INF	modal verb (possibility)	indirect directive (request)	'could you search?'	1;10
2;3	faut ouvrir must open.INF	impersonal modal verb (necessity)	indirect directive (speaker-external source of obligation)	'(one) must open'	1;8
2;3	a peux boire FILL can.2SG drink.INF	modal verb (possibility)	indirect directive (permission)	'(you) can drink'	1;8
2;9	tu peux pas prendre you can.2SG not take.INF	negative modal verb (negated possibility)	indirect directive (prohibition)	'you cannot take'	2;4

Table 7 (continued)

SOP Age	Verb forms	Linguistic means	Speech acts	Glosses	EMM Age
2;11	*tu dois ranger* you must.2SG tidy.INF	modal verb (obligation)	indirect directive	'you must tidy'	2;6
3;0	*tu vas chercher* you go.2SG search.INF	compound future	indirect directive	'you will look for'	2;4

Sophie starts with the compound future corresponding to a hortative, followed by the modal construction with *pouvoir* 'can' in a conventional indirect request, and only later uses an impersonal modal verb form of necessity for conveying an indirect directive. By contrast, Emma begins simultaneously with the two types of modal verbs of necessity and possibility expressing obligation and permission respectively, and the compound future emerges two months later. In both children prohibitions conveyed by a modal verb emerge later and deontic modals with a speaker-external source of obligation appear before the deontic modal with a speaker-internal source (cf. Stephany 1993: 136 for different findings on the acquisition of English and German modal verbs).

A time interval between the expression of obligation or prohibition by a modal form with a speaker-external source (*il faut* '(one) must)' and a speaker-internal one (*tu dois* 'you must') is also found in both parents' speech (Sophie's CDS 1;6 and 1;11; Emma's CDS 1;4 and 2;6) and accounts for the development in the children's speech. This interval is consistent with what we have found for the imperatives, i.e. parents do not use the strongest, most face-threatening directives towards their children in the early period (see Section 4.5).

There are two main differences between the CDS of both children which should be mentioned. First, prohibition expressed as a negated possibility (*tu peux pas* + INF) never occurs in the speech of Emma's parents, whereas it is common in Sophie's. Furthermore, Emma's father displays the regional use of *vouloir* 'want' for *aller* 'go' in compound future constructions, e.g. in prohibitions such as 1;5 *tu (ne) veux pas sortir* 'lit. you do not want to go out' for *tu (ne) vas pas sortir* 'you will not go out'. This form does not yet occur in the child's speech.

6 Conclusion

The main question of the present study has been which forms are used in the early data of two French-speaking children and their CDS for expressing deontic modality by direct and indirect directive speech acts which do not give the addressee the opportunity of not complying with them.

As is to be expected from the literature on the development of speech acts (see e.g., Bates 1976; Ninio and Snow 1996; Cameron-Faulkner 2014, among others, on the communicative importance of directives), the study has provided evidence that the category of directives conveying obligation and prohibition emerges from the very beginning of observation in the first half of the second year and soon begins to be expressed by a number of different grammatical forms. The data show that, besides imperatives and root infinitives, *tu*-forms may fulfill the function of positive or negative orders in certain contexts.

Our results demonstrate that there is no simple one-to-one (biunique) relation between forms and functions in CS or CDS and that forms which serve similar functions are in competition with each other from early on; however, variably in different developmental phases.

The main results are the following: root infinitives are rival forms of imperatives primarily in the early phase of development. *Tu*-forms, which are a rival category of the imperative and less frequently of root infinitives, are added only later to Sophie's speech, but occur from early on in Emma's (Table 8).

Table 8: Distribution of imperatives, root infinitives and *tu*-forms in CS throughout the recording period.

	Sophie	Emma
IMP	entire period	entire period
RI	early period (until 2;4)	early period (until 1;10)
tu-forms	2;7–2;11	1;8/2;1–2;11

Besides their competition in the expression of orders, the imperative and root infinitives have been shown to functionally supplement each other. Root infinitives may also replace modal verb constructions and correspond to indirect speech acts. In addition, some pragmatic specialization of root infinitives has been found in the expression of prohibitions throughout the entire period investigated: Sophie, and to a lesser extent Emma, prefers root infinitives to imperatives. In terms of meaning, there is thus variation between those root infinitives which convey positive or negative orders and those which express indirect directives.

The competition between these forms used for expressing deontic modality in child-directed speech has emphasized the relevance of variation sets involving imperatives and *tu*-forms. Such utterance sequences represent a major difference between caretakers' and child speech since they do not occur in the latter.

Another result concerning *tu*-forms is that, in the children's speech, they are pragmatically motivated by discourse type and discourse contrast. Nevertheless, in the investigated period, *tu*-forms do not serve functions entirely distinct from those of the imperative. What we have found with highly frequent verbs is that examples of alternations between imperative and *tu*-forms occur in identical contexts and convey the same meaning. In contrast to this, *tu*-forms tend to be used for prohibitions in CDS.

Competition has thus to be understood in two ways. In the early production of toddlers, competition between the imperative and root infinitives represents an undifferentiated use of these forms for expressing directives due to the children's limited pragmatic and linguistic knowledge. However, in the caretakers' speech, competition between the imperative and *tu*-forms rather corresponds to the ability of making a flexible use of tools for expressing similar contents in a given context. More generally, the data emphasize the range of meanings that each of the categories investigated may convey in context, from the strong illocutionary force of orders to more mitigated directive meanings.

Contextual factors which favor one form over the other are the kind of interaction, more specifically the type of exchange between caretaker and child (e.g., disagreement as a trigger of the imperative *regarde!* 'look!'), the discourse type (instructions expressed by *tu*-forms), discourse structure (contrast expressed by *tu*-forms), type of speech act (negative vs. positive, e.g., prohibitions expressed by root infinitives and *tu*-forms), type of register (imperatives which are more formal), the occurrence of a politeness marker (with *tu*-forms in Emma's corpus), the lexical specificity of the verb (e.g., pragmaticalized imperatives, *attends* 'wait' or *allez* 'go'). It is important to note that the actual meaning of a form and the illocutionary force it conveys are contextual in the sense that they can only be determined by taking the minutiae of the particular interaction at hand into consideration.

On the developmental level, a first conclusion is that various pragmatic meanings of imperatives and *tu*-forms are being taken up by the children so that they are able to use them in contextually adequate ways. The absence of variation sets in the children's speech suggests that there is less competition between these forms in their speech than in their caretakers'.

As far as the distinction between direct and indirect speech acts is concerned, our results confirm that the children use direct requests, as expressed by the imperative and root infinitives, from the beginning. However, attempts to use indirect requests appear shortly afterwards. This is indicated by examples of root infinitives that can be analyzed as truncations of modal constructions. The expression of indirect directives by complete finite constructions corresponds to the emergence of *tu-* and *on-*forms as well as modal verb constructions (Sophie 2;2, Emma 1;8). Politeness markers are documented in the data relatively late (Sophie 3;0, Emma 2;3).

The chronological sequence of different forms and functions of directive speech acts found in this study of two French-speaking children seems to be more strongly related to their linguistic development than to the pragmatic complexity of indirect speech acts (Zufferey 2015: 58). Indeed, when *tu-*forms have become recurrent (Sophie 2;7, Emma 2;4), main inflectional categories of verbs are used, verb paradigms have diversified and syntax allows relatively complex sentences with complements as well as subordinate clauses.

Although the function of strong directives points to competition between forms in CDS, the development of the speech act of order is not delayed. This contrasts with what has been found within the Competition model for ambiguous, hence competing cues at other linguistic levels such as morphology: low cue validity has been shown to slow case development down (see, e.g., Bates and MacWhinney 1989: 61; MacWhinney 2005). Our results are consonant with the findings of approaches emphasizing the role of CDS variation in the development of language (e.g., Küntay and Slobin 1996; Arnon and Clark 2011: 1), i.e. variation in form, meaning and communicative situations enhances children's generalizations about language. What this chapter especially emphasizes is that variation in CDS serves to foster language flexibility (cf. Berman 2004: 12), specifically the pragmatic flexibility that is merely emerging at this age and will develop with language proficiency (Berman 2004: 11).

In this way, our study is a contribution to acquisition studies focusing on the relation between input and output (see, among others, usage-based approaches, e.g., Tomasello 2003; Behrens 2009; Lieven 2014; see the Crosslinguistic Project on Pre- and Protomorphology in Language Acquisition, e.g. Bittner, Dressler and Kilani-Schoch 2003; Stephany and Voeikova 2009; Dressler, Ketrez and Kilani-Schoch 2017), and more specifically on the setting of interactional exchanges (e.g., Clark 2012; Veneziano 2014; Steinkrauss 2017) as the main resource of language learning.

On the general pragmatic level, the chapter raises the theoretical issue of the relation between order and request and suggests that in French a larger span of the scale dividing the two categories is ascribed to order than request in comparison with English. This issue, which bears on language-specific aspects of the typology of speech acts, deserves further research. As far as the French acquisition data are concerned, a preliminary step would be to extend the study to the entire category of directives and compare the realization and pragmatic distribution of requests in the strict sense, i.e. less strong directives, to that of strong directives investigated in this chapter. Another step would be to engage in a prosodic analysis of CDS and CS data (cf. Bassano and Mendes-Maillochon 1994).

Finally, the extensive use of *tu*-forms for expressing orders brought to the fore by the present study also sheds light on another issue of French linguistics that ought to be taken up in the future, i.e. diatopic variation in the expression of order.

Acknowledgements: The author is grateful to Sophie's and Emma's parents for collecting the data and checking the transcription, to Ursula Stephany and Ayhan Aksu-Koç, as well as to Maria D. Voeikova, for their numerous insightful suggestions and corrections, also of my English.

References

Aikhenvald, Alexandra Y. 2010. *Imperatives and commands*. Oxford: Oxford University Press.
Aikhenvald, Alexandra Y. 2016. Sentence types. In Jan Nuyts & Johan van der Auwera (eds.), *The Oxford handbook of modality and mood*, 141–165. Oxford: Oxford University Press.
Allen, Shanley. 2000. A discourse-pragmatic explanation for argument representation in child Inuktitut. *Linguistics* 38(3). 483–521.
Allen, Shanley, Barbora Skarabela & Mary Hughes. 2008. Using corpora to examine discourse effects in syntax. In Heike Behrens (ed.), *Corpora in language acquisition research: Finding structure in data*, 99–137. Amsterdam: John Benjamins.
Ambridge, Ben & Elena V. M. Lieven. 2011. *Child language acquisition: Contrasting theoretical approaches*. Cambridge: Cambridge University Press.
Arnon, Inbal & Eve V. Clark. 2011. Introduction. In Inbal Arnon & Eve V. Clark (eds.), *Experience, variation, and generalization: Learning a first language*, 1–11. Amsterdam: John Benjamins.
Avram, Larissa & Martine Coene. 2007. The root infinitive stage in a null subject language: Romance in the Balkans. *Bucharest Working Papers in Linguistics* 1. 231–245.
Bassano, Dominique. 2010. L'acquisition des verbes en français: Un exemple de l'interface lexique/grammaire. *Synergies France* 6. 27–39.

Bassano, Dominique & Isabelle Mendes-Maillochon. 1994. Early grammatical and prosodic marking of utterance modality in French: A longitudinal case study. *Journal of Child Language* 21(3). 649–675.

Bates, Elizabeth. 1976. *Language and context*. New York: Academic Press.

Bates, Elizabeth & Brian MacWhinney. 1989. Functionalism and the competition model. In Brian MacWhinney & Elizabeth Bates (eds.), *The crosslinguistic study of sentence processing*, 3–76. Cambridge: Cambridge University Press.

Behrens, Heike. 2009. Usage-based and emergentist approaches to language acquisition. *Linguistics* 47. 383–411.

Berman, Ruth A. 2004. Between emergence and mastery. In Ruth Berman (ed.), *Language development across childhood and adolescence* (Trends in Language Acquisition Research 3), 9–34. Amsterdam: John Benjamins.

Bittner, Dagmar, Wolfgang U. Dressler & Marianne Kilani-Schoch (eds.). 2003. *Development of verb inflection in first language acquisition* (Studies on Language Acquisition 21). Berlin & New York: Mouton de Gruyter.

Bybee, Joan L. 1985. *Morphology*. Amsterdam: John Benjamins.

Caët, Stéphanie & Aliyah Morgenstern. 2015. First and second person pronouns in two mother-child dyads. In Laure Gardelle & Sandrine Sorlin (eds.), *The pragmatics of personal pronouns*, 173–194. Amsterdam: John Benjamins.

Cameron-Faulkner, Thea. 2014. The development of speech acts. In Danielle Matthews (ed.), *Pragmatic development in first language acquisition*, 37–52. Amsterdam: John Benjamins.

Champaud, Christian, Dominique Bassano & Maya Hickmann. 1993. Modalité épistémique et discours rapporté chez l'enfant français. In Norbert Dittmar & Astrid Reich (eds.), *Modality in language acquisition*, 185–209. Berlin & New York: Mouton de Gruyter.

Choi, Soonja. 2006. Acquisition of modality. In William Frawley (ed.), *The expression of modality*, 141–172. Berlin & New York: Mouton de Gruyter.

Clark, Eve V. 2012. Children, conversation, and acquisition. In Michael J. Spivey, Ken McRae & Marc F. Joanisse (eds.), *Cambridge handbook of psycholinguistics*, 573–588. Cambridge: Cambridge University Press.

Dressler, Wolfgang U., F. Nihan Ketrez & Marianne Kilani-Schoch (eds.). 2017. *Nominal compound acquisition*. Amsterdam: John Benjamins.

Filipi, Ana. 2014. Conversation analysis and pragmatic development. In Danielle Matthews (ed.), *Pragmatic development in first language acquisition* (Trends in Language Acquisition Research 10), 71–86. Amsterdam: John Benjamins.

Gerhardt, Julie. 1991. The meaning and use of the modals HAFTA, NEEDTA and WANNA in children's speech. *Journal of Pragmatics* 16. 531–590.

Grosse, Gerlind, Tanya Behne, Malinda Carpenter & Michael Tomasello. 2010. Infants communicate in order to be understood. *Developmental Psychology* 46(6). 1710–1722.

Hickmann, Maya & Dominique Bassano. 2016. Modality and mood in first language acquisition. In Jan Nuyts & Johan van der Auwera (eds.), *Oxford handbook of modality and mood*, 430–447. Oxford: Oxford University Press.

Kerbrat-Orecchioni, Catherine. 2005. *Le discours en interaction*. Paris: Armand Colin.

Kilani-Schoch, Marianne, Ingrida Balčiunienė, Katharina Korecky-Kröll, Sabine Laaha & Wolfgang U. Dressler. 2009. On the role of pragmatics in child-directed speech for the acquisition of verb morphology. *Journal of Pragmatics* 41(2). 219–239.

Kilani-Schoch, Marianne & Wolfgang U. Dressler. 2002. Filler+infinitive and pre- and protomorphology demarcation in a French acquisition corpus. *Journal of Psycholinguistic Research* 30(6). 653–685.

Küntay, Aylin & Dan I. Slobin. 1996. Listening to a Turkish mother: Some puzzles for acquisition. In Dan I. Slobin, Julie Gerhardt, Amy Kyratzis & Jiansheng Guo (eds.), *Social interaction, social context and language: Essays in honor of Susan Ervin-Tripp*, 265–286. Mahwah, NJ: Lawrence Erlbaum.

Laaha, Sabine & Dominique Bassano. 2013. On the role of input for children's early production of bare infinitives in German and French. *Language, Interaction and Acquisition* 4(1). 70–90.

Lasser, Ingeborg. 2002. The roots of root infinitives: remarks on infinitival main clauses in adult and child language. *Linguistics* 40(4). 767–796.

Leech, Geoffrey N. 2014. *The pragmatics of politeness*. Oxford: Oxford University Press.

Lieven, Elena. 2014. First language development: A usage-based perspective on past and current research. *Journal of Child Language* 41(S1), 48–63.

Lyons, John. 1977. *Semantics*. 2 vols. Cambridge: Cambridge University Press.

MacWhinney, Brian. 2000. *The CHILDES project: Tools for analyzing talk*. Mahwah, NJ: Erlbaum.

MacWhinney, Brian. 2005. New directions in the competition model. In Michael Tomasello & Dan I. Slobin, *Beyond nature-nurture: Essays in honor of Elizabeth Bates*, 81–110. Mahwah: Lawrence Erlbaum.

Mueller Gathercole, Virginia C. M., Eugenia Sebastián & Pilar Soto. 2002. Negative commands in Spanish-speaking children: No need for recourse to relativized minimality. *Journal of Child Language* 29(2). 393–401.

Ninio, Anat & Catherine E. Snow. 1996. *Pragmatic development*. Boulder & Oxford: Westviews.

Phillips, Colin. 1995. Syntax at age two: Crosslinguistic differences. *MIT Working Papers* 26. 325–382.

Rojas Nieto, Cecilia. 2011. Developing first contrasts in Spanish verb inflection. In Inbal Arnon & Eve V. Clark (eds.), *Experience, variation, and generalization: Learning a first language*, 53–74. Amsterdam: John Benjamins.

Searle, John. 1976. A classification of illocutionary acts. *Language in Society* 5(1). 1–23.

Searle, John. 1977. Speech acts. In Andy Rogers, Bob Wall & John P. Murphy (eds.), *Proceedings of the Texas conference on performatives, presuppositions and implicatures*, 27–45. Arlington, VA: Center for Applied Linguistics.

Steinkrauss, Rasmus. 2017. L1 acquisition beyond frequency. In Jacqueline Evers-Vermeul & Elena Tribushinina (eds.), *Usage-based approaches to language acquisition and language teaching*, 117–141. Berlin & New York: Mouton de Gruyter.

Stephany, Ursula. 1993. Modality in first language acquisition: The state of the art. In Norbert Dittmar & Astrid Reich (eds.), *Modality in language acquisition* (Sociolinguistics and Language Contact 6), 133–144. Berlin & New York: Mouton de Gruyter.

Stephany, Ursula. 2013. The category of modality: A crosslinguistic study of its development. Department of General Linguistics, Institute of Linguistics, University of Cologne. Ms.

Stephany, Ursula & Maria D. Voeikova (eds.). 2009. *Development of nominal inflection in first language acquisition: A cross-linguistic perspective* (Studies on Language Acquisition 30). Berlin & New York: Mouton de Gruyter.

Stephany, Ursula & Maria D. Voeikova. 2015. Requests, their meanings and aspectual forms in early Greek and Russian child language. *Journal of Greek Linguistics* 15. 66–90.

Tomasello, Michael. 2003. *Constructing a language: A usage-based theory of language acquisition*. Cambridge, MA & London: Harvard University Press.

Veneziano, Edy. 2014. Conversation and language acquisition: Unique properties and effects. In Inbal Arnon, Marisa Casillas, Chigusa Kurumada & Bruno Estigarribia (eds.), *Language in interaction: Studies in honor of Eve V. Clark* (Trends in Language Acquisition Research 12), 83–100. Amsterdam: John Benjamins.

Wijnen, Frank, Masja Kempen & Steven Gillis. 2001. Root infinitives in Dutch early child language: An effect of input. *Journal of Child Language* 28(3). 629–660.

Zufferey, Sandrine. 2015. *Acquiring pragmatics*. London & New York: Routledge.

Larisa Avram and Andreea Gaidargi
On the acquisition of dynamic, deontic and epistemic uses of modal verbs in Romanian

Abstract: This study investigates the acquisition of dynamic, deontic and epistemic values conveyed by modal verbs in Romanian. It is based on the analysis of naturalistic speech from three longitudinal corpora of Romanian monolingual children (age range 1;8–3;0). The results show that subject-oriented dynamic values are the first to emerge and are, overall, more frequently used than the deontic ones. No epistemically used modal verb has been found for the period observed. The comparison of the use of modal verbs by children with that in child-directed speech reveals striking similarities. The developmental epistemic gap is accounted for in terms of language-specific properties. Adults preferentially use modal adverbs rather than modal verbs for expressing epistemic meanings, which results in uninformative input with respect to the epistemic use of modal verbs. Additionally, the early acquisition of epistemic adverbs is facilitated by the fact that they have one single inherent modal value, whereas modal verbs feature a range of modal meanings determined by the context in which they occur.

1 Introduction

A considerable number of studies which investigated the acquisition of the semantics of modal verbs provide evidence that children acquire subject-oriented dynamic and deontic values of modal verbs earlier than epistemic ones (Wells 1979, 1985; Shepherd 1982; Stephany 1986, 1993; Smoczyńska 1993; Bassano 1996, among many others). Some of these studies report that the acquisition of the full range of modal meanings may extend into middle childhood (Major 1974; Perkins 1983; Coates 1988).

The developmental priority of dynamic and deontic uses of modal verbs compared to epistemic ones is, however, challenged by the fact that children who are acquiring a language in which epistemic modality is expressed by suffixes use them as early as age two (Aksu-Koç 1988; Choi 1991, 1995, 2006).

Larisa Avram, Andreea Gaidargi, University of Bucharest

https://doi.org/10.1515/9781501504457-007

These findings indicate that the way in which epistemic modality is expressed in the language may modulate the acquisition route. Extending the investigation to other languages may shed light on the way in which language-specific properties can determine the order in which children acquire the contextual values of modal verbs.

The main aim of the present chapter is to study the acquisition of the semantics of modal verbs in Romanian. We focus on *a putea* 'can, may', *a trebui* 'need, must', and *a vrea* 'want'. The analysis is based on naturalistic speech from three longitudinal corpora of monolingual Romanian children and their caretakers (see Section 4).

For the analysis of modal verbs, we adopt a unitary meaning approach according to which they have one core meaning that gets contextually specified (Kratzer 1977, 2012; Perkins 1983; Hegarty 2016). In keeping with this view, one distinguishes "the contribution made by linguistically encoded information and inferential processes in the derivation of contextually attested interpretations of lexical items" (Papafragou 2000: 8). In terms of acquisition, this property of modal verbs has been shown to pose a learnability challenge since the child has to figure out under what conditions a particular modal value obtains (Hacquard and Cournane 2016).

Modals can express dynamic, deontic and epistemic meanings (Nuyts 2001; Palmer 2001). Dynamic modality is "concerned with properties and dispositions of persons, etc., referred to in the clause, especially by the subject NP" (Huddleston 2002: 178). Deontic modality concerns the sphere of duty, permission, appropriateness, and its interpretation may vary from more idealized to more realistic modal bases (Hegarty 2016: 66). According to Palmer (2001), subject-oriented dynamic modality[1] denotes real-world ability and willingness. Subject-oriented need or necessity has also been included in the category of subject-oriented dynamic modality (Palmer 1979; Huddleston and Pullum 2002; Nuyts 2006).

Subject-oriented dynamic modals (like English *can* and *will*, expressing ability and volition, respectively) have often been argued to actually ascribe a property to the entity in subject position (or "a property of the first argument of the predicate", Nuyts 2006: 3). Unlike deontic and epistemic modalities, the dynamic one is not "attitudinal" (Nuyts 2016: 46) and does not express subjective evaluation. This is reflected in the early acquisition of subject-oriented dynamic uses of modal verbs, i.e. of those that involve a realistic modal base.

In this first study of the acquisition of Romanian modal verbs we ask how their different contextual values are acquired. Section 2 offers a brief summary

---

[1] Nuyts (2006:3) calls this value "participant-inherent dynamic".

of previous findings on the acquisition of the semantics of modal verbs in different languages. The main properties of modal verbs in Romanian are presented in Section 3, where *a putea* 'can, may' and *a trebui* 'need, must', two modal verbs which feature various modal meanings, are compared to *a vrea* 'want', which expresses exclusively agent-oriented volition/desire. Section 4 contains the results of our longitudinal study of the acquisition of modal verbs in Romanian. The main findings are discussed in Section 5.

2 Previous studies on the acquisition of the semantics of modal verbs

Studies of developmental pathways in the domain of modal verbs offer a relatively uniform picture. A common finding resulting from analyses of longitudinal corpora is that modal verbs emerge before age three; but during the early stages they are used exclusively with dynamic and deontic values and occur in a limited number of syntactic environments (Brown 1973; Kuczaj and Maratsos 1975; Fletcher 1979; Wells 1979, 1985; Shepherd 1982; Stephany 1986, 1993; Shatz and Wilcox 1991; Smoczyńska 1993; Bassano 1996; Papafragou 1998; Cournane 2015). A significant number of studies offer data which show that modal verbs with subject-oriented dynamic values are attested earlier than those with deontic value. For English, it has been shown that ability and volition expressed by *can* and *will/wanna*, respectively, sometimes in the negative form, are the first to emerge before age 3 (see e.g. Brown 1973; Fletcher 1979; Bliss 1988; Stephany 1986; Hickmann and Bassano 2016).

Deontic meanings of modal verbs also emerge early. At age 2;6, the modal verb *can* is used to express both ability and permission (Wells 1979). Similar results have been reported for child French, where *pouvoir* 'can, may' is first found only with dynamic and deontic meanings (Bassano 1996). Also in Greek, during the early stages, before age 3, children use the verb *boró* 'can, may' only with a dynamic or deontic value (Stephany 1986).

The epistemic use of modal verbs is attested later than the dynamic and deontic ones across languages (see Hickmann and Bassano 2016 for an overview), with some differences from one study to another concerning age of emergence or full acquisition. However, the absence of epistemically used modal verbs during the early stages does not necessarily indicate that children have problems with epistemic modality in general. Epistemic adverbs and adjectives are attested very early. Bowerman (1986) and O'Neill and Atance (2000) show that two-year-old English-speaking children use epistemic adverbs such as *maybe* and *probably*. Similarly, Polish children begin to use epistemic adjectives at around age two (Smoczyńska 1993). For French, Bassano (1996) shows that epistemic utterances (with an epistemic adverb or in the conditional mood) are attested as early as age 2;7.

Such findings, which reveal the importance of the means by which epistemic modality is expressed, are further supported by results reported for the acquisition of languages in which epistemic/evidential modality is expressed by sentence-ending particles, such as Korean. Choi (1991, 1995, 2006) has shown that two-year-old Korean children can produce both epistemic/evidential and deontic modal expressions. Similar results have been discussed for Turkish, where epistemic modality is expressed by verbal inflection (Aksu-Koç 1988; Terziyan and Aksu-Koç, this volume). On the other hand, in Spanish, subjunctive morphology emerges early. The subjunctive is first produced exclusively with volitive and directive value; but the extension to contexts in which it is used with an evaluative value is delayed (Pérez-Leroux 1998). In Romanian as well subjunctive morphology is attested early, around age 2, and it is first used with volitive and directive values (Avram and Coene 2011). During the early stages, it occurs as a "surrogate" imperative, as the complement of modal verbs as well as in periphrastic future constructions. This means that the first subjunctives are found in (dynamic and deontic) obligatory contexts.

Such data are particularly telling. They show that when the means of expressing modality has a range of context-dependent modal values, allowing both deontic and epistemic uses, there is an epistemic gap. Along this line, Hacquard and Cournane (2016) distinguish between lexical modals (a class which, in their analysis, includes modal adverbs as well) and "grammatical" modal verbs. The latter get contextually specified for dynamic, deontic and epistemic values and they interact with tense and aspect depending on their modal interpretation. This context dependence for full semantic specification would explain why these modal verbs represent a learnability challenge.

If this line of reasoning is on the right track, it straightforwardly predicts cross-linguistic differences in the acquisition of the semantics of modal verbs.

3 Romanian modal verbs

In this section we offer a brief description of the most important properties of the modal verbs *a putea* 'can, may', *a trebui* 'must, need', and *a vrea* 'want'. The first two can express different modal values in a contextually determined way (Guțu-Romalo 1956; Avram 1999; Zafiu 2005, 2013), i.e. they correspond to the class of "grammatical" modals in Hacquard and Cournane's (2016) terms. *A vrea* 'want', on the other hand, is inherently dynamic.

A putea 'can, may' can express subject-oriented dynamic modality[2] (example 1a), deontic modality (example 1b) and epistemic modality (example 1c) (Avram 1999; Zafiu 2005).

(1) a. *Am putut să citesc cartea.*
have.PRS.1SG can.PTCP SBJV read.PRS.1SG book.DET
'I managed to read the book.'
b. *Pot să plec acum?*
can.1SG SBJV leave.1SG now
'May I leave now?'
c. *Copiii nu puteau fi în curte.*
children.DET not can.IPFV.PAST.3PL be in yard
'The children can't have been in the yard.'

The modal verb *a trebui* 'must, need' can be used with deontic (example 2a) and epistemic values (example 2b), but dynamic uses are very rare.

(2) a. *Trebuiau să plece imediat.*
must.PST.3PL SBJV leave.3PL immediately
'They had to leave immediately.'
b. *Trebuie să fi suferit mult.*
must.PRS.3SG SBJV be suffer.PTCP much
'They must have suffered a lot.'

A putea 'can, may' and *a trebui* 'must, need' can take both finite and non-finite clausal complements. They can be constructed with a subjunctive complement, irrespective of their modal value (see example 3, where the modals can have both a deontic and an epistemic interpretation). *A putea* 'can, may' can also take an infinitival complement (example 4), regardless of its modal value. Therefore, the complement type (subjunctive or infinitive) is not informative with respect to modal interpretation. It is inspection of the larger context which will provide clues with respect to the type of modality expressed by the verb.

---

2 We do not take Palmer's (2001) circumstantial dynamic modality into consideration.

(3) Trebuie/ poate să plece.
 must.PRS.3SG can.PRS.3SG SBJV leave.3SG
 'He must/may leave.'

(4) Poate ajunge acasă foarte repede.
 can.PRS.3SG arrive.INF home very fast
 'He can/may arrive home very fast.'

With *a trebui* 'must, need', however, some complementation patterns can offer a cue with respect to modal value. When *a trebui* 'must, need' takes a supine (example 5a) or a past participle complement with passive meaning (example 5b), the epistemic reading is blocked so that the construction can only be interpreted as deontic.

(5) a. Trebuie spus lucrurilor pe nume.
  must.PRS.3SG say.SUPINE things.DAT on name
  'One should speak frankly.'
 b. Cartea trebuie citită.
  book.DET must.PRS.3SG read.PTCP.FEM.SG
  'The book must be read.'

A trebui 'must, need' can also take an indicative clausal complement (example 6). In this pattern, the only available interpretation is an epistemic one. For possibility, an epistemic value can be conveyed only by the modal adverb *poate* 'maybe', homophonous with the third person singular of the present tense of the modal verb *a putea* 'can, may' with an indicative complement (example 7) (Avram 1999; Protopopescu 2012; Zafiu 2005, 2013).

(6) Trebuie că el a decis lucrul ăsta.
 must.PRS.3SG that he has decided thing.DET this
 'He must be the one who took this decision.'

(7) Ea poate că ajunge la timp.
 she maybe that arrive.PRS.3SG at time
 'She may arrive in time.'

A vrea 'want' exclusively expresses dynamic modality and can only occur with a subjunctive complement (example 8).

(8) *Mama   vrea   să   plece.*
    Mother want.PRS.3SG   SBJV   leave.3SG
    'Mother wants to leave.'

A remark is in order with respect to the actual use of modal verbs. Epistemically used modal verbs are rare in adult-directed speech.³ Epistemic modality is more frequently expressed by modal adverbs. Also, as mentioned above, modal verbs are frequently used with a subjunctive complement, which is uninformative with respect to the type of modality.

Given the role of input in the language acquisition process (e.g. Yang 2002), one could predict that the emergence of epistemically used modal verbs may be even more delayed in child Romanian than in other languages. First, because both *a putea* 'can, may' and *a trebui* 'must, need' can feature a range of context-dependent modal meanings whose acquisition requires inspection of syntactic structures which do not offer robust disambiguation cues. Second, because the frequency of epistemic modal verbs in the input is very low. Modal adverbs, on the other hand, whose modal value is not context-sensitive, are in addition more frequently used, facilitating their early acquisition.

4 The acquisition of the semantics of modal verbs in Romanian

4.1 Main questions

The main goal of the present study is to investigate the development of the modal verbs *a putea* 'can, may' and *a trebui* 'must, need' in early child Romanian. Their acquisition is compared to that of *a vrea* 'want', a modal verb which exclusively expresses subject-oriented dynamic modality, and to epistemic adverbs.

The first question to be addressed is whether dynamic uses of modal verbs, associated with subject orientation, are acquired earlier than their deontic uses. The second question is whether the epistemic use of Romanian modal verbs emerges later than their dynamic and deontic uses as found in other languages (Wells 1979, 1985; Perkins 1983; Stephany 1986, 1993; Bassano 1996; Cournane

---

3 The analysis of a transcript of 220 minutes of conversation among adults (the corpus in Dascălu-Jinga 2002) revealed that out of 57 tokens of *a trebui* 'must, need' with a clausal complement only one denoted epistemic necessity. We identified 73 tokens of *a putea* 'can, may', out of which only 2 were used epistemically.

2015). In order to evaluate to what extent language-specific input properties can account for the acquisition data we also analyze the use of modal verb meanings in child-directed speech (CDS) comparing it to child speech.

4.2 Data and method

The present study is based on three longitudinal corpora of child Romanian: Iosif (Stoicescu 2013), Bianca and Antonio (Avram 2001). The three children come from Bucharest families with different socio-economic backgrounds, including working class, lower middle class and upper middle class households. Antonio and Bianca are first-born children, while Iosif has an elder brother. All the corpora contain weekly 60-minute audio recordings made at home. They include non-structured conversations with family members in the presence of an investigator. Sessions were transcribed in CHAT format (MacWhinney 2000). For the present study, a total of 46 files were analyzed (one 60-minute file per month from each corpus) (see Table 1). The use of modals in CDS was also analyzed (see Table 2).

Table 1: Corpora of Romanian child speech.

Child	Age range	MLU range	No. of files	Utterance total	Utterances with MV
BIA	1;8–2;11	1.064–2.873	16	8,787	87
ANT	1;9–3;0	1.514–3.174	16	7,526	113
IOS	1;10–3;0	1.115–3.828	14[4]	7,981	152
TOTAL	1;8–3;0	1.064–3.828	46	24,294	352

MV = Modal verb.

Table 2: Corpora of CDS.

	No. of files	Utterances with MV
BIA	16	301
ANT	16	197
IOS	14	432
TOTAL	46	930

---

4 For Iosif, there is no recording available for age 2;3.

Each transcript was searched for utterances containing a modal verb (*a putea* 'can, may', *a trebui* 'must, need', or *a vrea* 'to want'). The meaning of each modal was analyzed taking into account the immediate conversational context (i.e. the interlocutor's preceding utterance). We coded each token for: (i) (subject-oriented) dynamic, (ii) deontic, and (iii) epistemic value. The few cases where the context did not provide sufficient information to allow the identification of the meaning were not included in the final analysis. For both *a putea* 'can, may' and *a trebui* 'must, need' we analyzed the syntactic context in which the modal occurred (i) with an omitted clausal complement (retrievable from the context), (ii) with a subjunctive clausal complement; (iii) with an infinitival complement; (iv) with a supine or a past participle, or (v) with an indicative clausal complement. The epistemic adverbs *poate* 'maybe' and *sigur* 'certainly' were also extracted from the corpora.

4.3 Results

4.3.1 The early use of modal verbs in child Romanian

The analysis of the meanings of the modal verbs found in child speech in the three longitudinal corpora reveals a similar acquisition path. *A putea* 'can, may' with a subject-oriented dynamic value is attested very early: at age 1;9 in Antonio's corpus (example 9a), at 1;10 in Bianca's (example 9b), and at 2;1 in Iosif's (example 9c).

(9) a. Antonio, 1;9
    Antonio   poate.
    Antonio   can.PRS.3SG
    'Antonio can (repair this toy).'
   b. Bianca, 1;10
    ADU: *Poți   și   tu   să   cauți*
         can.PRS.2SG and   you   SBJV search.2SG
         cu   mine?
         with   me
         'Can you look for it with me?'
    BIA: *Nu   poți,   mami.*
         not   can.PRS.2SG   Mummy
         'You cannot, Mummy.'
         (Intended meaning: 'I cannot do it; Mummy should.')

c. Iosif, 2;1
   Ăsta, nu pot.
   this not can.PRS.1SG
   'This, I cannot.'
   (Intended meaning: 'I cannot take this one out.')

Dynamic *a putea* 'can, may' emerges concurrently with the modal verb *a vrea* 'want' in Antonio's and Iosif's corpora (see examples 10a–b). With Bianca, no other modal verb besides dynamic *a putea* 'can, may' is found in the corpus in the period from 1;10 to 2;1; *a vrea* 'want' is first attested at 2;2.

(10) a. Antonio, 1;9
   ADU: *Spui?*
      say.PRS.2SG
      'Will you say it?'
   ANT: *Nu   vrei.*
      not   want.PRS.2SG
      'You don't want to.'
      (Instead of: 'I don't want to.')
   b. Iosif, 2;1
   ADU: *Tu vrei   să   mai arunci?*
      you want.PRS.2SG SBJV more throw.2SG
      'Do you want to throw it again?'
   IOS: *Da. Tu vrei?*
      yes you want.PRS.2SG
      'Yes. Do you want to?'

There is a time lapse of four months up to one year between the first subject-oriented uses of *a putea* 'can, may' marking ability and the first deontic uses of the same modal verb expressing permission (examples 11). The number of tokens of deontically used *a putea* 'can, may' is lower than that of the subject-oriented dynamic ones overall and also after the emergence of deontic uses.

(11) a. Antonio, 2;9
   ADU: *Stai   aici pe scăunel, frumos.*
      sit.IMP.SG here on chair.DIM nicely
      'Sit here on the chair, nicely.'

ANT: *Nu poți să stai și pe pat?*
not can.PRS.2SG SBJV sit.2SG and on bed
'May you not sit on the bed as well?'
(Instead of: 'May I not sit on the bed instead?')

b. Iosif, 2;5
Tu poți să iei aia.
you can.PRS.2SG SBJV take.2SG that
'You may take that one.'

c. Bianca, 2;7
Pot să intru în grajd?
can.PRS.1SG SBJV enter.1SG in stable
'May I enter the stable?'

The first spontaneous use of the modal verb *a trebui* 'need, must' with a deontic value is attested concurrently or almost so with the first deontic use of *a putea* 'can, may': at 2;7 in Bianca's corpus, at 2;8 in Iosif's and at 2;11 in Antonio's (examples 12).

(12) a. Bianca, 2;7
Trebuie să pun și eu asta.
must.PRS.3SG SBJV put.1SG and I this
'I must put this one too.'

b. Iosif, 2;8
Trebuie să mi dea tati cu d-ăsta.
must.PRS.3SG SBJV me.DAT give.3SG daddy with of-this
'Daddy must put this on my wound.'

c. Antonio, 2;11
De ce-ai pus cum nu trebuia?[5]
why that-have.PRS.2SG put.PTCP how not must.IPFV.PST.3SG
'Why did you put it the way you shouldn't have?'

Dynamic *a trebui* 'must, need' is absent from Iosif's and Antonio's corpora. The only context which allows a subject-oriented dynamic interpretation of *a trebui* 'must, need' is attested in Bianca's corpus at age 2;3 (example 13).

---

5 Antonio's mother has put a toy in the wrong place.

(13) Bianca, 2;3
(Wanting to look at a game that her father has arranged on the floor.)
Trebuie să văd.
must.PRS.3SG SBJV see.1SG
'I must see.'

While epistemically used modal verbs are not found in any of the CS files investigated, the corpora contain several epistemic/evidential adverbs which are used early and in an adult-like way. They are, however, attested only a few months after the first modal verbs with a dynamic value. In Antonio's corpus an isolated token of the epistemic adverb *poate* 'maybe' occurs as early as 2;3 (example 14a), but no other epistemic adverb is found until 2;11, when four tokens of *sigur* 'certainly' are used (example 14b).

(14) a. Antonio, 2;3
Poate n-a oprit.
maybe not-have.PRS.3SG stop.PTCP
'Maybe he did not stop.'
b. Antonio, 2;11
Sigur sînt alea.
certainly are those
'Those are certainly the ones.'

Iosif also occasionally uses epistemic modal adverbs. The first one is *parcă* 'apparently', attested as early as age 2;2 (example 15a). *Poate* 'maybe' is found later, at age 2;11 (example 15b).

(15) a. Iosif, 2;2
Parcă sînt a(i) mei.
apparently are DET mine
'They seem to be mine.'
b. Iosif, 2;11
Mai are două, poate.
more has two maybe
'Maybe he has two more.'

As has been found with the other two children, Bianca does not use modal verbs epistemically either during the period observed, but also uses epistemic modal adverbs instead: *poate* 'maybe' is first attested at 2;7 (example 16).

(16) Bianca, 2;7
    Poate   nu   mai   vine   gîndăcelu(l).
    maybe   not   more   comes   bug.DIM.DET
    'Maybe the little bug will not come anymore.'

Other epistemic modal adverbs besides *poate* 'maybe' are occasionally used: *parcă* 'apparently' (by Iosif) and *sigur* 'certainly' (by Antonio).

The results of the analysis of modal verbs are summarized in Table 3.

Table 3: Age of emergence and number of tokens of dynamic and deontic modal verbs in child speech.

Child		*putea* 'can, may'		*trebui* 'must, need'		*vrea* 'want'
		dynamic	deontic	dynamic	deontic	dynamic
BIA	Age	1;10	2;7	2;3	2;5	2;2
	Tokens	30	4	–	31	22
ANT	Age	1;9	2;9	–	2;11	1;9
	Tokens	47	3	–	10	51
IOS	Age	2;1	2;5	–	2;8	2;1
	Tokens	38	10	–	18	83

There are only two syntactic frames in which the modals *a putea* 'can, may' and *a trebui* 'must, need' are attested. They either occur with a contextually retrievable omitted clausal complement (illustrated in 17) or with a subjunctive complement (illustrated in 18).

(17) Antonio, 2;1
    Vrei   să   cazi.
    want.PRS.2SG   SBJV   fall.2SG
    'You want to fall down.'

(18) Antonio, 2;7
    Nu   mai   pot   să   mă   ridic.
    not   anymore   can.PRS.1SG SBJV   REFL   rise.1SG
    'I can't get up anymore.'

In terms of frequency, Bianca and Iosif preferentially use the modal verb *trebui* 'must, need' with a subjunctive complement and Iosif also does so with *putea* 'can, may'. In Antonio's corpus the modal verb with an omitted complement is the most frequently encountered pattern (see Table 4).

Table 4: Early modals: patterns of complementation.

Child	*putea* 'can, may'		*trebui* 'must, need'	
	omitted clausal COMP	SBJV COMP	omitted clausal COMP	SBJV COMP
BIA	23	11	5	26
ANT	31	19	8	2
IOS	18	30	4	14

4.3.2 Child-directed speech

One of the questions addressed in this study is to what extent the acquisition order of the contextual uses of modal verbs can be accounted for in terms of properties of the input. The analysis of CS has revealed that deontic *a trebui* 'must, need' and deontic *a putea* 'can, may' are attested later than the dynamic uses of *a putea* 'can, may'; the overall frequency of deontic use is much lower (see Table 3). The picture which emerges from the analysis of CDS is similar. One notices an asymmetry between agent-oriented *a putea* 'can, may', the most frequently encountered modal in child-directed speech across the three corpora (a total of 296 tokens), and agent-oriented *a trebui* 'must, need' (a total of 132 tokens).

The delayed acquisition of epistemically used modal verbs can also be accounted for in terms of properties of the input. The analysis of child-directed speech reveals a very low number of modal verbs used with an epistemic value (Table 5). In the input data of Iosif and Bianca, they amount to at most 5% of tokens and in Antonio's they are not found at all.

Table 5: Agent-oriented (dynamic and deontic) and epistemic use of modal verbs in CDS.

	A putea 'can, may'		*A trebui* 'must, need'	
	agent-oriented	epistemic	agent-oriented	epistemic
BIA	99	4	44	2
ANT	65	0	36	0
IOS	132	7	52	2

The adults in the three corpora investigated preferentially use adverbs to express epistemic modality. The adverb *poate* 'maybe' expressing epistemic possibility is used much more frequently than the corresponding verb (Table 6).

Table 6: Overall use of the epistemic modal verb *a putea* 'can' vs. the adverb *poate* 'maybe' in CDS.

	Epistemic verb *a putea* 'can, may'	Epistemic adverb *poate* 'maybe'
Iosif	7	20
Bianca	4	15
Antonio	0	5

5 Discussion and conclusion

The analysis of the modal verbs in the three longitudinal corpora of child Romanian has revealed that deontic and dynamic meanings of modal verbs are acquired before epistemic ones. While modal verbs with a subject-oriented dynamic value emerge very early, epistemically used modal verbs are not yet attested at age 3;0. In this respect, our results are similar to what has been reported for the acquisition of a variety of other languages (Wells 1979, 1985; Shepherd 1982; Bassano 1996, among many others). A number of researchers have accounted for this delay in terms of cognitive development (see Papafragou 2000 or Shatz and Wilcox 1991 for an overview). Besides evidence from many languages, the Romanian data challenge the cognitive development approach. Bianca and Antonio begin to use epistemic adverbs concurrently with or shortly after their first use of deontic modals, at a time when epistemic modal verbs are not yet attested. Iosif's epistemic adverb *parcă* 'apparently' is found at age 2;2. Although the number of such adverbs is relatively low, the fact that children use them correctly at a time when epistemic modal verbs are still absent from their speech suggests that epistemic modality per se does not actually lag behind. Since epistemic modal adverbs used in appropriate contexts are attested before age 3 in the corpora of the three Romanian children, a cognitive difficulty with the acquisition of epistemic modal meanings is excluded.

Another account links the delay in the acquisition of epistemic modal verbs to a delay in the acquisition of clausal complementation (see the discussion in Hegarty 2016). In Romanian, as shown in Section 3, deontic and epistemic modals occur with the same type of clausal complement. Both *a putea* 'can, may' and *a trebui* 'must, need' can take a subjunctive complement. Romanian children begin to use the subjunctive early, around age two (Avram and Coene 2011). They also use embedded clauses shortly after they turn two years of age (Avram and Coene 2006). Moreover, modal verbs in the longitudinal data which we investigated are frequently encountered with a subjunctive complement. Therefore, the delayed emergence of epistemically used modals cannot be accounted for in terms of a delay in the acquisition of clausal complementation.

Alternatively, one could look for a possible cause in input properties. The analysis of child-directed speech revealed a very low number of epistemic modal verbs. The Romanian data are not singular in this respect. Shatz et al.'s (1990) analysis of child-directed speech in American English and German revealed that epistemically used modals amount to less than 10% of the tokens of modal verbs. Interestingly, the caretakers of the Romanian children use even fewer modal verb tokens epistemically and prefer adverbs to express epistemic modality. The adverb *poate* 'maybe', for example, is found more frequently than the corresponding modal verb *a putea* 'can, may' for expressing epistemic possibility in child-directed speech.[6] We suggest that the complete absence of epistemic modal verbs in Romanian child speech during the early stages could be explained in terms of language-specific properties. These verbs have contextually determined modal values and they are rarely found in the input which children receive. The early emergence of epistemic adverbs in Romanian child speech (as in other languages) may be further facilitated by the fact that they are inherently epistemic and do not acquire this modal value contextually. This argument is in line with studies which argue that epistemic modality is delayed only with modal expressions conveying more than one contextual modal meaning (Hacquard and Cournane 2016). Our data show that the delay in the acquisition of epistemically used modals is tied to at least two factors: type of modal expression (context-dependent vs. context-independent) as well as the overall tendency in Romanian to use epistemic adverbs to the detriment of epistemic modal verbs. This account can also explain why in Romanian the epistemic delay with modal verbs is more significant than in other languages. In English, for example, epistemic uses of modal verbs are attested as early as age 2;3 (Cournane 2015). Gaidargi (2013) also reports early use of epistemic modal verbs in child English before age 3;0. But in the Romanian corpora no epistemic modal verb is attested before age three.

The second question which was addressed in the present study is whether a developmental asymmetry between subject-oriented dynamic and deontic uses of modal verbs is also found in child Romanian. Our results reveal that this is indeed

---

6 This is also true of adult-directed speech.

the case. In this respect as well the Romanian data are similar to those reported for other languages (Brown 1973; Fletcher 1979; Bliss 1988). Overall, modal verbs with subject-oriented dynamic meaning are attested before modal verbs used with deontic meaning. The order of acquisition is the same across the three longitudinal corpora investigated: subject-oriented dynamic *a putea* 'can, may' and *a vrea* 'to want' are the first modal verbs attested. The deontic meaning of *a putea* 'may, can' develops in the second half of the children's third year, more than half a year or even a full year after its dynamic meaning. This, however, does not mean that deontic meanings in general are not attested earlier in child Romanian. Bare subjunctives used as directives are attested as early as 1;10 in Bianca's corpus (see example 19a). Imperatives (though rarely found in the early data) are found in Antonio's corpus (see example 19b) at 2;4 (Avram and Coene 2011).

(19) a. Bianca, 1;10 (Avram and Coene 2011: 362)
Căutăm leul.
search.PRS.SBJV.1PL lion.DET
'Let's look for the lion.'
b. Antonio, 2;4 (Avram and Coene 2011: 363)
Dă o bomboană de-acolo!
give.IMP.SG a candy of-there
'Give a candy from over there.'

There is a slight delay only with deontic uses of modal verbs, not with deontic modality per se.

Dynamic modals ascribe properties; they do not involve the speaker's evaluation of situations. This may explain their early acquisition. The fact that dynamic *a trebui* 'need, must', which is infrequent in CDS, is also practically absent in child speech shows that frequency in child speech is similar to frequency in the input.

To summarize, in this chapter we have explored the path of acquisition of dynamic, deontic and epistemic uses of modal verbs in Romanian. We have compared the acquisition of *a putea* 'can, may' and *a trebui* 'must, need', which express dynamic and deontic as well as epistemic modality, to that of the modal verb *a vrea* 'to want'. In accord with results reported in several previous studies, the acquisition order for modality denoted by modal verbs is: (subject-oriented) dynamic > deontic > epistemic. Our data fully confirm the epistemic gap which has been previously observed for modal verbs in various other languages. The fact that the first instances of epistemic modality to be found in Romanian child data are adverbs rather than modal verbs can be attributed to language-specific properties.

Acknowledgements: We thank Ioana Stoicescu for generously allowing us to use her corpus of Iosif.

References

Aksu-Koç, Ayhan. 1988. *The acquisition of aspect and modality. The case of past tense reference in Turkish.* Cambridge: Cambridge University Press.

Avram, Larisa. 1999. *Auxiliaries and the structure of language.* Bucharest: Editura Universității din București.

Avram, Larisa. 2001. Early omission of articles in child Romanian and the emergence of DP. *Revue roumaine de linguistique* XLVI (1–4). 105–123.

Avram, Larisa & Martine Coene. 2006. The complementizer phrase in child Romanian: An early discourse-anchor. In Adriana Belletti, Elisa Bennati, Cristiano Chesi, Elisa Di Domenico & Ida Ferrari (eds.), *Language acquisition and development. Proceedings of GALA 2005*, 29–35. Newcastle upon Tyne: Cambridge Scholars Publishing.

Avram, Larisa & Martine Coene. 2011. Early non-finite forms in child Romanian. *Revue roumaine de linguistique* LVI (4). 347–370.

Bassano, Dominique. 1996. Functional and formal constraints on the emergence of epistemic modality: A longitudinal study on French. *First Language* 16 (46). 77–113.

Bliss, Lynn S. 1988. Modal usage by preschool children. *Journal of Applied Developmental Psychology* 9(3). 253–261.

Bowerman, Melissa. 1986. First steps in acquiring conditionals. In Dorothy Edgington (ed.), *On conditionals*, 285–308. Oxford: Oxford University Press.

Brown, W. Roger. 1973. *A first language: The early stages.* Cambridge, MA: Harvard University Press.

Choi, Soonja. 1991. Early acquisition of epistemic meaning in Korean: A study of sentence-ending suffixes in the spontaneous speech of three children. *First Language* 11 (31). 93–119.

Choi, Soonja. 1995. The development of epistemic sentence-ending modal forms and functions in Korean children. In Joan Bybee & Suzanne Fleischman (eds.), *Modality in grammar and discourse*, 165–203. Amsterdam: John Benjamins.

Choi, Soonja. 2006. Acquisition of modality. In William Frawley (ed.), *The expression of modality*, 141–171. Berlin: Walter de Gruyter.

Coates, Jennifer. 1988. The acquisition of the meanings of modality in children aged eight and twelve. *Journal of Child Language* 15(2). 425–434.

Cournane, Ailis. 2015. Modal development: Input-divergent L1 acquisition in the direction of diachronic reanalysis. Toronto: University of Toronto dissertation.

Dascălu-Jinga, Laurenția. 2002. *Corpus de română vorbită. Eșantioane.* [Corpus of spoken Romanian. Samples] Bucharest: Editura Academiei Române.

Fletcher, Paul. 1979. The development of the verb phrase. In Paul Fletcher & Michael Garman (eds.), *Language acquisition: Studies in first language development*, 261–284. Cambridge: Cambridge University Press.

Gaidargi, Andreea. 2013. Modal meanings in early child English. In Manuela Burada, Oana Tatu & Raluca Sinu (eds.), *Embracing multitudes of meaning: Proceedings of the 11th conference on British and American studies 2013*, 175–196. Newcastle-upon-Tyne: Cambridge Scholars Publishing.

Guțu-Romalo,Valeria.1956. Semiauxiliarele de mod [Semi-auxiliaries of mood]. *Studii de gramatică* [Grammar studies], vol. I, 57–81. Bucharest: Editura Academiei.

Hacquard, Valentine & Ailis Cournane. 2016. Themes and variation in the expression of modality. In Christopher Hammerly & Brandon Prickett (eds.), *NELS 46: Proceedings of the forty-sixth annual meeting of the North-East Linguistic Society*, vol. I, 21–42. Graduate Linguistics Student Association (GLSA), University of Massachusetts, Amherst.

Hegarty, Michael. 2016. *Modality and propositional attitudes*. Cambridge: Cambridge University Press.

Hickmann, Maya & Dominique Bassano. 2016. Modality and mood in first language acquisition. In Jan Nuyts & Johan van der Auwera (eds.), *The Oxford handbook of modality and mood*, 430–447. Oxford: Oxford University Press.

Huddleston, Rodney. 2002. The verb. In Rodney Huddleston & Geoffrey K. Pullum (eds.), *The Cambridge grammar of the English language*, 71–211. Cambridge: Cambridge University Press.

Huddleston, Rodney & Geoffrey K. Pullum (eds.). 2002. *The Cambridge grammar of the English language*. Cambridge: Cambridge University Press.

Kratzer, Angelika. 1977. What 'must' and 'can' must and can mean. *Linguistics and Philosophy* 1. 337–355.

Kratzer, Angelika. 2012. The notional category of modality. In Angelika Kratzer, *Modals and conditionals*, 27–69. Oxford: Oxford University Press.

Kuczaj, Stan & Michael Maratsos. 1975. What children can say before they will. *Merrill-Palmer Quarterly of Behavior and Development* 21. 89–111.

MacWhinney, Brian. 2000. *The CHILDES project: Tools for analyzing talk*. 3rd edn. Mahwah, NJ: Lawrence Erlbaum Associates.

Major, Diana. 1974. *The acquisition of modal auxiliaries in the language of children*. The Hague: Mouton.

Nuyts, Jan. 2001. *Epistemic modality, language and conceptualization: A cognitive-pragmatic The perspective*. Amsterdam: John Benjamins.

Nuyts, Jan. 2006. Modality: Overview and linguistic issues. In William Frawley (ed.), *The expression of modality*, 1–26. Berlin & New York: Mouton de Gruyter.

Nuyts, Jan. 2016. Analyses of modal meanings. In Jan Nuyts & Johan van der Auwera (eds.), *The Oxford handbook of modality and mood*, 31–49. Oxford: Oxford University Press.

O'Neill, Daniela, K. & Cristina M. Atance. 2000. "Maybe my daddy give me a big piano": The development of children's use of modals to express uncertainty. *First Language* 20 (58). 29–52.

Palmer, Frank R. 1979. *Modality and the English modals*. London: Longman.

Palmer, Frank R. 2001. *Mood and modality*, 2nd edn. Cambridge: Cambridge University Press.

Papafragou, Anna. 1998. The acquisition of modality: Implications for theories of semantic representations. *Mind and Language* 13(3). 370–399.

Papafragou, Anna. 2000. *Modality: Issues in the semantics-pragmatics interface*. Amsterdam: Elsevier.

Pérez-Leroux, Anna Teresa. 1998. The acquisition of mood selection in Spanish relative clauses. *Journal of Child Language* 25(3). 585–604.

Perkins, Mick R. 1983. *Modal expressions in English*. Frances Pinter & Norwood, NJ: Ablex.

Protopopescu, Daria. 2012. *The syntax of manner adverbs in English and Romanian*. Bucharest: Editura Universității din București.

Shatz, Marylin, H. Grimm, Sharon A. Wilcox & Karin Niemeier-Wind. 1990. Modal expressions in German and American mother-child conversations: Implications for input theories of language acquisition. University of Michigan, Ann Arbor: unpubl. ms.

Shatz, Marylin & Sharon A. Wilcox. 1991. Constraints on the acquisition of English modals. In Susan A. Gelman & James P. Byrnes (eds.), *Perspectives on language and thought*, 319–353. Cambridge: Cambridge University Press.

Shepherd, Susan. 1982. From deontic to epistemic: An analysis of modals in the history of English, creoles and language acquisition. In Anders Ahlvist (ed.), *Papers from the 5th international conference on historical linguistics*, 316–323. Amsterdam: John Benjamins.

Smoczyńska, Magdalena. 1993. The acquisition of Polish modal verbs. In Norbert Dittmar & Astrid Reich (eds.), *Modality in language acquisition*, 145–169. Berlin: Mouton de Gruyter.

Stephany, Ursula. 1986. Modality. In Paul Fletcher & Michael Garman (eds.), *Language acquisition. Studies in first language development*, 375–400. 2nd edn. Cambridge: Cambridge University Press.

Stephany, Ursula. 1993. Modality in first language acquisition: The state of the art. In Norbert Dittmar & Astrid Reich (eds.), *Modality in language acquisition*, 133–144. Berlin: Mouton de Gruyter.

Stoicescu, Ioana. 2013. *The acquisition of tense and aspect in Romanian*. Bucharest: Editura Universității din București.

Wells, Gordon. 1979. Learning and using the auxiliary verb in English. In Vivien Lee (ed.), *Cognitive development: Language and thinking from birth to adolescence*, 250–270. London: Croom Helm.

Wells, Gordon 1985. *Language development in the pre-school years*. Cambridge: Cambridge University Press.

Yang, D. Charles. 2002. *Knowledge and learning in natural language*. Oxford: Oxford University Press.

Zafiu, Rodica. 2005. Modalizarea [Modalization]. In Valeria Guțu-Romalo (ed.), *Gramatica limbii române* [Grammar of the Romanian language], vol. II, 673–697. Bucharest: Editura Academiei Române.

Zafiu, Rodica. 2013. Modality and evidentiality. In Gabriela Pană Dindelegan (ed.), *The grammar of Romanian*, 575–584. Oxford: Oxford University Press.

Ursula Stephany
Development of modality in early Greek language acquisition

Abstract: In this chapter, the development of agent-oriented (deontic and dynamic) and propositional (epistemic) modality in early Greek language acquisition is investigated. The study is based on audio-taped longitudinal data of monolingual Greek children growing up in Athens while interacting with their caretakers in natural speech situations. Five subjects come from the Stephany Corpus and one from the extraordinarily rich Katis Corpus. They were observed between 1;8 and 3;0 years. The main means for expressing deontic modal notions in Greek are the imperative and the subjunctive, but the principal devices for conveying dynamic meanings are lexical. The major expressions of epistemic notions to emerge early are epistemic adverbs while epistemically used modal verbs develop later. The chief aspects of the analysis are the early split of modal–non-modal expressions, the emergence of dynamic compared to deontic expressions, and the developmental asynchrony of agent-oriented and propositional modality. The study is based on usage-based approaches to language acquisition according to which "language structure emerges from language use" (Tomasello 2003: 327). Consequently, special attention is paid to the role of child-directed speech in the development of modality.

1 Introduction

As pointed out by Tomasello (2014: xx), "the overall function of language is communication in the sense that language evolved for purposes of communication phylogenetically, and it is learned for purposes of communication ontogenetically." The essential communicative possibilities offered by any language are to provide statements, command actions, and pose questions (Dixon 2016: 48–78). The three basic motives for communication are requesting, i.e., "getting others to do what one wants them to", offering help "by informing others of things" and an "expressive or sharing motive" (Tomasello 2010: 84–86). One of the earliest distinctions emerging in child language is that between statements and requests (Stephany 1985; see also Aksu-Koç and Stephany, this volume). Hence, modality is one of the most fundamental linguistic categories, not only

Ursula Stephany, University of Cologne

in the languages of the world, but also in the ontogenesis of language. Given the importance of requests for human social interaction, it is not surprising that "understanding and mastering directive speech acts [. . .] in a language is a key to successful communication" (Aikhenvald 2010: 331). In this chapter, the development of agent-oriented dynamic and deontic modality as well as propositional epistemic modality in early Greek language acquisition will be traced until the age of three years.

After a few remarks on the theoretical framework of the present study (section 1.1), a brief introduction into agent-oriented and propositional modality (section 1.2), a report on previous research on the acquisition of modality in Greek followed by a presentation of the aims of the present study (section 1.3) are given. Section 2 describes the forms and functions of the main inflectional and lexical devices for expressing agent-oriented and propositional modality in Modern Greek. The data on which the present study is based are presented in section 3. The main sections 4 and 5 of the chapter are devoted to the results of the analysis. While the more extensive section 4 deals with inflectional and lexical expressions of agent-oriented modality in early Greek child speech and child-directed speech, section 5 is concerned with propositional modality in the two registers. Section 6 contains a summary and a discussion of the main results of the study.

1.1 Usage-based theory of language and language acquisition

The present study is placed in the framework of usage-based theory of language considering the construction of grammatical knowledge to be based on input (Tomasello 2003, 2010: 313; Stephany 2012: 91; Lieven 2014). Put more precisely, "the most general point about acquisition is that the categories and schemas of a language are not given to children innately, [. . .] but rather that they are generalizations that children make on the basis of their own categorization skills working on the language they hear" (Tomasello 2014: xxv). In this view, language acquisition does not simply depend on the grammatical system of the mother tongue, but on the usage the grammatical form–function units are made of in child-directed speech. In the constructivist approach, "grammar is seen as a dynamic system of conventionalized form–function units, i.e., constructions, that children acquire based on domain-general learning mechanisms such as analogy, entrenchment, and automatization" (Diessel 2013: 348). Thus, type and token frequency of inflectional forms and syntactic constructions play a dominant role for productivity and entrenchment, respectively (Tomasello 2003: 238). According to the constructivist, usage-based approach "learning is a gradual process in which categories are acquired in a piecemeal fashion" (Diessel 2013: 348) and concrete inflectional forms are organized in emergent grammatical schemas which gradually become more abstract (Bybee 2010; Stephany 2012: 94). Ample evidence for this assumption rather than for across-the-board acquisition of grammatical categories describable by abstract rules has been found in the acquisition of Greek inflection and derivation (Stephany 1985; Thomadaki and Stephany 2007; Stephany and Thomadaki 2017).

1.2 Agent-oriented and propositional modality

The most fundamental distinction between the semantic domains of modality pertains to agent-oriented modality referring to actions (Bybee and Fleischman 1995: 6) and propositional modality "concerned with the speaker's attitude to the truth-value or factual status of the proposition" (Palmer 2001: 8). This differentiation has not only proved useful for the description of the modal systems obtaining in the languages of the world (see Nuyts and van der Auwera 2016) but also for the description of the acquisition of modal systems (Stephany 1986; Choi 2006; Hickmann and Bassano 2016). While agent-oriented modality includes deontic and dynamic meanings (Palmer 2001; Choi 2006), propositional modality refers to epistemic and evidential notions (Palmer 2001).[1]

Agent-oriented modality "encompasses all modal meanings that predicate conditions on an agent with regard to the completion of an action referred to by the main predicate, e.g., obligation, desire, ability, permission and root possibility" (Bybee and Fleischman 1995: 6). As pointed out by Lyons (1977: 826), "the origin of deontic modality [. . .] is to be sought in the desiderative and instrumental function of language: that is to say, in the use of language, on the one hand, to express or indicate wants and desires and, on the other, to get things done by imposing one's will on other agents. It is clear that these two functions are ontogenetically basic, in the sense that they are associated with language from the very earliest stage of its development in the child." Another important insight is that "deontic modality is concerned with the necessity or possibility of acts performed by morally responsible agents" (Lyons 1977: 823) and is therefore "associated with the social functions of permission and obligation" (Bybee and Fleischman 1995: 4).

As opposed to agent-oriented deontic modality, which refers to the obligation and permission of "events not yet actualized", epistemic modality indicates the speaker's "degree of confidence in a proposition" and therefore

---

[1] For more details see Stephany and Aksu-Koç, this volume, and Aksu-Koç and Stephany, this volume.

expresses the degree of certainty, necessity, probability, uncertainty, or possibility of a state of affairs (Boye 2016: 117), typically according to the speaker's opinion (Nuyts 2006: 6).

Modality may be expressed inflectionally or lexically. The main inflectional device is mood (e.g., imperative, subjunctive, optative, evidential, conditional) and the main lexical devices are modal verbs (e.g., *may, can, must*), verbs of desire (e.g., *want*) and mental verbs (e.g., *know, think, believe*) as well as epistemic adverbs (e.g., *necessarily, certainly, probably, possibly*) and adjectives (e.g., *necessary, certain*). Depending on the language, the burden of expression of certain modal meanings rests more on inflectional morphology or on the lexicon.

In language acquisition, the most important modal utterances are directives and expressions of desire and ability, belonging to deontic and dynamic agent-oriented modality, respectively. Directives may be defined as speech acts that attempt "to get the hearer to perform some action" (Nikolaeva 2016: 73). The major types of directives are orders (commands) and requests. "While orders imply telling someone else what to do, requests involve asking someone to do something, with an option for the addressee not to comply" (Aikhenvald 2016: 147).

In contrast to the main expressions of agent-oriented modality of Modern Greek, which are inflectional and occur very frequently in everyday usage, inflectional expressions of epistemic modality are to be found much more rarely. Furthermore, lexical expressions of epistemic modality are not very frequent either. Compared to agent-oriented modality, epistemic modality thus plays a minor role in Greek language acquisition and the development of its full potential lags behind. In early child Greek, it is mainly limited to a few epistemic adverbs expressing certainty or probability, a rare epistemic use of the two Greek modal verbs, and a few mental verbs (see sections 2.2 and 5).

1.3 Previous research on the acquisition of modality in Greek and aims of the present study

The early development of modality in Greek language acquisition has been investigated in a number of studies. It is one of the central topics of the detailed study of the development of verbal morphology, including mood, aspect, and tense as well as person–number forms of verbs, by Stephany (1985). The work is based on audiotaped data of five children (Stephany Corpus), four of whom were first observed at the respective ages of 1;8, 1;9, and 1;11. Two of them were observed a further two times at 2;3/2;5 and 2;9/2;11, and one more child, a late talker, was only observed twice at 2;3 and 2;9. An essential characteristic of the study of Stephany (1985) is that the mothers' (and in one case the grandmother's) speech directed to the children before the turn to their third year was analyzed and compared not merely with child speech but in addition with the mothers' adult-directed speech (ADS). One of the main results is that the registers of early Greek child speech (CS) and child-directed speech (CDS) are surprisingly uniform and that CDS is tuned to the developmental stage of the child (Stephany 1985: 198). A comparison of CDS to ADS has shown that the main difference between the two registers consists in the reduced complexity of the child's input language. The latter comprises a smaller number of verb form types, mainly restricted to the unmarked combinations of aspect with mood or tense. Thus, the imperfective non-past (present) tense, the perfective past, future, and subjunctive are more frequently used than the imperfective counterparts of the last three categories. As far as modal expressions are concerned, agent-oriented ones are preferred as compared to propositional ones (Stephany 1985: 199). These characteristics not only reduce the complexity of the input language, but increase the frequency of the most fundamental grammatical categories and functions, thereby supporting structure building on the one hand and entrenchment of forms on the other.

A comparison of the development of modality in Greek and English language acquisition shows that the Greek child "cannot, so to speak, escape the expression of inflectional categories, as they are a part of tightly knit lexical forms [. . .] [whereas] the structure of English makes it possible to concentrate first on the expression of lexical content" (Stephany 1986: 398). Stephany (1986: 397–398) concludes that "differences in the ontogenesis of languages must to a large extent be attributable to their structural differences."

The development of modality is also part of the more comprehensive description of early Greek language acquisition provided by Stephany (1997), which includes syntax besides morphology. The analysis mainly draws on Stephany (1985) and Katis (1984). Katis' work is based on the longitudinal data of a monolingual Greek girl observed from 2;6 to 4;0 and cross-sectional data from 21 subjects aged 2;0 to 4;11. Her findings include precursors to epistemic modality in pretend play and the development of non-counterfactual and counterfactual conditional expressions (see section 5 below).

A detailed analysis of the early development of verbal inflection by a monolingual Greek boy (Christofidou Corpus) and one girl (Stephany Corpus) has been provided by Christofidou and Stephany (2003). It shows that the first distinction to emerge as early as 1;8 in the boy's speech is that between non-modal non-past (present) and modal imperative forms. The subjunctive sets in at 1;11, outnumbering the imperative by far so that the imperfective non-past and the perfective subjunctive are the two most frequently occurring verbal categories up to 2;1 (Christofidou and Stephany 2003: 100). The authors show that there are not many differences between the two children concerning the early inflectional development of verbs with regard to the intake of TAM and person–number categories, something they consider to be evidence for a certain systematicity inherent even in early, largely lexically based inflectional acquisition (Christofidou and Stephany 2003: 118). As soon as paradigmatic patterns emerge, grammatical knowledge gains in systematicity.

One of the main results of the comparative study of direct and indirect requests in Greek and Russian first language acquisition by Stephany and Voeikova (2015) is "that children construct the grammatical distinctions of their language on the basis of its grammatical options as well as their usage by the caretakers" and "that language-specific factors affect acquisition from very early on" (Stephany and Voeikova 2015: 88).

Stephany (2017) studied the use of the two Greek modal verbs *boró* 'can, may' and *prépi* 'must' for expressing dynamic, deontic, and epistemic modal notions, comparing child speech with child-directed and adult-directed speech. The study is based on the exceptionally extensive Katis Corpus of CS and CDS, and on twenty dialogues among adults from the Corpus of Spoken Greek (Pavlidou, Kapellidi, and Karafoti 2014). The main finding is that CDS occupies an intermediate position between CS and ADS in a number of respects, one of them being the diversity of forms of modal verbs. As mentioned above, "the limited inventory of inflectional forms results in a relatively more frequent presentation of the most common grammatical types so that these get a better chance of becoming entrenched and the opportunity of discovering grammatical patterns is enhanced" (Stephany 2017: 95). Another result of this study is that the agent-oriented function of the two modal verbs "widely predominates in all three registers, but is most pronounced in CS and least so in ADS, with CDS occupying an intermediate position" (Stephany 2017: 96). Since the key features of ADS, CDS, and CS concern the most characteristic functions of Greek modal verbs, "the differences between the three registers are to a large extent quantitative rather than qualitative" (Stephany 2017: 98). Stephany (2017: 98) concludes that while the forms and use of the Greek modal verbs in ADS "may be taken to represent the goal the child has to reach in order to become a competent native speaker of the Greek language, the intermediate position between the size of the inflectional inventory, the occurrence of constructions of a modal verb with a complement verb and their agent-oriented vs. propositional use [in CDS] may be taken to smooth the way for children to achieve this goal."

In a comparison of the development of modality in first and second language acquisition, Stephany (1995: 116) points out that "the cognitively immature and socially dependent child is more concerned with deontic and dynamic modalities" while "epistemic modality is most relevant for the cognitively and socially mature adult."

In the present chapter, the development of modality in early Greek language acquisition is explored by bringing together findings from Stephany's earlier work on the acquisition of Greek verbal grammar (Stephany 1985, 1997) and more recent studies, which pay special attention to modal verbs (Stephany 2017), extending the analysis to epistemic adverbs and mental verbs. In particular, attention will be focused on main issues of the acquisition of modality, namely, the modal–non-modal split of verb forms, the relative emergence of dynamic vs. deontic modal expressions, the dominance of inflectional vs. lexical expressions, the asynchrony of the development of agent-oriented and propositional modality, and, finally, the role played by the input. The results relating to the development of modality in Greek language acquisition will be compared to other languages in the concluding section.

2 Forms and functions of agent-oriented and propositional modality in Modern Greek

In Modern Greek, agent-oriented modality is preferably expressed inflectionally and propositional modality lexically. The main inflectional means for expressing deontic meanings are the imperative and the subjunctive, while the present indicative, future, and conditional are of minor importance. The principal lexical means for rendering agent-oriented or propositional meanings are modal verbs (*boró* 'can, may' and *prépi* 'must'). Verbs of desire (*θélo* 'I want') and mental verbs (e.g., *kséro* 'I know', *nomízo* 'I think', *fénete* 'it seems, it appears') express dynamic and epistemic meanings, respectively.[2] Greek also provides a considerable number of epistemic modal adverbs, only a few of which occur in early Greek CS (e.g., *vévea* 'certainly' and *málon* 'probably').[3]

2.1 Inflectional expressions of modality in Modern Greek

Although Modern Greek has lost the infinitive, its verbal inflection is particularly rich, comprising the categories of mood, aspect, tense, and voice, as well as person and number. While aspect is marked on the verb stem, mood or tense

---

2 *Fénete* 'it seems, it appears' may be taken to have an evidential meaning.
3 For details on Modern Greek lexical expressions of modality see Clairis and Babiniotis (2005: 469–471).

and person–number are expressed by the verb ending. Aspect is the most important grammatical category of the verb, and nearly all verbs formally distinguish between an imperfective and a perfective verb stem. The main temporal distinction is that between past and non-past (present) (example 1a vs. 1b and 1c). One of the functions of the opposition between the perfective and the imperfective aspect in the past tense is the denotation of a specific action vs. habitual behavior (example 1b vs. 1c).[4]

(1) a. *févy-o   ja   Jermanía.*
       leave.IPFV-NONPST.1SG for Germany
       'I am leaving for Germany.'
    b. *xθes   é-fiy-a   stis   péde.*
       yesterday AUG-leave.PFV-PAST.1SG at.the five
       'Yesterday I left at five (o'clock).'
    c. *siníθos é-fevy-a   stis   tris.*
       usually AUG-leave.IPFV-PAST.1SG at.the three
       'Usually I left at three (o'clock).'

The future tense and subjunctive mood are expressed periphrastically by a future and a modal particle constructed with the perfective or imperfective non-past form of the verb (examples 2a and 2b vs. 2c and 2d). With verbs of the telic *aktionsart*, the perfective aspect is the unmarked form while the imperfective aspect is marked (e.g., expressing habitualness). The future tense is negated by a non-modal negating particle, whereas the subjunctive requires a modal one (example 2b vs. 2d). Since there is no negative form of the Greek imperative, negated requests are expressed by the subjunctive (example 2d).

(2) a. *θa   fiy-un   se líyo.*
       FUT.PTL leave.PFV-NONPST.3PL at little
       'They will leave soon.'
    b. *δen   θa   fiy-un.*
       NEG.NONMDL FUT.PTL leave.PFV-NONPST.3PL
       'They will not leave.'
    c. *na   fíj-is.*
       MDL.PTL leave.PFV-NONPST.2SG
       'You may/should leave.'

---

4 For a detailed description of Modern Greek aspect see Stephany (1985: 38–53).

d. *na   min   fij-is.*
   MDL.PTL NEG.MDL leave.PFV-NONPST.2SG
   'Don't leave.'

The aspectual perfective–imperfective distinction is often neutralized in the imperative (Mackridge 1985: 123–124; Stephany 1985: 102; Stephany and Voeikova 2015: 75–76). Since, partially due to the recording situation, the imperative singular occurs much more frequently than its plural counterpart in Greek CS and CDS, the imperative of most verbs consists in a single verb form, which is distinguished from the second person singular of the non-past indicative, future, and subjunctive in CS from an early age.

The second person singular endings of the non-past (present) coincide with those of the future and subjunctive, but differ from the second person singular of the imperative (Table 1 and examples 3). In the 2nd conjugation, the endings also depend on aspect.[5]

Table 1: Endings of the 2nd person singular non-past, future, and subjunctive vs. the imperative singular in the two Greek conjugations (see Christofidou and Stephany 2003: 94).

Non-past				Imperative		
PFV		IPFV		PFV	IPFV	
Class 1	Class 2	Class 1	Class 2	Class 1/2	Class 1	Class 2
-is	-is	-is	-as/-is	-e	-e	-a

(3) a. Perfective non-past vs. imperative 2SG, 1st conjugation
   θa/na   fij-is.
   FUT/MDL.PTL leave.PFV-NONPST.2SG
   'You will/shall, may leave.'
   fij-e!
   leave.PFV-IMP.2SG
   'Leave!'

---

5 The main difference between the two Greek conjugations is that verbs belonging to class 1 bear stress on the stem (e.g., *ayoráz-o* 'buy.IPFV-NONPST.1SG') while those of class 2 are stressed on the ending (e.g., *ayap-ó* 'love.IPFV-NONPST.1SG').

b. Imperfective non-past vs. imperative 2SG, 2nd conjugation
proxor-ás.
go.on.IPFV-NONPST.2SG
'You go on.'
proxór-a!
go.on.IPFV-IMP.2SG
'Go on!'

The imperative is the prototypical inflectional form for expressing direct requests or commands, which do not tolerate non-compliance. As pointed out by Stephany and Voeikova (2015: 78), it is to be expected that in cases where the perfective and the imperfective imperative are distinguished, the perfective imperative will be preferred in child-centered situations since it focuses on the result of a specific action.[6]

Statements of social or moral norms with a speaker-external deontic source are expressed by the 3rd person plural of the non-past (present) indicative (example 4). Such statements "are typically prohibitive, with the verb accompanied by the non-modal dependent negator *δen*" (Stephany and Voeikova 2015: 73).

(4) Mairi, 1;9, CDS (Stephany 1985: 193)
     (after Mairi has addressed the investigator by the imperative *éla!* 'come!')
     MOT: *δen*   *léne*   *'éla'*
           NEG.NONMDL   say.IPFV.NONPST.3PL 'come.IMP.2SG'
           ta   peδ-ákj-a.
           the child-DIM-PL
           'Little children don't say *come!*.'

In colloquial Greek, deontic modal meanings, such as direct or indirect requests for action, prohibitions, permission, warnings, and suggestions, as well as dynamic modal meanings, such as intentions, are commonly expressed by the subjunctive or future rather than by the modal verbs *boró* 'can, may' or *prépi* 'must' (V. Kantzou, p.c.). As compared to the imperative, conveying direct requests or commands, "the more courteous character of requests expressed by the subjunctive is consistent with a general cross-linguistic tendency according to which more polite forms express less forceful commands (Aikhenvald 2010: 221)" (Stephany and Voeikova 2015: 70). This is also the case in Greek, where "requests

---

[6] For further details on the functions of the imperative see Stephany and Voeikova (2015: 76–78).

expressed in the subjunctive are interpretable as advice and are therefore considered more polite" (Stephany 1997: 298, referring to Babiniotis and Kontos 1967: 181).

The meaning of modalized utterances with the verb in the subjunctive or future crucially depends on its person–number form. While the first person singular expresses the speaker's intentions (example 5a), the first person plural of the subjunctive (mostly accompanied by the modal particle *na*) has a hortative function conveying suggestions (example 5b), and the future may serve to make promises (example 5c).

(5) a. *na/θa   δjavás-o   éna vivlío.*
       MDL/FUT.PTL read.PFV-NONPST.1SG a   book
       'Let me/I shall read a book.'
    b. *(na)   páme   stis kúnjes.*
       MDL.PTL go.PFV.NONPST.1PL to.the swings
       'Let's go to the playground.'
    c. Anna, 2;7, CDS
       θa   páme   se oréo
       FUT.PTL go.PFV.NONPST.1PL to nice
       méros pu   θa   (e)çi polés varkúles.
       place where FUT.PTL has many boat.DIM.PL
       'We will go to a nice place where there are many little boats.'

The 3rd person singular or plural of the subjunctive or future may convey indirect requests concerning one or several third persons (example 6a). In early Greek CS or CDS, it may also refer to the speaker or addressee (example 6b).

(6) a. Anna, 2;0, CDS
       ekí   na   kimiθí.
       there MDL.PTL sleep.MP.PFV.NONPST.3SG
       'It shall sleep there.' (a doll)
    b. CS (Stephany and Voeikova 2015: 72)
       na   fái
       MDL.PTL eat.PFV.NONPST.3SG
       i   mamá líγo.
       the mommy little
       'Mommy shall eat a little bit.'

The most important form for conveying deontic modal meanings is the second person singular (or plural). While the subjunctive in example (7a) expresses an indirect request, the future form in (7b) functions as a command, which does not leave the addressee the choice of not complying. The modal strength of the future in (7b) is even greater than that of the imperative (*vále ta papútsja* (put. on.PFV.IMP.2SG the shoes) 'put on your shoes'). The reason is that the future literally predicts a future action. Examples (7c) and (7d) are prohibitions with different modal strength, where the modal strength of the future in (7d) is again greater than that of the subjunctive in (7c), which may be taken as an advice. Example (7e) is a directive giving a warning.

(7) a. na   vál-is   ta   papútsja.
       MDL.PTL put.on.PFV-NONPST.2SG the   shoes
       'Put on your shoes.'

   b. θa   vál-is   ta   papútsja.
       FUT.PTL put.on.PFV-NONPST.2SG the   shoes
       'You shall/will put your shoes on.'

   c. Na   min   vyál-is
       MDL.PTL NEG.MDL take.off.PFV-NONPST.2SG
       ta   papútsja.
       the   shoes
       'Don't take your shoes off.'

   d. δen   θa   vyál-is
       NEG.NONMDL FUT.PTL take.off.PFV-NONPST.2SG
       ta   papútsja.
       the   shoes
       'You shall/will not take your shoes off.'

   e. min   pés-is.
       NEG.MDL fall.PFV-NONPST.2SG
       'Don't fall down!'

Example (8) illustrates an interesting difference between the use of the imperative of *kitázo* 'to look (at)' and that of the subjunctive of *vlépo* 'to see' by Mairi's mother in the Stephany Corpus. She first uses the subjunctive of the verb *vlépo* 'to see' to attract her daughter's attention, a request which the child is likely to comply with because it is for her own benefit. Immediately afterwards the mother requests the child to look at a specific object (a toy horse) by using the imperative of the verb *kitázo* 'to look at' followed by an explanation of why this is interesting and thereby offering the child a reason for complying with her command.

(8) Mairi, 1;9, CDS (Stephany Corpus)
na   δis   eδó   káti
MDL.PTL see.PFV.NONPST.2SG   here   something
pu   éxo.   kíta,   to
that have.NONPST.1SG   look.IMP.2SG   the
aloγáki.   bíke   apáno   sto   tréno.
horse.DIM   enter.PFV.PAST.3SG on.top   on.the   train
'Come and see something I have here. Look, the horse. It went on top of the train.'

Inflectional forms serving to express epistemic modality are the future and the conditional (see section 5 below). According to Lyons (1977: 815, 820), the future is non-factive and has a modal character because, in contrast to the past, it cannot be known. Example (9a) fluctuates between the epistemic meaning of a more or less certain future action and the dynamic meaning of a third person's intention. Example (9b) issues a warning by stating a possible undesirable event.

(9) a. θa   fíji.
       FUT.PTL leave.PFV.NONPST.3SG
       'S/he will/may leave.'
    b. Janna, 1;11
       (θ)a   pési.
       FUT.PTL fall.PFV.NONPST.3SG
       'It will fall.'

2.2 Lexical expressions of modality in Modern Greek

The most important lexical means for expressing modality in Modern Greek are modal verbs and epistemic sentence adverbs. As is common in many languages, epistemic adverbs have a single inherent meaning while modal verbs may express agent-oriented (deontic and dynamic) or propositional (epistemic) modality. In contrast to languages such as German and English, which possess a series of modal verbs, Modern Greek has only two such verbs, *boró* 'can, may' and *prépi* 'must', situated at the poles of the scale of modality and expressing deontic or epistemic possibility and necessity, respectively (see nu. 10).

(10) Scale of modality (Stephany 1993: 134)
necessity   possibility
←--→
prépi   *boró*
'must'   'can, may'

The modal verb *boró* 'can, may' covers all person–number forms of the non-past (present), past, or future and distinguishes between the imperfective and perfective aspect, while *prépi* 'must' is a defective verb lacking aspectual distinctions and being limited to the 3rd person singular of the non-past, past, or future (Table 2).

Table 2: Selected forms of *boró* 'can, may' and *prépi* 'must'.

Forms	Morphemic translation	Gloss
bor-ó	can.IPFV-NONPST.1SG	'I can/may/am able to'
θa bor-és-is	FUT.PTL can-PFV-NONPST.2SG	'you will be able/allowed to'
bor-ús-ame	can-IPFV-PAST.1PL	'we were able/allowed to'
prép-i	must-NONPST.3SG	'it must/is necessary'
θa prép-i	FUT.PTL must-NONPST.3SG	'it will be necessary'
é-prep-e	AUG-must-PAST.3SG	'it was necessary'

The deontic/dynamic vs. epistemic meaning of modal verbs depends on a number of factors. While all person–number forms of the modal verb *boró* 'can, may' may occur in agent-oriented meanings (example 11a), only the 3rd person singular form (*borí* 'it can, may', *prépi* 'it must') is possible in epistemic use (example 11b). In deontic or dynamic use, the dependent lexical verb agrees with the modal verb in person and number (example 11a) while in epistemic use it may agree (in the 3rd person singular) but does not have to agree with the modal verb (example 11b). Constructions in which the modal verb and the dependent verb both occur in the 3rd person singular non-past are ambiguous between deontic/dynamic and epistemic use (example 11c). The dynamic and epistemic use of the modal verb *boró* 'can, may' can be readily observed in the adult-directed utterances of a Greek taxi driver quoted in example (12; from Stephany 2017: 90).

(11) a. *bor-úme   na   fíy-ume.*
      may.IPFV-NONPST.1PL MDL.PTL leave.PFV-NONPST.1PL
      'We can/may leave.'

b. *bor-í*   *na*   *fíɣ-ane.*
    may.IPFV-NONPST.3SG MDL.PTL leave.PFV-PAST.3PL
    'They may have left.'
c. *bor-í*   *na*   *fíj-i.*
    may.IPFV-NONPST.3SG MDL.PTL leave.PFV-NONPST.3SG
    'S/he can/may leave.'
    'It is possible that s/he will leave.'

(12) δόδεka óres   δe   bor-ó
    twelve hours NEG.NONMDL can.IPFV-NONPST.1SG
    na   *οδiɣáο*   *taksí.*
    MDL.PTL steer.IPFV.NONPST.1SG taxi.
    'I can't steer the taxi for twelve hours.'
    bor-í   *ja*   *to*   *ɣústo*   *mu*
    may.IPFV-NONPST.3SG for the pleasure of.me
    na   *οδiɣáο*   *ke*   *íkosi*   *óres.*
    MDL.PTL steer.IPFV.NONPST.1SG also twenty hours
    'I may drive for even twenty hours just for fun.'

Another factor which may determine the agent-oriented vs. propositional interpretation of modal verb constructions is the aspectual character (*aktionsart*) of the complement verb. Since agent-oriented meanings are excluded with stative verbs, example (13a; from Stephany 2017: 75) has an epistemic meaning. Finally, the modal interpretation may be determined by the tense of the complement verb. While a modal verb construction with the complement verb in the present tense may either have an agent-oriented or propositional modal meaning, only an epistemic meaning is possible with a complement verb in the past tense (example 13b vs. 13c; from Stephany 2017: 76; see also example 11b above). All this demonstrates the complexity of constructions of Greek modal verbs.

(13) a. *prépi/borí*   *na*   *íne élinas.*
        must/may.NONPST.3SG MDL.PTL is Greek
        'He must/may be Greek.'
    b. *prépi*   *na*   *mil-ís-i*
        must.NONPST.3SG MDL.PTL speak-PFV-NONPST.3SG
        sto   *sinéδrio.*
        at.the conference
        'S/he must speak at the conference.'
        ('S/he is obliged to speak at the conference' or 'It is likely that s/he will speak the conference')

c. *prépi*   *na*   *mílis/milús-e*
   must.NONPST.3SG MDL.PTL speak.PFV/IPFV-PAST.3SG
   sto   *sinéðrio.*
   at.the conference
   'S/he must have spoken at the conference.'

With the exception of the quasi-modal verb[7] *θélo* 'want' expressing dynamic and indirect deontic meanings, lexical verbs conveying modal notions are much less important in early Greek CS and CDS. The verb *kséro* 'know' has both a dynamic and an epistemic meaning (example 14a vs. 14b). It is often used in the negative form (*ðen kséro* (NEG.NONMDL know.NONPST.1SG) 'I don't know'). Verbs such as *nomízo* 'I think' and *fénete* 'it seems, appears' allow an epistemic and evidential qualification of statements, respectively.

(14) a. *kséro*   *na*   *kolibáo.*
   know.NONPST.1SG MDL.PTL swim.IPFV.NONPST.1SG
   'I can/know how to swim.'
   b. *kséro*   *óti*   *vréçi.*
   know.NONPST.1SG CONJ rain.IPFV.NONPST.3SG
   'I know that it rains/is raining.'

Although Greek is rich in epistemic adverbs expressing different degrees of necessity and possibility, only two of them play a certain role in our CS data. These are *vévea* 'certainly' and *málon* 'probably', expressing certainty and probability. The notions of certainty (epistemic necessity) and uncertainty (epistemic possibility) situated at the poles of the epistemic scale are expressed by the adverb *vévea* 'certainly' and the modal verb form *borí* 'it can, may', respectively, while the adverb *málon* 'probably' conveys an in-between value of epistemic strength.[8] An important difference between modal verbs and epistemic adverbs is that the latter have a single inherent meaning and that they need not be integrated into the structure of the sentence.

---

7 See Hickmann and Bassano (2016: 431) on the English quasi-modals *going to, want to*.
8 See Boye (2016: 117) on a more extended and detailed scale of epistemic meanings: "knowledge, certainty, epistemic necessity, probability, likelihood, uncertainty, epistemic possibility, doubt, unlikelihood, epistemic impossibility".

3 Data

The audio-taped CS and CDS data studied in the present chapter come from the Stephany Corpus (Tables 3 and 4) and the Katis Corpus (Table 5) of monolingual Greek children growing up in Athens, Greece, interacting with their caretakers, mostly their mothers, in natural speech situations.

Table 3: Handwritten transcription of the Stephany Corpus (recordings in min.) (Stephany 1985: 24).

Subjects	Natali	Spiros	Mairi	Janna	Maria
Age	1;8	1;9	1;9	1;11	–
Recordings	285	240	330	780	–
Age	–	–	2;3	2;5	2;3
Recordings	–	–	450	360	360
Age	–	–	2;9	2;11	2;9
Recordings	–	–	270	240	240
Total	285	240	1,050	1,380	600

Adult-directed speech as studied in Stephany (1985 and 2017) will only be marginally taken into consideration. While the ADS data analyzed in Stephany (1985) come from the children's mothers interacting with another adult, those in Stephany (2017) have been taken from the Corpus of Spoken Greek (CSG) containing naturalistic speech data among adults (Pavlidou, Kapellidi, and Karafoti 2014; Pavlidou 2016).

The children of the Stephany Corpus were observed at one to three different points in time: four of them before the end of the second year and three of them in the first and second half of their third year. The recordings amount to a total of slightly more than 59 hours (Table 3). The computerized transcription of the Stephany Corpus has been published in the CHILDES database (MacWhinney 2000). It represents the handwritten transcription only partially and amounts to a total of 16,000 word tokens of CS (Table 4). The children's interaction with their caretakers[9] and the investigator was tape-recorded in situations such as playing, looking at picture books, and daily routines.[10]

---

[9] The caretakers were mainly the mothers and in one case each a grandmother and a nanny.
[10] Major analyses of the handwritten transcript of the Stephany Corpus and of both the handwritten and the computerized parts are to be found in Stephany (1985) and Stephany (1997), respectively.

Table 4: Computerized part of the Stephany Corpus (CHILDES Database) (word tokens).[11]

Subjects	Natali	Spiros	Mairi	Janna	Maria
Age	1;8	1;9	1;9	1;11	–
CS	142	742	4,142	807	–
CDS	490	968	6,298	621	–
Age	–	–	2;3	2;5	2;3
CS	–	–	2,712	951	805
CDS	–	–	3,810	–	669
Age	–	–	2;9	2;11	2;9
CS	–	–	3,069	1,205	1,425
CDS	–	–	4,419	–	–
Total CS	142	742	9,923	2,963	2,230
Total CDS	490	968	14,527	621	669

The data of the Katis Corpus analyzed in the present study come from monthly tape recordings of one child from 1;8 to 3;0 and cover a total of 37 hours and 70,204 word tokens of CS (Table 5). This extraordinarily rich corpus includes the child's interaction with her mother in a wide variety of contexts. The transcription is in CHAT format but has not yet been grammatically coded.

Table 5: Katis Corpus (recordings and word tokens).

Anna's age	Recordings	Word tokens	
		CS	CDS
1;8–1;11	690 min.	15,886	52,988
2;0–2;6	1,050 min.	31,352	70,355
2;7–3;0	480 min.	22,966	28,843
Total	2,220 min.	70,204	152,186

The development of verb inflection by the boy Christos (Christofidou Corpus) from 1;7 to 2;1 has been studied by Christofidou and Stephany (2003) and will only be referred to occasionally in the present study.

---

[11] Only the input of the mothers, a grandmother, and a nanny have been included in CDS counts.

4 Forms and functions of agent-oriented modality in early Greek child speech and child-directed speech

4.1 Inflectional expressions of deontic and dynamic modality

While deontic modality is mainly expressed by verbal inflection in early Greek child language, dynamic modality is chiefly rendered by the quasi-modal verb *θélo* 'want' and the modal verb *boró* 'can'. The most important inflectional means for expressing deontic modal meanings in early Greek CS and CDS are the imperative and the subjunctive or future, conveying direct and indirect requests, respectively. The subjunctive not only expresses deontic meanings of indirect requests but also dynamic modal meanings of intention and desire. Other inflectional expressions conveying agent-oriented modal notions much more rarely in CS as well as CDS are the non-past (present) indicative and the imperfective past expressing the deontic notion of directives and the dynamic notions of unwillingness or inability, respectively.

4.1.1 The imperative vs. the subjunctive/future

Since the 2nd person singular of the imperative occurs much more frequently in interactions of mother–child dyads than the 2nd person plural and the aspectual distinction of the perfective and imperfective is often neutralized in the imperative mood, Greek children have to memorize only a single imperative form of many, if not most verbs. The five children observed by Stephany (1985: 103–104) between 1;8 and 2;11 use 94% to 97% correct forms of the 2nd person singular imperative on average (*n* = 943 tokens). Regular 2nd person singular imperative forms of the first conjugation and perfective ones of the second conjugation end in *-e*. The deletion of this ending in front of certain clitic personal pronouns may lead to consonant clusters which are often simplified in CS (e.g., *klís-e* (close.PFV-IMP.2SG), *klís-to* (close.PFV.IMP.2SG-it) > *klíto* 'switch it off!') (Stephany 1985: 104–105). Non-standard omission of the ending of singular imperative forms (*-e* or *-a*) is very rare in the speech of the children of the Stephany Corpus, decreasing from 5.6% before the turn to the third year to merely 3% at 2;9 and 2;11 (Stephany 1985: 108).

The perfective and imperfective imperative forms of verbs in which the aspectual distinction is not neutralized differ in meaning. Certain imperfective imperative forms are commonly used in the standard language because they express mitigated requests (e.g., *ksípn-a!* (wake.up.IPFV-IMP.2SG) vs. *ksípn-is-e!*

(wake.up-PFV-IMP.2SG) 'wake up!') (Stephany 1985: 173). The perfective imperative of a given verb is not yet contrasted with the imperfective form by any of the subjects in the Stephany Corpus, and the imperative of most verbs, especially telic ones, only occurs in the unmarked perfective form (Stephany 1985: 173).

As is common, the imperative is limited to dynamic verbs and is directed to the addressee. The two most frequently occurring singular imperative forms in CS in the Stephany Corpus are *kíta!* 'look!' and *éla!* 'come!' (Stephany 1985: 104). Other imperative forms often used by these children are *kátse!* or *kátsise!* 'sit down, remain seated, wait!' and *síko!* 'stand up!' (Stephany 1985: 172).[12] In Anna's data (Katis Corpus), the two imperatives *kíta!* 'look!' and *éla!* 'come!' amount to 90% of the total of 527 tokens of the most frequently used imperatives *kíta!* 'look!', *éla!* 'come!', and *kátse!* 'sit, wait!'.

Although the imperative expresses direct requests that do not give the addressee an option not to comply with the command, there are situations in which the imperative is more adequate than the subjunctive conveying indirect requests. Examples are *kátse!* (lit. sit) 'wait!' or *kíta!* 'look!' with which an addressee will naturally comply by courtesy or because this is to his or her own advantage (Stephany 1985: 173).

Requests containing a verb form are exclusively expressed by the imperative by three children of the Stephany Corpus before 2;0 and in 91% of tokens of the total of imperative and 2nd person singular subjunctive forms by the girl Mairi (1;9, n = 220). In the third year, indirect requests expressed by the 2nd person singular subjunctive increase in the speech of two subjects of the Stephany Corpus so that the imperative drops from 91% at 1;9 to 75% at 2;3 in Mairi's speech and from 100% at 1;11 to 54% at 2;5 in Janna's. In the second half of the third year, the percentage of requests expressed by the imperative in comparison to the 2nd person singular subjunctive amounts to 58% in both of these girls' speech. The late talker Maria, observed at 2;3 and 2;9, still expresses requests by the imperative in 80% or even 91% of the total of imperative and 2nd person singular subjunctive tokens. Mairi's and Janna's development shows that indirect requests expressed by the 2nd person singular subjunctive may increase considerably between the end of the second and the first half of the third year.

---

[12] In contrast to some Russian children who often use the imperative form *daj!* 'give!' (see Voeikova and Bayda, this volume), the form *dóse!* 'give!' is not among the most frequently used imperatives in Greek CS. According to the computerized part of the Stephany Corpus, three of four subjects either do not use the verb *díno* 'to give' at all or very infrequently. In Mairi's data (Stephany Corpus) 59% of the 42 tokens of this verb are in the 2nd person singular perfective imperative *dóse*, and in Anna's data (Katis Corpus) this form amounts to less than half of the 53 tokens of this verb.

Some interesting intersubjective and functional variation can be observed concerning the use of the subjunctive or the imperative for expressing requests (Stephany 1985: 173). While Janna (2;5), who spends half of her days in a kindergarten, expresses requests addressed to an adult rather frequently by the subjunctive, Maria (2;3), who is cared for by her grandmother during her mother's working hours, does so only rarely (Stephany 1985: 173). The imperative directly requires some immediate action, whereas the subjunctive softens requests (example 15a vs. 15b). Thus, Spiros (1;9) chooses the imperative for a request addressed to the investigator but prefers the subjunctive when turning to his mother (example 16a vs. 16b). Both forms may also be used in consecutive utterances in order to strengthen a request for action (example 17).

(15) Mairi, 2;3 (Stephany 1985: 175)
   a. (when another child is disturbing her at her play)
   fíj-e!
   go.away.PFV-IMP.2SG
   'Go away!'
   b. (addressing a neighborhood child)
   (n)a   fíj-is.
   MDL.PTL leave.PFV-NONPST.2SG
   'You shall leave.'

(16) Spiros, 1;9 (Stephany 1985: 174)
   a. (commanding the investigator to take off her watch)
   (to)   lolói [: *rolói*]*!*
   (the)   watch
   'The watch!'
   aláto [: *ja   vyál-to*]*!*
              MDL.PTL take.off.PFV.IMP.2SG-it
   'Take it off!'
   b. (asking his mother to remove the doll 'daddy' from a toy boat)
   láli . . . babás . . . típa.
   [: *(na)   vyál-i*
   (MDL.PTL)   take.out.PFV-NONPST.3SG
   (ton)   babá   (apó   tin)   trípa.]
   (the) daddy (from the) hole
   'She shall take daddy (out of the) hole.'
   láli   i   mamáli   típa.
   [: *(na)   vyál-i*
   (MDL.PTL)   take.out.PFV-NONPST.3SG

```
    i    mamá   (apó)  tin   trípa.]
    the  Mommy  (from) the   hole
```
'Mommy shall take (it out of) the hole.'

(17) Maria, 2;3 (Stephany 1985: 175)
(addressing the investigator, who is standing)
```
(n)a       káθ-e(s)e              káto.
MDL.PTL    sit.IPFV-MP.NONPST.2SG down
```
(after a short pause:)
```
káti    [: káts-e]    káto!
        sit-IMP.2SG   down
```
'You shall sit down. Sit down!'

The subjunctive may furthermore be chosen when the addressee's conduct is to be governed not so much by the speaker's subjective desire but by an objective necessity (example 18) (Stephany 1985: 173). Two of the three children in the Stephany Corpus observed at 2;9 and 2;11 use the subjunctive in requests relating to some distant future but the imperative when referring to the speech situation (examples 19) (Stephany 1985: 173).

(18) Janna, 2;11 (Stephany 1985: 174)
(asking the investigator to hold her while she is bending over to reach for an object on the floor)
```
na        me  k(r)at-ás              ómos.
MDL.PTL   me  hold.IPFV-NONPST.2SG   though
```
'Hold me though.'

(19) Janna, 2;11 (Stephany 1985: 175)
a. (discussing the investigator's next visit)
```
INV: éna  vrádi     θa       (e)rθ-ó.
     one  evening   FUT.PTL  come.PFV.MP-NONPST.1SG
```
'I will come some evening.'
```
JAN: ti   deftéra   ná        (er)θ-is.
     the  Monday    MDL.PTL   come.PFV.MP-NONPST.2SG
```
'Come on Monday.'

b. (addressing another child in kindergarten)
JAN: éla   lígoya [: γrίγora]!
      come.IMP.2SG quickly
      'Come quickly!'

As mentioned above, the Greek imperative cannot be negated. Negative requests such as prohibitions are therefore expressed by the subjunctive constructed with the modal negative particle *min*. Use of the non-modal negative particle *δen* in contrast to modal *min* may therefore allow to distinguish non-modal from modal expressions.[13] In example (20a), Mairi's mother asks her daughter to handle an object carefully using a subjunctive form negated by *min* while the child promises to do so by a future form negated by the non-modal negator *δen*. Example (20b) is a negative command which can be interpreted as a piece of advice or prohibition.

(20) a. Mairi, 2;3 (Stephany 1985: 156)
     MOT: na   min   to
          MDL.PTL   NEG.MDL it
          spas-is   ómos.
          break.PFV-NONPST.2SG however
          'But don't break it.'
     MAI: əm [: δen]   (θa   to)
          NEG.NONMDL   (FUT.PTL it)
          (s)pás-o.
          break.PFV-NONPST.1SG
          'I won't break it.'
  b. Maria, 2;3 (Stephany 1985: 158)
     (to a toy elephant which has fallen down)
     (m)i(n)   kle(s).
     NEG.MDL   cry.IPFV.NONPST.2SG
     'Don't cry.'

In CDS before 2;0 (Stephany Corpus),[14] the imperative is also much more frequently used for expressing requests than the subjunctive or future. Deontic

---

[13] However, the modally used future is constructed with the non-modal negative particle *δen* (e.g., *δen θa fíj-is* (NEG.NONMDL FUT.PTL leave.PFV-NONPST.2SG) 'you will/shall not leave'). The reason is that such requests are expressed by statements.
[14] Only the CDS of the first period of observation before 2;0 has been taken into consideration in Stephany (1985) and the present study (see Table 4 above).

modality conveyed by the non-past (present) indicative is least frequent as shown in number (21) (see also Stephany 1985: 185, 192).[15]

(21) Ranking of modally used TAM forms in CDS before 2;0
IMP > SBJV/FUT > NON-PAST
(IMP 54%, SBJV/FUT 33%, NON-PAST 13%; $n = 1{,}958$)

The imperative is exclusively used for commands while the modally used subjunctive, future, and present tense serve other modal functions besides expressing directives (see section 4.1.2 below). Example (22) not only illustrates use of the imperative for making a direct request but also various ways of conveying indirect ones (a question concerning the addressee's future behavior and the statement of a social norm).

(22) Janna, 1;11, CDS (Stephany 1985: 193)
(Janna is handing over an object to the investigator)
JAN: *pá(r)-to!*
take.PFV.IMP.2SG-it
'Take it!'
MOT: *ti   θa   pis?*
what FUT.PTL say.PFV.NONPST.2SG
'What will you say?'
(after a pause)
'oríste'   pes!
'please'   say.PFV.IMP.2SG
'Say "*please*"!'
ti   θa   pis,   mána   mu?
what FUT.PTL say.PFV.NONPST.2SG mother of.me
'What will you say, darling?'
ti   léne?
what   say.IPFV.NONPST.3PL
'What does one say?'

---

[15] As is to be expected, in the mothers' ADS, the frequency of the imperative is much lower than in their CDS (Stephany 1985: 185).

4.1.2 Modal use of the subjunctive and future

In Greek CS, the subjunctive is a more important category for expressing agent-oriented modal notions than the imperative because of its variety of functions. Besides the deontic notion of requests, it may also express the dynamic notions of intention or desire. Furthermore, the subjunctive is used in constructions with a modal or full verb (see section 4.2). The categories of the perfective subjunctive, the imperfective non-past (present) indicative, and the imperative are formally and functionally differentiated in Greek CS already before the end of the second year (see also section 4.1.1 above).

The perfective subjunctive is distinguished from the imperfective non-past (present) indicative by a modal (or future) particle and the combination of the perfective verb stem with a non-past (present) tense ending (e.g., *akú-o* (hear.IPFV-NONPST.1SG) 'I hear, listen' vs. *na/θa akú-s-o* (MDL/FUT.PTL hear-PFV-NONPST.1SG) 'that I listen, let me listen/I will listen'). More than 80% up to 99% of subjunctive forms occurring in the speech of five children in the Stephany Corpus throughout the observation period are perfective so that they are formally distinguished from the imperfective non-past indicative in spite of an as yet unreliable particle use before 2;0. At 1;8, 1;9, and 1;11, particles accompany subjunctive forms in only 12% to 57% of tokens (n = 572) depending on the child (Stephany 1985: 94). In cases where the particle is omitted in imperfective non-past forms, intonation, emphatic pronunciation, or context often allow to distinguish subjunctive from indicative forms (Stephany 1985: 95). During the third year, particle use rises to 82% or even 97% in three children's speech (Stephany 1985: 94).

While the subjunctive is quite well distinguished from the indicative (by aspect or particle use) in CS in the Stephany Corpus already before 2;0, this is not the case for the subjunctive and the future. The reason is that the modal and future particles *na* and *θa* are often either omitted or reduced to their vowel so that only 8% of subjunctive tokens are distinguished from future ones in three children's speech before the end of the second year and in 49% of tokens in the speech of a fourth child (Stephany 1985: 96). Nevertheless, there is some evidence for a distinction between a deontic or dynamic modal use and a more temporal or epistemic one of the perfective non-past even in cases where the subjunctive and future are not formally distinguished by particle use. While a deontic or dynamic modal use "occurs with animate subjects commonly referring to speaker or addressee, [a more temporal or epistemic use] is found in statements and questions about imminent situations uncontrolled by an agent or further removed from speech time" (Stephany 1997: 207) (examples 23).[16]

(23) a. Maria, 2;9 (Stephany 1985: 161)
(addressing the investigator)
ta   [: θa]   jín-is
FUT.PTL   become-NONPST.2SG
ke   mamá   esí.
and   mommy   you
'You'll also become a mommy.'
b. Marilena, 2;7 (Katis 1984, quoted by Stephany 1997: 300)
(θ)a   páme   θa   [: na]
FUT.PTL   go.PFV.NONPST.1PL   FUT.PTL   MDL.PTL
to   (s)kotós-ume   to   líko.
it   kill.PFV-NONPST.1PL   the   wolf
'We will go and kill the wolf.'

A cursory look at Anna's (uncoded) data (Katis Corpus) suggests that the girl uses the modal particle *na* (in a few cases reduced to [a]) in nearly all of her more than 300 tokens of subjunctive verb forms already before her turn to the third year (1;8–1;11). The same seems to be true for the future particle *θa* (often pronounced [ta] and rarely reduced to [a]) in the same period of observation (143 tokens). Anna therefore probably distinguishes the subjunctive from the future already by 1;8.

As mentioned above, the subjunctive expresses deontic as well as dynamic modal notions, namely indirect requests and desire or intention. Due to their subordinate social rank, children frequently announce their desires or intentions in order to get their wishes fulfilled, prevent some unwanted actions by their caretakers, or escape sanctions of their own actions (Stephany 1985: 155). Agent-oriented modal use of the subjunctive largely predominates during the entire period of observation of the children in the Stephany Corpus, but its more temporal (or epistemic) use and the occurrence in dependent clauses increase during the third year (Stephany 1985: 156).

Person-number forms are of utmost importance for distinguishing deontic from dynamic modal meanings of the subjunctive or future. The 1st person singular[17] usually expresses the child's intentions (example 24a) and desires (example 24b) or

---

[16] On the epistemic character of predictions see section 5 below.
[17] As is common in early CS, two subjects of the Stephany Corpus frequently use the 3rd person singular of the subjunctive for reference to the speaker before 2;0 (Stephany 1985: 100).

serves to inquire about the caretaker's opinion or advice concerning the child's action (example 24c). It may also be used to ask for permission (example 24d) or make promises (see example 20a above) (Stephany 1985: 156).

(24) a. Mairi, 1;9 (Stephany 1985: 156)
    (threatening an ugly toy monkey that she does not sympathize)

ekí	sururá	[: tin	urá]!
there		the	tail
sekóso	[: θa	su	kóps-o]
	FUT.PTL	you.GEN	cut.PFV-NONPST.1SG
ti	[: tin]	ururá	[: urá].
	the.ACC.SG		tail

'Your tail over there! I will cut your tail.'

b. Janna, 2;5 (Stephany 1985: 157)
    (wanting to continue playing with a doll after having been asked to put it back into the investigator's bag)

lígo	[: líyo]	na	kadzíso	[: kaθís-o].
a.little		MDL.PTL		sit.MP.PFV-NONPST.1SG

'I (would like to) continue a little more.'

c. Maria, 2;3 (Stephany 1985: 157)
    (asking for Granny's advice before inserting a jigsaw piece)

púndo	[: pu	na	to]	vál-o
	where	MDL.PTL	it	put.PFV-NONPST.1SG

a(f)tó?
this.one
'Where shall I put this one?'

d. Janna, 2;11 (Stephany 1985: 157)
    (asking for permission to look into the investigator's bag)

ja	na	δó?
MDL.PTL	MDL.PTL	see.PFV.NONPST.1SG

'May I look?'

In contrast to the 1st person singular, the 1st person plural of the subjunctive or future mainly expresses hortatives, suggesting some common action including speaker and addressee. Such utterances convey desires and are implicitly directive (examples 25) (Stephany 1985: 157).

(25) a. Natali, 1;8 (Stephany 1985: 157)
    badáki [: *peð-áki*]. (e)*kí*
        child-DIM   there
    pámi   [: (θa/na) *páme*]?
        FUT/MDL.PTL go.PFV.NONPST.1PL
    '(The) baby. Shall/will we go there?'
  b. Janna, 2;5 (Stephany 1985: 157)
    (wanting to see the babies in another room of the kindergarten)
    na   *zúme*   [: *δúme*]
    MDL.PTL   see.PFV.NONPST.1PL
    ta   *molá*   [: *morá*].
    the.N.PL   babies.N.PL
    'Let's see the babies.'

The 2nd person of the subjunctive or future nearly exclusively occurs in the singular and, with the exception of the child Mairi, only emerges during the third year in two other children's speech (Stephany 1985: 158). It expresses indirect requests (example 26a) or inquires about the addressee's intention (example 26b) (Stephany 1985: 158).

(26) a. Janna, 2;5 (Stephany 1985: 158)
    (addressing her aunt, whom she does not like)
    egó [: *eγó*] *sa* [: *θa*] *pá-o*
      I   FUT.PTL go.PFV-NONPST.1SG
    tikisía [: *stin eklisía*],
        in.the church
    k(e) *esí* *na*   *mín-is*,
    and you MDL.PTL stay.PFV-NONPST.2SG
    móni   *su*.
    alone.F.SG of.you
    'I will go to church and you shall stay, (and be left) alone.'
  b. Mairi, 2;3
    (after the investigator has announced that she will show her something)
    ti   *sa*   [: *θa*] *kán-is?*
    what   FUT.PTL do-NONPST.2SG
    'What are you going to do?'

In the earliest developmental period, the 3rd person singular of the subjunctive or future may refer to the speaker and serve for making indirect requests by implicitly expressing the child's desire (example 27a). Later on, such requests refer to a third person (example 27b).

(27) a. Spiros, 1;9 (Stephany 1985: 159)
(when the investigator fetches a book from her bag)

pío	[: (o)]	Spíros]
	the.M.SG	Spiros
vavási	[: (na/θa)]	δjavás-i].
	MDL/FUT.PTL	read.PFV-NONPST.3SG

'Spiros wants to/will read.'

b. Mairi, 2;9 (Stephany 1985: 159)
(addressing her mother when the investigator is about to put a fairytale book into her bag before leaving)

na	min	do
MDL.PTL	NEG.MDL	it
pár-i		aftó.
take.PFV-NONPST.3SG		this

'She shall not take this.'

Besides person–number distinctions, the differentiation between the perfective and imperfective aspect is an important characteristic of subjunctive or future forms. In Greek CS, the perfective aspect occurs more frequently with telic verbs and the imperfective one with atelic dynamic or stative ones. Both of these aspectual categories are adequately used with such verbs from the very beginning (Stephany 1985: 166). This can be explained by the affinity of the atelic and stative *aktionsart* with the imperfective aspect and that of the telic *aktionsart* with the perfective aspect (Stephany 1985: 166). Thus, Janna uses the telic verb *péfto* 'fall' in the perfective subjunctive but the atelic verb *kratáo* 'hold tight' in the imperfective (example 28). Errors with the use of the imperfective aspect with telic-punctual verbs persist until the end of the observation period (Stephany 1985: 170). In example (29), Spiros is referring to a single event so that the imperfective aspect is inappropriate.

(28) Janna, 2;11 (Stephany 1985: 167)
(referring to a book at which she is looking together with the investigator)
JAN: *na   mi   bési*
      MDL.PTL
      [from: *min   pés-i]   káto.*
                NEG.MDL fall.PFV-NONPST.3SG   down
      'It shall not fall down.'
INV: *δe(n)   θa   pés-i.*
      NEG.NONMDL FUT.PTL fall.PFV-NONPST.3SG
      'It will not fall.'
JAN: *sa [: θa]   to   krat-áo.*
        FUT.PTL   it   hold.IPFV-NONPST.1SG
      'I will hold it tight.'

(29) Spiros, 1;9 (Stephany 1985: 168)
(taking a ball which had previously rolled into a sleeve of the investigator's jacket by coincidence and putting it inside the sleeve after several futile attempts to insert it by throwing)
mésa.   tapéta   [: dzakéta].
inside   jacket
mésa   tapéta   [: dzakéta].
inside   jacket
na   bén-i   mésa.
MDL.PTL   enter.IPFV-NONPST.3SG   inside
for: *na   bi   mésa.*
     MDL.PTL   enter.PFV-NONPST.3SG   inside
tapéta   [: dzakéta].
             jacket
(putting the ball inside the sleeve)
ekí.
there
'Inside. Jacket. Inside jacket. It shall go inside. Jacket. There.'

Turning to CDS before 2;0 in the Stephany Corpus, the imperative exclusively expresses direct requests while the subjunctive and the future serve several deontic and dynamic functions. About one third of subjunctive forms occurring in main clauses in the speech of four mothers convey mitigated requests and are in the 2nd (or 3rd) person singular referring to the addressee (example 30a)

(Stephany 1985: 193). Requests in the future have a stronger illocutionary force than those in the subjunctive (example 30b).

(30) a. Spiros, 1;9, CDS (Stephany 1985: 194)
  edó   na   t(o)   aníks-is.
  here MDL.PTL it   open.PFV-NONPST.2SG
  'You shall open it here.'
 b. Janna, 1;11, CDS (Stephany 1985: 194)
  (after Janna has hit a doll)
  θa   to   afís-is
  FUT.PTL it   leave.PFV-NONPST.2SG
  tóra edó   péra   sti   karékla.
  now   here over.there on.the chair
  'You will now leave it over there on the chair.'

The caretakers most frequently use the subjunctive or future for announcing the speaker's intention (1st or 3rd person singular) (example 31a), inquiring about the addressee's intention or desire (mostly 2nd person singular) (example 31b), (seemingly) seeking his or her agreement, even for a caretaker's threatened action (mostly 1st person singular interrogative) (example 31c), or making suggestions (1st person plural) (example 31d) (see Stephany 1985: 193–195). Granting permission by the 2nd person singular of the subjunctive is a function only rarely found in the caretakers' speech (example 31e).

(31) a. Mairi, 1;9, CDS (Stephany 1985: 194)
  (after Mairi has asked Mother for some cake)
  θa   su   dós-i
  FUT.PTL you.GEN   give.PFV-NONPST.3SG
  i   mama.
  the   mommy
  'Mommy will give you.'
 b. Natali, 1;8, CDS (Stephany 1985: 194)
  sti(n)   bríza   [: príza]   na   to
  in.the   socket   MDL.PTL   it
  vál-is?
  put.PFV-NONPST.2SG
  'Are you going to put it into the socket?'

c. Spiros, 1;9, CDS (Stephany 1985: 194)
(after the Mother's threat to call the mouse, when Spiros continues to handle some toy carelessly)

na	to	fonáks-o?
MDL.PTL	it	call.PFV-NONPST.1SG

'Shall I call it?'

d. Mairi, 1;9, CDS

MOT:
ja	na	vál-ume
MDL.PTL	MDL.PTL	put.on.PFV-NONPST.1PL
poðítsa	ke	na	pár-ume
napkin	and	MDL.PTL	take.PFV-NONPST.1PL
metá	mazí	to	
afterwards	together	the	
pap-úli		na	
grandfather-DIM		MDL.PTL	
rot-ís-ume		ti	káni.
ask-PFV-NONPST.1PL		what	does

'Let's put on a napkin and afterwards call Grandfather together. Let's ask how he is doing.'

e. Natali, 1;8, CDS (Stephany 1985: 195)
(Natali announces that she is going to open the microphone case)

NAT:
a-aníto	[: na	(to)	aníks-o].
	MDL.PTL	(it)	open.PFV-NONPST.1SG

'I am going to open it.'

MOT:
ne.	na	to	aníks-is.
yes.	MDL.PTL	it	open.PFV-NONPST.2SG

'Yes. You may open it.'.

4.1.3 Modal use of the non-past (present) indicative

Although use of the non-past (present) indicative is primarily non-modal, modal uses of the 3rd person plural are found in both CS and CDS of the Stephany Corpus already before the turn to the third year. These are most frequently statements of social rules functioning as indirect requests. Others are questions about people's normal behavior asked by the caretakers (see example 22 above). Indirect requests expressed by the subjunctive or the future have a speaker-internal source of modality while that of deontic statements is speaker-external (Stephany 1985: 133). Such statements may be arranged on a scale reaching from a description of people's ordinary behavior with weak deontic modal strength (example 32a) to making such behavior the norm conferring deontic statements a stronger modal potential (example 32b) (Stephany 1985: 133).

(32) a. Spiros, 1;9 (Stephany 1985: 134)
(the investigator is describing a picture of a bear looking at a bird)
INV: eðó   i   arkúða   kitázi   to   pul-áki.
     here   the   bear   looks.at   the   bird-DIM
     'Here the bear is looking at the birdie.'
SPI: azoáki [: aiðon-áki]   ekí   (to)
                nightingale-DIM there   (it)
     léne.
     call.IPFV.NONPST.3PL
     'Nightingale there it is called.'
b. Mairi, 1;9 (Stephany 1985: 134)
(when Mother is moving her foot close to the toy monkey)
ze   [: ðen]   váz-un
         NEG.NONMDL   put.IPFV-NONPST.3PL
to   póði.
the   foot
'One doesn't put one's foot (there).'

The non-past (present) indicative may also convey dynamic modal meanings by expressing intentions of self or others (examples 33).

(33) a. Spiros, 1;9 (Stephany 1985: 136)
(announcing his intention to throw the investigator's book on the floor)
bedáo   [: (to)   petáo].
            (it)   throw.IPFV.NONPST.1SG
'I throw (it) down.'
b. Mairi, 1;9 (Stephany 1985: 136)
(when her aunt is making preparations for her departure)
jatí   févj-is?
why   leave.IPFV-NONPST.2SG
'Why are you leaving?'

Since all children of the Stephany Corpus express intentions, expectations, or concern much more frequently by the subjunctive or the future than by the non-past (present) indicative, the question is whether their meaning differs.

According to Stephany (1985: 138–139), the semantic difference between examples (33b) and (34) may be explained as follows. While (33b) is about the aunt's decision to leave, which is apparent from her present preparations, (34) is about a future undesirable situation.

(34) Mairi, 1;9 (Stephany 1985: 137–138)
(when her mother is leaving the room)
óši [: óçi] mamá   sa [: θa]   fíj-is!
no   Mommy FUT.PTL   leave.PFV-NONPST.2SG
for: δen   θa   fíj-is,   mamá!
     NEG.NONMDL   FUT.PTL   leave.PFV-NONPST.2SG   Mommy
'You shall not leave, Mommy!'

In her longitudinal as well as her cross-sectional data, Katis (1984; quoted by Stephany 1997: 303) found some expressions of the negated imperfective past at approximately 2;8 conveying the dynamic modal notions of unwillingness or inability (examples 35).

(35) a. Marilena 3;0 (Katis 1984, quoted by Stephany 1997: 304)
     δe(n)   stamátaj-e.
     NEG.NONMDL   stop.IPFV-PAST.3SG
     'He wouldn't stop.'
   b. Marilena 2;9 (Katis 1984, quoted by Stephany 1997: 304)
     δe(n)   tó-vrisk-e.
     NEG.NONMDL   it-find.IPFV-PAST.3SG
     'He couldn't find it.'

A comparison of modal and non-modal functions of the non-past (present) indicative occurring in CS and CDS shows a number of parallels. Thus, 20% of these forms used in CS before 2;0 express modal notions (n = 587) and 23.5% do so in CDS of the same period (n = 1,076). In both CS and CDS, deontic statements (or questions in CDS) occur much less frequently than deontic modal meanings expressed by the subjunctive or future and the imperative (Stephany 1985: 192). They amount to 10.5% in CS before 2;0 and to 13% in CDS (see number 21 above). In both CS and CDS, deontic statements are usually expressed by the 3rd person plural of the non-past indicative although a few instances of the 3rd person singular are found in one mother's speech (e.g., δen káni (NEG. NONMDL do.NONPST.3SG) 'this isn't possible/acceptable'). Deontic statements addressed to the children urge them to comply with social norms concerning their non-linguistic or linguistic behavior (example 36a vs. example 4, repeated as example 36b for the reader's convenience) (see also example 22 above). The children, in turn, criticize the caregivers' incorrect linguistic or non-linguistic behavior by such utterances (see examples 32 above).[18]

(36) Mairi, 1;9, CDS (Stephany 1985: 193)
    a. (when Mairi throws a toy on the floor)
        MOT: δen   to pet-áne
              NEG.NONMDL it throw.IPFV-NONPST.3PL
              ómos.
              however
              'One doesn't throw it down, however.'
    b. (when Mairi addresses the investigator by simply using the imperative éla 'come.IMP.2SG')
        MOT: δen   léne
              NEG.NONMDL say.IPFV.NONPST.3PL
              'éla'   ta   peδ-ákj-a.
              come.IMP.2SG the child-DIM-PL
              'Little children don't say *come!*.'

4.1.4 Comparison of child speech and child-directed speech

The prominent role of agent-oriented modal utterances in CS and CDS may be explained by the complementary social roles of mother and child (Stephany 1985: 155). The frequent use of directives in CDS is based on mothers' social role of guiding their children and their right to allow and duty to disallow certain of their actions while children's social dependence and physical immaturity necessitate the direct or indirect expression of requests.

A comparison of CS and CDS of the Stephany Corpus before 2;0 with respect to the use of inflectional expressions for conveying deontic and dynamic modal meanings shows that both registers are more or less uniform in a number of respects. The imperative expressing direct requests prevails in both of them while the subjunctive, which is primarily used for indirect ones is less prominent.

---

[18] Tomasello (2018: 157) points out that "only after three years of age will they [children] begin to identify with the particular social norms of their cultural group and so to construct a cultural morality." Examples (32) show that this development may even begin before children's turn to their third year.

Deontic statements only amount to little more than 10% of directives in both CDS and CS (Stephany 1985: 192).

As mentioned above (sections 2.1 and 4.1.2), person–number forms play an important role in verbalizing different meanings of the subjunctive and the future. While the 1st person singular expresses the speaker's intention in both CS and CDS, in CS it also serves for enquiring about the caretaker's opinion, asking for advice or permission, and making promises. In CDS, caretakers may also promise some action or seemingly seek the child's agreement for some threatening action by this person–number form. The most common functions of the 2nd person singular in both CS and CDS are indirect requests and questions about the addressee's intentions or desires. However, granting permission by this form is rare in CDS and does not occur in CS. Both the children and their caretakers may use the 3rd person singular referring to the speaker to announce their desires or intentions. The children also draw on this form to make indirect requests concerning third persons. In both registers, the 1st person plural of the subjunctive serves to express a hortative meaning suggesting an action that includes speaker and addressee.

In CDS as well as CS, the semantically unmarked perfective aspect of the subjunctive and future is much preferred in comparison with the imperfective one, which is semantically marked. This applies especially to telic verbs. However, the differences between CS, CDS, and ADS are gradual rather than categorical in this respect. While the perfective aspect of the subjunctive/future amounts to nearly 95% of tokens in CS before 2;0 (n = 614), it accounts for 93% in CDS (n = 1,130) but only 85% in ADS (n = 748) (Stephany 1985: 197). This shows that the tendency to prefer the unmarked perfective form of the subjunctive or future is more pronounced in CDS than in ADS and closer to its use in CS. This characteristic of CDS, which is especially strong with telic verbs, will favor children's development of the perfective aspect in the subjunctive and future, whereas there are fewer models for the semantically marked imperfective aspect to be found in the input (Stephany 1985: 197).[19]

---

[19] The tendency to prefer the unmarked perfective aspect is even stronger in the past tense in both CS and CDS, where it reaches 99% and 97% of tokens, respectively. In ADS it only amounts to 83% (Stephany 1985: 197).

4.2 Lexical expressions of dynamic and deontic modality

Although the two Greek modal verbs *boró* 'can, may' and *prépi* 'must' are used from early on by all Greek children studied in this chapter, their semantic functions are more limited than in the standard language. While both verbs admit of agent-oriented and propositional modal meanings in Modern Greek, only the former either exclusively or predominantly occur in Greek CS up to age 3;0.[20] Furthermore, the agent-oriented use of *boró* 'can, may' is limited to dynamic modality expressing ability or (mostly) inability in CS and does not yet include the deontic meaning of permission (Stephany 1985: 177, 2017: 80). Finally, dynamic *boró* 'can' expressing ability is more frequently used than deontic *prépi* 'must' conveying obligation although the difference between the number of tokens of each of the modals is much smaller in Anna's speech (Katis Corpus) (*boró* 53%, *prépi* 47%, *n* = 222) than in the speech of the children in the Stephany Corpus (*boró* 80%, *prépi* 20%, *n* = 36) (Stephany 2017: 78).[21] The dynamic modal meaning of desire is conveyed by the quasi-modal verb *θélo* 'want'. It appears in CS from the beginning of observation and its dynamic use expressing desire by far exceeds that of *boró* 'can' denoting ability (e.g., Anna, 1;8–3;0, *θélo* 88%, *boró* 12%, *n* = 1,057).

Anna mainly uses *θélo* 'want' in the first person singular of the non-past (*θél-o* (want.IPFV-NONPST.1SG) 'I want'; 76%, *n* = 928), which is documented from the beginning of observation at 1;8. The 3rd and 2nd person singular (*θél-i* (want.IPFV-NONPST.3SG) 's/he wants', *θél-is* (want.IPFV-NONPST.2SG) 'you want') emerge at 1;9 and amount to 19% of tokens while the three plural forms only account for 1% of tokens and first appear at 2;0 (*θél-ume* (want.IPFV-NONPST.1PL) 'we want') or in the second half of the girl's third year (2;6, *θél-ete* (want.IPFV-NONPST.2PL) 'you want'; 2;10, *θél-un* (want.IPFV-NONPST.3PL) 'they want').[22] As is common in early Greek CS as well as in other languages, the third person singular is sometimes used to refer to the speaker (e.g., 1;9, *e* [: *δen*] *sel-i* [: *θéli*] *i Anna* (NEG.NONMDL want.IPFV-NONPST.3SG the Ann) 'Anna doesn't want'). The frequencies of person–number forms of *θélo* show that Anna mainly uses this verb to express her own desires, but also refers to those of the addressee or third persons as well as the addressee and herself. The past of *θélo* 'want' amounting to nearly 3% of tokens emerges at 1;10 and more often refers to a third person

---

20 On propositional modality see section 5 below.
21 Spiros, who was observed only at 1;9, did not yet use either of the two modal verbs but only the quasi-modal *θélo* 'want' (Stephany 1985).
22 The remaining forms occur in the past (see below).

(*í-θel-e* (AUG-want.IPFV-PAST.3SG) 's/he wanted') than to the speaker (*í-θel-a* (AUG-want.IPFV-PAST.1SG) 'I wanted') (PAST.3SG, 20 tokens; PAST.1SG, 6 tokens).

In the beginning of Anna's development, *θélo* 'want' is often constructed with an object noun (example 37a) or an adverb, but very soon also constructions with a dependent verb are found (example 37b). Example (37c) illustrates the use of the past at the end of the girl's third year.

(37) a. Anna, 1;9
  θel-o   to γato mu!
  want.IPFV-NONPST.1SG the cat   of.me
  'I want my cat!'
 b. Anna, 1;10
  θel-o   na   to
  want.IPFV-NONPST.1SG MDL.PTL it
  katevas-o.
  put.down.PFV-NONPST.1SG
  'I want to put/take it down.'
 c. Anna, 2;11
  jati   *δen*   *i-θel-e*
  because NEG.NONMDL AUG-want.IPFV-PAST.3SG
  na   [//] *o*   *babas*   *mu*
  MDL.PTL   the daddy.NOM of.me
  na   *t(a)* *afis-i*   *eki.*
  MDL.PTL them leav.PFV-NONPST.3SG there
  'Because my Daddy didn't want to leave them there.'

As mentioned above, the five children of the Stephany Corpus also use the quasi-modal verb *θélo* 'want' to express their desires from the beginning of observation at 1;8, 1;9, 1;11, or 2;3. In their speech, this verb almost exclusively occurs in the non-past (present) indicative and mostly in the first person singular. While the first person singular is always used adequately before 2;0, the third person and even the second person[23] sometimes refer to the speaker. As with Anna, *θélo* 'want' is often constructed with a noun denoting the objective of the wish (examples 38a and 38b), but it is sometimes also used

---

[23] At 1;9, Spiros answers questions expressed by *θél-is* (want.IPFV-NONPST.2SG) 'do you want?' in an enthusiastic way in the affirmative by retaining the 2nd person form of the question (Stephany 1985).

without a complement (example 38c) and may even occur in complex sentences (example 38d) (Stephany 1985: 178).

(38) a. Mairi, 2;9
(being scared of a lotto card showing a lion)
δen	θél-o	(aftó)		
NEG.NONMDL	want.IPFV-NONPST.1SG	(that)		
me	to	liodári,	mamá.	
with	the	lion	Mommy	

'I don't want the one with the lion, Mommy.'

b. Janna, 2;11
(hearing a baby cry in another room of the kindergarten)
klé-i		jatí	
cry.IPFV-NONPST.3SG		because	
θél-i	ti	man-úla	tu.
want.IPFV-NONPST.3SG	the	mommy-DIM	his

'It is crying because it wants its mommy.'

c. Maria, 2;3
δen	θél-o	eγó.
NEG.NONMDL	want.IPFV-NONPST.1SG	I

'I don't want (to).'

d. Mairi, 2;9 (Stephany 1985: 179)
(when the investigator wants to take a fairytale book with her when leaving)
δe(n)	θél-o		na
NEG.NONMDL	want.IPFV-NONPST.1SG		MDL.PTL
mu	do	[: to]	pár-i.
of.me	it		take.PFV-NONPST.3SG

'I do not want her to take it away from me.'

The modal verb *boró* 'can', expressing the dynamic modal meaning of ability, is only found in one girl's data of the Stephany Corpus at 1;9 and in those of two other girls a year later (at 2;9 and 2;11). Besides a single token of the first person plural, only the first person singular of the non-past (present) indicative is found. This most commonly expresses the speaker's inability rather than her ability to perform some action (*δen boró* 'I can't'). In communicative exchanges, *boró* 'can' is most often used as an intransitive main verb, which is acceptable also in the adult language. In the CS data of the Stephany Corpus, *boró* 'can, may' is only exceptionally constructed with a complement verb (example 39a).

In Anna's speech (Katis Corpus), the agent-oriented use of this modal is also limited to the expression of ability or inability, but the verb occurs in four different person–number forms from 1;8 to 2;0 and in even eight inflections (mostly the non-past indicative) in the second half of the girl's third year. It is constructed with a complement verb in 60% of the tokens (*n* = 117) (example 39b) (Stephany 2017: 80).

(39) a. Mairi, 2;9 (Stephany 2017: 80)
      δen   bor-ó
      NEG.NONMDL can.IPFV-NONPST.1SG
      na   to   pjás-o.
      MDL.PTL it catch.PFV-NONPST.1SG
      'I can't catch it.'
   b. Anna, 1;10 (Stephany 2017: 80)
      (referring to a duckling)
      e [: δen]   bor-i   na
        NEG.NONMDL can.IPFV-NONPST.3SG MDL.PTL
      kolibis-i.
      swim.PFV-NONPST.3SG
      'It cannot swim.'

In contrast to the agent-oriented function of the modal verb *boró* 'can, may', which is limited to conveying a dynamic sense in early Greek CS, the agent-oriented use of the modal *prépi* 'must' expresses deontic necessity, i.e., obligation. There are only 7 tokens of this modal verb to be found in CS in the Stephany Corpus, first appearing in Mairi's speech at 1;9, in Janna's at 2;5 and in Maria's at 2;9 (Stephany 2017: 78, 79). Due to its defective character, *prépi* only occurs in the 3rd person singular. All instances are in the non-past indicative constructed with a complement clause, sometimes implied (examples 40).

(40) a. Janna, 2;11 (Stephany 1985: 176)
      (addressing the investigator, who is vainly trying to insert an element into an opening of a box in the wrong way)
      p(r)épi   na
      must.NONPST.3SG   MDL.PTL
      to jirís-is.
      it turn.PFV-NONPST.2SG
      'You must turn it.'

b. Maria, 2;3 (Stephany 1985: 177)
(looking for the appropriate opening in a box in order to insert an element)

MAR: pu   an   [: na]
      where   MDL.PTL
      (to)   vál-o   a(f)tó?
      (it)   put.PFV-NONPST.1SG   this
      'Where shall I put this?'

INV: eδó.
      'Here.'

MAR: eδó   na   (to)   vál-o.
      here   MDL.PTL   (it)   put.PFV-NONPST.1SG
      eδó   p(r)épi.
      here   must.NONPST.3SG
      'Let me put (it) here. Here (I) must (put it).'

With the exception of one past and one future form (*éprepe* 'it was necessary', *θa prépi* 'it will have to'), also Anna (Katis Corpus) uses *prépi* 'must' in the non-past (present) indicative constructing it with a main verb from 2;0 on. A particularly complex construction is presented in example (41). While 80% of the 117 tokens of *boró* 'can, may' are negated in Anna's speech, only 3 of the total of 105 tokens of *prépi* 'must' are in the negative form, with the scope of negation on the dependent verb (example 42) (Stephany 2017: 82).

(41) Anna, 2;8 (Stephany 2017: 82)
     omos   θa   prepi
     but   FUT.PTL   must.NONPST.3SG
     na   kaθis-un   se   mia   γonia
     MDL.PTL   sit.MP.PFV-NONPST.3PL   in   a   corner
     na   δune   ton   iljo
     MDL.PTL   see.PFV.NONPST.3PL   the.M.ACC   sun
     pu   pai   na
     which   go.PFV.NONPST.3SG   MDL.PTL
     kimiθ-i   piso   apo   to   vuno.
     sleep.MP.PFV-NONPST.3SG   behind   from   the   mountain
     'But they will have to sit in a corner in order to see the sun that goes to sleep behind the mountain.'

(42) Anna, 2;6 (Stephany 2017: 82)
    (δ)en   prepi   na
    not   must.NONPST.3SG   MDL.PTL
    vyune   ta   a(e)roplana.
    come.out.PFV.NONPST.3PL   the   planes
    'The planes must not come out.'

The analysis of the agent-oriented modal functions of the two Greek modal verbs *boró* 'can, may' and *prépi* 'must' occurring in CS has shown that their development starts from a principal form and central function. The basic forms are the 1st person singular non-past (present) indicative of *boró* and the 3rd person singular non-past (present) indicative of the defective verb *prépi*. The verbs convey the dynamic modal meaning of ability and the deontic meaning of obligation, respectively (Stephany 2017: 82–83). Since *boró* 'can, may' does not yet express the deontic meaning of permission and *prépi* 'must' is only used in an agent-oriented way (or nearly exclusively so), the functions of both modal verbs are still limited.

For lack of appropriate data in the Stephany Corpus, the analysis of the modal verbs in CDS in comparison to CS will be limited to the Katis Corpus. There are more than twice as many tokens of modal verbs found in CDS than in CS (553 vs. 222 tokens) (Stephany 2017: 78). Furthermore, the frequency of *boró* 'may, can' and *prépi* 'must' is reversed in the mother's speech as compared to the child's (CDS, *prépi* 54%, *boró* 46%, n = 553; CS, *prépi* 47%, *boró* 53%, n = 222) (Stephany 2017: 78, 83). Taking the respective social status of mother and child and their different abilities and responsibilities into consideration, this finding is noticeable but not surprising. While the child states ability (*boró*) more often than obligation (*prépi*), the mother favors the expression of obligation and prohibition (*prépi*) over ability and permission (*boró*).[24]

It is interesting to compare the use of *θélo* 'want' and *boró* 'can, be able to' conveying the dynamic modal notions of desire and ability, respectively, in CS and CDS. Both verbs emerge before 2;0 in the speech of three subjects of the Stephany Corpus, but desire is expressed much more frequently (and by a fourth child at 1;9 exclusively) than ability or inability through the third year by three subjects (with one exception at 2;11). In Anna's speech (Katis Corpus), there are 210 tokens of *θélo* 'want' before 2;0 as opposed to merely 13 tokens of *boró* 'can, be able to', i.e., 94% to 6%. In the second half of her third year, the difference decreases to 70% vs. 30% (n = 193). These relations mirror Anna's CDS,

---

24 For a comparison of the three registers of CS, CDS, and ADS see Stephany (2017).

where *θélo* 'want' amounts to 84% of the total of *θélo* and *boró* tokens (*n* = 1,612) in the entire period of observation. This shows that the expression of desire not only prevails over the expression of ability or inability in CS but also in CDS. However, use of the 1st and 2nd singular non-past (present) of *θélo* 'want' is complementary in Anna's speech and her input. While the child uses 89% of the total of these tokens (*n* = 795) in the 1st person singular non-past indicative, the 2nd person singular prevails in her mother's speech and amounts to 70% (*n* = 1,061). This discrepancy reflects the different social roles of mother and child. While the child primarily communicates her own desires, the mother inquires about her daughter's wishes.

5 Forms and functions of propositional modality in early Greek child speech and child-directed speech

As described in section 2, Modern Greek has inflectional as well as lexical means for expressing propositional modality. Compared to agent-oriented modality, expressions of propositional modality are very rarely found in early Greek CS. The future I and II, the conditional, epistemic adverbs, modal verbs, and a few mental verbs convey epistemic notions of certainty, probability, uncertainty, or possibility.

In spite of the fact that the epistemic use of Greek modal verbs emerges later than their deontic and dynamic use, "first hints at the development of epistemic modality appear early" (Stephany 1997: 207). These are found in predictions and pretend play. Stephany (1986: 381) considers predictions "as precursors to epistemically modalized statements representing a kind of 'null-degree' of epistemic modality" (see also Stephany 1985: 160, 1986: 397, 1993: 140, 1997: 207; Gee 1985).

The non-factive future tense is already quite well established in Anna's speech (Katis Corpus) in the beginning of observation at 1;8 and most of its 1,151 tokens up to 3;0 are formally distinguished from the subjunctive by the future particle *θa* (sometimes pronounced [ta] but rarely reduced to its vowel). Although the future most often conveys the dynamic modal notion of the speaker's intention or that of the addressee or third persons, it is also used epistemically for predicting the probability of future events (examples 43).[25]

---

[25] See also examples (23) in section 4.1.2 above.

(43) a. Anna, 1;9
   θa   pes-o.
   FUT.PTL fall.PFV-NONPST.1SG
   'I will fall.'
  b. Anna, 1;10
   a   [: θa]   vetsi [: vréks-i]
         FUT.PTL   rain.PFV-NONPST.3SG
   etso [: ékso].
         outside
   'It is going to rain outside.'

In cases where the subjunctive mood and future tense are formally distinguished by particle use, the functions of the future occurring in CS of the Stephany Corpus correspond to those found in Anna's data. A typical example is the expression of warnings against unpleasant future events that make an agent-oriented dynamic modal meaning unlikely (examples 44) (Stephany 1985: 160).

(44) a. Janna, 1;11 (Stephany 1985: 160)
   (θ)a   bési [: pés-i].
   FUT.PTL fall.PFV-NONPST.3SG
   'It will fall down.'
  b. Mairi, 2;3 (Stephany 1985: 160–161)
   (warning the investigator)
   MAI: Ulla, θa   spás-i.
        Ulla FUT.PTL break.PFV-NONPST.3SG
        'Ulla, it will break.'
   MOT: óçi. δen   spáz-i.
        no.   NEG.NONMDL   break.IPFV-NONPST.3SG
        mi   fováse.
        NEG.MDL   fear.MP.IPFV.NONPST.2SG
        'No. It won't break. Don't be afraid.'
   MAI: na   (s)pás-i,   íp-a.
        MDL.PTL   break.PFV-NONPST.3SG   say.PFV-PAST.1SG
        'It shall break, I said.'
     for: θa   spási,   ípa.
          FUT.PTL break.3SG I.said
          'It will break, I said.'

The future II, having an inferential and thus evidential meaning (see Mackridge 1985: 275), does not develop in Greek CS until 3;0. It only rarely occurs in the CDS of two children of the Stephany Corpus before 2;0 as well as in Anna's CDS throughout the observation period (examples 45) (Stephany 1985: 185).

(45) a. CDS (Stephany 1985: 192)
  θa   éçi   fíji.
  FUT.PTL has.3SG left.PP
  'S/he will have left.'

 b. Anna, 2;1, CDS
  kápu   θa   píje,
  somewhere FUT.PTL go.PFV.PAST.3SG
  mátja   mu.
  eyes   of.me
  'S/he will have gone somewhere, my darling.'

Although conditional sentences describing a contingent relationship between events are found in CS in the Stephany Corpus before 2;0 (example 46), the counterfactual conditional only emerged after 3;0 in Marilena's speech and is found with the 4-year-olds in Katis' cross-sectional data (Katis 1984) (example 47, quoted by Stephany 1997: 305).

(46) Natali, 1;8 (Stephany 1985: 163)
 (wanting to open the investigator's microphone case which she calls 'bed')
 əvátši nítšo,   malóni   babá.
 for: (áma)   aníks-o   to   kreváti,
         (if)   open.PFV-NONPST.1SG   the   bed
         (θa)   malón-i   (o)   babás.
         FUT.PTL   scold.IPFV-NONPST.3SG   (the) Daddy
 'If I open the bed, Daddy will shout.'

(47) Marilena, 3;2 (Katis 1984, quoted by Stephany 1997: 305)
 áma   kriv-ómuna   se mja spiljá,
 if   hide-MP.IPFV.PAST.1SG in a   cave
 θa   me é-vrisk-es?
 FUT.PTL me AUG-find.IPFV-PAST.2SG
 'If I hid in a cave, would you find me?'

In Katis' (1984) longitudinal data of the girl Marilena, "first instances of pretend play expressed by the imperfective past occur in the second half of the third year, and examples steadily increase during the fourth year" (Stephany 1997: 207). In the first examples, the verb is in the imperfective past, accompanied by the modal particle *na*. In the child's fourth year, "when counterfactual conditional sentences in which [the future particle] *θa* is constructed with imperfective past forms appear in Marilena's input, the particle *θa* gradually replaces *na* in the child's pretend play" (Stephany 1997: 304) (examples 48).

(48) a. Marilena, 3;0 (Katis 1984; quoted by Stephany 1997: 304)
    θes   esí   tóra   na
    want.IPFV.NONPST.2SG you.NOM.SG now MDL.PTL
    ísuna   pulakós   ke   na
    be.IPFV.PAST.2SG pulakós   and   MDL.PTL
    psóniz-es?
    buy.IPFV-PAST.2SG
    'Would you like to be a 'pulakós' and be shopping?'
  b. Marilena, 3;0 (Katis 1984; quoted by Stephany 1997: 305)
    kíta.   θa   kim-ótane
    look.IMP.2SG   FUT.PTL   sleep-MP.IPFV.PAST.3SG
    álos   sta   psémata.
    another   in.the   lies
    'Look. Someone else would be sleeping in pretend.'

Although Greek is rich in epistemic adverbs expressing different degrees of necessity and possibility, only two of them occur in Anna's data and her CDS. Epistemic adverbs and epistemic use of modal verbs have not yet emerged in the four children of the Stephany Corpus up to 2;9 or 2;11 and are almost absent from their CDS.

The epistemic adverbs found in Anna's data are *vévea* 'certainly' (CS, from 1;9 on, 14 tokens; CDS, from 1;8 on, 660 tokens) and *málon* 'probably' (CS, from 1;11 on, 2 tokens; CDS, from 1;9 on, 50 tokens), expressing certainty of a situation in the speaker's view on the one hand and the weaker epistemic degree of probability on the other. The different degrees of epistemic modal strength ranging from certainty through probability to mere possibility are expressed by the adverbs *vévea* 'certainly' and *málon* 'probably' and the modal verb form *borí* 'it may be/is possible'.

Epistemic or sentence adverbs occupy an initial or final position in the sentence and do not have to be integrated into its structure. In CDS, *vévea* 'certainly' usually confirms the child's statements (example 49a) while the girl often uses the adverb to give a strong positive response to her mother's question (example 49b).

(49) a. Anna, 1;9
    MOT: *íne aryá tóra.*
           it.is late now
           ás(e)   tis   tis   fotoɣrafíes,
           leave.IMP.2SG them the photographs
           ann-ula.
           Ann-DIM
           'It is late now. Leave the photographs alone, Ann darling.'
    ANN: *a(r)ɣa, ine a(r)ɣa Anna arɣa xxx.*
           late   it.is late Ann late
           'Late, it is late, Ann, late.'
    MOT: *ine   aryá,   vévea   íne   aryá,*
           it.is   late   certainly it.is   late
           kalá   pu   to   katálaves
           good that it   understood.2SG
           óti   in(e)   aryá.
           that it.is   late.'
           'It is late, certainly it is late, good that you understood that it is late.'
b. Anna, 2;5
    MOT: *ponái?*
           it.hurts
           'Does it hurt?'
    ANN: *ponai. vevea ponai.*
           it.hurts certainly it.hurts
           'It hurts. It certainly hurts.'
    MOT: *vévea ponái?*
           'It certainly hurts?'

The adverb *málon* qualifies a past or future situation as probable (example 50a). Example (50b) is particularly interesting because two degrees of modal strength, probability (expressed by a modal adverb) and mere possibility (expressed by a modal verb), occur in one and the same communicative exchange between Anna and her mother.

(50) a. Anna, 1;11
    MOT: *ti éjine i Andzela?*
          what became the.F.NOM Angela
          'What happened to Angela?'
    ANN: *malon to (x)tip-is-e*
          probably it.N hit-PFV-PAST.3SG
          <to ko> [//] to [/] to +...
          'Probably the, the... hit it.'
    MOT: *málon to xtíp-is-e*
          probably it hit-PFV-PAST.3SG
          to aftokínito málon?
          the.N car probably
          'Probably the car hit it probably?'
  b. Anna, 2;10 (Stephany 2017: 81)
    MOT: *éçi aplós sínefa.*
          it.has simply clouds.
          'There are simply clouds.'
    ANN: *malon θa vreks-i.*
          probably FUT.PTL rain.PFV-NONPST.3SG
          'It is probably going to rain.'
    MOT: *málon θa vréks-i,*
          probably FUT.PTL rain.PFV-NONPST.3SG
          alá bor-í ke
          but may.IPFV-NONPST.3SG also
          na mi(n) vréks-i.
          MDL.PTL NEG.MDL rain.PFV-NONPST.3SG
          'It is probably going to rain, but it may also not rain.'
    ANN: *bor-i.*
          may.IPFV-NONPST.3SG
          'Maybe.'

The most important lexical devices for expressing propositional modality besides epistemic adverbs are the modal verbs *boró* 'can, may' and *prépi* 'must'. In Anna's speech, the epistemic use of *boró* conveying mere possibility not only emerges 9 months later than its dynamic use (1;8 vs. 2;6) but also 9 to 11 months after the emergence of the epistemic adverbs *vévea* 'certainly' and *málon* 'probably' (1;9, *vévea*; 1;11, *málon*) (Stephany 2017: 80–81). The first two examples of the epistemic use of *borí* 'it may' in Anna's speech occur at 2;6 and 2;10 in response to her mother's utterances (example 50b above) and the first spontaneous instance is found at 2;11 (example 51).

(51) Anna, 2;11 (Stephany 2017: 81)
 θa bor-i na
 FUT.PTL may.IPFV-NONPST.3SG MDL.PTL
 spas-i to avγo.
 break.PFV-NONPST.3SG the egg
 'The egg may break.'

A more sophisticated example of the epistemic use of *borí* 'it may be' with the main verb in the imperfective past accompanied by the modal particle *na* is example (52) from Marilena's speech toward the end of her fourth year when an epistemic use of modal verbs is first attested in this girl's speech (Katis 1984, quoted by Stephany 1997: 207).

(52) Marilena, 3;9 (Katis 1984, quoted by Stephany 1997: 306)
 bor-í ke na fovótan-e.
 may.IPFV-NONPST.3SG also MDL.PTL fear.MP.IPFV-PAST.3SG
 'It is possible that she was scared.'

Among Anna's 105 tokens of *prépi* 'must' occurring during her third year, there is only a single clear example of epistemic use (example 53) besides a more doubtful one.

(53) Anna, 2;1 (Stephany 2017: 82)
 (commenting on some noise in the house)
 ANN: prepi na nine [: íne]
 must.NONPST.3SG MDL.PTL is
 o mastoras.
 the craftsman
 'It must be the craftsman.'
 MOT: ne. o mástoras prépi
 yes the craftsman must.NONPST.3SG
 na íne.
 MDL.PTL is
 'Yes. It must be the craftsman.'

It is difficult to estimate to what extent the development of the epistemic use of the two modal verbs in Anna's language is influenced by her input, where *borí* 'it may be' expressing epistemic possibility is much more often encountered than *prépi* 'it must be' expressing epistemic necessity (*borí*, 15% of tokens of *boró* (n = 269); *prépi*, 3% (n = 302)) (Stephany 2017: 96).

Besides the two modal verbs, several mental verbs convey different degrees of certainty on the part of the speaker in the CS of the Katis Corpus and the Stephany Corpus. These are *kséro* 'to know', *nomízo* 'to think', and evidential *fénete* 'it seems, appears'. *Kséro* 'to know' is used to express dynamic or epistemic modality, i.e., ability vs. inability for performing some action on the one hand and knowledge vs. ignorance of some state of affairs on the other. The 3rd person singular form *fénete* has the non-modal meaning 'it shows, can be seen' besides the evidential meaning 'it seems, appears'.

Nearly all of Anna's 15 tokens of the 1st person singular non-past (present) indicative of *kséro* 'I know' are negated. Since none of them is constructed with a dependent verb ('to know how to V'), they all seem to have an epistemic meaning (example 54). If a dependent clause is implied, example (54) may, however, also be interpreted dynamically expressing inability. Example (55) with the 3rd person form *kséri* 's/he knows' must rather be interpreted as a non-modal statement of a third person's knowledge.

(54) Anna, 1;11
    e [: δen]   dzero [: kser-o].
    NEG.NONMDL   know-NONPST.1SG
    ime   mik(r)-ula.
    I.am   small-DIM.F.SG
    'I don't know. I am small.'

(55) Anna, 1;11
    MOT: pjos   se   xteníz-i?
           who   you.ACC   comb.IPFV-NONPST.3SG
           'Who does your hair?'
    ANN: e   tseri   [: kser-i]
           FILL   know.IPFV-NONPST.3SG
           i   mama   mu.
           the.F   mommy of.me
           'My mommy knows.'

The verb *kséro* 'to know' emerges in Mairi's data (Stephany Corpus) at 1;9 and is first found in the speech of two other children at 2;3 and 2;5. It has begun to be used more frequently (21 to 43 tokens) by all three children at 2;9 or 2;11 (Stephany 1985). The first person singular non-past indicative of this verb most frequently expresses the child's ignorance (*δen kséro* 'I don't know') but the verb also occurs in questions about the knowledge of the addressee or self (e.g., *kséris* 'do you know?', *pu na kséro* 'how should I know?').

While there is only a single token each of the mental verb *nomízo* 'to think' expressing belief and thus uncertainty in the data of two children of the Stephany Corpus in their third year (example 56a) (Stephany 1997: 305–306), Anna (Katis Corpus) uses this verb in 12 instances from 2;0 to 3;0 (example 56b).

(56) a. Maria, 2;9 (Stephany 1997: 305–306)
 í(r)θ-e   i   mamá   mu.
 come.MP.PFV-PAST.3SG the mommy of.me
 íne i   jajá   mu.
 is   the granny of.me
 nómizə [: nómiz-a]   óti   ítan
         think.IPFV-PAST.1SG that it.was
 i   mamá   mu.
 the   mommy   of.me
 'My mommy came. It's my granny. I thought that it was my mommy.'
 b. Anna, 2;3
 nomiz-o   k(e) i   Vale(n)tini
 think.IPFV-NONPST.1SG also the Valentini
 ine   arosti.
 is   sick
 'I think that also Valentini is sick.'

The few tokens of *fénete* occurring in the data of two children of the Stephany Corpus as well as all but one of the 56 tokens of this verb emerging in Anna's speech during the last months of her second year have the non-modal meaning of 'it shows, can be seen'. The only instance of an inferential evidential interpretation is example (57) from Anna's data.

(57) Anna, 3;0
 afti   mu   fenete liyo   asçimi.
 this.one to.me seems   little ugly
 'It seems to me that this one is a little ugly.'

Turning to Anna's CDS, it must first be stated that agent-oriented modal meanings by far outnumber epistemic ones overall.[26] Still, epistemic expressions already occur before the child's second birthday (Stephany 2017: 84, 87). It is interesting to note that the epistemic use of the 3rd person singular form *borí* 'it may be', which is the only non-past form of *boró* 'can, may' conveying an epistemic meaning, rises from 19% of tokens of this verb before the girl's age 2;0 to 67% by age 3;0, so that the propositional use of this form predominates in the second half of the child's third year (*n* = 269) (example 58) (Stephany 2017: 97).

(58) Anna, 2;1, CDS (Stephany 2017: 84)
próseç-e   min   pés-un
be.careful.IPFV-IMP.2SG NEG.MDL fall.PFV-NONPST.3PL
aftá   óla. se   parakaló,
these all   you.ACC I.beg
annúla   mu,   jatí   bor-í
Ann.DIM of.me because may.IPFV-NONPST.3SG
na   jíni   meɣáli   zimjá   eδó.
MDL.PTL   become.NONPST.3SG big   damage   here
'Be careful not to let all these fall down. Please, Anna, because this may cause great damage here.'

The modal verb *prépi* 'must' is most often used in Anna's CDS for expressing the deontic meaning of obligation while epistemic meanings of certainty or high probability are very rare and amount to only 3% of tokens (*n* = 302) (examples 59) (Stephany 2017: 78, 87).

(59) a. Anna, 2;4, CDS (Stephany 2017: 87)
  (about a toy car)
  δen   éçi   timóni,   δe   fénete.
  NEG.NONMDL has   steering.wheel not   shows
  δen   prép-i   na   éçi.
  not   must-NONPST.3SG   MDL.PTL   has
  'It doesn't have a steering wheel, it doesn't show. It probably doesn't have one.'

---

26 In the CDS of the Stephany Corpus, modal expressions are totally limited to agent-oriented meanings or almost so (Stephany 1985: 192, 2017: 83).

b. Anna, 2;11, CDS (Stephany 2017: 87)
   prép-i   na   (e)xun
   must-NONPST.3SG   MDL.PTL   have.3PL
   klísi   i   tavérnes.
   closed.PP   the   restaurants
   'The restaurants must have closed.'

A comparison of the use of the Greek modal verbs in CS and CDS to ADS shows that adults use modal verbs more frequently in discourse among themselves than when addressing small children (Stephany 2017: 78, 88). However, the register of ADS corresponds to CS and CDS insofar as the agent-oriented use of both verbs by far exceeds their propositional use (ADS, 75% vs. 25% of tokens; n = 858) (Stephany 2017: 88). As has been found in CDS, the form *borí* 'can, may' is predominantly used epistemically expressing possibility of a state of affairs also in ADS (75% of tokens; n = 189) while *prépi* conveys epistemic certainty in less than 23% of tokens (n = 271) (Stephany 2017: 96).

The fact that the use of modal verbs in CDS is intermediate between ADS and CS may be taken as evidence that it assists children in achieving the goal of becoming competent native speakers of Greek (Stephany 2017: 98). The comparison of CS, CDS, and ADS also shows that children are aware of the basic features and most characteristic functions of Greek modal verbs from early on "so that the differences among the three registers are to a large extent quantitative rather than qualitative" (Stephany 2017: 98).

6 Discussion and conclusions

Since children acquire language for purposes of communication and by communicating with their conspecifics, the two fundamental functions of language of requesting actions from others and providing them with information are the first to develop ontogenetically. Accordingly, the imperative and the subjunctive are distinguished from the non-past (present) indicative (and the past) from an early age in Greek language acquisition. In CS of the Stephany Corpus before 2;0, utterances in which agent-oriented modality is expressed by the future/subjunctive or the imperative amount to 62% and non-modal non-past or past utterances to 38% (n = 1,580) (see Stephany 1985: 192). In CDS of the same period, modal utterances exceed non-modal ones nearly as much as they do in CS (modal 58%, non-modal 42%; n = 2,933; see Stephany 1985: 192). These relative frequencies show that the basic communicative functions of requesting and informing are both firmly established before 2;0 in CS mirroring the picture presented by CDS.

The modal domain developing earliest in Greek language acquisition is agent-oriented modality, including the deontic and dynamic sub-domains. Due to their physical and social dependence, children frequently ask for help or announce their desires and intentions in order to get their wishes fulfilled. While the deontic modal expressions of requests function to get "others to do what one wants them to" (Tomasello 2010: 84), dynamic expressions of desire may do so more indirectly. It is therefore not surprising that both deontic and dynamic expressions emerge early.

Expressions of deontic and dynamic modal notions are documented in the speech of each of the five children of the Stephany Corpus and the single child of the Katis Corpus before the end of the second year. Although both semantic types emerge simultaneously in Greek language acquisition, the type of formal devices for their expression differs. Deontic modal notions are typically expressed inflectionally by the imperative or the subjunctive/future, whereas dynamic notions are mainly rendered by the quasi-modal verb *θélo* 'want' and the modal verb *boró* 'can, be able to'. While *boró* 'can, may' is only used dynamically for expressing ability (or inability) but not yet deontically for granting permission, certain uses of *θélo* 'want' may be interpreted as indirectly deontic, implying a request. Although the main functions of the subjunctive/future are deontic, some uses of the first person singular convey the dynamic notion of intention from early on.

Summarizing the findings regarding the development of deontic and dynamic modality in early Greek CS, the inflectional expressions of deontic modal notions (imperative and subjunctive/future) emerge simultaneously with lexical expressions of dynamic notions (*boró* 'can' and *θélo* 'want') before the end of the second year. Inflectional deontic expressions precede the emergence of lexical ones (*prépi* 'must') by at least three months. While the imperative and the subjunctive/future are documented before 2;0 in Anna's and the other children's data, *prépi* 'must' is only found in Anna's speech from 2;0 on.[27] In Anna's CDS, dynamic and deontic modal notions lexically expressed by the verbs *θélo* 'want', *boró* 'can, may', and *prépi* 'must' occur from the beginning of observation around 1;9. Since *prépi* 'must' is used more frequently than *boró* 'can, may' (*prépi* 298 tokens, *boró* 255 tokens), frequency of occurrence in CDS cannot underlie the later emergence of the modal verb *prépi* as compared to

---

[27] In the Stephany Corpus, only a single token of deontic *prépi* 'must' is found in Mairi's speech at 1;9 and a few tokens are first documented in Maria's and Janna's speech a year later.

boró in Anna's speech. Rather, this must be due to the competing inflectional devices for expressing deontic notions, the imperative and the subjunctive/future, which are firmly established from early on.

In the CS of the Stephany Corpus as well as the Katis Corpus, expressions of the dynamic modal notion of desire occur much more frequently than those of ability. A predominance of tokens of *θélo* 'want' over those of *boró* 'can, be able to' is also attested by CDS in the Katis Corpus. This shows that desire is a communicatively more important category than ability for both partners in mother–child interactions. Complementary communicative needs of mother and child are demonstrated by the preference of the 1st person singular non-past of *θélo* 'want' by the child Anna in contrast to the mother's 2nd person singular non-past. As mentioned above, this reflects the different social roles of mother and child.

One of the most controversial questions regarding the development of modality in first language acquisition is the order of development of agent-oriented and propositional modality. Although deontic and dynamic modal expressions have emerged at the beginning of observation before 2;0, a rash conclusion that the development of agent-oriented modality precedes propositional modality in Greek language acquisition would be misguided. Rather, there is evidence that agent-oriented and propositional modality do not simply develop successively, but in a closely intertwined way. Precursors of epistemic meanings are found in the use of the future for predicting events, which emerges before the end of the second year, as well as pretend play appearing in the second half of the third year in Greek language acquisition. Some lexical devices for the expression of propositional modality, namely epistemic adverbs, emerge as early as the main devices of deontic and dynamic notions or nearly so. In Anna's speech (Katis Corpus), they do so before 2;0. As mentioned above (section 5), the adverb *vévea* 'certainly', expressing certainty, is first found at 1;9 preceding *málon* 'probably', conveying probability and occurring two months later at 1;11. The fact that epistemic sentence adverbs do not need to be integrated into sentence structure and have an inherent context-independent meaning can explain their precocious emergence as compared to the epistemic use of modal verbs. The usage of these verbs to convey either agent-oriented or epistemic meanings depends on a number of features of sentence structure and is therefore a later development. After Anna has been accustomed to expressing agent-oriented meanings by the Greek modal verbs *boró* 'can, may' and *prépi* 'must' from 1;8 and 2;0 on, the form *borí* 'it may be' is first used with an epistemic meaning only 10 months later at 2;6, and there is a single clear example of the epistemic use of *prépi* 'it must be the case that' to be found at 2;1 in her data, one month after its first deontic use.

Mental verbs expressing epistemic meanings are only very rarely documented in Anna's speech (Katis Corpus) and in the speech of three subjects of the Stephany Corpus. The earliest occurrences are mainly found in the third year of the children's development. The future II and counterfactual conditionals are also later developments only found in Marilena's fourth year (Katis 1984).

All in all, these findings suggest that the question of a gap between the development of agent-oriented and propositional modality in Greek language acquisition cannot simply be answered in the affirmative. Rather, the development of the two sub-domains of modality is intricate and statements about chronological order presuppose that different types of devices are taken into consideration. Thus, the propositional use of the Greek modal verbs clearly succeeds their agent-oriented use.

There are both similarities and differences of the development of modality in early Greek language acquisition and other languages. The early development of a contrast between modal and non-modal expressions has also been observed in a number of typologically different languages of various genetic affiliations studied in this volume, namely Russian (Voeikova and Bayda), German (Korecky-Kröll), French (Kilani-Schoch), Finnish (Laalo), Turkish (Terziyan and Aksu-Koç), Hebrew (Uziel-Karl), and Korean (Choi). These results show that this contrast is pragmatically fundamental independently of language families and language structure.

According to Hickmann and Bassano (2016: 431), an important result of naturalistic studies of the acquisition of modality noted in the literature[28] is a "clear-cut" "developmental asynchrony" of the production of agent-oriented and propositional modality, "particularly in languages that rely mostly on modal auxiliaries and mental verbs to express modality." While it is certainly true that children express agent-oriented modality much more frequently than epistemic modality, at least in languages in which epistemic modality is not grammaticized, a clear developmental precedence of agent-oriented modality can only be found in certain domains of modal expressions. There is thus no doubt that in languages in which modal verbs are available for the expression of both agent-oriented and epistemic meanings, the former develop earlier than the latter. However, when epistemic adverbs are compared to epistemically used modal verbs, the former may emerge earlier, namely in the second year of life. This is not only the case in Greek, but also in, e.g., Hebrew and Turkish. In Russian and Romanian, epistemic sentence adverbs are however only found in the third year.

---

28 See Stephany (1986, 1993) and Choi (2006) as well as studies on English, French, Greek, Polish, and Spanish quoted in Hickmann and Bassano (2016).

The most remarkable state of affairs is that in languages in which epistemic notions are grammaticized, such as Turkish and Korean, epistemic inflections already emerge in the second half of the second year. While there may be individual variation among children with respect to the development of lexical, non-grammaticized devices for the expression of epistemic modality, in languages in which such expressions are grammaticized, they emerge as early as expressions of agent-oriented modality. However, in languages in which the expression of epistemic modality is not grammaticized, precursors to epistemic statements referring to nearby future events also emerge early.

Since children construct their native language while using it and by using it, their achievements largely depend on input, first from their caretakers, and later on from peers and school education. The complex domain of modality will continue to develop during all these years in which young learners will gradually approach the target of becoming competent native speakers.

Acknowledgements: I would like to thank Demetra Katis for giving me access to the rich corpus of child speech she collected from her elder daughter Anna. Thanks also go to Ayhan Aksu-Koç for helpful comments on earlier versions of this chapter.

References

Aikhenvald, Alexandra Y. 2010. *Imperatives and commands*. Oxford: Oxford University Press.
Aikhenvald, Alexandra Y. 2016. Sentence types. In Jan Nuyts & Johan van der Auwera (eds.), *The Oxford handbook of modality and mood*, 141–165. Oxford: Oxford University Press.
Babiniotis, Georgios & Panajotis Kontos. 1967. *Synchroniki grammatiki tis koinis neas ellinikis: Theoria, askiseis* [Synchronic grammar of Common Modern Greek: Theory, exercises]. Athens.
Boye, Kasper. 2016. The expression of epistemic modality. In Jan Nuyts & Johan van der Auwera (eds.), *The Oxford handbook of modality and mood*, 117–140. Oxford: Oxford University Press.
Bybee, Joan. 2010. *Language, usage and cognition*. Cambridge: Cambridge University Press.
Bybee, Joan & Suzanne Fleischman. 1995. Modality in grammar and discourse. In Joan Bybee & Suzanne Fleischmann (eds.). 1995. *Modality in grammar and discourse*, 1–14. Amsterdam: John Benjamins.
Choi, Soonja. 2006. Acquisition of modality. In William Frawley (ed.), *The expression of modality*, 141–171. Berlin: Walter de Gruyter.
Christofidou, Anastasia & Ursula Stephany. 2003. Early phases in the development of Greek verb inflection. In Dagmar Bittner, Wolfgang U. Dressler & Marianne Kilani-Schoch (eds.), *Development of verb inflection in first language acquisition: A cross-linguistic perspective* (Studies on Language Acquisition 21), 89–129. Berlin & New York: Mouton de Gruyter.

Clairis, Christos & George Babiniotis (in cooperation with Amalia Moser, Ekaterini Bakakou-Orfanou & Stavros Skopeteas). 2005. *Grammatiki tis neas ellinikis: Domoleitourgiki-epikoinoniaki* [A Grammar of Modern Greek: Structural–functional and communicative]. Athens: Ellinika Grammata.

Diessel, Holger. 2013. Construction grammar and first language acquisition. In Thomas Hoffmann & Graeme Trousdale (eds.), *The Oxford handbook of construction grammar*, 347–364. Oxford: Oxford University Press.

Dixon, Robert M. W. 2016. *Are some languages better than others?* Oxford: Oxford University Press.

Gee, Gerhardt J. 1985. An interpretive approach to the study of modality: What child language can tell the linguist. *Studies in Language* 9(2). 197–229.

Hickmann, Maya & Dominique Bassano. 2016. Modality and mood in first language acquisition. In Jan Nuyts & Johan van der Auwera (eds.), *The Oxford handbook of modality and mood*, 430–447. Oxford: Oxford University Press.

Katis, Demetra. 1984. *The acquisition of the Modern Greek verb: With special reference to the imperfective past and perfect classes*. Reading: University of Reading dissertation.

Lieven, Elena V. M. 2014. First language development: A usage-based perspective on past and current research. *Journal of Child Language* 41(Suppl. 1). 48–63.

Lyons, John. 1977. *Semantics*. 2 vols. Cambridge: Cambridge University Press.

Mackridge, Peter. 1985. *The Modern Greek language: A descriptive analysis of Standard Modern Greek*. Oxford: Clarendon Press.

MacWhinney, Brian. 2000. *The CHILDES project: Tools for analyzing talk*. 3rd edn. Mahwah, NJ: Lawrence Erlbaum.

Nikolaeva, Irina. 2016. Analyses of the semantics of mood. In Jan Nuyts & Johan van der Auwera (eds.), *The Oxford handbook of modality and mood*, 68–85. Oxford: Oxford University Press.

Nuyts, Jan. 2006. Modality: Overview and linguistic issues. In William Frawley (ed.), *The expression of modality*, 1–26. Berlin & New York: Mouton de Gruyter.

Nuyts, Jan & Johan van der Auwera (eds.). 2016. *The Oxford handbook of modality and mood*. Oxford: Oxford University Press.

Palmer, Frank R. 2001 [1986]. *Mood and modality*. 2nd edn. Cambridge: Cambridge University Press.

Pavlidou, Theodossia-Soula (ed.). 2016. *Katagrafontas tin elliniki glossa* [Making a record of the Greek language]. Thessaloniki: Aristotle University of Thessaloniki. http://ins.web.auth.gr/index.php?option=com_content&view=article&id=1074:greek-language-katagrafontas&catid=93&lang=en&Itemid=270

Pavlidou, Theodossia-Soula, Charikleia Kapellidi & Eleni Karafoti. 2014. The corpus of spoken Greek (CSG). In Şükriye Ruhi, Michael Haugh, Thomas Schmidt & Kai Wörner (eds.), *Best practices for spoken corpora in linguistic research*, 56–74. Newcastle upon Tyne: Cambridge Scholars Publishing.

Stephany, Ursula. 1985. *Aspekt, Tempus und Modalität: Zur Entwicklung der Verbalgrammatik in der neugriechischen Kindersprache* (Language Universals Series 4). Tübingen: Gunter Narr Verlag.

Stephany, Ursula. 1986. Modality. In Paul Fletcher & Michael Garman (eds.), *Language acquisition: Studies in first language development*, 375–400. 2nd edn. Cambridge: Cambridge University Press.

Stephany, Ursula. 1993. Modality in first language acquisition: The state of the art. In Norbert Dittmar & Astrid Reich (eds.), *Modality in language acquisition/Modalité et acquisition des langues* (Soziolinguistik und Sprachkontakt/Sociolinguistics and Language Contact 6), 133–144. Berlin & New York: Walter de Gruyter.

Stephany, Ursula. 1995. Function and form of modality in first and second language acquisition. In Anna Giacalone Ramat & Grazia Crocco Galèas (eds.), *From pragmatics to syntax: Modality in second language acquisition* (Tübinger Beiträge zur Linguistik 405), 105–120. Tübingen: Gunter Narr Verlag.

Stephany, Ursula. 1997. The acquisition of Greek. In Dan I. Slobin (ed.), *The crosslinguistic study of language acquisition*, vol. 4, 183–333. Mahwah, NJ & London: Lawrence Erlbaum.

Stephany, Ursula. 2012. Selecting a theoretical framework fitting acquisition data is no easy matter. In Zoe Gavriilidou, Angeliki Efthymiou, Evangelia Thomadaki & Penelope Kambakis-Vougiouklis (eds.), *Selected papers of the 10th international conference of Greek linguistics*, 89–100. Komotini: Democritus University of Thrace.

Stephany, Ursula. 2017. Forms and functions of Greek modal verbs in child speech, child-directed speech and adult-directed speech. In Anastasia Christofidou (ed.), *Opseis tis somatokeimenikis glossologias: Arches, efarmoges, prokliseis* [Aspects of corpus linguistics: Principles, implementations, challenges]. Bulletin of Scientific Terminology and Neologisms 14. 69–111. Athens: Academy of Athens.

Stephany, Ursula & Evangelia Thomadaki. 2017. Compounding in early Greek language acquisition. In Wolfgang U. Dressler, Nihan Ketrez & Marianne Kilani-Schoch (eds.), *Nominal compound acquisition* (Language Acquisition and Language Disorders 61), 119–143. Amsterdam & Philadelphia: John Benjamins.

Stephany, Ursula & Maria D. Voeikova. 2015. Requests, their meanings and aspectual forms in early Greek and Russian child language. *Journal of Greek Linguistics* 15(1). 66–90.

Thomadaki, Evangelia & Ursula Stephany. 2007. Diminutives in Greek child language. In Ineta Savickienė & Wolfgang U. Dressler (eds.), *The acquisition of diminutives* (Language Acquisition and Language Disorders 43), 89–123. Amsterdam & Philadelphia: John Benjamins.

Tomasello, Michael. 2003. *Constructing a language: A usage-based theory of language acquisition*. Cambridge, MA & London: Harvard University Press.

Tomasello, Michael. 2010 [2008]. *Origins of human communication*. Paperback edn. Cambridge, MA & London: The MIT Press.

Tomasello, Michael (ed.). 2014. *The new psychology of language: Cognitive and functional approaches to language structure*. Vol. 1. New York & London: Psychology Press, Taylor & Francis Group.

Tomasello, Michael. 2018 [2016]. *A natural history of human morality*. Paperback edn. Cambridge, MA & London: Harvard University Press.

Reili Argus
Acquisition of requests in Estonian

Abstract: The main objective of the study is to identify the linguistic means that are most frequently employed by Estonian children to express requests and the paths through which they develop. The analysis is based on 25 hours of recorded spontaneous speech of two monolingual Estonian children between the ages 1;3 and 3;0 and their caregivers. All requests in the material were classified according to the type (direct vs. indirect requests such as commands, prohibitions vs. suggestions) at a first level and according to the linguistic means used (such as imperative, modal verbs) at a second level. One of the main results of the study is that rather than clear-cut periods of development there is a continuous order of emergence of different linguistic means children use for forming requests. They start with cognitively and grammatically less complex requests where the source of modality is within the speaker (e.g. commands). Requests with a source of modality external to the speaker (such as statements of desired actions by quoting social norms) are acquired later. The impact of child-directed speech is reflected most clearly in the order of appearance of the first indirect requests in the children's speech: the most frequent types of indirect requests occurring in child-directed speech, namely appeals for joint action and statements of the addressee's desired action, emerge first.

1 Introduction

The literature dealing with modality and requests in Estonian is quite substantial (see Uuspõld 1989; Tragel 2001; Torn-Leesik 2007; Metslang 2004; Pajusalu 2014). However, studies regarding their acquisition are scarce: There is a limited amount of work on the acquisition of epistemic modality, mainly evidentiality, based on experimental data (Argus et al. 2014a; Argus et al. 2014b; Kazakovskaya and Argus 2016; Tamm et al. 2015). Furthermore, there is one study on requests in child-directed speech (Kõrgesaar 2014) and another one on directives in the speech of a father and his daughter during a one-hour conversation (Rääbis 2012). The focus of the study by Kõrgesaar (2014) was on the quantity of requests in the parents' speech, namely 13–14% of all utterances. Rääbis (2012) found that the main devices for the expression of directives in the speech of a father and his daughter are modal auxiliaries constructed with full verbs and the imperative.

Reili Argus, Tallinn University

The present study is a first attempt to describe the acquisition of agent-oriented modality (as opposed to epistemic/evidential modality) in Estonian, more specifically requests, on the basis of longitudinal data of two children between the ages of 1;3 and 3;0.

Requests are important speech acts in everyday communication and are acquired early by children learning different languages (Aikhenvald 2010: 326; Stephany and Voeikova 2015). Expressions of modality develop toward the end of their second year. Children start with agent-oriented modality, pointing to what they want and need before they talk about what others want or need (Choi 2006: 165). The ways of making acceptable requests may vary from culture to culture and therefore require both linguistic and cultural knowledge on the part of the speaker. Requests may thus differ with regard to the degree of directness and the linguistic means used.

This paper provides a description of the acquisition of requests in Estonian from a pragmatic point of view. The term "request" refers to speech acts used in directive situations, i.e. in situations where the speaker's goal is "to get others to do what one wants them to" (Tomasello 2010: 84). In short, requests are intended to induce the addressee to some action. According to Mauri and Sansò (2011: 3), directive situations are situations in which the speaker wishes a state of affairs to become true and conveys an appeal to the addressee to help make it true. The performer of the action required to bring about the desired state of affairs may coincide with the addressee (as in the imperative clause *Come!*), the addressee together with the speaker, a third party or any possible combination of the three. For example, in the cohortative request *Let's do it* the performer is the speaker together with an addressee and in the jussive request *Let her be there* the performer is the addressee with a third party (*she*). It would seem that requests where performer and addressee coincide would be the easiest for a child to acquire and those where the performer is the addressee together with the speaker would be more difficult, while requests in which the performer is a third party would seem most difficult of all and would therefore be expected to be acquired later.

Besides the scales of grammatical complexity there is a scale of cognitive complexity of different types of requests. Furthermore, increasing indirectness of requests is accompanied by increasing politeness and also increasing grammatical complexity. A command is a direct request because it is an explicit call for action to be performed by the addressee. With a command the addressee does not have the choice not to comply with the request, whereas a statement of desire like "I want" may function as an indirect request by the speaker, which may or may not be fulfilled by the addressee. Questions could similarly be met by a verbal answer rather than the performance of action, but are interpreted as requests on pragmatic grounds. Interpreting questions such as *Can you pass the salt?* as questions for information and answering them verbally by *Yes* or *No* or *Of course* is pragmatically inadequate since they function as indirect requests for action (namely to pass the salt). Statements of social rules functioning as requests may be considered to constitute the most abstract type of requests because the source of modality is speaker-external.

In the present paper, the term "request" will be used to refer to a range of speech acts including prohibitions and preventions (warnings). These include both direct and indirect ways of conveying directive meaning, from intense commands and prohibitions, instructions and requests to less intense suggestions, appeals for joint action, wishes, warnings, and the like.

The main issue of the present study is to identify the linguistic means which are most frequently employed by the children studied for expressing requests in the course of their development. By taking different periods of child speech and child-directed speech into consideration it is hoped to gain an understanding of the developmental paths of requests in Estonian language acquisition. Following Christofidou and Stephany (2003: 117) who have found "smoothly gliding developmental phases" of inflectional development in Greek rather than different stages of morphological development marked by "turning points" in language development, it can be expected that there will not be clear-cut stages in the development of linguistic means used by children acquiring requests in Estonian but rather a continuous developmental path.

The study is based on the main assumption of usage-based approaches to first language acquisition, namely "that language structure emerges from language use" (Tomasello 2009: 85). In the constructivist, usage-based approach, grammatical knowledge is taken to emerge "from the categorization of experienced utterances" (Bybee 2010: 78). The acquisition of language thus crucially depends on the linguistic input to the child. Therefore, both CS and CDS will be analysed in this chapter.

The main types of requests in Estonian, along with grammatical means used for each type, are presented in section 2. An overview of the methodology of investigation and information concerning the data analysed is provided in section 3. Section 4 deals with the development of requests in early child Estonian. The development of requests is described according to pragmatic types of requests (direct vs. indirect) and grammatical means used for expressing them. In the concluding section the results of the study are discussed.

2 Requests in Estonian

There is a continuum of requests in colloquial Estonian, ranging from strict commands and prohibitions to mild suggestions or warnings. Request types can be ordered according to pragmatic factors of directness: While direct requests require obedience, with indirect requests there is (at least hypothetically) a possibility for the addressee to refuse to comply with them (see Table 1).

Table 1: Types of requests and their linguistic expressions in Estonian CDS.[1]

Types of requests	Linguistic expression
Direct positive requests (commands)	Imperative
	Verbless utterances
Direct negative requests (prohibitions)	Negative imperative
Indirect prohibitions	Negative constructions with the modal verb *tohtima* 'may'
	Negative constructions with the verb *lubama* 'permit'
Statements of an action desired by the speaker	Indicative second person singular
	Indicative third person singular
	Jussive construction (*las* 'let') with a 3rd person verb form or the infinitive
Obligations	Constructions with the modal verb *pidama* 'must' or the phrasal verb *vaja olema* 'is necessary'
Suggestions	Complement clauses introduced by the verbs *vaata, näe, kuule* 'look/see, see, hear'
	Conditional in the main clause
	Conditional in the subordinate clause
Appeals for joint action	Hortative (1st person plural)
Statements of social rules	Impersonal constructions
	Constructions with modal verbs
	Questions
Speaker's wishes	Verbs *tahtma, soovima* 'want, wish'

Request types may also be ordered according to grammatical complexity. The formally simplest types of requests are positive commands expressed by imperatives. Negative commands containing a negative auxiliary or particle are slightly more complex (see below).

---

[1] The subcategories of requests are partially based on Stephany and Voeikova (2015: 70–74) and for Estonian on Metslang (2004: 243–256). Examples in this chapter have been taken from the child-directed speech studied.

Prototypical direct requests are commands expressed by a verb in the imperative (example 1).

(1) tule   siia!
    come.IMP.2SG here.ILL
    'come here!'

The simplest form of the Estonian verbal paradigm is the 2nd person singular imperative, which consists of an unmarked verb stem without suffixes[2] (see Viitso 2003: 58). Although imperative verb forms represent the simplest and most direct way to express requests in Estonian, they are only used with close friends, while more indirect types of requests, such as conditionals and questions, are preferred when addressing other people (Pajusalu 2014: 251). Imperatives may be rendered more polite by adding the particle *palun* 'please' (e.g., *palun tule siia!* 'please come here!').

Commands may also be expressed by verbless utterances typically consisting of an object noun and adverb (example 2).

(2) kork   peale!
    cap.NOM   onto
    '(put) the cap on (the bottle)!'

One way to express negative imperatives is to combine the imperative of the negative auxiliary *ära*[3] 'not' with the corresponding imperative form of the main verb[4] (example 3).

(3) ära   tule   siia!
    NEG.IMP.2SG come.CNG here
    'don't come here!'

Another possibility is to use the negative particle *ei* 'no' (example 4).

---

2 An unmarked verb stem can occur only in the imperative and negative, in all other forms it occurs with tense or person suffixes, e.g. *tule-b* 'go-PRS.2SG'. In the negative the verb stem occurs with the negative particle *ei* 'no'. In this article the verb stem occurring in the negative is marked as connegative (see Tamm 2015).
3 The imperative forms of *ära* are: *ära* NEG.IMP.2SG, *ärgem* NEG.IMP.1PL, *ärge* NEG.IMP.2PL.
4 The form of the imperative is identical with the connegative (see Tamm 2015: 405).

(4) *ei   tee!*
     NEG do.CNG
     'don't do it!'

Prohibitions with the negative particle *ei* are formally negative declarative sentences, which receive their interpretation as prohibitions mainly by intonation and the context. Such prohibitions are very strong orders and characteristic of a close relationship between interlocutors. They may even be considered as impolite.

Prohibitions may furthermore be expressed by the deontic use of the modal verb *tohtima* 'may' in the negative and the verb in the infinitive with an objective, external source of modality (example 5).

(5) *nuppe   ei   tohi vajuta-da.*
     buttons.PARTIT.PL no   may   press-INF
     'it's not allowed to press buttons.'

In child-directed speech, prohibitions are also usually rendered by a negated sentence with the verb *lubama* 'permit' having a speaker-internal source of modality. The child is asked to refrain from some action as in example (6).

(6) *ma   ei   luba.*
     I   not   permit.CNG
     'I don't permit (to do it).'

There are many ways to express indirect requests in Estonian. Speakers' statements of some future action to be carried out by the addressee or a third party are considered to be strong requests. They are grammatically more complex than positive or negative commands in the imperative, but less complex than the constructions with *tohtima* 'may' described above, which consist of a modal auxiliary and a main verb in the infinitive. The strongest requests among indirect ones, which are not considered as very polite, are grammatically quite simple since they are expressed by the 2nd person singular present indicative (example 7).

(7) *kõigepealt ütle-d   tere.*
     first   say-PRS.2SG hello
     'first you say hello.'

Milder requests can be expressed by the third person singular present indicative (example 8).

(8) Martina   võta-b   pudruampsu   ka.
     Martina.NOM take-PRS.3SG porridge.mouthful.PARTIT also
     'Martina will take a mouthful of porridge also.'

Indirect requests as statements of future actions may also be expressed by a jussive construction consisting of *las* 'let', a frozen, particle-like uninflected verb form, used for marking either causativity or deontic modality. Such constructions contain a first or third person verb form in addition to the form *las* (example 9).

(9) las teised maga-vad.
     let others sleep-PRS.3PL
     'let others sleep.'

In such indirect requests, the verb can also be in the *da*-infinitive.[5] In both cases (examples 9 and 10) the situation in question has to be made possible, initiated or continued by the addressee, who is supposed not to interfere with the state or the action of the subject of the situation (Metslang 2001: 373).

(10) las see   arvuti   oll-a.
     let it.NOM computer.NOM be-INF
     'let the computer be (there).'

In everyday Estonian speech, polite indirect requests, such as appeals for joint action, may be expressed by hortatives with the verb in the first person plural (example 11).

(11) läh-me   nüüd maga-ma.
     go-PRS.1PL now sleep-SUP
     'let's go to sleep now.'

A further construction used for making indirect requests consists of the particle-like verb (or fossilized imperative) *vaata* 'look' followed by a complement clause (example 12).

---

[5] There are two infinitive forms in Estonian, the *ma*-infinitive (supine) and the *da*-infinitive. The *da*-infinitive has three allomorphs (-*da*, -*a*, and -*ta*).

(12) vaata,   kas sa   saa-d   ise   teh-a.
    look.IMP.2SG if you.NOM can-PRS.2SG yourself make-INF
    'see/try if you can do it yourself.'

In such constructions, *vaata!* 'look!' does not have the literal meaning of making the addressee look at something or getting his attention, but functions to prompt some of his actions.

Obligations may be expressed by the modal verb *pidama* 'must' (example 13).

(13) sa   pea-d   se-da   tege-ma.
    you must-PRS.2SG it-PARTIT do-SUP
    'you must do it.'

In obligations with an objective source of modality external to the speaker the phrasal verb *vaja olema* 'be necessary, need' may be used (example 14).

(14) käe-d   on vaja   ka   pes-ta.
    hand-NOM.PL is necessary also wash-INF
    'it is necessary to also wash your hands.'

Conditionals and conditional clauses (examples 15 and 16) can be used for expressing suggestions. Example 16 expresses a very mild indirect request, namely the condition to be fulfilled so that the action mentioned in the main clause may be realized.

(15) sa   pea-ksi-d   tooli   too-ma.
    you should-COND-2SG chair.GEN bring-SUP
    'you should bring a chair.'

(16) kui sa   supi   ära   söö-d,
    if   you.NOM soup.GEN PFV.PTL eat-PRS.2SG
    saa-d   magustoitu.
    get-PRS.2SG dessert.PARTIT
    'If you finish your soup, you'll get dessert.'

Questions may be used as indirect requests implying that the addressee stops an action or refrains from doing it. In addition, they may be used in cases where the speaker supposes that the addressee is not reluctant to comply with his suggestion (see also Metslang 1981: 101). Thus, example (17) is not used for getting information but suggests to the recipient to put the boy on the floor.

(17) miks sa   ta   sülle   tõsta-d?
      why   you.NOM he.GEN lap.ILL   raise-PRS.2SG
      'why do you take him on your lap?'

In Estonian, as in many other languages, statements of social rules may function as indirect requests. One possibility is to use the impersonal voice (example 18).

(18) käsi   pesta-kse   enne   sööki.
      hand.PARTIT.PL   wash-IMPRS   before meal.PARTIT
      'one washes one's hands before a meal.'

Another way of expressing such requests is to use a construction with the modal verb *pidama* 'must' in the 3rd person singular present as in example (19).

(19) käsi   pea-b   pese-ma.
      hand.PARTIT.PL   must-PRS.3SG   wash-SUP
      'one must wash one's hands.'

Statements of social rules may also be expressed by questions reminding the addressee (e.g., the child) of a socially acceptable response (example 20). Such questions may either be formed with the 2nd person singular present form or, in child-directed speech, also with the 3rd person singular (this form addresses the child as a member of a social class, which strengthens the request).

(20) mis   laps   ütle-b,
      what   child.NOM   say-PRS.3SG
      kui   kommi   saa-b?
      when   candy.PARTIT   get-PRS.3SG
      'What does a child say when she gets a candy?'

Another way to form a polite indirect request is by stating a speaker's wish (example 21).

(21) ma taha-n   kartuli-t.
      I   want-PRS.1SG potato-PARTIT
      'I want some potatoes.'

There are several possibilities of expressing negative indirect requests such as warnings or statements of undesired actions ("preventives"), the strongest of which are constructions with the pronoun of the 2nd person singular (example 22).

(22) sina   se-da   ei võta.
you.NOM.SG it-PARTIT no take.CNG
'you will not take it.'

Warnings may also be expressed by statements in the present indicative, which also refers to the near future in Estonian. In example (23) the speaker warns the addressee about an object likely to fall down.

(23) see kuku-b maha.
it fall-PRS.3SG down
'it will fall down.'

Yet another way to express a warning is to use a preventive construction consisting of a clause with the particle-like verb *vaata* 'look' (example 24) or the particle *muidu* 'otherwise' (example 25). Both of these constructions draw the addressee's attention to a possible danger.

(24) vaata, et sa ei kuku.
look that you.NOM no fall.CNG
'make sure you don't fall.'

(25) muidu kuku-b maha.
otherwise fall-PRS.3SG down
'otherwise it will fall down.'

3 Data, methodology and research questions

The present analysis is based on the speech of two monolingual Estonian children between the ages of 1;3 and 3;0, in interaction with their parents. There are 11 hours of recordings from the girl Martina and 14 hours from the boy Andreas. Each recording session lasted about 60 minutes and there was usually one session per month (see Tables 2 and 3). The data were transcribed according to the CHAT conventions of the CHILDES Project (MacWhinney 2000) and form a part of the Estonian database in CHILDES (subcorpora Vija and

Table 2: Total number and percentage of requests in Martina's CS and CDS.

Age	CS			CDS		
	Utterances	Requests	Percentage	Utterances	Requests	Percentage
1;3	416	7	1.7	443	37	8.4
1;5	456	14	3.1	471	41	8.7
1;6	240	5	2.1	242	30	12.4
1;9	334	10	0.3	409	38	9.3
1;10	378	12	3.2	454	57	12.6
1;11	312	33	10.6	444	49	11.0
2;1	400	34	8.5	388	87	22.4
2;3	184	15	8.2	257	44	17.1
2;4	154	14	9.1	189	33	17.5
2;7	280	28	10.0	246	45	18.3
3;0	279	16	5.7	268	68	25.4
Total/average	3,432	188	5.7	3,811	529	14.9

Table 3: Total number and percentage of requests in Andreas' CS and CDS.

Age	CS			CDS		
	Utterances	Requests	Percentage	Utterances	Requests	Percentage
1;7	431	13	3.0	522	42	8.1
1;8	347	0	0	325	67	20.6
1;9	224	24	10.7	257	44	17.1
1;10	224	17	7.6	323	63	19.5
1;11	114	10	8.8	132	22	16.7
2;0	484	53	11.0	454	113	28.9
2;1	306	31	10.1	283	64	22.6
2;3	179	45	25.2	127	38	28.3
2;4	307	44	14.3	433	36	8.3
2;5	140	22	15.7	118	25	21.2
2;6	348	45	12.9	221	34	15.4
2;7	387	114	29.5	280	24	8.6
2;8	257	45	17.5	191	30	15.7
3;0	516	79	15.3	454	55	12.1
Total/average	4,264	542	13.0	4,120	657	17.4

Kapanen[6]). Although the biological ages of the children were different in their first recordings (Martina 1;3, Andreas 1;7) the linguistic development may be considered to have been approximately at the same level since the MLU values of both children were similar (> 2.2 words per utterance).

All directive speech acts in the children's and their interlocutors' speech were included in the analysis. Turns consisting of two requests were analysed separately. Thus, example (26) contains a command and a prohibition.

(26) Andreas, 2;4
　　MOT: *räägi,　　　　aga　ära　se-da*
　　　　　speak.IMP.2SG,　but　not　it-PARTIT
　　　　　suhu　　　　pane.
　　　　　mouth.ILL　　put.CNG
　　　　　'speak, but don't put it into your mouth.'

On a first level, requests were classified according to type of function (command, prohibition, suggestion etc.) and on a second level according to the linguistic means used (imperative, modal verbs etc.).

In connection with the general aims of the present study mentioned in Section 1, the following more specific research questions have been addressed:
- What type of requests (e.g., direct or indirect) emerge first in the speech of Estonian children and in what order?
- Do the categories of addressee vs. performer of directives play a role in their order of development? In particular, will the first requests emerging in the child's speech be those in which the performer coincides with the addressee? Will requests in which the addressee, together with the speaker, are the performers appear next? And will requests where the performer is a third party develop last? Is the hypothesized order of emergence corroborated by an increasing linguistic complexity of requests of the three functional types mentioned?
- The forms and functions of direct and indirect requests occurring in CDS as well as their type and token frequencies, important for pattern recognition and entrenchment respectively, will be analyzed and related to what is found in CS.

---

6 http://childes.psy.cmu.edu/browser/index.php?url=Other/Estonian/ (4.07.2016)

4 The development of requests in early child Estonian

In this section the development of requests in child Estonian will first be traced by a description of the amount of requests occurring in the two children's speech as well as the emergence of different types of direct and indirect requests. These findings will subsequently be compared to those in CDS.

The absolute numbers and percentages of requests occurring in CS and CDS are presented in Tables 2 and 3 above (see Section 3).

The number of requests occurring in CS as well as CDS varies greatly in different recordings and is partially due to the types of situations being recorded. Thus, at 2;7, Andreas and his mother were involved in a photo-shooting game in which the child was playing the role of the photographer so that he gave a lot of commands to his mother. Another factor is age, since requests are more rarely found before 1;9 than from 1;9 or 1;11 onward.

4.1 Emergence of direct requests in child Estonian

Both children already used requests in their first recordings. Andreas at first only made verbless requests consisting of the name of an object in the partitive. In example (27) he asked for some cake reaching out his hand.

(27) Andreas, 1;7
 kooki.
 cake.PARTIT
 'some cake.'

In another request (example 28) he used the interjection *aitäh* 'thanks' with the name of the object in the partitive.

(28) Andreas, 1;7
 kommi   aitää [: *aitäh*].[7]
 candy.PARTIT thanks
 'some candy thanks.'

---

[7] The standard form is given in square brackets.

All first partitives used as objects were suffixless forms and they already occurred in the first recordings.

(29) *palun   kommi!*
     please   candy.PARTIT
     'some candy please.'

At 1;11 Andreas started to make requests consisting of the name of an object in the partitive constructed with the adverb *veel* 'more' and, in a retracing, adding an adjectival attribute (example 30).

(30) Andreas, 1;11
     veel   saia,
     more   bread.PARTIT
     kõva   saia   veel.
     hard.PARTIT bread.PARTIT more
     '(give me) more bread, more hard bread.'

At this age case-marking has started to become productive[8] in Andreas' speech and the partitive was used with several nouns and contrasted with other case forms.

Requests containing a verb in the second person singular imperative emerged somewhat later than verbless requests in the boy's speech, namely at 1;9 (example 31).

(31) Andreas, 1;9
     emme   tule.
     mommy.NOM   come.IMP.2SG
     'mommy, come (with me).'

Negative direct requests with the verb in the imperative appeared shortly after positive ones (example 32).

---

8 First three-member miniparadigms (sets of at least three inflectional forms of the same lexeme produced spontaneously in contrasting contexts, see Bittner, Dressler & Kilani-Schoch 2003: xvi) of nouns were found in the child's speech at age 2;0, but he had already used several oppositions of two case forms of the same noun before that age (Argus 2009).

(32) Andreas, 1;10
    äla [: ära] leika [: lõika].
    not   cut.CNG
    'don't cut.'

As far as Martina's early speech is concerned, there is a verbless request with the noun in the illative found at 1;3 (example 33).

(33) Martina, 1;3
    kätte.
    hand.ILL
    '(I want it/give it to me) in my hand.'

However, this example co-occurs with requests containing imperative verb forms, partially constructed with an object in the partitive,[9] in the same recording (examples 34 and 35).

(34) Martina, 1;3
    näita   mängu.
    show.IMP.2SG game.PARTIT
    'show (me) the game.'

(35) Martina, 1;3
    emme   buue [: loe].
    mommy.NOM   read.IMP.2SG
    'mommy, read (to me).'

In spite of her precocious use of imperative verb forms, verbless requests consisting of a noun in the partitive or genitive persist through 1;5 in Martina's speech (examples 36 and 37). Case-marked nouns used at age 1;3 are likely to be frozen forms, but the usage of both the partitive and genitive of one and the same noun give evidence of productivity at age 1;5. In most cases an elliptic use of requests such as those in examples (36) and (37) is not justified by the preceding context.

---

[9] The partitive form used in the example may be a rote-learned form, since Martina's first miniparadigms emerged only 2 months later. However, the girl's development of noun inflection has not yet been studied in detail.

(36) Martina, 1;5
tomati-t.
tomato-PARTIT
'(I want/give me) some tomato.'

(37) Martina, 1;5
tommati [: *tomati*]   *ka.*
tomato.GEN   also
'(I want to have one) tomato also.'

Negative requests in the imperative functioning as prohibitions only emerged at 2;0 in Martina's speech, seven months after their positive equivalents, but their constructions were much more complex than those produced by Andreas at 1;10 (example 38 vs. 32).

(38) Martina, 2;0
äla [: *ära*] *pane   se-da   patsi   kõvasti.*
not   put.CNG it-PARTIT pigtail.PARTIT tight
'don't tie this pigtail tightly.'

Summarizing our findings so far, it can be stated that the earliest direct requests produced by Estonian children are either verbless expressions consisting of a noun in the partitive (or the genitive) referring to a desired object or contain a verb in the imperative, sometimes constructed with a noun in the partitive or the negative particle or both.

The development of imperatives differed in the two children. In spite of her younger age, Martina's imperatives emerged simultaneously with verbless requests, while Andreas started to use imperatives two months after the first verbless requests. However, negative imperatives emerged shortly after the first positive ones in Andreas' speech, while Martina started to use negative imperatives only six months after positive ones, the latter of which appeared very early at 1;3.

4.2 Development of indirect requests in child Estonian

In the beginning of speech production, both Andreas (1;7–2;0) and Martina (1;3–1;5) only used direct requests. Andreas' indirect requests first occurring at 2;0 are more complex both formally and semantically than the direct requests he used earlier. Some of these requests are hortatives which consist of the 1st person plural present form of the verb, refer to speaker and addressee and function as suggestions (example 39).

(39) Andreas, 2;0
läh-me   noonista-me [: *joonista-me*] *k(r)iidi-ga.*
go-PRS.1PL draw-PRS.1PL   chalk-COM
'let's go and draw with chalk.'

Besides the hortative (example 39), the boy even used a wish (example 40) in the same recording. His first two wishes did not, however, contain the verb *tahtma* 'want', but were mere infinitive constructions with an object in the partitive or an adverbial complement (examples 40 and 41).

(40) Andreas, 2;0
Andsu [: *Andreas*] *muna   süi-ja* [: *süüa*].
Andsu.NOM   egg.PARTIT eat-INF
'Andreas (wants) to eat an egg.'

(41) Andreas, 2;0
ma-ha   tul-la.
down-ILL   come-INF
'(I want) to come down.'

It is unclear whether grammatically complete wishes containing the modal verb *tahtma* 'wish' emerged subsequently to mere infinitive constructions or simultaneously with them. Anyhow, a grammatically complete example occurred in the recording at 2;1 after the elliptic examples found at 2;0 (example 42).

(42) Andreas, 2;1
Antsu [: *Andreas*] *taha-b   se-da.*
Andsu.NOM   want-PRS.3SG it-PARTIT
'Andreas wants this.'

As is common with young children, Andreas used the 3rd person singular instead of the 1st person to refer to himself until 2;4, when the first uses of *tahtma* 'wish' in the 1st person emerged (example 43).

(43) Andreas, 2;4
(The child asks his father to hand the recorder over to him and let him listen to the recording.)
anna,   mina   taha-n   Antsu-t.
give.IMP.2SG   I   want-PRS.1SG   Antsu-PARTIT
'give, I want (to listen to the recording of) Antsu.'

Although Martina also started to use indirect requests only after having developed direct ones, she did so much earlier than Andreas. Both a hortative and a wish occurred in one and the same recording at 1;6 (examples 44 and 45).

(44) Martina, 1;6
(l)äh-me   õue.
go-PRS.1PL   outside.ILL
'let's go outside.'

(45) Martina, 1;6
taha-(n)   leib [: *leiba*].[10]
want-PRS.1SG   bread
'(I) want (some) bread.'

Unlike Andreas, Martina used the verb *tahtma* 'want' constructed with an object noun already in her first wishes while infinitive constructions without the modal verb did not occur in her speech. In her early wishes at 1;6, she usually omitted the inflectional suffix and only produced the verb stem (example 45).

Starting from age 2;0 Andreas used statements with the verb in the 3rd person present indicative expressing a desired action to be performed by the addressee. He used the 3rd person singular to refer not only to the speaker but also to the addressee thereby keeping reference constant and avoiding shifters. The first of these statements were negative requests (example 46). Such indirect negative requests became more frequent in the boy's speech only at 3;0.

---

10 Martina uses an incorrect nominative instead of a partitive form of the object noun.

(46) Andreas, 2;0
    emme   ei   läpi [: näpi].[11]
    mommy.NOM   no   touch.CNG
    'mommy does not touch (the recorder).'

Statements asking the addressee to either cause or admit a state of affairs of an object or a person only emerged at about 2;3 in the boy's speech, i.e. three months later than negative requests. Such jussive constructions with the particle *las* are quite complex since in addition to the particle they require a subject noun either in the nominative or the adessive case and the verb in the present indicative or the *da*-infinitive. The subject of these constructions can be either animate or inanimate. At first Andreas only used inanimate subjects in the nominative case in his *las*-constructions (e.g. to refer to the recorder in example 47) with the verb in the *da*-infinitive; animate subjects and a present indicative verb form were used only from 3;0 on (example 48).

(47) Andreas, 2;3
    las   ta   ol-la   maa-s.
    let   it.NOM   be-INF   floor-ILL
    'let it (recorder) be on the floor.'

(48) Andreas, 3;0
    las   ma   maitse-n.
    let   I   taste-PRS.1SG
    'let me taste (some chocolate).'

Besides the types of indirect requests mentioned so far, there were also a few examples of suggestions in Andreas' speech expressed by the modal verb

---

11 There are no person endings in present indicative negative forms. The negative imperative and negative indicative can only be differentiated by the negative particle *ära* in the imperative and *ei* in the indicative.

	Positive	Negative
Indicative	*tule-n* 'come-PRS.1SG'	*ei tule* 'no come.CNG'
Imperative	*tule* 'come.IMP.2SG'	*ära tule* 'no come.CNG'

construction v*aja olema* 'necessary be' (example 49). The conditional makes the request sound more polite.

(49) Andreas, 2;6
kõrvale   ole-ks   vaja   kommi.
beside   be-COND   necessary   candy.PARTIT
'It would be necessary to have a candy (put) beside (the main dish).'

Much as with Andreas' development, Martina also started to use statements with the verb in the 3rd person present indicative expressing a desired action to be performed by the addressee some time later than she expressed wishes. Thus, when she did not want to obey her father's request to pick up the pieces of a game, she directed this activity to her father (example 50).

(50) Martina, 1;10
FAT: *pane   siis   kiisumäng   kokku.*
       put.IMP.2SG then   cat.game.NOM together
       'put the pieces of the cat game together.'
CHI: *issi   pane-b.*
       daddy.NOM   put-PRS.3SG
       'daddy puts.'

Statements of the addressee's desired action expressed with *las*-constructions emerged after statements with the verb in the 3rd person present indicative. In contrast to Andreas, Martina used finite verb forms in her *las*-constructions from the very beginning. In example (51) the child wanted her mother not to switch the light off.

(51) Martina, 1;11
a   las see   tuli   põle-b.
but   let   this.NOM light.NOM light-PRS.3SG
'but leave this light on.'

The first and only statement of a social rule functioning as an indirect request appeared in Martina's speech at 2;1 (example 52). There are no examples of this type to be found in Andreas' speech.

(52) Martina, 2;1
 aken-t pu(h)asta-takse selle-ga.
 window-PARTIT clean-IMPRS.PRS it-COM
 'one cleans the window with this.'
 (wanting to get a window cleaning spray)

In spite of the age differences concerning the development of different types of requests in the two children's speech, the order of emergence is quite similar, as can be observed in Table 4.

Table 4: Emergence of different types of requests in CS.

Andreas		Martina	
Age	Type of request	Age	Type of request
		1;3	Verbless commands
			Commands (IMP)
		1;6	Hortatives (PRS.1PL)
			Wishes (*tahtma* 'want' in PRS.1SG)
1;7	Verbless commands		
1;9	Commands (IMP)	1;9	Negative commands (NEG.IMP)
1;10	Negative commands (NEG.IMP)	1;10	Statements of speaker's desired action (verb in PRS.3SG)
		1;11	Statements of speaker's desired action (*las*-construction with the verb in PRS.3SG)
2;0	Hortatives (PRS.1PL)		
	Wishes (without the verb *tahtma* 'want')		
	Statements of speaker's desired action (verb in NEG.PRS.3SG)		
2;1	Wishes (the verb *tahtma* 'want' in PRS.1SG)	2;1	Social rules (verb in IMPRS.PRS)
2;3	Statements of speaker's desired action (*las*-construction with the verb in INF)		
2;6	Suggestion (verb in COND)		

Both children start with verbless constructions and direct requests in the imperative, namely commands, followed by indirect requests such as hortatives and wishes. The order of emergence of more complex types of indirect requests such as the statement of social rules slightly differs. A statement of a social rule with an impersonal verb form was used only once by Martina, but not at all by

Andreas. On the other hand, a suggestion containing a conditional verb form only occurred once in Andreas' speech. Statements with impersonal constructions and constructions with a conditional verb form are generally acquired later by Estonian children: The impersonal between 2;3 and 3;0 (Vija, Torn-Leesik and Pajusalu 2009) and the conditional at 2;6 (Pajusalu et al. 2011: 141).

4.3 Input-output relationships in the acquisition of Estonian requests

It has been shown that children are very efficient pattern recognizers in that they can derive linguistic structure from the language they hear (Tomasello 2003). In order to get an insight into the way in which the children's language relates to the changing distributional properties of the input language in the course of development, two issues will be addressed in this section: the form and function as well as the frequency of direct and indirect requests in the input and the reflection of their distribution in the children's language.

As is to be expected, the inventory of different patterns of requests is larger in CDS than in CS. Warnings, obligations and indirect prohibitions are used by the caretakers, but not by the children (see Figures 1–2). Warnings (only one or two examples) emerged only at the end of the observation period in the speech of both parents. For example, Martina's mother used the particle *vaata* 'see' to express a warning (example 53).

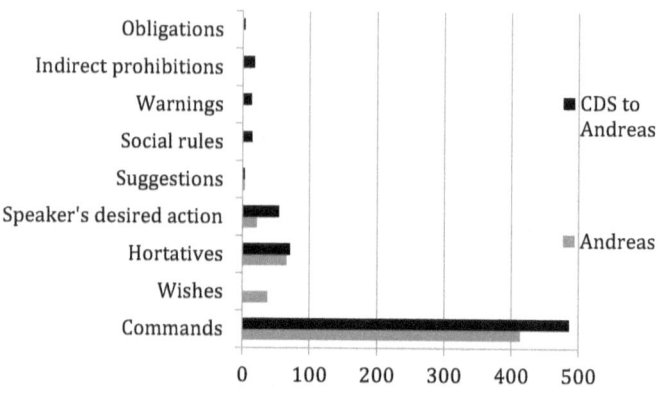

Figure 1: Distribution of types of requests in Andreas' CS and CDS (absolute numbers, entire period of observation).

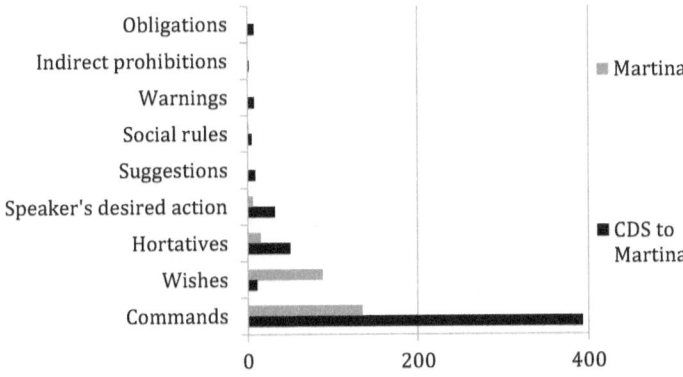

Figure 2: Distribution of types of requests in Martina's CS and CDS (absolute numbers, entire period of observation).

(53) Martina's mother, 2;3
 vaata   et   sa   ei   kuku,   hoia   tasakaalu.
 see.IMP.2SG that you no fall.CNG hold.IMP.2SG balance
 'see that you will not fall, hold balance.'

The difference between CDS and CS is even more pronounced if the form of requests is taken into consideration. While verbless commands are quite frequent in the children's speech, they rarely occur in the adults'. The caretakers use both *las*-constructions with the verb in the infinitive or the 3rd person singular present indicative for expressing statements of the speaker's desired action, while each of the children uses only one of these constructions (Martina the 3rd person present singular and Andreas the *da*-infinitive).[12]

The third person present forms in statements of the addressee's desired action were used by both caretakers and children. However, the strongest forms of request among the statements of a speaker's desired actions, second person singular forms, were used only by the adults (example 54). Direct requests, i.e. commands with the verb in the second person singular imperative, clearly predominate in the CDS of both children overall (Figures 1 and 2).

---

[12] One must not forget that the collected data only represent a small fraction of the input so that the child may very well have had the opportunity of detecting the respective patterns.

(54) Martina's mother, 2;1
　　siis　　tule-d　　　　võta-d　　　　ühe.
　　then　come-PRS.2SG　take-PRS.2SG　one.GEN
　　'then you (have to) come and take one.'

The most frequent types of indirect requests are hortatives, wishes expressed with *tahtma* 'want', and the speaker's desired actions with a full verb in the third person present. Other types of indirect requests such as obligations, suggestions, statements of social rules, warnings and indirect prohibitions are represented by only three to ten examples each. Social rules with an impersonal verb form were observed later in CDS, namely from 2;3 in Andreas' CDS and from 1;10 in Martina's. Based on these data, the late emergence of the latter type of requests in CS is to be expected.

Although both children's CDS was quite similar, a difference concerns the number of prohibitions among commands. These amounted to 11% in Andreas' CDS but to only 6% in Martina's. The amount of prohibitions expressed by the negative auxiliary *ära* in the imperative (see example 4) largely exceeded that with the negative particle *ei* 'no' (see example 5) in the speech of both parents. The order of emergence as well as the frequency of the two different patterns of prohibitions in CS is clearly influenced by CDS. Both children acquired prohibitions with the negative auxiliary *ära* first (Martina at 1;9, Andreas at 1;10) and used this type of prohibitions frequently. There were only some examples with the negative particle *ei* 'no' to be found in the speech of Andreas, but none in Martina's.

Table 5: Number of requests (tokens) and percentages of direct and indirect requests in Martina's CS and CDS.

	CS			CDS		
Age	Number of requests	Direct requests (%)	Indirect requests (%)	Number of requests	Direct requests (%)	Indirect requests (%)
1;3	7	100	0	37	73	27
1;5	17	47	53	41	68	32
1;6	5	40	60	29	86	16
1;9	10	50	50	38	92	8
1;10	12	33	67	57	81	19
1;11	33	7	93	49	69	31
2;1	34	56	44	87	74	26
2;3	15	47	53	44	77	23
2;4	14	35	65	33	73	27
2;7	28	25	75	38	81	19
3;0	16	69	31	68	76	24

Table 6: Number of requests (tokens) and percentages of direct and indirect requests in Andreas' CS and CDS.

Age	CS			CDS		
	Number of requests	Direct requests (%)	Indirect requests (%)	Number of requests	Direct requests (%)	Indirect requests (%)
1;7	13	100	0	42	81	19
1;8	0	0	0	67	88	12
1;9	24	100	0	44	63	37
1;10	17	82	18	63	78	22
1;11	10	100	0	22	95	5
2;0	53	17	83	113	74	26
2;1	31	74	26	64	66	34
2;3	43	86	14	38	87	13
2;4	44	54	46	36	83	17
2;5	22	59	41	25	60	40
2;6	45	62	38	34	76	24
2;7	114	79	21	24	58	42
2;8	45	73	27	30	67	33
3;0	79	77	23	55	73	27

As far as the dynamics of different types of requests occurring in CDS in the course of the children's development during the observational period are concerned, no notable changes were found either in the relation of direct to indirect requests or in that of positive vs. negative commands. As shown in Tables (5) and (6), the percentage of direct requests by far exceeded that of indirect ones in both children's CDS throughout the observational period (with a minor exception at Andreas' age 2;7). While indirect requests like warnings and suggestions were used from the very first recordings on by Martina's mother, Andreas' mother started to use them later (after 2;0).

In contrast to CDS, the percentage of direct requests as compared to that of indirect ones differs in the two children. While direct requests largely predominate in all of Andreas' recordings (Table 6), in Martina's speech the relation between both types of requests is much more balanced from 1;5 on, with a few exceptions in which indirect requests even outnumber direct ones depending on the activities in the recorded situation (Table 5). Thus, in the recording at 1;11, Martina was sitting at the breakfast table and expressed a lot of wishes in order to get different kinds of food by using the verb *tahtma* 'want' (27 times), sometimes repeating this verb several times in one and the same utterance (example 55).

(55) Martina, 1;11
taha-n,   taha-n,   taha-n   baan [: *banaani*]
want-PRS.1SG,   want-PRS.1SG,   want-PRS.1SG,   banana
süi-a   saa-da   saa-da   kätte.
eat-INF   get-INF   get-INF   hand.ILL
'I want to eat banana and get it in my hand.'

Martina's frequent use of wishes containing the modal verb *tahtma* 'want' thereby expressing indirect requests may be considered as an individual strategy of this child which not only represents a main difference between the two children studied, but also the effect of CDS. Questions consisting of the verb *tahtma* 'want' such as "What do you want?" were used by her mother approximately 10 times during each recording session.

5 Discussion and conclusion

One of the main findings of our study is that different types of requests emerge in almost the same order in the speech of both children. They started by using direct requests, namely commands and prohibitions. Later on, the first indirect requests emerged in the form of wishes and at the same time as appeals for joint action expressed by hortatives. Statements of the speaker's desired actions followed in both children's development. Indirect requests stating social rules (with an impersonal verb form) and suggestions containing modal particles or conditionals were the latest to emerge.

The early development of direct requests has mainly two reasons: their frequency in CDS and the grammatical simplicity of imperatives. Children hear a great number of direct requests (see Tables 5 and 6) and the verb form used in commands is the simplest one in the entire Estonian verbal paradigm. Imperatives do not only play an important role in Estonian (Argus 2004; Salo 1995: 13), but are also typically the first verb forms (or among the first) to emerge in many other languages, for example in Finnish (Laalo 2003: 330), Spanish (Aguirre 2003: 5, 21), Croatian (Katičić 2003: 246), Lithuanian (Wojcik 2003: 409), Greek[13] and Russian (Stephany and Voeikova 2015: 79; Gagarina 2003: 146).

---

[13] In Greek the imperative emerges together with indicative verb forms so that the contrast between modal and non-modal verb forms is the first to develop (e.g., Christofidou and Stephany 2003).

According to the present study, commands expressed by the imperative are the first type of requests to emerge in Estonian language acquisition and remain the main type of direct requests throughout the observational period. The high proportion of direct requests may result not only from the simplicity of their form, but also from the close social and affective relationship between the child and the parent. The percentage of direct requests was also high in the CDS of both children and this percentage did not change noticeably during the observation period.

Negative direct requests, mostly containing a negated imperative verb form and expressing prohibitions, also emerged quite early in both children's speech although in a different order. While Andreas acquired them shortly after positive direct requests, they appeared in Martina's speech only after hortatives and wishes.

First indirect requests were appeals for joint action expressed by the hortative (1st person plural present indicative) and wishes for objects or actions to be performed (1st person singular present indicative of *tahtma* 'want'). In some recordings, Martina used wishes even more frequently than direct requests. Our findings on Estonian agree with what Stephany (1986: 391) reports on English: "The earliest indirect requests are probably desiderative utterances containing *want* (*to*) used as a main verb or semi-auxiliary."

Statements of a speaker's desired action emerged at the same time as hortatives. They were first expressed by constructions with the verb in the 3rd person singular present indicative referring to the addressee and later on by *las* constructions with the verb in the 3rd person singular present indicative or the infinitive. The order of emergence of these two types of constructions can be explained by the greater complexity of *las* constructions as compared to those simply containing a present tense form.

The statement of social rules functioning as indirect requests and suggestions in the conditional emerged much later. There was only one example of such a suggestion in Andreas' speech at 2;6. Reasons for the rareness and the late development of this type of suggestions in CS are their structural complexity (conditional form of the main verb constructed with the phrasal verb *vaja olema* 'need') and their low frequency in CDS. The conditional has also been found to be a relatively late acquisition in other languages (Stephany 1993: 140–141), one reason being that it is not frequently used in CDS (for Greek see Stephany 1993: 141). The same is true of impersonal forms expressing social rules in Estonian CDS and their late emergence and infrequent use in CS.

The order of emergence of different types of requests in Estonian CS can be summarized as follows: Children start with direct requests where the performer of the desired action is the addressee (commands), subsequently they make indirect requests where the performer is the addressee together with the speaker (appeals for joint action expressed by hortatives), and finally indirect requests where the performer is the addressee together with a third party appear (statements of the speaker's desired action in situations where there is a speaker, a listener and a third party). Statements of social rules functioning as requests may be considered to constitute the most abstract type of requests because the source of modality is speaker-external rather than speaker-internal.

The impact of CDS was reflected most clearly in the extremely high frequency of direct requests (commands expressed by the imperative) in CDS and the order of emergence of different types of indirect requests in the speech of the children: The most frequent types of indirect requests in CDS, namely appeals for joint action and statements of the speaker's desired action, emerged first in the speech of the children. Infrequent request types in CDS such as statements of social rules were acquired late.

In conclusion, it can be argued that the acquisition of different types of requests in Estonian language acquisition follows the scale of frequency and grammatical complexity as well as abstractness of different types of requests. Although the children gave evidence for a gradual approximation of the adult distribution of different types of requests up to the end of the observation period, several types of requests used in CDS were still missing from CS, namely obligations, indirect prohibitions and warnings. However, by age 3;0, Estonian children seem to have acquired the most commonly used conventional means for expressing requests.

References

Aguirre, Carmen. 2003. Early verb development in one Spanish-speaking child. In Dagmar Bittner, Wolfgang U. Dressler & Marianne Kilani-Schoch (eds.), *Development of verb inflection in first language acquisition: A cross-linguistic perspective* (Studies on Language Acquisition 21), 1–25. Berlin & New York: Mouton de Gruyter.

Aikhenvald, Alexandra. 2010. *Imperatives and commands*. Oxford: Oxford University Press.

Argus, Reili. 2004. Verbi esimestest eelkäijatest esimeste miniparadigmadeni: eesti ja soome keele andmetel [From first pre-verbs to first mini-paradigms: Estonian and Finnish]. In Maria-Maren Sepper & Jane Lepasaar (eds.), *Toimiv keel. II: töid rakenduslingvistika alalt* (2. rakenduslingvistika konverentsi ettekanded: 24.-25. aprill 2003, Tallinn) [Papers on Applied Linguistics (presentations of the 2nd conference of Estonian Applied Linguistics, April, 24–25, 2003, Tallinn)], 37–52. Tallinn: Tallinna Ülikool.

Argus, Reili. 2009. The early development of case and number in Estonian. In Ursula Stephany & Maria D. Voeikova (eds.), *Development of nominal inflection in first language acquisition. A cross-linguistic perspective* (Studies on Language Acquisition 30), 111–152. Berlin & New York: Mouton de Gruyter.

Argus, Reili, Kadri Suurmäe, Andra Kütt & Anne Tamm. 2014a. Eesti keele evidentsiaalsuse omandamisest: mõistmiskatse tulemused [Acquisition of evidentiality in Estonian: The results of a comprehension task]. *Tallinna eesti keele ja kultuuri instituudi toimetised* [Proceedings of the Institute of Estonian Language and Culture of Tallinn University] 16, 83–101. Tallinn: Tallinna Ülikooli Kirjastus.

Argus, Reili, Kadri Suurmäe & Anne Tamm. 2014b. Evidentsiaalid: kas uskuda või mitte? Teabe vormi mõju eesti koolieelikute käitumisele [Evidential sentences guiding Estonian preschoolers' exploration of novel objects and their properties]. *Emakeele Seltsi aastaraamat* [Papers of Estonian Mother Tongue Society] 59. 244–261.

Bittner, Dagmar, Wolfgang Uwe Dressler, Marianne Kilani-Schoch. 2003. Introduction. In D. Bittner, W. U. Dressler & M. Kilani-Schoch (eds), *Development of verb inflection in first language acquisition: A cross-linguistic perspective* (Studies on Language Acquisition 21), vii–xxxvii. Berlin & New York: Mouton de Gruyter.

Bybee, Joan. 2010. *Language, usage, and cognition*. Cambridge: Cambridge University Press.

Choi, Soonja. 2006. Acquisition of modality. In William Frawley (ed.), *The expression of modality*, 141–172. Berlin & New York: Mouton de Gruyter.

Christofidou, Anastasia & Ursula Stephany. 2003. Early phases in the development of Greek verb inflection. In Dagmar Bittner, Wolfgang U. Dressler & Marianne Kilani-Schoch (eds.), *Development of verb inflection in first language acquisition: A cross-linguistic perspective* (Studies on Language Acquisition 21), 89–129. Berlin & New York: Mouton de Gruyter.

Gagarina, Natalia. 2003. The early development and demarcation of stages in three Russian-speaking children. In Dagmar Bittner, Wolfgang U. Dressler & Marianne Kilani-Schoch (eds.), *Development of verb inflection in first language acquisition: A cross-linguistic perspective* (Studies on Language Acquisition 21), 131–169. Berlin & New York: Mouton de Gruyter.

Katičić, Antigone. 2003. Early verb development in one Croatian-speaking child. In Dagmar Bittner, Wolfgang U. Dressler & Marianne Kilani-Schoch (eds.), *Development of verb inflection in first language acquisition: A cross-linguistic perspective* (Studies on Language Acquisition 21), 239–267. Berlin & New York: Mouton de Gruyter.

Kazakovskaya, Victoria & Reili Argus 2016. Acquisition of epistemic marking in Estonian and Russian. *Eesti Rakenduslingvistika Ühingu aastaraamat* [Estonian Papers in Applied Linguistics] 12. 57–80.

Kõrgesaar, Helen. 2014. Eesti isade-emade hoidjakeel: kes küsib, kes käsutab, kes räägib rohkem? [Estonian fathers' and mothers' child-directed speech: who asks more questions, who gives orders, who speaks more?]. *Tallinna eesti keele ja kultuuri instituudi toimetised* [Proceedings of the Institute of Estonian Language and Culture of Tallinn University] 16, 59–81. Tallinn: Tallinna Ülikooli Kirjastus.

Laalo, Klaus. 2003. Early verb development in Finnish: A preliminary approach to miniparadigms. In Dagmar Bittner, Wolfgang U. Dressler & Marianne Kilani-Schoch (eds.), *Development of verb inflection in first language acquisition: A cross-linguistic perspective* (Studies on Language Acquisition 21), 323–350. Berlin & New York: Mouton de Gruyter.

MacWhinney, Brian. 2000. *The CHILDES project. Tools for analyzing talk*. Mahwah, NJ: Lawrence Erlbaum Associates.

Mauri, Caterina & Andrea Sansò. 2011. How directive constructions emerge. Grammaticalization, constructionalization, cooptation. *Journal of Pragmatics* 43.

3489–3521. (http://www.sciencedirect.com/science/article/pii/S0378216611002189). (accessed 30. 10.2017)

Metslang, Helle. 1981. *Küsilause eesti keeles* [The interrogative clause in Estonian]. Tallinn: Valgus.

Metslang, Helle. 2001. Eesti *las*-imperatiivivormist partikliks [Estonian *las* – from imperative verb form to particle]. In Congressus Nonus Internationalis Fenno-Ugristarum: 7. – 13.8.2000, Tartu: Pars V, Dissertationes sectionum: Linguistica II / redegit: Tõnu Seilenthal; curaverunt: Anu Nurk, Triinu Palo, 1372–1377. Tartu: Tartu University.

Metslang, Helle. 2004. Imperative and related matters in everyday Estonian. *Linguistica Uralica* XL(4). 243–256.

Pajusalu, Renate. 2014. Palved eesti, soome ja vene keeles: grammatika pragmaatika teenistuses [Requests in Estonian, Finnish and Russian: grammar serves pragmatics]. *Eesti Rakenduslingvistika Ühingu aastaraamat* [Estonian Papers in Applied Linguistics] 10. 241–257.

Pajusalu, Renate, Pirkko Tõugu, Maigi Vija & Tiia Tulviste. 2011. Konditsionaali omandamisest eesti lapsekeeles [The acquisition of the Estonian conditional in child language]. *Eesti Rakenduslingvistika Ühingu aastaraamat* [Estonian Papers in Applied Linguistics] 7. 141–156.

Rääbis, Andriela. 2012. Direktiivisekventsid isa ja tütre suhtluses: juhtumianalüüs. [Directive sequences in a conversation of father and daughter: A case study]. *Eesti Rakenduslingvistika Ühingu aastaraamat* [Estonian Papers in Applied Linguistics] 8. 213–230.

Salo, Age. 1995. Eesti keele verbivormistiku omandamine vanuses 1;5–3;1 [Acquisition of Estonian verbal inflection at age 1;5–3;1]. Tartu: Tartu ülikool, Tartu University MA thesis.

Stephany, Ursula. 1986. Modality. In Paul Fletcher & Michael Garman (eds.), *Language acquisition: Studies in first language development*, 375–400. 2nd edn. Cambridge: Cambridge University Press.

Stephany, Ursula. 1993. Modality in language acquisition: The state of the art. In Norbert Dittmar & Astrid Reich (eds.), *Modality in language acquisition*, 133–144. Berlin & New York: Walter de Gruyter.

Stephany, Ursula & Maria D. Voeikova. 2015. Requests, their meanings and aspectual forms in early Greek and Russian child language. *Journal of Greek Linguistics* 15(1). 66–90.

Tamm, Anne. 2015. Negation in Estonian. In Matti Miestamo, Anne Tamm & Beáta Wagner-Nagy (eds.), *Negation in Uralic languages*, 399–432. Amsterdam: John Benjamins.

Tamm, Anne, Reili Argus, Andra Kütt, Airi Kapanen & Kadri Suurmäe. 2015. Evidentsiaalsuse ja episteemilise modaalsuse suhetest eesti lastekeeles käitumiskatsete põhjal [Evidentiality and epistemic modality are combined in the Estonian morpheme *-vat* but are different categories in acquisition: experimental evidence]. *Eesti Rakenduslingvistika Ühingu aastaraamat* [Estonian Papers in Applied Linguistics] 11. 236–280.

Tomasello, Michael. 2003. *Constructing a language. A usage-based theory of language acquisition*. Cambridge, MA & London: Harvard University Press.

Tomasello, Michael. 2009. The usage-based theory of language acquisition. In Edith L. Bavin (ed.), *The Cambridge handbook of child language*, 69–87. Cambridge: Cambridge University Press.

Tomasello, Michael. 2010. *Origins of human communication*. Cambridge, MA: MIT Press.

Torn-Leesik, Reeli. 2007. Voice and modal verbs in Estonian. *Linguistica Uralica* XLIII (3). 176–186.

Tragel, Ilona. 2001. Eesti *saama* ja *võima* ning soome *saada* ja *voida*. Tähendused ja vastavused kognitiivse grammatika vaatenurgast [Estonian *saama* and *võima* and Finnish *saada* and *voida*. Meanings and counterparts from the perspective of cognitive grammar]. *Keel ja Kirjandus* [Language and Literature] 2. 99–110.

Uuspõld, Ellen. 1989. Modaalsusest ja modaalsest predikaadist eesti keeles [Modality and modal predicates in Estonian]. *Keel ja Kirjandus* [Language and Literature] 8. 468–477.

Viitso, Rein. 2003. Structure of Estonian language. Phonology, morphology and word formation. In Mati Erelt (ed.), *Estonian Language* (Linguistica Uralica, Supplementary Series 1), 9–129. Tallinn: Estonian Academy Publishers.

Vija, Maigi, Reeli Torn-Leesik & Renate Pajusalu. 2009. Tegumood eesti lapsekeeles [Voice constructions in Estonian child language]. *Eesti Rakenduslingvistika Ühingu aastaraamat* [Estonian Papers in Applied Linguistics] 7. 329–344.

Wojcik, Pavel. 2003. Early verb inflection in Lithuanian. In Dagmar Bittner, Wolfgang U. Dressler & Marianne Kilani-Schoch (eds.), *Development of verb inflection in first language acquisition: A cross-linguistic perspective* (Studies on Language Acquisition 21), 401–420. Berlin & New York: Mouton de Gruyter.

Klaus Laalo
Directives in Finnish language acquisition

Abstract: This article examines the means of expressing agent-oriented modality in Finnish from a developmental perspective with particular attention to directives, especially requests. For this purpose the spontaneous speech of two children, aged 1;7–2;6, as well as that of their caregivers is analyzed. The kinds of formal means used in early child language as well as their functions are traced in the course of time. The results show a wide variety of expressions with directive functions in child-directed speech as well as child speech. The first directives to emerge in child speech are 2nd person singular imperatives and verbless requests followed soon by simple passive forms. Modal expressions occurring in child speech include most of the types found in child-directed speech, excluding certain more indirect and polite expressions such as conditional forms, suggestions formulated as questions, and passive forms mitigated in different ways.

1 Introduction

In the present article, the development of directives, especially requests, in Finnish child language is examined in the speech of two children. The child-directed speech (CDS) of their caregivers is also studied in order to determine the models made available to the children as well as the directive types to emerge later in child speech (CS). The aim of the study is to give a comprehensive overview of the development of the forms and functions of directives in early Finnish language acquisition until the age of 2;6 or 2;10.

Directives are speech acts used in situations where the speaker's goal is to get others to do what he wants them to. This is a fundamental human communicative motive (Tomasello 2010: 84). Directives not only include commands (direct requests for action), but also mitigated requests such as suggestions and invitations (indirect requests). These speech acts constitute a functional category expressed by a variety of lexical, inflectional and syntactic means.

The theoretical background of this study is constructivist and usage-based. The child is assumed to learn the language by observing and comprehending the linguistic means used by others interacting with him or her (input) and producing utterances which are in the beginning rote-learned and directly based

Klaus Laalo, Tampere University

https://doi.org/10.1515/9781501504457-010

on the models offered by the input; later the child proceeds to a more creative stage and starts to produce analogical formations and other novel expressions. In the framework of pre- and protomorphology the analogical innovations and the miniparadigms (paradigms consisting of at least three different forms of the same lexeme) are regarded as important steps in the child's language development (Dressler, Kilani-Schoch and Klampfer 2003).

Forms and functions of Finnish directives are presented in section 2 as far as these are relevant for the description of early CS and CDS. Previous studies on the acquisition of modality in Finnish are reported in section 3. After the presentation of the data in section 4, the means of expressing requests and other directives are examined in the longitudinal data of two children and their CDS in section 5. In section 6, the results are summarized and some general conclusions are drawn.

2 Forms and functions of agent-oriented modality in Finnish

2.1 Forms and functions of directives

Directives are modalized utterances that fall under the scope of deontic modality, one of the two domains of agent-oriented modality. While deontic modality is concerned with obligation and permission, dynamic modality covers volition and capability.

The most important means for expressing directives in Finnish are certain forms of full verbs and a group of modal verbs. However, especially in early child language, verbless directives consisting of a noun or adverb also occur. Furthermore, there are several ways of expressing directives in an indirect way, especially so in adult language. A comprehensive presentation of modal expressions in standard Finnish is to be found in Kangasniemi (1992).

Each Finnish finite verb form can carry at most one modal or temporal suffix attached to the active or passive stem and in addition a final personal suffix as well as clitics, for example the interrogative clitic *–kO*. The major Finnish verb forms expressing deontic modality are the imperative, the conditional, passive forms and the third infinitive illative constructions, which may express both singular and plural (Table 1). These devices will be described in the following sections.

Table 1: Major Finnish verb forms expressing deontic modality.

	SG	PL
IMP	*syö!* eat.IMP.2SG 'eat!' *syö-kö-ön* eat-IMP-3SG '(s)he shall eat'	*syö-kää!* eat-IMP.2PL 'eat!' *syö-kö-öt* eat-IMP-3PL 'they shall eat'
COND	*tul-isi-t-ko?* come-COND-2SG-CLIT 'would you come?'	*tul-isi-tte-ko?* come-COND-2PL-CLIT 'would you come?'
PASS		*men-nään* go-PASS 'let's go!' *men-nään-kö?* go-PASS-CLIT 'shall we go?'
INF3-ILL	*syö-mä-än* eat-INF3-ILL 'come and eat!' *nukku-ma-an* sleep-INF3-ILL 'you must go to bed'	

2.2 Finnish imperatives

Imperative forms are the most important means for expressing deontic modality in Finnish. There are two imperative systems in the language: the formal paradigm and the colloquial paradigm of contemporary spoken Finnish (Table 2). The colloquial imperative paradigm is used in CDS and CS.

While the two paradigms are identical in the 2nd and 3rd persons, their most important difference is that in colloquial Finnish the first person plural is replaced by the passive.

Second person imperatives form a productive part of verb inflection and are used to express direct requests (commands). Third person imperatives are especially used in frozen idioms such as congratulations (example 1).

(1) *Onne-ksi   ol-ko-on!*
    luck-TRANSL be-IMP-3SG
    'Congratulations!'

Table 2: The imperative paradigm of colloquial Finnish.

	SG	PL
1	–	syö-dään eat-PASS 'let's eat'
2	syö eat.IMP.2SG 'eat'	syö-kää eat-IMP.2PL 'eat'
3	syö-kö-ön eat-IMP.3SG '(s)he may eat'	syö-kö-öt eat-IMP.3PL 'they may eat'

In the first person plural of the colloquial paradigm the passive used with a hortative function expresses suggestions rather than commands. As is common with hortatives in other languages (Aikhenvald 2010: 52–53) this form has an inclusive meaning implying the participation of both the addressee and the speaker. In contrast to the passive used with a hortative meaning in colloquial Finnish, the formal 1st person plural imperative carrying the imperative suffix -kAA is used almost exclusively in ceremonial phrases and certain conventional expressions (example 2).

(2) otta-kaa-mme   esimerki-ksi.
     take-IMP-1PL   example-TRANSL
     'Let us take as an example.'

Lauranto (2013: 178) found that in recorded telephone conversations the function of the first person plural inclusive imperative was nearly exclusively expressed by the passive rather than the formal -kAAmme form (1 in 57 tokens).

In spoken Finnish 3rd person singular and plural imperatives are often confounded. This may have originated in affective speech but is nowadays quite general. Thus, the third person plural imperative may be used in referring to a singular argument as in the lexicalized 3rd person plural imperative *olkoot* 'never mind' in example (3) (literally 'let it be', instead of the singular *olkoon* with the same meaning). Illustrative examples from adult spoken Finnish concerning this tendency to mix up the singular and plural third person imperatives are found in Yli-Vakkuri (1986: 60).

(3) Boy, 3;10 (from Toivainen 1980: 35)
   tämä on-kin   rikki.   ol-ko-ot.
   this be.3SG-CLIT broken be-IMP-3PL
   'Oh, this is broken. Never mind.'

The forms preferably used in both CDS and CS are the colloquial 2nd person singular and plural imperatives as well as the passive. The latter mainly functions as the 1st person plural inclusive imperative.

In about one third of the languages of the world the 2nd person singular imperative is identical to the verb stem (Aikhenvald 2010: 18). Although this is also mainly the case in Finnish, in the spoken language an additional marker of the imperative may be present. Thus, if the word following a 2nd person singular imperative form begins with a consonant, this consonant is realized as the final sound of the imperative, for example *annas se minu-lle* 'give it to.me-ALL'. But this consonant gemination is not realized in early child speech so that the bare stem is used, e.g. *anna* 'give.IMP.2SG', *sano* 'say.IMP.2SG', *tule* 'come.IMP.2SG'.

The negated imperative expressing prohibitions consists of the negative auxiliary constructed with a main verb. Negative 2nd person imperatives are formed with *älä* (2SG) or *älkää* (2PL) 'don't', the latter of which carries an imperative ending (example 4). In the 2nd person singular negative imperative main verbs only have the weak stem (e.g. *älä nuku* 'don't.2SG sleep'), but in the 2nd person plural the suffix *-kO* is attached to the strong stem of the main verb (e.g. *älkää nukku-ko* 'don't sleep'). In the 2nd person singular, there is no *kO*-suffix on the main verb and the auxiliary has no suffix either (example 5).

(4) Boy, 3;10 (from Toivainen 1980: 35)
   äl-kää   tul-ko!
   AUX.NEG-IMP.2PL come-IMP.NEG
   'Don't come!' (plural)

(5) Boy, 3;10 (from Toivainen 1980: 35)
   älä   tule!
   AUX.NEG.2SG come.IMP.NEG
   'Don't come!' (singular)

In colloquial speech, negative imperatives of both the 1st person plural and the passive are expressed by a combination of the basic form of the negation verb *ei* (3rd person singular indicative, also grammaticalized as a negative adverb) and the passive stem of the verb, e.g. *ei men-nä* (NEG go-PASS 'let's not go') (Table 3).

Table 3: The colloquial paradigm of the Finnish negative imperative (prohibitive).

	SG	PL
1	–	ei syö-dä NEG eat-PASS 'we shall not eat'
2	älä syö ~ e-t syö NEG eat.IMP ~ NEG-2SG eat.IMP 'don't eat'	äl-kää syö-kö ~ e-tte syö NEG-IMP.2PL eat-IMP ~ NEG-2PL eat.IMP 'don't eat'
3		äl-kö-ön syö-kö ~ äl-kö-öt syö-kö NEG-IMP-3SG eat-IMP ~ NEG-IMP-3PL eat-IMP '(s)he ~ they shall not eat'
PASS		ei syö-dä NEG eat-PASS 'let's not eat'

Negated second person singular and plural present indicative forms are used as alternatives of negated imperatives, e.g. *e-t mene* (NEG-2SG go.NEG) 'you don't go'. Both negated 3rd person imperative and passive forms are neutral with regard to the number distinction. In contrast to 1st and 2nd person imperatives, third person imperative forms are only infrequently found in CS and CDS.

2.3 Other forms used with directive functions

Conditional forms are a more polite way to express directives. These forms distinguish the second and third person singular and plural (see Table 1 above).

The so-called Finnish "passives", which are actually pseudopassives, are important forms for expressing indirect requests. They are 4th person indefinite verb forms which presuppose an actor and are neutral to the distinction between singular and plural. These forms are often used in spoken Finnish in the function of 1st person plural forms for expressing hortatives including the speaker and the addressee and are suggestions rather than commands (see Seppänen 1989: 202–207). Directives in the passive may be mitigated by the conditional as for example in *men-tä-isi-in-kö* (go-PASS-COND-PASS-CLIT) 'should we go?'.

Another way to express hortatives are illative forms of the 3rd infinitive (see Table 1). These are formed by the *mA*-suffix with the illative case suffix added and express motion towards some place (e.g. *syö-mä-än* (eat-INF3-ILL) 'let's go and eat'). An example of this construction typically used in daily routines in CDS is *nukku-ma-an* (sleep-INF3-ILL) 'let's go and sleep'.

Besides the inflectional forms of full verbs discussed so far, Finnish also possesses modal verbs for expressing different degrees of modal strength. The constructions illustrated by examples (6) convey deontic necessity, i.e. an obligation to act. These expressions can be used for a generally admitted necessity. If the relevant parameters are specified in the context, it is possible to eliminate a complement (examples 6a–d) or specify the performer of the action by a noun phrase in the genitive (examples 6e–g). In many constructions the main verb is in the first infinitive form, which is the basic infinitive without any case suffix.

(6) a. *pitä-ä   teh-dä.*
       must-3SG do-INF1
       'One must do.'
    b. *täyty-y   teh-dä.*
       must-3SG do-INF1
       'One has to do.'
    c. *on   pakko   teh-dä.*
       be.3SG necessity do-INF1
       'It is necessary to be done.'
    d. *on   teh-tä-vä.*
       be.3SG do-PASS-PRS.PTCP
       'It must be done.'
    e. *Ulla-n   pitä-ä   teh-dä.*
       Ulla-GEN must-3SG do-INF1
       'Ulla must do.'
    f. *sinu-n   täyty-y   teh-dä.*
       you-GEN   must-3SG do-INF1
       'You have to do.'
    g. *minu-n   on   pakko   sano-a.*
       I-GEN   be.3SG necessity say-INF1
       'I must say.'

The modal verb *saada* 'may' expresses the deontic notion of permission (example 7a) and *voida* 'can' may render both deontic possibility and dynamic ability (example 7b). When these verbs are negated they convey prohibition (example 7c) or impossibility (example 7d).

(7) a. *saa teh-dä.*
 may do-INF1
 'One may do.'
 b. *voi teh-dä.*
 can do-INF1
 'It can be done.'
 c. *ei saa teh-dä.*
 NEG may do-INF1
 'It must not be done.'
 d. *ei voi teh-dä.*
 NEG can do-INF1
 'It cannot be done.'

From early on, children often use a two-syllabic variant of the 3rd person singular form of the verb *haluta* 'want', namely *halu-u* (full form *halua-a*) (want-3SG) 'wants' to express their desires. Such expressions may function as indirect requests (example 8). As has been found in many languages, young children commonly refer to themselves by the 3rd person singular before having acquired the so-called shifters of the 1st and 2nd person.

(8) *halu-u leikki-mä-än.*
 want-3SG play-INF3-ILL
 'He/she wants to play.' (= 'I want to play.')

Verbless requests are also commonly found in early Finnish child data as well as in colloquial Finnish. Thus, the adverb *uudelleen* 'again' may be used when one wants something to be repeated. Other verbless directives consist of nouns in certain case forms including partitives such as *maito-a* (milk-PARTIT) 'some milk' and illatives, e.g. *syli-in* (lap-ILL) 'into the lap'.

3 Previous studies on the acquisition of modality in Finnish

Although the acquisition of modality by Finnish children has not been the subject of intensive studies so far, there are a number of interesting observations to be found in Toivainen's and Kauppinen's work (Toivainen 1980, 1997; Kauppinen 1982, 1998). Toivainen (1980) examines the acquisition of suffixes occurring in directives such as the imperative and the passive. Toivainen (1997: 107, 110–111) in addition presents some other means of expressing modality in Finnish.

Kauppinen (1982: 150–156) discusses different types of negation in the early speech of a Finnish-speaking boy. In Kauppinen (1998) she analyzes the functions of conditional forms in Finnish CS, e.g. in play situations when planning and suggesting something. The conditional is used in suggestions occurring in children's role play in much the same way as e.g. the past tense in English: *You were mother and she didn't want you to go* (Lodge 1978).

The development of certain directive expressions is reported in detail in Kauppinen 1998. In her data (Kauppinen 1998: 60), the verb *haluta* 'want' is first used at the age of 1;11 in a simplified, suffixless form *alu* (< *haluu* ~ *haluaa*). At 2;0–2;4, the 3rd person singular form appears, once at 2;0 in a shortened form *alu* accompanied by the first person singular personal pronoun. Finally, starting at 2;4, the 1st person singular ending is used (*halua-n* 'want-PRS.1SG', 'I want to').

Toivainen's and Kauppinen's findings will be discussed in more detail below, along with the analysis of the data on which the present study is based.

It has been noted that the earliest functional distinction of verb forms is that between modal and non-modal ones (for Greek see Stephany 1985: 115 and for Turkish Terziyan and Aksu-Koç, this volume). Finnish children typically first distinguish between 2nd person singular imperatives and 3rd person singular indicatives (Toivainen 1980: 44–48). Similar results have also been found for Spanish (Aguirre 2003: 5, 21), Croatian (Katičić 2003: 246), Lithuanian (Wojcik 2003: 409), and Russian (Gagarina 2003: 146). In German (Klampfer 2003: 306–307) and Russian (Voeikova and Bayda, this volume) infinitives used in both a modal and non-modal function are among children's first verb forms. Due to their formal complexity Finnish infinitives are acquired only later.

4 The data

The data in the present study consist of recordings and diary material from two Finnish-speaking children, a girl called Mari and a boy called Tomi.[1] The data are basically the same as those analyzed in Laalo (2003) and Laalo (2011). The number of utterances of the diary data and the duration of the recording sessions are presented in Tables 4a and 4b. Other materials, such as the recordings of 25 Finnish-speaking children aged 1–3 years (Toivainen 1980), will be used for comparison.

---

[1] Mari and Tomi are pseudonyms for the children's real names used in former studies.

Table 4a: Diary data of Mari and Tomi.

Age range	Mari	Tomi
	utterances	
until 1;8	1,000	1,000
1;9–1;11	1,500	1.000
2;0–2;6	2,000	1,300

Table 4b: Recordings of Mari and Tomi.

Age	Mari	Tomi
	minutes	
1;6		30
1;7	96	30
1;8	120	30
1;9	90	60
1;10	30	60
1;11	90	60
2;0		60
2;1	120	30
2;2	105	60
2;3	30	60
2;4	60	60
2;5	90	60
2;6	90	60
2;8	60	
2;9	60	
2;10	60	

5 Results

5.1 Directives in CDS

Although CDS provides important models for language acquisition, only certain aspects are adopted by the children so that important differences exist between CS and CDS. One of these is that requests are softened by questions and turned into suggestions in CDS but not in CS. Such mitigations typically consist of conditional forms of full verbs used in the passive and of modal verb constructions.

Tables 5 and 6 present the different expressions of directives found in the early recordings of Mari's and Tomi's CDS.

Table 5: Expressions of directives in Mari's CDS (tokens).

	1;7	1;8	1;9	1;10	1;11
PASS	1	≤4	≥5	1	≤4
PASS + Q	≤4	≤4	≥5	1	≥5
PASS NEG					1
PASS COND + Q					≤4
COND					1
COND + Q		1			
PRS.2/3SG + Q	2SG ≤4	3SG ≤4			3SG ≥5
IMP.2SG		1	≥5	≥5	1	≥5
IMP.2SG NEG					1
IMP.3SG			1		
MDL.V	1	≥5	≤4	1	≥5
MDL.V COND	1	≥5		1	≥5
MDL.V NEG					≤4
haluaa 'wants to'	1	1	≤4		≥5
tahtoo 'wants to'		3SG ≤4	≤4		2SG 1
*tahto.*COND 'would like to'			≤4		2SG 1

Table 6: Expressions of directives in Tomi's CDS (tokens).

	1;7	1;8	1;9	1;10	1;11	2;0
PASS	1	≤4	≤4		≤4	1
PASS + Q	≤4	≤4	1	1	1	1
PASS NEG			1			1
PASS COND						1
COND NEG					1	
PRS.2/3SG + Q	3SG≤4	3SG 1			2SG≤4	2SG 1
MDL.V	≥5	≥5	≥5	≥5	≥5	
MDL.V NEG			≤4	1	1	
MDL.V COND	1	1	≤4		≤4	
IMP.2SG	≥5	≤4	≥5	≥5	≥5	≥5
IMP.2SG NEG		1			≤4	
IMP.3SG						1
haluaa 'wants to'		≤4				
tahtoo 'wants to'					1	

Directives expressed by passive forms or modal verb constructions are found in CDS in all these recordings. They are typically used in suggestions for actions where both the speaker and the addressee are involved. The suggestions are often formulated as questions, thus having the interrogative enclitic particle *–kO* attached to the passive form. Passives used in suggestions may also carry other enclitic particles for mitigating purposes; for example, the particle *-pA(s)*, e.g. *ote-taan-pas* (take-PASS-CLIT) 'let us take'. Example (9) is a typical mitigated directive chosen from CDS.

(9) CDS, Mari, 1;11
  (referring to a stone collection)
  FAT: *ruve-tta-(i)s(iin)-ko me tutki-ma-an Tuuliki-n*
  start-PASS-COND-CLIT we study-INF3-ILL Tuulikki-GEN
  kiv-i-ä?
  stone-PL-PARTIT
  'Should we start to examine Tuulikki's stones?'

Prohibitions are usually expressed by negated 3rd person singular present forms of modal verbs such as *ei saa* 'must not', *ei voi* 'cannot' and *ei tarvitse* 'need not'. In a few instances negated forms of the passive and conditional are used. The most direct way of expressing prohibitions is by the negated form of the 2nd person singular imperative. There are more negated 2nd person singular imperative forms to be found in Tomi's CDS (especially at 1;11) than in Mari's. The reason is that with Mari, a greater number of softer directives expressed by the conditional are used than with Tomi.

Some forms occur only once or twice. For example, the 3rd person imperative is used in concessive-type expressions such as *ol-koon nyt* (be-IMP.3SG ADV) 'let it be'.

The 2nd person singular imperative is the most frequent form used for requests in CDS and occurs in at least one instance in each of both children's recordings. An especially frequent imperative form found in both children's recordings is *kato* 'look.IMP.2SG' meaning 'note, be aware' and drawing the child's attention to something. In addition, *kuule* 'listen' is frequent in Tomi's CDS from 1;6–1;8 and 1;10–1;11 but is absent from Mari's. Both of these imperatives, requesting actions for the addressee's rather than the speaker's benefit, are also generally used in adult-directed speech (about *kato* in this function see Hakulinen and Seppänen 1992).

Since only one of the two siblings was present during each of the recordings, 2nd person plural imperatives do not occur in CDS, although they are found in Mari's data when she is speaking to her toys (recordings 2;3, 2;6, 2;8 and 2;9).

Jussives expressed by the third person imperative are only rarely used by the caretakers. The first recorded instance is found in the mother's speech at Mari's age 1;9 (example 10).

(10) CDS, Mari, 1;9
   MOT: *no ol-ko-on   kala sitten vielä tä-ssä.*
         so be-IMP-3SG fish then   still here-INESS
         'Well, let the fish then still be here.' (referring to a toy)

In both children's CDS, directives are frequently expressed by modal verb constructions (see Tables 5 and 6 above). The modal verb *pitää* 'must' denoting deontic necessity is commonly used not only in CDS but also in spoken Finnish more generally (example 11).

(11) CDS, Mari, 1;8
   MOT: *miks nalle-n   pitä-ä   nukku-u?*
         why teddy.bear-GEN must-3SG sleep-INF1
         'Why must the teddy bear sleep?'

Several other ways of expressing indirect directives besides softened passives (see example 9 above) belong to CDS but are scarcely used by the children. For example, questions such as "can you reach the milk?" or "could you open the window?" must be pragmatically interpreted as requests for action rather than information.

Directives expressed by 3rd infinitive illative forms are typically used by the caretakers in daily routines: e.g., *syö-mä-än* (eat-INF3-ILL) 'come and eat' (invitation call) or 'let's go and eat' (suggestion or request), *nukku-ma-an* (sleep-INF3-ILL) 'let's go to sleep', *katso-ma-an* (look-INF3-ILL) 'come and see'. These forms are not observed in the recording sessions of CDS but only in CS when the children give instructions to their toy animals. In the early periods, the children use these forms only of a few verbs: e.g. Mari 1;6 *työmää* [for *syömään*] 'let's go and eat' and Tomi 1;8 *kattommaa* [for *katsomaan*] 'come and look', *ukkummaa* [for *nukkumaan*] 'let's go to sleep'.

5.2 The development of directive expressions in Mari's speech

5.2.1 The emergence of Mari's directive verb forms

The first two verb forms used by Mari were second person singular imperative and third person singular present indicative. From a formal point of view they may be taken to be basic verb forms because they are short and morphologically simple and may be used as building blocks in more complex forms to be acquired later. These forms are also basic from a functional point of view since the 3rd person singular indicative is the most neutral verb form being used for informing the interlocutor while the 2nd person singular imperative is the most simple verb form serving the instrumental use of language.

The first directive verb forms in Mari's speech are 2nd person singular imperatives, which were first recorded at 1;7. However, in the diary data, examples of imperative forms are found even earlier: 1;0 (k)ato 'look', 1;3 avaa 'open', 1;4 anna 'give', pa(ne) 'put on' (the light), 1;5 ota 'take', pese 'wash' and 1;6 pelaa 'play'. From 1;7 on, Mari enlarges her inventory of verbs used in the 2nd person singular imperative every month; e.g. 1;7 notta [for nosta] 'lift', pyyhi 'wipe off', 1;8 tule 'come', työ [for syö] 'eat', mene 'go'.

The next verb forms Mari uses in requests in addition to imperatives are passive and 3rd infinitive illative forms. According to the diary data, her first passive form with a directive function already emerged at 1;4, namely the formulaic men-nään (GO-PASS) 'let's go' (Laalo 2003: 327, 332). After several months during which this had been her only passive form, the girl added negative passives with a modal meaning (see below).

Typical early passives in Finnish CS are 1;4 katotaa [for katsotaan] 'let's watch', 1;4 mennään 'let's go' (Laalo 2003: 327, 332), and 1;8 luetaan 'let's read' (Toivainen 1980: 56–57, 1997: 106).

A typical colloquial way of using the passive for making suggestions is in negated forms of the first person plural. Such examples occur in Mari's speech from 1;11 on, yet the diary data show that she already used them at 1;8 (examples 12 and 13).

(12) Mari, 1;8
     ei   lähde-tä vielä.
     NEG go-PASS yet
     'Let's not leave yet.'

(13) Mari, 1;8
    ei   men-nä tinne [for *sinne*].
    not go-PASS   there
    'Let's not go there.'

Another type of verb forms used with a directive function to emerge early in Mari's speech is the 3rd infinitive illative. An example occurring in the diary data from 1;6 on is *syö-mä-än* (eat-INF3-ILL) 'let's go and eat' used by Mari when calling her toy animals for meals. A likely reason for the early acquisition of such infinitives is that they are frequently used in CDS during daily routines. In the recordings 3rd infinitive illatives occur when Mari engages in performing daily routines with her toys.

Finally, another important verb form category developing in Mari's speech for expressing directives is the 2nd person plural imperative. As described in section 2, with many verbs the 2nd plural imperative is formed by just adding the suffix *-kAA* to the 2nd person singular imperative, but there are numerous exceptions for several verb types which require stem alternations before this suffix. Children, however, initially often use the simple principle of just adding the suffix to the 2nd person singular imperative of all verbs (Laalo 2011: 243–244) and so did Mari. As is common in child speech, she only started to overgeneralize such imperative forms after first having used the correct forms imitated from CDS. Mari's first 2nd person plural imperative is the correct reproduction of the standard form *pysy-kää* (stay-IMP.2PL) 'stay (here)' noted in the diary data at 1;8 and also at 1;9 in the expression *pysy-kää tässä* (stay-IMP.2PL here) 'stay here'. In the recordings this form does not occur until 2;3.

In view of the fact that the formation of the 2nd person plural imperative is complicated, Mari produced some interesting analogical forms. In verbs with consonant gradation, 2nd person singular imperatives have weak grade but 2nd person plural imperatives strong grade, e.g. *anna* 'give' (2SG, weak grade *nn*) vs. *anta-kaa* 'give' (2PL, strong grade *nt*). In verbs having both a consonantal and a vowel stem the final stem vowel *e* is preserved in the 2nd person singular (vowel stem with final *e*) but dropped in the 2nd person plural imperative (consonantal stem without *e*) in front of the *-kAA* suffix (e.g., *tule* 'come.IMP.2SG', *tul-kaa* 'come-IMP.2PL'). Even more complex alternations of stem formation occur in the imperative of contracted verbs such as *irtoa* 'get loose (IMP.2SG)' vs. *irrot-kaa* 'get loose (IMP.2PL)', *haukkaa* 'take a bite (IMP.2SG)' vs. *haukat-kaa* 'take a bite (IMP.2PL)'.

The first 2nd person plural imperatives were repetitions of standard forms. Later the child constructed her own analogical forms resulting from the overuse of the principle of forming 2nd person plural imperatives by simply adding the suffix *–kAA* to the singular form. This is theoretically interesting because it shows that the child starts to actively process linguistic material. Examples of Mari's analogical formations of contracted verbs are presented in (14) and (15).

(14) Mari, 2;7
 nyt   leego-t   irto-kaa [for irrot-kaa].
 now   lego-PL   loosen-IMP.2PL
 ne   irto-s.
 they loosen-PST
 'Now lego bricks, come loose.
 They came loose.' (after separating them)

(15) Mari, 2;10
 haukkaa-kaa [for haukat-kaa]   ruoka-a.
                bite-IMP.2PL   food-PARTIT
 'Now take a bite of the food.'

An example of an analogical formation of the negated 2nd person plural imperative, which is also quite intricate in standard Finnish, is *äl-kää tule* [for *äl-kää tul-ko*] (NEG-IMP.2PL come-IMP.NEG) 'don't come' at 1;11. The model for this analogical formation is the 2nd person singular imperative negated form *älä tule* (NEG.IMP.2SG come.IMP.NEG) 'don't come'. Mari uses the same verb correctly in the simpler positive imperative *tul-kaa* 'come-IMP.2PL'.

Third person imperatives rarely occur in Mari's data. In one of the infrequent but typical examples (16) she repeats her mother's utterance word for word making an indirect request of eating some biscuits.

(16) Mari, 2;5
 ol-koon   nyt näin joulu-n   alla.
 be-IMP.3SG now so   Christmas-GEN   under
 'Let it be so before Christmas.'

Mari expresses indirect prohibitions constructed with the 3rd person singular indicative form of the negation verb *ei* and the negated form of the main verb in a standard form from age 1;8 on (examples 17 and 18).

(17) Mari, 1;8, diary data
 ei   äiti   auta.
 NEG.3SG   mother help.NEG
 'Mother does not help.' (meaning 'mother must not help')

(18) Mari, 1;8, diary data
   ei   isi   auta.   Tuuti itte   keinu-u.
   NEG.3SG father help.NEG   Tuuti herself swing-PRS.3SG
   'Father does not help (= must not help). Tuuti is swinging by herself.'[2]

Directive verb forms occurring in Mari's recordings from 1;7 through 2;10 are presented in Table 7 (see Laalo 2003: 327). As far as passives and 3rd infinitive illatives are concerned, only instances used as directives have been included in the counts[3] (example 19).

Table 7: Mari's directive verb forms (types/tokens).

Age	IMP 2SG	INF3 ILL	PASS	PASS NEG	IMP 2PL	IMP 2SG NEG	IMP 3SG	COND
1;7	3/3	–	–	–	–	–	–	–
1;8	8/12	1/2	3/9	–	–	–	–	–
1;9	3/3	–	2/3	–	–	–	–	–
1;10	3/3	1/1	4/5	–	–	–	–	–
1;11	4/5	–	7/9	1/1	–	–	–	–
2;1	7/11	–	–	1/1	–	3/3	–	–
2;2	5/6	1/1	11/24	–	–	2/2	–	–
2;3	3/13	–	–	–	1/1	–	–	–
2;4	1/1	1/1	1/6	–	–	–	–	–
2;5	2/7	1/5	6/16	2/2	–	–	1/1	1/1
2;6	5/9	1/1	3/6	2/3	1/1	–	–	–
2;8	3/14	–	6/20	–	1/1	–	–	–
2;9	6/8	–	5/8	–	1/1	–	–	–
2;10	5/9	–	4/6	–	–	–	–	–

(19) Mari, 2;5
   hei   nyt   nukku-ma-an.
   hey   now   sleep-INF3-ILL
   'Now let's (go and) sleep.'

Many early directive verb forms, above all 2nd person singular imperatives, passives in a hortative function, and the 3rd infinitive illatives are so frequently used in Finnish CS that they are often included in the first miniparadigms of

---

[2] Tuuti is a nickname for Mari; the child is here referring to herself.
[3] In Laalo (2003) all verb forms are included, not only those used in directive function.

verbs emerging in the children's language. Four miniparadigms found in Mari's language at 1;8 are presented in Table 8 (based on Table 1 in Laalo 2011: 25).

Table 8: Mari's early miniparadigms at 1;8.

IMP.2SG	PRS.3SG	PST.3SG	PRS.PASS	PST.PASS	PASS.NEG
anna 'give'	anta-a give-3SG 'gives'	anto-i give-PST.3SG 'gave'			
mene 'go'	mene-e go-3SG 'goes'	men-i go-PST.3SG 'went'	men-nään go-PRS.PASS 'let's go'	men-tiin go-PST.PASS 'we went'	ei men-nä go-PASS.NEG 'let's not go'
syö 'eat'	syö eat.3SG 'eats'	sö-i eat-PST.3SG 'ate'	syö-dään eat-PRS.PASS 'let's eat'	syö-tiin eat-PRS.PASS 'we ate'	
tule 'come'	tule-e come-3SG 'comes'	tul-i come-PST.3SG 'came'		tul-tiin come-PST.PASS 'we came'	

5.2.2 Verbless directives in Mari's speech

In early Finnish child language (as well as in many other languages) directives are often expressed by verbless one-word utterances consisting of a noun or adverb. Such simple expressions may allow for more specific requests than the use of a verb in the imperative (e.g. *leipää!* 'bread.PARTIT!' vs. *anna!* 'give. IMP.2SG!'). The following adverbs and case forms of nouns expressing directives in Mari's speech are typical of early Finnish CS more generally:
a) The partitive of mass nouns denoting nourishments, such as *vet-tä* 'water-PARTIT' or *leipä-ä* 'bread-PARTIT';
b) illatives such as *koti-in* (home-ILL) '(let's go) home';
c) the partitive of the lexicalized adverb *lisä-ä* 'more-PARTIT';
d) other adverbs such as *uudelleen* 'again' (when the child wants some activities to be repeated), *luo* 'close', *hiljaa* 'quiet' and *pois* 'away' (when the child wants to leave or wants something to be removed).

Such one-word utterances in which the verb is omitted are often expanded by the caretakers so that e.g. *vet-tä* 'water-PARTIT' becomes *otetaan lisää vettä* 'let's have some more water', *pois* 'away' becomes *mene ~ mennä(än) pois* 'go ~ let's go away', and *uudelleen* 'again' becomes *lasketaan uudelleen* 'let's slide downhill again'.

Requests for food containing a noun in the partitive are used by Mari from early on (examples 20).

(20) a. Mari, 1;6
 bana-a [for banaani-a]
 'banana-PARTIT'
 b. Mari, 1;7
 vet-tä
 'water-PARTIT'
 c. Mari, 1;7
 lisää liha-a
 'more meat-PARTIT'

Desired actions to be performed with the help of a certain object may be expressed by naming the object in question in the partitive (example 21).

(21) Mari, 1;7
 (wanting to read a book in the livingroom)
 killa-a [for kirja-a] olohuone.
 book-PARTIT living.room
 'book in the living room.'

Requests or wishes for motion towards some place are expressed by the illative form of nouns (examples 22).

(22) a. Mari, 1;5
 koti-in
 home-ILL
 'home'
 b. Mari, 1;6
 syli-in
 lap-ILL
 'onto the lap'
 c. Mari, 1;6
 tä-hän
 this-ILL
 'here' (= put this here)

d. Mari, 1;7
   pois   kaappi-i(n)
   away   cupboard-ILL
   'away, into the cupboard'
e. Mari, 1;8
   äilin tylii [for *äidi-n   syli-in*]
                      mother-GEN lap-ILL
   'onto mother's lap'
f. Mari, 1;8
   yläkentaa [for *yläkerta-an*]
                    upstairs-ILL
   'upstairs' (wanting to climb upstairs)

Among the adverbs which Mari uses in her early requests are *ei* 'no(t)', *hiljaa* 'slowly, quietly', *lisää* 'more', *luo* 'close to', *pois* 'away', and *uudelleen* 'again'. These express negation, a way of acting, amount, direction, and repetition.

The first of these adverbs occurring in a request is *pois* 'away' at 1;4 (diary data, also in truncated forms such as *po, poo* etc.). Examples (23) and (24) illustrate the use of *pois*.

(23) Mari, 1;7
     kivi   pois.
     stone away
     '(Take) the stone away (from the avocado).'

(24) Mari, 1;8
     kello   pois   Tuuti(n)   käte-e(n)   vaihta-a.
     watch   away   Tuuti's   hand-ILL   switch-3SG
     'The watch away (from mother's hand), move (it) to Tuuti's hand.'

Mari also constructs *pois* with nouns in the elative expressing the source of the movement (example 25).

(25) Mari, 1;8
     pois   tuu-tta. [for *suu-sta*]
     away   mouth-ELAT
     'Away from the mouth.' (referring to a toy)

Verbless directives also include prohibitions and refusals. The simplest way to express them is by the negator *ei* 'no'. Mari sometimes intensified such requests by repeating the negator, e.g., *ei ei ei* at 1;6. A similar use of the negator by a boy aged 1;7 has been reported by Kauppinen (1982: 146–147). In CS, the expression *ei enää* 'no longer' used for stopping an activity may be shortened to the one-word utterance *enää*.

In sum, verbless directives play an important role in the early stages of language acquisition because a great number of quite different meanings may be simply expressed by one-word utterances. From 1;9 on, verbless directives are no longer used frequently because Mari has acquired additional means for expressing requests, above all many new verb forms. Also, from then on, adverbs are constructed with verbs rather than used in one-word utterances.

5.2.3 Directives expressed by modal verbs in Mari's speech

Mari started to use modal verb constructions with *pitää* 'must' and *ei saa* 'must not' already by 1;8. Such constructions are modeled on CDS since they are grammatically correct from the very beginning. Examples (26) and (27) from the diary data illustrate prohibitions expressed by a construction consisting of the negation particle *ei* and the modal verb *saa* 'may' in the 3rd person singular meaning 'must not'. This kind of prohibitions is typical of everyday speech.

(26) Mari, 1;8, diary data
 ei saa Juuso tönii.
 NEG must Juuso push
 'Juuso must not push.'

(27) Mari, 1;8, diary data
 ei äiti taa [for saa] nostaa Tuuti-a.
 not mother must lift Tuuti-PARTIT
 'Mother must not lift Tuuti.'

Examples such as (28) belong to daily routines and reflect behavioral rules occurring in CDS.

(28) Mari, 1;11, diary data
 pitä-ä puhalta-a.
 must-3SG blow-INF1
 'One must blow.' (noticing that the food is too hot)

5.2.4 Indirect requests with the verbs *haluta* 'want to' or *tahtoa* 'want to'

Wishes expressing indirect requests are found in Mari's speech from early on. A frequently occurring verb of desire is *haluta* 'want' (*haluu* ~ *haluaa* 'wants to') used in the 3rd person singular present indicative referring to the speaker (examples 29). The synonymous verb *tahtoa* 'want' (*tahtoo* 'wants to') is used with the same function (example 30).

(29) a. Mari, 1;8, diary data
Tuuti halu-u juutto-o.
Tuuti want-3SG cheese-PARTIT
'Tuuti wants some cheese.'
b. Mari, 1;8, diary data
äilim [for *äidi-n*] *massu(-lle) halu-u Tuuti.*
mother-GEN belly(-ALL) want-3SG Tuuti
'Tuuti wants (to lie) on mother's tummy.'

(30) Mari, 1;10, diary data
tahto-o syö-mä-ä(n) pöytä-ä(n).
want-3SG eat-INF3-ILL table-ILL
'(Mari) wants to eat at the table.'

5.3 The development of directive expressions in Tomi's speech

5.3.1 The emergence of Tomi's directive verb forms

The overall development of agent-oriented modality emerging from Tomi's data is quite similar to Mari's. The first directive verb forms to occur are 2nd person singular imperatives, passive forms with a hortative function, and 3rd infinitive illative forms (cf. Laalo 2011: 82–84). Frequently used imperatives are *anna* 'give' and *auta* 'help' (examples 31).

(31) Tomi
1;0 *anna* 'give', *avaa* 'open'
1;5 *auta* 'help', *tu(le)* 'come'
1;7 *istu* 'sit', *kat(s)o* 'look'
1;8 *puha(lla)* 'blow'

Passive present indicative forms in the function of the 1st person plural hortative expressing a joint action involving both the speaker and the addressee(s) are illustrated by examples (32).

(32) Tomi
    1;6 *pettää* [for *pestään*] 'we shall wash' (formulaic)
    1;8 *mennään* 'let's go'

3rd infinitive illatives expressing the child's suggestions to go in some direction and reach a goal or state are presented in examples (33).

(33) Tomi
    1;8 *katso-ma-an* (watch-INF3-ILL) 'let's watch'
    1;8 *nukku-ma-an* (sleep-INF3-ILL) 'let's sleep'

The grammatical categories of directive verb forms occurring in Tomi's recordings are presented in Table 9. The first verb forms used in requests are the three 2nd person singular imperatives found at 1;7. A month later, Tomi also uses passive present forms. 3rd infinitive illative forms occur at 1;9 in indirect requests.

Table 9: Tomi's directive verb forms (types/tokens).

Age	IMP. 2SG	INF3. ILL	PRS. PASS	PASS NEG	IMP.NEG. 2SG	PRS. 3SG
1;7	3/6	–	–	–	–	–
1;8	1	–	1	–	–	–
1;9	3/3	1/5	–	–	1/2	–
1;10	3/5	2/4	4/9	–	–	–
1;11	3/4	–	2/3	1/2	–	–
2;0	5/7	–	1/1	–	–	1/1
2;1	2/2	3/4	3/4	1/3	1/1	–
2;2	2/6	2/4	5/18	1/1	–	–
2;3	3/3	–	3/3	–	–	–
2;4	9/11	–	3/4	–	–	–
2;5	8/14	1/1	6/38	–	–	–
2;6	4/4	2/2	6/13	2/2	–	–

Second person singular imperatives as well as the 3rd infinitive illative are members in two verbal miniparadigms having developed in Tomi's language at the age of 1;8 (Table 10, based on Laalo 2011: 90).

Table 10: Tomi's early miniparadigms at 1;8.

IMP.2SG	PRS.3SG	PST.3SG	PASS.PST	INF3.ILL
auta 'help'	autta-a help-3SG 'helps'	autt-i (for auttoi) help-PST 'helped'		
kat(s)o 'look'	katso-o look-3SG 'is looking'		katsot-tiin look-PASS.PST 'we looked'	katso-ma-an look-INF3-ILL 'let's go and look'

5.3.2 Tomi's verbless directives

Tomi uses verbless directives similarly to Mari, namely partitive (examples 34 and 35) and illative forms of nouns and certain adverbs.

(34) Tomi, 1;7
    pipa-a   (for *pipari-a*)
                    bisquit-PARTIT
    pookka-a (for *porkkana-a*)
                    carrot-PARTIT

(35) Tomi, 1;8
    puukka-a (for *puolukka-a*)
                    lingonberry-PARTIT

Illatives express requests for motion toward locations and often occur in daily dressing routines (examples 36a and b).

(36) a. Tomi, 1;3
      (wanting to have his shoes put on)
      kaaka-a(n)   (for   *jalka-an*)
                                foot-ILL

b. Tomi, 1;6
   (wanting to have his gloves put on)
   käte-e(n)
   hand-ILL

In Tomi's diary material many different adverbs serving a number of directive functions have been noted very early (examples 37). Thus, in example (37a) the boy either expresses his wish to get rid of some food he dislikes, to move from the baby-chair, or to get help with getting undressed.

(37) a. Tomi, 1;4
   poo (< pois)
   'away'
   b. Tomi, 1;8
   tähä(n)
   'here' (wanting berries to be added to his porridge)
   c. Tomi, 1;6–1;8
   toho(o) (< t[u]o-hon)
   'there'

The very early *too*-variant for 'there' was elaborated to *toho(o)* in the course of time and was used for example when wanting some building bricks to be fastened or something to be moved to a certain place.

5.3.3 Tomi's use of modal verbs in directive function

Modal verb constructions expressing directives emerge in Tomi's speech at 2;1 and thus much later than verbless directives and certain inflected forms of full verbs (Table 9). As has been found with Mari, also Tomi uses modal verbs correctly from the very beginning (examples 38a and 38b). The boy's development of shifters is difficult to follow because he does not use them often, but in these examples he correctly addresses his father in the 2nd person singular.

(38) a. Tomi, 2;1
   FAT: *saa-n-ko   autta-a?*
         may-1SG-CLIT help-INF1
         'May I help?'

TOM: *saa-t.*
    may-2SG
    'You may.'

b. Tomi, 2;6
    FAT: *saa-n-ko mä omena-n syö-dä?*
        may-1SG-CLIT I apple-ACC eat-INF1
        'May I eat the apple?'
    FAT: *saa-t ja pipari-n saa-t syö-dä.*
        may-2SG and bisquit-ACC may-2SG eat-INF1
        'You may and you may also eat the biscuit.'

The negated form of the modal verb *saada* 'may' is used in the 3rd person singular in prohibitions with a generic meaning (example 39).

(39) Tomi, 2;1
    ei saa men-nä sii-he(n).
    NEG may.3SG go-INF1 DEM-ILL
    '(One) must not go there.'

Examples (40) and (41) illustrate prohibition and permission addressed to the boy's sister using the 3rd person singular form to clarify who is addressed.

(40) Tomi, 2;1
    ei saa sisko men-nä!
    NEG may.3SG sister go-INF1
    'The sister may not go.'

(41) Tomi, 2;1
    kohta saa sisko sii-hen men-nä ui-ma-an.
    soon may.3SG sister there-ILL go-INF1 swim-INF3-ILL
    'The sister may soon go and swim there.'

Another modal verb expressing permission or prohibition is *voida* 'can, may' (examples 42 and 43).

(42) Tomi, 2;2
    keltase-sta voi lähte-e. [for *lähte-ä*]
    yellow-ELAT may.3SG go-INF1
    'When yellow, one may start.'

(43) Tomi 2;2
   punase-sta ei   voi   lähte-e. [for lähte-ä]
   red-ELAT   not may.3SG   go-INF1
   'When red, one may not start.'

A third modal verb emerging in Tomi's data at 2;4 is *pitää* 'must' expressing obligations (example 44).

(44) Tomi, 2;4
   (building a toy train with his father)
   tää   pitä-ä   pan-na   kiinni   sii-hen.
   this must-3SG   fasten-INF1   closed   it-ILL
   'This must be fastened to that one.'

Although Tomi's development is similar to Mari's in many respects, there are two differences. Unlike Mari, Tomi uses 2nd singular forms of modal verbs (examples 38 above) but does not express indirect requests by the 3rd singular of the verb for 'want'.

5.4 Similarities and differences between CDS and CS

Most directives containing a verb and occurring in both CDS and CS are either 2nd singular imperative, passive, or modal verb constructions. All of them are also used in negated forms conveying prohibitions. The marked 3rd singular imperative is found only twice in CDS.

While certain verb forms are limited to CDS, others only occur in CS. Since only one of the children at a time was present during the recording sessions, the 2nd plural imperative does not occur in the audiotaped data of CDS. It is, however, used by Mari in addressing her toy animals.

Among the verb forms typical of CDS are mitigated directives, i.e. active or passive conditional forms of main verbs or conditional forms of modal verbs, some of them constructed with a question particle. An active conditional form of a full verb only occurs once in Mari's speech at 2;5.

Directives expressed by illative forms of the 3rd infinitive are typically used by the children when they are playing with dolls or animals. In CDS, these infinitive forms are constructed with another verb, especially in the passive (e.g., *men-nään nukku-ma-an* (go-PASS sleep-INF3-ILL) 'let's go to sleep').

The verbs *haluta* 'want to' and *tahtoa* 'want to' are used in the 3rd person singular form when the child is referring to herself. CDS offers a model for this, because these forms are typically used when addressing the child (examples 45a and b). As has also been noted for other languages, use of the 3rd person instead of the 1st or 2nd is a common strategy of babytalk keeping personal deixis constant and avoiding the problem of shifting the communicative roles of the interlocutors.

(45) a. Mari 1;8
 äiti autta-a.
 mother help-PRS.3SG
 'The mother helps.'
b. Mari 1;9
 tahto-o-ko Mari?
 want-3SG-Q Mari
 'Does Mari want to?'

The verbless directives typical of early CS are often expanded by the caretakers (example 46).

(46) Mari, 1;8
 MAR: uulellee [for uudelleen].
 'Again.'
 MOT: uudelleen kerro-taan mitä siinä teh-dään.
 again tell-PASS what there do-PASS
 'Let's tell again what is done there.'

Although directives of CS containing a verb form may be taken to be modeled by CDS, verbless requests of CS consisting of a noun do not occur in the recorded material of CDS and those consisting of an adverb such as *uudelleen* 'again' are only rarely found.

6 Discussion and conclusions

The earliest functional distinction of verb forms found in the acquisition of a number of languages is that between modal and non-modal forms (see section 3). In Finnish this contrast is materialized between 2nd person singular imperative and 3rd person singular present indicative verb forms expressing directives and statements, respectively.

In early Finnish child speech directives are expressed by 2nd person singular imperatives or verbless utterances. The early emergence of the 2nd person singular imperative can be explained by its important communicative function on the one hand and its short and simple form coinciding with the verb stem on the other. Furthermore, this form is frequently modeled in CDS.

In the beginning, the lexical inventory of verbs used in the imperative is quite limited. Verbs occurring in the imperative much more frequently than others are *anna* 'give' and *katso* 'look' getting the addressee to execute an action in his or her favor and drawing his or her attention to something of interest, respectively. These results not only coincide with Toivainen (1980: 33) for Finnish but also with Stephany (1997) for Greek, Gagarina (2003) and Voeikova and Bayda, this volume, for Russian and Aguirre (2003) for Spanish. This shows that the exchange of objects as well as the linguistic successor of the early pointing gesture are significant in the communication of children and their caregivers.

Besides imperatives, another way to express requests and wishes which emerges early in Finnish language acquisition are verbless utterances containing certain case forms of nouns or adverbs. Nouns in the partitive are used for requesting various kinds of food and illatives indicate places to go. Requests expressed by nouns have more specific meanings than those rendered by bare imperatives (e.g. *vettä!* 'water!' vs. *anna!* 'give!').

Another form of directives which also develops early is the inclusive imperative expressed by the passive and having a hortative meaning. Examples are *men-nään* (go-PASS) 'let's go' and *pes-tään* (wash-PASS) 'let's wash', which also frequently occur in CDS.

An important type of non-finite directives are illative forms of the 3rd infinitive such as *syö-mä-än* (eat-INF3-ILL) 'let's go and eat' (or 'come and eat') and *nukku-ma-an* (sleep-INF3-ILL) 'let's go to sleep', which belong to daily routines and are regularly used in CDS. But because the recordings were made in situations of free play, these forms only occur in CS when the children are speaking to toy animals or dolls.

The 2nd person plural imperative is a verbal category giving rise to analogical formations (examples 14 and 15 above). Such formations are evidence of the child's active processing of inflectional verb forms. Since 2nd person plural imperatives are not only quite complex and rarely occur in CDS (outside the recording sessions when more people are addressed at the same time), these imperatives do not easily become entrenched and are therefore acquired slowly. Only three tokens of this form were found by Toivainen (1980: 34–35) in his recordings of 25 Finnish-speaking children aged 1–3 years.

Several means for softening requests are used in CDS; for example, passives are mitigated by interrogative clitics or conditional forms. In CS there are some means to soften requests, e.g. conditional forms are used for making suggestions, such as distributing the roles in imaginary play situations. Another way of softening directives found early in CS are indirect requests, such as expressing desires by the verb *tahtoa* 'want to' or its synonym *haluta*. This type of requests has also been found in other languages (Stephany 1986: 391).

As shown by the present study, the use of directives in CDS offers models for developing their expression in CS. Many directive types, such as illative forms of the 3rd infinitive and modal verb constructions, are easily acquired and show no particularly childlike features, but some – for example the 2nd person plural imperative – are morphologically complex and give rise to analogical formations.

Further studies of the acquisition of the vast and communicatively important domain of modality should not only enlarge the number of subjects and extend their age range considerably but must also take the development of epistemic modality into consideration.

Acknowledgements: I thank Ayhan Aksu-Koç and Ursula Stephany for their critical editorial comments on the earlier versions of this paper and for brushing up my English. I also thank Elina Kost for technical assistance in the editing process.

References

Aguirre, Carmen. 2003. Early verb development in one Spanish-speaking child. In Dagmar Bittner, Wolfgang U. Dressler & Marianne Kilani-Schoch (eds.), *Development of verb inflection in first language acquisition: A cross-linguistic perspective* (Studies on Language Acquisition 21), 1–25. Berlin & New York: Mouton de Gruyter.

Aikhenvald, Alexandra. 2010. *Imperatives and commands*. Oxford: Oxford University Press.

Dressler, Wolfgang U., Marianne Kilani-Schoch & Sabine Klampfer. 2003. How does the child detect morphology? Evidence from production. In R. Harald Baayen & Robert Schreuder (eds.), *Morphological structure in language processing*, 391–425. Berlin: Mouton de Gruyter.

Gagarina, Natalia. 2003. The early development and demarcation of stages in three Russian-speaking children. In Dagmar Bittner, Wolfgang U. Dressler & Marianne Kilani-Schoch (eds.), *Development of verb inflection in first language acquisition: A cross-linguistic perspective* (Studies on Language Acquisition 21), 131–169. Berlin & New York: Mouton de Gruyter.

Hakulinen, Auli & Eeva-Leena Seppänen. 1992. Finnish *kato*: From verb to particle. *Journal of Pragmatics* 18. 527–549.
Kangasniemi, Heikki. 1992. *Modal expressions in Finnish* (Studia Fennica Linguistica 2). Helsinki: Suomalaisen Kirjallisuuden Seura [The Finnish Literature Society].
Katičić, Antigone. 2003. Early verb development in one Croatian-speaking child. In Dagmar Bittner, Wolfgang U. Dressler & Marianne Kilani-Schoch (eds.), *Development of verb inflection in first language acquisition: A cross-linguistic perspective* (Studies on Language Acquisition 21), 239–267. Berlin & New York: Mouton de Gruyter.
Kauppinen, Anneli. 1982. Kuinka negaatio kasvaa [The development of negation]. *Virittäjä* 86. 140–163.
Kauppinen, Anneli. 1998. *Puhekuviot, tilanteen ja rakenteen liitto*. [Speech figures, the union of situation and structure] (Suomalaisen Kirjallisuuden Seuran Toimituksia 713). Helsinki: Suomalaisen Kirjallisuuden Seura [The Finnish Literature Society].
Klampfer, Sabine. 2003. Emergence of verb paradigms in one Austrian child. In Dagmar Bittner, Wolfgang U. Dressler & Marianne Kilani-Schoch (eds.), *Development of verb inflection in first language acquisition: A cross-linguistic perspective* (Studies on Language Acquisition 21), 297–321. Berlin & New York: Mouton de Gruyter.
Laalo, Klaus. 2003. Early verb development in Finnish: A preliminary approach to miniparadigms. In Dagmar Bittner, Wolfgang U. Dressler & Marianne Kilani-Schoch (eds.), *Development of verb inflection in first language acquisition: A cross-linguistic perspective* (Studies on Language Acquisition 21), 323–350. Berlin & New York: Mouton de Gruyter.
Laalo, Klaus. 2011. *Lapsen varhaiskielioppi ja miniparadigmat* [Protogrammar and miniparadigms in child language] (Suomalaisen Kirjallisuuden Seuran Toimituksia 1309). Helsinki: Suomalaisen Kirjallisuuden Seura [The Finnish Literature Society].
Lauranto, Yrjö. 2013. Suomen kielen imperatiivi – yksi paradigma, kaksi systeemiä [The imperative in Finnish – one paradigm, two systems]. *Virittäjä* 117. 156–200.
Lodge, Ken R. 1978. The use of the past tense in games of pretend. *Journal of Child Language* 6. 365–369.
Seppänen, Eeva-Leena. 1989. Henkilöön viittaaminen puhetilanteessa [Referring to person in speech situations]. *Kieli* 4. 195–222. Helsinki: University of Helsinki.
Stephany, Ursula. 1985. *Aspekt, Tempus und Modalität: Zur Entwicklung der Verbalgrammatik in der neugriechischen Kindersprache* (Language Universals Series 4). Tübingen: Gunter Narr.
Stephany, Ursula. 1986. Modality. In Paul Fletcher & Michael Garman (eds.), *Language acquisition: Studies in first language development*, 375–400. 2nd edn. Cambridge: Cambridge University Press.
Stephany, Ursula. 1997. The acquisition of Greek. In Dan I. Slobin (ed.), *The crosslinguistic study of language acquisition*, vol. 4, 183–333. Mahwah, NJ: Lawrence Erlbaum.
Toivainen, Jorma. 1980. *Inflectional affixes used by Finnish-speaking children aged 1–3 years*. Helsinki: Suomalaisen Kirjallisuuden Seura [The Finnish Literature Society].
Toivainen, Jorma. 1997. The acquisition of Finnish. In Dan I. Slobin (ed.), *The crosslinguistic study of language acquisition*, vol. 4, 87–182. Mahwah, NJ: Lawrence Erlbaum.
Tomasello, Michael. 2010. *Origins of human communication*. Cambridge, MA: MIT Press.

Wojcik, Pavel. 2003. Early verb inflection in Lithuanian. In Dagmar Bittner, Wolfgang U. Dressler & Marianne Kilani-Schoch (eds.), *Development of verb inflection in first language acquisition: A cross-linguistic perspective* (Studies on Language Acquisition 21), 401–420. Berlin & New York: Mouton de Gruyter.

Yli-Vakkuri, Valma. 1986. *Suomen kieliopillisten muotojen toissijainen käyttö* [The secondary use of Finnish grammatical forms]. (Publications of the Department of Finnish and General Linguistics of the University of Turku 28). Turku.

Sigal Uziel-Karl
Modality in child Hebrew

Abstract: The present paper examines the acquisition of modality in child Hebrew from a usage-based perspective, comparing child speech with child-directed speech. Although the paper touches on epistemic modality, its focus is on the early forms and functions of agent-oriented modality (dynamic and deontic modality). The study is based on the analysis of naturalistic speech samples of two Hebrew-speaking girls, aged 1;5–3;0, and their primary caretakers. The findings reveal that the acquisition of modality proceeds gradually. Modal expressions denoting agent-oriented modality appear earlier than epistemic ones. The girls start out with modal inflection, relying heavily on the imperative. Across development the frequency of modal inflection decreases, giving way to lexically expressed modal verbs, adjectives and adverbs. At the outset, only one or two of these are used but, over time, their frequency and diversity increase. Parental input as well as communicative factors were found to affect the development of modality in the acquisition of Hebrew.

1 Introduction

The present study examines the early development of modality in child Hebrew, with a focus on agent-oriented modal expressions, taking into consideration the emergence of epistemic notions where relevant and comparing child speech (CS) with child-directed speech (CDS).

As stated already by Bybee and Fleischman (1995: 6) "agent-oriented modality encompasses all modal meanings that predicate conditions on an agent with regard to the completion of an action referred to by the main predicate, e.g. obligation, desire, ability, permission and root possibility".[1]

Agent-oriented modality includes both dynamic and deontic modality. Dynamic modality ascribes to the first-argument participant of the verb the capacity or ability to realize or effectuate the state of affairs expressed in the clause and to indicate a need or a necessity (Nuyts 2006: 3). Dynamic modality is described as participant-internal, denoting ability (*he can stand on his head*)

---

[1] Bybee and Fleischman (1995: 5) define 'root possibility' as predicating "general enabling conditions (e.g., *it can take three hours to get there*)".

Sigal Uziel-Karl, Achva Academic College

and volition (*he won't go*) as its main functions. Dynamic modality was found to be the earliest and the most prominent type of modality found in early language development, with ability and volition playing a central role (Hickmann and Bassano 2016: 431).

In contrast, deontic modality is concerned with the necessity or possibility of acts performed by morally responsible agents (Lyons 1977: 823) with reference to norms (Stephany 1986: 375) and is associated with the social functions of permission and obligation (Bybee and Fleischman 1995). Deontic modality is considered participant-external with obligation (*you must go*) and permission (*you may leave*) as its main functions (van der Auwera and Plungian 1998).[2]

Agent-oriented modality contrasts with propositional modality, which is "concerned with the speaker's attitude to the truth-value or factual status of the proposition" (Palmer 2001: 8). Propositional modality includes epistemic and evidential modality. Epistemic modality indicates the speaker's "degree of confidence in a proposition" (Boye 2016: 117). It expresses the speaker's assessment about the truth of a proposition, as well as the degree of probability of a state or event, typically based on the speaker's opinion (Nuyts 2016: 38). The speaker may estimate that the event or state expressed in the main predicate is possible, probable or certain. The difference between epistemic and evidential modality is that "with epistemic modality speakers express their judgments about the factual status of the proposition" while "with evidential modality they indicate the evidence they have for its factual status" (Palmer 2001: 8–9, 24–69).

Cross-linguistic studies on the acquisition of modality reveal that children start producing agent-oriented modality before epistemic modality, with few exceptions. For example, Choi (1995, 2006) reports that in Korean modal sentence-ending particles were used for expressing epistemic meanings from early on. Nonetheless, agent-oriented modality was found to be much more frequent than epistemic modality (Hickmann and Bassano 2016). Based on an examination of naturalistic longitudinal data, Shatz and Wilcox (1991) report that the acquisition of English modals begins gradually with a single negative form (e.g., *can't*) in a limited syntactic environment. Under experimental conditions, children perform better with modal words that are familiar to them (e.g., *has to, can't*) than with more formal words (e.g., *might*) (Byrens and Duff 1989). Wells (1979) has found that children aged 1;3–3;6 acquire the deontic use of modal verbs earlier than their epistemic one (see also Brown 1973; Pea, Mawby, and MacKain 1982 among

---

[2] It should be noted that van der Auwera and Plunigan (1998) use the word "participant" in "participant-external" to refer to the addressee and not to the speaker or to both. A more viable alternative would be to use the term "agent" akin to Bybee (1995: 6; cf. 1985: 166).

others). Similar findings were reported by Stephany (1986, 1993, 1995). Children begin to produce epistemic markers before or well after 2 years of age, depending on the semantic and morphological nature of the markers in the target language, but they take several years to be mastered. Children acquire the notion of certainty earlier than various degrees of uncertainty (i.e., possibility or probability). Uncertainty involves the cognitively more demanding act of representing and evaluating unactualized states of affairs which may be said to rest on a gradual cognitive development in the level of abstraction (Choi 2014: 199).

Stephany and Aksu-Koç (this volume) note that the distinction between verb forms marked for agent-oriented modality and non-modal forms (e.g., imperative vs. present or past tense) is the first to emerge in the acquisition of different languages. Agent-oriented modality (especially directives) has been found to play a central communicative role in mother–child interactions before the age of 3;0 years.

The early preference for agent-oriented modality is attributed to pragmatic and linguistic factors. Pragmatic factors constitute an essential component of the acquisition and use of modality, since young children are more concerned with norms for actions (the main concern of agent-oriented modality), with the possibility of performing them (dynamic modality), and with expressing desired states of affairs (dynamic modality) than with worrying about their relative certainty (epistemic modality) (Stephany 1993). The expression of agent-oriented modality may also be linguistically less demanding than that of epistemic modality (Hickmann and Bassano 2016: 432).

Languages may express modality using different structural means: inflectional, syntactic or lexical. The main inflectional device to express modality is mood (e.g., imperative, subjunctive). The main syntactic and lexical devices are modal verbs (e.g., *may, can, must*), verbs of desire and belief (e.g., *want, think, know*), adverbs (e.g., *probably, possibly*) and adjectives (e.g., *certain, necessary*) (Hickmann and Bassano 2016: 431; Stephany and Aksu-Koç, this volume).

Regarding language acquisition, the two most important domains of agent-oriented modality are ability/volition and directives (Stephany and Aksu-Koç, this volume). The expression of ability may involve modal verbs (e.g., *I can run a marathon*), inflection, or more frequently, negative forms conveying inability. Volition may be expressed with the verb 'want' as well as certain inflected forms of full verbs (e.g., the optative). Such utterances may function as indirect requests (*I wanna eat ice-cream*) or denote intention (*I won't read this book*).

Directives are speech acts that attempt to get the hearer to perform some action. The two main types of directives are orders (commands) and requests. Orders involve telling someone what to do, whereas requests involve asking someone to do something, with an option for the addressee not to comply (Aikhenvald 2016: 147). Two early directive types are the need statement (*want/need* ...), an indirect request, and the imperative (*give me* ...), a command which the child uses to refer to a desired action or object.³ Around age 3, English-speaking children begin to use some modal verbs in indirect requests (*could you give me a* ... ?), in permissive directives (*can/may I have a* ... ?), and question directives (*may I have a* ... ?) (Owens 2012: 240–241). Indirect requests may be expressed using modal verbs, certain inflected forms of full verbs and certain sentence types (e.g., *shouting is not allowed in the mall*).

The present paper is organized a follows: Section 2 provides an overview of the expression of modality in Modern Hebrew; Section 3 describes the state of the art of the acquisition of agent-oriented modality in Hebrew and outlines the goals of the study; Section 4 sketches the theoretical framework of the study; Section 5 describes the data and method of analysis; Section 6 is devoted to the analysis of child speech (CS) and child-directed speech (CDS), and Section 7 offers a discussion of the findings and the conclusions.

2 Modality in Modern Hebrew

Modern Hebrew lacks a dedicated, grammatically distinct set of modal auxiliaries like English *can, may, must, shall* and *will*. Instead, it relies on a set of modal predicates that are often morphologically anomalous (in that they have a defective paradigm) and are invariably followed by a verb in the infinitive, e.g., agent-oriented *yaxol* 'can, is able to' and *carix* 'have to, should', as well as epistemic adjectives like *asuy* 'is likely to' and *alul,* 'is liable to' (Berman 2011, 2014; Reilly et al. 2002; see also Boneh 2015; Coffin and Bolozky 2005: 300–313; Dromi 1980).

Hebrew modal predicates belong to one of three main lexical groups – verbal, adjectival or adverbial, the first two expressing agent-oriented modality and the third mostly epistemic modality. Verbal modals, e.g., *roce* 'want' and *yaxol* 'can, be able to', are inflected for tense, number, gender and person.⁴ In

---

3 As noted by Nikolaeva (2016: 75), the imperative may also serve to make recommendations and to give advice and permission. However, these functions are more commonly evident in CDS than in CS.

4 In Hebrew, verbs are distinct from adjectives or nouns in that they have infinitive forms and are inflected for past and future or the imperative. In contrast to the past and future, present tense forms are not exclusive to verbs but are also used with many nouns and adjectives, especially 'present participle' (deverbal) adjectives, and nouns (Glinert 1989: 458). Thus, verb forms like *roce* 'want.PRS.M.SG' or *yaxol* 'may.PRS.M.SG', called *beynoni*, are participles, characterized as non-finite verb forms inflected for a combination of verbal and nominal features.

terms of function, the verb *roce* 'want' is used to express volition and desires that may be fulfilled or could have been fulfilled in the past (example 1). When combined with the verb *lihyot* 'to be' in the past tense, it is used to express a wish or a craving akin to an impossible condition (example 2).

(1) *Dani   roce/   raca/   yirce*
     Danny   want.PRS.M.SG/ want.PST.M.3SG/ want.FUT.M.3SG
     leʔexol glida.
     eat.INF ice-cream
     'Danny wants/wanted/would want to eat ice-cream.'

(2) *Dani   haya   roce   leʔexol axshav glida.*
     Danny   be.PRS.M.3SG   want.PRS.M.SG eat.INF now   ice-cream
     'Danny would have liked to eat ice-cream right now.'

The verb *yaxol* 'can, be able to', conjugated in the present tense and followed by a verb in the infinitive, is used to express ability/capability (example 3) or to make indirect requests (examples 4 and 5).

(3) *Dani   yaxol   likroʔ   maher.*
     Danny   can.PRS.M.SG   read.INF fast
     'Danny can read fast.'

(4) *ani   yaxol   lavoʔ   itxem?*
     I   may.PRS.M.SG   come.INF   with.you.M.PL
     'May I come with you?'

(5) *ani   yaxol   lekabel   ʕod   xatixat   uga?*
     I   may.PRS.M.SG   get.INF   another   piece.of   cake
     'May I get another piece of cake?'

Adjectival modals, e.g., *carix* 'have to, should', *xayav* 'obliged' (example 6), *mux-rax* 'must' are inflected only for number and gender (e.g., *carix* 'have.to.M.SG', *crix-a* 'have.to.F.SG', *crix-im* 'have.to.M.PL', *crix-ot* 'have.to.F.PL'). These modals

---

When they function as primary predicates of a main clause, they correspond to the present tense in European languages, but they are like nouns and adjectives in taking suffixes for number and gender, although not for person (Berman 2014: 5).

require an overt form of the verb *lihyot* 'to be' in the past or future tense (e.g., *haya carix* 'be.PST.M.3SG have.to.M.SG', *yihye carix* 'be.FUT.M.3SG have.to.M.SG').

(6) Dani   xayav/   haya   xayav/
    Danny be.obliged.PRS.M.SG/ be.PST.M.3SG obliged/
    yihye   xayav   lishtof   yadayim.
    be.FUT.M.3SG obliged wash.INF hands
    'Danny is obliged/was obliged/will be obliged to wash (his) hands.'

In Hebrew, certain adjectival modals exhibit a particular anomaly insofar as they may enter (often defective) paradigms in the form of verbs (e.g., *hictarex* 'have.to.PST.M.3SG', *hitxayev* 'commit.PST.M.3SG').[5] Example (7) illustrates this with the use of *yaxol* 'be able to', which should be conjugated as *haya yaxol* according to the norms of formal Hebrew, but alternates with the verbal form *yaxal* 'can.PST.M.3SG' in colloquial Hebrew. Thus, these modals are typically members of defective or suppletive paradigms.

(7) Dani   haya   yaxol/   yaxal
    Danny be.PST.M.3SG able.PRS.M.SG/ can.PST.M.3SG
    lomar   et   ha-ʔemet.
    tell.INF ACC   the-truth
    'Danny could tell the truth.'

Adjectival modals like *rashay* 'allowed', *carix* 'have to, should', *muxrax* 'must', and *xayav* 'obliged' are used in Hebrew to denote varying degrees of obligation, from weak to strong (example 8). The adjectival modal *carix* 'have to, should' also marks obligation when used in impersonal constructions followed by a main verb in the infinitive (example 9).

(8) Dani   rasahy/   carix/   muxrax/
    Danny allowed.M.SG/ have.to.M.SG/ must.M.SG/
    xayav   lilmod   la-mivxan.
    be.obliged.M.SG to.study.INF   for.the-test
    'Danny is allowed/ has to/ must/ is obliged to study for the test.'

---

5 Unlike other adjectival modals like *asuy* 'is likely to' or *alul* 'is liable to' which may not supplement verbal paradigms.

(9) carix   lifnot   la-mishatara be-mikre shel te?una.
    necessary turn.INF   to.the-police in-case   of   accident
    '(It is) necessary to turn to the police in case of (an) accident.'

The epistemic adjectival modals *asuy* 'is likely to' and *alul* 'is liable to' are used to denote likelihood or positive/negative assessment of a possibility, respectively. The adjectival modals *mesugal* 'is capable' and *muxan* 'ready' express dynamic modality. While the former marks ability/capability, the latter indicates readiness and willingness.

Adverbial modals like *efshar* 'possibly' or *keday* 'worthwhile' are used in impersonal constructions, followed by a main verb in the infinitive. As is typical of adverbs, they have an invariable form and neither take gender nor number inflection, as shown in examples (10) and (11). Adverbial modals are used in Hebrew to mark deontic or epistemic possibility (*efshar* 'possibly'), desirability in indirect requests (*keday* 'worthwhile'), permission and prohibition (*mutar* 'allowed', *asur* 'forbidden').

(10) efshar   le?exol   glida   bli   letaftef   al   ha-ricpa.
     possibly to.eat   ice-cream without drip.INF   on   the-floor
     '(One can) possibly/(it is) possible to eat ice-cream without dripping on the floor.'

(11) keday   laxzor   habayta ba-zman.
     worthwhile   return.INF home   on-time
     'It is worthwhile to return home on time.'

Modality in Modern Hebrew is also expressed inflectionally through mood. Irrealis mood is manifest in imperatives, infinitives and future tense (Berman 2014), which together form a 'modal cluster' (Ravid 2010). In terms of form, imperatives are uniformly inflected for 2nd person. Gender and number are marked by the suffix *–i* for feminine singular as in *kxi* 'take.IMP.F.2SG' and by *–u* for plural as in *kxu* 'take.IMP.2PL'. The masculine singular form does not carry a suffix, e.g., *kax* 'take.IMP.M.2SG' (Berman 1985). Canonical imperatives are used for giving direct orders and instructions. However, the imperative is characterized as a high-register form, not commonly used in everyday oral communication. Imperatives occur in formal settings like court trials, with the military, in written instructions, e.g. cookbooks, etc. What is used in colloquial Hebrew instead is a so-called future-imperative form (see below).

The future tense is formed by attaching a set of agreement affixes to a temporal stem formed by interlineating a consonantal root into a pattern (*binyan*).[6] Agreement features on future tense forms split between prefixes and suffixes. The future-tense prefixes *ʔ-*, *y-*, *t-*, *n-* mark person and number (in the 3rd person singular they mark gender as well), as in *ʔelex* 'go.FUT.1SG', *yelex* 'go.FUT.M.3SG', *telex* 'go.FUT.M.2SG'/'go.FUT.F.3SG', and *nelex* 'go.FUT.1PL', whereas the future tense suffixes *-i* and *-u* mark feminine and plural agreement, respectively, akin to the imperative, e.g., *telxi* 'go.FUT.F.2SG', *telxu* 'go.FUT.2PL'. The future tense is used to make predictions or declarations about future events, to express conditions, and to provide a more polite or attenuated alternative for giving orders (Bolozky 2009).

In colloquial Hebrew, imperative forms occur mainly with the 2nd person future prefix *t-* as in *tikax* 'take.FUT.IMP.M.2SG', so that both *kax* 'take.IMP.M.2SG' and *tikax* 'take.FUT.IMP.M.2SG' can be contextually interpreted as masculine forms of the imperative.[7] However, unlike the canonical imperative, the latter form, also termed the future imperative, is a mitigated form for giving orders or making direct requests frequently used in CDS and CS.

Lastly, the infinitive consists of a verb stem preceded by the preposition *le-* as in *leʔexol* 'to eat' and is used mainly to give generic orders or instructions, without referring to any particular addressee. In CDS infinitives are used mostly for prohibitions while in CS these forms also serve to make indirect requests.

---

6 Thus, to form the future tense of the Qal pattern, a consonantal root is inserted into the temporal stem of the future tense, i.e., *PiCCoC* (where *P* marks a prefix which represents the temporal/agreement features of the future tense and the capital Cs represent the slots of the root consonants). For example, to form *nikfoc* 'jump.FUT.1PL', the root *k-f-c* 'jump' is inserted into *PiCCoC* to yield *Pikfoc* and *P* is replaced by the prefix *n-* 'FUT.1PL'. For a detailed description of the system see Ravid (2010) and Ashkenazi (2015: 5–6).

7 "Future imperative" is not a formal inflectional category in Hebrew as are the future or the imperative. Rather, it is a form used in colloquial Hebrew combining the inflection of the future tense with the illocutionary force of the imperative. This form is sometimes referred to as the "new imperative" in work on Hebrew morphology (e.g., Bolozky 2009).

3 The acquisition of agent-oriented modals in Hebrew: State of the art

Agent-oriented modality is only briefly discussed in research on the early acquisition of Hebrew.[8] Armon-Lotem and Berman (2003) report that among the early verbs that Hebrew-speaking children acquire, there are a few stative ones which are usually used with a modal meaning, e.g. *roce* 'want', *yaxol* 'can, be able to', and *macliax* 'manage'. This suggests that expressions of dynamic modality emerge early. These verbs are initially acquired in the present tense and a single number-gender form (PRS.M.SG or PRS.F.SG) depending on the child's gender and are used by the child to refer to the speaker. These are also the forms used by children's caretakers to address them. Ravid (1997), who studied the development of verbal morphology in a pair of Hebrew-speaking twins, reports that in the pre-morphological stage (1;11–2;1) the children had only the modal verb *roce* 'want' at their disposal, which they used in the singular feminine (the girl) or singular masculine (the boy) form of the present tense. In the proto-morphological stage (2;1–2;4) the twins acquired the gender contrasts *roce/roca* 'want.M/F' and *yaxol/yexola* 'can, be able to. M/F'.[9] Already Berman (1985) notes that Hebrew-speaking children initially use stative verbs like *roce* 'want' and *yodea* 'know (how to)' in the present tense to denote the dynamic notions of desire and ability. These verbs occur in addition to other early verbs denoting durative activities such as *boxe* 'is.crying' and *mesaxek* 'is.playing'. The early emergence of the verb *roce* 'want' has also been confirmed in a longitudinal study of four Hebrew-speaking children (3 girls and 1 boy, observed from 1;5 to 3;0) by the author (Uziel-Karl 2001). Each of the four children used this verb in the present tense, with the girls restricting themselves to the feminine form *roca* 'want.F' and the boy to the masculine form *roce* 'want.M'. Finally, Ashkenazi (2015) investigated CS–CDS relations in Hebrew

---

8 The acquisition of epistemic modality in Hebrew has not been studied before.
9 The pre- and proto-morphological approach to language acquisition distinguishes three developmental stages: Pre-morphology, proto-morphology and morphology proper (Dressler and Karpf 1995). The pre-mophological stage is assumed to rely on general cognitive knowledge, as the morphological module has not yet been formed. At this stage, children produce only isolated rote-learned word forms so that each verb occurs in a single form, with no inflectional oppositions (Bittner, Dressler and Kilani-Schoch 2003: xxi; Stephany and Voeikova 2009: 4). In the protomorphological stage, grammatical oppositions start to emerge, developing into mini-paradimgs with at least 3 different inflectional forms of a given lemma (Stephany and Voeikova 2009: 4). Finally, in the stage of morphology proper, children construct a considerable number of morphological rules and gradually acquire adult morphology with all of its basic typological properties (Dressler and Karpf 1995).

verb acquisition based on a dense corpus of natural conversational interaction in two dyads (caregiver and boy/girl, aged 1;8–2;2). She reports that grammatically unspecified (mostly modal) frozen or unanalyzed verb stems were present only in CS and that the number of these verb forms decreased over time.

In CDS, the modal cluster of imperative, infinitive and future forms of main verbs had higher token frequencies than non-modal present and past tense forms, suggesting that modal inflectional prefixes and suffixes present stable initial and final word boundaries for acquisition, increasing verb salience and facilitating learning despite internal stem opacity. Ashkenazi (2015) further notes that the children were each exposed to more forms relating to their own gender and also preferentially produced such forms. Finally, she remarks that modal semantics and pragmatics dominate in CDS as well as CS (2nd person future, infinitive and imperative forms of verbs as well as the present tense form of the verb of desire *roce* 'want'), functioning as a central pragmatic anchor in early parent–child interaction.

Several studies discuss the syntactic properties of agent-oriented modals in child Hebrew. Berman (1985) notes that in verb-complement structures, early verb–verb combinations (where the second verb is infinitival) initially appear with *roce* 'want' and are later followed by other types of modal verbs such as *yaxol* 'can, is able to', *carix* 'should', and *yodea* 'know (how to)' which also take infinitival complements. Ninio (1999) argues that *want* is a path-breaking verb, since it is the earliest and most frequently used verb in Hebrew V OBJ and SBJ V OBJ structures both in CS and CDS. Uziel-Karl (2001) points out that the modal verb *want* is not only frequently used in CS but also in CDS from early on. It mostly occurs in the present tense, with gender marking, but without an overt subject, as shown in example (12).[10]

(12) Smadar's mother (Smadar 1;6)
 roca she ani asaper lax shuv?
 want.PRS.F.SG that I tell.FUT.F.1SG you again
 '(Do you) want me to tell you (the story) again?'

---

10 Note that pro-drop is not grammatically licensed in the present tense in Hebrew so that sentence (12) is structurally ungrammatical since the main clause has no overt subject. However, in spoken colloquial Hebrew, in a discourse setting, when both the speaker and the hearer are present, it is quite common and acceptable for a speaker to ask the hearer about his desires using an interrogative construction in which the verb *want* appears without an overt subject.

Parental language input is claimed to be the most important mediating variable between SES and children's linguistic proficiencies (Huttenlocher et al. 2010). Several studies (Hart and Risley 1995; Hoff, Laursen and Tardif 2002) show that parental conversation style is closely related to SES: Parents from high SES (HSES) backgrounds were found to be more responsive to their children's verbalizations, to initiate and sustain conversation with their children more frequently, to encourage them to talk by asking questions (Hoff 2003), and to formulate indirect requests, e.g., "Why don't you pick up the toys for me?" (Hart and Risley 1995: 57). In contrast, parents from low SES (LSES) backgrounds tend to focus on goal-directed caretaking settings and to use more behavior-regulating speech acts like direct commands and prohibitions, e.g., "Put it here!", "Don't touch it!" (Hoff-Ginsberg 1991).

A study by Zimmermann (2012) comparing the linguistic input to two Hebrew-speaking children of different socio-economic backgrounds confirms that LSES input is more directive than HSES input. While HSES input consisted of about 11% directive vs. more than 20% elaborative utterances, the LSES input was composed of about 48% directive vs. 1% elaborative utterances.[11] The highly directive nature of LSES input is characterized by a high proportion of deontic modal verb tokens (80%) as well as 2nd person forms (over 60%), as compared to less than 30% 2nd person and only 50% modal verb tokens in HSES input. Concomitantly, the HSES corpus contained close to 40% present-tense verbs, expressing commentaries on ongoing activities and states or their elaborations, as compared to less than 15% of such utterances in LSES. Another finding relating to modal usage suggests that whereas one third of all adjective tokens in the LSES input consist of the prohibitive *asur* 'forbidden', a third of all adjective tokens in the HSES input is made up of the confirmatory *naxon* 'right, correct'.

In view of the available research, the present study has two major goals: (1) to provide a comprehensive description of the development of dynamic, deontic and epistemic modality in child Hebrew, and (2) to examine the potential influence of the input on the early acquisition of modal expressions.

4 Usage-based theories of language acquisition

The present study is set within the theoretical framework of the constructivist, usage-based approach to language acquisition. One of the major tenets of this approach is that language learning is based on experience – "language structure

---

11 Elaborative utterances are utterances which echo, detail, and expand on the child's speech.

emerges from language use" (Tomasello 2003: 327); that is, a speaker's linguistic system is grounded in concrete usage events or utterances (Langacker 1987). With an increase in linguistic experience, more abstract linguistic patterns may evolve. Within this framework, grammatical development is described as a continuum rather than a stage-based process. Children are considered to be active learners, engaged in extracting words and morphemes from the speech stream, detecting patterns, and forming linguistic generalizations helped by socio-cognitive abilities (Saffran 2003; Tomasello 2003, 2006, 2009). Thus, schemas and abstract categories gradually emerge, based on the items children have learned and the distributional and frequency properties of the input (Behrens 2006; Lieven 2008; Tomasello 2004, 2006).

In the present paper, the development of modal expressions will be traced in order to show that children initially start with constructing small item-based schemas and gradually expand the variety and frequency of modal expressions in their language. The nature of the input and its possible effects on the development of agent-oriented modality will also be examind. In particular, the forms of different kinds of direct and indirect requests occurring in CS and CDS as well as their functions will be analyzed.

5 Data and method

The database for the present study comes from naturalistic longitudinal speech samples of two Hebrew-speaking girls, aged 1;5–3;0, and their mothers, who were also their primary caretakers. The girls come from middle-class families living in the vicinity of Tel Aviv, in the central region of Israel. The girls and their caretakers were audio-recorded in intervals of 10–14 days, in different settings (meal time, storytelling, play time, etc.).

Table 1 presents information about the participants and the database and Table 2 includes the token distribution of the two main formal categories of modal expressions studied here, namely, those containing forms of main verbs (imperative and future imperative), on the one hand, and modal verbs, adjectives and adverbs (deontic and epistemic) on the other. Forms of main verbs (e.g., past, present or future) expressing non-modal meanings are excluded from Table 2.[12]

---

[12] Since the present study focuses on modal predicates, predicateless requests like one-word utterances containing a noun or an adjective were not taken into consideration.

Table 1: Participants and database.

Participant*	Age range	MLU range	No. of transcripts	Total no. of utterances
SMD	1;6–2;4	1.5–4.5	16	3,753
SMD-MOT				3,363
LIO	1;5–2;9	1.0–3.5	32	6,691
LIO-MOT				7,778

Table 2: Verb tokens and modal forms.

Participant	Total no. of verbs	Total no. of main verbs with modal forms (IMP, INF, FUT.IMP)	Total no. of agent-oriented and epistemic modal Vs, ADJs and ADVs
SMD	1,019	213	176
SMD-MOT	1,455	550	246
LIO	1,573	387	667
LIO-MOT	4,322	1,449	848

The recordings were transcribed, coded and analyzed using CHILDES as adapted to Hebrew (MacWhinney 2000; Uziel-Karl 2001). All utterances containing predicates were isolated and predicates were coded for their inflection. Modal predicates were singled out and further coded for type of modality (deontic, dynamic, epistemic), function (volition, ability, necessity, possibility, permission, intention, probability) and lexical category (verb, adjective, adverb). Examples of the coding scheme are provided in Table 3.

Table 3: Data coding scheme.

Modal	Gloss	Type	Function	Lexical category	Inflected form
roce	'want'	dynamic	volition	V	PRS.F.SG
carix	'have to, need'	deontic	necessity	ADJ	F.SG
efshar	'possibly'	epistemic	probability	ADV	–

6 Results

In this section, expressions of dynamic, deontic and epistemic modality in the children's course of development will be analyzed and compared to CDS. We first describe modal meanings expressed by verb forms in Hebrew CS and CDS (6.1), then modal meanings expressed by modal verbs, adjectives and adverbs in both varieties (6.2), and lastly, the early development of the modal verb 'want' (6.3).

6.1 Development of inflectionally expressed modal meanings in Hebrew CS in comparison to CDS

Directives, including direct requests (commands) and indirect ones, have been noted to play a central role in the early acquisition of agent-oriented modality, with the imperative as their early and most prominent morphological manifestation (Stephany and Aksu-Koç, this volume).[13] Figures (1)–(4) display the distribution of modal verb forms (in percentages) across all modally used full verbs in CS and CDS throughout the sampling period. In the Figures, IMP and FUT.IMP are counted only when functioning as directives or denoting requests and INF is counted when used modally to express commands or prohibitions.

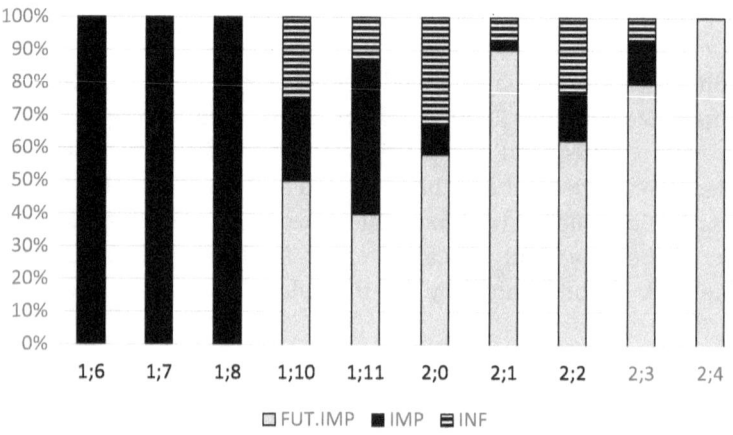

Figure 1: Distribution of verb forms across all modal predicates in Smadar's CS.

Figures (1) and (2) reveal that the girls use members of the "modal cluster", i.e., the imperative, the future imperative and the infinitive throughout the sampling period. Both rely on forms of the "modal cluster" to express deontic modal notions

---

[13] It should be noted that verbless requests such as *milk! ball!* were not taken into consideration in the present study.

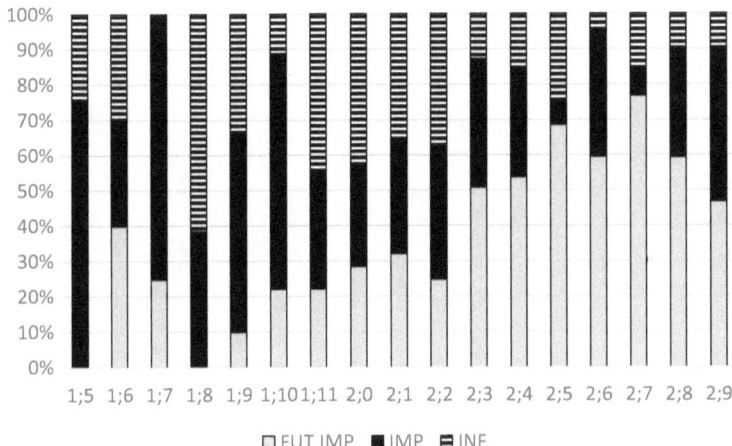

Figure 2: Distribution of verb forms across all modal predicates in Lior's CS.

in commands, other requests and prohibitions, yet they differ in the overall distribution of these forms across development.

Figure (1) shows that between ages 1;6–1;8 Smadar uses verbs only in the imperative form. Her early imperatives are initially limited to a small set of transfer and motion verbs (examples 13). She uses the imperative to express requests and ask her mother to perform desired actions. From age 1;10 onward, Smadar starts using the two additional members of the "modal cluster", the infinitive and the future imperative while reducing the number of imperatives. She uses the infinitive rather sparsely throughout the sampling period mainly to express her own desires (example 14), to make requests for her own benefit (example 15), or to express prohibitions (examples 16). The future imperative and the imperative have similar functions. Smadar uses both to get her mother to act (examples 17) and to make direct requests (example 18).

(13) a. Smadar 1;6
    kxi!
    take.IMP.F.2SG
    'Take!'
  b. *boi!*
    come.IMP.F.2SG
    'Come!'

(14) Smadar 1;10
    leʔexol.
    eat.INF
    'Eat.'

(15) Smadar 2;0
    ʕod   lasim.
    more   put.INF
    'Put more.'

(16) a. Smadar 2;0
        loʔ lishpox.
        not spill.INF
        'Don't spill.'
    b. Smadar 2;1
        loʔ lisgor.
        not close
        'Don't close.'

(17) a. Smadar 2;11
        ima, teshvi   al ha-sapa.
        mom, sit.FUT.IMP.F.2SG on the-sofa
        'Mom, sit on the sofa.'
    b. Smadar 2;0
        tesadri!
        arrange.FUT.IMP.F.2SG
        'Tidy up!'

(18) Smadar 2;0
    taʕazri   li.
    help.FUT.IMP.F.2SG   to.me
    'Help me.'

Unlike Smadar, Lior makes use of the three members of the "modal cluster" right from the start (Figure 2). At the outset, she uses the imperative to make direct requests for things (example 19) or to get her mother to act (example 20). The number of imperatives in her data starts to decrease at age 1;11. Between 1;8–2;2 Lior uses the infinitive rather extensively to make requests (example 21a), express desires (example 21b) and prohibitions (example 22).

From age 2;3 onward, the number of infinitives in her sample decreases drastically, giving way to the future imperative. Lior uses this form to make direct requests (example 23) and to draw her mother's attention to various objects and people (example 24).

(19) Lior 1;6
 tni et ze!
 give.IMP.F.2SG ACC this
 'Give (me) this!'

(20) Lior 1;6
 bo, bo!
 come.IMP.M.2SG come.IMP.M.2SG
 'Come, come!'

(21) a. Lior 1;6
  liftoax.
  open.INF
  'Open.'
 b. Lior 1;8
  lishon.
  sleep.INF
  'Sleep.'

(22) Lior 1;11
 lo? laʕalot!
 not go.up.INF
 'Don't go up!'

(23) Lior 1;9
 taviʔi yad!
 bring.FUT.IMP.F.2SG hand
 'Give (me a) hand!'

(24) Lior 1;10
 tirʔi!
 look.FUT.IMP.F.2SG
 'Look!'

The data suggest that at the outset of the sampling period, the use of modal verb forms by the girls is verb-specific, i.e., each verb gets only one of the three modal forms (IMP or INF or FUT.IMP) (cf. Armon-Lotem and Berman 2003). The girls appear to differentiate the early function of the infinitive from the one of the imperative and the future imperative. They seem to use the imperative and future imperative to make direct, personalized requests of the addressee (objects or actions), while using the infinitive in more general and often impersonal requests, mostly to express their own needs and desires. The number of imperatives decreases dramatically in Smadar's speech from 1;10 and in Lior's from 1;11 on, giving way mainly to modal verb forms in the future imperative.

Unlike CS, in CDS the distribution of verb forms belonging to the "modal cluster" remains relatively stable over time (Figures 3 and 4). The two mothers use the imperative rather moderately during the sampling period, with slightly more occurrences at the outset. It is used with certain transfer and motion verbs to express deontic meanings like making requests or to make the girls carry out some action (examples 25).

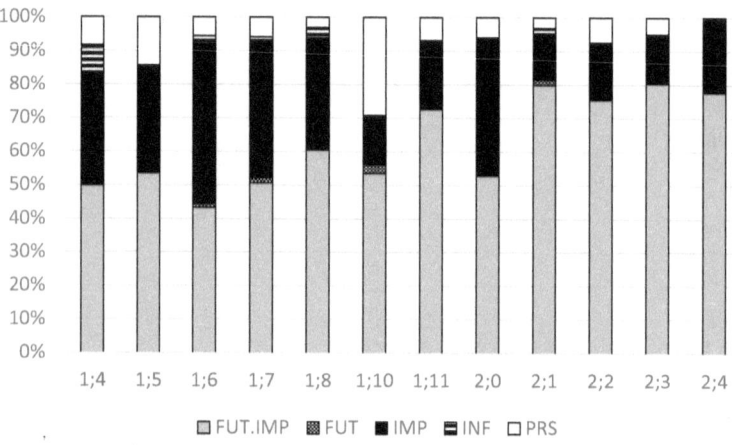

Figure 3: Distribution of verb forms across all modal predicates in Smadar's CDS.

(25) a. Smadar's mother (Smadar 1;5)
lexi!
go.IMP.F.2SG
'Go!'

b. Smadar's mother (Smadar 1;6)
   simi!
   put.IMP.F.2SG
   'Put!'

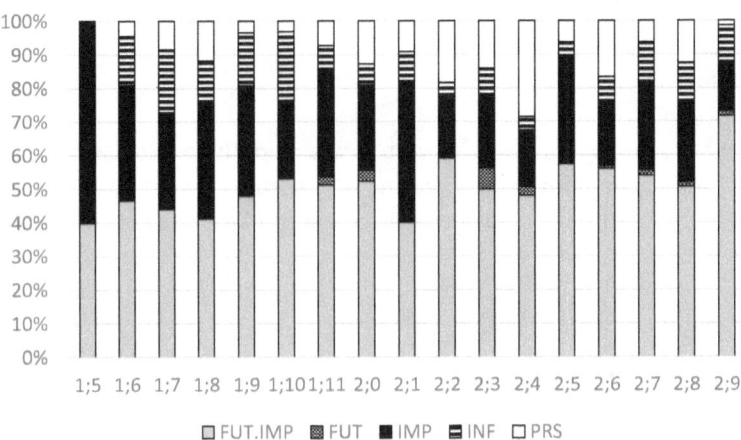

Figure 4: Distribution of verb forms across all modal predicates in Lior's CDS.

The mothers make extensive use of the future imperative throughout the sampling period mainly for instructing their daughters what to do and how to behave. In contrast, they use the canonical future later in development and extremely sparsely to express dynamic modal notions like intentions, and unlike the girls, to express epistemic modal notions of different degrees of certainty or uncertainty (example 26). The two mothers differ from each other in the extent to which they use the infinitive for expressing modality. While Smadar's mother resorts to infinitives only sporadically, they occur rather frequently and more consistently in the language of Lior's mother throughout the sampling period. In both mothers' CDS the infinitive mainly serves to express prohibitions (examples 27).

(26) Lior's mother (Lior 2;7)
   ulay   nelex   maxar   le-gan.xayot.
   perhaps   go.FUT.1PL   tomorrow   to-zoo
   'Perhaps we'll go to (the) zoo tomorrow.'

(27) a. Lior's mother (Lior 1;6)
    loʔ   lagaʕat!
    not   touch.INF
    'Don't touch!'
  b. Smadar's mother (Smadar 2;1)
    asur   laʕalot!
    forbidden   go up.INF
    '(It is) forbidden to go up.'

The two mothers use present indicative verb forms modally to express deontic meaning in prohibitions rendered by stating social rules (example 28) or to convey epistemic modality by using cognitive verbs like 'know' and 'think' (examples 29–31).

(28) Smadar's mother (Smadar 1;11)
    loʔ potxim   et   ze!
    not open.PRS.M.PL ACC this
    'One doesn't open this!'

(29) Lior's mother (Lior 1;6)
    at   yodaʕat, ani xoshevet   she Nican
    you.F.SG know   I   think.PRS.F.SG that Nican
    hitʕorer.
    wake.up.PST.M.3SG
    'You know, I think that Nican woke up.'

(30) Smadar's mother (Smadar 1;5)
    ani xoshevet   she loʔ meʕanyen otax.
    I   think.PRS.F.SG that not interests   you
    'I think that it doesn't interest you.'

(31) Lior's mother (Lior 1;7)
    LIO: mi   baʔ
           who come.PST.M.3SG
           'who came?'

MOT: *ani   lo? yodaʕat   im misheu*
     I   not know.PRS.F.SG   if someone
     ba?.
     come.PST.M.3SG
     'I don't know if someone came.'

Although both mothers use present indicative verb forms to express modality, most occurrences of present verb forms in CDS as well as CS are non-modal. Non-modal uses of the present indicative of full verbs include questions for clarification (example 32), questions for information (example 33), confirmation or description of a state or activity (perhaps to facilitate future transcription of the situation as the girls were only audio-recorded) (examples 34–35), and expression of emotions. Finally, past forms expressing past desires and intentions occur rarely in CDS (example 36).

(32) Lior's mother (Lior 1;6)
Itamar mitragez   ve   boʕet
Itamar get.angry.PRS.M.SG   and   kick.PRS.M.SG
ba-delet?
on.the-door
'Does Itamar get angry and kick the door?'

(33) Lior's mother (Lior 1;6)
ma   at   osa?
what   you.F.2SG   do.PRS.F.SG
'What (are) you doing?'

(34) Smadar's mother (Smadar 1;5)
hine, at   macbiʕa   al ha-teyp, naxon?
here   you.F.2SG point.PRS.F.SG   at   the-tape   right
'Here, you are pointing at the tape, right?'

(35) Smadar's mother (Smadar 1;5)
axshav at   lo?   macbiʕa   at
now   you.F.SG   not   point.PRS.F.SG   you.F.SG
rak   mar?a   li,   ken.
just   show.PRS.F.SG   to.me   yes
'Now you are not pointing, you are just showing me, right?'

(36) Lior's mother (Lior 3;0)
    ani davka raciti   laʕasot itax   mashehu.
    I   rather want.PST.1SG do.INF with.you.F.2SG something
    axer.
    else
    'I rather wanted to do something else with you.'

To summarize, as has been found in CS, during the entire sampling period there is also quite an extensive use of "modal cluster" verb forms expressing deontic modal notions in CDS. In addition, the two mothers use present verb forms modally rather sparsely to express deontic and epistemic modality. Use of the canonical future and past verb forms to express modality is almost nonexistent.[14]

6.2 Modal meanings expressed by modal verbs, adjectives and adverbs in Hebrew CS and CDS

In this section the emergence of modal verbs, adjectives and adverbs in CS as compared with their early use in CDS are examined. The token frequency of agent-oriented vs. epistemic modals out of the total number of modal verbs, adjectives and adverbs for each participant is presented in Figure 5.

Figure 5 reveals (1) that overall, agent-oriented modal verbs, adjectives and adverbs are considerably more prominent than epistemic modals in the language of the girls and their mothers, and (2) that the percentage of agent-oriented modal verbs, adjectives and adverbs in the girls' language is slightly higher than in the mothers' language, whereas the percentage of epistemic modals in the mothers' language is higher than in the girls'.

---

14 Non-modal present verb forms are used in CS extremely sparsely and hence are not described at length in this section. Nonetheless, it should be noted that non-modal uses of present verb forms appear in the girls' language earlier than modal uses of these forms. The girls use the present to describe a variety of states (physical, cognitive, emotional), e.g., *Kushi omed kaxa* (Kushi stand.PRS.M.SG like that) 'Kushi (a dog) stands like that' (Smadar 1;7), *koʕes* 'angry.PRS.M.SG' (Lior 1;8), and activities, e.g., *ose an-an* (make.PRS.M.SG an-an) 'making (a sound) an-an' (Smadar 1;7), *tusa* (you.F.2SG.do.PRS.F.SG) 'you do'. Non-modal past and canonical future verb forms occur extremely scarcely. Past verb forms mainly describe past activities or changes of state, e.g., *nafal* 'fall.PST.M.3SG' (Lior 1;6). Canonical future forms convey future plans and activities, e.g., *anaxnu nesader* 'we tidy.up.FUT.1PL', and concerns, e.g., *she loʔ yipol* 'that not fall.FUT.M.3SG' (Smadar 2;0).

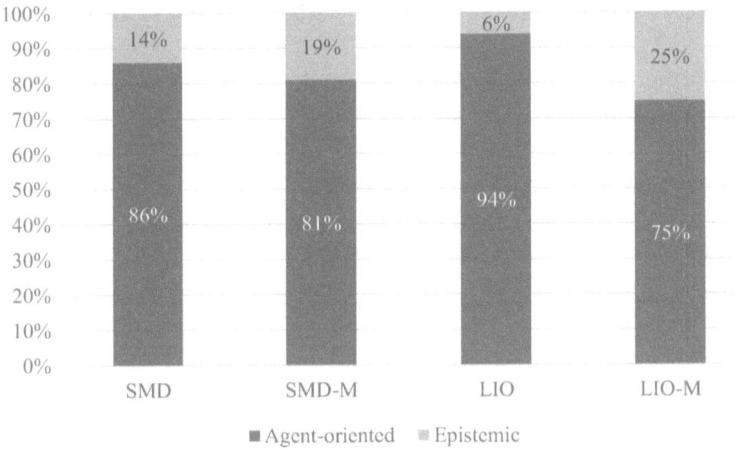

Figure 5: Distribution of agent-oriented vs. epistemic modal verbs, adjectives and adverbs in CS and CDS.

Table 4 lists the number of tokens of agent-oriented vs. epistemic modal verbs, adjectives and adverbs for each participant and presents the percentage of each type of modality out of the total number of these parts of speech.

Table 4: Tokens and percentages of agent-oriented and epistemic modal verbs, adjectives and adverbs in CS and CDS.

Type of Modality	LIO	LIO-MOT	SMD	SMD-MOT
Agent-oriented	626	639	152	200
	(94%)	(75%)	(86%)	(81%)
Epistemic	41	209	24	46
	(6%)	(25%)	(14%)	(19%)

As shown in Figure 5 and Table 4, lexical expressions of agent-oriented modality occur much more frequently than epistemic ones. The development of the agent-oriented use of lexical expressions will be described in section 6.2.1 and their epistemic use in section 6.2.2.

6.2.1 The development of agent-oriented modal verbs, adjectives and adverbs

Table 5 presents the overall frequencies of dynamic vs. deontic modal verbs, adjectives and adverbs for each participant.

Table 5: Deontic vs. dynamic modals in CS and CDS (tokens).

Modal category	Modal	Gloss	Lex. cat.	SMD	S-MOT	LIO	L-MOT
Dynamic	roce	'want'	V	115	134	553	304
	yaxol	'be able to'	V	17	15	32	149
Deontic	carix	'have to'	ADJ	17	45	39	164
	xayav	'obliged'	ADJ	0	0	1	18
	mutar	'allowed'	ADV	0	4	0	1
	asur	'forbidden'	ADV	3	2	1	3
Total				152	200	626	639

The following observations arise from Table 5: (1) The girls and their mothers use *roce* 'want' and *yaxol* 'can, be able to' considerably more often than the modal adjectives *carix* 'have to', *xayav* 'obliged' and the modal adverbs *mutar* 'allowed' and *asur* 'forbidden'. Thus, the two dynamic modal verbs constitute most agent-oriented modal predicates in the girls' as well as the mothers' speech. (2) Within the category of deontic modality, the girls and mothers express obligation most frequently and permission least frequently (see the adjectival predicate *carix* 'have to' and the adverbial predicate *mutar* 'allowed', respectively). (3) The girls' and the mothers' speech match with regard to the relative frequency of modal verbs, adjectives and adverbs.

Figures (6)–(9) show the development of the four most frequently occurring agent-oriented modal verbs and adjectives in CS and CDS.

The first modal verb expressing the dynamic notion of desire (*roce* 'want') in Smadar's speech emerges at 1;7, i.e. two months after the beginning of observation (Figure 6). Until 1;11, the two modal expressions *yaxol* 'can, be able to' and *carix* 'should, ought to' rendering the dynamic notion of ability (example 37) and the deontic notion of necessity (example 38), respectively, are added. Smadar uses all three modal expressions for the first time in a single session at age 1;11. At age 2;0 the token frequency of these modal expressions increases dramatically, with *roce* 'want' being by far the most frequent one. The frequency of modal verbs and adjectives expressing dynamic and deontic notions remains high for several months (until 2;3). After first using *yaxol* 'can, be able to' to express dynamic

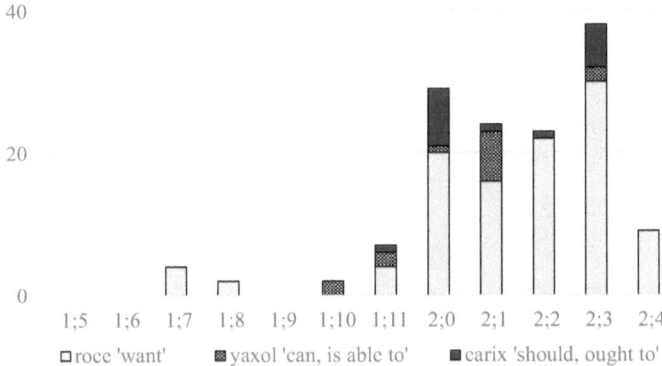

Figure 6: Smadar's acquisition of agent-oriented modal verbs and adjectives (tokens).

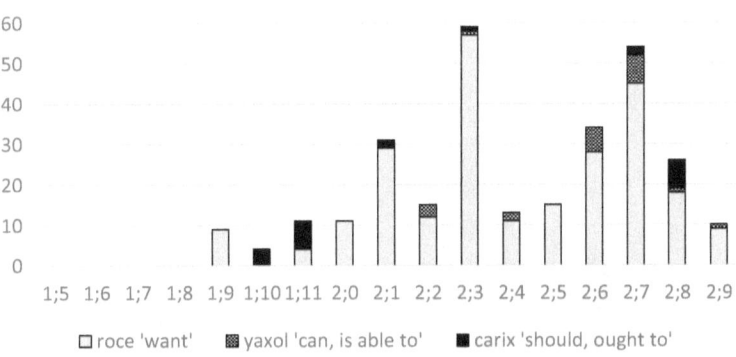

Figure 7: Lior's acquisition of agent-oriented modal verbs and adjectives (tokens).

modality at age 2;3, Smadar employs this modal verb to make polite indirect requests (example 39). To summarize, Smadar's development of lexically expressed agent-oriented modality starts with an expression of dynamic modality being joined by those for deontic modal notions later. The girl uses the modal verb *roce* 'want' considerably more often than any other modal verb or adjective.

(37) Smadar 1;10
    ani lo? yexola.
    I   not can.PRS.F.SG
    'I can't.'

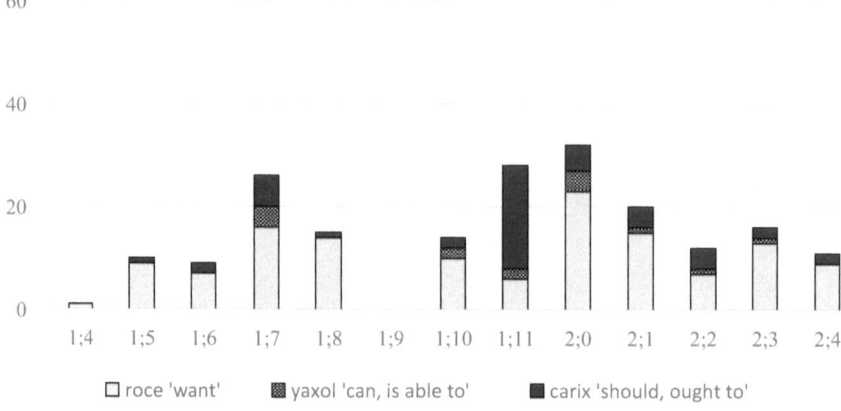

Figure 8: Agent-oriented modal verbs and adjectives in Smadar's mother's CDS (tokens).

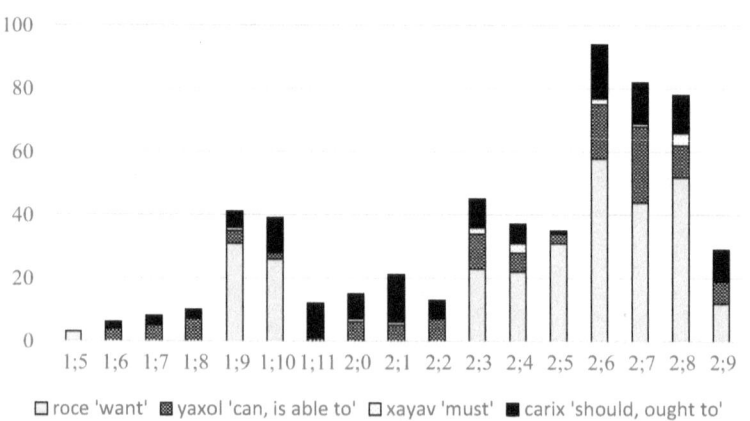

Figure 9: Agent-oriented modal verbs and adjectives in Lior's mother's CDS (tokens).

(38) Smadar 2;0
 Carix lenakot.
 necessary.M.SG clean.INF
 'It is necessary to clean.'

(39) Smadar 2;3
 ulay ata yaxol lexakot?
 perhaps you.M.SG can.PRS.M.SG wait.INF
 'Perhaps you can wait?'

Between 1;9 and 2;0, Lior uses only one or two modal verbs and adjectives per sampling period at a rather low frequency (Figure 7). As with Smadar, the earliest modal predicate in her language is the modal verb *roce* 'want' expressing volition. Lior's earliest uses of 'want' are expressions of unwillingness or refusal i.e., *loʔ (ro)ca* (not want.PRS.F.SG) 'don't wanna'. At age 1;10 she starts using the modal adjective *carix* 'should, ought to' to express deontic necessity, but until 2;0 all her uses of this adjective include the negator *loʔ* 'not', e.g., *loʔ carix* 'not necessary' (example 40). From age 2;1 onward, Lior no longer limits her expression of deontic necessity to negative contexts (examples 41 and 42).

(40) Lior 1;11
MOT: *at roca et ha-kesef?*
you.F.SG want.PRS.F.SG ACC the-money
'Do you want the money?'
LIOR: *loʔ carix.*
not necessary
'Not necessary.'

(41) Lior 2;1
Carix lilbosh naʕalayim.
Necessary wear.INF shoes
'It is necessary to wear shoes.'

(42) Lior 2;3
sandalim carix.
sandals necessary.M.SG
'(It is) necessary (to wear) sandals.'

Lior starts using modal verbs and adjectives later than Smadar and shows dramatic peaks in the frequency of modal verbs and adjectives at ages 2;1, 2;3, and 2;7. These peaks may be due to the nature of the interactions between her mother and herself; while some interactions may elicit more modals (e.g., a conversation about Lior's preferred dinner menu), others may elicit less, or none (e.g., a joint book reading activity). At age 2;2, Lior first uses *yaxol* 'can, be able to' to denote dynamic ability in much the same way as Smadar (example 37). Lior has been found to use three modal expressions in a single session only at age 2;7 expressing the dynamic and deontic notions outlined above.

To summarize the development of lexical expressions of agent-oriented modality in CS, dynamic notions are observed in the girls' data prior to deontic ones and are highly frequent in the language of both girls.

Turning to CDS, Smadar's mother uses only one or two modals expressing agent-oriented meanings with very low frequency in the early period from 1;4 to 1;6 (Figure 8). The earliest modal predicate in her speech is the modal verb *roce* 'want' expressing dynamic modality, which is also the most frequently used modal throughout the sampling period. When Smadar is 1;5, the adjectival modal *carix* 'should, ought to' expressing deontic necessity is introduced by her mother. However, initially, this verb is used in negative constructions such as *lo? carix lisgor et ha-delet* (not necessary close.INF the-door) 'it is not necessary to close the door'. When the child is 1;7, her mother's speech shows an increase in the number of modal lexemes and their token frequency. At this age, the mother also starts using the modal verb *yaxol* 'can, be able to'. This verb is primarily used to express the dynamic notion of (in)ability, and to a lesser extent, the deontic notion of possibility. Between ages 1;10–2;3, Smadar's mother uses all three modal predicates in each sampling period, with dynamic modality being significantly more frequent than deontic modality. As far as the functions of modal predicates are concerned, they mainly relate to her daughter's desires, inquire about the child's abilities or inabilities and make statements about her expected behavior.

As is the case with Smadar's mother, Lior's mother uses only one or two modal lexemes very infrequently between the child's ages 1;5 and 1;8 (Figure 9). These modal predicates include *roce* 'want', *yaxol* 'can, be able to' and *carix* 'should, ought to'. At 1;9, the modal adjective *xayav* 'obliged' expressing deontic obligation is added. Lior's mother only sporadically uses this adjective to talk about norms of behavior or social obligations throughout the entire sampling period (e.g., *at halaxt yexefa baxuc, xayavim lehitkaleax* (you.F.2SG walk.PST.F.2SG barefoot outside, obliged.M.PL shower.INF) 'you walked barefoot outside, (one) must shower'). During the two periods in which modal frequency is low (1;5–1;8 and 1;11–2;2), Lior's mother uses the modal verb *yaxol* 'can, be able to' and the modal adjective *carix* 'should, ought to' almost exclusively. *Yaxol* expresses ability and permission (example 43) and *carix* 'should, ought to' as well as *xayav* 'obliged' deontic necessity. During the periods in which modal frequency is high, *roce* 'want' is used to express the child's volition or inquire about it.

(43) Lior's mother (Lior 1;8)
    ha-pil   *lo? yaxol*   *lasheve po.*
    the-elephant not be.able.PRS.M.SG sit.INF here
    'The elephant cannot (=is not allowed to) sit here.'

As pointed out above, agent-oriented use of modal verbs, adjectives, and to a lesser extent adverbs, is much more prominent than epistemic use in both CDS and CS. Within agent-oriented modality, dynamic modality is realized by the modal verb *roce* 'want' and slightly less by *yaxol* 'can, be able to'. The former is not only more prominent throughout but also emerges earlier in the language of the mothers and the girls. Whereas the girls use *roca* 'want.PRS.F.SG' primarily to express their own desires or (un)willingness to do things, the mothers use this verb form to ask the girls questions about their desires, make indirect requests (example 44), or ask for confirmation and clarification. Both mothers use *yaxol* 'can, be able to' to talk about the girls' abilities or inabilities (example 45) as well as about their own, e.g., *ani yexola laʕazor lax* (I can.PRS.F.SG help.INF to.you.F.2SG) 'I can help you' (Lior's mother, when Lior is 1;10). Smadar's mother also uses *yaxol* 'can, be able to' to express dynamic possibility, and Lior's mother to express permission. The mothers differ from each other in that, later, only Lior's mother uses it to express epistemic possibility. The girls' language displays the same variability in the use of *yaxol* 'can, be able to'. Finally, both the mothers and the girls use the modal adjective *carix* 'should, ought to' to express deontic necessity. Yet, the inventory of modal lexemes is not exploited to the same extent in the speech of the two dyads. Thus, the modal adjective *xayav* 'obliged' is used to express deontic necessity only by Lior and her mother but not by Smadar and her mother. A general observation on the use of modal lexemes by the mothers is that they seem to respond to the girls' needs and wants when they are younger and to comment more on their behavior and abilities introducing social norms as they get a bit older.

(44) Lior's mother (Lior 1;6)
 roca   lesaper le-ima   sipur?
 wanna.PRS.F.SG tell.INF to-Mommy story
 'Wanna tell Mommy (a) story?'

(45) Smadar's mother (Smadar 1;7)
 tensi   tenasi   at   yexola.
 try.PRS.F.2SG try.PRS.F.2SG   you can.PRS.F.SG
 'Try, try you can.'

6.2.2 The development of epistemic verbs, adjectives and adverbs

In Hebrew, a few modal verbs and adjectives can be used to denote both agent-oriented and epistemic modality. When followed by the copula 'be' in the infinitive the following modal predicates denote increasing degrees of certainty on the epistemic scale: *yaxol lihyot* (may be.INF) 'possibly, maybe', *carix lihyot* (should be.INF) 'probably, should be' and *xayav lihyot* (must be.INF) 'certainly, must be'. Epistemic uses of these modal predicates emerge after their agent-oriented uses and are relatively scarce in both CS and CDS, as described in what follows.

Epistemic modal expressions appear in the girls' language later than agent-oriented ones (about a month later in Smadar's language and about five months later in Lior's). Smadar's first epistemic modal is found at 1;7 with the use of the modal adverb *ulay* 'perhaps' to express possibility. At 1;10, she uses *betax* 'surely' for the first time to mark certainty and, at 2;0, she starts using *efshar* 'possibly' to express possibility in addition to *ulay* 'perhaps'. In contrast to modal adverbs, Smadar does not show evidence of using modal verbs epistemically during the entire sampling period. Lior's first use of an epistemic modal expression is found at 1;11, when she expresses possibility by *ulay* 'perhaps'. At 2;0, she first uses *ʔi-efshar* 'impossible'. At 2;4, Lior starts using the modal verb *yaxol* 'can, be able to' epistemically to express possibility or probability (example 46). At 2;7, she first uses the modal adverb *betax* 'surely' to mark certainty and, at 2;9, she expresses impossibility by *loʔ yaxol lihyot* (not may.PRS.M.SG be.INF) 'it is not possible'.

(46) Lior 2;4
 ze yaxol lihyot.
 it may.PRS.M.SG be.INF
 'It may be.'

To summarize, the two girls differ in the onset of epistemic forms in their language and in using modal verbs in addition to modal adjectives and adverbs for expressing epistemic notions. They resemble each other in that both of them first use epistemic modals to express possibility and only later certainty. The epistemic notion of (im)probability is expressed last, but only by Lior.

Smadar's mother uses the epistemic modal adverb *ʔi-efshar* 'impossible' when the girl is 1;4 and *ulay* 'perhaps' when she is 1;7. The epistemic adverb *betax* 'surely' is found in Smadar's mother's speech when her daughter is 1;10, and *efshar* 'possibly' when she is 1;11. The same adverbs are also used by Lior's mother: *ulay* 'perhaps' when Lior is 1;6, *betax* 'surely' at 2;2, and *efshar* 'possibly' at 2;6. Finally, when Lior is 2;9, her mother uses the two additional epistemic modal expressions *yaxol lihyot* 'possibly, maybe' and *carix lihyot* 'probably, should be'. Thus, both mothers first express the epistemic functions of (im)possibility and certainty, introducing probability last. In both CDS and CS, modal adverbs appear before pairings of a modal adjective with the copula 'to be'. As is to be expected, the mothers use a slightly larger variety of epistemic modals than the girls.

6.3 The early development of *roce* 'want'

Dynamic modality has been found to play a prominent role in the early development of modality in many languages as far as lexical expressions of agent-oriented modality are concerned (Hickmann and Bassano 2016). In the acquisition of Hebrew, dynamic modality is most often expressed by the verb *roce* 'want', reported to emerge early and to function as the first modal verb in the early lexicon of Hebrew-speaking children (Armon-Lotem and Berman 2003; Uziel-Karl 2001). This has also been confirmed by the present study. Since *roce* 'want' occurs very frequently both in CS and CDS throughout the entire period of observation, the development of its inflected forms and their functions is interesting and will be described in detail in the present section. The verb *roce* 'want' has also been reported to be the earliest verb used with different argument structures (V OBJ, NEG V, SBJ V, SBJ V V and SBJ V OBJ, respectively), as illustrated in examples (47)–(51) (see Uziel-Karl 2001). The early use of *roce* 'want' in multiple-word constructions suggests that children use this verb as a path-breaking verb to move beyond the one-word stage into syntax (Ninio 1999; Uziel-Karl 2001).

(47) Smadar, 1;7
 roca sakin.
 want.PRS.F.SG knife
 'I want a knife.'

(48) Smadar 1;8
 lo? roca!
 not want.PRS.F.SG
 'I don't want!'

(49) Lior, 1;9
 ani roca!
 I want.PRS.F.SG
 'I want!'

(50) Smadar, 2;0
   ani   roca   lirʔot.
   I   want.PRS.F.SG   see.INF
   'I want to see.'

(51) Smadar, 2;2
   ani   roca   ʕod   harkava.
   I   want.PRS.F.SG   another   puzzle
   'I want another puzzle.'

Since both subjects of the present study are girls, the earliest and most frequently used form of *roce* 'want' is the feminine singular of the present indicative *roca* referring to the speaker (Table 6). This is also the form commonly used by the mothers when addressing their daughters.

Table 6: Forms of *roce* 'want' in CS (tokens).[15]

AGE	raciti PST.1SG		roce PRS.M.SG		roca PRS.F.SG		rocim PRS.M.PL	
	LIO	SMD	LIO	SMD	LIO	SMD	LIO	SMD
1;7						4		
1;8			1			1		
1;9					9			
1;10					3			
1;11			1	2	3	1		
2;0			2	4	9	16		
2;1		5			29	11		
2;2			1	2	11	18		2
2;3		3	5		52	27		
2;4					11	9		
2;5			4		7		4	
2;6			6		22			
2;7			1		44			
2;8	1		1		14		2	
2;9			1		8			

---

15 Smadar's data are only available until age 2;4.

A qualitative analysis of the data reveals that, at an early stage, the girls use *roca* 'want.PRS.F.SG' with no overt subject, primarily to express their own desires (example 47) or (un)willingness to do things (example 48). For example, Lior uses *lo? (ro)ca* 'don't wanna' to reject objects offered to her or refuse activities in which her mother tries to engage her against her will. Since Hebrew does not mark person on present tense forms (see section 2), *roca* 'want.PRS.F.SG' may be interpreted as referring to the girls themselves or to other female participants in the conversational setting (the hearer or a third party). Although the present tense normally requires an explicit subject, subjectless sentences may nevertheless be discourse appropriate. Shortly after the null subject phase, the girls start using *roca* 'want.PRS.F.SG' with a personal pronoun, e.g., *ani* 'I', *at* 'you.F.SG', *hi* 'she' etc. to overtly indicate the referent. These utterances, too, exhibit only partial argument structure in that they do not contain a complement (see examples 49 and 50 above). Nonetheless, they may be pragmatically adequate in the discourse context, e.g., when functioning as responses to direct questions. Soon after age 2;0, the girls are able to express their desires and intentions using grammatically complete sentences (see example 51 above). Around the same time, they start using subjectless sentences with *roca* 'want.PRS.F.SG' to ask the interlocutor for their desires or to make indirect requests, e.g., *roca lesaxek?* (want.PRS.F.SG play.INF) 'do you want to play?'.

Since our two subjects are girls, it is to be expected that they start using the feminine singular form *roca* before the masculine form *roce* 'want.PRS.M.SG'. The latter form serves to make indirect requests by expressing the desires of animate or inanimate male beings in their environment, e.g., Lior's brother, father, the family dog or inanimate cartoon figures (example 52). A further function of this form is to ask males questions about their desires (example 53).

(52) Lior 2;2
 hu roce la-ʕagala.
 he want.PRS.M.SG to.the-stroller
 'He wants (to get) on the stroller.'

(53) Lior 2;8
 Pinuki, ma ata roce?
 Pinuki what you.M.SG want.PRS.M.SG
 'Pinuki, what do you want?'

Additional inflected forms of the verb *roce* 'want' are acquired later and used very infrequently. One of these is the past form *raciti* 'want.PST.1SG' describing the girls' past desires or intentions (example 54). The present masculine plural form *rocim* 'want.PRS.M.PL' is used to pose indirect requests to a group of people in the girls' environment (example 55) or to state their desires (example 56).

(54) Smadar 2;3
    ani   raciti   lehaklit,   ani   raciti
    I   want.PST.1SG record.INF, I   want.PST.1SG
    ledaber   im   ha-teyp.
    speak.INF   with the-tape.recorder
    'I wanted to record, I wanted to talk with the tape-recorder.'

(55) Smadar 2;2
    rocim   lir?ot   she ani markiva
    want.PRS.M.PL see.INF that I   assemble.PRS.F.SG
    et-ze?
    ACC-this
    'Do you want to see that I am assembling this?'

(56) Lior 2;5
    anashim rocim   le?exol.
    people   want.PRS.M.PL eat.INF
    'The people want to eat.'

As in the girls' speech, the present feminine singular form *roca* 'want' is also the most frequent form of *roce* occurring in the mothers' speech throughout the sampling period (Table 7).

The mothers use *roca* 'want.PRS.F.SG' to ask questions about the girls' desires (examples 57 and 58), to achieve clarity (example 59) and to obtain confirmation (example 60).

(57) Lior's mother (Lior 2;1)
    at   roca   neshika?
    you.F want.PRS.F.SG kiss
    'Do you want a kiss?'

(58) Lior's mother (Lior 2;5)
    az ma   at   roca?
    so what you.F.SG want.PRS.F.SG
    'So what do you want?'

Table 7: Forms of *roce* 'want' in CDS (tokens).[16]

AGE	*roce* PRS.M.SG		*roca* PRS.F.SG		*racit* PST.F.2SG		*rocim* PRS.M.PL	
	LIO	SMD	LIO	SMD	LIO	SMD	LIO	SMD
1;4				1				
1;5		1	3	8				
1;6			40	7				
1;7		1	12	14				1
1;8	1		15	14				
1;9	5	2	26	8				
1;10	2	1	23	5			1	
1;11	1	1	14	22				
2;0	3		29	14		1		
2;1	1		58	7	2			
2;2	2		15	12		1		
2;3			21	9	2			
2;4			22	1				
2;5	8		20				3	
2;6	10		46				2	
2;7	7		32		4		1	
2;8	5		37		2		5	
2;9	4		4		2		1	

(59) Smadar's mother (Smadar 2;1)
 kaxa at roca leharkiv?
 like.this you.F.SG want.PRS.F.SG put.together.INF
 'This is how you want to put it together?'

(60) Lior's mother (Lior 2;6)
 at roca lelamed oto lo?
 you.F.SG want.PRS.F.SG teach.INF him not
 lixʕos alav, naxon?
 be.angry.INF with.him right
 'You want to teach him not to be angry with him, right?'

The next most frequent form after the present feminine singular occurring in CDS is the masculine singular *roce* 'want.PRS.M.SG'. Lior's mother uses this form

---

[16] No data are available for Smadar's mother after the child's age 2;4.

to make assertions about the desires of male beings (e.g., her son, her husband or the family dog), for indirect requests (e.g., trying to make her children sit down) (example 61), or for getting information about a male individual's needs (example 62). Smadar's mother uses *roce* 'want.PRS.M.SG' mainly in statements about the desires of animate beings or even inanimate entities and objects in Smadar's environment (example 63).

(61) Lior's mother (Lior 2;1)
 mi roce lashevet?
 who want.PRS.M.SG sit.INF
 'Who wants to sit?'

(62) Lior's mother (Lior 2;2)
 ma ata roce?
 what you.M.2SG want.PRS.M.SG
 'What do you want?'

(63) Smadar's mother (Smadar 1;11)
 ha-teyp roce lirʔot ma she at
 the-tape.recorder want.PRS.M.SG see.INF what that you.F.2SG
 osa.
 do.PRS.F.SG
 'The tape recorder wants to see what it is that you are doing.'

Over time, the mothers increase the number of inflected forms of *roce* 'want' including several forms which do not occur in the girls' speech, namely *racit* 'want.PST.F.2SG', *raca* 'want.PST.M.3SG', and *raciti* 'want.PST.1SG', which is sparsely used only by Lior's mother. These forms serve to talk about their own past intentions or desires and about those of others. They are most steadily used by Lior's mother after her daughter's age 2;5.

To summarize, the verb of desire *roce* 'want' primarily expressing dynamic modality emerges early in both CS and in CDS. Since both of our subjects are girls and their main caretakers are the mothers, the most frequent form of this verb in both CS and CDS is *roca* 'want.PRS.F.SG'. However, unlike the girls, who use this form to express their own desires or (un)willingness to act, it primarily serves to inquire about the girls' needs and desires in the mothers' speech. The next frequent form in both CS and CDS is *roce* 'want.PRS.M.SG', used by the girls as well as their mothers to ask about the desires of male beings in their environment. Over time, the mothers produce more different forms of this verb with additional functions than the children.

7 Discussion and conclusions

In the present study the development of modality in child Hebrew was examined. To this end the forms and functions of early directives expressed inflectionally or by modal verbs, adjectives and adverbs in the language of two Hebrew-speaking girls and their mothers were analyzed.

The findings suggest that both girls make a clear distinction between modal and non-modal verb forms from the very beginning of the observation period in the end of the first half of their second year. They use modal verb forms like the imperative and the future imperative to make direct requests, alongside with non-modal present indicative and past forms for statements. As in other languages, the proportion of modal as compared to non-modal forms changes over time (see, e.g., Stephany 1985 for Greek), with the imperative becoming less frequent in comparison to present and past forms. The early modal/non-modal distinction may be explained by two of the most basic motives for communication which according to Tomasello (2010: 84–86) include requests, i.e. "getting others to do what one wants them to" and offering help "by informing others of things".

A comparison of the use of modal verb forms in CS and CDS shows that the mothers' use of such forms remains relatively stable throughout the sampling period, while the proportion of imperative vs. future imperative verb forms in the girls' language undergoes drastic changes over time. This may be due to a number of factors: (1) Since the girls only have a restricted verbal lexicon at their disposal in the beginning, each verb is initially used in a unique form which most often echos the most salient verb form in the input so that the frequent use of certain verbal lexemes entails a more frequent occurrence of their particular forms; (2) unlike the girls, the mothers start out with a larger verb repertoire, which contributes to the stability of their verb form usage over time; (3) most of the early verbs that the girls initially use in the imperative are general purpose verbs like 'come', 'go', 'give', 'take' and 'put'. As they grow older and expand their verb lexicon, the girls add more specific verbs to their repertoire, the imperative forms of which are more high-register and less common in colloquial language; consequently, these latter verbs are used in the future imperative rather than the canonical imperative to express similar functions; (4) finally, Hebrew imperatives are shorter than future imperative forms and thus may be easier to pronounce early on.

By contrast, the mothers, being more attentive to the girls' needs, use more attenuated ways of addressing them. As stated in section 3, HSES parents tend to be more responsive to their children's verbalizations and to use indirect requests, whereas LSES parents make more extensive use of direct requests and prohibitions. In the present study, both mothers were found to use the future imperative, a softened form for giving orders and making direct requests, considerably more often than the canonical imperative form for expressing commands. In addition, they used to echo their daughters' actions verbally, elaborate on their utterances, and express some opinion or emotion by non-modal present tense verb forms.

To summarize our findings, the development of agent-oriented modality was found to precede that of epistemic modality in the language of two Hebrew-speaking girls. The girls start out with modally inflected verb forms expressing deontic meanings relying heavily on imperative and future imperative forms. Across development, the frequency of modal inflections of main verbs decreases, giving way to modal verbs, adjectives and adverbs, used primarily to express dynamic modality. At the outset, only one or two modal verbs or adjectives are used, but the frequency and diversity of lexical modal expressions gradually increase in the girls' repertoires. The most frequent lexical expressions of agent-oriented modality are *roce* 'want', *yaxol* 'can, be able to', and *carix* 'should, ought to'. The first two express dynamic modality reflecting the girls' desires and abilities while the third one serves to express deontic meanings like general rules of behavior and expectations or obligations. While these lexical items express the speaker's desires in CS, they serve to inquire about the addressee's in CDS. It is important to note that, due to the fact that person remains unmarked, the verb form used for these functions in CS and CDS is identical, namely the feminine singular of the present indicative. Our findings corroborate Budwig's (2002) results on English-speaking children aged 1;6 to 3;0, who were found to use the verb *want* to express their own desires while their mothers used it mainly to inquire about their children's desires.

Towards the end of the observation period, the girls start to express (im)probability. Thus, the modal *yaxol* 'can, be able to' is first used for expressing dynamic ability or deontic possibility (Smadar at age 1;11 and Lior at age 2;2) and only later for expressing epistemic probability (only by Lior at 2;4). This order of acquisition may be explained by the fact that the more abstract evaluation of states of affairs in terms of likelihood of occurrence must wait for further cognitive development.

The present case study has only barely scratched the surface of the different factors involved in the acquisition of modality in Hebrew. Further research with more subjects and a wider age range will be needed to determine the contribution of factors like frequency in the input, SES, function, cognitive development as well as structural factors like the morpho-phonological structure or the inflectional complexity of a verb to the acquisition process.

References

Aikhenvald, Alexandra Y. 2016. Sentence types. In Jan Nuyts & Johan van der Auwera (eds.), *The Oxford handbook of modality and mood*, 141–165. Oxford: Oxford University Press.
Armon-Lotem, Sharon & Ruth A. Berman. 2003. The emergence of grammar: Early verbs and beyond. *Journal of Child Language* 30(4). 845–862.
Ashkenazi, Orit. 2015. *Input – output relations in the early acquisition of Hebrew verbs*. Tel Aviv: Tel Aviv University dissertation.
Behrens, Heike. 2006. The input – output relationship in first language acquisition. *Language and Cognitive Processes* 21. 2–24.
Berman, Ruth A. 1985. Acquisition of Hebrew. In Dan I. Slobin (ed.), *The cross-linguistic study of language acquisition*, vol. 1, 255–371. Hillsdale, NJ: Erlbaum.
Berman, Ruth A. 2011. Revisiting impersonal constructions in Modern Hebrew: Discourse-based perspectives. In Andrej Malchukov & Anna Siewierska (eds.), *Impersonal constructions: A cross-linguistic perspective*, 323–356. Amsterdam: John Benjamins.
Berman, Ruth A. 2014. Acquiring and expressing temporality in Hebrew: A T/(M/A) language. *SKASE Journal of Theoretical Linguistics* 11(2). 2–29.
Bittner, Dagmar, Wolfgang U. Dressler & Marianne Kilani-Schoch. 2003. Introduction. In Dagmar Bittner, Wolfgang U. Dressler & Marianne Kilani-Schoch (eds.), *Development of verb inflection in first language acquisition: A cross-linguistic perspective* (Studies on Language Acquisition 21), vii–xxxvii. Berlin & New York: Mouton de Gruyter.
Bolozky, Shmuel. 2009. Colloquial Hebrew imperatives revisited. *Language Sciences*, vol. 31. 136–143. http://works.bepress.com/shmuel_bolozky/4/ [accessed 13 August 2017]
Boneh, Nora. 2015. Mood and modality: Modern Hebrew. In Geoffrey Khan (ed.), *Encyclopedia of Hebrew language and linguistics*. Brill Online. http://referenceworks.brillonline.com/entries/encyclopedia-of hebrew-language-and-linguistics/mood-and-modality-modern-hebrew-EHLL_COM_00000137 [accessed 10 August 2017]
Boye, Kasper. 2016. The expression of epistemic modality. In Jan Nuyts & Johan van der Auwera (eds.), *The Oxford handbook of modality and mood*, 117–140. Oxford: Oxford University Press.
Brown, Roger. 1973. *A first language: The early stages*. Cambridge, MA: Harvard University Press.
Budwig, Nancy. 2002. A developmental-functionalist approach to mental state talk. In Eric Amsel & James P. Byrnes (eds.), *Language, literacy and cognitive development: The development and consequences of symbolic communication*, 59–86. Mahwah, NJ: Erlbaum.
Bybee, Joan. 1985. *Morphology: A study of the relation between meaning and form*. Amsterdam & Philadelphia: John Benjamins.
Bybee, Joan & Suzanne Fleischman. 1995. Modality in grammar and discourse. In Joan Bybee & Suzanne Fleischman (eds.), *Modality in grammar and discourse* (Typological Studies in Language 32), 1–14. Amsterdam: John Benjamins.
Byrens, James & Mishelle Duff. 1989. Young children's comprehension of modal expressions. *Cognitive Development* 4. 369–387.
Choi, Soonja. 1995. The development of epistemic sentence-ending modal forms and functions in Korean children. In Joan Bybee & Suzanne Fleischman (eds.), *Modality in grammar and discourse*, 165–204. Amsterdam: John Benjamins.
Choi, Soonja. 2006. Acquisition of modality. In William Frawley (ed.), *The expression of modality*, 141–171. Berlin & New York: Mouton de Gruyter.

Choi, Soonja. 2014. Epistemic markers. In Patricia Brooks & Vera Kempe (eds.), *Encyclopedia of language development*, 198–199. SAGE Publications.

Coffin Amir, Edna & Shmuel Bolozky. 2005. *A reference grammar of Modern Hebrew*. Cambridge: Cambridge University Press.

Dressler, Wolfgang U. & Annemarie Karpf. 1995. The theoretical relevance of pre- and proto-morphology in language acquisition. In Jreet Booji & Jaap van Marle (eds.), *Yearbook of morphology 1994*, 99–122. Dordrecht: Kluwer Academic Publishers.

Dromi, Esther. 1980. Modality in Modern Hebrew. In Patricia Hamel and Ronald Schaefer (eds.), *Kansas Working Papers in Linguistics* 5. 99–115.

Glinert, Lewis. 1989. The Grammar of Modern Hebrew. Cambridge: Cambridge University Press.

Hart, Betty & Todd R. Risley 1995. *Meaningful differences in the everyday experience of young American children*. Baltimore: Brookes.

Hickmann, Maya & Dominique Bassano. 2016. Modality and mood in first language acquisition. In Jan Nuyts & Johan van der Auwera (eds.), *The Oxford handbook of modality and mood*, 430–447. Oxford: Oxford University Press.

Hoff, Erika. 2003. Causes and consequences of SES-related differences in parent-to-child speech. In Marc H. Bornstein & Robert H. Bradley. (eds.), *Socioeconomic status, parenting, and child development*, 147–160. Mahwah, NJ: Erlbaum.

Hoff, Erika, Brett Laursen & Twila Tardif. 2002. Socio-economic status and parenting. In Marc H. Bornstein (ed.), *Handbook of parenting*, 231–252. 2nd edn. Mahwah, NJ: Erlbaum.

Hoff-Ginsberg, Erika. 1991. Mother–child conversation in different social classes and communicative settings. *Child Development* 62(4). 782–796.

Huttenlocher, Janellen, Heidi Waterfall, Marina Vasilyeva, Jack Vevea & Larry V. Hedges. 2010. Sources of variability in children's language growth. *Cognitive Psychology* 61. 343–365.

Langacker, Ronald W. 1987. *Foundations of cognitive grammar: Theoretical prerequisites*, vol. 1. Stanford, CA: Stanford University Press.

Lieven, Elena. 2008. Learning the English auxiliary: A usage-based approach. In Heike Behrens (ed.), *Corpora in language acquisition research: History, methods, perspectives*, 61–98. Amsterdam: John Benjamins.

Lyons, John. 1977. *Semantics*. 2 vols. Cambridge: Cambridge University Press.

MacWhinney, Brian. 2000. *The CHILDES project: Tools for analyzing talk*, 3rd edn. Mahwah, NJ: Lawrence Erlbaum Associates.

Ninio, Anat. 1999. Path-breaking verbs in syntactic development and the question of prototypical transitivity. *Journal of Child Language* 26. 619–653.

Nikolaeva, Irina. 2016. Analyses of the semantics of mood. In Jan Nuyts & Johan van der Auwera (eds.), *The Oxford handbook of modality and mood*, 68–85. Oxford: Oxford University Press.

Nuyts, Jan. 2006. Modality: Overview and linguistic issues. In William Frawley (ed.), *The expression of modality*, 1–26. Berlin & New York: Mouton de Gruyter.

Nuyts, Jan. 2016. Analyses of modal meanings. In Jan Nuyts & Johan van der Auwera (eds.), *The Oxford handbook of modality and mood*, 31–49. Oxford: Oxford University Press.

Owens, Robert E. Jr. 2012. *Language development: An introduction*. 8th edn. New Jersey: Pearson.

Palmer, Frank R. 2001. *Mood and modality*. 2nd edn. Cambridge: Cambridge University Press.

Pea, Roy, Ronald Mawby & Sally MacKain. 1982. World-making and world-revealing: Semantics and pragmatics of modal auxiliary verbs during the third year of life. Paper presented at the 7th Annual Boston Conference on Child Language Development, October 8–10, 1982.

Ravid, Dorit. 1997. Early morphological development a duo: Pre- to proto-morphology in Hebrew-speaking twins. *Papers and Studies in Contrastive Linguistics* 33. 79–102.
Ravid, Dorit. 2010. The emergence of the Hebrew verb category. *Literacy and Language* 3. 131–160. [in Hebrew]
Reilly, Judy S., Elisheva Baruch, Harriet Jisa & Ruth A. Berman. 2002. Propositional attitudes in written and spoken language. *Written Language and Literacy* 5. 183–218.
Saffran, Jenny R. 2003. Statistical language learning: Mechanism and constraints. *Current Directions in Psychological Science* 12(4). 110–113.
Shatz, Marilyn & Sharon Wilcox 1991. Constraints on the acquisition of English modals. In Susan Gelman & James Byrnes (eds.), *Perspectives on language and thought: Interrelations in development*, 319–353. Cambridge: Cambridge University Press.
Stephany, Ursula. 1985. *Aspekt, Tempus und Modalität: Zur Entwicklung der Verbalgrammatik in der neugriechischen Kindersprache* (Language Universals Series 4). Tübingen: Gunter Narr.
Stephany, Ursula. 1986. Modality. In Paul Fletcher & Michael Garman (eds.), *Language acquisition*, 375–400. 2nd edn. Cambridge: Cambridge University Press.
Stephany, Ursula. 1993. Modality in first language acquisition: The state of the art. In Norbert Dittmar and Astrid Reich (eds.), *Modality in language acquisition*, 133–144. Berlin & New York: Mouton de Gruyter.
Stephany, Ursula. 1995. Function and form of modality in first and second language acquisition. In Anna Giacalone Ramat & Grazia Crocco Galeas (eds.), *From pragmatics to syntax: Modality in second language acquisition*, 105–120. Tübingen: Gunter Narr.
Stephany, Ursula & Maria D. Voeikova. 2009. Introduction. In Ursula Stephany & Maria D. Voeikova (eds.), *Development of nominal inflection in first language acquisition: A crosslinguistic perspective* (Studies on Language Acquisition 30), 1–14. Berlin & New York: Mouton de Gruyter.
Tomasello, Michael. 2003. *Constructing a language: A usage-based theory of language acquisition*. Cambridge, MA: Harvard University Press.
Tomasello, Michael. 2004. Learning through others. *Dedalus* 133. 51–58.
Tomasello, Michael. 2006. Acquiring linguistic constructions. In Robert Siegler & Deanna Kuhn (eds.), *Handbook of child psychology*, 255–298. New York: Wiley.
Tomasello, Michael. 2009. The usage-based theory of language acquisition. In Edith L. Bavin (ed.), *The Cambridge handbook of child language*, 69–88. Cambridge: Cambridge University Press.
Tomasello, Michael. 2010. *Origins of human communication*. Cambridge, MA: MIT Press. [first printing 2008]
Uziel-Karl, Sigal. 2001. *A multi-dimensional perspective on the acquisition of verb-argument structure*. Tel Aviv: Tel Aviv University dissertation.
Van der Auwera, Johan & Vladimir Plungian. 1998. Modality's semantic map. *Linguistic Typology* 2(1). 79–124.
Wells, Gordon. 1979. Learning and using the auxiliary verb in English. In Viviane Lee (ed.), *Language development*, 250–270. London: Croom Helm.
Zimmerman, Anael. 2012. *Input to two toddlers from different SES backgrounds: A study in Hebrew*. Tel Aviv: Tel Aviv University MA thesis.

Victoria V. Kazakovskaya
Epistemic modality in Russian child language

Abstract: The chapter studies the acquisition of epistemic modality, i.e., propositional attitude to situations and linguistic means of its expression in the early stages of Russian first language acquisition. The results are based on naturalistic observations of three typically developing monolingual children recorded from 1;5 to 4;0 years. Acquisition of epistemic semantics and the basic means of its expression (epistemic markers) in Russian start to develop in the third year of life with the marking of the semantic domain of uncertainty. The findings indicate an expansion of epistemic evaluation from objective situations in the physical world to the mental world. The emergence of epistemic markers in children's speech is investigated in relation to their occurrence in child-directed speech. A comparison of epistemic marking in child speech and child-directed speech has revealed that both the frequency of a marker in the target system and the degree of certainty or uncertainty (modal strength) of use influence its emergence and further development.

1 Introduction

The present chapter studies the early stages of the development of epistemic modality in Russian language acquisition taking into consideration the meanings of certainty and uncertainty and their basic means of expression, i.e., epistemic markers (EM). The goals of this study based on the data of adult–child spontaneous dialogues are to analyze the emergence and further development of EM in child speech (CS) in relation to their use in child-directed speech (CDS).

Epistemic modality (along with the category of evidentiality) relates to the speaker's attitude concerning the probability status of the proposition and contrasts with agent-oriented or event modality that includes dynamic and deontic modality (Choi 2006: 142; Hickmann and Bassano 2016: 431; see also Palmer 2001; Plungjan 2000: 311; Haßler 2016). Epistemic modality indicates the degree of the speaker's certainty of the reliability, authenticity and accuracy of what he/she is saying, i.e., the speaker's degree of certainty about the truth of propositions (Lyons 1977: 800; Palmer 2001: 8). The analysis of epistemic modality in Russian

Victoria V. Kazakovskaya, Russian Academy of Sciences

child language in the present study is based on the description of the target system in the Russian academic grammar (*Russkaja Grammatika* (RG) 1980).

The acquisition of epistemic modality in Russian has been little investigated so far. A few references to this process can be found in Gvozdev (1949, I: 113, II: 36), Stoljarova (1992), Kazakovskaya (1997, 2011, 2019: 145–175) and Švec (2007). These studies are mostly based on diary data and do not contain any examination of caregiver speech. The first experimental studies of epistemic modality in CS of older Russian children (aged 6 to 11 years) are those by Ovčinnikova, Uglanova and Krauze (1999) and Krauze (2004).

We will begin this chapter with a brief overview of the target system of epistemic modality in Russian (§2), thereafter summarize the previous results of its study in acquisition (§3), describe our data and methodology (§4) and present the results of our investigation (§5). The chapter will be concluded by a discussion of our results and some final remarks (§6).

2 Epistemic modality in Russian

The theoretical background for the study of the acquisition of epistemic modality in the Russian language adopted in the present study is the theory of modality proposed by Russian academic grammar (Vinogradov 1947: 725–744, 1975, 1986; RG 1980: 214–236) and developed further in different linguistic frameworks (Belošapkova 1997: 768–775; Lekant 2002: 127, 130; see also Bulygina and Šmelev 1982, 1993; Iordanskaja and Mel'čuk 2002; Jakovleva 1994), including the theory of functional grammar proposed by Bondarko (Bondarko 1990: 62; Beljaeva 1990: 157–170). This description of Russian epistemic modality involves formal (means of expression), semantic, and pragmatic features (i.e., discourse functions) of this phenomenon. The semantic and formal features and their connection with the pragmatic problem of "the speaker's point of view" are relevant for the study of its acquisition as well. According to the theory of modus (Bally 1965), each utterance has an objective (dictum) and a subjective (modus) semantic sphere. Epistemic modality belongs to the modus part of utterance, i.e. to the subjective sphere of semantic structure which contrasts with the dictum part (*p*, or *that p*) (Kolosova 1980: 69–70; Arutjunova 1988: 109–152; Beljaeva 1990: 159; Kazakovskaya 1996).

The semantic structure of epistemic modality is represented by two domains or "polar fields" of certainty (confidence) and uncertainty (probability) (Vinogradov 1947: 739; Bondarko 1990: 62; Beljaeva 1990: 163). Epistemic modality represented by respective markers can be construed as a gradual scale in the order of decreasing degrees of uncertainty and, consequently, increasing degrees of certainty (from uncertainty to categorical certainty) of the speaker's judgment regarding the likelihood of a given state of affairs (Lekant 2002: 125; Beljaeva 1990: 163, 165; Krauze 2004: 137; see also Stephany 1993: 134 for a similar scale of modality and Palmer 2001: 34, 52 for other languages). Certainty is categorized in terms of simple certainty ("neutral statements", i.e., modally unmarked statements of fact), categorical certainty and problematic certainty (Belošapkova 1997: 773; Lekant 2002: 128, 132; see also Lyons 1977: 809); whereas the domain of uncertainty is represented by high, medium and low degrees (Panfilov 1977; Beljaeva 1990; see also Gatinskaja 2015: 152) (see Figure 1).

Certainty <---------------------------------|--------------------------------> Uncertainty
　　　　　　　　　　　　Turning point

categorical certainty	problematic certainty	low uncert.	medium uncert.	high uncert.
konečno	vrjad.li	po-moemu	možet.byt'	navernoe
dejstvitel'no	edva.li	podi	možet	vidimo
na.samom.dele	vrode.by	nebos'	vozmožno	očevidno
pravda	kak.budto		verojatno	po-vidimomu
bessporno				dolžno.byt'
		kažetsja	požaluj	

Figure 1: The scale of explicit epistemic modality with some examples of Russian EM.[1]

While categorical certainty borders on factual knowledge it cannot be considered equal to it. It is usually expressed by *konečno* 'of course', *dejstvitel'no* 'really', etc. Problematic certainty arises in conditions of incomplete knowledge, which may be due to an imperfection of memory, lack of perception, or incomplete information. Its main means of expression are modal particles (e.g., *vrjad li* 'hardly, unlikely') and a modal word *kažetsja* '(it) seems'. A low degree of uncertainty is manifested in weakly reasoned and poorly evidenced statements,

---

[1] Since only some EM are described in the text following Figure 1, the English translations of the other markers are given in the following list: *edva.li* 'scarcely, hardly, unlikely', *vrode.by* '(it) seems, seemingly, it looks as if', *kak.budto* 'apparently, it would seem', *podi* '(very) likely, probably' (colloquial), *nebos'* 'very likely' (colloquial), *verojatno* '(very) likely, probably', *očevidno* 'obviously, clearly, apparently, manifestly', *po-vidimomu* 'apparently, appear to, seemingly', *dolžno.byt'* 'probably' (see also section 5.2.2).

e.g., *kažetsja* '(it) seems'.[2] A medium degree of uncertainty occurs in suggestions, assumptions and suppositions of the speaker; it is expressed by *možet byt'* 'maybe' or its colloquial version *možet* lit. 'may', etc. A high degree of uncertainty concerning the speaker's deductions may in turn be expressed by *navernoe* 'probably, most likely' or its colloquial variant *naverno*, etc. (Panfilov 1977: 49; Beljaeva 1990: 165; Gatinskaja 2011: 247).

While uncertainty must be explicitly expressed in Russian, simple certainty is implicitly rendered, as in other languages. However, certainty may be explicitly conveyed if it needs to be stressed. As will be shown below, the category of unmarked simple certainty emerges first in Russian child language. In Russian, epistemic meanings are expressed by special intonation, parenthetical modal words,[3] modal particles, and syntactic constructions (RG 1980: 215, 224–226; Vinogradov 1947: 731; Lekant 2002: 129; Birjulin and Kordi 1990: 68; Beljaeva 1990: 159). The modal words and their combinations are considered as EM, i.e., the main (prototypical) means of expressing epistemic modality (Vinogradov 1947: 731; Beljaeva 1990: 159).

EM are a historically heterogeneous class and their number has been increased by the inclusion of words from different grammatical classes (RG 1980: 228–230; Xolodov 1996: 275; Gatinskaja 2007: 18), mainly adverbs (e.g., *navernoe* 'probably'), but also adjectives (e.g., *verojatno* '(most) likely'), nouns (e.g., *pravda* lit. 'truth'), verbs (e.g., *možet byt'* 'may be', *kažetsja* '(it) seems'), and even pronouns (e.g., *samo soboj* 'self by itself' derived from *samo soboj razumeetsja* 'it goes without saying'). When these modal words are used parenthetically, they are not integrated into the syntactic structure of the sentence (i.e., EM are not syntactically obligatory (Vinogradov 1947: 725; Lekant 2002: 131; Beljaeva 1990: 159; Xolodov 1996: 274)) and express the speaker's epistemic evaluation of the proposition so that their scope is on the entire sentence (Vinogradov 1947: 741; Xolodov 1996: 275; Miloslavsky 1997: 595). Thus, *pravda* functions as a predicate noun in example (1) while it is used as a propositional EM in example (2).

---

[2] Due to the semantic continuity (or graduality) of epistemic modality, the adjacent divisions of this scale partially overlap: e.g., *kažetsja* 'it seems' is interpreted as a low degree of uncertainty and, at the same time, as a problematic certainty (depending on the context); see also *požaluj* 'very likely, perhaps, it may be', etc.

[3] This term partially corresponding to "sentence level adverbs" and "modal adjuncts" is widely used in Russian academic grammatical tradition. An adjective "parenthetical" emphasizes its special state, i.e., the absence of a formal connection with the structure of the sentence (see also Urmson 1970: 228 for parenthetical verbs and adverbs in English).

(1) eta istorija čist-aja pravd-a.
    this story clear-FEM.SG truth-NOM
    'this story (is) true.'

(2) on, pravda, prixodi-l.
    he truth.EM go-PST.MASC
    'he really went there.'

Parenthetical EM can occupy any place of the sentence: central (example 2 above), initial (example 3) or final (example 4).

(3) navernoe, p 'probably.EM p'.

(4) p, možet byt' 'p maybe.EM'.

Moreover, in colloquial dialogues, EM are often used in responses within adjacent pairs (Vinogradov 1955: 403, 413), e.g., minimal question–reply units, see example (5).

(5) Liza, 1;6
    MOT: kak Stepaša tancuet?
         'how is Stepaša dancing?'
    CHI: lja-lja-lja.ONOM
    MOT: nu konečno.
         well of.course.EM
         'well, of course.'

EM relate to the entire proposition since they express the speaker's commitment to the factuality of the information (Lyons 1977: 809), see examples (6) and (7).

(6) konečno, p 'of.course.EM p'.

(7) ja znaju, (čto) p 'I know (that) p'.

Epistemic modality concerns the sphere of mental modus (knowledge, opinion, thinking, evaluation) which establishes the connection between a judgment and the person who issues it (Arutjunova 1988: 109–152; Dmitrovskaja 1988). Epistemic evaluation as a point of view or "authority", in terms of Vinogradov (1975: 268) and Zolotova (1973: 263), may refer to the speaker or to "another person": e.g., *po-moemu* 'in my opinion' (authority of the 1st person) — *po-tvoemu* 'in your opinion' (authority of the 2nd person) — *po ego mneniju* 'in his opinion' (authority of the 3rd person).

3 Previous investigations of the development of epistemic modality in Russian child language

Despite the fact that epistemic modality has an impressive history of investigation in Russian philological tradition (see section 2), the ontogenesis of this category has been little explored so far. Previous studies of the acquisition of epistemic modality (or even references to it) are mostly based on diary data, including the famous diary of Gvozdev (1949) (Stoljarova 1992; Kazakovskaya 1997, 2019: 145–173; Švec 2007[4]). A few experimental studies were conducted with older children, covering the age range of 6 to 11 (Ovčinnikova, Uglanova, and Krauze 1999; Krauze 2004, 2007).

The longitudinal observations based on diary data mentioned above have shown that in Russian epistemic modality emerges later and is less frequently expressed than deontic modality. Markers of deontic modality emerge before 2;0 (Gvozdev 1949; Wiemer 1992; Oficerova 2005; Voeikova and Bayda, this volume), whereas EM usually occur after this age. The earliest case of epistemic modality use (at 1;8) based on diary data was noted in Kazakovskaya (2019: 146, 154), where it is observed that both the emergence of epistemic modality and the repertoire of epistemic expressions show variability across children (2019: 149, 160). It was also noted that the list of certainty markers is smaller than the one of uncertainty markers (Kazakovskaya 2019: 163).

While utterances expressing deontic modality serve to request actions from the interlocutor, utterances of epistemic modality express the child's own point of view or that of another person (Kazakovskaya 2011, 2019: 167). Actually, children start to express their "authority" or point of view and evaluate states of affairs by the use of EM quite early (about 2;0) (Kazakovskaya 2019: 159–165). Complex sentences with a dependent clause under the scope of a main clause

---

4 The results presented in Švec (2007) are mainly based on a diary collected by herself (2007: 167). Since her notion of epistemic modality and its expression is rather broad, including interrogatives (2007: 170–171) as well as non-modal items (2007: 175–178), Švec's results have not been included in the present chapter.

expressing the speaker's judgment (examples 8 and 9) only occur around 2;6–3;0 years (Kazakovskaya 2019: 150–151, 166).[5]

(8) *ja dumaju, (čto) p* 'I think (that) p'.

(9) *ty dumaješ, (čto) p* 'you think (that) p'.

The expression of epistemic modality is important not only for children's communicative competence but also for their cognitive development. Research has shown that epistemic items such as the mental verbs *think, know, remember* (e.g., Shatz, Wellman, and Silber 1983; Moore et al. 1994; Tardif and Wellman 2000) are crucial for the development of a theory of mind concerning "the ability to attribute to oneself and others mental representations" (Papafragou 2002: 185; see also Choi 2006: 142; Wellman 1990; Flavell 2000; Mandler 2004; for Russian see Sergienko, Lebedeva, and Prusakova 2009). As pointed out by Hickmann and Bassano (2016: 433), "children's capacity to use mental verbs (*want, know, think, believe, remember*) to talk about the self and others' mental states indicates the development of a 'theory of mind'." Russian EM play a similar functional role as mental verbs since, expressing the speaker's judgment, they also serve to reveal children's viewpoint or their attitude to the proposition and thereby demonstrate their mental state (Kazakovskaya 1997, 2011, 2016, 2019: 145–173; see Kazakovskaya and Argus 2016: 58 for Russian and Estonian).

Experimental studies conducted with Russian children aged 6, 8 and 11 years have examined the development of children's understanding of EM based on their perception of the epistemic force of modal words (Ovčinnikova, Uglanova, and Krauze 1999: 132; Krauze 2004: 136, 2007). These studies have shown that the development of comprehension of EM is more delayed than production and is determined by age and gender. Boys coped with the task of evaluating EM more successfully than girls, but these differences were smoothed out at the age of 11. The authors propose that "the idea of epistemic modality" and its lexical and prosodic expressions are achieved by the age of 11 (Ovčinnikova, Uglanova, and Krauze 1999: 132; Krauze 2004: 137).

So far, the early development of epistemic modality in a longitudinal corpus of spontaneous Russian CS including input has not been investigated. Our

---

[5] In the developmental literature complement constructions with verbs of cognition such as *think, guess, know, believe, see* are observed "typically around the third birthday" (Tomasello 2003: 225).

study aims to fill this gap taking the possible influence of caregiver speech on CS into consideration.

4 Data and method

Spontaneous speech data of three typically developing monolingual Russian children have been analyzed. Two boys, named Vanja and Vitja, and one girl Liza were audio-recorded in interaction with their main caregivers in their homes within the age range of 1;5–4;0 (Table 1). The data comprising approximately 162 hours of recorded speech were transcribed according to the CHAT conventions of the CHILDES project (MacWhinney 2000).

Table 1: Russian corpora.

Subject	Age	Hours of recordings	Number of words (CS/CDS)	Number of utterances (CS/CDS)
Vanja	1;5–3;6, 4;0	80	88,408/209,965	44,122/62,136
Liza	1;6–3;0, 3;5–3;7, 3;10, 4;0	38	20,677/59,247	9,277/17,502
Vitja	2;0–4;0	44	24,978/49,980	10,509/13,595
Total		162	134,063/319,192	63,908/93,233

These corpora were analyzed with regard to the frequency of tokens and diversity of lemmas of EM occurring in CS and CDS (including the relationship between the two registers), the order of emergence of these markers in CS as well as the development of expressions of different degrees (modal strength) of certainty/uncertainty. Other points taken into consideration in the analysis are the position of EM in the children's and caregivers' sentences as well as the meaning and illocutionary types of such sentences. Furthermore, some individual differences in the children's acquisition of epistemic modality were taken into account. The qualitative analysis includes not only the inventory of lemmas but also their different functions, i.e., degrees of certainty/uncertainty.

5 Results

5.1 Development of epistemic modality in Russian CS

This section aims at providing a general overview of epistemic development in CS based on the Russian data described above. It presents information about the quantity of explicit markers of certainty[6] and uncertainty, about the age and sequence of their emergence and the main characteristics of the initial epistemic repertoire in the speech of the three children and their CDS.

Uncertainty markers mostly dominate in the conversation of the adult–child dyads starting at 1;5 in CDS and 2;1 in CS. Figure 2 shows the overall distribution of EM for each dyad.

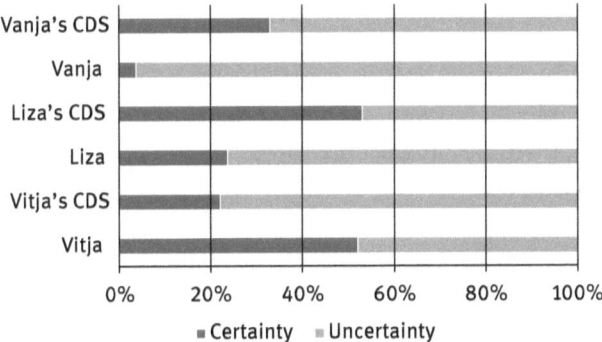

Figure 2: Distribution of certainty and uncertainty markers in CS and CDS (% of all EM tokens in a given individual's speech).

Each of the three children started to use EM during the third year of life by expressing uncertainty (see Table 2). Statements expressing "simple certainty" (see Section 2) are modally unmarked. As stated by Stephany (1993: 134), "accepting the factuality of the proposition expressed by a statement and expecting the hearer to agree, the speaker sees no need to qualify the validity of his utterance."

The delay between the first marking of uncertainty in CDS and its emergence in CS is shorter than that of the respective occurrence of EM expressing certainty. For uncertainty markers it ranges between 7 months with Vitja and 15

---

6 Modally unmarked statements (expressing so-called simple certainty) have not been counted.

months with Vanja and for certainty markers between 9 months with Vitja and 28 with Liza.

Table 2: Age of emergence of EM in CS and CDS.

Subject	Uncertainty		Certainty	
	CS	CDS	CS	CDS
Vanja	2;8	1;5	3;4	1;8
Liza	2;2	1;6	3;10	1;6
Vitja	2;7	2;0	2;10	2;1

Liza begins to use uncertainty markers at 2;2, much earlier than the boys. These are *navernoe* 'probably' and *po-moemu* 'in my opinion' (4 tokens during the first recording of their emergence) (examples 10 and 11).

(10) Liza, 2;2
    MOT: *navernoe, tam čelovečki, mal'čiki,*
            probably.EM there little.people boys
           devočki guljaj-ut.
           girls walk-PRS.3PL
           'probably little people, boys, girls are walking there.'
    CHI: *eto, navernoe, guljaj-ut Lizočk-oj.*
           this probably.EM walk-PRS.3PL Liza.DIM-INS
           'these are probably girls walking with little Liza.'

(11) Liza, 2;2
    MOT: *davaj rasskaž-i etu sčitaločk-u.*
           let tell-IMP.2SG this counting.rhyme.DIM-ACC
           'do tell (me) this small counting-rhyme.'
    CHI: *ne ta, po-moemu.*
           not that in-mine.EM
           'this is not the same in my opinion.'

The boys Vitja and Vanja use their first uncertainty markers about half a year later than Liza, namely at 2;7 (Vitja, 1 token of *po-moemu* 'in my opinion') and 2;8 (Vanja, 2 tokens of *navernoe* 'probably') (examples 12 and 13).

(12) Vitja, 2;7
    MOT: *gde   u   tebj-a   pečka, Viten'ka?*
            where at you-GEN stove Vitja.DIM
            'where is your stove, little Vitja?'
    CHI: *vot pečka, po-moemu.*
            this stove in-mine.EM
            'here is the stove in my opinion.'

(13) Vanja, 2;8
    MOT: *kak ty   dumaj-eš,   kto eto takoj?*
            how you think-PRS.2SG who this such
            'what do you think who this is?'
    CHI: *eto takoj volk,   navernoe.*
            this such   wolf   probably.EM
            'it is a kind a wolf probably.'

Explicit markers of certainty occur later than those of uncertainty in the children's speech (2;10–3;10). Vitja starts to use them at 2;10 with 5 tokens during the first recording of their emergence (example 14).

(14) Vitja, 2;10
    (He is looking at his hand.)
    eto y menj-a, konečno,   pal'cy.
    this at I-GEN   of.course.EM fingers
    'these are, of course, my fingers.'

Vanja and Liza make first use of certainty markers about half a year or even a year later than Vitja, namely at 3;4 (1 token) and 3;10 (2 tokens), respectively (examples 15 and 16).

(15) Vanja, 3;4
    MOT: *teper' koleso   spusti-l-o.*
            now   wheel   deflate-PST-N
            'now the tire has been deflated.'
    CHI: *u   menj-a, konečno,   est'   nasos.*
            at   I-GEN of.course.EM have pump
            'I have of course a pump.'

(16) Liza, 3;10
    MOT: *oj,   poln-aja   skovorodka, Lizka.*
          oh   full-FEM   frying.pan   Lizka
          'oh, the frying pan is full, Lizka.'
    CHI: *poln-aja   skovorodka,   dejstvitel'no.*
          full-FEM   frying.pan   really.EM
          'the frying pan is full, really.'

Certainty is expressed by a single marker in Vanja's speech at 3;4 (*konečno* 'of course'; see example 15 above), but Liza and Vitja possess three lemmas serving this function, namely *dejstvitel'no* 'really' (examples 16 above and 17 below), *na samom dele* 'actually' (example 18) and *pravda* 'truly' (lit. 'truth') (example 19).

(17) Vitja, 2;10
    dzjdzj,   malyš   s   nami   poexa-l,   dejstvitel'no.
    ONOM   kid   with us   go-PST.MASC   really.EM
    'brmbrm, a kid went with us, really.'

(18) Liza 3;10
    (Talking about russula mushrooms)
    syroežečk-i   prosto   inogda   syrye,   na.samom.dele,   net.
    russula.DIM-PL   just   sometimes   raw   actually.EM   not
    'small russulas are just sometimes raw, actually (they are) not.'

(19) Vitja 2;11
    eto,   pravda,   korzinočka.
    this   truth.EM   basket.DIM
    'this is truly a small basket.'

Despite the differences in the age of emergence, the developmental sequence of the EM in the children's speech is quite similar. Table 3 shows the individual differences in the age of emergence of EM as well as their repertoire in a given CS. For example, in Vitja's speech *po-moemu* 'in my opinion' emerges before *navernoe* 'probably' while *možet byť* 'maybe' is absent. In Vanja's speech, however, *možet* lit. 'may' emerges before *po-moemu* 'in my opinion' and *dejstvitel'no* 'really' is not observed at all.

Among the uncertainty markers frequently used by each of the children in the course of the third year are *navernoe* 'probably', *po-moemu* 'in my opinion' and *možet* lit. 'may' (derived from *možet byť* 'maybe'); whereas *možet byť* 'maybe' is documented only in Vanja's and Liza's speech. As to the most frequent certainty

Table 3: The sequence of emergence of EM in CS.

Age	Vanja	Liza	Vitja
2;2		navernoe 'probably', po-moemu 'in my opinion'	
2;5		možet lit. 'may' (from možet byt' 'maybe')	
2;7			po-moemu 'in my opinion'
2;8	navernoe 'probably'		navernoe 'probably'
2;9	možet lit. 'may' (from možet byt' 'maybe')	možet byt' 'maybe'	
2;10			možet lit. 'may' (from možet byt' 'maybe'), konečno 'of course', dejstvitel'no 'really'
2;11	po-moemu 'in my opinion'		pravda 'truly' (lit. 'truth')
3;3	možet byt' 'maybe'		
3;4	konečno 'of course'		
3;10		konečno 'of course', dejstvitel'no 'really', na samom dele 'actually'	

markers such as *konečno* 'of course' and *dejstvitel'no* 'really', they emerge in the end of the third year in Vitja's speech and in the fourth year in Liza's.

It is no coincidence that the first uncertainty and certainty markers to emerge in Vanja's and Liza's speech express a high degree of modal strength (see Section 2). All EM are correctly used by the children from the very beginning. The first sentences containing them generally refer to the observable situation, the here and now. These statements usually have a zero copula (examples

14, 16, 18 and 19 above). A typical context for using EM in statements is in reply to a caregiver's question (example 20).

(20) Liza, 2;
    MOT: *kto s   Lizočk-oj guljaj-et?*
           who with Liza.DIM-INS walk-PRS.3SG
           'who is taking a walk with little Liza?'
    CHI: *devočki eto,   navernoe.*
           girls   this   probably.EM
           'it is girls, probably.'

An analysis of the sentence types containing EM shows that the children first use them in statements (examples 10–16). Vanja marks interrogative utterances epistemically only six months after statements (at 3;4, see example 21).

(21) Vanja, 3;4
    ili, možet.byt', ja kuplj-u   tebe   ljagušek?
    or maybe.EM I buy-FUT.1SG you.DAT frogs
    'or maybe I will buy you frogs?'

In Liza's speech this period is much longer, namely 16 months (example 22) and Vitja does not use EM in interrogatives at all.

(22) Liza, 3;6
    a možet, pojdj-om pokataemsja na gorke sejčas?
    or may.EM go-FUT.1PL ride   on hill   now
    'or maybe we'll go ride on the hill now?'

As for the sentential position of EM, it is observed that the three children use them in all possible positions – initial (example 22), internal (examples 10, 14, 15, 19) and final (examples 11–13, 16, 17); but the position preferred above all is the sentence internal one (Table 4).

Table 4: Positions of EM in CS (tokens and percentage).

Subject	Sentence -initial	%	Sentence -internal	%	Sentence -final	%
Vanja	12	15.2	38	48.1	29	36.7
Liza	1	2.9	18	52.9	15	44.1
Vitja	2	9.5	12	57.1	7	33.3

The children start to use EM in both sentence-internal and sentence-final positions. The first EM in initial position emerging several months later is mainly the uncertainty marker *možet* 'may' (from 'maybe'). It is first found in Vanja's and Vitja's speech at 2;10 and in Liza's only at 3;6. The most typical contexts for EM in initial sentence position are questions proposing activities to be carried out together with the addressee (example 22). EM used in sentence-initial or sentence-final position often evaluate the entire proposition (examples 23 and 24).

(23) Vitja, 2;10
 i možet, mašina prid-et, bak.
 and may.EM car go-FUT.3SG tank
 'and maybe, the car will move, (which is a) tank.'

(24) Liza, 3;10
 a u Lizy bolit život, navernoe?
 and at Liza ache stomach probably.EM
 'does Lisa probably have a stomach ache?'

Placed in the middle of a sentence, EM express certainty/uncertainty in relation to immediately adjacent sentence constituents, i.e., they epistemically evaluate the components which are placed immediately after (examples 25 and 26) or before them (example 27).

(25) Liza, 2;9
 (referring to an object belonging to grandfather)
 vot et-a, navernoe, deduškin-a.
 here this-FEM probably.EM grandfather-FEM
 'this one, probably, is grandfather's (object).'

(26) Vitj'a, 2;11
 ja vzja-l, konečno, rybk-u.
 I take-PST.MASC of.course.EM fish.DIM-ACC
 'I took, of course, the small fish.'

(27) Vitja, 4;0
 vse uže, ostyla, navernoe, jaičnica.
 all already cool.down probably.EM scrambled.eggs
 'everything is ready, the scrambled eggs have probably cooled down.'

More definitive conclusions could only be reached by taking the intonational contour of utterances of CS into consideration.[7] An unambiguous interpretation of the children's utterances is also complicated due to the briefness of responses occurring in spontaneous dialogue. A positional analysis of EM in CDS has shown similar results in all the corpora under observation: All caregivers prefer to use EM in an internal sentence position (Figure 3). It can, therefore, be said that children use EM with the same preferences as their caregivers.

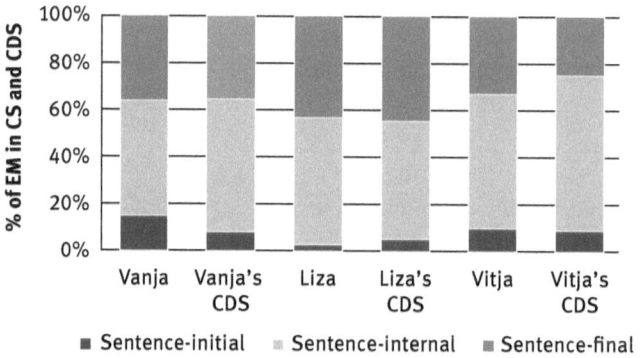

Figure 3: Positional preferences of EM in adult–child dyads.

Speakers' preferences for placement of EM noted in the CS and CDS under observation reflect common positional characteristics of EM in adult-directed speech (ADS) (RG 1980).

The children's use of EM shows that they have started to reflect on the relation of their statements to the reality they describe. In the beginning, children epistemically modalize propositions concerning the existence (example 15) or identity (in a broad sense) of objects (example 13). Later on, the EM may refer to such attributes of objects as their size,[8] color (example 28) or quantity (example 29).

---

7 This is not possible, since this study is based on transcripts which have not yet been linked to the sound tier.
8 Although we know of examples of epistemic evaluation of object size from child Russian (Kazakovskaya and Argus 2016: 63), they do not occur in our recorded material.

(28) Vanja, 2;10
(The boy and his grandmother looking at colorful balloons)
CHI: *eto   sinij,   navernoe,   takoj.*
     this   blue   probably.EM   such
     'this balloon is probably such a blue one.'
GRA: *da,   eto   sinij.*
     'yes, this is blue.'

(29) Vanja, 2;10
(trying to recite a dialogue from a fairytale by K. Čukovsky)
skol'ko   emu   prislat'?
how.many   him   send.INF
'how many (poods) should we send him?'
možet,   pjat',   možet,   tri.
may.EM   five   may.EM   three
'may(be) five, may(be) three.'

Still later children may focus on the epistemic evaluation of states and activities (usually of third persons) including different circumstances, such as time, cause (example 30) or location (example 31).

(30) Liza, 2;9
(lifting the mould when trying to make "mud pies" from dry sand)
CHI: *ne polučilos'.*
     '(it) did not work out.'
MOT: *ne polučilos', da?*
     '(it) did not work out, right?'
CHI: *takoj   syxoj   pesok,   navernoe.*
     such   dry   sand   probably.EM
     '(because of) such dry sand, probably.'

(31) Vanja, 2;10
(about his parents in a dialogue with his grandmother)
eto   oni   v   teatr-e,   navernoe.
this   they   at   theatre-LOC   probably.EM
'they are at the theatre, probably.'

Children use EM not only in their judgements about a situation and its different components, but also about animate beings (e.g., relatives or animals) and their activities (examples 32 and 33).

(32) Liza, 2;9
 (about words usually uttered by her grandfather)
 da, eto deduška, navernoe, skaza-l.
 yes this grandfather probably.EM say-PST.MASC
 'yes, grandfather probably said this.'

(33) Vanja 2;9
 (while playing)
 tut, možet, myšonok budet begat'.
 here may.EM little.mouse will run
 'here maybe a little mouse will run.'

At the end of their third year of life, children also use EM in utterances referring to their own actions or states (example 34 and example 24 above), proposals including imaginary situations when playing (example 21 above) and joint activities with a dialogue partner (example 22 above).

(34) Vanja, 2;11
 eto ja, navernoe, ee kida-l.
 this I probably.EM it.FEM.ACC throw-PST.MASC
 'this is me probably who threw it.'

From the end of the fourth year onwards, children use EM in utterances about the mental states or activities of the interlocutor (examples 35 and 36).

(35) Liza, 3;10
 i tebe, navernoe, nočju tak prisni-l-o-s'.
 and you.DAT probably.EM night so dream-PST-N-REFL
 'and you probably dreamt so at night.'

(36) Vanja, 4;0
 ty, navernoe, znaj-eš.
 you.2SG probably.EM know-PRS.2SG
 'you probably know.'

In summary, children first make epistemic evaluations about objects and their properties, subsequently about their own and others' actions, and finally about their own and others' (typically their interlocutors') mental states. With increasing age, propositions by which children convey their subjective attitude to their interlocutors become ever more frequent. Such changes in epistemically modalized utterances may be interpreted as indications of advances in theory of mind revealing children's attempts to reflect upon the mental state of other persons.

5.2 Input–output relationship in the acquisition of epistemic modality

5.2.1 Frequency of EM in Russian CS and CDS

The data analysed provide evidence that there are individual differences in the frequency of EM usage, both among the children and their caregivers. The largest number of EM comes from Liza's dialogues with her main caregiver. The percentage of epistemically marked utterances in her CS (.37%) and CDS (1.66%) is higher than the corresponding percentages in the boys' corpora (Table 5).

Table 5: Frequency of utterances with EM in relation to the total number of utterances for each CS and CDS pair.

Subject	CS		CDS	
	EM	% of utterances	EM	% of utterances
Vanja	79	0.17	283	0.46
Liza	34	0.37	291	1.66
Vitja	21	0.20	162	1.19
Total	134		736	

An overview of the emergence and frequency of EM in the course of the children's development shows that, with Vanja and Liza, they emerge in the third year and increase noticeably in the fourth year. Vitja hardly uses any EM in his third year and even less so in the fourth. As far as CDS is concerned, a comparison of the percentages of utterances marked for EM with the total of utterances occurring in a given period of time shows that this index increases with each of the three children.

As shown in Figure 4, the growing use of EM in CDS is paralleled by an increase of their occurrence in Vanja's and Liza's speech, but not in Vitja's. There is thus variation among the children, with the child Vitja making little use of his six different EM until 3;0 (see Table 3 above).

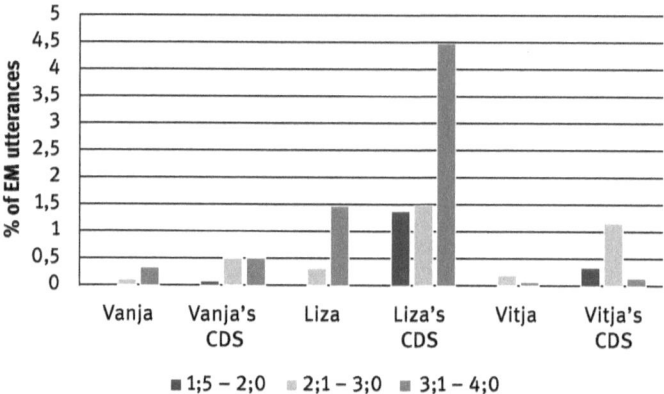

Figure 4: Percentage of EM utterances in relation to all utterances in CS and CDS.

5.2.2 Diversity of EM in Russian CS and CDS

As is to be expected, the lexical diversity of EM in CDS is somewhat greater than in CS (on average 9 vs. 6 lemmas, as shown in Table 6). Furthermore, the usage made of each EM in CDS is twice as high or even more than six times higher than in CS, a characteristic which may lead to further entrenchment of EM in the children's language.

Table 6: Diversity and frequency of EM in CS and CDS.

Subject	CS		CDS	
	lemmas	tokens	lemmas	tokens
Vanja	5	79	10	283
Liza	7	34	9	291
Vitja	6	21	8	162

While the lexical inventory of EM in Vitja's and Liza's speech is only slightly smaller than that of their caregivers, Vanja's is only half as large. Although Liza's corpus is smallest (see Table 1 above), she has developed a slightly more diverse list of EM than the boys. Among the four uncertainty and three certainty markers each in Liza's speech (see Table 3 above), the uncertainty marker *navernoe* 'probably' (examples 20, 24, 25, 30, 32 and 35 above) is the most frequent one (78%) among all uncertainty tokens documented in her speech.

Table 7: EM of uncertainty: Relationship between emergence in CS and frequency in CDS.

EM	Age of emergence in CS[9]	Vanja's CDS	Liza's CDS	Vitja's CDS	Total
naverno(e) 'probably'	2;2–2;8	140	54	88	282
možet(byt') 'may(be)'	2;5–3;3	32	28	31	91
po-moemu 'in my opinion'	2;2–2;11	16	52	6	74
kažetsja '(it) seems'	–	1	6	2	9
požaluj 'very likely'	–	2			

There are considerably fewer markers of certainty than uncertainty in Liza's utterances. The former constitute 24% of all EM tokens and are expressed most frequently by *konečno* 'of course' (75% of all her certainty tokens), followed by *dejstvitel'no* 'really' (example 16 above) and *na samom dele* 'actually' (example 18 above).

Tables 7 and 8 show the token frequencies of uncertainty and certainty markers used by each caregiver and the age of emergence of these EM in CS. The relation between their emergence in CS and frequency in CDS can be interpreted as follows: EM used continuously from early on and therefore occurring more frequently than others in CDS emerge earlier in CS. In particular, the uncertainty marker *naverno(e)* 'probably' that is the most frequent in CDS and emerges earliest in CS is used by all children and is cumulatively more frequent than the others (see the last column in Table 7). On the other hand, the EM *kažetsja* '(it) seems', for instance, is rarest in CDS and absent from CS during the entire period of observation.

---

9 This column represents age periods for the three CS corpora collapsed together; for individual information concerning each child see Table 3 above (the same for the second column of the Table 8).

This observation is also valid in relation to EM of certainty: *konečno* 'of course', the most frequent certainty marker in CDS, emerges earlier than other EM of this category (Table 8). According to its frequency in CDS and its consequent entrenchment in CS, *konečno* 'of course' is used more frequently than e.g. *dejstvitel'no* 'really' also in CS.

Table 8: EM of certainty: Relationship between emergence in CS and frequency in CDS.

EM	Age of emergence in CS	Vanja's CDS	Liza's CDS	Vitja's CDS	Total
konečno 'of course'	2;10–3;10	49	85	20	154
dejstvitel'no 'really'	2;10–3;10	31	47	2	80
pravda 'truly' (lit. 'truth')	2;11	8	14	12	34
na samom dele 'actually'	3;10	4	5	1	10

Most importantly, *naverno(e)* 'probably' and *konečno* 'of course', the two most frequent EM in CDS and the earliest to emerge in CS, occupy the extreme poles of the epistemic continuum and express a high degree of uncertainty and certainty, respectively (see Figure 1 above). Markers with a low degree of certainty or uncertainty are documented mostly in CDS. However, they are used infrequently and occur later than those with a higher modal strength. Accordingly, such EM emerge late in CS. Thus, the marker *kažetsja* '(it) seems', which expresses low uncertainty, is found in CDS only after 3;0 (example 37).

(37) Liza, 3;0
    (Liza is sitting on a small shovel and playing)
    CHI: *eto*   *lošadka.*
             this   horse.DIM
             'this is a small horse.'
    MOT: *kažetsja,*   *lopatka.*
             it.seems.EM   shovel.DIM
             'it seems that this is a small shovel.'

Among the certainty markers found in CDS which are rare and late to emerge in CS are *na samom dele* 'actually' (example 18 above) and *pravda* 'truly' lit. 'truth' (example 38).

(38) Liza, 1;7
(Liza's mother is showing a pineapple)
MOT: *ty   nikogda ne e-l-a,   pravda.*
     you never   not eat-PST-FEM truth.EM
'it is true that you have never eaten (it).'

Figures 5 and 6 present the distribution of uncertainty and certainty markers in the speech of each child (% of all respective tokens). It is observed that children continue to use certain EM constantly after they have emerged so that EM that emerge earlier in CS tend to be used more frequently. Particularly in the domain of uncertainty (Figure 5), two out of the three children (Vanja and Liza, see Table 3 above) start with *navernoe* 'probably'. *Po-moemu* 'in my opinion', *možet* lit. 'may'[10] and *možet byt'* 'maybe' emerge subsequently. The distribution of these forms in CS shows that *možet byt'* and *možet* 'maybe' rank second after *navernoe* 'probably', with *po-moemu* 'in my opinion' being least frequent.

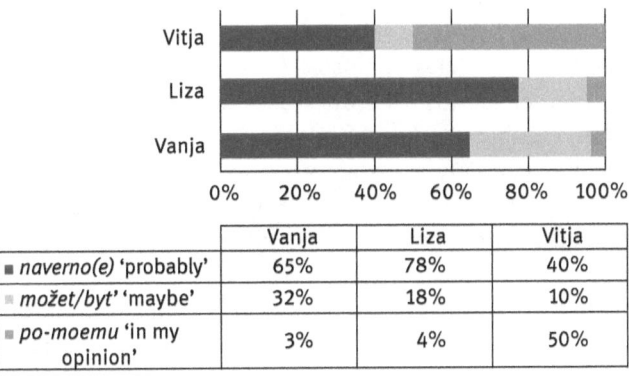

	Vanja	Liza	Vitja
■ *naverno(e)* 'probably'	65%	78%	40%
možet/byt' 'maybe'	32%	18%	10%
■ *po-moemu* 'in my opinion'	3%	4%	50%

Figure 5: Distribution of uncertainty markers in CS.

Figure 6 shows the frequency of certainty markers in the speech of each child. Acquisition of markers of explicit certainty (see Table 3 above) begins with *konečno* 'of course' followed by *dejstvitel'no* 'really', *na samom dele* 'actually' and *pravda* 'truly' lit. 'truth'.

---

10 Since children learn the language from the language variety spoken in their environment, the colloquial version of *možet byt'* 'maybe', namely *možet*, is the first to be acquired by the children studied in this paper. The standard version is used from 2;7 on, three months after the colloquial one.

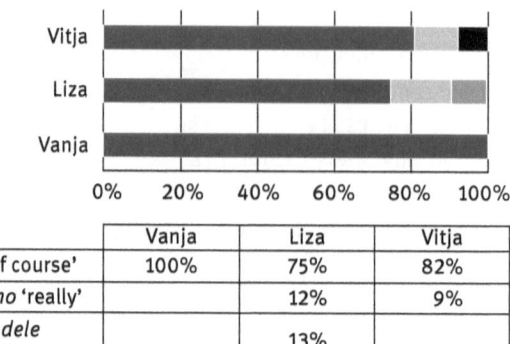

	Vanja	Liza	Vitja
■ *konečno* 'of course'	100%	75%	82%
▪ *dejstvitel'no* 'really'		12%	9%
▪ *na samom dele* 'actually'		13%	
■ *pravda* lit. 'truth'			9%

Figure 6: Distribution of certainty markers in CS.

Our data have also shown that infrequent markers in CDS, such as *kažetsja* '(it) seems' and *požaluj* 'very likely', are not adopted by the children (see Figure 7). In summary, it has been observed that the relative age of emergence of uncertainty and certainty markers in CS is closely related to their frequency in CDS. In turn, the EM acquired earlier are also the ones used with the highest frequency in CS. Furthermore, children start epistemic marking with the markers that express a high degree of uncertainty or certainty.

Comparing the diversity of EM occurring in CDS to the one in ADS it is found that it is more limited in the former than the latter (RG 1980: 230; see also Kazakovskaya and Argus 2016 for the Russian National Corpus[11]) so that CDS occupies an intermediate position between CS and ADS in this respect. EM such as *bessporno* 'undoubtedly', *bezuslovno* 'certainly', *vozmožno* 'perhaps', *vidimo* 'apparently', *samo soboj razumeetsja* 'it goes without saying' do not occur in either CDS or CS.

---

[11] The analysis of EM in ADS is based on the data of the main corpus of the Russian National Corpus (www.ruscorpora.ru, http://search1.ruscorpora.ru/search.xml?env=alpha&mycorp=&mysent=&mysize=&mysentsize=&mydocsize=&dpp=&spp=&spd=&text=lexform&mode=main&sort=gr_tagging&lang=ru&nodia=1&req=%EA%EE%ED%E5%F7%ED%EE&p=2&docid=106945 (25.03.2016)). The total number of EM is 330,086 tokens. The distribution of the tokens of uncertainty and certainty markers is almost equal (53% vs. 47%). The most frequent EM are *možet byt'* 'maybe' and its colloquial version *možet* 'may' (19%), *konečno* 'of course' (16%), *pravda* 'truly' lit. 'truth' (11%), *kažetsja* 'it seems' (9%), *dejstvitel'no* 'really' (7%), *navernoe* and its colloquial variant *naverno* 'probably' (5%) (Kazakovskaya and Argus 2016: 72). 26% of EM tokens occurring in ADS are not found in CDS.

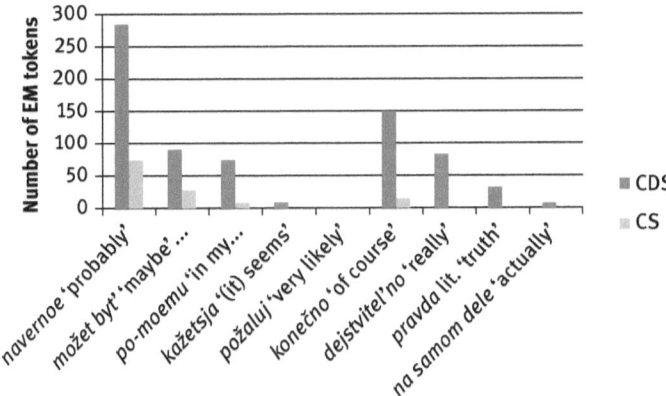

Figure 7: Distribution of EM in CDS and CS (tokens).

The specific relation between the use of EM in CDS and CS can be understood in more detail by a study of the uncertainty markers occurring in the large corpus of the dyad caregiver–Vanja. Vanja starts to use EM later than the other children (see Table 2 above). Comparing the developmental curves of his speech with CDS there are two simultaneous peaks of EM usage at 2;10 and 3;3 (Figure 8).

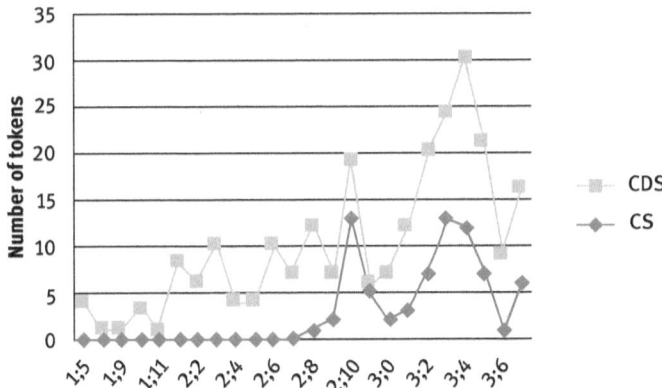

Figure 8: Uncertainty markers in the dyad caregiver–Vanja (tokens).

Although such peaks, which can also be found in the other two dyads studied, may be taken as evidence for fine-tuning of CDS to the children's development, it must be pointed out that, in our data, the children use EM either in response to their presence in the preceding utterance of the caregiver or in the wider conversational context. Another factor stimulating the use of EM in CS is the topic of adult–child interaction and the nature of the ongoing activity. Thus, in Vanja's corpus, the adult's questions about the unexpected states of objects in a play context generate plausible explanations by the child marked for epistemic modality (examples 39–42).

(39) Vanja, 3;2
    (Vanja and his grandmother are playing with a car)
    GRA: *ne zavoditsja?*
        'will it not start?'
        net.
        'no.'
    CHI: *benzin-a, navernoe, net.*
        gasoline-GEN probably.EM not
        'gasoline probably has run out.'
    GRA: *nu prover'.*
        'well, check.'

(40) Vanja, 3;2
    GRA: *oj, da, fara razbitaja.*
        'oh, yes, the headlight is broken.'
    GRA: *v avariju popala?*
        'did the car get into an accident?'
    CHI: *da, naverno, popa-l-a.*
        yes, probably.EM get.into-PST-FEM
        'yes, probably the car got into an accident.'

(41) Vanja, 3;3
    (speaking about the place where a roaster was made)
    tože, navernoe, v Šveci-i delaj-ut.
    also probably.EM in Sweden-LOC make-PRS.3PL
    'they also probably make it in Sweden.'

(42) Vanja, 3;3
    možet.byt', beževyj tvoj "Moskvič", da.
    maybe.EM beige your "Moskvič" yes
    'maybe, your "Moskvič" is beige, yes.'

6 Discussion and conclusions

The present study has investigated the emergence of epistemic modality and its gradual development in Russian children's speech. Summarizing our findings on the development of so-called parenthetical modal words for marking epistemic modality in Russian, it must first be noted that although both uncertainty and certainty markers emerge early they occur infrequently until the age of 4;0 in the speech of the children studied. The first marker to emerge in each of the fields of uncertainty and certainty (*navernoe* 'probably' and *konečno* 'of course', respectively) tends to become the one most frequently used in the repertoire of epistemic modality at the disposal of a child.

Early utterances with epistemic marking are multi-word statements describing the situation in the here and now. The children begin to mark epistemic modality by evaluating some situation about third persons and move on to reflections concerning their interlocutor. This may be taken to demonstrate their developing capacities in theory of mind that involve reflections on others' as well as one's own mental states.

For one of the three children studied in the present chapter, there is evidence for the development of epistemic modality as compared to agent-oriented modality. Based on analyses of Liza's spontaneous speech, Voeikova and Bayda (this volume) have shown that the girl starts to use imperatives for expressing direct requests from the beginning of the observation period at 1;6, whereas her first epistemically marked utterances representing the propositional modality of uncertainty (EM *navernoe* 'probably' and *po-moemu* 'in my opinion') are registered later, at 2;2. At this time Liza is already able to use both imperatives and infinitives for expressing directives and infinitives for the expression of her own intentions and suggestions. Additionally, she manages to use indirect requests (especially hortatives) so that her repertoire of deontic modality is quite rich, with infinitives expressing indirect requests being functionally distinguished from imperatives conveying direct requests.

Considered together, Voeikova and Bayda's and our own study of Liza's development of modality support earlier findings concerning the sequence of development of agent-oriented and epistemic modality based on parental diaries (Gvozdev 1949; Wiemer 1992; Oficerova 2005). These findings are also confirmed by studies on other languages and are particularly true "in languages that rely mostly on modal auxiliaries and mental verbs to express modality" (Hickmann and Bassano 2016: 431). The developmental asynchrony between agent-oriented and epistemic modality can first of all be accounted for by pragmatic factors (Stephany 1986, 1993; Hickmann and Bassano 2016: 431–432) and "is also due to interrelated cognitive and linguistic factors" (Hickmann and Bassano 2016: 432; see also Hickmann and Bassano 2016: 444–445; Matsui 2014: 297).

As far as the development of epistemic modality is concerned, the present study has shown that Russian children start to explicitly mark uncertainty prior to certainty. In contrast to French, where EM expressing certainty are acquired before those of uncertainty (Choi 2006: 147 reporting on work by Bassano), a contrastive study of Russian and Estonian has shown that children acquiring either of these genetically unrelated languages start by marking uncertainty (Kazakovskaya and Argus 2016: 62). This leads us to the conclusion that the acquisitional sequence of epistemic modality from certainty to uncertainty may not be universal.

Comparing CDS to CS it is to be noted that the inventory of EM in the former is only insignificantly larger than in the children's speech and much more limited than the one found in ADS. As far as input–output relations of EM are concerned, not only their frequency in CDS but also their diversity and positional features seem to have a certain impact on CS. This may be taken to provide some evidence for a usage-based theory of EM acquisition. The order of emergence of different EM reflects their 'modal strength' (i.e., the degree of certainty or uncertainty), which is supported, in turn, by the frequencies of such EM in CDS. Specifically, the first markers to be acquired by the children are those occurring most frequently in CDS and expressing a high degree of certainty or uncertainty. They are the most prototypical ones of their respective categories. It seems natural that EM which are early acquired are the ones to be best understood in later years (Ovčinnikova, Uglanova and Krauze 1999; Krauze 2004).

References

Arutjunova, Nina D. 1988. *Tipy jazykovyx značenij (ocenka, sobytie, fakt)* [Types of linguistic meanings (assessment, event, fact)]. Moscow: Nauka.
Bally, Charles 1965. *Linguistique générale et linguistique française*. Bern: Francke.
Beljaeva, Elena I. 1990. Dostovernost' [Reliability]. In Aleksandr V. Bondarko (ed.), *Teorija funkcional'noj grammatiki: Temporal'nost'. Modal'nost'* [Theory of functional grammar. Temporality. Modality], 157–170. Leningrad: Nauka.
Belošapkova, Vera A. 1997. Smyslovaja organizacija prostogo predloženija [The semantic organization of a simple sentence]. In Vera A. Belošapkova (ed.), *Sovremennyj russkij jazyk* [Modern Russian Language], 764–785. Moscow: Azbukovnik.
Birjulin, Leonid A. & Elena E. Kordi. 1990. Osnovnye tipy modal'nyx značenij, vydeljaemyx v lingvističeskoj literature [Main types of modal meanings allocated in linguistic literature]. In Aleksandr V. Bondarko (ed.), *Teorija funkcional'noj grammatiki: Temporal'nost'. Modal'nost'* [Theory of functional grammar. Temporality. Modality], 67–71. Leningrad: Nauka.

Bondarko, Aleksandr V. 1990. Vstupitel'nye zamečanija [Introductory remarks]. In Aleksandr V. Bondarko (ed.), *Teorija funkcional'noj grammatiki: Temporal'nost'. Modal'nost'* [Theory of functional grammar. Temporality. Modality], 59–67. Leningrad: Nauka.

Bulygina, Tatjana V. & Aleksej D. Šmelev. 1982. Dialogičeskie funkcii nekotoryx tipov voprositel'nyx predloženij [Dialogic functions of some interrogative sentences]. *Izvestija AN SSSR. Serija literatury i jazyka* [News of the Russian Academy of Sciences. Series of literature and language] 41(4). 314–326.

Bulygina, Tatjana V. & Aleksej D. Šmelev. 1993. Gipoteza kak myslitel'nyj i rečevoj akt [Hypothesis as a mental and speech act]. In Nina D. Arutjunova & Nadežda K. Rjabceva (eds.), *Logičeskij analiz jazyka. Mental'nye dejstvija* [Logical analysis of language. Mental actions], 78–82. Moscow: Nauka.

Choi, Soonja. 2006. Acquisition of modality. In William Frawley (ed.), *The expression of modality*, 141–171. Berlin: Walter de Gruyter.

Dmitrovskaja, Maria A. 1988. Znanie i dostovernost' [Knowledge and reliability]. In Nina D. Arutjunova (ed.), *Pragmatika i problemy intensional'nosti* [Pragmatics and the problems of intentionality], 166–187. Moscow: Institute of Linguistics Press.

Flavell, John H. 2000. Development of children's knowledge about the mental world. *International Journal of Behavioral Development* 24(1). 15–23.

Gatinskaja, Nadežda V. 2007. Modal'no-ocenočnye slova v istoričeskom i sovremennom kontekste [Modal and evaluation words in a diachronic and contemporary context]. *Vestnik RUDN* 1. 17–24.

Gatinskaja, Nadežda V. 2011. Semantičeskaja struktura modal'nyx slov v svjazi s ix proisxoždeniem [Semantic structure of modal words in connection with their origins]. In Nadežda K. Onipenko (ed.), *Voprosy russkogo jazykoznanija. Grammatika i tekst (K jubileju Galiny Aleksandrovny Zolotovoj)* [Issues of Russian linguistics. Grammar and text (Festschrift Galiny Aleksandrovny Zolotovoj)], 244–257. Moscow: Moscow State University Press.

Gatinskaja, Nadežda V. 2015. Semantičeskij analiz modal'nyx slov v diaxroničeskom aspekte [Semantic analysis of modal words in a diachronic aspect]. *Vestnik RUDN* 1. 89–95.

Gvozdev, Aleksandr N. 1949. *Formirovanie u rebenka grammatičeskogo stroja russkogo jazyka* [The formation of the Russian grammatical system in the child]. 2 vols. Moscow: Academy of Pedagogical Science of the Russian Federation Press.

Haßler, Gerda 2016. *Modality and evidentiality in European languages*. Paper presented at the Department of General Linguistics, St. Petersburg State University, 27 April 2016.

Hickmann, Maya & Dominique Bassano. 2016. Modality and mood in first language acquisition. In Jan Nuyts & Johan van der Auwera (eds.), *The Oxford handbook of modality and mood*, 430–447. Oxford: Oxford University Press.

Iordanskaja, Lidia N. & Igor' A. Mel'čuk. 2002. Tekstovye konnektory v raznyx jazykax: francuzskoe *en effet* i russkoe *v samom dele* [The text connectors in different languages: French *en effet* and Russian *v samom dele*]. *Semiotika i informatika* 37. 78–115. Moscow: All-Union Institute of Scientific and Technical Information of the Russian Academy of Sciences Press.

Jakovleva, Ekaterina S. 1994. *Fragmenty russkoj jazykovoj kartiny mira (modeli prostranstva, vremeni i vosprijatija)* [Fragments of the Russian language picture of the world (models of space, time and perception)]. Moscow: Gnozis.

Kazakovskaya, Victoria V. 1996. *Sposoby vyraženija avtorstva v structure predloženija* [The means of authorship expression within utterance structure]. Moscow: Moscow Pedagogical University dissertation.

Kazakovskaya, Victoria V. 1997. Modusnaja ramka v ontogeneze [A modus frame in the ontogenesis of language]. In Stella N. Ceitlin (ed.), *Problemy detskoj reči 1997* [Problems of child language 1997], 21–22. St. Petersburg: The Institute of Early Intervention Press.

Kazakovskaya, Victoria V. 2011. K voprosu ob ontogeneze ramočnyx sredstv [On the question of the ontogenesis of frame means]. In Nadežda K. Onipenko (ed.), *Voprosy russkogo jazykoznanija. Grammatika i tekst (K jubileju Galiny Aleksandrovny Zolotovoj)* [Issues of Russian linguistics. Grammar and text (Festschrift Galiny Aleksandrovny Zolotovoj)], 258–282. Moscow: Moscow State University Press.

Kazakovskaya, Victoria V. 2016. Input–output relations in early epistemic modality in Russian: a corpus-based approach. In Li Chen (ed.), *Proceedings of the 3rd International Conference on Applied Social Science Research* (Advances in Intelligent System Research 105), 423–426. Paris, Amsterdam & Beijing: Atlantis Press. DOI: 10.2991/icassr-15.2016.80.

Kazakovskaya, Victoria V. 2019. *Vopros i otvet v dialoge "vzroslyj–rebenok": Psixolingvističeskij aspekt* [Questions and answers in "adult–child" dialogue: Psycholinguistic aspect]. Moscow: Knižnyj dom «LIBROKOM».

Kazakovskaya, Victoria V. & Reili Argus. 2016. Acquisition of epistemic marking in Estonian and Russian. *Estonian Papers in Applied Linguistics* 12. 57–80. DOI: 10.5128/ERYa12.04.

Kolosova, Tatjana A. 1980. *Russkie složnye predloženija asimmetričnoj struktury* [Russian complex sentences of asymmetric structure]. Voronež: Voronež State University Press.

Krauze, Marion. 2004. Modal'nye markery v reči detej: Stanovlenie funkcij i sistemy [Modal markers in child speech: Development of functions and system]. In Stella N. Ceitlin (ed.), *Detskaja reč kak predmet lingvističeskogo issledovanija* [Children's speech as an object of linguistic research], 136–139. St. Petersburg: Nauka.

Krauze, Marion. 2007. *Epistemische Modalität. Zur Interaktion lexikalischer und prosodischer Marker*. Wiesbaden: Harrassowitz Verlag.

Lekant, Pavel A. 2002. *Očerki po grammatike russkogo jazyka* [Essays on the grammar of the Russian language]. Moscow: Moscow State Pedagogical University Press.

Lyons, John. 1977. *Semantics*. 2 vols. Cambridge: Cambridge University Press.

MacWhinney, Brian. 2000. *The CHILDES project: Tools for analyzing talk*. Hillsdale, NJ & London: Lawrence Erlbaum.

Mandler, Jean M. 2004. Thought before language. *TRENDS in Cognitive Sciences* 8(11). 508–513.

Matsui, Tomoko. 2014. Children's understanding of linguistic expressions of certainty and evidentiality. In Danielle Matthews (ed.), *Pragmatic development in first language acquisition*, 295–316. Amsterdam: John Benjamins.

Miloslavsky, Igor' G. 1997. Modal'nye slova [Modal words]. In Vera A. Belošapkova (ed.), *Sovremennyj russkij jazyk* [The modern Russian language], 595–596. Moscow: Azbukovnik.

Moore, Chris, David Furrow, Loraine Chiasson & Maria Pitriquin. 1994. Developmental relationships between production and comprehension of mental terms. *First Language* 14. 1–17.

Oficerova, Ekaterina A. 2005. *Vyraženie modal'nyx značenij vozmožnosti i neobxodimosti v russkoj detskoj reči* [The expression of modal meanings of possibility and necessity in

Russian child speech]. St. Petersburg: Institute for Linguistic Studies of the Russian Academy of Sciences dissertation.

Ovčinnikova, Irina G., Inna A. Uglanova & Marion Krauze. 1999. Ob ocenke det'mi dvux vozrastnyx grupp stepeni uverennosti/neuverennosti vyskazyvanija [On estimation of the certainty/uncertainty degree of utterances by children of two age groups]. In Stella N. Ceitlin (ed.), *Problemy ontolingvistiki 1999* [Problems of ontolinguistics 1999], 132–133. St. Petersburg: Hertsen University Press.

Palmer, Frank R. 2001. *Mood and modality*. 2nd edn. Cambridge: Cambridge University Press.

Panfilov, Vladimir Z. 1977. Rol' modal'nosti v konstruirovanii predloženija i suždenija [The role of modality in the construction of sentence and judgment]. *Voprosy jazykoznanija* 4. 37–48.

Papafragou, Anna. 2002. Modality and theory of mind: Perspectives from language development and autism. In Sjef Barbiers, Frits Beukema & Wim van der Wurff (eds.), *Modality and its interaction with the verbal systems*, 105–204. Amsterdam & Philadelphia: John Benjamins.

Plungjan, Vladimir A. 2000. Modal'nost' i naklonenie [Modality and mood]. In Vladimir A. Plungjan. *Obščaja morfologija: Vvedenie v problematiku* [General morphology: Introduction to problematic issues], 308–329. Moscow: Editorial URSS.

Russkaja grammatika [Russian Grammar]. 1980. Vol. 2. Moscow: Nauka.

Sergienko, Elena A., Evgenia I. Lebedeva & Ol'ga A. Prusakova. 2009. *Model' psixičeskogo kak osnova ponimanija sebja i drugogo v ontogeneze čeloveka* [Theory of mind as the basis for understanding self and other in human ontogenesis]. Moscow: Institute of Psychology of the Russian Academy of Sciences Press.

Shatz, Marilyn, Henry Wellman & Sharon Silber. 1983. The acquisition of mental verbs: A systematic investigation of the first reference to mental state. *Cognition* 14. 301–321.

Stephany, Ursula. 1986. Modality. In Paul Fletcher & Michael Garman (eds.), *Language acquisition*, 375–400. 2nd edn. Cambridge: Cambridge University Press.

Stephany, Ursula. 1993. Modality in first language acquisition: The state of the art. In Norbert Dittmar & Astrid Reich (eds.), *Modality in language acquisition*, 133–144. Berlin & New York: Walter de Gruyter.

Stoljarova, Irina V. 1992. Vyraženie sub"ektivno-modal'nyx otnošenij v detskoj reči [Expressing subjective and modal relations in child speech]. In Stella N. Ceitlin (ed.), *Detskaja reč: Lingvističeskij aspect* [Child language: Linguistic aspect], 86–95. St. Petersburg: Obrazovanie.

Švec, Varvara M. 2007. Sub'ektivnaja (epistemičeskaja) modal'nost' i ee vyraženie v detskoj reči [Subjective (epistemic) modality and its expression in child spech]. In Stella N. Ceitlin (ed.), *Semantičeskie kategorii v detskoj reči* [Semantic categories in child speech], 161–180. St. Petersburg: Nestor.

Tardif, Twila & Henry M. Wellman. 2000. Acquisition of mental state language in Mandarin- and Cantonese-speaking children. *Developmental Psychology* 36. 25–43.

Tomasello, Michael. 2003. *Constructing a language: A usage-based theory of language acquisition*. Cambridge, MA & London: Harvard University Press.

Urmson, James O. 1970. Parenthetical verbs. In Charles E. Caton (ed.), *Philosophy and ordinary language*, 220–240. Urbana, Chicago & London: University of Illinois Press.

Vinogradov, Viktor V. 1947. Modal'nye slova i časticy [Modal words and particles]. In Viktor V. Vinogradov, *Grammatičeskoe učenie o slove* [Grammatical doctrine of the word], 725–744. Moscow & Leningrad: Učpedgiz.

Vinogradov, Viktor V. 1955. Osnovnye voprosy sintaksisa predloženija [Basic issues of syntax]. In Viktor V. Vinogradov (ed.), *Voprosy grammatičeskogo stroja* [Issues of grammatical structure], 389–435. Moscow: Soviet Union Academy of Sciences Press.

Vinogradov, Viktor V. 1975. *Izbrannye trudy. Issledovanija po russkoj grammatike* [Selected works. Research on Russian grammar]. Moscow: Soviet Union Academy of Sciences Press.

Vinogradov, Viktor V. 1986. Modal'nye slova i časticy. Ix razrjady [Modal words and particles. Their classes]. In Viktor V. Vinogradov. *Russkij jazyk (grammatičeskoe učenie o slove)* [Russian language (grammatical doctrine of the word)], 594–608. Moscow: High School.

Wellman, Henry M. 1990. *The child's theory of mind*. Cambridge, MA: MIT Press.

Wiemer, Björn 1992. Ovladenie modal'nymi značenijami v ontogeneze (na materiale russkogo i anglijskogo jazykov) [Acquisition of modal meanings during ontogenesis (based on Russian and English)]. In Stella N. Ceitlin (ed.), *Detskaja reč: Lingvističeskij aspect* [Child language: Linguistic aspect], 131–144. St. Petersburg: Obrazovanie.

Xolodov, Nikolaj N. 1996. Modal'nye slova [Modal words]. In Pavel A. Lekant (ed.), *Sovremennyj russkij literaturnuj jazyk*, [The modern Russian literary language], 274–275. Moscow: High School.

Zolotova, Galina A. 1973. *Očerk funkcional'nogo sintaksisa russkogo jazyka* [An essay on the functional syntax of the Russian language]. Moscow: Nauka.

Treysi Terziyan and Ayhan Aksu-Koç
Epistemic and evidential modality in early Turkish child speech

Abstract: Turkish expresses epistemic modality, which concerns the speaker's evaluation of the factual status of a proposition, and evidentiality, which has to do with the grounds for that judgment, both inflectionally and lexically. In this study, we investigate the emergence of the expression of these modal notions in the speech of two monolingual Turkish-speaking children between the ages of 1;3–2;0 and 1;6–2;10 and their caregivers. Our results show that both types of modality emerge around 1;8–2;0 years; however, the use of evidential utterances is more frequent than epistemic ones. First evidential utterances occur in contexts of encountering new information and in those of story-telling, whereas use that refers to how the information was acquired (source) follows somewhat later. Children's first epistemic utterances express either a high or low degree of certainty, values at the two opposite poles of the epistemic scale. Use of adverbs along with multifunctional epistemic inflections indicates a preference for forms that carry a unique modal value. The frequency and order of emergence of formal means of expression in children's speech is highly reflective of the frequency of forms used by their caregivers. As for functions, the frequency of types of epistemic functions children express differs from that of the caregivers, whereas the frequency of the types of evidential functions match those of the caregivers somewhat more closely. These findings indicate that while language input is an important factor, children's cognitive capacities and language typology also play a role.

1 Introduction

Modal expressions allow speakers to indicate their subjective perspective on states of affairs. The notions of necessity and possibility are recognized as basic for defining the different categories of modality among which deontic and epistemic modalities stand out (Boye 2016; Lyons 1977; Palmer 2001; Stephany 1986, 1993). Developments in the last three decades have witnessed an increased attention to another notional category, evidentiality, which concerns indicating the factual status of the information by specifying its source (Aikhenvald 2004; Chafe and

Treysi Terziyan, Tilburg University
Ayhan Aksu-Koç, Boğaziçi University

Nichols 1986; Johanson and Utas 2000). While debates as to whether it is a modal category (Palmer 2001) or not (Aikhenvald 2004; de Haan 1999) have yet to be resolved, the close relationship between evidentiality and epistemic modality is well recognized (Dendale and Tasmowski 2001; Faller 2002; Palmer 2001; Plungian 2001 among others). In the present study, we explore the emergence and early use of the expression of epistemic and evidential modalities in Turkish, where both of these notions are grammaticized in the verbal morphology. For this purpose, we examine longitudinal data from two children between the ages of 1;3–2;0 and 1;6–2;10 in spontaneous interaction with their caregivers and trace the order of acquisition of the formal means used and the modal notions expressed. In doing so, we consider the relations between children's speech (CS) and child-directed speech (CDS) with a focus on the possible input factors and cognitive constraints that may guide the discovery of form–function relations by the child.

The chapter is organized as follows. In Section 2 we discuss briefly the theoretical positions that guide our investigation, the usage-based approach for acquisition (Bybee 2010; Tomasello 2003) and Palmer's (2001) framework for modality. In Section 3, we present the means of expression of epistemic and evidential modalities in Turkish, limiting ourselves to what is observed in child and caregiver speech. We describe the data and our coding in Section 4 and present the results of our analysis in Section 5. Section 6 includes the discussion and conclusions.

2 Frameworks for analysis

2.1 Usage-based approach

The usage-based functional approach to language acquisition maintains that "language structure emerges from language use" (Tomasello 2003: 327). In this view, children use their domain-general cognitive mechanisms in deciphering the structure of their language by working on the sequences of speech they receive as input (Bybee 2010; Theakston and Lieven 2017; Tomasello 2003). Among these mechanisms are pattern recognition, imitation, abstraction by analogy from stored exemplars, generalization, recognition of variations and "a generative capacity that allows the imitated sequences to be used productively in new situations" (Bybee 2010: 15; also Behrens 2006; Tomasello 2009).

Among the properties of the input that support these processes are frequency of use, consistency of form–function relations and complexity and variability of structure (Behrens 2006; Küntay and Slobin 1996). Caregivers take on an active role and provide feedback by repeating what the child has said to affirm his/her linguistic choices or to model the correct version of those choices (Tarplee 2010). Repetition also serves to inquire about the child's intentions and build on what the child has said with new information (Clark and Bernicot 2008). Caregivers often repeat the child's utterance only partially, substituting a novel element in place of what is not repeated in order to create a coherent linguistic interaction (du Bois 2014). Such partial repetitions, which resonate (du Bois 2014: 367; Choi, this volume) what the child has said, result in high frequency of occurrence of the structures repeated and are functional in the entrenchment of what the child is integrating into his/her system.

2.2 The categories of epistemic and evidential modality

Epistemic and evidential modalities are concerned with the speaker's stance on the truth value of a proposition. Epistemically modalized utterances express the speaker's judgment about the factual status of the proposition whereas evidential utterances indicate the evidence for this factual status (Palmer 2001: 8–9, 24–69).

Epistemic modality covers a range of judgments on a scale of 'necessity–possibility' (Lyons 1977; Stephany 1993: 135) and epistemic markers indicate the degree of speaker certainty regarding the factuality of the state of affairs referred to (Boye 2016: 117; Palmer 2001: 25). While epistemic judgments express varying degrees of possibility, probability or inferred certainty, statements unmarked for modality are neutral; they simply assert "without indicating the reasons for that assertion or the speaker's commitment to it" (Palmer 2001: 64; Bybee, Perkins, and Pagliuca 1994).

A modal notion related to epistemic modality, if not overlapping at times (Palmer 2001: 24), is evidentiality. While epistemic modality concerns the speaker's evaluation of the truth of a proposition, evidential modality concerns the question of how the speaker acquired the information behind the proposition, that is, its source. Examples of modes of information acquisition marked by evidential languages are visual, auditory, inference, general knowledge and hearsay. Evidential languages differ in what combination of these notions they include under the non-modal, the epistemic and the evidential domains and in the number of distinct markers they use (e.g., over four in Tibetan vs. one in Turkish) (Aikhenvald 2004; Palmer 2001; Plungian 2001). In short, the boundaries between evidentials, epistemics and non-modal categories as well as the fineness of the formal distinctions are language specific.

In view of the crosslinguistic differences and lack of clear-cut boundaries between epistemic and evidential modalities, it has been suggested that the two semantic domains are independent (Aikhenvald 2004; Bybee, Perkins, and

Pagliuca 1994; de Haan 2006), independent but intersecting (Plungian 2001: 354) or are closely related as subcategories of propositional modality (Choi 2006: 142; Nuyts 2006: 10–11; Palmer 2001: 8). We think that the way Turkish carves the domain of epistemic and evidential modalities is in line with the latter conceptualization and is best analyzed within Palmer's (2001) general framework (Aksu-Koç 2016: 143–144).

Palmer (2001) proposes two major categories, event modality and propositional modality. Event modality concerns the speaker's stance on prospective events, which have not yet been realized but might be, and includes deontic and dynamic modalities.[1] Propositional modality, on the other hand, refers to the speaker's perspective about the truth or factual status of a proposition and comprises epistemic and evidential modalities. The functions of epistemic and evidential modalities are presented in Table 1.

Table 1: Palmer's categorization of propositional modality.[2]

Propositional Modality	Epistemic	Speaker's judgment about the factual status of a proposition Functions: Deduction: The only possible conclusion (inferred certainty) Assumption: Reasonable, probable conclusions (probability) Speculation: Possible conclusions (possibility)
	Evidential	The evidence the speaker provides for a proposition's factual status (direct or indirect) Functions: Sensory: Firsthand evidence gathered via senses Reported: Evidence obtained from a third party or general/folk knowledge

3 Expression of propositional modality in Turkish

Turkish has SOV order and agglutinating morphology. The verb root is followed by a string of affixes that indicate voice, negation, tense-aspect-modality[3]

---

[1] "Event modality" corresponds to the category of "agent-oriented modality" more widely used in the literature (e.g., Bybee, Perkins, and Pagliuca 1994). For the sake of consistency with the terminology used in this volume, we also use "agent-oriented modality".
[2] See Palmer (2001: 6, 22, 24–25).
[3] Since both mood and modality are primarily expressed by suffixation in Turkish, the appropriate terminology to designate this category is "modality" (Taylan 2015: 171, 173–174; see also Göksel and Kerslake 2005: 283–321).

(TAM) and person-number (Göksel and Kerslake 2005: 50, 283–321; Taylan 2015: 173–174). Modal categories are primarily expressed morphologically through multifunctional TAM inflections on the verb that may convey temporal and aspectual meanings as well as modal ones. The expression of modal categories is compositional since a combination of TAM suffixes is used to express complex temporal-aspectual-modal perspectives. These inflections are (i) the tense-aspect-modality suffixes that constitute the TAM-I paradigm, plus the modal suffix -*Abil*, and (ii) copular clitics that constitute the TAM-II paradigm, plus the generalizing modality marker -*DIr* (Göksel and Kerslake 2005: 284). TAM-I suffixes attach only to verbal predicates, whereas TAM-II clitics attach to nonverbal predicates as well as verbal predicates inflected for TAM-I.

To illustrate the compositional nature of the expression of tense-aspect-modality on the verb, we refer to Taylan's (2001: 101) presentation of the affix order and her example in (1) below:

(1) Verb +(voice) +(negation) +(*Abil*) +TAM-I (TAM-II) +agreement
     çağır -ıl   -ma   -yabil   -ir   -miş   -iz.
     call   -PASS   -NEG   -PSB   -AOR   -EVID.CL -1PL
     'Apparently it is possible that we may not be called (invited).'

As can be observed in example (1) there are two slots for the finite verb of a main clause that have to be filled. These are the TAM-I and agreement slots, all others (within parentheses), being optional. In example (1), six of these slots are occupied: The verb is followed by the passive suffix -*Il*, then the negation marker -*mA* and the modal suffix -*Abil*. The TAM-I slot is occupied by the aorist -(*A/I*)*r* and the TAM-II slot is filled in by the evidential -*ImIş*.[4]

The TAM suffixes and clitics[5] functional in the expression of epistemic and evidential modality, either singularly or compositionally, are presented in Table 2. The examples illustrate the temporal, aspectual and modal meanings of these forms. We refer to Table 2 in our explanation of the specific epistemic and evidential uses of these forms in sections 3.1 and 3.2 below.

---

[4] Affixes alternate according to the rules of vowel harmony, which operate in terms of the high/low, front/back and rounded/unrounded phonological contrasts. Consonant assimilation and other regular morphophonological processes also apply. Alternating vowels and consonants are represented by uppercase characters.

[5] Henceforth, we will refer to TAM-I suffixes as "TAM suffixes" and TAM-II suffixes as "clitics".

Table 2: Tense-aspect-modality markers expressing propositional modality.

Suffixes & Clitics	Forms	TAM functions	Examples with the verb *otur* 'sit'	Gloss
NEUTRAL				
Past	-*DI*	perfective past	a. *otur-du* sit-PST	'(s/he) sat'
Imperfective	-*Iyor*	imperfective present	b. *otur-uyor* sit-IPFV	'(s/he) is sitting'
MODAL				
Possibility	-*Abil*	epistemic/ deontic/ dynamic	c. *otur-abil-ir* sit-PSB-AOR	'(s/he) might sit' '(s/he) may sit' '(s/he) can sit'
Probability (Aorist)	-*(A/I)r*	epistemic/ habitual	d. *otur-ur* sit-AOR	'(s/he) will probably sit' '(s/he) sits'
Future	-*AcAk*	epistemic/ dynamic	e. *otur-acak* sit-FUT	'(s/he) will certainly sit' '(s/he) can sit'
Necessitative	-*mAlI*	epistemic/	f. *otur-uyor ol-malı* sit-IPFV be-NEC	'(s/he) must be sitting'
		deontic	g. *otur-malı* sit-NEC	'(s/he) must sit'
Evidential	-*mIş*	perfective past evidential	h. *otur-muş* sit-EVID	'(s/he) has sat'
CLITICS				
Past	-*IDI*	past	i. *otur-uyor-du* sit-IPFV-PST.CL	'(s/he) was sitting'
Evidential	-*ImIş*	evidential	j. *otur-uyor-muş* sit-IPFV-EVID.CL	'(s/he) was reportedly sitting'
Generalizing modality	-*DIr*	epistemic	k. *otur-uyor-dur* sit-IPFV-GM	'(s/he) must be sitting'

While propositional modality is expressed with the rich verbal morphology obligatorily, the language also makes use of lexical means to denote epistemic and evidential notions. These are adverbs (e.g., *belki* 'perhaps'), adjectives (e.g., *lazım* 'necessary'), verbs (e.g., *san-* 'suppose') and nouns (e.g., *olasılık* 'possibility') (Taylan 2014).

3.1 Means of expression of epistemic modality

A verbal clause that is marked with the perfective past *-DI* (example a, Table 2) and the imperfective *-Iyor* (example b) and a nominal clause that is unmarked or marked with the clitic *-IDI* (example i) are modally neutral. Epistemically modalized utterances have a main clause marked by one of the following suffixes: the possibility *-Abil*, the aorist *-(A/I)r*, the future *-AcAk*, the necessitative *-mAlI* and the generalizing *-DIr* or some combination of these. The interpretation of their modal strength on the epistemic continuum depends on context, linguistic and situational.

The modal suffix *-Abil* (example c, Table 2) comes after the verb stem and has to be followed by a TAM suffix. Depending on what it combines with and the context, *-Abil* expresses either dynamic ability/potentiality, deontic permission or epistemic possibility. All three interpretations are possible when *-Abil* is combined with the aorist (V-*Abil-Ir*); the epistemic interpretation depends on the presence of an adverb, the semantics of the main verb or the discourse context (Taylan 2015: 176); first example of (c) in Table 2 is a speculation referring to a possible state of affairs. Epistemic statements with the aorist *-(A/I)r*, which is also the habitual aspect marker, may express assumptions/predictions regarding probable events (example d) as well as generalizations and deductions of a stronger modal value. Example (2) below illustrates its use in the expression of a deduction.

(2) Mine, 1;11, Phase 3
 CDS: yok o-na dokun-mak. boz-ul-ur.
 exist.NEG that-DAT touch-INF break-PASS-AOR
 'No touching that (= you are not allowed to touch that). It will break.'

In its epistemic use the future suffix *-AcAk* conveys a prediction (example e, Table 2) and in combination with *-Abil*, it expresses a speculative possibility (Göksel and Kerslake 2005). The necessitative *-mAlI* is purely modal and denotes deontic or epistemic necessity, depending on context (example f) (Göksel and Kerslake 2005: 298–299). Finally, the generalizing modal clitic *-DIr* may assume different values on a scale of 'necessity–possibility'. These range from factual generic statements about the characteristics of a class to nonfactual statements such as deductive inferences and assumptions based on general knowledge and habitualities (example k) (Aksu-Koç 1995; Göksel and Kerslake 2005: 295–297; Tura 1986). A typical non-modal use is for eliciting class labels for objects as in *bu nedir?* 'what is this?'. Statements marked with *-(A/I)r* and *-DIr* are usually modified with an adverb which expresses "the strength of the speaker's confidence in the soundness of the assumption" (Göksel and Kerslake 2005: 298). This is illustrated in example (3), where the epistemic adverb *belki* 'perhaps' modulates the meaning of the *-DIr* assertion and decreases its strength from an assumption to a speculation.

(3) Mine, 2;1, Phase 3
 CDS: *belki   Ali deniz-e git-miş-tir.*
       perhaps Ali sea-DAT go-PFV-GM
       'Perhaps Ali went to the sea.'

3.2 Means of expression of evidential modality

The evidential suffix *-mIş* and the clitic *-ImIş* (examples h and j, Table 2) indicate that the information conveyed is based on knowledge acquired indirectly (Aksu-Koç 1988; Johanson 2000; Slobin and Aksu 1982). In Table 2, the evidential past in example (h) *otur-muş* (sit-EVID) 'evidently (s/he) sat/has sat' contrasts with the past of direct experience in example (a) *otur-du* (sit-PST) '(s/he) sat' on modal grounds. That is, the evidential past *-mIş* and clitic *-ImIş* are in obligatory opposition with the neutral past *-DI* and clitic *-IDI* and Turkish speakers are expected to specify whether the information they are conveying is taken to be factual or has been acquired indirectly.[6]

When it is the only inflection on the verb, *-mIş* denotes perfective aspect, past tense and evidentiality. If the speaker wants to present an indirectly accessed event from another aspectual perspective than perfective, then the clitic *-ImIş*, which is just modal with no inherent aspectual or temporal value, is appended to the verb marked for tense-aspect-modality with a TAM suffix as in example (j) *otur-uyor-muş* (sit-IPFV-EVID.CL) 'evidently (s/he) is/was sitting'. Nominal predicates that refer to entities or their properties and are therefore inherently stative, also require the use of the clitic *-ImIş*. When a verb inflected with *-mIş* is followed by one of the clitics (*-IDI, -IsA, -DIr*) as in example (j) *otur-muş-tu* (sit-PFV-PST.CL) '(s/he) had sat', its evidential meaning is cancelled

---

[6] The suffixes *-DI* and *-mIş* and the clitics *-IDI* and *-ImIş* are similar in phonological form, but stress patterns and other phonological constraints differentiate the two sets. TAM affixes receive stress whereas clitics are unstressable but assign stress to the preceding variable. Phonologically, clitics require the palatal glide /j/ as a buffer when they are attached to words ending in vowels while there is no such requirement in case of TAM affixes (Nakipoğlu and Yumrutaş 2009).

(Aksu-Koç 1988; Göksel and Kerslake 2005: 75, 295; Slobin and Aksu 1982: 194; Taylan 2001: 102).

The functions of *-mIş/-ImIş* that fall under Palmer's (2001) sensory category are new information (Aksu-Koç 1988; Slobin and Aksu 1982), i.e., information assessed as new or unexpected despite direct perceptual access,[7] and inference, i.e., information deduced from consequences of an unobserved past process, that is, a resultant state. Turkish subsumes such inferences that express "information new for unprepared minds" (Slobin and Aksu 1982: 197–198) or put differently, the "cognitive awareness of the perception of some aspect of the situation" (Choi, this volume) under evidentiality but deductive inferences from knowledge well assimilated in the speaker's mind, marked by *-DIr*, under the epistemic domain (Aksu-Koç 1995, 2016).[8] The functions of *-mIş/-ImIş* that fall under Palmer's reported category are reports of information based on the statement of a third party, hearsay, narrative and, by pragmatic extension, utterances referring to the nonfactual realm (e.g., pretend play, behavior regulating requests attributed to a third party) (Aksu-Koç 1988; Slobin and Aksu 1982; Uzundağ et al. 2018; see also Göksel and Kerslake 2005: 309–311). In reporting information obtained from someone else, the speaker has to modify the inflectional form of the original speaker's utterance by replacing it with the suffix *-mIş* or by adding the clitic *-ImIş*.

In short, Turkish has a single form that denotes the modal category of evidentiality, or more precisely, indirectivity (Johanson 2000), rather than several distinct forms to mark different types of information source. Therefore, the interpretation of the above functions depends on the semantics of the predicate that *-mIş/-ImIş* is attached to, the temporal and/or aspectual composition of the TAM markers on the verb and the discourse context.[9] Although a direct correspondence between form and function does not hold, new information and reports are often conveyed by a nominal-*ImIş* (NML-*ImIş*) and a verb-TAM-*ImIş*

---

[7] Plungian (2001: 355) also argues that such "mirative" use of evidentials is modal as they involve a special kind of judgment, one concerning the speaker's expectations. In fact, here, the Turkish evidential and epistemic modalities have fuzzy boundaries.

[8] Languages differ in what types of inferences they treat as epistemic or evidential. Some include both inference from observable evidence and inference from general knowledge under the evidential category whereas others such as Turkish treat the former under the evidential and the latter under the epistemic domain (Aikhenvald 2004; Aksu-Koç 1995).

[9] The form–function relations indicated by the *-mIş/-ImIş* forms is a matter of debate among linguists. The various analyses include those that argue for a single form with multiple functions (Slobin and Aksu 1982), a single form with a basic meaning (Johanson 2000), and for two homophonous forms with different functions (Şener 2011). In the present study, we follow Slobin and Aksu (1982), accepting a single form with multiple functions the specifics of which are understood from the grammatical and discourse context.

(V-TAM-*ImIş*) construction whereas the verb-*mIş* (V-*mIş*) construction may express all the above functions. In example (4) new information is expressed with the clitic *-ImIş* appended to a nominal predicate, in example (5) inference is conveyed by the suffix *-mIş* appended to a verb and in (6) reference is made to a future event as learned through the report of another person, marked with the clitic *-ImIş*. An example for use in a narrative utterance is given in (7).

(4) Deniz, 1;3, Phase 1, looking at picture book
CDS: *aa, ora-da   da   bi   miyav*
oh   there-LOC also one   cat
var-mış.
exist-EVID.CL
'Oh, it appears that there is a cat there.'

(5) Deniz, 1;3, Phase 1, referring to the torn page of a book
CDS: *evet, ora-sı   da   yırt-ıl-mış.*
yes   there-POSS.3SG also tear-PASS-EVID
'Yes, it has also been torn there, evidently.'

(6) Mine, 1;6, Phase 1
CDS: *gel-ecek-miş.*
come-FUT-EVID.CL
'(S/he) will come, reportedly/it is said.'

(7) Deniz 1;6, Phase 1, mother reading a story book
CDS: *birgün   Dingo spor   yap-ma-ya   karar   ver-miş.*
one.day   Dingo sports do-NMLZ-DAT   decision   give-EVID
'One day Dingo decided to exercise.'

This overview of epistemic and evidential categories in Turkish shows that the modal system presents the child a complex combination of perspectives to be expressed.

3.3 Previous research on the acquisition of epistemic and evidential modalities in Turkish

Previous research shows that children first acquire the neutral markers *-DI* and *-Iyor* and then the future *-AcAk*, the aorist *-(A/I)r* and the evidential *-mIş* sometime between 1;6 to 2;6 years (Aksu-Koç 1988, 1998; Aksu-Koç and Ketrez 2003;

Aksu-Koç and Slobin 1985; Ekmekçi 1982; Ketrez 1999; Savaşır and Gee 1982 among others). The developmental trajectory of these multifunctional suffixes and the clitics -*IDI*, -*ImIş* and -*DIr* show that children first pick up a single function of a given form (e.g., aspect) extending its use to other functions gradually (e.g., tense and modality). Notionally, children first express deontic (commands) and dynamic modality followed by evidential and epistemic modalities. The emergence of deontic expressions of obligation and permission is observed subsequently (Aksu-Koç 1988; Aksu-Koç, Terziyan, and Taylan 2014; Terziyan 2013).

Studies that particularly focus on the acquisition of epistemic and evidential modalities in Turkish language acquisition are not many. The emergence of the different modal functions of a given form show that the aorist *-(A/I)r* is used first for dynamic modality and then epistemically, around 2;0 (Aksu-Koç 1998). *-DIr* is observed between 2;0 and 3;0 years and is first used non-modally in a generic sense (asking for labels of objects) then modally to express gradations of epistemic notions (Aksu-Koç, Ögel-Balaban, and Alp 2009: 17). Experimental evidence for the comprehension of generic *-DIr* (Ataman 2018; Tamm et al. 2014) and of epistemic *-DIr* (Aksu-Koç and Alıcı 2000) show that 4-year-old children have already grasped these functions.

Research on the evidential *-mIş/-ImIş* shows that its different functions emerge between 1;8–2;6. Its first uses are marking new or unexpected information in contexts of joint attention with an adult and telling stories in the narrative genre. Uses to express inferences and reports/hearsay are observed subsequently (Aksu-Koç 1988; Uzundağ et al. 2018). Experimental studies on the production of *-mIş/-ImIş* reveal similar findings (Ünal and Papafragou 2016), however with successful performance at older ages, arguably due to task demands (Aksu-Koç 1988; Ögel 2007; Öztürk and Papafragou 2008). Controversial results on whether the inference (Aksu-Koç 1988) or the reportative function (Öztürk and Papafragou 2008) emerges first have raised questions about the effects of input frequency versus cognitive complexity of the two functions. The semi-dense corpus study of Uzundağ et al. (2018) has shown that although the inferential use is more frequent in the input than the reportative use, children do not display any consistent order of acquisition between these two functions, suggesting that input frequency is not the only determining variable. As for cognitive factors, Öztürk and Papafragou (2008) have argued for the complexity of inference over hearsay, defining the former in terms of the ability to make logical deductions from knowledge, which however does not correspond to the less demanding inferences from perceptual evidence that the Turkish evidential *-mIş/-ImIş* encodes (Aksu-Koç 1988).

In the present study, we take a more detailed look at the development of the expression of propositional modality by tracing the emergence and use of both epistemic and evidential modalities in the speech of two children. Our research questions are as follows:
1. When is propositional modality first accessible to children?
   a. What is the order of emergence of epistemic and evidential notions?
   b. How do children express these notions?
2. In what ways may input frequency and cognitive factors affect the acquisition of propositional modality?

4 Method

4.1 Participants

Our data come from two monolingual girls between the ages 1;3–2;0 (Deniz) and 1;6–2;10 (Mine) and their caregivers. The parents of both girls are professionals. The data consist of samples of naturalistic speech audio recorded during playtime at home. The recordings are about 30–40 minutes long each and three to four weeks apart. The number of recordings for Deniz is 21 and for Mine 17.

4.2 Coding and Data

Coding was done in CHAT format and the analyses were performed with the CLAN programs of the CHILDES Project (MacWhinney 2000). All intelligible utterances of child speech and child-directed speech were coded according to their morphological composition and modal function.[10] For morphological composition, the constituents of the utterance were coded for their word class if words, or functions if suffixes. Only utterances with an overt modal form were coded as expressing a modal notion; otherwise, they were deemed non-modal. Modal utterances were coded for their type, namely epistemic, evidential, deontic or dynamic, and specific function (e.g., speculation).

The criteria adopted for the onset of productivity were the use of an inflection in obligatory contexts with at least two different verbs that also occurred either in non-inflected form or with another inflection in the same session.

---

[10] In order to differentiate the epistemic, deontic and dynamic uses of the multifunctional inflections, we coded for deontic and dynamic modality as well.

Children's speech was analyzed in terms of mean length of utterance (MLU in morphemes), syntactic complexity (mean number of verbs per utterance), productivity of verbs (number of verbal lemmas that paradigmatically appear with more than one TAM marker) and productivity of verbal inflections (number of TAM markers that appear with more than one verb). The results of these analyses revealed four developmental phases in the speech of Deniz and Mine. Table 3 presents these phases for the two children.

Table 3: Developmental phases in the speech of Deniz and Mine.

	Age range	MLU	Total number of utterances	Number of verbs per utterance	Productive verbs % (lemmas)
Deniz					
Phase 1	1;3–1;6	< 1.6	372	.105	40 (6)
Phase 2	1;7–1;8	< 3.0	1011	.537	71 (35)
Phase 3	1;9–1;10	< 3.5	1300	.801	61 (51)
Phase 4	1;11–2;0	> 3.5	1056	.698	65 (53)
Mine					
Phase 1	1;6–1;7	< 1.6	77	.325	13 (1)
Phase 2	1;8–1;10	< 2.5	192	.505	27 (8)
Phase 3	1;11–2;4	< 3.0	1022	.503	55 (44)
Phase 4	2;5–2;10	> 3.5	856	.575	53 (54)

In the first phase, children have very few verbs and the majority of them are not used productively. They are either unmarked or occur with the perfective past suffix -DI, indicating a modal vs. non-modal distinction since the bare verb represents the imperative in Turkish. In the second phase, for Deniz both the number and the proportion of verbs used productively increase with the entry of other verbal inflections, namely the optative -A, imperfective -Iyor and future -AcAk. The epistemic aorist -(A/I)r and the evidential -mIş/-ImIş are also observed in Phase 2. In the case of Mine, these developments are observed in Phase 3, where her verbal repertoire becomes more diverse and each verb is used with more than one inflection on the paradigmatic axis. Her first utterances marked by the epistemic aorist -(A/I)r and the evidential -mIş/-ImIş are also observed in Phase 3. In the fourth phase, children become more skilled in combining the clitics with verbal inflections to denote complex meanings regarding tense, aspect and modality. Although Deniz is younger, she is a precocious talker compared to Mine, who exhibits a somewhat slower progress at the beginning of this early period of development.

5 Results

5.1 Overview

The analysis of children's speech into phases allows us to give an overall picture of their linguistic skills during the period under investigation and to capture progress more concisely in what we regard to be a continuous development. Table 4 presents information about the modal utterances in the CS and the CDS of the two children.

Table 4: Modal utterances in CS and CDS.

	Total number of utterances	Modal utterances % (token)	Epistemic utterances % (token)	Evidential utterances % (token)
Deniz CS				
Phase 1	372	3 (13)		
Phase 2	1011	36 (365)	3 (11)	6 (23)
Phase 3	1300	54 (696)	1 (6)	3 (23)
Phase 4	1056	42 (442)	1 (4)	2 (11)
Deniz CDS				
Phase 1	1515	33 (499)	5 (24)	11 (55)
Phase 2	2008	38 (768)	5 (37)	12 (95)
Phase 3	2014	42 (838)	5 (46)	14 (116)
Phase 4	1706	42 (711)	9 (64)	10 (72)
Mine CS				
Phase 1	77	5 (4)		
Phase 2	192	13 (25)		
Phase 3	1022	19 (201)	5 (10)	19 (38)
Phase 4	856	26 (233)	5 (12)	39 (91)
Mine CDS				
Phase 1	333	41 (135)	8 (11)	9 (12)
Phase 2	551	29 (160)	4 (7)	23 (37)
Phase 3	1605	37 (592)	7 (43)	17 (103)
Phase 4	828	36 (295)	10 (30)	19 (56)

In CDS, the proportion of utterances expressing propositional modality is quite low in the period covered by our analysis. Among all modal utterances (agent-oriented and propositional) these comprise only about 18% in Deniz's and 25%

in Mine's CDS and about 5% in Deniz's and 33% in Mine's CS. For each child, the first epistemic and evidential utterances are observed within the same phase of development indicating that the two categories of propositional modality co-emerge, in Phase 2 for Deniz (evidential at 1;7 and epistemic at 1;8) and in Phase 3 for Mine (both at 2;0). However, the children do not produce epistemic and evidential utterances with equal frequency; for both, the number of evidential utterances, particularly in the narrative function, clearly exceeds the number of epistemic utterances. This pattern also holds true for their CDS. Since reading books or telling stories are common activities of playtime during which the recordings were made, the high proportions of evidential modality might be inflated in our data. However, findings of the semi-dense longitudinal study of six children between 8–36 months also indicate that narratives and pretense talk are highly common activities between children and their caregivers early on (Uzundağ et al. 2018).

In the sections that follow we present the results for epistemic and evidential modalities separately. For each modal category, we show the developments in the CS of each child and relate it to her CDS. We first compare the two registers (CS and CDS) in terms of form, then in terms of function (Tables 5 to 18).

5.2 Emergence of epistemic modality: Forms and functions

5.2.1 Deniz's CS and CDS

Deniz uses lexical before inflectional means for the expression of epistemic modality. Her first epistemic utterances are marked by adverbs at 1;8, followed by the aorist V-*(A/I)r* inflection at 1;9 and the V-*Abil*-*(A/I)r* construction at 2;0. Since the suffixes -*(A/I)r* and -*Abil* may also be used non-modally or to express agent-oriented modality, we present their relative ages of emergence in different types of utterances in Table 5. It is observed that the epistemic uses of -*Abil* and -*(A/I)r* emerge slightly later than or at the same time as their use in dynamic and

Table 5: Age of emergence of verb inflections denoting non-modal and modal functions in Deniz's CS.

TAM Marker	Epistemic	Dynamic	Deontic	Non-modal
-*Abil*	2;0	1;10	1;10	
-*(A/I)r*	1;9	1;8	1;9	1;11
-*AcAk*		1;8	2;0	1;9
-*DIr*				1;9

deontic contexts, whereas -*AcAk* and -*DIr* are not used epistemically even though the suffixes themselves have been acquired.

Tables 6 and 7 display the frequency and token percentage of lexical and inflectional means used in Deniz's CS and CDS for denoting the three types of epistemic functions, i.e., speculations about possible states of affairs, assumptions about probable ones and deductions about situations almost certain to occur. Since the meaning of an utterance containing these constructions also depends on the semantics of the main verb, the compositional structure of the verb complex and the discourse context, they may express the different functions interchangeably.

Table 6: Frequency of forms expressing epistemic modality by function and phase in Deniz's CS (% (type/token)).

Phase	Function	Lexical	-Abil	-(A/I)r
2	Speculation	100 (1/8)		
	Assumption			
	Deduction	100 (2/3)		
3	Speculation			
	Assumption			100 (2/6)
	Deduction			
4	Speculation	50 (1/1)	50 (1/1)	
	Assumption			100 (2/2)
	Deduction			

Table 7: Frequency of forms expressing epistemic modality by function and phase in Deniz's CDS (% (type/token)).

Phase	Function	Lexical	-Abil	-(A/I)r	-AcAk	-DIr
1	Speculation	60 (1/3)	20 (1/1)		20 (1/1)	
	Assumption	19 (3/3)	6 (1/1)	56 (5/9)		19 (3/3)
	Deduction		100 (2/3)			
2	Speculation	95 (5/20)				5 (1/1)
	Assumption	25 (2/3)		58 (7/7)	17 (2/2)	
	Deduction	25 (1/1)		75 (3/3)		
3	Speculation	92 (7/11)			8 (1/1)	
	Assumption	29 (3/8)	11 (3/3)	61 (12/17)		
	Deduction	17 (1/1)	17 (1/1)	67 (4/4)		
4	Speculation	75 (11/15)	20 (3/4)			5 (1/1)
	Assumption	29 (9/11)	5 (2/2)	58 (17/22)		8 (3/3)
	Deduction	17 (1/1)	17 (1/1)	17 (1/1)	17 (1/1)	33 (2/2)

Epistemic utterances are quite scarce in Deniz's speech (Table 6). The first examples expressed with the adverbs *acaba* 'I wonder' often used in a game routine with the mother and *gerçekten* 'really' convey, respectively, speculation (example 8) and deduction (example 9), corresponding to uncertainty and certainty, notions at the two extremes of the epistemic scale.

(8) Deniz, 1;8, Phase 2, looks for a book
    CS: *acaba   ner-de* [=*nere-de*]?
        I.wonder   where-LOC
        'I wonder where it is?'

(9) Deniz, 1;8, Phase 2, expresses her surprise when she finds a bird picture in a book contrary to her expectation
    CS: *getteden* [=*gerçekten*] *ba:* [=*var*].
        really   exist
        'There really is (one).'

In Deniz's speech these adverbs only occur in utterances with nominal predicates, whereas in adult speech they may be used in combination with verbal morphology to clarify the meaning of the multifunctional TAM suffixes. In example (10) from Deniz's mother, the presence of the adverb gives a speculative reading to what would otherwise be a non-modal question.

(10) Deniz, 1;9, Phase 3, Deniz's mother prepares milk for her
     CDS: *Deniz iç-ecek   mi acaba?*
          Deniz drink-FUT Q I.wonder
          'I wonder if Deniz will drink (this)?'

Inflectional expression of epistemic modality is observed in Phase 3 of Deniz's development with the aorist -*(A/I)r* used to convey assumptions as in example (11).

(11) Deniz, 1;9, Phase 3, warns her mother not to get her hand stuck in chest of drawers
     CS: *el-in   dıgıd-ıy* [=*sıkış-ır*]   *el-in.*
         hand-POSS.2SG   get.stuck-AOR hand-POSS.2SG
         'Your hand will get stuck, your hand.'

In phase 4, Deniz attempts an utterance with the -*Abil*-*(A/I)r* construction to express possibility but fails to add -*(A/I)r* as the finite TAM marker to complete the speculative meaning (example 12) even though her mother's preceding utterance provides an example.

(12) Deniz, 1;11, Phase 4, tries to put a piece of puzzle in place
    CS: *bu-nun.*
             this-GEN
             'This one's.'
    CDS: *ol-abil-ir.*
             be-PSB-AOR
             'It may be (the case).'
    CS: *bu-nun   ol-abil-*Oir.*
             this-GEN be-PSB-*OAOR
             'It may belong to this.'

Deniz does not produce any inflectional combinations to affect compositional epistemic meanings although her CDS displays examples as in (13), where *-Abil -(A/I)r* together denote possibility while the clitic *-IDI* defines the temporality of the utterance as past.

(13) Deniz, 1;3, Phase 4, Her mother explains the possible consequence of Deniz's actions to her
    CDS: *ama kır-ıl-abil-ir-di.*
             but   break-PASS-PSB-AOR-PST.CL
             'But (it) could have been broken.'

An inspection of Table 7 for the forms used in CDS across the four phases shows that adverbs have the highest frequency for speculations while the aorist *-(A/I)r*, followed by adverbs, has the highest frequency for assumptions. Forms denoting deductions become more diverse across the stages with *-(A/I)r* being the most frequent overall. The *-Abil-(A/I)r* construction, the future *-AcAk* and the generalizing clitic *-DIr*, which occur with relatively low frequency, are observed for all three functions.

There is a close correspondence between CS and CDS in terms of the forms used for particular functions although CS displays a restricted range of forms despite the variability in CDS. Both the child and the mother rely on the use of adverbs as much as inflectional marking. The most frequent form–function combinations observed in both registers are adverbs for speculations and the aorist *-(A/I)r* for assumptions.

Table 8 displays the frequency of epistemically modalized utterances by function per phase in Deniz's CS and CDS.

Table 8: Frequency of epistemic functions in Deniz's CS and CDS by phase (% (tokens)).

		Phase 1 1;3–1;6	Phase 2 1;7–1;8	Phase 3 1;9–1;10	Phase 4 1;11–2;0
Deniz CS	Speculation		73 (8)		50 (2)
	Assumption			100 (6)	50 (2)
	Deduction		27 (3)		
Deniz CDS	Speculation	21 (5)	57 (21)	26 (12)	31 (20)
	Assumption	67 (16)	32 (12)	61 (28)	59 (38)
	Deduction	13 (3)	11 (4)	13 (6)	9 (6)

The overall distribution of epistemic utterances differs between CDS and CS in terms of function. In CDS, assumptions are the most frequent category, deductions the least frequent and speculations are in between. In CS, however, speculations occur with the highest frequency followed by deductions. Speculations express the child's wonderings about the location of objects and people and deductive utterances affirm their existence or location. Their contrast in terms of modal strength may ease children's acquisition. On the other hand, the few assumptions observed in the children's speech are repetitions of what they have heard from adults, something that is not surprising in view of their limited experience concerning the likelihood of events. In short, the child's epistemic evaluations during this early period convey her subjective orientation to her environment with an inquisitive attitude revealing curiosity and a desire to learn. For example, her use of the adverb *acaba* 'I wonder' expresses "a sub-type of uncertainty" regarding knowledge about the world similar to the early uses of the "negative of the verb *savoir*" by French children (Hickmann and Bassano 2016: 434).

5.2.2 Mine's CS and CDS

In Mine's speech, inflectional expressions of epistemic modality precede lexical ones. Utterances using the aorist -(A/I)r are observed at 2;0 and expressions with adverbs at 2;1, both at the beginning of Phase 3. Table 9 shows that both the aorist -(A/I)r and the generalizing clitic -DIr are used non-modally at the same age as they are used for epistemic modality while -(A/I)r is used for dynamic ability about two months later. Epistemic uses of -Abil and -AcAk are not observed during the period of sampling.

Table 9: Age of emergence of verb inflections denoting modal and non-modal functions in Mine's CS.

TAM Marker	Epistemic	Dynamic	Deontic	Non-modal
-Abil		2;1	2;0	
-(A/I)r	2;0	2;2		2;0
-AcAk		1;7		1;8
-DIr	2;1			2;1

Tables 10 and 11 present the means of expression Mine and her caregiver use to express epistemic modality.

Table 10: Frequency of forms expressing epistemic modality by function and phase in Mine's CS (% (type/token)).

Phase	Function	Lexical	-(A/I)r	-DIr
3	Speculation	100 (3/4)		
	Assumption		33 (1/1)	67 (2/2)
	Deduction		67 (2/2)	33 (1/1)
4	Speculation	100 (3/8)		
	Assumption		100 (1/1)	
	Deduction		100 (2/3)	

Table 11: Frequency of forms expressing epistemic modality by function and phase in Mine's CDS (% (type/token)).

Phase	Function	Lexical	-Abil	-(A/I)r	-AcAk	-DIr
1	Speculation			67 (2/2)	33 (1/1)	
	Assumption			50 (3/3)	50 (2/3)	
	Deduction		100 (2/2)			
2	Speculation	100 (1/1)				
	Assumption	50 (1/2)		25 (1/1)	25 (1/1)	
	Deduction	50 (1/1)			50 (1/1)	
3	Speculation	42 (3/5)	33 (1/4)	8 (1/1)		17 (2/2)
	Assumption	35 (4/6)		53 (8/9)	6 (1/1)	6 (1/1)
	Deduction	8 (1/1)	17 (2/2)	75 (6/9)		
4	Speculation	46 (3/6)		54 (5/7)		
	Assumption	22 (1/2)		56 (5/5)	11 (1/1)	11 (1/1)
	Deduction	13 (1/1)		88 (6/7)		

Mine uses the aorist -(A/I)r (example 14) and the generalizing clitic -DIr to convey her assumptions about probable states of affairs and deductions made with near certainty, reserving adverbs for speculation about possibilities (Table 10).

(14) Mine, 2;0, Phase 3, tries to grab her lamp but her mother asks her not to touch it and Mine responds by saying it would break
 CS: *kıl-ıl-ıl* [=*kır-ıl-ır*].
   break-PASS-AOR
   '(It) would break.'

The child uses adverbs to modalize utterances comprising modally neutral verbal inflections (example 15) or to fine-tune the modal strength of an utterance expressed with a modal inflection. In example (16) the adverb *mesela* 'for instance' weakens the assumptive meaning conveyed by the clitic -DIr to a speculation.

(15) Mine, 2;1, Phase 3, looking at a picture taken at the sea resort that she had been to with her mother
 CS: *belki   de   ben   o   kaya-lar-ı*
   perhaps   too   I   that   rock-PL-ACC
   sev-me-di-m.
   like-NEG-PST-1SG
   'Maybe, I did not like those rocks.'

(16) Mine, 2;5, Phase 3, mother and child are playing and pretending there are other children with them
 CS: *şuya-ya* [=*şura-ya*] *gel-miş-ler-dir   mesela.*
   there-DAT   come-PFV-3PL-GM   for.instance
   '(They) might have come there, for instance.'

Such use of adverbs for sentential modification differs in linguistic complexity from the first uses of adverbs by Deniz that occur in utterances with nominal predicates (see examples 8 and 9), which is not surprising since her examples come from a younger age (2;0) than do Mine's (2;5).

Mine's adverbs are also semantically more sophisticated. Examples observed in Phase 4 (*yoksa* 'or/if not' and *sence* 'in your opinion') contrast with those in Phase 3 (*acaba* 'I wonder' and *belki* 'maybe/perhaps') indicating that she can now consider the other's point of view (*sence* 'in your opinion') and entertain different possibilities (*yoksa* 'if not') in her evaluation of experience (example 17).

(17) Mine, 2;10, Phase 4, Mine and her mother are trying to stick a book spine together but have trouble finding out which scrap of paper belongs where
CS: *adaba* [=*acaba*] *bu   mu?*
    I.wonder this Q
    ba:mı [=*var mı*] *sen-ce   bu?*
    exist Q   you-ADVR this
    'I wonder if this is it? Do you think there is one (a match)?'

A comparison of Tables 10 and 11 for form–function mappings shows a close match between Mine's CS and CDS. In CDS, speculations are expressed with adverbs or -*(A/I)r*, assumptions with -*(A/I)r* and also with adverbs, and deductions primarily with -*(A/I)r*. This distribution of forms per function is observed in CS as well. Moreover, -*Abil* and the future -*AcAk*, which occur with low frequency in CDS, are not observed in CS.

Table 12 presents the frequency of the functions of the epistemically modalized utterances in Mine's CS and CDS.

Table 12: Frequency of epistemic functions in Mine's CS and CDS by phase (% (token)).

		Phase 1 1;6–1;7	Phase 2 1;8–1;10	Phase 3 1;11–2;4	Phase 4 2;5–2;10
Mine CS	Speculation			40 (4)	67 (8)
	Assumption			30 (3)	8 (1)
	Deduction			30 (3)	25 (3)
Mine CDS	Speculation	27 (3)	14 (1)	29 (12)	43 (13)
	Assumption	55 (6)	57 (4)	42 (17)	30 (9)
	Deduction	18 (2)	29 (2)	29 (12)	27 (8)

The most frequent function in Mine's CS is speculation, where she offers possible explanations for past events, asks who carried out an action and where an object is located. Assumptions are the least frequent and express hypotheses about the most probable location of an object or a person and the consequence of an action. The few deductions concerning similar topics fall between speculations and assumptions in frequency. The overall distribution of epistemic functions in Mine's CDS differs from that in CS. Assumptions have the highest frequency, speculations the next and deductions are the least frequent.

In summary, the children's speech mirrors child-directed speech in terms of frequency of formal means of expression used per type of epistemic function but not in terms of the frequency of type of function expressed. Both children's data show that they produce speculations and deductions that express low and high degrees of certainty, respectively, rather than assumptions that qualify assertions in terms of probability, which their caregivers seem to prefer. This might be a function of children's limited life experience, hence their restricted knowledge repertoire to base their predictions and assumptions on, contrary to that of adults.

5.3 Emergence of evidential modality: Forms and functions

5.3.1 Deniz's CS and CDS

The type/token frequency and token percentage of the inflectional constructions used to denote the different evidential functions in Deniz's CS are presented in Table 13. As explained in section 3.2, the type of construction used depends on the aspectual or temporal perspective the event is presented from, the verb type and the discourse context rather than the specific function expressed.

Table 13: Frequency of evidential constructions by function and phase in Deniz's CS (% token (type/token)).

Phase	Function	V-mİş	NML-İmİş	V-TAM-İmİş
2	New Info		100 (2/5)	
	Inference			
	Report			
	Narrative	55 (4/10)	28 (1/5)	17 (2/3)
3	New Info		100 (2/3)	
	Inference	100 (3/3)		
	Report			
	Narrative	75 (10/12)		25 (4/4)
4	New Info			
	Inference	100 (2/5)		
	Report			100 (1/1)
	Narrative	100 (3/4)		

All three types of constructions (V-mİş, NML-İmİş and V-TAM-İmİş) are observed in Deniz's CS starting from Phase 2, when evidential modality emerges in her speech. What develops through phases is the appearance of new functions denoted by the different constructions in line with the principle that old forms come to express new functions (Slobin 1973: 184). In Phase 2, Deniz uses NML-İmİş to mark new information or surprise, typically in stative contexts directly accessible to perception (example 18).[11] She also uses all three constructions to denote the narrative function: NML-*ImIş* often describes states, V-*mIş* completed events and V-TAM-*ImIş* ongoing activities. Example (19) illustrates the use of V-*mIş* with a change-of-state verb to denote a completed event represented in her story book.

(18) Deniz, 1;7, Phase 2, is looking for a scarf and finds it under the carpet
    CDS: *nere-de-ymiş?*
           where-LOC-EVID.CL
           'Where was (it)?'
    CS: *buy-da:-mış* [=*bura-da-ymış*].
           here-LOC-EVID.CL
           '(It is/was) here.'

(19) Deniz, 1;8, Phase 2, looking at a picture book with mother and describing the picture in narrative genre
    CDS: *bur-da   na:pmış* [=*ne yap-mış*] *ayı-sı-nı?*
           this-LOC   what do-EVID   bear-POSS.3SG-ACC
           'Here, what did s/he do to his/her teddy?'
    CS: *kuda-a-na* [=*kuca-ğı-na*] *a:-mış* [=*al-mış*].
           lap-POSS.3SG-DAT   take-EVID
           '(S/he) took it on his/her lap.'

In Phase 3, the new function observed is inference, which is expressed by V-*mIş*. In example (20) the presence of an agent plus the use of the causative affix on a change-of-state-verb provides evidence for the inferential interpretation.

(20) Deniz, 1;10, Phase 3, observes that her book has been mended
    CS: *abla   buya-yı* [=*bura-yı*]
           sister   here-ACC
    yapıt-tıy-mıt [=*yapış-tır-mış*].
           stick-CAUS-EVID
           'Sister has glued it together, evidently.'

The last function to develop is the reportative in Phase 4. In example (21), the construction V-TAM-*ImIş*, where the clitic is attached to a stative verb marked

---

[11] In her sample at age 1;8 Deniz produces 7 repetitions of *Ebru getir-miş* (Ebru bring-EVID) 'Ebru brought it' for which the context does not provide enough evidence for interpretation, either as new information or report. It was therefore not included in the counts.

for imperfective aspect, conveys information heard from someone else in the context of pretense play.

(21) Deniz, 1;11, Phase 4, tells her mother what her teddy bear just told her
 CS: kazak   itti-yo-muş [=isti-yor-muş].
      sweater   want-IPFV-EVID.CL
      '(S/he) wants a sweater (s/he said).'

The fact that Deniz can use all three types of construction from Phase 2 onwards indicates that the compositional use of TAM suffixes and clitics does not pose a problem with the expression of evidential functions in contrast to her failed attempt to attach the aorist -(A/I)r to -Abil observed in the case of her expressions of epistemic modality. This discrepancy between her linguistic skills in the two modal domains might be related to the fact that the homophonous -mIş/-ImIş inflections exclusively denote evidential modality and are the only forms that do so. They are, therefore, more frequent and prominent in the input in contrast to several multifunctional inflections that may express non-modal and agent-oriented modal notions in addition to epistemic modality. Furthermore, epistemic adverbs have a high frequency in the input (28% of all the epistemic utterances in Deniz's CDS) and provide an alternative means of expression for epistemic meanings early on. In contrast, evidential adverbs are extremely scarce in the input possibly because inflectional marking of evidentiality does not necessitate further specification of meaning.

The frequency of evidential constructions by function in Deniz's CS and CDS is presented in Table 14.

As can be observed, the form–function relations in CDS are more flexible than in CS. New information is expressed using both NML-*ImIş* and V-*mIş*

Table 14: Frequency of evidential constructions by function in Deniz's CS and CDS (% (token)).

	Function	V-*mIş*	NML-*ImIş*	V-TAM-*ImIş*
CS	New Info		100 (8)	
	Inference	100 (8)		
	Report			100 (1)
	Narrative	68 (26)	13 (5)	18 (7)
CDS	New Info	40 (41)	57 (59)	3 (3)
	Inference	96 (72)	3 (2)	1 (1)
	Report	47 (8)	12 (2)	41 (7)
	Narrative	67 (95)	15 (21)	18 (26)

constructions, inferences are almost exclusively conveyed by V-*mIş* and reports by V-*mIş* or V-TAM-*ImIş*. The frequency of the evidential constructions used per function in CS reflects almost directly those form–function associations that occur with the highest frequency in CDS. The narrative function, where the correspondence is striking, provides even clearer evidence of how the frequency patterns in CS reflect those in CDS.

Table 15 displays the frequency of the four evidential functions in Deniz's CS and CDS.

Table 15: Frequency of evidential functions in Deniz's CS and CDS by phase (% (token)).

		Phase 1 1;3–1;6	Phase 2 1;7–1;8	Phase 3 1;9–1;10	Phase 4 1;11–2;0
Deniz CS	New Info		22 (5)	14 (3)	
	Inference			14 (3)	50 (5)
	Report				10 (1)
	Narrative		78 (18)	72 (16)	40 (4)
Deniz CDS	New Info	30 (16)	29 (28)	21 (25)	47 (34)
	Inference	42 (23)	20 (19)	11 (13)	28 (20)
	Report	2 (1)	3 (3)	3 (3)	14 (10)
	Narrative	26 (14)	48 (45)	65 (75)	11 (8)

The overall distribution of the evidential functions in CDS is closely matched by that in CS in terms of relative frequency. Narrative utterances occur with the highest frequency in both registers except for Phase 4. The function with the next highest frequency in CDS is new information and then inference, whereas the total number of times these functions occur in the child's speech is equal, new information being observed in Phase 2 and Phase 3, and inference in Phase 3 and Phase 4. The frequency of reports is quite low in CDS and only one instance is found in CS.

5.3.2 Mine's CS and CDS

Expressions of evidential modality are first noted in Mine's Phase 3, where she displays examples of narrative, new information and inferential utterances.[12]

---

[12] A single utterance expressing new information is observed at 1;8 in Mine's Phase 2, where she responds to the routinized question of *kim gel-miş?* (who come-EVID) 'who is it that came?' when the doorbell rings with a contextually inappropriate *anne gel-miş* (mother come-EVID) 'mother has arrived', although her mother is sitting next to her and asking the question. Since

The reportative function is observed in Phase 4. Table 16 presents the construction types used for the different evidential functions in Mine's CS.

Table 16: Frequency of evidential constructions by function and phase in Mine's CS (% token (type/token)).

Phase	Function	Lexical	V-*mIş*	NML-*ImIş*	V-TAM-*ImIş*
3	New Info		50 (1/1)	50 (1/1)	
	Inference		100 (3/4)		
	Report				
	Narrative		100 (20/32)		
4	New Info			100 (2/2)	
	Inference	10 (1/1)	90 (7/9)		
	Report		70 (6/7)	30 (2/3)	
	Narrative		99 (40/68)		1 (1/1)

In the course of the observation period, Mine utilizes all construction types as well as lexical means to denote evidential modality. In Phase 3, she uses V-*mIş* and NML-*ImIş* to denote new information, V-*mIş* to express inference and also to tell narratives. Example (22) illustrates the use of V-*mIş* in an utterance expressing new information with the verb *ol* 'be' and example (23) an inference with the change-of-state verb *gir* 'go in'.

(22) Mine 2;0, Phase 3, showing mother her toy with a broken foot
 CS: bu yol:-muş [=ne ol-muş] anne bak ayağ-a:
  this what be-EVID mother look foot-DAT
  no:l-muş [=ne ol-muş] anne?
   what be-EVID mother
  'What (seems to have) happened to this? Mother look! What (seems to have) happened to its foot, mother?'

(23) Mine, 2;1, Phase 3, looking at pictures from the summer, she infers that her brother did not go into the swimming pool because she alone appears in the picture
 CS: Ali ciy-me-miş [=gir-me-miş] buya-ya [=bura-ya].
  Ali go.in-NEG-EVID here-DAT
  'Ali did not go in here, evidently.'

---

the next observation of an evidential utterance is made four months later, this singular instance was considered as unproductive and the beginning of the expression of evidentiality was dated as Phase 3 with the first example at 2;0.

Phase 4 demonstrates the emergence of a new evidential function, namely the reportative, with the use of NML-*ImIş* as in example (24).

(24) Mine, 2;8, Phase 4, refers to the big serving of food at the restaurant, which she was told was for grown-ups
 CS: *büyük-ler için-miş   o-nun*
  big-PL for-EVID.CL that-GEN
  için çok doy-du-k.
  for much full-PST-1PL
  '(It) is/was for grown-ups, (they said); therefore, we were very full.'

Moreover, two new forms of evidential modality are observed in Phase 4: an adverb and V-TAM-*ImIş*. Mine uses the evidential adverb *demek* 'it seems/evidently' for expressing inference (example 25). Her CDS presents two instances of the same adverb plus two others that render the meaning of an utterance evidential. On the other hand, V-TAM-*ImIş* is used in a narrative utterance.

(25) Mine, 2;7, Phase 4, after having announced twice that she is thirsty, she uses an inferential adverb with the same verb form (-*DI* past for direct experience)
 CS: *demek   susa-dı-m.*
  evidently thirsty-PST-1SG
  'It seems/evidently I am thirsty.'

The distribution of the evidential constructions by function in CS and CDS is presented in Table 17.

Table 17: Frequency of evidential constructions by function in Mine's CS and CDS (% (token)).

	Function	Lexical	V-*mIş*	NML-*ImIş*	V-TAM-*ImIş*
CS	New Info		25 (1)	75 (3)	
	Inference	7 (1)	93 (13)		
	Report		70 (7)	30 (3)	
	Narrative		99 (100)		1 (1)
CDS	New Info		42 (8)	58 (11)	
	Inference	5 (3)	91 (60)	2 (1)	3 (2)
	Report		60 (18)	23 (7)	17 (5)
	Narrative	1 (1)	88 (80)	4 (4)	7 (6)

The frequency of evidential constructions per function in Mine's CDS shows that new information is marked by NML-*ImIş* and V-*mIş*, inference predominantly by V-*mIş* and much less frequently by NML-*ImIş* and V-TAM-*ImIş*. Reported speech and narrative utterances are conveyed by all three types of constructions but the latter predominantly by V-*mIş*. A comparison of the two registers indicates that CS displays the same relative ranking of V-*mIş* and NML-*ImIş* in terms of frequency as CDS, but comprises only one instance of V-TAM-*ImIş* used in the narrative genre.

Table 18 presents the distribution of evidential functions in Mine's CS and CDS by phase.

Table 18: Frequency of evidential functions in Mine's CS and CDS by phase (% (token)).

		Phase 1 1;6–1;7	Phase 2 1;8–1;10	Phase 3 1;11–2;4	Phase 4 2;5–2;10
Mine CS	New Info			5 (2)	2 (2)
	Inference			11 (4)	10 (9)
	Report				11 (10)
	Narrative			84 (32)	77 (69)
Mine CDS	New Info	17 (2)	20 (7)	9 (9)	2 (1)
	Inference	66 (8)	43 (15)	30 (30)	19 (10)
	Report	17 (2)	9 (3)	8 (8)	31 (17)
	Narrative		28 (10)	53 (54)	48 (26)

It is observed that the overall frequency ranking of evidential functions in Mine's CS reflects that in her CDS: Narrative utterances occur with the highest frequency, followed by inferential and then reportative utterances, with new information being the least frequent.

This close match between CS and CDS observed in both children's speech is possibly due to the fact that the contexts that promote evidential talk in early mother–child interaction are more subject to activities in the here-and-now, such as novel objects or states of shared attention, pretend play, book reading and story-telling, than to contexts of epistemic judgments.

To sum up, Deniz's and Mine's speech are characterized by three features concerning the acquisition of evidentiality. First, the earliest functions observed in both children's speech are new information and narrative, neither of which are typically evidential since they do not indicate 'information source'. Second, highly frequent forms and functions in CDS are also frequent in CS. Third, narrative productions usually outnumber other evidential functions due to the types of activity prevailing in mother–child play contexts.

5.4 Relations between CS and CDS

In a previous study, we demonstrated a robust relationship between frequency of TAM inflections expressing non-modal as well as modal meanings in CDS and their order of emergence in CS of the same children as the ones in the present study (Aksu-Koç, Terziyan, and Taylan 2014). The forms most frequently occurring in the input were found to be the first to emerge in the children's speech and those occurring least frequently in CDS were the last forms to appear in CS. In order to investigate whether a similar relationship holds when particular modal categories are considered, the figures below were constructed. They show the relationship between age of emergence of a specific form for a specific modal category in CS and frequency of occurrence of that form for that category in CDS, for each child.

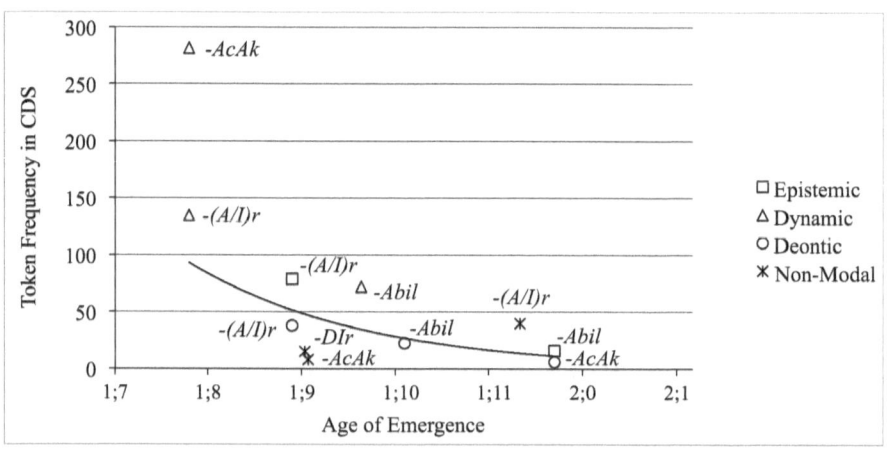

Figure 1: Distribution of -(A/I)r, -Abil, -AcAk and -DIr by frequency and function in CDS and by age of emergence in CS for Deniz.

As can be observed in Figure 1,[13] the age the children start using a multifunctional inflection for a specific function (non-modal or modal) corresponds to the frequency of use of that inflection for that function in CDS. For example, in Deniz's

---

[13] The frequencies were calculated over the total number of modal utterances observed in CDS during the period of observation since their relative frequency is found to be stable over time, particularly across phases 2–4 (see Table 4). It has also been demonstrated in Terziyan (2013) that the relative frequencies of the suffixes in CDS are stable over the period of observation.

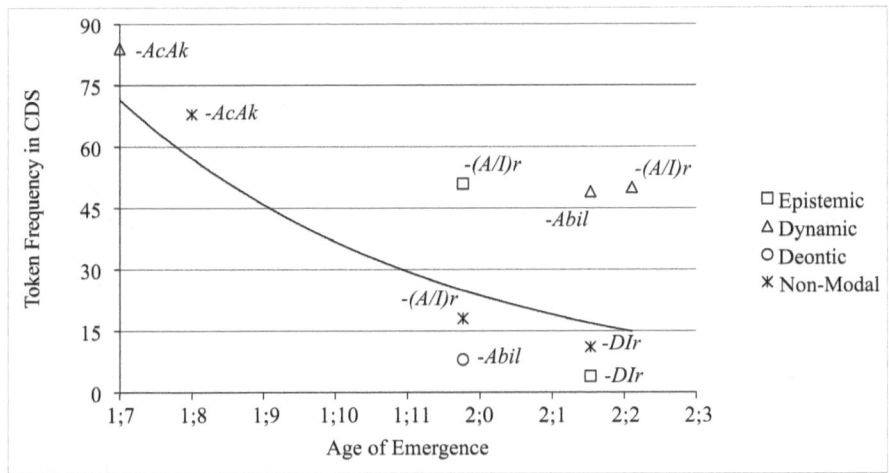

Figure 2: Distribution of -(A/I)r, -Abil, -AcAk and -DIr by frequency and function in CDS and by age of emergence in CS for Mine.

CDS, the aorist -(A/I)r is used with highest frequency to denote dynamic, then epistemic meanings and with lowest frequency for deontic and non-modal meanings, and this order shows quite a close match to the order of emergence of -(A/I)r for dynamic and epistemic functions in her CS. The relationship between Mine's CS and CDS shown in Figure 2 holds directly for the future -AcAk and the generalizing clitic -DIr. -AcAk occurs with the highest frequency in CDS expressing dynamic modality and is used earliest for this function in CS, whereas -DIr has very low frequency in CDS for both epistemic and non-modal functions and appears late in CS for both of these functions. For -(A/I)r, which is used with highest frequency to convey epistemic modality in CDS, the relationship is less tight as it emerges for epistemic and non-modal functions at the same age in CS.

The effect of frequency of formal means in CDS on CS is also quite directly observed in the first expressive means of epistemic modality the two children adopt, which are adverbs for Deniz and inflections for Mine. The frequency of adverbs is almost three times as high in Deniz's CDS (77 tokens) as compared to their frequency in Mine's (25 tokens).

6 Discussion and conclusions

The present study is the first to investigate the emergence of both epistemic and evidential modality morphologically and lexically in the spontaneous speech of children acquiring Turkish in relation to the input they receive. Our findings reveal that children express epistemic and evidential modalities first around age 1;8–2;0 and that the two categories of propositional modality co-emerge within a time span of about one month.

In case of epistemic modality, inflectional expressions emerge earlier than adverbial ones in the speech of one child, whereas the order is reversed for the other. This difference between the two children can be explained by their input since the CDS of the child who initially favors adverbs displays them three times more often than the CDS of the child who starts off inflectionally. Speculations and deductions conveying, respectively, the polar notions of uncertainty and near certainty are expressed with higher frequency than assumptions, which are statements of intermediate degrees of modal strength. While speculations and deductions are preferentially expressed lexically with adverbs, assumptions are marked mainly inflectionally. Findings indicating that children first differentiate contrastive notions on the epistemic scale have also been reported for languages which employ modal verbs for epistemic meanings (Hickmann and Bassano 2016; see also Avram and Gaidargi, this volume, for Romanian).

In case of evidential modality, all expressions are almost exclusively conveyed inflectionally by both of our subjects. New information and narrative functions are the ones to be observed first. New information utterances indicate surprise or rather the cognitive realization of a perceptually available state and reflect the child's perspective on events. They are therefore more attitudinal or 'stance marking' than evidential. Narrative utterances, on the other hand, express a specific 'discourse genre' the scope of which includes the realm of the nonfactual, including pretense play. In neither of these functions does evidential morphology directly encode source of information. Inferential utterances that refer to a past process on the basis of a present resultant state and reportative utterances that convey information obtained from someone else's report, on the other hand, do indicate 'source of information', namely, that the speaker's mode of knowledge acquisition is indirect (Aksu-Koç 1988).

Considered within the broader domain of propositional modality, the functions that are acquired late by both children are epistemic assumption, evidential inference and the reportative. Both assumptions and inferences require children to draw conclusions from past experiences, whether based on their knowledge repertoire or on observed evidence. Reportative utterances are late both because they rely on memory representations of linguistic messages and because they introduce the perspective of another person into the discourse. Finally, both the inferential and the reportative uses as markers of indirectly acquired information involve a choice between the evidential vs. the neutral/direct forms. In short, the cognitive load of these functions may be the reason for their somewhat later acquisition.

When considered together, the developmental sequences of the expression of epistemic and evidential modalities show that children first differentiate between new and old knowledge, subsequently between certain and uncertain knowledge and eventually between direct and indirect sources of knowledge, a pattern also observed in Korean (Choi, this volume). This intertwined development of the expression of epistemic and evidential notions supports our view that the way Turkish carves the epistemic and evidential domains is most congruent with Palmer's (2001) framework, which subsumes the two categories under propositional modality.

It has been noted in the literature that in languages where epistemic notions are expressed inflectionally, children produce them at an earlier age as compared to children acquiring languages where they are expressed lexically by multifunctional modal verbs (e.g., Bulgarian, Korean, Turkish vs. Greek, Romanian, see the Introduction and the Conclusions, this volume; see also Choi 2006; Hickmann and Bassano 2016). While the present study supports this view by providing evidence for the primacy of inflection and an early age of emergence, it also demonstrates that even in these languages, children use lexical means, namely adverbs, to express epistemic notions if the inflectional means are multifunctional as they are in Turkish. In the present study, adverbs were observed to be used early and most frequently to convey epistemic meanings of certainty and uncertainty by both children, whereas they were not found in the evidential domain where the inflectional means of expression are specific to evidential modality. Avram and Gaidargi (this volume), who observe that Romanian children use adverbs before modal verbs to convey epistemic meanings, argue that adverbs emerge early because they have a single inherent modal meaning as opposed to multifunctional modal verbs that may be interpreted dynamically and deontically as well as epistemically. The same explanation applies in the case of Turkish, where the multifunctional TAM inflections, each with a range of meanings, are not dedicated to specific modal notions whereas the unifunctional adverbs are semantically transparent. Considering that unifunctional forms that map onto one meaning are easier to learn than those that are multifunctional (Dressler et al. 2007; Slobin 1985, 2001), it is not surprising that adverbs appear earlier than or along with multifunctional suffixes in the speech of young children.

Concerning the role of input, the present study has shown that epistemic and evidential forms that occur with highest frequency in CDS emerge earliest and have the highest frequency in CS. The grammaticized nature and thus obligatory use of inflectional means of expression can be taken to be the most important factor contributing to the frequency in input. However, functions with high frequency in CDS do not always emerge early or occur with high frequency in CS, suggesting that cognitive and pragmatic factors modulate what children pick up from the input. Lack of a direct relationship between frequency of a function in CDS and the relative timing of its emergence in CS has also been reported for other languages (see the chapters in this volume; Uzundağ et al. 2018).

In addition to presenting a relatively simplified inventory of formal means with frequent repetitions, input also displays the diversity and complexity of the structure of the language being acquired (Aksu-Koç, Terziyan, and Taylan 2014; Küntay and Slobin 1996; Stephany 1985; Xanthos et al. 2011). The frequency relations between CDS and CS reflect the processes in adult–child discourse where caregiver utterances support the discovery of form–function relations by introducing specific forms in appropriate contexts on the one hand and help to entrench these form–function associations by repeating the child's utterance fully or partially on the other hand, thereby increasing the frequency of their occurrence (Choi, this volume; Dąbrowska and Szczerbiński 2006; Dressler 1997; MacWhinney, Bates, and Kliegl 1984; Slobin 1985; Tomasello 2003 among others).

To conclude, the emergence of propositional modality is highly influenced by the frequency of forms in CDS, but the developmental trajectory of the notions expressed is governed by the children's cognitive capacities, their communicative needs and, above all, the structure of the language being acquired, most significantly, by whether the means of expression of a category are grammaticized and thus obligatory or optional.

Acknowledgements: The data analyzed in this study are part of a larger project "A longitudinal study of the acquisition of Turkish" (Project no: 96S0017) supported by a grant from the Boğaziçi University Research Fund to Ayhan Aksu-Koç. We thank Deniz and Mine and their caregivers, who did a lot of talking and made it possible for us to use it as data. We also thank Ursula Stephany for her valuable comments on the paper; errors that remain are ours.

References

Aikhenvald, Alexandra. Y. 2004. *Evidentiality*. Oxford: Oxford University Press.
Aksu-Koç, Ayhan. 1988. *The acquisition of aspect and modality: The case of past reference in Turkish*. Cambridge: Cambridge University Press.

Aksu-Koç, Ayhan. 1995. Some connections between aspect and modality in Turkish. In Pier Marco Bertinetto, Valentina Bianchi, Östen Dahl & Mario Squartini (eds.), *Temporal reference, aspect and actionality*, vol. 2: *Typological perspectives*, 271–287. Torino: Rosenberg & Sellier.

Aksu-Koç, Ayhan. 1998. The role of input vs. universal predispositions in the emergence of tense–aspect morphology: Evidence from Turkish. *First Language* 18(54). 255–280.

Aksu-Koç, Ayhan. 2016. The interface of evidentials and epistemics in Turkish: Perspectives from acquisition. In Mine Güven, Didar Akar, Balkız Öztürk & Meltem Kelepir (eds.), *Exploring the Turkish linguistic landscape: Essays in honor of Eser Erguvanlı-Taylan* (Studies in Language Companion Series 175), 143–156. Amsterdam & Philadelphia: John Benjamins.

Aksu-Koç, Ayhan & Didem Mersin Alıcı. 2000. Understanding sources of beliefs and marking of uncertainty: The child's theory of evidentiality. In Eve V. Clark (ed.), *Proceedings of the 30th annual child language research forum*, 123–130. Stanford: CSLI Publications.

Aksu-Koç, Ayhan & F. Nihan Ketrez. 2003. Early verbal morphology in Turkish: Emergence of inflections. In Wolfgang U. Dressler, Dagmar Bittner & Marianne Kilani-Schoch (eds.), *Development of verb inflection in first language acquisition: A cross-linguistic perspective* (Studies on Language Acquisition 21), 27–52. Berlin: Mouton de Gruyter.

Aksu-Koç, Ayhan, Hale Ögel-Balaban & Ercan İ. Alp. 2009. Evidentials and source knowledge in Turkish. In Stanka A. Fitneva & Tomoko Matsui (eds.), *Evidentiality: A window into language and cognitive development* (New Directions for Child and Adolescent Development 125), 13–28. San Francisco: Jossey Bass.

Aksu-Koç, Ayhan & Dan I. Slobin. 1985. The acquisition of Turkish. In Dan I. Slobin (ed.), *The crosslinguistic study of language acquisition*, vol. 1: *The data*, 845–878. Hillsdale, NJ: Lawrence Erlbaum Associates.

Aksu-Koç, Ayhan, Treysi Terziyan & Eser Erguvanlı Taylan. 2014. Input offers and child uptakes: Acquiring mood and modal morphology in Turkish. *Language, Interaction and Acquisition* 5(1). 62–81.

Ataman, Merve. 2018. *The effect of language on generic knowledge understanding and source reliability: A developmental study*. Istanbul: Boğaziçi University MA thesis.

Behrens, Heike. 2006. The input–output relationship in first language acquisition. *Language and Cognitive Processes* 21(1–3). 2–24.

Boye, Kasper. 2016. The expression of epistemic modality. In Jan Nuyts & Johan van der Auwera (eds.), *The Oxford handbook of modality and mood*, 117–140. Oxford: Oxford University Press.

Bybee, Joan. 2010. *Language, usage and cognition*. Cambridge: Cambridge University Press.

Bybee, Joan L., Revere Dale Perkins & William Pagliuca. 1994. *The evolution of grammar: Tense, aspect, and modality in the languages of the world*. Chicago: University of Chicago Press.

Chafe, Wallace & Johanna Nichols (eds.). 1986. *Evidentiality: The linguistic coding of epistemology*. Norwood, NJ: Ablex.

Choi, Soonja. 2006. Acquisition of modality. In William Frawley (ed.), *The expression of modality*, 141–171. Berlin: Mouton de Gruyter.

Clark, Eve V. & Josie Bernicot. 2008. Repetition as ratification: How parents and children place information in common ground. *Journal of Child Language* 35(2). 349–371.

Dąbrowska, Ewa & Marcin Szczerbiński. 2006. Polish children's productivity with case marking: The role of regularity, type frequency, and phonological coherence. *Journal of Child Language* 33. 559–597.

De Haan, Ferdinand. 1999. Evidentiality and epistemic modality: Setting boundaries. *Southwest Journal of Linguistics* 18(1). 83–101.

De Haan, Ferdinand. 2006. Typological approaches to modality. In William Frawley (ed.), *The expression of modality*, 27–69. Berlin: Mouton de Gruyter.

Dendale, Patrick & Liliane Tasmowski. 2001. Introduction: Evidentiality and related notions. *Journal of Pragmatics* 33(3). 339–348. Doi: 10.1016/S0378-2166(00)00005-9.

Dressler, Wolfgang U. (ed.). 1997. *Studies in pre- and protomorphology*. Wien: Verlag der Österreichischen Akademie der Wissenschaften.

Dressler, Wolfgang U., Ursula Stephany, Ayhan Aksu-Koç & Steven Gillis. 2007. Discussion and conclusion. In Sabine Laaha & Steven Gillis (eds.), *Typological perspectives on the acquisition of noun and verb morphology* (Antwerp Papers in Linguistics 112), 67–72. Antwerp: Universiteit Antwerpen.

Du Bois, John W. 2014. Towards a dialogic syntax. *Cognitive Linguistics* 25(3). 359–410.

Ekmekçi, F. Özden. 1982. Acquisition of verbal inflections in Turkish. *METU Journal of Human Sciences* 1(2). 227–241.

Faller, Martina. 2002. *Semantics and pragmatics of evidentials in Cuzco Quechua*. Stanford: Stanford University dissertation.

Göksel, Aslı & Celia Kerslake. 2005. *Turkish: A comprehensive grammar*. London: Routledge.

Hickmann, Maya & Dominique Bassano. 2016. Modality and mood in first language acquisition. In Jan Nuyts & Johan van der Auwera (eds.), *The Oxford handbook of modality and mood*, 430–447. Oxford: Oxford University Press.

Johanson, Lars. 2000. Turkic indirectives. In Lars Johanson & Bo Utas (eds.), *Evidentials: Turkic, Iranian and neighboring languages*, 61–87. Berlin: Mouton de Gruyter. Doi: 10.1515/9783110805284

Johanson, Lars & Bo Utas (eds.). 2000. *Evidentials: Turkic, Iranian and neighboring languages*. Berlin: Mouton de Gruyter.

Ketrez, F. Nihan. 1999. *Early verbs and the acquisition of Turkish argument structure*. Istanbul: Boğaziçi University MA thesis.

Küntay, Aylin & Dan I. Slobin. 1996. Listening to a Turkish mother: Some puzzles for acquisition. In Dan I. Slobin, Julie Gerhardt, Amy Kyratzis & Jiansheng Guo (eds.), *Social interaction, social context and language: Essays in honor of Susan Ervin-Tripp*, 265–286. Hillsdale, NJ: Lawrence Erlbaum.

Lyons, John. 1977. *Semantics*. 2 vols. Cambridge: Cambridge University Press.

MacWhinney, Brian. 2000. *The CHILDES project: Tools for analyzing talk*, 3rd edn. Mahwah, NJ: Lawrence Erlbaum.

MacWhinney, Brian, Elizabeth Bates & Reinhold Kliegl. 1984. Cue validity and sentence interpretation in English, German, and Italian. *Journal of Memory and Language* 23. 127–150.

Nakipoğlu, Mine & Neslihan Yumrutaş. 2009. Acquisition of clitics. In Sıla Ay, Özgür Aydın, İclal Ergenç, Seda Gökmen, Selçuk İşsever & Dilek Peçenek (eds.), *Essays on Turkish linguistics: Proceedings of the 14th international conference on Turkish linguistics, August 6–8, 2008* (Turcologica 79), 331–340. Wiesbaden: Harrassowitz Verlag.

Nuyts, Jan. 2006. Modality: Overview and linguistic issues. In William Frawley (ed.), *The expression of modality*, 1–26. Berlin: Mouton de Gruyter.

Ögel, Hale. 2007. *Developments in source monitoring and linguistic encoding of source.* Istanbul: Boğaziçi University MA thesis.
Öztürk, Özge & Anna Papafragou. 2008. The acquisition of evidentiality in Turkish. *University of Pennsylvania Working Papers in Linguistics* 14(1). 297–309.
Palmer, Frank Robert. 2001. *Mood and modality*, 2nd edn. Cambridge: Cambridge University Press.
Plungian, Vladimir A. 2001. The place of evidentiality within the universal grammatical space. *Journal of Pragmatics* 33(3). 349–357.
Savaşır, İskender & Julie Gee. 1982. The functional equivalents of the middle voice in child language. In Monica Macaulay & Orin D. Gensler (eds.), *Proceedings of the eighth annual meeting of the Berkeley Linguistics Society*, 607–616. Berkeley: Berkeley Linguistics Society.
Şener, Nilüfer. 2011. *Semantics and pragmatics of evidentials in Turkish.* Storrs: University of Connecticut dissertation.
Slobin, Dan I. 1973. Cognitive prerequisites for the development of grammar. In Charles A. Ferguson & Dan I. Slobin (eds.), *Studies of child language development*, 175–208. New York: Holt, Rinehart and Winston.
Slobin, Dan I. 1985. Crosslinguistic evidence for the language-making capacity. In Dan I. Slobin (ed.), *Crosslinguistic study of language acquisition*, vol. 2: *Theoretical issues*, 1157–1256. Hillsdale, NJ: Lawrence Erlbaum.
Slobin, Dan I. 2001. Form–function relations: How do children find out what they are? In Melissa Bowerman & Steve Levinson (eds.), *Language acquisition and conceptual development*, 406–449. Cambridge: Cambridge University Press.
Slobin, Dan I. & Ayhan Aksu. 1982. Tense, aspect, and modality in the use of the Turkish evidential. In Paul J. Hopper (ed.), *Tense-aspect: Between semantics and pragmatics*, 185–201. Amsterdam & Philadelphia: John Benjamins.
Stephany, Ursula. 1985. *Aspekt, Tempus Modalität: Zur Entwicklung der Verbalgrammatik in der neugriechischen Kindersprache* (Language Universals Series 4). Tübingen: Gunter Narr.
Stephany, Ursula. 1986. Modality. In Paul Fletcher & Michael Garman (eds.), *Language acquisition*, 2nd edn., 375–400. Cambridge: Cambridge University Press.
Stephany, Ursula. 1993. Modality in first language acquisition: The state of the art. In Norbert Dittmar & Astrid Reich (eds.), *Modality in language acquisition*, 133–144. Berlin & New York: de Gruyter.
Tamm, Anne, Leyla Roksan Çağlar, Ayhan Aksu-Koç & Gergely Csibra. 2014. Generic grammar makes Turkish preschoolers generalize statements and tolerate exceptions. Poster presented at the Budapest CEU Conference on Cognitive Development, Central European University, 9–11 January 2014.
Tarplee, Clare. 2010. Next turn and intersubjectivity in children's language acquisition. In Hilary Gardner & Michael Forrester (eds.), *Analysing interactions in childhood: Insights from conversation analysis*, 3–22. Oxford: Wiley-Blackwell.
Taylan, Eser Erguvanlı. 2001. On the relation between temporal/aspectual adverbs and the verb form in Turkish. In Eser Erguvanlı Taylan (ed.), *The verb in Turkish*, 97–128. Amsterdam & Philadelphia: John Benjamins.
Taylan, Eser Erguvanlı. 2014. A modality map of Turkish. Paper presented at the 17th International Conference on Turkish Linguistics, University of Rouen, 3–5 September 2014.

Taylan, Eser Erguvanlı. 2015. *The phonology and morphology of Turkish*. Istanbul: Boğaziçi University Press.
Terziyan, Treysi. 2013. *Acquisition of modality in Turkish*. Istanbul: Boğaziçi University MA thesis.
Theakston, Anna & Elena Lieven. 2017. Multiunit sequences in first language acquisition. *Topics in Cognitive Science* 9(3). 588–603.
Tomasello, Michael. 2003. *Constructing a language: A usage-based theory of language acquisition*. Cambridge, MA: Harvard University Press.
Tomasello, Michael. 2009. The usage-based theory of language acquisition. In Edith L. Bavin (ed.), *The Cambridge handbook of child language*, 69–88. Cambridge: Cambridge University Press.
Tura, Sabahat Sansa. 1986. DIR in modern Turkish. In Ayhan Aksu-Koç & Eser Erguvanlı Taylan (eds.), *Proceedings of the Turkish linguistics conference, 9–10 August 1984*, 145–158. Istanbul: Boğaziçi University Publications.
Ünal, Ercenur & Anna Papafragou. 2016. Production–comprehension asymmetries and the acquisition of evidential morphology. *Journal of Memory and Language* 89. 179–199.
Uzundağ, Berna, Süleyman S. Taşçı, Aylin C. Küntay & Ayhan Aksu-Koç. 2018. Functions of Turkish evidentials in early child–caregiver interactions: A growth curve analysis of longitudinal data. *Journal of Child Language* 45(4). 878–899.
Xanthos, Aris, Sabine Laaha, Steven Gillis, Ursula Stephany, Ayhan Aksu-Koç, Anastasia Christofidou, Natalia Gagarina, Gordana Hržica, F. Nihan Ketrez, Marianne Kilani-Schoch, Katharina Korecky-Kröll, Melita Kovačević, Klaus Laalo, Marijan Palmović, Barbara Pfeiler, Maria D. Voeikova, Wolfgang U. Dressler. 2011. On the role of morphological richness in the early development of noun and verb inflection. *First Language* 31. 461–479.

Soonja Choi
The development of sentence-ending epistemic/evidential markers in young Korean children

Abstract: Korean has a large number of sentence-ending modal suffixes that express evidentiality and epistemic modality. These suffixes also convey the speaker's assessment of an event/state in relation to the listener's current state of knowledge. The present study examines the development of the sentence-ending modal system in five children from 1;8 (year; months) to 4;0. The database consists of several sets of longitudinal spontaneous speech data of mother–child interaction. From the one-word stage on, Korean children produce sentence-ending suffixes appropriately in discourse interaction and by age four, they acquire (or start to acquire) seven suffixes in a specific order. With these suffixes, children distinguish between new and old knowledge (−*ta* vs. −*e*), degree of certainty, which derives from shared information with the listener (−*ci*), source of information (−*tay*), and degree to which they agree or disagree with the listener's assessment of the situation (−*ci* vs. −*(nu)ntey*). As they acquire these functions, children also become competent conversational partners, building a common knowledge basis with their caregivers. A systematic investigation into possible mechanisms for the particular developmental pattern reveals that several factors contribute to the acquisition process: input frequency, discourse-pragmatic and cognitive factors as well as degree of structural resonance.

1 Introduction

Korean grammar has a large number of sentence-ending (SE) modal suffixes that express varying degrees of modal strength on the epistemic scale and different types of evidentiality. Many of these suffixes also express the speaker's assessment of an event/state in relation to the listener's current state of knowledge Given these complex features of the modal suffixes, children learning Korean need to acquire not only the forms and their meanings, but also the discourse-pragmatic aspects of these suffixes. Thus, a systematic study of the development of modal suffixes in young Korean children will provide some valuable insight into the general mechanisms by which children acquire the complex grammatical

---

Soonja Choi, San Diego State University and University of Vienna

https://doi.org/10.1515/9781501504457-014

system and its usage. With this perspective in mind, in this chapter, I examine the development of SE suffixes in five Korean children from 1;8 (year; months) till 4;0 based on sets of naturalistic speech data collected while mother and child spontaneously interacted in a home environment.

The study asks two specific questions: (a) What is the developmental order of acquisition for SE in Korean? (b) How can the particular order be explained? More specifically, what types of mechanism facilitate some forms to be acquired earlier than others? To answer these questions, I adopt a usage-based analysis of language acquisition (Ambridge and Lieven 2015; Lieven, Salomo, and Tomasello 2009) as well as the theory of dialogic syntax (Du Bois 2014) and investigate four possible factors: input frequency, discourse-pragmatic and cognitive factors, and structural factors.

The chapter is organized as follows: Section 1 provides general descriptions of Korean grammar for SE suffixes and presents key issues of the study. Sections 2 and 3 provide detailed analyses of the development of SE suffixes in two sets of children from 1;8 to 4;0. Section 4 evaluates the four types of mechanism as possible explanations for the development, and Section 5 concludes the chapter with a discussion of the results.

1.1 Sentence-ending (SE) suffixes in Korean

Korean is an SOV language with an agglutinating morphology. Thus, in Korean, sentences typically end with a verb or a predicative adjective with a number of grammatical suffixes following it. As shown in examples (1) and (2), suffixes, such as honorific, tense and aspect markers, are added after the predicate stem (*sin-* 'put.on' or *ippu-* 'pretty'). SE suffixes,[1] the topic of this chapter, occur in the final position,[2] after a tense/aspect marker. The SE suffixes denote mood and modal meanings and are, for the most part, independent of tense and aspect.

---

1 Researchers have used various terms for sentence-ending suffixes in Korean, such as sentence-final (or sentence-ending) particles and sentence enders. In this chapter, I will use the term 'SE suffixes' and 'SE particles' interchangeably.
2 The only possible form that can occur after a SE suffix is a 'low formal' (Lee 1989) or 'low polite' ending form *-yo*. The form *-yo* is regularly used among acquaintances to show respect for each other. It is a typical polite form for children to use to parents. Mothers may also use it to their children to teach them the polite form.

(1) *Cinderella-ka kwutwu-lul sin-ess-e.*
    Cinderella-SBJ shoes-OBJ put.on-PST-SE
    'Cinderella put shoes on.'

(2) *Cinderella-ka ippu-0-ta.*[3]
    Cinderella-SBJ pretty-PRS-SE
    'Cinderella is pretty.'

The category of SE suffixes has two characteristics. First, it is an obligatory grammatical class. A sentence (or an utterance containing a verb) without a SE suffix would be considered incomplete and ungrammatical. Second, among the categories of verbal suffixes, SE suffixes have the largest number of members in the spoken language (Choi 1929; Lee 1991). More than twenty forms, most of which are short one-syllable morphemes, frequently occur in colloquial Korean (e.g., *−ta, −e, −ci, −kwun, −tay, −ney*). These SE suffixes are typically used in spoken discourse during informal and spontaneous conversation. They are not used in written reports or formal speeches.

Traditional analyses have suggested that the category of SE suffixes fulfills two functions, mood and speech register. Thus, in Choi (1929) SE suffixes are grouped according to different moods: indicative, interrogative, imperative, and hortative (see also Lee 1989). Within each mood category, the suffixes are grouped into five different speech registers ranging from the most formal to the least formal forms. However, the system of SE suffixes is actually more complex than is presented in the traditional analysis, because it is often the case that one form is used for several categories (both in terms of mood and speech register), and one category has several forms. For example, the suffix *−ci* (marking certainty or shared information, see below) can be used in the indicative mood as well as in the interrogative mood as in (3) and (4).

(3) *Halmeni-ka   onul Seoul-ey tochakha-si-ess-ci.*
    grandmother-SBJ today Seoul-LOC arrive-HON-PST-SE
    'Grandmother arrived in Seoul today.'

---

[3] For a predicative adjective (e.g., *ippu-* 'pretty'), the present tense takes the zero form, while the past tense takes the same form, *-ess*, as for a verbal predicate.

(4) (with a rising intonation)
 Halmeni-ka   onul   Seoul-ey   tochakha-si-ess-ci?
 grandmother-SBJ today Seoul-LOC arrive-HON-PST-SE
 'Did grandmother arrive in Seoul today?'

Thus, what had remained unexplained in these traditional analyses was the meaning and function of individual forms in discourse. Over the last two decades, a number of studies in the semantic and pragmatic domains (and particularly within the framework of Conversational Analysis (e.g., Goodwin 1981; Sacks, Schegloff, and Jefferson 1974) have uncovered some of the discourse-pragmatic functions of the SE suffixes (e.g., Lee 1991; Strauss 2005). Overall, the particles express various types of modal meaning, especially conveying the speaker's viewpoints on the epistemicity and/or evidentiality of the core proposition. Epistemicity concerns indication of degree of certainty about the truth of a proposition (Boye 2016; Nuyts 2006), whereas evidentiality has to do with specifying source of information (e.g., direct witness, hearsay, inference) (Aksu-Koç, Balaban, and Alp 2009; Chafe and Nichols 1986). For example, the particles express the speaker's assessment of the status of information (e.g., whether the information is new or old/well established), source of information (e.g., whether knowledge about the event/state of affairs has been directly or indirectly obtained), or whether the information is shared or not shared with the listener. In response, the listener also uses a specific suffix, indicating whether he/she agrees or disagrees with the speaker's assessment or providing a different viewpoint on the information. Through such negotiation of the modal and interactional aspects of the information, the speaker and the hearer reach a common assessment of the event or state of affairs in question.

1.2 Sentence-ending suffixes to be examined in this study

In this chapter, I examine seven SE suffixes that occur either in the indicative or interrogative mood: *–e, –ta, –ci, –tay, –(nu)ntey,*[4] *–ney,* and *–kwuna*. These suffixes are used (with varying degrees of frequency) during spontaneous

---

4 The two forms, *–nuntey* and *–ntey*, are phonological variants: *–nuntey* is used when the preceding morpheme ends in a consonant (e.g., *mek-* 'eat' -> *mek-nuntey*), but *–ntey* is used when it ends in a vowel (e.g., *ippu-* 'pretty' -> *ippu-ntey*). *–(Nu)ntey* can also be used as a relational conjunction at the end of a subordinate clause connecting to the main clause that follows it, or as a SE suffix of a single-clause utterance. In this paper, only the latter type is analyzed since children of the age range studied in this paper (3;0–4;0) use *–(nu)ntey* predominantly in single-clause utterances.

interaction between mother and child, and children acquire many of them by four years of age. Examples 5 through 11 illustrate the suffixes with the core proposition *Cinderella is pretty* and a general meaning is indicated for each suffix.

(5) Generic/factual information (*It is the case that* . . .)
    Cinderella-ka ippu-e.
    Cinderella-SBJ pretty-SE

(6) Direct evidence/new information (*I have just noticed that* . . .)
    Cinderella-ka ippu-ta.
    Cinderella-SBJ pretty-SE

(7) Shared knowledge/certainty (*It is certain and we both know that* . . .)
    Cinderella-ka ippu-ci.
    Cinderella-SBJ pretty-SE

(8) Hearsay/story-telling (*Someone said that* . . .)
    Cinderella-ka ippu-tay.
    Cinderella-SBJ pretty-SE

(9) Contrastive/conflicting information (*But/On the contrary,* . . .)
    Cinderella-ka ippu-ntey.
    Cinderella-SBJ pretty-SE

(10) Perceptual awareness/inference (*I have just realized/seen that* . . .)
    Cinderella-ka ippu-ney.
    Cinderella-SBJ pretty-SE

(11) Inference
    Cinderella-ka ippu- kwuna. (*I infer/understand that* . . .)
    Cinderella-SBJ pretty-SE

Previous studies have shown that these forms mark the status of the speaker's (and listener's) knowledge about the proposition and source of information. While the precise functions of these forms are still much investigated and discussed, some general characteristics can be stated based on the available research (e.g., Choi 1991; Lee 1991; Lee 1993; Strauss 2005):
– The suffix –*e* is a generic marker that informs about factual and established information. It is considered as an unmarked form and thus is used most frequently.

- The suffix *–ta* indicates new and noteworthy information that comes from immediate perceptual evidence.
- *–Ci* indicates that the information is certain and shared by both the speaker and the listener. Lee (1999) argues that *–ci* also expresses the speaker's commitment to the truth of the proposition.
- The suffix *–tay* informs the listener that the statement is based on indirect evidence (e.g., hearsay or reported speech). *–Tay* is also used for events/states that come from storybooks. There are individual differences among mothers in terms of frequency of using *–tay* during story-telling (Choi 1991; see also section 3.1 below).
- The suffix *–(nu)ntey* presents information that contrasts with the preceding utterance or provides some background information that would lead to a different perspective from the preceding discourse (Park 1999).

It is important to note that the generic/unmarked form *–e* is ubiquitous and can be used in lieu of all other forms. Use of a marked form (e.g., *–ci*, *–(nu)ntey*) rather than the generic form *–e* is for the speaker to signal or add to the core proposition a specific semantic/pragmatic meaning that would be appropriate in the on-going discourse interaction and/or that would clarify the speaker's perspective.

In the following conversation (12), Mother and child (JW) negotiate about whether one can see things through the video camera. During this negotiation, they use three different SE suffixes, *–ta*, *–(nu)ntey*, and *–ci*.

(12) JW, 3;9
 (JW and Mother are adjusting the video camera for recording. JW is looking through the video lens.)
 JW: an   po-i-n-ta.   (direct evidence/new information)
      NEG   see-PASS-PRS-SE
      '(It) is not seen. (= (I) do not see.)'
 M: po-i-nuntey.   (conflicting information)
      see-PASS-SE
      '(It) is seen. (= (I) see.)'
      (JW looks through the camera again.)
 JW: ta   cokumakey   po-i-n-ta.   (direct evidence)
      all   small   see-PASS-PRS-SE
      'All are seen small. (= (I) see all small.)'
 M: cokumakey   po-i-ci?   (certain and shared information)
      small   see-PASS-SE
      '(They) are seen small, right? (= (You) see them small, right?)'

In the above example, JW first tells M that he does not see anything. He uses the suffix *–ta* for his statement, expressing the new and noteworthy (Lee 1991) information that he has just perceived. Then, M responds to JW repeating the same core proposition *po-i*, but in an affirmative construction, using the suffix *–(nu)ntey*. The suffix conveys that her assessment conflicts with JW's. M's conflicting information prompts JW to look into the video camera again. JW apparently can see things now and thus repeats the mother's positive statement with the particle *–ta* (which again expresses that the information is new and directly perceived). M then validates the fact with the particle *–ci* expressing that the information is certain and shared. By using an interrogative, rising intonation in this sentence M additionally wants to re-confirm the information with JW.

In the above conversation (12), M and JW initially exchange contrasting statements but resolve the issue after some negotiation about the fact of the matter. In the process, M and JW use three SE particles: Reporting a state of affairs newly obtained from direct evidence with *–ta*, a presentation of conflicting information with *–(nu)ntey*, verification of the information given and finally agreement of the fact with *–ci*. These suffixes, then, denote a number of aspects: the speaker's assessment of the situation, how the speaker obtained the information (i.e. source of information) and they also express how the speaker's assessment relates to the conversation partner's assessment.

There are two other SE suffixes, *–ney* and *–kwuna* (see examples 10 and 11 above), to be examined in this chapter. These two suffixes are intriguing (and have been the subject of much research) because there is a fair amount of overlap in their uses (i.e. either suffix is acceptable in many cases), although they are not always interchangeable. Both encode the speaker's cognitive realization of some aspect of the current situation, either through direct perception or by inference. There is also a certain degree of mirativity in these suffixes (Strauss 2005). The difference between them has to do with the degree to which they encode a current perceptual state of affairs and the degree to which the utterance is directed to the addressee for a conversational purpose. More specifically, *–ney* is typically used to describe an event/state that the speaker actually sees, smells or feels (i.e. cognitive awareness of perception) and it can also mark inference derived from current perceptual evidence (Ha 2016). Thus in example (13) below, HS's mother (M) uses *–ney* as she recognizes that the tower has now become tall. With *–ney* she in addition conveys her surprise that HS did it quite fast. The form *–kwuna* also marks perceptual evidence, but more often expresses an inference derived from perceptual evidence (examples 14 and 15) and it does so at a more speaker-internal level. That is, the inference made by *–kwuna* is directed to the speaker's self more than to the addressee (Ha 2016). For example, in (15), seeing JW close his eyes, M infers that JW is sleepy. M marks her inference with –*kwuna*. As we will see, the mothers in the present study use –*ney* more often than –*kwuna* when they talk to young children (see section 3).

(13) HS, 3;6
(HS is stacking Lego pieces to make a tower. M now sees a tall tower.)
M: *kapcagi nopha-ci-ess-ney.*
suddenly tall-become-PST-SE
'(It) suddenly got tall.'
HS: *ung.*
yes
'Yes.'

(14) JW, 3;5
JW: *emma kongyong sa-cwu-l-kka-yo?*
mommy dinosaur buy-give-FUT-Q-POL
'Shall I buy you a dinosaur?'
M: *kongyong caymi eps-e.*
Dinosaur interest not.exist-SE
'Dinosaurs are not interesting.'
ne-nun emma-ka mwe cohahanun-ci
you-TOP mommy-SBJ what like-CONN
molu-nun-kwuna.
not.know-CONN-SE
'(I see that) you don't know what Mommy wants.'

(15) JW, 3;8
(JW is closing his eyes.)
M: *ne colip-kwuna.*
you sleepy-SE
'You are sleepy.'

In summary, the seven SE suffixes reviewed in this section (–*ta*, –*e*, –*ci*, –*tay*, –(*nu*)*ntey*, –*ney*, –*kwuna*) serve to construct a shared/common basis of knowledge between conversation partners by explicitly expressing a variety of epistemic/evidential and other types of modal meanings: (a) degree of novelty of information, (b) degree of certainty of knowledge about events/states, (c) source of information, (d) cognitive awareness and inference from the current situation, (e) agreement with or challenge to the listener's current knowledge. Using such suffixes, the conversation partners understand each other's mental state as well as the dynamics of the information exchange that is taking place: The interaction often progresses from self-awareness of a given situation to sharing the conversationally relevant information, i.e. from non-shared individual experience to shared experience and confirmation. Thus, a common goal in using these particles is to construct shared knowledge about a topic at hand and discover the substance of the matter in collaboration. The particles reveal and specify the process by which such shared knowledge comes about.

1.3 Structural resonance in discourse interaction

What is noteworthy in example (12) above, is the extensive syntactic repetition that is taking place in the conversation: JW initiates the conversation with the core proposition, *po-i* (lit. see-PASS) 'be seen/visible'. In each of the ensuing three conversational turns, M or JW repeat the form of the core proposition while varying the SE suffix.

Partial or full repetition of prior syntactic structure in discourse interaction is termed 'syntactic resonance' in Du Bois' (2014) theory of Dialogic Syntax. Du Bois (2014) defines 'syntactic resonance' as follows: "One speaker constructs an utterance based on the immediately co-present utterance of a conversational partner. Words, structures, and other linguistic resources invoked by the first speaker are selectively reproduced by the second. This strategy can be applied when the second speaker's meaning is parallel or opposed to that of the first" (Du Bois 2014: 360).

According to Du Bois (2014) syntactic resonance plays a critical role in adults' discourse structure and also in children's language acquisition. Because the resonance takes place within a short span of discourse interaction, the syntactic structure is still in the language learners' working memory to perform necessary cognitive operations on it. Thus, syntactic resonance – also called 'dialogic resonance' because the resonance is accomplished between two conversational partners – can facilitate language acquisition (Clancy 2009). In fact, it can be a powerful strategy in the acquisition of grammar.[5] Structural resonance between mother and child and the analogies it implies (when the resonance is partial) give the child a rich environment for learning new forms and their functions.[6] As we will see in the present study, syntactic (or structural)

---

5 In this study resonance will be termed 'structural' rather than 'syntactic' because no syntactic analysis of resonance is conducted in the current study.
6 For a study of the early development of complement constructions in English-learning toddlers within the dialogic bootstrapping framework see Köymen and Kyratzis (2014). Of relevance here is also a usage-based theory of acquisition (e.g., Lieven, Salomo, and Tomasello

resonance can in part explain the acquisition order of SE suffixes in Korean: The suffixes that children acquire early, for example –*ci* and –*(nu)ntey*, tend to have a higher degree of dialogic resonance in mother-child interaction.

In the following sections, I will first examine the order in which Korean children develop the SE suffixes from 1;8 till 4;0 and investigate the factors that facilitate this development.

2 The development of SE suffixes in Korean at early stages (1;8–3;0): Previous studies

In previous work (Choi 1991, 1995), I examined the development of SE particles in three children, starting from the one-word stage (1;8) till 3;0. During this early stage, the children acquired four SE suffixes, –*ta*, –*e*, –*ci*, –*tay* in the order mentioned, with clear semantic distinctions (see also Kim 1997).

From the one-word stage, the children spontaneously produce SE suffixes at the end of an utterance. Initially, for the first month or so (1;8–1;9/1;10), they use two suffixes –*ta* and –*e*, each form for a specific type of mood: –*e* for requests (i.e. direct requests) (16) and –*ta* for statements (17).

(16) –*e* (request) (Choi 1991: 102)
TJ, 1;9
(TJ is with a friend)
TJ: *ilwu o-a.*[7]
here come-SE
'Come here.'

(17) –*ta* (statement) (Choi 1991: 103)
TJ, 1;9
(Mother asks TJ about the bird picture on the wall, but TJ doesn't see it at first.)
M: *say eti iss-ni?*
bird where exist-SE

2009) that highlights the role of frequency (in mother and/or child's speech) at all levels of lexicon, morphology and syntax.

7 –*E* and –*a* are allomorphs. –*E* occurs after high and mid-high vowels and after consonants. –*A* occurs following low and mid-low vowels.

'Where is the bird?'
(TJ looks for it and finds it.)
TJ: *chac-ass-ta.*
find-PST-SE
'(I) found (it).'

However, from 1;10, the children use the suffix *-e* also for statements juxtaposing it with *-ta*. The function of *-e* in statements contrasts with *-ta* in terms of degree of assimilation of information in the child's mind.

The suffix *-ta* is used for immediate perceptual information. The events/states that *-ta* expresses are ones that the children have just perceived (typically visually) in the here-and-now (example 17 above). Choi (1991) argues that the suffix *-ta* expresses information that the child is still processing in his/her mind. In contrast, the events/states that *-e* expresses are old information that has been assimilated in the child's mind, e.g., past events or intentions that the child has created in her mind as in example (18).

(18) *-e* (statement) (Choi 1991: 107)
TJ, 2;2
(TJ is in the middle of reading a book with the mother, but wants to stop.)
TJ: *eps-e.*
not.exist-SE
'(There) is none.'

In the next phase (between 2;0 and 2;2), the children start using the suffix *-ci*. The contexts for *-ci* are distinct from the others in that it is primarily used: (a) when reiterating the information described in the preceding utterances either by the child herself or by the adult (thus the truth of the information has become certain), or (b) when making a statement about an event/state which has some evidence (e.g., perceptual evidence) to support the truth of the reference. Example (19) illustrates both features of (a) and (b). In most of the *-ci* contexts, evidence for certainty could be found in the preceding discourse where the information has been repeated several times during the conversations with the caregiver. In fact, Choi (1995) found that the propositions with *-ci* in the children's speech often had structural resonance with previous utterances. The function of *-ci* marking shared knowledge also relates to indicating certainty of the shared information. In example (19) below, the investigator first describes to HS that the coin got stuck (line a). In line (b), HS repeats the proposition in the form of a question to confirm it with the investigator. In line (c), the investigator tells HS that the register machine is not broken. (It is not entirely clear why the investigator brings up the issue of 'not being broken', but it seems that she does not want HS to associate 'being stuck' with 'being broken'.) In line (d), HS disagrees with the investigator and says *kocang na-ss-e* '(It)'s broken' using a generic marker *–e*. Notice that in line (d), HS challenges the investigator's statement and thus, at this point 'being broken' is simply HS's opinion and its certainty is not established. But after seeing another coin getting stuck the girl repeats the proposition *kocang-na* ('be broken') using *–ci* this time to mark certainty (example 19, line g). In this discourse interaction, one readily observes structural resonance between the investigator and the child.

(19) *-ci* (Choi 1995: 191)
   HS, 2;9
   (HS is playing with a toy cash register machine with the investigator (Inv.). One coin chip gets stuck in the cash register.)
   a. Inv.: *kelye-ss-cyana.*
       stuck-PST-SE
       '(It's) stuck.'
   b. HS: *kelye-ss-e?*
       stuck-PST-SE
       '(It's) stuck?'
   c. Inv.: *kocang   an   na-ss-e.*
       broken   NEG   arise-PST-SE
       '(It) is not broken.'
   d. HS: *kocang   na-ss-e.*
       broken   arise-PST-SE
       '(It)'s broken.'
   (Inv. tries again but it still gets stuck)
   e. HS: *an   tway.*
       NEG   become
       '(It) doesn't work.'
   f. Inv.: *an   tway.*
       NEG   become
       '(It) doesn't work.'
   g. HS: *kocang   na-ss-ci.*
       broken   arise-PST-SE
       '(It)'s broken.'

From about 2;5 on, the children begin producing *–tay* for hearsay (20) and for events in pretend-play (21) or a story.

(20) −*tay* (hearsay) (Choi 1995: 195)
HS, 2;5
(HS and her older sister are coloring.)
HS's sister: *nay-ka   saykchil hay   cwu-kkey.*
              I-SBJ   coloring do   give-SE
              'I will color (it) for you.'
(HS immediately reports to the Investigator:)
HS: *enni-ka   saykchil hay   cwu-n-tay.*
     sister-SBJ coloring do   give-PRS-SE
     '(My) sister says that she will color (it) for me.'

(21) −*tay* (hearsay in pretend play) (Choi 1995: 195)
TJ, 2;4
(TJ is looking at a picture of Ernie (= a character in 'Sesame Street') jumping)
Inv.: *jumphu-ha-e?*
      jump-do-SE
      '(Is he) jumping?'
TJ: *pal   ayaya   ha-n-tay.*
     foot   ayaya[8]   do-PRS-SE
     '(He) says (his) feet are hurt.'
Inv.: *ung.*
      yes
      'I see.'

To summarize, Korean children acquire several epistemic/evidential SE suffixes and use them appropriately at an early stage. Specifically, between 1;8 and 3;0, children learn four SE suffixes to mark distinct meanings:
1. The information has been recently acquired by the child through direct experience and is in the process of being assimilated to the child's knowledge system (−*ta*);
2. The information has been assimilated to his/her knowledge system (−*e*);
3. The information is certain and shared by the conversation partner (−*ci*);
4. The information is hearsay or part of story-telling (−*tay*).

Choi (1991, 1995) explains the order of acquisition in terms of general cognitive development (see Figure 1) at two levels. First, referring to Piaget's (1955) classical theory of 'decentration', namely that children think about their own perspective

---

[8] An onomatopoeic word referring to the sound made when one is hurt.

before they can incorporate other people's points of view, Choi (1991, 1995) proposes that Korean learners start out by marking newly perceived information that interests them and which they are still in the process of assimilating to their own knowledge system. Such information marked by –ta is directed to the self more than the listener.

Subsequently, –e is acquired to contrast the new knowledge with old/assimilated knowledge. As –ci is acquired, a new component, the feature of shared knowledge, is added to the SE modal system. Finally, as –tay is added to the modal system, another layer in modal dimension, namely source of information, is distinguished.[9] This developmental order suggests that as each new modal form and its corresponding function(s) are acquired, a new dimension of epistemic modality is added to the existing one(s), as shown in Figure (1).

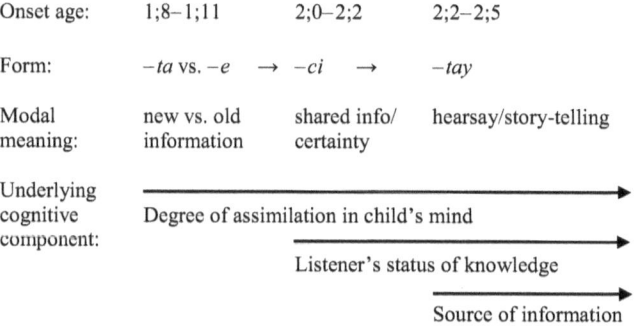

Onset age:	1;8–1;11	2;0–2;2	2;2–2;5
Form:	–ta vs. –e →	–ci →	–tay
Modal meaning:	new vs. old information	shared info/ certainty	hearsay/story-telling

Underlying cognitive component:

Degree of assimilation in child's mind ⟶

Listener's status of knowledge ⟶

Source of information ⟶

Figure 1: Development of SE suffixes in Korean children from 1;8 till 3;0: Forms, meanings, and underlying cognitive components (adapted from Choi 1991, 1995).

Recall that the unmarked/generic form –e can be used ubiquitously in almost all contexts in statements and questions. So, for example, it is acceptable to use –e in place of –ci in example (19) and of –tay in examples (20) – (21). What marked SE forms such as –ci and –tay do then is to add or specify a modal component (e.g., certainty or sharing of information, source of information) to the core proposition for communicative purposes (i.e. for better or clearer communication). Thus, development of marked SE forms in children's speech means that as children grow they make advances in understanding the diverse and intricate modal concepts encoded in the SE suffixes and express them in their

---

9 –Tay may also signal that the information conveyed could be unknown to the listener.

speech for the purpose of building common knowledge and sharing information with the addressee.

While it is impressive that children learn and use several suffixes productively during this early period, they still need to acquire many more of them (e.g., *-(nu)ntey, -ney*) in order to master the full range of meanings and functions that the Korean SE suffix system offers and become skilled conversation partners. The present study examines the next stage in the development of the SE modal system with new sets of data.

3 The development of SE suffixes in later stages (3;1–4;0): The present study

To examine the further development of SE particles in young Korean learners, new sets of data that span from age 3;1 to 4;0 were analyzed. The database is spontaneous speech of two children, JW (boy) and SH (girl). Both children were growing up in monolingual Korean homes in Taegu,[10] South Korea, and were attending preschool in the morning. During the observational period, the children were video-recorded regularly once a month for 30 minutes while they interacted with their mothers. The onset ages of the data collection were slightly different between the two children: JW's recordings were started at 3;1 while SH's began at 3;4. For JW the monthly recordings till 4;0 amounted to a total of 12 recording sessions and for SH there were 10 sessions.[11]

At each recording session, the mother and the child engaged in two or three of the following joint activities or conversation topics:
a) Child's everyday school experiences: The mother asks the child about what s/he did at the preschool, about his/her school friends, etc.
b) Pretend play: The mother and the child engage in different kinds of pretend play, such as exchanging roles of mother and child or impersonating the figurines that they play with together.
c) Playing games together, e.g., coloring, jigsaw puzzle, Lego blocks.
d) Telling stories from books.
e) Other topics, e.g., past experiences, planning future activities.

---

10 A major city that is located south of Seoul, South Korea.
11 There were two recording sessions (which were three weeks apart) for SH when she was 3;11.

All verbal interactions in the recordings were transcribed in Korean along with relevant contextual notes using an Excel program.

Table (1) shows the total number of utterances produced during the recordings as well as the number of utterances with SE suffixes that mark epistemicity or evidentiality. These suffixes consist of –ta, –ci, –tay, –(nu)ntey, –ney, and –kwuna. The majority of utterances (50%–70%) carry the unmarked, generic marker –e. The marked suffixes constitute about 16.5%–18% in the mothers' speech and about 8.5%–12% in the children's. The remaining utterances are one-word utterances (e.g., adverbs, nouns) and incomplete phrases without a verb and do not contain any SE suffixes. In Table (1), we observe that the two mothers produce almost the same amount of utterances and marked SE suffixes overall. But the two children differ: SH is much less talkative than JW (as shown in the two children's total numbers of utterances in Table 1) and she accordingly produces much fewer utterances marked with SE suffixes. In addition, many of SH's utterances are one-word utterances that do not require a SE suffix, such as reading the Korean alphabet letters one by one, saying words syllable by syllable, or engaging in a word game with her mother.

Table 1: Database.

Subject		Age	Recording time	Total Utterances[1]	Utterances with marked SE suffixes (% based on total utterances)
JW	Mother		30 minutes/month	3520	624 (17.7%)
	Child	3;1–4;0	6 hours total	3048	375 (12.3%)
SH	Mother		30 minutes/month	3387	557 (16.4%)
	Child	3;4–4;0	5 hours total	1808	160 (8.84%)

[1]One-word utterances of exclamation (e.g., ah!), response (e.g., ung 'yes'), and calling someone's name as well as unintelligible or interrupted utterances were excluded from the utterance counts.

In this study, analyses are conducted on the six SE suffixes that are epistemically and evidentially marked: –ta, –ci, –tay, –(nu)ntey, –ney, and –kwuna. (Their functions have been illustrated above by examples 3 through 15). The suffix –e is excluded from the present analysis, as it is an unmarked and generic suffix that the mothers and the children use predominantly to exchange information.

To assess the developmental pattern of the other six suffixes, the data are divided into three age periods: 3;1–3;3 (Period I), 3;4–3;7 (Period II) and 3;8–4;0 (Period III). (Since SH's recording began at 3;4, only JW's data are available for Period I.) Tables (2a) and (2b) report a breakdown of the database by age period, showing the total number of utterances in each period in the mothers' and the children's speech, respectively. The tables also present the raw frequencies and the percentage distribution of the six suffixes in the mothers' and the children's speech for each period based on the total number of utterances.

The data show that both the mothers and the children produce the marked suffixes increasingly more often from one period to the next in both token frequency and percentage of use. The two mothers increase their input of the six suffixes by an average of 2.5% as their children advance in age from one period to the next (Table 2a). By Period III JW's mother uses the suffixes about 20% in her overall speech while SH's mother uses them slightly less often, about 18%.

Table 2a: Token frequencies and percentages of the six marked SE suffixes in the mothers' speech by child age period.

Subject		Total recording time	Total Utterances	Utterances with marked SE suffixes (% based on total utterances)
	Age period			
JW Mother	I. 3;1–3;3	1.5 hrs. (3 sessions)	1109	168 (15.15%)
	II. 3;4–3;7	2 hrs. (4 sessions)	1080	189 (17.50%)
	III. 3;8–4;0	2.5 hrs. (5 sessions)	1331	266 (19.98%)
	Total	6 hours (12 sessions)	3520	624 (17.70%)
SH Mother	II. 3;4–3;7	2.5 hrs. (5 sessions)	1460	218 (14.93%)
	III. 3;8–4;0	2.5 hrs. (5 sessions)	1927	339 (17.59%)
	Total	5 hours (10 sessions)	3387	557 (16.40%)

The two children also increase their use of the suffixes as they advance in age (Table 2b). In JW's speech, both the token frequencies and the percentage uses of the suffixes jump steeply from Period I to Period II. From Period II to Period III, JW shows a modest increase, ending with 15.33% of usage at Period III, which approaches the frequency rate of his mother. SH also shows a modest increase from Period II to III, i.e., from 8.21% to 9.34%. The increase in the

Table 2b: Token frequencies and percentages of the six marked SE suffixes in the children's speech by age period.

Subject		Age period	Total recording time	Total Utterances	Utterances with marked SE suffixes (% based on total utterances)
JW Child		I. 3;1–3;3	1.5 hrs. (3 sessions)	766	41 (5.35%)
		II. 3;4–3;7	2 hrs. (4 sessions)	938	128 (13.65%)
		III. 3;8–4;0	2.5 hrs. (5 sessions)	1344	206 (15.33%)
	Total		6 hours (12 sessions)	3048	375 (12.30%)
SH Child		II. 3;4–3;7	2.5 hrs. (5 sessions)	791	65 (8.21%)
		III. 3;8–4;0	2.5 hrs. (5 sessions)	1017	95 (9.34%)
	Total		5 hours (10 sessions)	1808	160 (8.84%)

amount of the suffixes reveals that, as the age advances, the children mark events/states more frequently with some epistemic/evidential qualification.

SH's overall usage rates are, however, not only much lower than JW's but also as compared to her mother's rate. As mentioned earlier, SH was not very talkative and often produced one-word utterances that did not require a SE suffix.

Despite the difference in frequency rate for marked SE suffixes, however, we will see that JW and SH show a similar developmental pattern in the way they acquire marked SE suffixes.

In order to examine how individual SE suffixes develop over time, I assessed the frequency distribution of the suffixes by age period. The results are shown in Table (3). The percentages are based on the total number of occurrences of the six suffixes in each period, thus showing which suffixes are used more often than others in the child's speech during a given period. It should be noted that like the children studied for earlier periods (Choi 1991, 1995; see also Kim 1997), the children in the present study used SE suffixes with remarkably few errors. JW and SH each made a total of 5 errors[12] in the entire dataset.

Overall, the two children are remarkably similar in their distributive use of the suffixes in Periods II and III. One exception is –*tay* (hearsay/storytelling) which JW uses far more frequently (18.75%) during the 3;4–3;7 period than SH does (1.54%). In the data, the use of –*tay* is dependent on context in

---

[12] A SE suffix was coded as an 'error' when it could not be considered appropriate in any way in the conversational context where it was used.

that the majority of its uses occur when telling stories from picture books. JW engages in storybook narratives much more often than SH. (See ii below for more discussion about –*tay*.) During the fourth year (3;1–4;0), two new forms appear in the speech of both children: *–(nu)ntey* (contrastive/conflicting information; example 12 above), and *–ney* (perceptual awareness/inference; example 13). The suffix *–kwuna*, (inference; example 14) which also emerges in period II, is scarcely used, however.

The two children show the following developmental patterns:

i. As discussed above with Table (2b), the two children increase their use of the suffixes both as far as token frequencies and percentage of uses of the markers are concerned.

ii. As can be expected from the previous findings on an earlier stage (summarized in Section 2 above), the two children use the 'early-acquired' forms – in particular *–ta* and *–ci* – with relatively high frequency (cf. Table 3). The children also produce *–tay* but, as mentioned above, with much variability in frequency within and between the two children. The variability is in large part due to the fact that the frequency of story-telling situations, in which *–tay* can be used, varies between the two children. The use of *–tay* in such contexts is optional.

Table 3: Distribution of percentages (and token frequencies) of six SE suffixes in the children's speech.

SE suffix (Approximate meaning/function)		–*ta* (direct evidence)	–*ci* (shared info/ certainty)	–*tay* (hearsay/story-telling)
Child	Age			
JW	I. 3;1–3;3[1]	31.70% (13)	39.02% (16)	4.87% (2)
	II. 3;4–3;7	20.31% (26)	36.71% (47)	18.75% (24)
	III. 3;8–4;0	14.08% (29)	44.17% (91)	1.46% (3)
SH	II. 3;4–3;7	18.46% (12)	46.15% (30)	1.54% (1)
	III. 3;8–4;0	14.74% (14)	34.74% (33)	5.26% (5)

Table 3 (continued)

		−ntey (contrastive information)	−ney (perceptual awareness/inference)	−kwuna (inference)	TOTAL
Child/Period					
JW	I.	9.75% (4)	14.63% (6)	0.00% (0)	100% (41)
	II.	15.62% (20)	7.03% (9)	1.56% (2)	100% (128)
	III.	34.47% (71)	4.37% (9)	1.46% (3)	100% (206)
SH	II.	24.62% (16)	7.69% (5)	1.54% (1)	100% (65)
	III.	38.95% (37)	6.31% (6)	0.00% (0)	100% (95)

[1]Data for this period is available only from JW.

In Period II, during which JW produces −tay most often (Table 3), JW engages in story-telling (with figurines or books) at almost every recording session, amounting to a total of 110 story-telling utterances. JW produces −tay in 22 of those utterances, mostly during two sessions, at 3;4 and 3;5. In contrast, SH engages in such activity only occasionally. In Period II, she produces a total of 28 story-telling utterances but does not use −tay in any of them. The one −tay token she uses in Period II is to express hearsay, retelling her mother what another person said. In Period III, however, SH produces −tay twice in story-telling contexts.

It should be noted that both mothers produce −tay optionally in story-telling contexts as well. During Period II, JW's mother uses −tay 13 times out of her 31 story-telling utterances and SH's mother uses it in 11 out of 41 story-telling utterances.

JW and SH also use −tay to mark an indirect source of information (i.e. hearsay) in Periods II and III. JW expresses hearsay with −tay appropriately twice in Period II and once in Period III. SH does so once in Period II and three times in Period III. −Tay is also produced for the hearsay function by the two mothers in both periods: 9 times by JW's mother and 14 times by SH's mother.

Based on the previous findings about the acquisition of −tay (Choi 1991) as well as the present study, it may be assumed that the two children use −tay in the story-telling context as well as to convey hearsay appropriately.

iii. For the five suffixes, –ta, –ci, –(nu)ntey, –ney, and –kwuna, the following developmental changes are observed from Period I/II to Period III in both children:
  (a) Use of –ta (direct evidence) decreases (proportionately in relation to the other suffixes) over time.
  (b) Use of –ci (shared info/certainty) is dominant throughout the three age periods, ranging between 35% and 46% of the marked SE suffixes.
  (c) Occurrence of the suffix –(nu)ntey (contrastive/conflicting information) increases noticeably from Period I/II to Period III.
  (d) The suffix –ney (perceptual awareness/inference) is proportionately used somewhat more frequently in JW's speech in Period I as compared to Periods II and III. But the raw frequency counts of –ney are small for both children in all three periods, ranging between 5 to 9 occurrences in each period. In JW's speech 6 utterances with -ney in Period I result in 14.6% of the total number of marked suffixes, but it is based on a total of only 41 utterances, a small sample size, so that its frequency rate may not be generalizable to a bigger sample. Furthermore, two of the six examples with –ney were 'errors'. (For example, at 3;3 JW used –ney inappropriately referring to a non-perceivable thought.) In Periods II and III –ney occurs between 4%–8% (of the marked SE suffixes) for both children. Thus, the children use the suffix –ney only occasionally, suggesting that they do not fully acquire its function during the fourth year.
  (e) The scarcity of –kwuna (inference) suggests that it is not acquired during the fourth year.

As the two children's developmental patterns are very similar, I have collapsed their data of Periods II and III and provided a chart (Figure 2) for an easier grasp of their development. What is immediately apparent in Figure (2) is that –ta decreases over time. As mentioned earlier –ta is directed to the speaker him/herself more than to the listener as it expresses speaker's own realization of status of affairs. Taking into account the interactional nature of SE markers in conversation, the decrease of –ta can be explained in terms of its relative lack of dialogic motivation.

Figure (2) shows that –ci, on the other hand, remains the most frequently produced suffix throughout the age periods, and –(nu)ntey increases impressively from Period I/II to Period III. As a result, in Period III (3;8–4;0) both –ci and –(nu)ntey are prominent in the children's production of marked SE suffixes.

In contrast, –ney and –kwuna are used only occasionally (–ney) or scarcely (–kwuna). The persistent salience of –ci and rapid acquisition of –(nu)ntey are

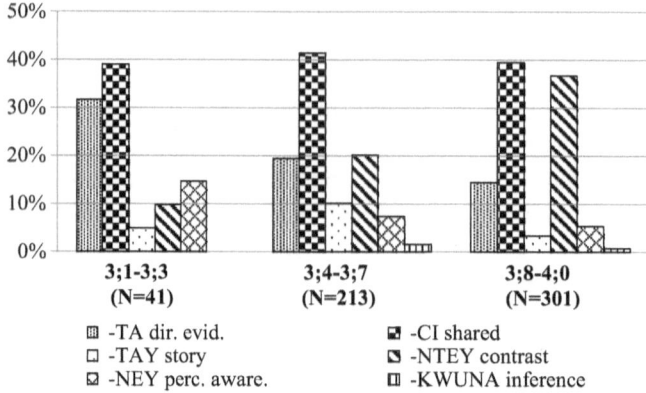

Figure 2: Frequency distribution of the six SE suffixes in the children's speech by age period.

intriguing from the perspective of the theory of language acquisition in that they raise the question about the underlying mechanisms.

Thus, in the remainder of the paper, I will focus on investigating possible mechanisms for the development of the two dominant suffixes, *–ci* and *–(nu) ntey* in the children's speech during the fourth year (3;1–4;0). The specific questions are: What are the factors that facilitate the maintenance of *–ci* and the acquisition of *–(nu)ntey*? In answering these questions, several aspects of the two suffixes will be compared with the other four suffixes examined in this study.

4 Mechanisms for the development of SE suffixes

As the function and use of SE markers are deeply embedded in conversational interaction, they correspond well to a usage-based theory of language, which emphasizes analysis and explanation of language at all levels (e.g., morphology, syntax, semantics) in relation to actual use of language in discourse (Bybee 2006). Taking this approach to explain acquisition (Ambridge and Lieven 2015; Lieven 2010; Lieven, Somalo, and Tomasello 2009), and based on previous findings on development of SE suffixes (Choi 1991, 1995), I explore four possible factors for the early acquisition of the two suffixes: Frequency in mothers' input, discourse-pragmatic and cognitive factors as well as structural ones in the input.

4.1 Input frequency

We first examine the frequency rates of the six suffixes in the input and relate them to the children's. Table (4) shows the two mothers' input frequencies. The frequency rates for the six suffixes in Periods II and III are quite consistent within each mother (except –*tay* in JW's mother, who frequently engaged in story-telling activities with JW in Period II, cf. Section 3.1.i) and they are also remarkably similar between the two mothers. Thus, in Figure (3), the data of the two mothers have been collapsed to provide an average pattern.

Table 4: Distribution of percentages (and token frequencies) of six SE suffixes in the mothers' speech.

SE suffix (Approximate meaning/ function)	Child Age	–*ta* (direct evidence)	–*ci* (shared info/ certainty)	–*tay* (hearsay/story-telling)
JW Mother	I. 3;1–3;3	13.61% (23)	43.79% (74)	2.96% (5)
	II. 3;4–3;7	22.75% (43)	26.98% (51)	10.05% (19)
	III. 3;8–4;0	14.66% (39)	30.08% (83)	2.63% (7)
SH Mother	II. 3;4–3;7	10.09% (22)	39.91% (87)	8.72% (19)
	III. 3;8–4;0	8.26% (28)	43.36% (147)	6.79% (23)

Child/Period		–*ntey* (contrastive information)	–*ney* (perceptual awareness/ inference)	–*kwuna* (inference)	TOTAL
JW Mother	I.	20.12% (34)	11.24% (19)	8.28% (14)	100% (168)
	II.	15.34% (29)	20.12% (38)	4.76% (9)	100% (189)
	III.	22.18% (59)	20.68% (55)	9.77% (26)	100% (266)
SH Mother	II.	24.31% (53)	16.05% (35)	0.92% (2)	100% (218)
	III.	22.71% (77)	18.29% (62)	0.59% (2)	100% (339)

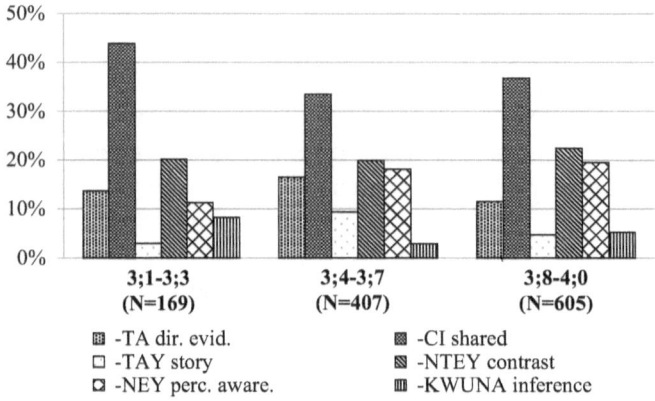

Figure 3: Frequency distribution of SE suffixes in the mothers' speech by age periods.

Comparing the mothers' frequency rates with those of the children, it is found that the children's frequency rates relate to the mothers' for *–ci*, the most frequent SE, and *–kwuna*, the least frequent one. On the other hand, input frequency rates are noticeably different from the children's concerning the forms *–(nu)ntey* and *–ney*: While the two mothers use *–ney* about 16%–20% in their speech (in Periods II and III), the two children use it only 4%–7%. In contrast, while the mothers use *–(nu)ntey* only 15%–24%, its frequency in the children's speech goes up to 34%–38% in Period III. In other words, whereas the two mothers provide *–(nu)ntey* and *–ney* with similar frequency rates, the children acquire *–(nu)ntey* much faster than *–ney*. Input frequency, then, does not explain the children's rapid acquisition of *–(nu)ntey* and their slow acquisition of *–ney*. We need to consider other possible factors, namely, discourse-interactional and cognitive factors as well as structural ones. In the next section, discourse-interactional and cognitive factors will be examined together because they are closely interrelated.

4.2 Discourse-interactional and cognitive factors

In Choi (1991, 1995), the developmental order of SE suffixes from 1;8 to 3;0 was explained in terms of cognitive development (cf. Figure 1): Children first express the event that they have just noticed (unassimilated knowledge) and juxtapose it with the event that is already known or has been established (assimilated) in their mind (*–ta* vs. *–e*). Later on, they go on to take the listener's knowledge into consideration, using *–ci* to express shared information. From 2;5 on, children start conveying to the listener that the information has been obtained indirectly, namely through hearsay or a storybook, using the marker *–tay*. From a pragmatic point of view, we observe that, at each developmental step, the conversation between mother and child becomes more interactional. The child talks increasingly more in response or in relation to the mother's speech or state of knowledge. This process of discourse interaction getting tighter continues through the fourth year (3;1–4;0): During this period, children use *–ta* less and less often but continue to make use of *–ci* frequently. They also rapidly acquire *–(nu)ntey*, a suffix that is inherently interactional in that it expresses a contrastive/conflicting opinion from the listener's point of view. Accordingly, in the present data, *–(nu)ntey* often occurs as a direct response to the preceding utterance in both the mother's and the child's speech, as illustrated in example (22) (a copy of example 12 above) as well as in (23).

(22) JW, 3;9
   (JW and Mother are adjusting the video camera for recording. JW is looking through the video lens.)
   JW: *an   po-i-n-ta.*   (direct evidence)
       NEG   see-PASS-PRS-SE
       '(I) cannot see.'
   M: *po-i-nuntey.* (conflicting information)
       see-PASS-SE
       '(I) can see.'
   (JW looks through the camera again.)
   JW: *ta   cokumakey po-i-n-ta.*   (direct evidence)
       all small   see-PASS-PRS-SE
       'I can see all (of them) small.'
   M: *cokumakey po-i-ci?*   (certain and shared information)
       small   see-PASS-SE
       'You can see (them) small, right?'

(23) JW, 3;5
   (M and JW are playing with a toy dinosaur.)
   M: *kongyong-un   mwusewu-e-yo.*
       Dinasaur-TOP   scary-SE-HON
       'Dinosaurs scare me.'
   JW: *na-nun   an   mwusewu-ntey.*
       I-TOP   NEG   scary-SE
       'They don't scare me.'

The developmental progress made in the early and later stages converges on children's increased ability and interest in becoming competent conversation partners as they pay attention and respond to what the listener says or knows. Integration of the listener's statement/knowledge into one's own speech takes cognitive sophistication. In this way, in learning SE modal suffixes in Korean, discourse interaction and cognitive components go hand in hand.

A high degree of discourse interaction may be revealed by a high degree of structural resonance (cf. Section 1.3). Therefore the extent of structural resonance between mother and child when using particular SE suffixes is investigated next.

4.3 Structural resonance

One important aspect of *–ci* and *–(nu)ntey* is that these markers are highly contingent upon the preceding utterance: They mark agreement and disagreement, respectively, with what the conversation partner has just stated (see examples 22 and 23 above). This feature of aligning with the conversation partner's statement may occur not only at the discourse-pragmatic level but also at the syntactic one. That is, utterances in which *–ci* and *–(nu)ntey* are used may also have a high degree of structural resemblance with the preceding utterance. Thus, I hypothesize that, in the mothers' speech, we find more structural resonance with *–ci* and *–(nu)ntey* than with *–ney* and *–kwuna*. The hypothesis is based on the assumption that a high degree of structural resonance in the mothers' input will enhance the children's acquisition of the markers, because in such a discourse environment, i.e. one in which the structure of the core proposition is repeated with only the SE suffix being changed, children can pay more attention to learning new items, in this case SE markers that vary between utterances. To illustrate, in (24), JW's mother understands that JW does not want to do a video session. She expresses her empathy by fully repeating the child's verb phrase and changing only the SE suffix to *–ci* in order to denote her understanding. In (25), she encourages JW to play with the dinosaur by repeating the verb *noh-* 'put.on' and partially changing the child's demonstrative adverb *ilehkey* 'like.this' to *kulehkey* 'like that.' She also adds the adverb *nophi* 'highly' to the utterance to convey her encouragement and, most importantly, changes the suffix to *–ci* expressing her agreement with the child's play.

(24) JW, 3;6
   (JW doesn't want to do a video session.)
   JW: an   ha-ko   siph-e.
        NEG   do-CONN   want-SE
        '(I) don't want to do (it).'
   M: an   ha-ko   siph-ci?
        NEG   do-CONN   want-SE
        '(You) don't want to do (it), right?'

(25) JW, 3;1 (JW is putting a toy dinosaur on top of a table.)
   M: mwe   ha-e?
        what   do-SE
        'What are you doing?'
   JW: ilekey   noh-a.
        like.this   put.on-SE
        'I put (it) on like this.'
   M: kulay, kulekey nophi   noh-aya-ci.
        right, like.that highly   put.on-OBLIG-SE
        'Right. You should put (it) on high like that.'

In the above discourse contexts in which M repeats JW's core propositions, JW's task of understanding M's speech is reduced to paying attention to and processing the new items, i.e. the SE suffixes and a couple of adverbs. It should be much easier for JW to do so in a structurally resonant discourse context (such as that of examples 24 and 25) than in a context where both the proposition and the SE suffixes are new. It is thus hypothesized that higher frequency rates of 'structural resonance' in mothers' input will enhance acquisition of those SE suffixes.

To test this hypothesis, I have examined frequency rates of structural resonance for each of the six SE suffixes in the two mothers' speech. I counted those of the mothers' utterances that reproduced the preceding utterance[13] fully or partially as illustrated in examples (24) and (25), respectively, within the span of five previous conversational turns.

For each suffix, the percentage of syntactic resonance was calculated based on the total number of occurrences of the given suffix (Figure 4). As

---

[13] The preceding utterance could be produced by either the child or the mother. The important point here is that the child has been exposed to the core proposition in a recent section of the conversation and thus is already familiar with it.

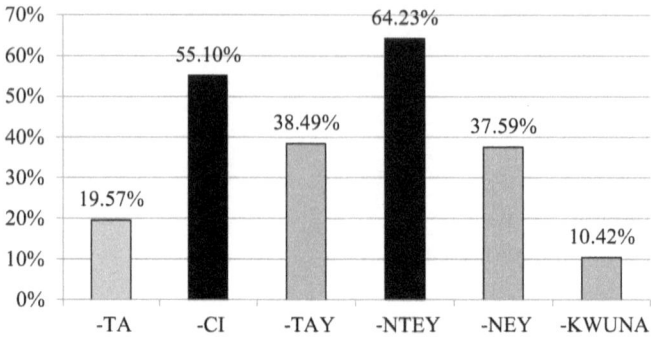

Figure 4: Percentages of structural resonance in the mothers' input.

hypothesized, –*ci* (55%) and –*(nu)ntey* (64%) have much higher proportions of 'structural resonance' than the other four suffixes. The results support the hypothesis in that –*kwuna*, the suffix that the children of the present study rarely produce, has the lowest degree of structural resonance in their mothers' speech. Unlike –*kwuna*, –*ci* and –*(nu)ntey* are more advantageous than the other suffixes as far as structural resonance is concerned.

I also examined the rate of structural resonance of the suffixes in the children's speech. Here, one would also expect that, as they begin to learn a new form, children use it with structural resonance. That is, it would be easier for them to produce a new SE form in a familiar structure than with a new structure. More importantly for the present aim of the study, one would expect more frequent structural resonance for the forms –*ci* and –*(nu)ntey*, whose functions (i.e. shared vs. contrastive information) relate closely to the conversation partner's utterance, and which have the highest rates of structural resonance in the mothers' speech.

This prediction was also met. In the children's speech, –*ci* and –*(nu)ntey* have the highest frequency of structural resonance among the six suffixes: In the two children's data taken together, –*ci* shows 52% of structural resonance and –*(nu)ntey* 70%. These percentages are impressively similar to the frequency rates in the mothers' speech.

The following examples illustrate the children's use of structural resonance for –*ci* (example 26) and –*(nu)ntey* (example 27). In example (26), JW repeats his mother's structure almost fully, changing the SE suffix from the generic –*e* to –*ci* to express shared information and certainty. In example (27), SH repeats her mother's utterance but changes from a negative to a positive statement replacing the generic –*e* of the mother's utterance with –*(nu)ntey* to denote a contrastive meaning.

(26) JW, 3;3
(JW and M are constructing a car together with car parts. M picks up a wheel.)
M: *ike-to   philyoha-e?*
   this-too   necessary-SE
   'Is this necessary, too?'
JW: *ike   philyoha-ci.*
    This   necessary-SE
    'This is necessary.'

(27) SH, 3;6
(SH and M are making a doll house together.)
M: *emma   pang-ey   chimtay   an   mantul-e*
   Mommy   room-LOC   bed   NEG   make-CONN
   cwu-e?
   give(BEN.AUX)-SE
   'Are (you) not making a bed in mommy's room for mommy?'
SH: *emma   chimtay   mantul-e   cwu-lkke-ntey.*
    Mommy   bed   make-CONN   give(BEN.AUX)-FUT-SE
    '(I) will make mommy's bed for mommy.'

The present analysis supports the hypothesis that degree of structural resonance in mothers' input is a factor that facilitates children's acquisition of SE suffixes. Given the complexity of discourse-pragmatic functions of the SE suffixes, which are highly grammaticalized, it is not surprising that children will acquire those suffixes with a high degree of structural resonance in the input earlier than others.

5 Discussion

Korean grammar has a large number of sentence-ending suffixes that express varying degrees of epistemicity and different types of evidentiality. Many of these suffixes also express the speaker's assessment of an event/state in relation to the listener's current knowledge about the event/state. Thus, in order to acquire the system of SE suffixes, Korean children need not only to acquire semantic but also discourse-pragmatic aspects of the suffixes.

In this chapter, previous studies on the early development of epistemic/evidential SE suffixes in Korean from 1;8 till 3;0 (Choi 1991, 1995) have been reviewed and further development from 3;1 till 4;0 has been examined with new sets of data. The studies have shown that Korean children start producing SE suffixes appropriately from the one-word period onwards and acquire a number of them before they reach four years of age. At the very beginning, Korean children mark an event that they experience in the immediate perceptual context with *–ta*, which does not have much of a discourse component in relation to the conversational partner. But soon, from 2;2 onward, children take the status of the listener's knowledge into account, express shared knowledge (*–ci*) or give new information to the listener by marking its source (*–tay*). In the fourth year, children become even more skillful in discourse interaction: One third or more of their utterances occur with *–ci* (35%–46%), a marker that signals that the information is certain and shared with the listener. During this time, children also rapidly increase the production of *–(nu)ntey*. Its function is inherently discourse interactional as it conveys information that contrasts with or challenges the listener's assessment of an event/state.

Four possible factors that could explain the order of acquisition of SE suffixes have been examined: Input frequency, discourse-pragmatic and cognitive factors as well as structural ones. The results show that all four types contribute to the acquisition process. First, an analysis of the mothers' input frequencies of the suffixes shows that while those for *–ci* (the most frequent SE suffix) and *–kwuna* (the least frequent one) relate well to the children's rates, there are important differences between the mothers and the children for the suffixes *–(nu)ntey* and *–ney*: While the mothers use the two suffixes with comparable rates, the children produce *–(nu)ntey* far more frequently than *–ney*, thus acquiring it earlier. Consequently, input frequency explains acquisition order only partially (Lieven 2010).

The earlier acquisition of *–(nu)ntey* can be explained by a discourse-pragmatic factor, one that relates to the ability to use language appropriately in a social context for more efficient communication. This suffix is a valuable linguistic device for exchanging differential views between conversational partners. Along with the prominent use of *–ci* that is already in place, appropriate use of *–(nu)ntey* helps children build common knowledge with their caregivers. Furthermore, this process enhances the bond between mother and child.

As has been argued, the particular order of acquisition of SE suffixes has a cognitive component as well. Korean children acquire SE suffixes first to express their own knowledge status (*–ta* for newly perceived information vs. *–e* for old/established information) and subsequently to incorporate the listener's knowledge status. Talking about information that relates to the child's own knowledge status should be cognitively less demanding than relating to the listener's (cf. Piaget 1955). Later, when children are cognitively able to take the listener's perspective into account, they acquire the marker that agrees with the listener's knowledge (*–ci*) before the one that conflicts with it (*–(nu)ntey*). For young children, agreement should be cognitively easier to process than disagreement, because the latter implicates an alternative viewpoint.

Although children learn impressively many SE suffixes within four years, they are far from having mastered the entire system of SE suffixes in colloquial Korean. The present data show that at 4;0 the two children still lack markers expressing inference, such as *–ney* and *–kwuna*, in their productive repertoire. While one can explain the scarcity of *–kwuna* in the children's speech by the correspondingly infrequent use of the suffix in the mothers' input, one cannot do so to account for the children's infrequent production of *–ney*: The mothers in the present data produce *–ney* 16%–20% of the time (compared to children's production of 4%–7%) (compare Table 4 to Table 3).

One possible explanation is that the inferential function of *–ney* (and *–kwuna*) is cognitively difficult for children to fully acquire by 4;0 since making an inference requires a mental operation beyond what is directly perceivable in the here-and-now, e.g., thinking about a probable cause or consequence of the current situation (cf. examples 14 and 15 above). However, it is interesting to note that Aksu-Koç (1988) reports an early acquisition of the inference marker *–mIş/(–y)mIş*, in Turkish children (example 28). Similar to Korean, Turkish is an SOV language marking epistemicity and evidentiality at the end of a sentence by a verbal suffix. Aksu-Koç (1988) reports that Turkish children start expressing inference by the marker *–mIş/(–y)mIş* from around 2;2, which is much earlier than the onset age for Korean children.

(28) Turkish
CHILD, 2;6 (from Aksu-Koç 1988: 98)
(Experimenter shows a toy's legs to Child)
EXP: *Bunun ayakları nasıl?*
       'How are the feet of this one?'
CHI: *Bu-nun   ayak-lar-ı.*
       this-GEN   foot-PL-POSS
       'This one's feet.'
       Kır-mış-lar.
       break-mIs-3PL
       'They broke it (evidently).'

A possible explanation for this crosslinguistic difference may have to do, at least in part, with degrees of input frequency and multi-functionality of the markers. In Turkish, the form *–mIş/(–y)mIş* is frequent in the input because it is a past tense marker and has a number of functions including past tense, reported speech/story-telling function, and inference. It is possible that once the form is in place in the children's inventory carrying a given function, it will facilitate children's acquisition of additional functions of the form. In contrast, the inference markers *–ney/–kwuna* in Korean occur much less frequently in the mothers' input during the early years and also their function is more restricted and cognitively complex, namely inference or the cognitive conclusions that the speaker can draw from the currently observable state (Ha 2016).

Last but not least, in the present study it was found that structural resonance plays an important role in facilitating the acquisition of SE suffixes. Thus, *–ci* and *–(nu)ntey* have a much higher degree of structural resonance in mothers' input than any other suffixes. That is, when mothers use the two suffixes, the core proposition tends to be either a partial or full repetition of a prior utterance. For language learners, such resonance will simplify their task of learning new linguistic materials embedded in a sentence (Lieven, Samolo, and Tomasello 2009; Pine et al. 2008): Once children have become familiar with the core structure of an utterance, they can focus their learning efforts on its variable elements such as SE suffixes. Thus, the higher the degree of structural resonance for a SE suffix, the faster children can learn its meaning.

In conclusion, starting from the one-word stage, Korean children acquire a number of SE suffixes in a particular order, using them in socially appropriate ways with almost no errors. By four years of age, they produce at least seven different suffixes, each with distinct epistemic/evidential or other types of modal functions: Children distinguish between new and old knowledge, degree of certainty which derives from shared information with the listener, source of information, and degree to which they agree or disagree with the listener's assessment of the situation. As they acquire these functions, they become progressively more competent conversational partners. In this paper, possible mechanisms for the particular developmental pattern observed have been investigated: The results have shown that the early-acquired suffixes relate to children's sensitivity to discourse-pragmatic functions, input frequency, and degree of structural resonance in the mothers' speech. The order of acquisition is also in line with general cognitive factors. Future research should examine further development of SE suffixes to discover how Korean children acquire SE suffixes marking inference.

Acknowledgement: I sincerely thank Professor Hyunjin Lee and the mothers of the children for generously allowing me to use the database (JW and SH) for research purposes.

References

Aksu-Koç, Ayhan. 1988. *The acquisition of aspect and modality: The case of past reference in Turkish.* Cambridge: Cambridge University Press.

Aksu-Koç, Ayhan, Hale Ögel-Balaban & I. Ercan Alp. 2009. Evidentials and source knowledge in Turkish. In Svenka Fitneva & Tomoko Matsui (eds.) *Evidentiality: A window into language and cognitive development* (New Directions for Child and Adolescent Development 125), 13–28. San Francisco: Jossey-Bass.

Ambridge, Ben & Elena V. M. Lieven. 2015. A constructivist account of child language acquisition. In Brian MacWhinney and William O'Grady (eds.), *The handbook of language emergence*, 479–510. Oxford: John Wiley & Sons.

Boye, Kasper. 2016. The expression of epistemic modality. In Jan Nuyts & Johan van der Auwera (eds.), *The Oxford handbook of modality and mood*, 117–140. Oxford: Oxford University Press.

Bybee, Joan. 2006. From usage to grammar: The mind's response to repetition. *Language* 82. 711–733.

Chafe, Wallace & Johanna Nichols (eds.). 1986. *Evidentiality: The linguistic coding of epistemology.* Norwood, NJ: Ablex.

Choi, Hyun-Bae. 1929. *Uli malpon* [Our Grammar] (6th edition, 1977). Seoul: Chongum Publication.

Choi, Soonja. 1991. Early acquisition of epistemic meanings in Korean: A study of sentence-ending suffixes in the spontaneous speech of three children. *First Language* 11. 93–119.

Choi, Soonja. 1995. Early acquisition of epistemic sentence-ending modal forms and functions in Korean children. In Joan Bybee & Suzanne Fleischman (eds.), *Modality in grammar and discourse*, 165–204. Amsterdam: John Benjamins.

Clancy, Patricia M. 2009. Dialogic priming and the acquisition of argument marking in Korean. In Jiansheng Guo, Elena Lieven, Nancy Budwig, Susan Ervin-Tripp, Kei Nakamura, & Şeyda Özçalişkan (eds.), *Crosslinguistic approaches to the psychology of language: Research in the tradition of Dan Isaac Slobin*, 105–117. New York: Psychology Press.

Du Bois, John. 2014. Towards a dialogic syntax. *Cognitive Linguistics* 25(3). 359–410.

Goodwin, Charles. 1981. *Conversational organization: Interaction between speakers and hearers.* New York: Academic Press.

Ha, Kyoungmi. 2016. Assessment sequences in Korean conversation: A corpus analysis of the sentence-ending suffix *–ney.* Unpubl. manuscript. University of California Los Angeles.

Kim, Young-joo. 1997. The acquisition of Korean. In D. I. Slobin (ed.), *The crosslinguistic study of language acquisition*, vol. 4, 335–443. Mahwah, NJ: Lawrence Erlbaum Associates.

Köymen, Bahar & Amy Kyratzis. 2014. Dialogic syntax and complement constructions in toddlers' peer interactions. *Cognitive Linguistics* 25(3). 497–521.

Lee, Hansol H. B. 1989. *Korean grammar.* Oxford: Oxford University Press.

Lee, Hyo Sang. 1991. *Tense, aspect, and modality: A discourse-pragmatic analysis of verbal affixes in Korean from a typological perspective.* Los Angeles, CA: University of California Los Angeles dissertation.

Lee, Hyo Sang. 1999. A discourse-pragmatic analysis of the committal *–ci* in Korean: A synthetic approach to the form-meaning relation. *Journal of Pragmatics* 31. 243–275.

Lee, Kee-Dong. 1993. *A Korean grammar on semantic-pragmatic principles.* Seoul: Hankuk Munhwasa.

Lieven, Elena. 2010. Input and first language acquisition: Evaluating the role of frequency. *Lingua* 120. 2546–2556.

Lieven, Elena, Dorothé Salomo & Michael Tomasello. 2009. Two year-old children's production of multiword utterances: A usage-based analysis. *Cognitive Linguistics* 20(3). 481–507.

Nuyts, Jan. 2006. Modality: Overview and linguistic issues. In William Frawley (ed.) *The expression of modality*, 1–26. Berlin and New York: Mouton de Gruyter.

Park, Yong-Yae. 1999. The Korean connective *nuntey* in conversational discourse. *Journal of Pragmatics* 31. 191–218.

Piaget, Jean. 1955. *The language and thought of the child*. New York: Meridian Books.

Pine, Julian, Gina Conti-Ramsden, Kate Joseph, Elena Lieven & Ludovica Serratrice. 2008. Tense over time: Testing the agreement/tense omission model as an account of the pattern of tense-marking provision in early child English. *Journal of Child Language* 35. 55–75.

Sacks, Harvey, Emanuel A. Schegloff & Gail Jefferson. 1974. A simplest systematics for the organization of turn-taking in conversation. *Language* 50. 696–735.

Strauss, Susan. 2005. Cognitive realization markers in Korean: A discourse-pragmatic study of the sentence-ending particles *–kwun, –ney* and *–tela*. *Language Sciences* 27(4). 437–480.

Barbara Pfeiler and Alejandro Curiel
The acquisition of evidentiality in two Mayan languages, Yukatek and Tojolabal

Abstract: Most Mayan languages have rather robust evidential systems for expressing up to four semantic contrasts: non-specified source of information, reported evidence, quotations, and information inferred through the senses. Evidentials are not only used for expressing the source of information but for a number of metapragmatic uses such as the marking of narrative speech-genres, the expression of vividness, or the indexicals of narrative climaxes. Both Tojolabal and Yukatek use morphological, syntactic, and lexical devices for expressing these meanings. This study investigates the acquisition of the grammatical means for expressing quoted and reported information in Yukatek and Tojolabal. Spontaneous longitudinal data of two Yukatek children between 1;1 and 3;3 and cross-sectional data of six Tojolabal children between 2;0 and 3;7 as well as four schoolchildren between 5;6 and 11;1 have been analyzed. Despite the fact that reportatives and quotatives are quite generally used in adult speech of both Mayan languages, our study shows a scarce use of these evidentials in child-directed speech and child speech. While in child-directed speech quotatives particularly serve to prompt children's utterances, reportatives occur in settings related with orders, wishes, or commitments presented from the perspective of another party. Our data show that Mayan children learn to mark source of information from an early age on. They first systematically produce quotatives. Reportatives emerge later than quotatives in both languages. The fact that evidentials are grammaticized in Mayan and their usage as prompts by caretakers facilitate their acquisition.

1 Introduction

In his description of Kwakiutl, Franz Boas (1947) proposed the existence of a category for specifying the source of information and labeled it evidentiality. Although Boas' finding caught the attention of Jakobson (1957), the category did not receive consistent consideration. Some theoretical approaches have proposed

Barbara Pfeiler, Universidad Nacional Autónoma de México
Alejandro Curiel, Vienna, Austria

that evidentiality is a subphenomenon of modality (Palmer 2001; Plungian 2001; Portner 2009). However, cross-linguistic evidence has led to refutation of this view (Givón 1982; Mithun 1986; Chafe and Nichols 1986; Dendale and Tasmowski 2001; Aikhenvald 2004). Since evidentials in Mayan form a semantically and lexically independent category which is clearly distinguished from modals, we take the latter view.

The acquisition of evidentials has been studied both in terms of cognitive and linguistic aspects (Keenan 1977; Wimmer and Hogrefe 1988; Papafragou and Li 2002; Papafragou and Ozturk 2007; Papafragou et al. 2007; Peterson 2010). Studies in a number of languages such as Bulgarian (Fitneva 2008), Korean (Choi 1991, 1995; Papafragou and Ozturk 2007; Ozturk and Papafragou 2016), Tibetan (de Villiers et al. 2009), and Turkish (Aksu-Koç and Slobin 1986; Aksu-Koç, Ögel-Balaban and Alp 2009) have revealed information about the emergence and mastery of the different semantic and pragmatic functions that are covered by the category of evidentials. The present study is the first of its kind on Mayan languages.

In this paper we study the acquisition and use of two evidential contrasts, reports and quotations, in Yukatek and Tojolabal. The chapter is organized as follows: After a presentation of the most salient grammatical features of Yukatek and Tojolabal, with special emphasis on the grammar of evidentials, the Yukatek corpus consisting of the data of two Yukatek children and their input and the Tojolabal corpus consisting of the data of eight children are presented and analyzed. The input not only contains child-directed speech (henceforth CDS), but also speech among adults. Following the analysis of the Yukatek data we turn to Tojolabal child speech (henceforth CS). Subsequently, our findings on narrative data collected from schoolchildren are presented, discussing the relevance of evidentials in the grammatical and rhetorical structures of Tojolabal. In a final section, our results are summarized and the data of early acquisition in both Mayan languages are compared with the acquisition of the evidential category in other languages.

2 The expression of evidentiality in Yukatek and Tojolabal

Yukatek and Tojolabal are two Mayan languages of southeastern Mexico. Yukatek is spoken by more than 800,000 inhabitants of Yucatan, Quintana Roo and Campeche (INEGI 2010) while Tojolabal is spoken by about 50,000 inhabitants (INALI 2014) in the east of Chiapas.

Whereas Yukatek belongs to the Yukatekan branch of the Mayan family (Kaufman 1972), the classification of Tojolabal is controversial. According to

Kaufman (1972), Tojolabal is a member of the Q'anjob'alan branch, although lexical, phonological, morphological, and syntactic evidence have led to several alternative proposals, namely that Tojolabal is a subsection of Tseltalan (Robertson 1977) or that it is a mixed language (Law 2014).

Yukatek and Tojolabal are strictly head-marking languages (Nichols 1986), i.e. both languages use ergative markers to cross-reference the subject of transitive verbs and nominal possessors. Tojolabal has a rigid ergative-absolutive alignment in which the argument of an intransitive verb and the object of a transitive verb are marked by the same morphological means, namely absolutive morphology, while the agent of a transitive verb is marked with an ergative prefix. Yukatek also holds ergative-absolutive alignment but has a nominative-accusative split in certain syntactic environments (Bricker 1981). The split is triggered by aspect and mood morphology (Bohnemeyer 2004). Both languages possess all features reported for predicate-initial languages (Dryer 2007).

Evidentials constitute a central part of Mayan grammar. As do a number of other Mayan languages, Yukatek (Lucy 1993a, 1993b; Hanks 1993; AnderBois 2014) and Tojolabal (Curiel 2018) express four evidential contrasts, namely non-specified source of information, reported speech, quoted information, and information inferred through the use of the senses. The functional category of Mayan evidentials can be coded lexically, morphologically, or syntactically. Unlike other languages, neither Yukatek nor Tojolabal encode multiple meanings in the same morpheme. An overview of the Yukatek and Tojolabal evidential systems is presented in Table 1.

Table 1: Evidential systems of Yukatek and Tojolabal.

Language	Reportative	Quotative	Sensorial
Yukatek	=b'in	k-	DEICTICS
Tojolabal	=b'i	chi'	[COMPLEMENT CLAUSE] + SENSORIAL VERB

Clauses with a non-specified source of information are unmarked for evidentiality in both Yukatek and Tojolabal as in examples (1a) and (1b).

(1) a. Yukatek (Dzul Poot and Pfeiler 2000: 22)
   Tumen   le=ka'ach   úuch=o'   mina'an   sak   bu'ul.
   because DET=formerly in.the.past=DEICT NEG.EXIST white bean
   'Since long ago there have not been any white beans.'

b. Tojolabal
Ja'xa ta=Moyses ja=jun bwelta il=i
TOPS CLF.M=Moyses DET=one turn DEM=TOP
wan=xa x-s-k'ux-a-Ø kan
INCOMPL=DISC INCOMPL-ERG.3-bite-TR-ABS.3 definitely
ja=y-ej-e'=i.
DET=POSS.3-mouth-3PL=TOP
'As for Moyses, they managed to bite their whole mouths already once.'

Clauses encoding hearsay information are usually marked with a reportative morpheme in both languages as in examples (2a) and (2b). This means that the information asserted in these sentences has not been attested by the speaker but was obtained from the report of someone else.

(2) a. Yukatek (Hanks 1990: 213)
Yan=b'in u=taal.
OBLIGATIVE=REPORT ERG.3=come
'He is to come. So it is said.'
b. Tojolabal
Kechan=b'i kan-Ø mot-an ja=s-nuk'=i.
only=REPORT stay-ABS.3 stuck-STAT DET=POSS.3-neck=TOP
'Her neck just got stuck. So it is said.'

A significant difference between the evidential systems of Yukatek and Tojolabal is the grammatical status of reportatives. While the Yukatek reportative =*b'in* is part of a small set of clitics which may occur at the end of any prosodic word (AnderBois 2017), the Tojolabal reportative =*b'i* is part of a set of second position clitics consisting of an inventory of six bound morphemes which obligatorily follow the first prosodic word in the sentence. The second position clitics in Tojolabal can form a clitic chain occupying up to three positions that occur immediately after the verbal auxiliary, as shown in Table 2. Since the members of a class contrast with each other, only one member of each class can occur in a second position clitic chain as in examples (3a) to (3d).

Table 2: Second position clitics in Tojolabal.

ADVERBS	EMPHATIC	EVIDENTIAL	MODALS
=xa 'already' DISCONTINUATIVE	=ni EMPHATIC	=b'i REPORTATIVE	=ma POLAR INTERROGATIVE
=to 'still' CONTINUATIVE			=k'a DUBITATIVE

(3) a. *Wan-Ø=to=ni=b'i*   *way-el.*
       PROG-ABS.3=still=EMPH=REPORT sleep-NFIN
       'Definitely, s/he is still sleeping. So it is said.'
     b. *El-an=b'i*   *ij-ito.*
       go.out-IMP.INTR=REPORT grand.child-DIM
       '"Go out, grandchild!" So it is said.'
     c. *La'=b'i*   *oj=xa*   *y-il-Ø-e.*
       DESIDERATIVE=REPORT IRR=DISC ERG.3-see-ABS.3-IRR.SG
       'He's longing to see him soon. So it is said.'
     d. *I'-aj-Ø=b'i*   *nan lima.*
       carry-TR-ABS.3=REPORT CLF.F lime
       'Take one lime. So it is said.'

In neither language can reportatives be inflected for person encoding the original speaker nor can they be accompanied by an oblique phrase encoding an addressee. This suggests that utterances marked by =b'in or =b'i do report hearsay but not the specific source from which the information has been obtained. Thus, in both languages, utterances marked by the reportative may only be attributed to the state of knowledge of the current speaker as in examples (2). They often occur immediately after the verbal auxiliary which expresses an obligation, a wish, or an assertion as in examples (2a) and (3c).

Quotatives are a metapragmatic[1] means for presenting others' discourse in Yukatek (Lucy 1993a, 1993b) as well as in Tojolabal (Curiel 2018). Like the third person form of a verb of saying implying the communicating subject, quotatives encode the reporter by pointing at that person as the source of information.

---

[1] Metapragmatics, a term introduced by Silverstein (1976), allows participants to describe how the effects and conditions of language use themselves are an object of discourse by allowing the participants to signal what is going on in an interaction. For further discussion, see Lucy (2004).

Quotatives are marked by different formal means in the two languages. In Yukatek the quotative stem *k-* inflects for the communicating subject, i.e. for person, and can be followed by a dative complement marking the recipient of the report, as shown in example (4a). Unlike standard verbs, the Yukatek quotative cannot bear tense, aspect, or mood marking. Quotatives cannot be questioned, negated, or adverbially modified in any way to qualify the reported utterance (Hanks 1990). They obligatorily follow the reported act of communication. Due to its restricted morphosyntactic properties the quotative has been described as a defective verb (Lehmann 2016), a grammatically intermediate form between a verbal element and a particle (Lucy 1993b), or a grammaticized 'parenthetical' quotative marker (AnderBois 2017).

In contrast to Yukatek, the Tojolabal quotative *chi'* 'say' is a fully inflected verb with some paradigmatic gaps in aspect marking (example 4b). For instance, *chi'* does not inflect for either progressive or perfective aspect.

(4) a. Yukatek (Lucy 1993b: 92)
     Tu'ux k-a=bin   k-en   t-i'.
     where INCOMPL-ERG.2=go QUOT-ABS.1 DAT-PRO.3
     '"Where are you going?", I said to him.'
  b. Tojolabal
     Pwes wa-kumpare   y-al-a-Ø
     well POSS.2-godfather ERG.3-say-TR-ABS.3
     ke=a'-Ø   y-i'
     COMP=give-ABS.3 POSS.3-DAT
     x-chi'-Ø.
     INCOMPL-QUOT-ABS.3
     'Well, your godfather said that... He said: "Do it!"'

In contrast with the regular verb of speaking "the quotative is especially suited to presenting the nonreferential pragmatic values of individual utterance tokens" (Lucy 1993b: 99). Quotatives do not only report speech but also screams, animal noises or even nonauditory communications such as someone's gesture or facial expression (Lucy 1993b: 92). Quoted speech is used in Yukatek conversation for a variety of purposes, such as correcting the speech of the interlocutor, putting words into the mouth of the interlocutor by attributing an utterance to her which she did not make but should have made, or poking fun at an addressee (Hanks 1990: 213). The quotative form *kih* 'says.he' can be used in combination with the reportative *=b'in* 'so it is said' as shown in example (5). In this example the reportative =b'in alludes to hearsay, the speech event projected by the quotative.

(5) Yukatek (Hanks 1990: 207)
    Yan   in=taal   k-ih=b'in.
    OBLIGATIVE ERG.1=come QUOT-ABS.3=REPORT
    '"I will come", he says. So it is said.'

Tojolabal quotatives form a closed class of verbs. Its only members are the intransitive verbs *chi'* 'say' and *chikan* 'quote' and the transitive *ut* 'say aloud'. These verbs obligatorily follow the quotation as shown in example (4b). Unlike Yukatek, quotatives in Tojolabal normally inflect not only for person but also for aspect. However, these verbs show some morphological idiosyncrasies: (a) unlike the rest of intransitive verbs, *chi'* and *chikan* do not take the intransitive vowel *-i*, (b) unlike other non-derived transitive verbs, *ut* 'say aloud' takes *-aj* as a transitive suffix rather than copying the stem vowel, (c) the intransitive *chi'* and *chikan* can only be inflected for imperfective aspect and irrealis mood, and (d) *ut* does not have a perfect form. Furthermore, quotatives do not occur with directional and aspectual adverbs. Similar to Yukatek, quotatives in Tojolabal may represent speech but also ideophones and gestures. They cannot be negated although they can be questioned.

In both Yukatek and Tojolabal, evidentials are not only used for expressing the source of information but also for marking narrative speech genres, the expression of vividness, or narrative climaxes through indexicals, etc. (Lucy 1993b; Hanks 1993; Curiel 2018). In the narrative speech genre, they are used for building a dialogical basis for the narration as well as for indexing linguistic competence (Curiel 2018).

The two languages mark inferences made by use of the senses in different ways. While Yukatek uses deictics for expressing such meanings as in example (6a), in Tojolabal inference is expressed by a fronted complement clause with one of the matrix verbs of perception *il* 'see' or *ab'i* 'feel' as in example (6b).

(6) a. Yukatek (Hanks 1990: 275)
    Piilar=e'   tu=pak'ach   héeb'e'.
    Pilar=TOP PROG.ERG.3=make.tortillas OSTEN.DEICT
    'Pilar is making tortillas. There! Listen!'

b. Tojolabal
[*ay-Ø   yal   loj-ito*]_{COMPLEMENT CLAUSE}
EXIST-ABS.3 DIM twin-DIM
wa   x-k-il-a-Ø-tik-on.
INCOMPL INCOMPL-ERG.1-see-TR-ABS.3-1PL-EXCL
'We realize visually that there are little twins.'

As far as language acquisition is concerned, we assume that quotatives may emerge earlier than reportatives because of their unambiguous function to "present speech as a replica which draws from some specific communicative event" (Lucy 1993b: 99) in contrast to reportatives which mark indirectly accessed information. Quotatives may also be acquired early due to their pragmatic function such as prompting routines found in CDS. Furthermore, we expect the fixed position of reportatives in Tojolabal clause structure in comparison to their variable position in Yukatek to facilitate the timing of acquisition.

3 The data

The Yukatek data for this study come from two children, the boy Armando (ARM) and the girl Sandi (SAN), who belong to the same extended family and live in the same plot of land. They were usually recorded twice a week, Armando from age 1;1 to 2;8 and his older cousin Sandi from 1;9 to 3;3 (Table 3). The households are monolingual with polydiadic interactions between mothers (MOT), grandmothers (GRA), aunts, and the children. The children were recorded while performing everyday activities. Both children were present in almost all the recordings.

Table 3: The Yukatek corpus.

ARMANDO		SANDI		CDS
Age	Number of utterances	Age	Number of utterances	Number of utterances
1;1	47	1;9	270	233
1;2	33	1;10	397	353
1;3	88	1;11	405	282
1;4	41	2;0	291	84
1;5	98	2;1	198	123
1;6	34	2;2	30	18
1;7	8	2;3	312	118

Table 3 (continued)

ARMANDO		SANDI		CDS
Age	Number of utterances	Age	Number of utterances	Number of utterances
1;8	253	2;4	167	364
1;9	160	2;5	288	297
1;10	160	2;6	59	182
1;11	121	2;8	233	136
2;0	153	2;9	92	170
2;1	290	2;10	160	292
2;2	272	2;11	148	266
2;3	150	3;0	262	211
2;4	212	3;0	286	196
2;5	361	3;1	116	167
2;6	320	–	–	186
2;7	347	3;3	401	186
2;8	187	3;4	326	192

Among the communicative events having been recorded there are the following: daily routines such as taking a bath, eating, sweeping the floor or feeding animals, but also looking at pictures, pretend play and playing with toys.

For the Tojolabal data (Table 4), the communicative interaction of eight children aged between 2;0 and 3;7 with an adult native speaker was video-recorded in the fall of 2014 in Buenavista Bahuitz, Chiapas, where Tojolabal is the first language. The recordings were made with the help of Bertha Sántiz, a native speaker of Tojolabal and relative to all of the children. In addition, four schoolchildren from San Miguel Chiptic, Altamirano, Chiapas, were recorded. The latter recordings mainly concern the production of 231 invented narratives in a competition game.

Table 4: The Tojolabal corpus.

Child	Age	Number of utterances
Deysi	2;0	137
Yuri	2;0	67
Mario	2;0	480
Daniel	2;6	249
Karla	2;10	267
Gleydi (twin sister of Karla)	2;10	781

Table 4 (continued)

Child	Age	Number of utterances
Brenda	3;4	888
Ana	3;7	1400
Citlalli	5;6	507
Moisés	9;0	635
Juan	9;3	620
Patricia	11;1	593

4 Evidentials in Yukatek child speech and child-directed speech

In this section we will analyze the use of quotatives and reportatives in Yukatek CDS as well as the children's speech. Contrary to colloquial adult speech, where reportatives and quotatives are frequently found, these evidentials only very scarcely occur in CDS. Since they do, however, constitute an important aspect of the acquisition of this language, we will first study their use in the input in order to prepare a proper usage-based background for focusing on their emergence and use in the children's speech. Evidentials found in adult speech directed to both children reach as much as 5 percent in relation to the total of utterances (201 tokens in 4,056 utterances). We assume that the relatively small amount of evidentials found in our CDS data may be attributed to the type of interaction between adults and small children. Mayan caregivers direct "more speech to upright babies who now understand and will obey some directives" (Gaskins 1996: 352). The input consists of directives above all, no stories or narratives are transmitted to the children. Furthermore, Mayan caregivers are not used to comment on or correct children's utterances (Gaskins 1996; Pfeiler 2012). Analogously to what is found in CDS, the children's use of evidentials is also scarce. Thus, only 0.5% of Armando's utterances ($N = 3,335$) contain an evidential marker and 1% of Sandi's ($N = 4,441$).

4.1 Usage of evidentials in the Yukatek input

Adults use quotatives for presenting others' discourse but also as a device for prompting children to communicate, for controlling their behavior, and socializing them in culturally appropriate ways (Pfeiler 2007). The form *k-ech* 'you should say' serves the purpose of making children talk in a communicatively appropriate way. In example (7), Armando's grandmother shows the boy how to answer her question by using this prompt. The form *k-ech-ti'* 'you should say to her/him' is used for prompting children to direct themselves to a third conversational participant. In example (8) Sandi's mother tells her daughter to let her cat know about its food.

(7) Armando, 1;8.7
GRA: *Kux   túun   a=mama'?*
     what.about so.then POSS.2=mom
     'What about your mom?'
GRA: *Tuy=ichkil   k-ech!*
     PROG.ERG.3=bath QUOT-ABS.2
     '"She is taking a bath", you should say.'
ARM: *Ichki.* (for: *tuy=ichkil*)
                     PROG.ERG.3=bath
     'She is taking a bath.'

(8) Sandi, 2;3.8
MOT: *Aw=ooch   k-ech-t-i'!*
     POSS.2=food QUOT-ABS.2-DAT-PRO.3
     '"Your food", say to him!'
SAN: (*aw=*)   *Oochmiix je'ela'.*
     (your=) food cat   DEM
     'Cat, here is (your) food.'

Prompts are used by caregivers especially at earlier ages. There is evidence that both children understand prompts before using them themselves since they respond to the prompted utterances with partial success (omitting part of the verb phrase) but never (inadequately) by repeating the quotatives occurring in the adult's utterance (see examples 7 and 8).

Though Mayan caregivers usually do not correct children's utterances (Gaskins 1996; Pfeiler 2012), Sandi's mother uses the form *kih* 'he.says' to reformulate her daughter's utterance as shown in example (9). This will at the same time facilitate the interpretation of child speech by other listeners such as the interviewer.

(9) Sandi, 1;9.27
    SAN: *Mari waye'.*
            Mari here
            'Mari, here!'
    MOT: *Mari ko'oten waye' k-ih.*
            Mari come here QUOT-ABS.3
            '"Mari, come here!", she says.'

In adult speech, the quotation marker *kih* is also used with ideophones (example 10). Furthermore, quotations are usually performed with due observance of the gestures accompanying the sentence quoted.

(10) Sandi's CDS, 1;10.17
    MOT: *Sandi ko'oten aw=il mehen miis.*
            Sandi come.IMP ERG.2=see small cat
            'Sandi, come to see the kitty!'
    GRA: *Miau k-ih.*
            meow QUOT-ABS.3
            '"Meow", she says.'

In contrast to the quotative *kih*, which is particularly used for making children attend to specific objects or activities, the reportative *=b'in* 'so it is said' occurs in speech acts reporting wishes or commands as if they were issued by a third party. Thus, in example (11), when Armando refers to a whining pig in the yard, his aunt uses this reportative indexing information about what the reporter (the aunt) wants to happen or to have happened.

(11) Armando, 2;0.12
    ARM: *Chéech k'eni'* (for: *chéech k'éek'en=i'*).
            whining pig=LOC
            'The whining pig there.'
    AUNT: *Le=k'éek'en=o' tséen-t-Ø=b'in.*
            DET=pig=DEIC feed-TR-IMP=REPORT
            '"Feed the pig!", so it is said.'

Reportatives and quotatives can be used together in the same utterance. In example (12), Sandi's aunt, by reproducing the girl's inaccurate utterance, presents its nonreferential pragmatic value and, by adding the reportative particle *=b'in*, she alludes to the speech event projected by the quotative.

(12) Sandi, 1;10.17
 MOT: *Ba'ax t-a=ts'íib-t-ah beya' hm?*
    what PFV-ERG.2=write-TR-COMPL like.this hm
    'What did you write like this, hm?'
 SAN: *Chíi* (for: *ts'íib*).
        writing
 AUNT: *Ah chíi k-ih=b'in.*
    ah writing QUOT-ABS.3=REPORT
    '"Ah. Writing", she says. So it is said.'

Reportatives are more frequent than quotatives in the speech of the children's caregivers. There are some individual differences to be observed among them, however. While Sandi's mother is more concerned with quoting, reformulating and interpreting her daughter's unclear utterances, using *k-ih* and *=b'in* across the entire period of observation, Armando's mother and grandmother more often use *=b'in*, but they only sporadically reproduce Armando's utterances using the quotative *k-ih*. While reportatives occurring in CDS primarily serve to render commands and wishes given by a third party, quotatives are mainly used to explain to the researcher what the child tried to say with his either inaccurate pronounciation or incomplete utterances.

4.2 Evidentials in Yukatek child speech

As mentioned above, evidentials are scarcely observed in the child data. Tokens are summarized in Table 5.

Table 5: Frequency of reportatives and quotatives in Yukatek child speech (tokens).

ARMANDO			SANDI		
Age	Quotative *k-ih*	Reportative *=b'in*	Age	Quotative *k-ih*	Reportative *=b'in*
2,0	2	0	2;1	1	0
2;1	2	0	2;5	1	3
2;3	0	3	2;9	1	1
2;4	2	0	2;10	9	3
2;5	2	1	2;11	1	7
2;6	4	0	3;0	4	4
2;8	1	0	3;1	0	1
			3;3	2	8
Total	13	4		19	27

Armando's little use of evidentials must be attributed to his young age. Although his recordings start at 1;1, evidentials begin to occur only at age 2;0. Most of them correspond to the quotative *k-ih* and only a few of them to the reportative *=b'in*. No prompts were registered in Armando's speech.

All but one example of the quotative *k-ih* in Armando's speech refer to quotations of an aforementioned utterance (example 13).

(13) Armando, 2;4.2
 INT: *Tu'ux yaan?*
 where EXIST
 'Where is it (the duck)?'
 SAN: *Sáat-Ø-ih.*
 get.lost-COMPL-ABS.3
 'It got lost.'
 MOT: *Sáat-Ø-ih?*
 get.lost-COMPL-ABS.3
 'It got lost?'
 ARM: *Hm, sáat-Ø-ih k-ih.*
 yes get.lost-COMPL-ABS.3 QUOT-ABS.3
 '"Yes, it got lost", she says.'
 MOT: *Sáat-Ø-ih k-ih.*
 get.lost-COMPL-ABS.3 QUOT-ABS.3
 '"It got lost", she says.'

From 2;10 on, Sandi behaves like an adult towards Armando and uses reportatives in the same way as her caretakers. In example (14) Armando and Sandi are playing with a toy bear called Osina. After Armando has fallen down, Sandi is making fun using *=b'in* to pretend that it was Osina that threw Armando down.

(14) Sandi, 2;9.24
 INT: *Máax lúub-s-ech?*
 who fall-CAUS-ABS.2
 'Who threw you down?'
 SAN: *Oxina=b'in Oxina=b'in.*
 Oxina=REPORT Oxina=REPORT
 'It was Osina. So it is said. It was Osina. So it is said.'
 SAN: *U=meen-t-ik-ubah il-eh.*
 ERG.3=make-TR-INCOMPL-REFL.3 look-IMP
 'He is pretending, look!'

SAN: *Láat'-eh   láat'-eh.*
      Raise.up-IMP   raise.up-IMP
      'Raise him up! Raise him up!'

In the same recording Sandi uses the quotative *k-ih* to either repeat Armando's whole utterances or individual words when both children are playing with toys as in example (15). After a mere repetition of the boy's incorrect pronounciation of the verb *taas* 'bring' the girl adds the quotative particle and the addressee of the boy's request.

(15) Sandi, 2;9.24 and Armando, 2;1.7
  ARM: *Taxeh, taxeh, taxeh.* (for: *taas-eh*)
                                     bring-IMP
       'Bring it, bring it, bring it!'
  SAN: *Tax-eh!*
       bring-IMP
       'Bring it!'
  SAN: *Tax-eh   k-ih-t-een.*
       bring-IMP   QUOT-ABS.3-DAT-PRO.1SG
       '"Bring it!", he says to me.'

In example (16), Sandi does not want to drink atole (a hot drink) and pretends being ill, using the reportative. Her mother takes up the argument and pretends to send Sandi to the doctor.

(16) Sandi, 2;11.6
  SAN: *Ma' inw=uk'-ik.*
       NEG ERG.1=drink-INCOMPL
       'I don't drink it.'
  SAN: *K'oha'an-en=b'in.*
       ill-ABS.1=REPORT
       'I'm ill. So it is said.'
  MOT: *K'oha'an-ech?*
       ill-ABS.2
       'Are you ill?'

Prompts addressed to younger children and even pets are found only in Sandi's data, starting from age 2;8. The girl uses the prompt *k-ech(-ti')* spontaneously for encouraging her little brother and younger cousin to talk as in example (17). It is remarkable that Sandi never addresses this kind of request to adults but only to her peers.

(17) Sandi, 3;0.17
SAN: *Días   k-ech-t-een.*
Morning   QUOT-ABS.2-DAT-PRO.1.SG
'"(Good) morning!", you should say to me!'

A comparison between the children's data during the overlapping period from 2;0 to 2;8 indicates that both children use few evidential forms. There are not sufficient data in Armando's corpus to attest their full acquisition because observation stopped at 2;9 while Sandi's continued through 3;3. Although her data are also scarce, Sandi distinguished between reportative and quotative evidentials and, from about 2;11 on, used quotatives as prompts as well.

Sandi distinguishes the different linguistic forms as indicators of informational perspectives and metapragmatic awareness, suggesting competence in source marking at age 3;0. Her use of the reportative from age 2;10 on is close to that observed in her input, which usually serves to comment on the child's utterances helping the interviewer or other caretakers to find their possible meaning.

5 Evidentials in Tojolabal child-directed and child speech

In this section we will explore the acquisition of the Tojolabal reportative second position clitic *=b'i* and the quotative predicate *chi'*. Since the Tojolobal data are cross-sectional, it is not possible to present token frequencies and percentages for quotatives and reportatives in child-directed speech. Their use will instead be illustrated with examples. By comparing our cross-sectional data on preschool children with those on schoolchildren we hope to be able to trace the development of evidentials in Tojolabal from early childhood to the schoolyears.

5.1 Evidentials in Tojolabal child-directed speech

In contrast to Yukatek CDS, the quotative *chi'* is widely used in Tojolabal CDS. However, reportatives occur considerably less frequently in spontaneous speech than in narratives (Curiel 2018). In example (18) a Tojolabal mother uses the reportative *=b'i* for coding information based on hearsay.

(18) Mother to Ana, 3;7
    Ja'=b'i   wan-Ø   s-job'-j-el
    FOC=REPORT PROG-ABS.3   POSS.3-ask-PASS-NFIN
    ja=s-b'i'il   ja=wa-wats=i.
    DET=POSS.3-name   DET=POSS.2-elder.sibling=TOP
    'What she is asking for is the name of your elder sister. So it is said.'

Similar to Yukatek, quotatives in Tojolabal CDS are not restricted to their evidential meaning but are also used as a device for prompting the child to talk, as shown by (19). The example is a clear illustration of a Tojolabal mother reformulating her child's unclear expression by using the quotative verb *chi'* after five unsuccessful attempts by the child.

(19) Ana, 3;7
    Ana: *Majkule?* (for: *ma'   s-k'ul-an-Ø?*)
                              who   ERG.3-do-TR-ABS.3
            Majkulo?
            Majkulu?
            Ma'ojkulu'?
            'Who did it?'
    Bertha: *Ja'sa?*
            'What?'
    Ana: *Maj   kulu?* (for: *ma'   s-k'ul-an-Ø?*)
                                 who   ERG.3-do-TR-ABS.3
            'Who did it?'
    MOT: *Ma'   s-k'ul-an-Ø*
            who   ERG.3-make-TR-ABS.3
            x-chi'-Ø?
            INCOMPL-QUOT-ABS.3
            '"Who did it?", she says.'

When her little daughter starts screaming because she has been unintentionally kicked by one of her elder sisters while crawling on the kitchen floor, the mother verbalizes the child's reaction by an utterance marked by the quotative *chi'* as in example (20).

(20) Rosa Luz, 0;6
    (The child is screaming)
    MOT: *Mok   wa-b'at-Ø   k-i'*
           NEG.IMP   ERG.2-step-ABS.3   POSS.1-DAT

> *j-k'ab'* *x-chi'-Ø.*
> POSS.1-hand INCOMPL-QUOT-ABS.3
> '"Do not step on my hand!", she says.'

Tojolabal caretakers also use quotatives very frequently for framing sentences to be used by their children. In (21), a Tojolabal mother presents her child a sentence marked by a quotative inflected for the imperative.

(21) Yuri, 2;0
    Bertha: *Jasu wa x-a-k'ul-an-Ø*
            what INCOMPL INCOMPL-ERG.2-make-TR-ABS.3
            wa'xa?
            long.ago
            'What did you do long ago?'
    Yuri: [babbling]
    Bertha: *Ja'?*
            'What?'
    MOT: *j-lo'-o-Ø ko'san*
          ERG.1-eat.something.soft-TR-ABS.3 chayote.tuber
          chi'-an.
          QUOT-IMP.INTR
          '"I ate chayote tuber. Say so."'
    Yuri: *Kox [//] koxan.*
          'Cha [//] chayote tuber.'

5.2 Evidentials in early Tojolabal child speech

The tokens of the quotative *chi'* and the reportative *=b'i* or both together occurring in Tojolabal child speech are summarized in Table 6.

The frequency of quotatives and reportatives in CDS seems to lead children to use them successfully as early as age 2;10. In example (22), Gleydi prompts her twin sister Karla to ask the interviewer Bertha to bring them a TV set on her next visit. The quotative is correctly inflected for the imperative and follows the quoted material. There are no examples in our Tojolabal child data with quotatives wrongly placed.

Table 6: Frequency of the quotative *chi'* and the reportative =*b'i* in Tojolabal child speech (tokens).

Child	Age	chi'	=b'i	chi'=b'i
Deysi	2;0	0	0	0
Yuri	2;0	0	0	0
Mario	2;0	1	0	0
Daniel	2;6	2	0	1
Karla	2;10	0	0	0
Gleydi (twin sister of Karla)	2;10	1	4	0
Brenda	3;4	8	0	0
Ana	3;7	3	0	1

(22) Gleydi, 2;10
I' jan jun tele, chi'-an.
(for: i'-aj-Ø jan
carry-TR-ABS.3 DIREC.towards.speaker
k-i'-tik-on jun j-tele-tik-on.)
POSS.1-DAT-1PL-EXCL one POSS.1-TV.set-1PL-EXCL
'"Bring us a TV set!", you should say.'

By age 3;7, Tojolabal children seem to have also grasped the adult use of quotatives as grammatical devices for indexing source of information (example 23).

(23) Ana, 3;7
Bertha: Jas x-chi'-Ø wa-tat=i?
what INCOMPL-QUOT-ABS.3 POSS.2-father=TOP
'What does your father say?'
Ana: Jex a'pani! (for: jel x-ajb'an-i-Ø).
INTENS INCOMPL-be.tasty-INTR-ABS.3
Mta, mta, oj k-u'-Ø t'un-uk
yum yum IRR ERG.1-drink-ABS.3 a.little-IRR
a=it=i x-chi'-Ø.
DET=DEM=TOP INCOMPL-QUOT-ABS.3
'"It's delicious! Yum, yum, I'll drink a little of this.", so he said.'

However, examples like (24) suggest that, in spite of the fact that the core function of quotatives (i.e. marking the source of information) occurs early in

Tojolabal child speech, their entire set of metapragmatic functions develops only slowly. In this example, which is the earliest token of self-quotations in our data, Brenda quotes herself telling what she dreamt the night before. Self-quotations in Tojolabal are a sophisticated rhetorical device used not only for framing a quotation but also for lending liveliness to both narratives and conversations. Since narrations are constructed dialogically in Tojolabal (Brody 1986), the caretaker Bertha responds to the child's last utterance by framing it with the quotative *chi'*. It is noteworthy that neither this child nor any other seem to have any problems with the verbal inflection of the quotative. Also, Tojolabal children seem to be aware of the morphological and syntactic idiosyncrasies of these verbs, such as gaps in verbal inflection (Curiel 2018).

(24) Brenda, 3;4
    Brenda: *Waj-y-on   b'a   nana   Rapa.*
                go-INTR-ABS.1 PREP elder.woman Rapa
                'I went to auntie Rapa.'
    Bertha: *Waj-y-a?*
                go-INTR-ABS.2
                'Did you?'
    Brenda: *A'ja.*
                INTERJECTION
                'Yep!'
    Bertha: *Jas   x-chi'-Ø   a=nana*
                what INCOMPL-QUOT-ABS.3 DET=elder.woman
                Rapa   wa   la-k'ot-i-Ø?
                Rapa INCOMPL INCOMPL.SAP-arrive.there-INTR-ABS.2
                'What did auntie Rapa say when you got there?'
    Brenda: *Ti   ay-a   la-chi'-y-on?*
                DEICT EXIST-ABS.2 INCOMPL.SAP-QUOT-EPEN-ABS.1
                '"Are you there?", I said.'
    Bertha: *Ti=ma   ay-a   nana*
                DEICT=Q EXIST EXIST-ABS.2SG elder.woman
                la-chi'-y-on.
                INCOMPL.SAP-QUOT-EPEN-ABS.1
                '"Are you there, auntie?", I said.'

As for the acquisition of the reportative =b'i, Tojolabal children appear to start using it later than the quotative chi'. Example (25) is our earliest record (see Table 6). In this example, Daniel uses the reportative after a quotative verb. It is important to point out that the use of both a quotative verb and a reportative does not signal that a quotation was obtained from someone else but is a sophisticated way of strengthening the illocutionary force of the quotation. This kind of metapragmatic use of quotations and reportatives is typical of adult speech. For further discussion see Curiel (2018).

(25) Daniel, 2;6
    Jas   *s-b'i'il-Ø*   *ja=men*   *Ber?*
    what   POSS.3-name-ABS.3   DET=CLF.F   Ber
    exchib'i (for: *x-chi'-Ø=b'i*).
                                INCOMPL-QUOT-ABS.3=REPORT
    '"What's Ber's name?", she said. So it is said.'

Reportatives in Tojolabal seem to be used later than the other second position clitics, such as the temporal adverbials =xa 'already' and =to 'still', and the emphatic =ni. Mario is the youngest child in the Tojolabal corpus using second position clitics. In his repertoire, there are examples with the emphatic =ni and the adverbials =xa and =to but not a single one with the reportative =b'i. Although Mario seems to be using the reportative (=pi instead of =b'i) in the reformulation of the interlocutor's utterance in example (26), he uses the distal enclitic =a in addition, which can only be triggered by the emphatic =ni.

(26) Mario, 2;6
    Bertha: *Ja=ta'*   Oli,   *wa*
                 DET=CLF.M   Oli   INCOMPL
                 x-tajni-Ø   *sok*   *a=Kike?*
                 INCOMPL-play-ABS.3   with   DET=Kike
                 wan=ni   *a=Oli?*
                 INCOMPL=EMPH   DET=Oli
                 'As for Oli, does Kike play with him? I mean with Oli?'
    Mario: *Mipi, mini'ay, mini'a.* (probably for: *mi=ni=a*)
                                                      NEG=EMPH=DIST
               'Not at all!'

5.3 The use of evidentials in narrative texts by Tojolabal schoolchildren

In this section, one of a collection of 231 micro-narrations belonging to the sub-genre *lom lo'il* ('vain discourse') performed by three Tojolabal children aged between 5;6 and 9;3 will be analyzed in order to achieve at least some preliminary results on the way Tojolabal-speaking schoolchildren use evidentials in narrative texts.

A *lom lo'il* narrative is a kind of verbal contest where several children try to show their rhetorical skills. First, one child tells a funny invented story about the other competitors. After that, another child retells the same story using a different, usually more sophisticated rhetorical apparatus. In this way, Tojolabal children may chain up as many as six texts in a *lom lo'il* competition. At the end of a chain, the best performer is chosen by the competitors together with the audience (see Curiel 2012).

The narrative chain analyzed here was produced by Juan (9;3), Moisés (9;0), and Citlalli (5;6). All children are native speakers of Tojolabal with a low level of competence in Spanish. They belong to the same extended family but live in two different domestic units and attend a monolingual Spanish primary school.[2] None of them can write or read Tojolabal.

The first narrative in the chain, performed by Juan (9;3), is presented in example (27). As in all Tojolabal narratives, the opening is a deictical frame (line 1) and the closing frame consists of the adverb *kechan* 'only' (line 5). In line 3, Juan creates a feeling of suspense by interrupting the narrative (line 3a) and using an epistemic marker, the dubitative proclitic *se=*, denoting that he was surprised by the event (line 3b). Juan does not use any evidentials in his story.

(27) Juan, 9;3 *Ja sb'ajtanil le'uj xolob'i* ('The first crab fishing')

1 *Ja'xa ta Moyses ja jun bwelta ili' wajtikon le'u xolob'.*   As for one time Moisés and I we went to look for crabs.
2 *Wajtikon le'u xolob'.*   We went to look for crabs.
3a *Ja'xa jawa' se. . .*   And then . . .!
3b *Se je. . .*   And then I really. . .!
3c *Se junta joko ko' yi' yanswelo'.*   I really threw his hook down.
4 *Wokolto el k'en a yanswelo'.*   It was very difficult for his hook to get out here.
5 *Kechan.*   Only.

---

2 It is to be noted that Spanish is taught by Tojolabal teachers with a poor knowledge of that language.

The second narrative (example 28) was performed by Moisés (9;0), who also framed his tale in the usual way (lines 1 and 4). Unlike Juan, Moisés makes use of the quotative *xchi'* in line (3c) for framing the direct speech occurring in lines (3a) and (3b). By quoting the voice of a protagonist, Moisés increases the vividness of his narrative and manages to introduce the last participant in the competition, Citlalli, into this chain. Moisés also uses the dubitative proclitic *se=* (line 2). According to our Tojolabal associates, dubitative proclitics *se(n)=* and *na'=* are grammatical devices related to vividness (Curiel 2018).

(28) Moisés, 9;0 *Ja xchab'il le'uj xolob'i* ('The second crab fishing')
1   *Ja'xa jun bwelta il a Sitlali'*   As for one time, Citlalli and I,
    wajtikon le'u xolob' chajkil.   we also went to look for crabs.
2   *Se waj ko' ja' ya yanswelo'!*   Her little hook went down
                                              to the water!
3a *'Tanik jan ki' wego ya kanswelo,*   'Give me my little hook fast!
3b *wa la'ok'yon ta mi xawa'wex ki'i',*   I will cry if you guys don't
3c *xchi a Sitlali'.*   give it to me.'
                                              That's what Citlalli said.
4   *Kechan.*   Only.

The last of the three texts constituting the *lom lo'il* was produced by Citlalli (5;6) and was the winning episode (example 29).

(29) Citlalli, 5;6 *Ja yoxil le'uj xolob'i* ('The third crab fishing')
1   *Ja'xa jun bwelta ta Moysesi' se se se*   As for one time, Moisés and I, we
    waj ka' eltikon k'en nan kandrejo'.   went to bring crabs down here.
2   *Nan kandrejo waj jle'tikon.*   Crabs is what we went to look
                                              for.
3   *Tixta b'a Kanyada, Moy?*   Was it in the Ravine, Moy?
4   *Tixta b'a Kanyada.*   Yes, it was in the Ravine.
5   *Jmjm.*   Hm.
6   *Jta'atikon jun niwan lek.*   We found a very big one.
7   *Ya' ka'l jun...*   He (i.e. Moisés) gave a little...
8a *Ja' s...*   What happened is that he...
8b *Ja' wa stu...*   What happened is that...
8c *Ojb'i...*   He was going to... So it is said.
8d *Ojb'i ya' k'e' k'en a...*   He was going to fish it off... So
8e *Ojb'i...*   it is said.

8f	Ja' stuch'unej k'en a sti' a nan kandrejo'.	He was going to... So it is said. What happened is that a female pinched his mouth.
9	Yajni ke jawa' el juts'ilita.	A little bit later.
10a	Teyxa b'a...	It was already in...
10b	Ja b'a b'a ixta k'ote.	On this side.
10c	Textani'a.	There it was.
11a	K'uxji yu.	It bit him.
11b	K'uxji a sk'ab'i'.	It bit his hand.
12a	Yajni ke jaw,	When that happened:
12b	"mamito mmmm."	"Mommy, mmm."
12c	xchi' a Moysesi'.	That's what Moisés said.
13	Kechan.	Only.

Citlalli's narrative is the most sophisticated one of the chain, not only structurally but also as far as the use of evidentials is concerned. The text is about three times the length of that of the other two competitors. Like her siblings, Citlalli frames her narrative by conventional phrases occurring at the beginning and the end (line 1, "as for one time"; line 13, "only"). It is interesting to note that the by far youngest narrator uses both Tojolabal evidentials in her retelling. In lines (8c–e), the source of information, namely Moisés' report, is marked by the reportative =b'i and in line (12c), a direct quotation constituting the climax of the story is framed by the quotative verb chi'. Citlalli's skilled use of evidentials in this text was judged by our Tojolabal adult consultants to be one of the reasons why the girl won the entire competition.

However, the fact that Citlalli was selected as the winner of this *lom lo'il* chain does not mean that she has reached full adult narrative competence. Five ill-formed sentences occur in her narrative (lines 7, 8a, 8b, 8c, 8e), something not found in the texts of her older competitors. In line 7, Citlalli utters an ungrammatical transitive clause in which the object position is occupied by an incomplete noun phrase consisting of the indefinite determiner *jun*. Lines (8a) to (8d) are infelicitous contractions. The utterances in lines (8a) and (8b) have a focus marker *ja'* and a 3rd person ergative prefix but do not have a predicate. Line (8b) contains the incompletive marker *wa* without an inflected verb. Lines (8c) and (8e) consist of an irrealis marker and the reportative enclitic without a verb. Although the verb occurring in line (8d) is fully inflected, the incomplete noun phrase *a* . . . shows that Citlalli was unable to finish her utterance. Also, Citlalli's way of interrupting her narrative by asking Moisés a question (line 3) is not typical of Tojolabal narrative texts.

A rich use of evidentials has been reported as a core part of the desired skills that a proficient narrator needs to have in other oral traditions such as Mexicano

(Briggs 1988), Wasco (Moore 1993), Yukatek (Hanks 1993), Mam (England 2009) as well as Tojolabal (Curiel 2018). The last story shows that children start using evidentials in narratives even at preschool age, suggesting a growing awareness of the high value attached to evidentials (Curiel 2018), which form a central part in Tojolabal grammar.

Although the texts analyzed in this section show that young schoolchildren are aware of the metapragmatics of evidentials used in narratives, it must be left to future research to trace the development of the complex functions of evidentials in Tojolabal language acquisition through the later school years.

6 Summary and discussion

In this chapter two methodological approaches have been applied for studying the acquisition of evidentials in Yukatek and Tojolabal. On the one hand, in a longitudinal study on Yukatek, the use of evidentials in the input has been compared to the speech of two children whose ages range from 1;1 to 3;3, and on the other, cross-sectional data of six Tojolabal children between 2;0 and 3;7 as well as three schoolchildren between 5;6 and 9;3 have been analyzed.

It has been shown that Yukatek and Tojolabal caretakers in interaction with children use quotatives and reportatives not only for expressing the source of information but also for metapragmatic purposes. Caretakers employ quotatives to guess at the meaning of children's utterances or for prompting them. Reportatives occurring in the caretakers' speech characterize indirect information, i.e. information obtained by hearsay. Both Yukatek and Tojolabal children are exposed to both types of evidentials in the input from early on.

Mayan children start using quotatives around age 2;0 in a fashion similar to the way they occur in CDS. Their status as predicates in sentence-final position as well as the fact that they retain person marking (see Section 2) may ease children's analysis. The fact that, in contrast to Yukatek, in Tojolabal quotatives are fully inflected verbs does not seem to provide any advantage with respect to the timing of acquisition since they emerge in both languages at the same age. An early emergence of grammatically coded evidentials has also been reported in Korean (Choi 1991; Rhoades-Ko 2013), Turkish (Aksu-Koç 1988; Aksu-Koç, Ögel-Balaban and Alp 2009) and Bulgarian (Fitneva 2018).

The fact that Mayan children start to use reportatives later than quotatives may be due to the cognitively more challenging character of the former. Speech events that have just taken place in the presence of the quoter are easier to process than reported information that cannot be attested by the speaker and is obtained from the report of someone else. By using a quotative the speaker points to the utterance of a specific person as the source of information, whereas a reportative often indicates a vaguer source of information, namely some undetermined person. Also, the explicit person marking with quotatives but not with reportatives may be a factor which leads to their early use. The fixed position of reportatives in Tojolabal clause structure in comparison to their variable position in Yukatek does not seem to influence the timing of acquisition.

The low frequency of evidentials in the input, the specific recording situation with an interviewer being present and the unusual practice of Yukatek caretakers to explain child speech resulting from these circumstances make it difficult to draw any conclusions about the effects of the input on children's development.

The cross-sectional data from Tojolabal confirm the early use of quotatives in spontaneous child speech. In addition to the data obtained by elicitation, the analysis of *lom lo'il*, a ludic narrative sub-genre performed exclusively by children, show that, at least from age 5;6 on, children use evidentials in the same way as adults would.

In spite of the fact that Mayan children use reportatives in their own utterances and respond efficiently to prompts framed by quotatives from early on, early child data of spontaneous speech cannot provide evidence for the acquisition of the full range of functions of the grammatical devices expressing evidentiality in Yukatek and Tojolabal since these only develop in the course of time. An additional reason is that, in Mayan, evidentials occur less frequently in spontaneous speech than in narratives (Lucy 1993a, 1993b; Curiel 2018).

Due to the low frequency of quotatives and reportatives in the children's early spontaneous speech the present analysis can only offer initial information on the emergence and gradual development of elements marking source of information in Yukatek, so that further studies of Yukatek language development beyond age 3;0 are needed. Since, in Tojolabal, evidentials occur considerably less frequently in spontaneous speech than in narratives, Tojolabal narratives were analyzed in order to show how children of different ages use quotatives and reportatives as markers of narrative speech genres, expressing vividness or indicating the climax. Our analysis has shown that Tojolabal children start to use evidentials as sophisticated devices closely related to the rhetoric structure of narrative genres from an early age (5;6). Although we do not have enough data to discuss the way in which Tojolabal children achieve full mastery of evidentials, the analysis of more than 200 narratives leads us to think that this might be happening quite early in contrast to Tibetan children (de Villiers et al. 2009), whose full mastery of the evidential system is achieved as late as 9;0. More research is clearly needed for crosslinguistic comparisons.

To summarize, the Mayan data suggest that the morphological and metapragmatic distinction between the forms of quotatives and reportatives plays a central role in the development of what may appear to be a cognitively rather challenging category such as evidentiality. Children succeed to distinguish between quotative and reportative marking due to their different forms, their distinct metapragmatic uses and the conceptualization of different types of speech events.

References

Aikhenvald, Alexandra. 2004. *Evidentiality*. Oxford: Oxford University Press.
Aksu-Koç, Ayhan. 1988. *The acquisition of aspect and modality: The case of past reference in Turkish*. Cambridge: Cambridge University Press.
Aksu-Koç, Ayhan, Hale Ögel-Balaban & I. Ercan Alp. 2009. Evidentials and source knowledge in Turkish. In Stanka A. Fitneva & Tomoko Matsui (eds.), *Evidentiality: A window into language and cognitive development* (New directions in child and adolescent development 125), 13–28. San Francisco: Jossey Bass.
Aksu-Koç, Ayhan & Dan I. Slobin. 1986. A psychological account of the development and use of evidentials in Turkish. In Wallace Chafe & Johanna Nichols (eds.), *Evidentiality: The linguistic coding of epistemology*, 159–167. Norwood, New Jersey: Ablex.
AnderBois, Scott. 2014. On the exceptional status of reportative evidentials. *Proceedings of Semantics and Linguistic Theory* 24. 234–254.
AnderBois, Scott. 2017. An illocutionary account of reportative evidentials in imperatives. Paper presented at the 27th Meeting of Semantics and Linguistic Theory. The University of Maryland, 12–14 May, 2017.
Boas, Franz, 1947. Kwakiutl grammar, with a glossary of the suffixes. *Transactions of the American Philosophical Society* 37. 201–377.
Bohnemeyer, Jürgen. 2004. Split intransitivity, linking, and lexical representation: The case of Yukatek Maya. *Linguistics* 42(1). 67–107.
Bricker, Victoria R. 1981. The source of the ergative split in Yucatec Maya. *Journal of Mayan Linguistics* 2. 83–127.
Briggs, Charls. 1988. *Competence in performance: The creativity of tradition in Mexicano verbal art*. Philadephia: University of Pennsylvania Press.
Brody, Jill. 1986. Repetition as a rhetorical and conversational device in Tojolabal (Mayan). *International Journal of American Linguistics* 52(3). 255–274.
Chafe, Wallace & Nichols, Johanna (eds.). 1986. *Evidentiality: The linguistic coding of evidentiality*. Norwood, New Jersey: Ablex.
Choi, Soonja. 1991. Early acquisition of epistemic meanings in Korean: A study of sentence-ending suffixes in the spontaneous speech of three children. *First Language* 11. 93–119.
Choi, Soonja. 1995. The development of epistemic sentence-ending modal forms and functions in Korean children. In Joan Bybee & Suzanne Fleischman (eds.), *Modality in grammar and discourse*, 165–204. Amsterdam: John Benjamins.
Curiel, Alejandro. 2012. Contar mentiras para aprender a decir la verdad. El *lom lo'il*, un género de habla infantil en maya Tojol-ab'al. *Revista Digital Universitaria* 13. http://www.revista.unam.mx/vol.13/num11/art111/ (accessed 12 May, 2016).

Curiel, Alejandro. 2018. *Evidencialidad y texto narrativo en tojolabal*. Mexico City: Universidad Nacional Autónoma de México.

Dendale, Patrick & Liliane Tasmowski. 2001. Introduction: Evidentiality and related notions. *Journal of Pragmatics* 33. 339–349.

de Villiers, Jill G., Jay Garfield, Harper Gernet-Girard, Tom Roeper & Margaret Speas. 2009. Evidentials in Tibetan: Acquisition, semantics, and cognitive development. In Stanka A. Fitneva & Tomoko Matsui (eds.), *Evidentiality: A window into language and cognitive development* (New directions in child and adolescent development 125), 29–47. San Francisco: Jossey Bass.

Dryer, Matthew. 2007. Word order. In Timothy Shopen (ed.), *Clause structure, language typology and syntactic description*, vol. 1, 61–131, 2nd edn. Cambridge: Cambridge University Press.

Dzul Poot, Domingo & Barbara Pfeiler. 2000. *Cuentos Mayas*. Hannover: Horus Presse, Verlag für Ethnologie.

England, Nora. 2009. To tell a tale: The structure of narrated stories in Mam, a Mayan Language. *International Journal of American Linguistics* 75(2). 207–31.

Fitneva, Stanka A. 2008. The role of evidentiality in Bulgarian children's reliability judgements. *Journal of Child Language* 35. 845–868.

Fitneva, Stanka A. 2018. The acquisition of evidentiality. In Alexandra Y. Aikhenvald (ed.), The Oxford handbook of evidentiality, 185–202. Oxford: Oxford University Press.

Gaskins, Suzanne 1996. How Mayan parental theories come into play. In: Sara Harkness & Charles M. Super (eds.), *Parents' cultural belief systems. Their origins, expressions, and consequences*, 345–363. New York/London: The Guilford Press.

Givón, Talmy 1982. Evidentiality and epistemic space. *Studies in Language* 6(1). 23–49.

Hanks, William F. 1990. *Referential practice: Language and lived space among the Maya*. Chicago: University of Chicago Press.

Hanks, William F. 1993. Metalanguage and pragmatics of deixis. In John Lucy (ed.), *Reflexive language: Reported speech and metapragmatics*, 127–157. Cambridge: Cambridge University Press.

Instituto Nacional de Estadística y Geografía (INEGI). 2010. *México en cifras*. Aguascalientes, Mexico, INEGI. http://www.inegi.gob.mx/inegi/default.aspx (accessed April 10, 2015). (accessed 12 February, 2016).

Instituto Nacional de Lenguas Indígenas (INALI). 2014. Proyecto de Indicadores Sociolingüísticos de las Lenguas Indígenas Nacionales. http://www.inali.gob.mx/component/content/article/62-indicadores-basicos. (accessed 13 May, 2016).

Jakobson, Roman. 1957. *Shifters, verbal categories, and the Russian verb*. Harvard: Harvard University.

Kaufman, Terrence. 1972. *El proto-Tzeltal-Tzotzil. Fonología comparada y diccionario reconstruido*. Mexico City: Universidad Nacional Autónoma de México.

Keenan Ochs, Elinor 1977. Conversational competence in children. *Journal of Child Language* 1. 163–183.

Law, Danny. 2014. *Language contact, inherited similarity and social difference: The story of linguistic interaction in the Maya lowlands*. Amsterdam: John Benjamins.

Lehmann, Christian. 2016. La lengua maya de Yucatán. http://www.christianlehmann.eu/ling/sprachen/maya/index.php (accessed 24 March, 2016).

Lucy, John A. 1993a. Reflexive language and the human disciplines. In John Lucy (ed.), *Reflexive language: Reported speech and metapragmatics*, 9–33. Cambridge: Cambridge University Press.

Lucy, John A. 1993b. Metapragmatic presentationals: Reporting speech with quotatives in Yucatec Maya. In John Lucy (ed.), *Reflexive language: Reported speech and metapragmatics*, 91–125. Cambridge: Cambridge University Press.

Lucy, John A. 2004. Language, culture, and mind in comparative perspective. In Michel Achard & Suzanne Kemmer (eds.), *Language, culture, and mind*, 1–21. Stanford, CA: Center for the Study of Language and Information Publications.

Mithun, Marianne. 1986. Evidential diachrony in northern Iroquoian. In Wallace Chafe & Joanna Nichols (eds.), *Evidentiality: The linguistic coding of epistemology*, 89–112. Norwood, New Jersey: Ablex.

Moore, Robert E. 1993. Performance form and the voices of characters in five versions of the Wasco Coyote Cycle. In John Lucy (ed.), *Reflexive language: Reported speech and metapragmatics*, 213–240. Cambridge: Cambridge University Press.

Nichols, Johanna. 1986. Head-marking and dependent-marking grammar. *Language* 62(1). 56–119.

Ozturk, Ozge & Anna Papafragou. 2016. The acquisition of evidentiality and source monitoring. *Language Learning and Development* 12(2). 199–230.

Palmer, Frank R. 2001. *Mood and modality*. 2nd edn. Cambridge: Cambridge University Press.

Papafragou, Anna & Peggy Li. 2002. Evidential morphology and theory of mind. *Proceedings of the 26th Annual Boston University Conference on Language Development*, 510–520. Somerville, MA: Cascadilla Press.

Papafragou, Anna, Peggy Li, Youngon Choi & Chung-hye Han. 2007. Evidentiality in language and cognition. *Cognition* 103. 253–299.

Papafragou, Anna & Ozge Ozturk. 2007. The acquisition of evidentiality in Turkish. *University of Pennsylvania Working Papers in Linguistics* 11(1). 1–12.

Peterson, Tyler. 2010. Examining the mirative and nonliteral uses of evidentials. In Tyler Peterson & Uli Sauerland (eds.). *Evidence from evidentials*. University of British Columbia Working Papers in Linguistics 28. 129–159.

Pfeiler, Barbara. 2007. "Lo oye, lo repite y lo piensa". The contribution of prompting to the socialization and language acquisition in Yukatek Maya toddlers. In Barbara Pfeiler (ed.), *Learning indigenous languages: Child language acquisition in Mesoamerica*, 183–202. Berlin: Mouton de Gruyter.

Pfeiler, Barbara. 2012. Creencias parentales y la interacción verbal en el desarrollo de niños mayas de Yucatán. *Ketzalcalli* 2. 3–21.

Plungian, Vladimir. 2001. The place of evidentiality within the Universal Grammar space. *Journal of Pragmatics* 33. 349–357.

Portner, Paul. 2009. *Modality*. Oxford: Oxford University Press.

Rhoades-Ko, Yun-Hee. 2013. *Second language acquisition of Korean evidentiality in expressions of psychological state of mind*. Manoa, Hawaii: University of Hawaii at Manoa dissertation.

Robertson, John S. 1977. A proposed revision in Mayan subgrouping. *International Journal of American Linguistics* 43(2). 105–120.

Silverstein, Michael. 1976. "Shifters, linguistic categories, and cultural description." In Keith Basso and Henry A. Selby (eds.), *Meaning in Anthropology*, 11–55. Albuquerque: University of New Mexico Press.

Wimmer, Heinz & Jürgen Hogrefe. 1988. Children's understanding of informational access as a source of knowledge. *Child Development* 59. 386–396.

Ayhan Aksu-Koç and Ursula Stephany
Conclusions

1 Introduction

Modality not only plays an important role in the basic motive for human communication of "getting others to do what one wants them to" but also in "informing others of things" (Tomasello 2010: 84–86). In the latter case, reliability of the information transmitted as well as its source both matter for smooth communication. Consequently, devices for expressing requests directly by giving commands or indirectly by communicating one's wishes constitute an important domain of linguistic structures. In addition, certain linguistic communities consider ways of marking the certainty, probability, possibility, or unlikeliness of the states of affairs communicated and of indicating whether the modes of information acquisition are visual, auditory, inference, general knowledge, or hearsay (Aikhenvald and Dixon 2003) as essential and provide inflectional or lexical means of their expression.

The language chapters in the present volume focus on the deontic/dynamic (agent-oriented), the epistemic/evidential (propositional), or on both domains and provide detailed descriptions of these communicatively fundamental types of modality by (usually) case studies of a number of genetically and typologically diverse languages in most of which the acquisition of modality is systematically studied for the first time.

This chapter starts with evidence gained for an initial split between modal and non-modal expressions in child speech (CS). In the following section results concerning the development of agent-oriented and propositional modality as well as their sub-domains (dynamic/deontic and epistemic/evidential) are considered. The final section deals with new insights offered into the development of modality by the interrelation of input and cognition as well as pragmatics and social factors.

2 Modal vs. non-modal meanings in early language development

In Halliday's (1975: 87) classical distinction between the two semiotic modes of "language as action, and language as reflection", the pragmatic and the

---
Ayhan Aksu-Koç, Boğaziçi University
Ursula Stephany, University of Cologne

mathetic mode, the former is considered as "the source of the mood system of the adult language" (Halliday 1975: 104). One of the earliest achievements of early child language is the split between these two semiotic modes, with modal expressions conveying directives or wishes and non-modal ones statements or questions of information. In this section, we briefly summarize at which point of development and by which expressive means the distinction between modal and non-modal modes is realized in child speech in the languages studied.

The data analyzed in this volume come from an early age bracket of children acquiring 14 languages, some starting as young as 1;3 and going up to 3;0 or even 4;9 years. The split between modal and non-modal utterances is observed to take place within the second year of life. Although this is the first contrast to develop among verb forms, no particular attention has so far been paid to the fact that it constitutes a major developmental milestone. Instead, most studies of early child speech have focused on the early contrast of the perfective/imperfective aspect or past/present tense (see the classical study by Antinucci and Miller 1976 among others), which either develops later than the modal/non-modal contrast or is at least less prominent than the latter (see Stephany 1985, 1986 among others). The present volume is the first to provide evidence on the emergence of the modal/non-modal distinction and the subsequent development of the modal domain in more than a dozen of genetically and typologically varying languages.

In the longitudinal data from 29 German-speaking children between 2;11–4;9 years, Korecky-Kröll found that the infinitive is used assertively for expressing wishes and deontically for requests through the second half of the fifth year, although significantly less frequently than in the fourth year. Clearer evidence for the modal/non-modal split in German language acquisition comes from a girl's speech with the first contrast between the present indicative form *ich habe* 'I have' and the infinitive *haben* '(to) have' emerging at 1;10, the former expressing a non-modal meaning and the latter a modal one conveying wishes. Such contrasts become more systematic from 2;3 onwards (Kollndorfer 2009, cited by Korecky-Kröll).

For Russian, Voeikova and Bayda provide rich information about the modal/non-modal split from the literature. Modal meanings rendered by the imperative or the infinitive emerge prior to declaratives in Ženja's speech (Gvozdev 1990: 24) while with other Russian children requests for objects and the naming function were found to develop in parallel and the opposition of modal and non-modal verb forms emerged around age 2;0 (Ceitlin 2008). Poupynin (1996) found that the imperative and the infinitive start to specialize already before 2;0, serving modal vs. (most often) non-modal functions. In their own analysis of the speech of two children, Voeikova and Bayda show that modal utterances conveying directives by imperatives or bare infinitives are already attested at 1;6 in both children's speech and that modal (imperative) forms are distinguished from non-modal ones (present or past) at 1;7 and 1;8.

In Croatian (Hržica, Palmović, and Kovacevic), one-word utterances consisting of the bare infinitive emerge early (1;5–1;7) and convey both modal and non-modal meanings. However, in the second half of the second year, the children also use the imperative for modal utterances and the present indicative for non-modal ones so that a modal/non-modal split of verb forms is observed.

Modern Greek (Stephany) lacks an infinitive and thus mainly relies on finite verb forms for expressing tense-aspect-mood (TAM) categories. Evidence for the modal/non-modal split, found at the beginning of observation in the last part of the second year, comes from four children of the Stephany Corpus, who express modal meanings by the (mostly perfective) subjunctive or the imperative and non-modal ones by the imperfective non-past (present). These three categories rank above the perfective past in mean frequency of use (Stephany 1986: 379; for details see Stephany 1985). A distinction between the perfective subjunctive and the imperative for expressing deontic modality and the imperfective non-past (and marginally the perfective past) used non-modally was also found to emerge before the end of the second year in the speech of a Greek boy studied by Christofidou and Stephany (2003: 100–101).

The data of two French-speaking girls documenting the development of deontic modality and studied by Kilani-Schoch with a focus on obligation and prohibition also provide evidence of an early distinction between modal and non-modal expressions marked by the imperative (or root infinitives) and the present indicative, respectively. In the data of one of the girls, the first present indicative forms (*p(l)eut* '(it) rains', *aime* '(I) like') have even been found earlier (at 1;6) than imperatives and root infinitives (*donne* give.IMP.2SG 'give', *donner* give.INF 'give') (at 1;8).[1] Since root infinitives vary between non-modal statements and modal dynamic or deontic meanings, they do not furnish clear evidence of the modal/non-modal split.

An early distinction between modal and non-modal meanings (around 1;6) is also observed by Laalo in the speech of two children acquiring Finnish who use the 2nd person singular imperative for directives and the third person singular present indicative for statements. In addition, verbless utterances containing case-marked (partitive or illative) nouns or adverbs as well as those expressed by the inclusive imperative with a hortative meaning are among the earliest forms conveying directives.

The modal/non-modal distinction is also found early in Hebrew, namely toward the middle of the 2nd year. The two girls studied by Uziel-Karl use the

---

[1] Kilani-Schoch does not mention the use of non-modal present forms by the other girl.

imperative and future imperative to express direct requests alongside with the present indicative and past forms conveying statements.

In Turkish (Terziyan and Aksu-Koç), the split between modal and non-modal utterances is observed at 1;5 and 1;6 in the speech of two girls with the emergence of the past perfective and the present imperfective for statements contrasting with the use of the imperative and later the optative (inclusive imperative with hortative meaning) for directives (Aksu-Koç and Ketrez 2003, cited by Terziyan and Aksu-Koç).

Finally, in Korean (Choi), modal and non-modal expressions are initially distinguished between 1;8–1;9/1;10 years. Children use sentence-ending modal suffixes, which are obligatory in everyday conversation, such that –e marks direct requests while –ta expresses statements about events that are experienced in the immediate perceptual context.

Although the nine languages for which information on the modal/non-modal split is provided[2] belong to five genetic affiliations (Indo-European, Finno-Ugric, Semitic, Altaic, and Korean), the modal/non-modal split of verb forms already emerges within the second half of the children's second year or around the turn to their third year in all of them. This may be taken as evidence that the contrast between agent-oriented (primarily deontic) modal and non-modal utterances, i.e., those commanding action and those providing information, concerns a communicatively fundamental distinction. In seven of these languages (Russian, Croatian, Greek, French, Finnish, Hebrew, and Turkish), the second person singular of the imperative conveying deontic modal meanings is contrasted with the present (or past) indicative used for statements. In Greek, the (mostly perfective) subjunctive plays an important role for expressing modal meanings. In early German, Russian, Croatian, and French child speech, the infinitive may serve modal as well as non-modal functions so that the interpretation of such utterances must rely on context. Finally, in Korean, a sentence-ending suffix denoting direct requests is distinguished from a suffix marking statements about events experienced in the immediate perceptual context. In many, if not all of the languages studied, early requests may also be expressed by verbless utterances consisting of a noun or adverb. The case-marking of such nouns (e.g., the partitive) in languages like Estonian and Finnish indicates their deontic function more explicitly than in languages without such case forms.

---

[2] No information on the modal/non-modal split is available in the chapters on Lithuanian (Kavaliauskaitė-Vilkinienė and Dabašinskienė), Romanian (Avram and Gaidargi), Estonian (Argus) and Yukatek/Tojolabal (Pfeiler and Curiel).

3 Development of agent-oriented and propositional modality

It has been found that in many languages agent-oriented modality develops prior to propositional modality. This finding may not, however, be generalized since in certain languages both domains of modality develop in parallel from early on. The decisive factor is whether notions of propositional modality are grammaticized and thus obligatorily expressed in the language acquired or not. Further questions concern the order of emergence of the subdomains of dynamic vs. deontic agent-oriented modal notions and epistemic vs. evidential propositional ones.

3.1 Dynamic and deontic modality

Information on the distinction between dynamic and deontic modality and their relative emergence is found in 10 studies of the 14 languages included in this volume, 7 Indo-European ones belonging to 5 language families, 2 Finno-Ugric languages, and a Semitic one. In all languages studied, agent-oriented modal meanings may be expressed inflectionally or lexically. Dynamic and deontic meanings can only be distinguished in utterances containing a verb form. One-word utterances consisting of a noun or adverb (e.g., *book!*, *more!*) fluctuate between dynamic wishes and deontic requests.

A major inflectional device for expressing commands which predominates in many languages is the imperative. It is found in nearly all languages in which the development of inflectional means has been taken into consideration.[3] Its early emergence and deontic function is explicitly stated in the chapters on Lithuanian, Russian, Croatian, French, Greek, Estonian, Finnish, and Hebrew. In Finnish (Laalo), first imperatives are found in a girl's diary data at 1;0 and in her recorded data at 1;7. Forms used in Hebrew child speech (Uziel-Karl) for expressing (mostly) deontic meanings are the imperative, the infinitive, and the so-called future imperative. In Greek (Stephany), direct requests are expressed by

---

3 Since the study of Romanian (Avram and Gaidargi) is limited to modal verbs, the development of inflectional devices for conveying modal meanings has not been taken into consideration. Although German (Korecky-Kröll) takes both inflectional and lexical expressions into account, the relative first emergence of the different means of expression cannot be determined since the children studied are nearly 3;0 years and older.

the imperative and indirect ones by the (mostly perfective) subjunctive.[4] Both forms are amply used by Greek children from the beginning of observation in the second half of the second year (at 1;8, 1;9, and 1;11) onwards. Modally used subjunctive verb forms in the 1st or 3rd person singular referring to the speaker or the 1st person plural referring to speaker and addressee have a desiderative function while those in the 2nd or 3rd person singular forms referring to the addressee or a third person convey indirect requests. In Lithuanian (Kavaliauskaitė-Vilkinienė and Dabašinskienė), the infinitive and the future tense are additional means for expressing direct requests besides the imperative and so is the 2nd person singular present indicative in French (Kilani-Schoch). In Russian (Voeikova and Bayda) as well as German (Korecky-Kröll) and French, the infinitive is an as yet unspecialized, multipurpose verb form conveying not only non-modal meanings but also deontic and dynamic agent-oriented modal ones, i.e., requests or wishes, the latter of which may be taken to express indirect requests. In Croatian (Hržica, Palmović, and Kovacevic) and Hebrew (Uziel-Karl), the infinitive expresses the dynamic modal meanings of desire and intention.

While the imperative expresses direct requests, other forms may convey direct or indirect ones. In Finnish, directives with a hortative meaning rendered by 3rd infinitive illative forms are not only used by the caretakers in daily routines, but also by two children when talking to their toy animals already at 1;6 and 1;8. The future imperative in Hebrew and the future tense in Lithuanian (and in Greek child-directed speech) are additional inflectional devices conveying deontic meanings. In French, even the 2nd person present indicative may express requests. Due to its unspecialized, multipurpose character, the infinitive is an inflectional device which, besides non-modal meanings, may convey the deontic meaning of request or the dynamic meaning of desire. The latter may, however, be interpreted deontically as expressing indirect requests. A distinction between the dynamic desiderative function and the deontic directive one is achieved by Greek subjunctive forms referring to the speaker or the speaker and addressee on the one hand or to either the addressee or a third person on the other.

With lexically expressed agent-oriented modal meanings the two types of dynamic and deontic modality are distinguished from early on. A frequently used expression of desire is a modal or quasi-modal verb for 'want' (or more rarely 'need'). The verbs for 'want' emerge in the second half of the second year in Lithuanian and Croatian. Wishes become more frequent in Lithuanian by the end of the second year when also expressions of inability ('I can't') are found. A Russian

---

[4] As mentioned above, Modern Greek has lost the infinitive so that modal and non-modal meanings are expressed by finite verb forms.

boy uses the verb *xotet'* 'want' at 1;11, most often declaring his unwillingness to perform certain actions. The modal verb of desire *vouloir* 'want' is first found at 1;7 in the speech of one French-speaking girl and at 2;2 in that of another one. In Romanian (Avram and Gaidargi), the inherently dynamic modal verb *a vrea* 'want' expressing desire emerges concurrently with the modal verb expressing ability in three children's speech at 1;9, 2;1, and 2;2. Four Greek children first observed at 1;8, 1;9, and 1;11 express their desires by the lexical verb *θélo* 'want'. Although lexical expressions of ability (or inability) emerge concurrently with those of desire in three of these four children, the latter are used much more frequently. In Estonian (Argus), wishes expressed by 'want' are first found in a girl's speech at 1;6 and in a boy's at 2;1. In a recording at 1;11, influenced by the mother's questions concerning her daughter's wishes, the girl uses 'want' very frequently to ask for different kinds of food. According to their diary data, one of two Finnish children first expresses wishes by the modal verbs *haluta* 'want' and *tahtoa* 'want' at 1;8 and 1;10 (the other child first uses verbless utterances for this function). The modal verb of desire *roce* 'want' emerges early also in Hebrew language acquisition and is first documented in the speech of three children at 1;7, 1;11, and 2;1.

In the languages in which lexical expressions of both dynamic notions of desire and ability have been studied, it has been found that verbs expressing desire either emerge earlier than or simultaneously with those expressing ability and tend to be used more frequently than the latter. Thus, in Croatian, the dynamic notion of ability conveyed by the modal verb for 'can' begins to become increasingly frequent only in the last months of the second year. In Romanian, *a putea* 'can, may' with a subject-oriented dynamic value expressing ability or inability emerges concurrently with the modal verb *a vrea* 'want' expressing desire around the turn to the third year in three children's speech. In Greek as well, the modal verb *boró* 'can, may' expressing ability (or inability) is attested in the data together with the full verb of desire *θélo* 'want' in three of four Greek children first observed at 1;8, 1;9, and 1;11. However, *θélo* 'want' is used much more frequently than *boró* 'can, may'. In three Hebrew-speaking children, the modal verb *yaxol* 'can, be able to' emerges at 1;11, 2;1, or 2;4 and thus two to four months later than *roce* 'want' expressing desire. At least with one of these children, lexical expressions of desire occur considerably more frequently than expressions of ability.[5]

Turning to lexical expressions of deontic modality, the notions of permission and request are first expressed by the modal verbs *pouvoir* 'can, may' and (defective) *falloir* 'must' at 1;8 by one French-speaking girl and at 2;2 by another. The modal

---

[5] The lexical expressions of the dynamic modal meanings of ability or inability have not been taken into consideration in the chapters on Russian, French, Estonian, and Finnish.

devoir 'must' develops later (at 2;6 and 2;11). In Lithuanian, deontic meanings expressed by modal verbs appear only in the beginning of the third year ('can I?' asking for permission). In Russian, the verb *xotet'* 'want' not only expresses dynamic meanings of desire but also deontic ones of indirect requests. The Romanian modal verb *a putea* 'can, may' is used more often for conveying dynamic than deontic notions. The first spontaneous use of the modal *a trebui* 'need, must' with a deontic value is attested concurrently or almost so with *a putea* 'can, may' at 2;7, 2;8, or 2;11. In Greek, deontic modality is mainly, and in the beginning totally, expressed inflectionally. While the modal verb *boró* 'can, may' only conveys dynamic meanings in the children's agent-oriented use, the (defective) modal verb *prépi* 'must' expressing deontic modality has only been documented in children's data at 1;9, 2;5, and 2;9, respectively. The Finnish modal verb *voida* 'can, may' renders deontic expressions of permission or prohibition. Negated constructions of prohibition already occur by 1;8 in a girl's diary data, affirmative ones a little later at 1;11. In a boy's speech, both types of functions date from the beginning of his third year. In Hebrew, the modal verb *carix* 'should, ought to' is first found at 1;11 in one girl's speech.

Table 1: Emergence of inflectionally and lexically expressed deontic and dynamic modality.

Languages	DEONTIC/DYNAMIC, INFL/LEX
Lithuanian	DEO.INFL = DYN.LEX
	DYN.LEX < DEO.LEX
	DEO.INFL < DEO.LEX
Russian	DEO.INFL < DYN.LEX
Croatian	DEO.INFL < DYN.LEX
	DEO.INFL = DYN.INFL
French	DEO.INFL < DYN.LEX
	DYN.LEX = DEO.LEX
	DEO.INFL </= DEO.LEX
Romanian	DYN.LEX < DEO.LEX
Greek	DEO.INFL = DYN.LEX
	DEO.INFL/DYN.LEX < DEO.LEX
Estonian	DEO.INFL < DYN.LEX
	DYN.LEX < DEO.LEX
	DEO.INFL < DEO.LEX
Finnish	DEO.INFL </= DYN.LEX
	DEO.INFL/DYN.LEX </= DEO.LEX
Hebrew	DEO.INFL < DYN.LEX
	DYN.LEX < DEO.LEX
	DEO.INFL < DEO.LEX

Legend: x < y 'x emerges earlier than y'; x = y 'x emerges (almost) simultaneously with y'

The findings on the role played by inflectional and lexical means of expression of agent-oriented modal notions as well as their deontic and dynamic subtypes in development are summarized in Table 1. Most importantly, there is no evidence for deontic modality emerging before dynamic modality (or vice versa) as such in any of the languages studied. Corroboration of deontic meanings developing before dynamic meanings or vice versa can only be found if inflectional and lexical means of expression are both taken into account. When attention is limited to lexical expressions of agent-oriented modality as in the study on Romanian, there is evidence for dynamic notions of desire and ability developing earlier than deontic ones such as permission. Lexical expressions of dynamic modality have also been found to emerge earlier than or simultaneously with lexical expressions of deontic modality in Lithuanian, French, Greek, Estonian, Finnish, and Hebrew. However, if both inflectional and lexical means of expression of dynamic and deontic modal notions are taken into consideration, the opposite order or simultaneous development is found. Thus, in all languages in which inflectional as well as lexical devices have been studied (Lithuanian, Russian, Croatian, French, Greek, Estonian, Finnish, and Hebrew), inflectional deontic utterances such as commands expressed by the imperative develop prior to or concurrently with lexical dynamic ones conveying desire or ability expressed by modal or full verbs. Six languages (Lithuanian, French, Greek, Estonian, Finnish, and Hebrew) show that deontic meanings expressed inflectionally precede these same meanings expressed by lexical means.[6] In five languages (Lithuanian, Croatian, Romanian, Greek, and Hebrew), there is evidence that lexical expressions of the dynamic meaning of desire emerge before or simultaneously with those conveying ability. Most importantly, there are no counterexamples to any of the regularities summarized in (1) in the acquisition of any of the nine languages in which the early development of deontic and dynamic modality has been studied.

(1)   a.   DYN.LEX   </=   DEO.LEX
       b.   DEO.INFL   </=   DYN.LEX
       c.   DEO.INFL   </=   DEO.LEX
       d.   DYN.LEX.DESIRE   </=   DYN.LEX.ABILITY

Since the development of deontic and dynamic modal meanings is closely intertwined with their inflectional or lexical means of expression, cognitive

---

[6] In French, the two types of expression emerge simultaneously in one of the children studied.

development or pragmatic needs cannot exclusively account for their development. Grammaticized inflectional forms take precedence over lexical ones.

3.2 Epistemic and evidential modality

Information on the distinction between epistemic and evidential modality and their relative emergence is available in only two of the fourteen languages included in this volume (Turkish and Korean), on epistemic modality in four (Russian, Romanian, Greek, and Hebrew), and on evidential modality in another two (Yukatek, Tojolabal). While all these languages have some lexical or inflectional means to express epistemic and evidential modality, these notions are only grammaticized in the inflectional systems of Turkish, Korean, and the two Mayan languages.

The major lexical means for the expression of epistemic and evidential notions in Indo-European languages are modal verbs and modal adverbs, with mental verbs and adjectives also playing a role. Russian (Kazakovskaya) uses a large inventory of sentence adverbs called "parenthetical" words. Adverbs expressing uncertainty (e.g., *navernoe* 'probably', *možet* lit. 'may') are first observed at 2;2, 2;7, and 2;8 in the speech of three children and adverbs of certainty (e.g., *konečno* 'of course', *dejstvitel'no* 'really') somewhat later, between 2;10–3;10. The verbal construction *možet byt'* 'maybe' is documented at 2;9 and 3;3 in the speech of two children, whereas *kažetsja* '(it) seems' with epistemic/evidential meaning is absent from their data.

In Romanian (Avram and Gaidargi), the modal verbs *a putea* 'can, may' and *a trebui* 'need, must' may express epistemic as well as agent-oriented meanings. However, their epistemic use is not observed in the speech of three children, where *a putea* 'can, may' conveys dynamic and deontic meanings (at 1;9, 1;10, 2;1, and 2;9, 2;7, 2;5, respectively) and the verb *a trebui* 'need, must' deontic ones (at 2;11, 2;5, 2;8). Instead, epistemic possibility/uncertainty is conveyed by the adverb *poate* 'maybe' observed at the ages of 2;3, 2;7, and 2;11, after the dynamic use of the verb *a putea* and either before, concurrently with, or after the expression of deontic notions. The adverb *sigur* 'certainly' indicating the stronger modal degree of certainty is observed at 2;11 and the epistemic/evidential adverb *parcă* 'apparently' at 2;2 in the speech of two of the children.

In Greek (Stephany), main lexical devices for expressing modal notions are the two modal verbs *boró* 'can, may' and (defective) *prépi* 'must', epistemic adverbs, and mental verbs. While the modal verb *prépi* 'must' is only used to convey deontic modality by four children observed until the last part of their third year, *boró* 'may' is first used for rendering the notion of epistemic possibility by only one child at 2;11. Two epistemic modal adverbs (*málon* 'probably' and *vévea* 'certainly') are found in the data of the same child emerging before 2;0. The mental verb *kséro* 'to know' expressing the notions of dynamic ability and epistemic certainty only begins to be used quite frequently by three children at 2;9 or 2;11, often conveying ignorance.

In Hebrew (Uziel-Karl) adverbs expressing uncertainty (*ulay* 'perhaps', *efshar* 'possibly') are observed at 1;7 and 2;0 while *betax* 'surely' expressing certainty is noted at 1;10 in the speech of one girl. In the speech of the other one, the two adverbs of uncertainty are observed at 1;11 and 2;0, and *betax* 'surely' at 2;7. Modal verb constructions with adjectival predicates conveying epistemic possibility (*yaxol lihyot* 'may be.INF') and impossibility (*lo? yaxol lihyot* 'it is not possible') are used at 2;4 and 2;9, respectively, by only one of the children.

Turkish (Terziyan and Aksu-Koç) lacks modal verbs and the main lexical means for the expression of propositional modality are adverbs and mental verbs. The notions of uncertainty and certainty are first conveyed by the adverbs *acaba* 'I.wonder' and *gerçekten* 'really' at 1;7 and 1;8, respectively, by one child and by more varied adverbs such as *belki* 'perhaps' at 2;1, *sence* 'in your opinion' and *yoksa* 'if not' at 2;10 by the other, who also produces the only evidential adverb observed, *demek* 'apparently', at 2;7. Mental verbs are not attested in the children's speech.

For the Mayan languages Yukatek and Tojolabal (Pfeiler and Curiel) information is available only with respect to evidentiality, which is grammaticized and expressed predominantly by inflections or clitics. However, quotatives, considered as evidential, are expressed lexically by verbs of saying and encode the original reporter, thereby specifying the exact source of information. The verb stem *k-* for 'say' in Yukatek and the verbs *chi* 'say', *chikan* 'quote', *ut* 'say aloud' in Tojolabal are used for this purpose. Quotatives emerge around 2;0–2;1 in both Yukatek and Tojolabal children's speech and they are constructed with dative complements at 2;9 (Yukatek *tax-eh k-ih-t-een* (bring-IMP QUOT-ABS.3-DAT-PRO.1SG) '"bring it!", he says to me').

In summary, in almost all of the languages considered, the first means of expression observed in children's speech are epistemic adverbs expressing uncertainty and certainty, the use of modal verbs to convey epistemic meanings being a subsequent development.

Evidence for inflectional expression of epistemic and evidential meanings is available for Turkish, Korean, and for evidential modality for Mayan. In Turkish, epistemic statements are expressed by TAM inflections which may be interpreted dynamically, deontically, or epistemically. The first examples marked by the suffix *-(A/I)r* referring to highly probable events are found in the speech of the two children at 1;9 and 2;0, respectively. The *-Abil+(A/I)r* construction expressing possibility is observed at 2;0 in the speech of one child and examples of the clitic -*DIr* conveying epistemic certainty ('must be') at 2;2, in the speech of the other. The evidential suffix/clitic -*mIş*/-*ImIş* that marks an obligatory distinction between direct vs. indirect experience is first used to express novel information and the narrative/pretense mode, at 1;7 by one child and at 2;0 by the other, before and concurrently with epistemic utterances. Use of the evidential as a source marker, as in case of inferential and reportative utterances, is observed subsequently, the former at 1;9 and 2;1 and the latter at 2;0 and 2;8 in the speech of the two children.

Korean has a set of obligatory sentence-ending modal suffixes that express varying degrees of epistemicity and different types of evidentiality, several of which children acquire until age 4;0. Starting around 1;10, the suffix -*ta* denoting new information is used contrastively with the suffix -*e* for already assimilated information. At 2;0–2;2, the suffix -*ci* affirms information that is certain either because it has been shared in discourse with the interlocutor or because there is perceptual evidence for it. From 2;5 onwards, -*tay* encodes information that is hearsay, part of pretend-play, or story-telling, thereby marking source. The suffix -*(nu)ntey* conveying information that contrasts with or challenges the listener's assessment of an event or state and -*ney* that marks inference through direct perception are acquired during the fourth year (3;1–4;0). These suffixes also convey the speaker's assessment of an event or state in relation to the listener's current state of knowledge.

The Mayan languages Yukatek and Tojolabal express reportatives inflectionally. Reportatives (=*b'in* in Yukatek and =*b'i* in Tojolabal), which convey secondhand information but not its exact source, are first observed in Yukatek at 2;3 and 2;5 in the speech of two children and in Tojolabal at 2;6 in the speech of one. Children distinguish reportative and quotative evidentials in terms of source marking within the first half of the fourth year.[7]

It is interesting to note that, in both Turkish and Korean, epistemic and evidential modality markers either co-emerge or emerge in close succession. However, their intertwined developmental paths suggest that the two types of modality differentiate[8] gradually. Children first try to ascertain the factuality of knowledge by evaluating states of affairs in terms of possibility (uncertainty) and necessity (certainty) and subsequently attend to source of knowledge. This

---

[7] In the chapter contained in the present volume there is only information on quotatives and reportatives.
[8] For the close relation between epistemic and evidential meanings see Palmer (2001) and Plungian (2001) among others.

is indicated by the relatively later emergence of inferential and reportative functions in the Mayan languages as well as in Turkish and Korean.

Table 2 presents a summary of the findings on the emergence of lexical and inflectional means of expression by type of propositional modality and language. Although it is difficult to draw any definite conclusions on the primacy of inflectional over lexical expression or of epistemic over evidential modality on the basis of the available evidence, the following generalizations can be made.

Table 2: Emergence of inflectionally and lexically expressed epistemic and evidential modality.

Languages	EPST/EVID, MV/ADV, INFL/LEX
Russian	EPST.LEX.ADV < EPST.LEX.MV
Romanian	EPST.LEX.ADV < EPST.LEX.MV
Greek	EPST.LEX < EPST.INFL
	EPST.ADV < EPST.MV
Hebrew	EPST.LEX.ADV < EPST.LEX.MV
Turkish	EVID.INFL </= EPST.INFL
	EVID.INFL < EVID.LEX
	EVID.INFL < EPST.LEX
	EPST.LEX </= EPST.INFL
	EPST.LEX < EVID.LEX
Korean	EPST.INFL < EVID.INFL
Mayan (Yukatek & Tojolabal)	EVID.LEX.QUOT < EVID.INFL.REPORT

Legend: x < y 'x emerges earlier than y'; x = y 'x emerges (almost) simultaneously with y'

Among the eight languages where propositional modality has been analyzed, the primary means of expression is lexical in Russian, Romanian, Greek, and Hebrew and the findings indicate the primacy of adverbs over modal verbs, adjectival predicates, and mental verbs. In these languages, no evidence has been attested regarding the emergence of evidential modality (for example with the use of adverbs) in children's speech during the period of observation between 1;8–3;0.

In the two Mayan languages, Yukatek and Tojolabal, only two subtypes of evidential modality, quotatives and reportatives, have been examined and quotatives expressed lexically precede reportatives expressed with verbal clitics in children's speech.

The primary means of expression of epistemic and evidential notions in Turkish and Korean is inflectional. In Turkish, the inflectional expression of evidential modality emerges before or concurrently with the inflectional marking of epistemic modality, whereas in Korean inflectional expressions of epistemic notions appear before those of evidential modality. In Turkish, lexical expressions of epistemic modality emerge before or concurrently with inflectional ones, however, no information is available on lexical expressions of propositional modality in Korean. The early emergence of inflectional means in these two languages indicate that, where epistemic/evidential distinctions are grammaticized and thus obligatorily marked, the notions of propositional modality are easily accessible to the child and that their expression is not delayed in comparison to the expression of agent-oriented modality.

The acquisition of expressions of agent-oriented and propositional modality, however, is not only dependent on their status in the grammatical system of the language and the type of expressive device but also on the cognitive demands and pragmatic constraints on their use and their frequency in the speech directed to children (Stephany 1993; Hickmann and Bassano 2016), factors which we consider briefly in the next section.

4 The interrelation of input, cognition, and pragmatics in the development of modality

An important consequence of a means of expression being grammaticized and thus obligatory is its occurrence with high frequency in child-directed speech (CDS). A significant aspect of the studies in the present volume is that the forms and functions of the expression of agent-oriented and propositional modality analyzed in CS have also been examined in CDS in terms of frequency of occurrence. CDS is particularly tailored to provide a learning ground for abstracting the structure and meaning of the speech units children receive as input (Tomasello 2003; Bybee 2010; Theakston and Lieven 2017). Among the properties of CDS that support this process are frequency of use, consistency of form–function relations, variability of structure (Stephany 1985; Küntay and Slobin 1996; Weizman and Snow 2001; Huttenlocher et al. 2002; Behrens 2006; Brodsky, Waterfall, and Edelman 2007) as well as a discourse context where new words and constructions are introduced and feedback is provided for existing ones by full or partial repetitions (Clark and Bernicot 2008; du Bois 2014). In short, CDS is infused with processes that make diversity and frequency important parts of the language acquisition process. While diversity of forms is important for pattern recognition and acquisition of new structures, repetition is important for entrenchment of what is acquired into the existing system.

It is also well accepted that the effect of input frequency is closely intertwined with cognitive and pragmatic constraints through which it is filtered. The domain of modality is particularly rich with examples of the role played by these factors as illustrated in the studies on this early period of development. We will therefore touch upon some of the findings regarding the effects of frequency and thereafter upon those related to cognitive and pragmatic factors as revealed in the present studies.

4.1 Frequency of form and function of modal expressions in child speech and child-directed speech

The order of emergence of the forms of expression in CS is closely related to the frequency of their occurrence in CDS. Structurally simple forms which frequently occur in CDS and are most functional for the child are taken over or extracted from the input. This is demonstrated by the prominence of imperative and (bare) infinitive verb forms – typically the simplest forms in most languages – and their emergence as the earliest means of expression of verbal directives in CS in all our languages where the acquisition of agent-oriented modality has been studied (German, Russian, Croatian, French, Romanian, Lithuanian, Greek, Estonian, Finnish, Hebrew). In case of the languages examined for propositional modality, again the highly frequent forms in CDS – inflectional markers of epistemic/evidential modality – emerge early in CS (Turkish and Korean). Another example where frequency and structural simplicity go together is the high frequency of epistemic adverbs relative to the lower frequency of epistemically used modal verbs in CDS and the emergence of adverbs as the first markers of epistemic notions in CS, where epistemic use of modal verbs is scarcely observed (Russian, Romanian, Greek, and Hebrew). Epistemic adverbs are syntactically simpler since they do not have to be integrated into the structure of the sentence. They are also semantically simpler because they have a single inherent meaning as compared to modal verbs that have dynamic and deontic interpretations as well. Conversely, forms that are structurally complex occur with low frequency in CDS and are late to appear in CS. Thus, in Estonian, suggestions, which are indirect requests expressed by a complex construction comprising the conditional form of the main verb plus a phrasal verb, are found with low frequency in CDS and emerge late in CS.

Another observation is that highly frequent formal means of expression (for a specific function) in CDS also tend to be used with high frequency (for that function) in CS. Such a correspondence between CDS and CS is reported for almost all the languages analyzed. For example, in Hebrew a close match is observed between the mothers' and the children's speech in terms of the relative frequency of modal verbs, adjectives, and adverbs, such that the use of these forms expressing agent-oriented modality is much more prominent than their use for epistemic modality both in CDS and in CS. In Turkish as well, the relative frequencies of adverbs and different inflections expressing epistemic notions in the two registers of CDS and CS are equal.

Mere frequency of grammatical forms in CDS does not, however, necessarily result in early acquisition. Children select from the inventory in the input what is functionally relevant for them and may ignore what is not, even if it is frequent and structurally simple. The following are among the examples that have been noted. In order to prompt their children to talk, Russian mothers use verbs of saying ('say', 'tell') in the imperative with high frequency. Children, however, do not use these verbs, instead favoring verbs of giving and taking, asking for actions rather than speech (Voeikova and Bayda). Similarly, in Yukatek, children frequently hear quotative utterances with verbs of saying but start using them only towards the end of their third year and just to address children younger than themselves to stimulate them to talk. Among the most frequent types of indirect requests in Estonian CDS are appeals for joint action and these emerge first in children's speech, whereas warnings, prohibitions, and obligations, also highly frequent in CDS, are not used by children as they are not appropriate for their social role vis-à-vis adults. While the modal verb *moći* 'can' is more often used deontically for permission or prohibition in Croatian CDS, it expresses the dynamic notion of ability in CS.

4.2 Cognitive factors and discourse mechanisms

Research so far converges on the fact that expressions of deontic and dynamic modality emerge in children's speech before expressions of epistemic meanings (Choi 2006; Hickmann and Bassano 2016; but see section 3.2 above and Stephany, this volume). While there has been a lot of concern about the cognitive prerequisites of epistemic modality, the cognitive correlates of the expressions of deontic and dynamic modality, which convey children's requests for action as well as their desires and intentions or abilities, have not received as much attention. However, the sequence of development of directives as the earliest expressions of deontic modality in children's speech observed in the studies of the present volume are revealing in this respect. An example in point is the progress observed in Estonian children's directives from issuing commands that call for the action of a single person (the addressee) to appeals for joint action that involve two persons (the speaker and the addressee) and finally to indirect requests that call for the action of the speaker, the addressee, and a third party, thus gradually increasing the number of participants in the envisaged action.

Explanations of developments in the domain of epistemic modality have been closely associated with developments in theory of mind enabling the representation of the mental states of the self and the other around age 4;0 (Nelson 1996; Astington and Baird 2005; Choi 2006 among many others). However, in line with the gradual progress in the differentiation of perspectives beginning at the end of the first year of life (Tomasello, Kruger, and Ratner 1993), precursors of epistemic evaluations are found already between 1;8–3;0 as demonstrated by the studies on propositional modality of the present volume. For example, Russian children's epistemic expressions show gradual changes in terms of the content of the propositions evaluated, shifting from those about objects and their properties to those about their own and others' actions, and finally to their own and others' mental states (Kazakovskaya).

In languages where the coding of epistemic and evidential notions is obligatory, as in Korean and Turkish, developments in the use of the epistemic/evidential suffixes indicate that children first attend to developing a knowledge base, marking new knowledge contrastively with old, which they then evaluate for factuality on the basis of whether others attest to it with certainty or uncertainty. Finally, they take into account the source of information that would form the grounds for the assessments of reliability. Evidence for another gradual process, namely, the differentiation of degrees of modal strength, is found in the chapters on Russian, Romanian, Greek, and Hebrew, which show that children first contrast the notions of uncertainty and certainty and only later express in-between values such as (im)probability within the third year of life, before the full manifestation of theory of mind skills. These results agree with those of earlier studies (see Stephany 1993: 142–143) that expressions placed at the poles of the modal scale reaching from necessity to possibility begin to develop before the end of the fourth year. The developmental trajectories that have been summarized reveal successive differentiations in children's understanding of knowledge and its reliability, providing another example of the fact that acquisition of the full range of functions of linguistic means of expressions proceeds slowly (Berman and Slobin 1994).

These advances, both linguistic and cognitive, take place in the context of discourse with adults, where children encounter new forms and learn their functions through use. The analysis of the acquisition of epistemic/evidential suffixes in Korean shows how the impact of input frequency is interactively determined by progress in cognitive and pragmatic skills. Increased sophistication in children's perspective-taking abilities enables them to make their contributions to discourse by taking the knowledge state of their interlocutors into account. Adults, in turn, reinforce and modify children's contributions by repeating the core proposition in their utterance, replacing its modal suffix with the pragmatically appropriate one.

4.3 Pragmatic constraints and social factors

Finally, a number of studies of the present volume provide information on how individual differences and differences in social class condition the frequency of occurrence of modal structures and their functions. Individual differences in parenting styles reflected in the speech patterns of mother–child dyads show that one mother may prefer an explanatory, guiding style, whereas another may pursue a controlling strategy using many directives and prohibitions, or one mother may prefer mitigating polite requests while another employs more direct forms. Such differences are observed between mothers from the same high socio-economic background (Russian: Voeikova and Bayda; Lithuanian) as well as between mothers of high vs. low socio-economic status (German). The behavior-directing style of mothers from low socio-economic backgrounds is reflected in their more frequent use of imperatives and infinitives with imperative meaning compared to parents from high socio-economic backgrounds. However, differences in the frequency of types of directives are found mainly in CDS but are not as yet reflected in the speech of children, indicating that children's needs, which are similar in both groups, are more important than input frequency as a determining factor.

To conclude, the studies in the present volume approach the problem of the acquisition of modality from multiple perspectives, taking into account the type of expressive device, its status in the grammatical system of the language, the cognitive underpinnings, pragmatic constraints, discourse processes, and the social context, which interactively determine the frequency of modal devices in the speech directed to children and what children pick up from the input.

References

Aikhenvald, Alexandra Y. & Robert M. W. Dixon. 2003. Evidentiality in typological perspective. In Alexandra Y. Aikhenvald & Robert M. W. Dixon (eds.), *Studies in evidentiality* (Typological Studies in Language 54), 1–31. Amsterdam: John Benjamins.

Aksu-Koç, Ayhan & F. Nihan Ketrez. 2003. Early verbal morphology in Turkish: Emergence of inflections. In Wolfgang U. Dressler, Dagmar Bittner & Marianne Kilani-Schoch (eds.),

Development of verb inflection in first language acquisition: A cross-linguistic perspective (Studies on Language Acquisition 21), 27–52. Berlin: Mouton de Gruyter.

Antinucci, Francesco & Ruth Miller. 1976. How children talk about what happened. *Journal of Child Language* 3. 167–190.

Astington, Janet W. & Jodie A. Baird. 2005. Why language matters for theory of mind. In Janet W. Astington & Jodie A. Baird (eds.), *Why language matters for Theory of Mind*, 3–25. Oxford: Oxford University Press.

Behrens, Heike. 2006. The input–output relationship in first language acquisition. *Language and Cognitive Processes* 21. 2–24.

Berman, Ruth A. & Dan I. Slobin. 1994. *Relating events in narrative: A crosslinguistic developmental study*. Hillsdale, NJ & Hove, UK: Lawrence Erlbaum.

Brodsky, Peter, Heidi Waterfall & Shimon Edelman. 2007. Characterizing motherese: On the computational structure of child-directed language. In Danielle S. McNamara & J. Gregory Trafton (eds.), *Proceedings of the 29th meeting of the Cognitive Science Society*, 833–838. Austin, TX: Cognitive Science Society.

Bybee, Joan. 2010. *Language, usage and cognition*. Cambridge: Cambridge University Press.

Ceitlin, Stella N. 2008. Vyraženie pobuždenija v detskoj reči [Expression of requests in child language]. In Alexandr V. Bondarko & Sadje A. Shubik (eds.), *Problemy funkcionalnoj grammatiki: kategorizacija semantiki* [Problems of functional grammar: categorization of semantics], 309–330. Saint Petersburg: Nauka.

Choi, Soonja. 2006. Acquisition of modality. In: William Frawley (ed.), *The expression of modality*, 141–171. Berlin: Walter de Gruyter.

Christofidou, Anastasia & Ursula Stephany. 2003. Early phases in the development of Greek verb inflection. In Dagmar Bittner, Wolfgang U. Dressler & Marianne Kilani-Schoch (eds.), *Development of verb inflection in first language acquisition: A cross-linguistic perspective* (Studies on Language Acquisition 21), 89–129. Berlin & New York: Mouton de Gruyter.

Clark, Eve V. & Josie Bernicot. 2008. Repetition as ratification: How parents and children place information in common ground. *Journal of Child Language* 35(2). 349–371.

Du Bois, John W. 2014. Towards a dialogic syntax. *Cognitive Linguistics* 25(3). 359–410.

Gvozdev, Aleksandr N. 1990. *Razvitie slovarnogo zapasa v pervye gody žizni rebjonka* [Development of the lexicon in the first years of the child's life]. Saratov: Saratov University Press.

Halliday, Michael A. K. 1975. *Learning how to mean: Explorations in the development of language*. London: Edward Arnold.

Hickmann, Maya & Dominique Bassano. 2016. Modality and mood in first language acquisition. In Jan Nuyts & Johan van der Auwera (eds.), *The Oxford handbook of modality and mood*, 430–447. Oxford: Oxford University Press.

Huttenlocher, Janeellen, Marina Vasilyeva, Elina Cymerman & Susan Levine. 2002. Language input and child syntax. *Cognitive Psychology* 45. 337–374.

Kollndorfer, Kathrin. 2009. Entwicklung der Modalität im Erstspracherwerb des Deutschen. Vienna: University of Vienna MA thesis.

Küntay, Aylin & Dan I. Slobin. 1996. Listening to a Turkish mother: Some puzzles for acquisition. In Dan I. Slobin, Julie Gerhardt, Amy Kyratzis & Jiansheng Guo (eds.), *Social interaction, social context and language: Essays in honour of Susan Ervin-Tripp*, 265–286. Hillsdale, NJ: Lawrence Erlbaum.

Nelson, Katherine. 1996. *Language in cognitive development: The emergence of the mediated mind*. Cambridge & New York: Cambridge University Press.

Nikolaeva, Irina. 2016. Analyses of the semantics of mood. In Jan Nuyts & Johan van der Auwera (eds.), *The Oxford handbook of modality and mood*, 68–85. Oxford: Oxford University Press.

Palmer, Frank R. 2001. *Mood and modality*. 2nd ed. Cambridge: Cambridge University Press.

Plungian, Vladimir A. 2001. The place of evidentiality within the universal grammatical space. *Journal of Pragmatics* 33. 349–357.

Poupynin, Yuri. 1996. Usvoenie sistemy russkix glagol'nyx form rebenkom (rannie etapy) [Acquisition of the system of Russian verb forms by a child (the early stages)]. *Voprosy jazykoznanija* 3. 84–95.

Stephany, Ursula. 1985. *Aspekt, Tempus und Modalität: Zur Entwicklung der Verbalgrammatik in der neugriechischen Kindersprache* (Language Universals Series 4). Tübingen: Gunter Narr.

Stephany, Ursula. 1986. Modality. In Paul Fletcher & Michael Garman (eds.), *Language acquisition: Studies in first language development*, 375–400. 2nd ed. Cambridge: Cambridge University Press.

Stephany, Ursula. 1993. Modality in first language acquisition: The state of the art. In Norbert Dittmar & Astrid Reich (eds.), *Modality in language acquisition/Modalité et acquisition des langues*, 133–144. Berlin & New York: Walter de Gruyter.

Theakston, Anna & Elena Lieven. 2017. Multiunit sequences in first language acquisition. *Topics in Cognitive Science* 9(3). 588–603.

Tomasello, Michael. 2003. *Constructing a language: A usage-based theory of language acquisition*. Cambridge, MA: Harvard University Press.

Tomasello, Michael. 2010 [2008]. *Origins of human communication*. Paperback edn. Cambridge, MA & London: The MIT Press.

Tomasello, Michael, Ann C. Kruger & Hilary H. Ratner. 1993. Cultural learning. *Behavioral and Brain Sciences* 16(3). 495–511.

Weizman, Zehava O. & Catherine E. Snow. 2001. Lexical input as related to children's vocabulary acquisition: Effects of sophisticated exposure and support for meaning. *Developmental Psychology* 37. 265–279.

List of Contributors

Ayhan Aksu-Koç
Boğaziçi University
Department of Psychology
Bebek
34342, Istanbul, Turkey
koc@boun.edu.tr

Reili Argus
Tallinn University
School of Humanities
Narva mnt 25
Tallinn, Estonia
reili.argus@tlu.ee

Larisa Avram
University of Bucharest
Faculty of Foreign Languages
010451 Bucharest, Romania
larisa.avram@lls.unibuc.ro

Kira Bayda
Russian Academy of Sciences
Institute for Linguistic Studies
Department of Grammatical Theory
Tuchkov per. 9
199053 Saint Petersburg, Russia
kira.bayda@gmail.com

Soonja Choi
San Diego State University
Department of Linguistics and Asian/
Middle-Eastern Languages
5500 Campanile Drive
San Diego, CA 92182, USA
and
University of Vienna
Department of Linguistics
Sensengasse 3a
A-1090 Vienna, Austria
soonja.choi@univie.ac.at

Alejandro Curiel
Meldemannstraße 24/3702
A-1200 Vienna, Austria
alejandrocuriel@yahoo.com

Ineta Dabašinskienė
Vytautas Magnus University
Department of Lithuanian Studies
V. Putvinskio str. 23-206
LT-44243 Kaunas, Lithuania
ineta.dabasinskiene@vdu.lt

Andreea Gaidargi
University of Bucharest
Doctoral School of Languages and Cultural
Identities
010451 Bucharest, Romania
deea.andreea86@yahoo.com

Gordana Hržica
University of Zagreb
Department of Speech and Language
Pathology
Borongajska cesta 83f
10000 HR Zagreb, Croatia
gordana.hrzica@erf.unizg.hr

Viktorija Kavaliauskaitė-Vilkinienė
Vytautas Magnus University
Department of Lithuanian Studies
V. Putvinskio str. 23-206
LT-44243 Kaunas, Lithuania
viktorija.kavaliauskaite-vilkiniene@vdu.lt

Victoria V. Kazakovskaya
Russian Academy of Sciences
Institute for Linguistic Studies
Department of Grammatical Theory
Tuchkov per. 9
199053 Saint Petersburg, Russia
victory805@mail.ru

Marianne Kilani-Schoch
University of Lausanne
Department of Language and Information Sciences
CH-1015 Lausanne, Switzerland
marianne.kilanischoch@unil.ch

Katharina Korecky-Kröll
University of Vienna
Department of German Studies
Universitätsring 1
A-1010 Vienna, Austria
katharina.korecky-kroell@univie.ac.at

Melita Kovacevic
University of Zagreb
Department of Speech and Language Pathology
Laboratory for Psycholinguistic Research
Borongajska cesta 83f
10000 HR Zagreb, Croatia
melita.kovacevic@unizg.hr

Klaus Laalo
Tampere University
PinniB 4028
33014 Tampereen yliopisto, Finland
klaus.laalo@tuni.fi

Marijan Palmović
University of Zagreb
Department of Speech and Language Pathology
Laboratory for Psycholinguistic Research
Borongajska cesta 83f
10000 HR Zagreb, Croatia
marijan.palmovic@erf.unizg.hr

Barbara Pfeiler
Universidad Nacional Autónoma de México
Centro Peninsular en Humanidades y Ciencias Sociales
Ex Sanatorio Rendón Peniche
Calle 43 s/n entre 44 y 46,
col. Industrial
C.P. 97150 Mérida, Yucatán, Mexico
bpfeiler@prodigy.net.mx

Ursula Stephany
University of Cologne
Institute of Linguistics
D-50923 Cologne, Germany
stephany@uni-koeln.de

Treysi Terziyan
Tilburg University
Department of Culture Studies
Warandelaan 2
NL 5037 AB Tilburg, The Netherlands
T.Terziyan@uvt.nl

Sigal Uziel-Karl
Achva Academic College
Early Childhood Program,
Dept. of Hebrew Language
and Dept. of Communication Disorders
Arugot, 7980400, Israel
sigaluk@gmail.com

Maria D. Voeikova
Russian Academy of Sciences
Institute for Linguistic Studies
Department of Grammatical Theory
Tuchkov per. 9
199053 Saint Petersburg, Russia
and
Saint Petersburg State University
Philological Faculty
Chair of Russian Language
Universitetskaja nab. 11
199034 Saint Petersburg, Russia
maria.voeikova@gmail.com

Subject Index

Abbreviations for language codes

Cr	Croatian	Ko	Korean
Es	Estonian	Li	Lithuanian
Fi	Finnish	Ma	Yukatek Maya, Tojolabal
Fr	French	Ro	Romanian
Ge	German	Ru	Russian
Gk	Greek	Tu	Turkish
He	Hebrew		

ability/capability/inability 5, 7, 9, 560, 561, 563, 565, 570, **Cr** 159, 173, 183, 187, **Fi** 348, 353–354, **Fr** 191–192, 202, **Ge** 33, **Gk** 257, 258, 273, 288, 291, 293–294, 296–297, 304, 308–309, **He** 379–380, 381, 383, 385, 387, 391, 402–403, 405, 406, 407, 416, **Li** 104, **Ro** 236, 237, 244, **Tu** 459, 471 *see also* dynamic modality
adjectives 564, 570, **He** 382, 390fn *see also* modal adjectives
adult-directed speech (ADS) **Fi** 358, **Ge** 29, 30, 35, **Gk** 259, 260, 268–269, 271, **Ma** 525, 526, 534, 536, 545, **Ro** 241, 250fn, **Ru** 135, 436, 444, 448, **Tu** 469
adverbials/adverbs 557, 558, 564–565, 567, 569, 570, **Es** 319, 328, 331, **Fi** 348, 354, 364, 366–367, 370, 371, 374, 375, **Fr** 200, 215–216, **Ko** 506, 516–517, **Li** 79, 86, 91, 94–95, 108, **Ma** 529, 530, 531, 545, 546 *see also* modal adverbials
agent-oriented modality 3, 4, 5, 8, 559–564, 568, 569, 570, **Cr** 159, 161–163, 164, 173, 178–180, 185–186, 187, **Es** 316, **Fi** 347, 348, 368, **Fr** 191–192, 200, **Gk** 257–258, 261, 273, 297, 306, 307, 308, 309–310, **He** 379, 380, 381, 382, 387, 388, *391*, 392, 400, **401**, 402, **403–404**, 405–406, 407, 408, 416, **Li** 79, **Ro** 248, **Ru** 421, 447–448, **Tu** 456fn, 467, 477 *see also* deontic modality; dynamic modality; event modality
aktionsart **Gk** 262, 269, 283 *see also* aspect

Altaic *2*, 558
analogy **Fi** 348, 361–362, 375, 376, **Gk** 256, **Tu** 454 *see also* overgeneralization
aorist **Cr** 162, **Tu** 457, *458*, 459–460, 462–463, 465, 467, 469–470, 471, 472, 473, 474, 477, 482–483
aspect 556, **Gk** 261–262, 269, **Ko** 492, **Ro** 238, **Ru** 147–151, **Tu** 456–457, *458*, 460, 461, 463, 465, 475
– continuative/discontinuative **Ma** 529
– habitual **Gk** 262, **Tu** *458*, 459
– imperfective 556, 557, 558, **Cr** 162–163, **Gk** 262, 283–284, 290, **Ru** 116fn, 117–118, *128–129*, 133, 134, 138–139, 151, **Tu** *458*, 459, 465, 476–477
– imperfective vs. perfective 556, **Gk** 263, 268, 273, **Ru** 139, 147–148, 149–150, 152
– perfective 556, 557, 558, **Cr** 161, 162–163, **Gk** 262, 283–284, 290, **Ru** 116fn, 117–118, 119–120, 133, 134, 137, **Tu** *458*, 459, 460, 465
auxiliaries **Cr** 162, 163
– future **Ru** 129–130
– modal **Cr** 162, **Es** 320, **Ru** 119, 129–130
– negative **Es** 318, 319, 338, **Fi** 351
– semi-auxiliary **Fr** 197, 210fn *see also* modal verbs; negator

Baltic *2*
Bulgarian 38, 485, 526

case marking 557, 558, **Es** 328, 329, **Fi** 354, 364, 375
- absolutive **Ma** 527
- accusative **Cr** 162, 163, **Li** 91, **Ru** 114
- adessive **Es** 333
- dative 565
- elative **Fi** 366
- ergative **Ma** 527, 548
- ergative-absolutive **Ma** 527
- genitive **Cr** 160, 162, 163, **Es** 329, 330, **Fi** 353, **Li** 91, **Ru** 114
- illative 557, 560, **Es** 329, **Fi** 348, 352–353, 354, 364, 365–366, 370–371, 375
- nominative **Es** 332fn, 333, **Li** 91, **Ru** 114
- nominative-accusative split **Ma** 527
- partitive 557, 558, **Es** 327–328, 329–330, 331, 332fn, **Fi** 354, 364–365, 370, 375, **Ru** 114 *see also* infinitive, 3rd infinitive illative

certainty/uncertainty 6, 7, 9, 555, 564, 565–566, 571, **Cr** 159, 161, **Ge** 38, **Gk** 257–258, 270, 297, 300–301, 302, 304, 305, 306, 307, 309, **He** 380, 381, 397, 408–409, **Ko** 491, 493–494, 495, 496–497, 498, 501–502, 503, **504**, *509*, 511, *513*, 515, 518–519, 520, 522, **Ru** 421, 422–425, 426, 428, **429**, 430–435, *441–442*, **443–444**, **445**, 447, 448, **Tu** 453, 455, *456*, 469, 471, 473, 474–475, 484, 485 *see also* epistemic modality; modal adjectives; modal adverbials

child-directed speech (CDS) 3, 568, 569–570, **Cr** 159, 161, 162, 163, *164*, 172, 173, *180–181*, 182–*183*, **184**–185, 186–187, **Es** 315, 317, *318*, 320, 323, *325*, 326, 327, 336, 337, *338–339*, 340–342, **Fi** 347, 349, 351, 352, 353, 356–359, 361, 367, 373–374, 375–376, **Fr** 191, 194, 199, 200, 202fn, 203, 204, 207, 209fn, 218–223, 224–226, 227, 228, 229, 230, **Ge** 26–27, 30, 33, 34, 35–36, **Gk** 256, 259, 260, 270, 272, 273, 277–278, 284–286, 288–290, 296–297, 299, 300–301, 306–307, 308, 309, **He** 379, 382fn, 386, 387–388, 389, 392, **396**–400, **401**, *402*, **404**, 406, 407, 408–409, *413*–414, 415–416, **Li** 79, 82fn, 104–105, 108, **Ma** 525, 526, 532, 534, 537, 540–541, 542, 549, **Ro** 235, 242, 248–249, 250, 251, **Ru** 113, 115, 119–120, *121–122*, **123**, 124, 127, *128*–129, *130–131*, 132–133, 135–*136*, 137, 139–*141*, *142*, 144–145, *146*, 147–148, 149, **150**–151, 152, 421, *428*, **429**, *430*, **436**, 439–443, 444–446, 448, **Tu** 454, *466*–467, *468*, 470, *471*, *472*, 474–475, *477*–478, *480–481*, **482–483**, 484, 485–486
- high vs. low socio-economic status **Ge** 25, 26–27, 39–40, **He** 389, 415–416
- prompting/prompts **Li** 100, **Ma** 525, 532, 534–535, 538, 539, 540, 541, 542, 549, 550
- reformulation **Fr** 201, **Ma** 535–536, 537, 541, 545
- repetition 568–569, 572, **Ko** 496–497, 499, 501, 502, 516–517, 518–519, 522, **Ru** 120, 128, **Tu** 454–455, 486
- routines **Fi** 353, 359, 361, 367, 370–371, 375, **Ma** 532, 533, **Tu** 469 *see also* fine-tuning; gender-related communication; input; input–output relation; parenting style; socio-economic status; structural resonance; variation set

clitics 9, 10, 565–566, 567, **Fi** 348, 358, 376, **Fr** 195, 217, **Ge** 31, **Ma** 528–529, 540, 545, **Tu** 457–462, 463, 465, 470, 473, 477, 483
- adverbial **Ma** 530, 545
- distal **Ma** 545
- emphatic **Ma** 529, 545
- enclitics **Ma** 545, 548
- epistemic/generalizing **Tu** 457, *458*, 459–460, 461, 463, *467–468*, 470, *471–472*, 473, 482–483
- evidential 565–566, 567, **Ma** 528–529, **Tu** 457, *458*, 460, 461–462, 463, 465, *475–476*, *477–478*, *479*, *480*–481
- modal **Ma** 529
- proclitics **Fr** 195, **Ma** 546, 547
- temporal **Ma** 545 *see also* evidentials; particles; pronouns; sentence-ending modal suffixes

cognition/cognitive development 1, 3, 563–564, 568, 569, 570–572, **Cr** 159, **Ge** 26, **He** 381, 387fn, 390, 416, **Ko** 491,

492, 497, 498, 499, 503-**504**, 512, 514-516, 520-522, **Ma** 526, 549, **Ro** 249, **Ru** 427, 447-448, **Tu** 453, 454, 461, 463, 464, 484-485, 486
- cognitive complexity **Es** 315, 316, **Fr** 207-208, **Tu** 463, 485

command/order 1, 8, 555, 558, 559-560, 563, 570-571, **Cr** 159, 161, 167, 180, 181, 183, 186, **Es** 315, 316, 317, *318*-320, 326, 327, *335*, 336-339, 340-342, **Fi** 347, 349, 350, 352, **Fr** 191, 192-193, *195*, 196-197, 198, 200-202, 203, 207, 208, 209, 212, 214, 217, 222, 223, 224, 228-229, 230, 231, **Ge** 27, 30, 34fn, 35, 39, 63, **Gk** 255, 258, 264, 266, 274, 275, 277, **He** 381-382, 389, **392-393**, 415-416, **Li** 81, 83, 85-86, 91, 94-95, 102-103, 106-107, 108, **Ma** 525, 536, 537, **Ru** 114, 120, 127, 129-130, 141, 152, **Tu** 463 *see also* deontic modality; directives; imperative; requests

communication/conversation partners **Ko** 491, 498-499, 503, 505, 516, 518, 520, 522
- addressee/hearer/listener 8, 11, 560, 570-571, **Cr** 175, 177, 180, 181, 185, **Es** 315, 316, 318, 320, 321-323, 324, 326, 332-333, 334, 341-342, **Fi** 358, 375, **Fr** 191, 192-193, *195*, 196-197, 198, 200, 201, 206, 207, 215, 217, *226*, 228, **Ge** 30, 33-34, 35, 52fn, **Gk** 258, 265, 266, 274, 276, 278, 281, 282, 284-285, 290, 291, 297, 305, **He** 380fn, 381, 386, 388fn, 396, 411, 416, **Ko** 494, 497-498, **504**, 511, 514-516, 518, 519, 520-521, 522, **Li** 80, 83, 84fn, *85*, 86-88, 97-98, 102, 103-104, **Ru** 114, 116, 119, 125, 132, 138-139, 141, 144-145
- performer **Es** 316, 326, 332, 334, 341-342, **Fi** 353, **Fr** 197, 201, **Ru** 116, 132
- speaker 560, 571, **Cr** 159, 175, 185, **Es** 316, *318*, 320, 322-323, 324, 332, *335*, **336-337**, 338, 340, 341, 342, **Fi** 347, 368, **Fr** 192, 196-198, 200, 201, 217, 223, **Ge** 30, 34, 35, **Gk** 257-258, 265, 280fn, 283, 285, 290, 291, 292, 293, 300, 304, **He** 380, 387, 388fn, 410, 416, **Ko** 491, 494, 495, 496, 497-498, 499, 511, 519, 522, **Li** 80, *85*, 86-87, 88, *97*, *99-100*, 106, **Ru** 114, 116, 135, 140, 421, 422, 423, 424-427, 429, **Tu** 453, 455, *456*, 459-460, 461, 484
- speaker and addressee/hearer/listener 560, 570-571, **Cr** 177, 180, 185, **Es** 315, 317, *318*, 321, 326, 331, 340, 341, 342, **Fi** 350, 352, 358, 369, **Fr** 197, *226*, **Ge** 37, **Gk** 281-282, 290, **Ko** 491, 494, 495, 496, 498, 504-505, **Li** 83, 87, **Ru** 117, 118fn, 135, 435
- third person/party 560, **Es** 316, 320, 321, 326, 342, **Gk** 265, 267, 283, 290, 291-292, 297-298, 304, **He** 411, **Ru** 137, 144-145, 437, 447, **Tu** 456, 461 *see also* jussive; source of modality

communicative function 1, 3, 555, 569, 570, 571, **Cr** 159, 160, 162, 163, *169*, 172, 173, 177, 180, 181-182, 183-184, 185, 186-187, **Es** 316-317, 322, 323, 326, 330, 331, 334-335, 341, 342, **Fi** 375, **Fr** 192, 193-194, *195*, 197, 198, 200, 204, 207, 208, 209, 210, 211, 212, 213, 215, 217fn, 218-226, 228, 229, 230, **Ge** 30, 33-38, 49-61, **Gk** 255, 257, 307-308, 309, **He** 379-380, 381-382, 383, 388, *391*, 392, 393-394, 396, 406, 409, 411, 414, 415, 416, **Ko** 491, 493, 494, 495, 499, 501, 504, 505, 506, *509-510*, 511, 512, *513-514*, 518, 519, 520, 521-522, **Li** 79, 80, 82fn, 86, 88, 90, 91, 92, 93, 95, 108, **Ru** 114, 115, 118, 119, 120fn, 125, 126, 129, 130, 132, 133, 137, 138-139, 145, 151, 152, 153, 422, 427, 428, 447, **Tu** 453, 486 *see also* discourse; pragmatics

competition of grammatical forms **Fr** 208, 213, 214-215, 222, 226, 228, 229-230, **Gk** 308-309, **Ru** 134-135
- reformulation **Fr** 200-201, 202, 213-214, 215 *see also* child-directed speech; communicative function

concessive **Fi** 358 *see also* imperative, third person

conditional 569, **Cr** 161, 162, 182, **184**, 185, 186, **Es** *318*, 319, 322, 334, 336, 340,

341, Fi 348–349, 352, 355, 356, *357*, 358, 373, 376, Fr 204fn, Ge 32, Gk 258, 261, 267, 297, 299, Li 83, 84, *85*, 88, 96, 105, Ro 238 *see also* counterfactual constructions/structures 13, 568–569, Fi 348, 352–353, Gk 256–257, He 388, 409, 411
- elliptic Cr 170–171, Es 329–330, 331, Fr 198, 210, 212–213, Li 86, 91, 92, 94, *95*, Ru 127–*128*, 129, 139, 152
- impersonal Cr 162, Es *318*, 323, 335–336, 338, 340, 341, Fr *195*, 197, *226*, 227, He 384–385, 396
- modal Cr 159, 160, 163, 166, 173–*177*, *178*–**179**, 182, **184**, 185, 186, 187, Fi 353, 356, 358, 359, 367, 371, 373, 376, Fr 210, 211, 212, 214–215, 217, 220, *226*–*227*, 228, 230, Ge 31, 32–33, 39, 46, Gk 268–270, 292, Li 84, *85*, 87–88, 96, 101, 105, 107, Ru 113, 114, 115–116, 119–120, 127–129, 135–*142*, 144–147, 149, 150–151, 152–153 *see also* modal adverbials; modal verbs; schema
conversation/conversational/discourse interaction Fr 191, 192, 204, 206, 207–208, 214, 218–219, 222, 223–224, 229, 230, He 389, 405, Ko 491, 493, 494–495, 496–497, 498–500, 502, 505, 508fn, 511, 512, 514–516, 517, 520, Li 80, 81, 84, *97*, 108, Ru 142, 148, 429, 445–446 *see also* communication partners
conversation style, *see* parenting/ conversation style
counterfactual Cr 162, Gk 299–300, 310 *see also* conditional; irrealis; subjunctive II
Croatian 2, 13, 15–16, 108, 159–189, 340, 355, 557, 558, 559, 560, 561, *562*, 563, 569, 570

deictic(al) Fr 206, Ma 527, 531–532, 546
deontic modality 1, 4–5, 6, 7, 556–558, 559–564, 570, Cr 159, 160, 163, 173, 175, 180, 183–184, 186–187, Es 321, Fi 348, *349*, Fr 191, 192, *195*, 200, 208–209, 210, 227, 228, 229, Ge 38, Gk 257, 273, 291–297, 308–309, He 379, 380, 389, 390, 391, 400, 402, 406, 416, Ro 235, 236, 237, 238, 239–240, 241, 243, 244–246, 247–248, 249, 250–251, Ru 116, 119, 421, 426, 447, Tu 453, 456, *458*, 459, 463, *467*–468, *472*, 483, 485 *see also* command; directives; imperative; modal verbs; requests
desire/desiderative/wish 4, 5, 555, 556, 559, 560–561, 563, 570, Cr 159, 162, 172, 173, 174–175, 183, 187, Es 315, 316, *318*, 324, 330, 332, 334, *335*, **336–337**, 338, 340, 341–342, Fi 354, 365–366, 375, 376, Fr 191–192, 197, 198, 200, 201–202, Ge 30, 33, 35, 39, Gk 257, 258, 273, 276, 279, 280–282, 283, 285, 290, 296–297, 308, 309, He 379, 381, 382, 383, 387, 388, 393–395, 396, 399, 402, 406, 407, 411–412, 414, 416, Li 79, 80–81, 91, 94, 96, 97–99, *100*, 101, 105, 106–107, 108–109, Ma 525, 529, 536, 537, Ro 237, Ru 114, 115, 122, 127–128, 132, 142–143, 152–153 *see also* dynamic modality; verbs of desire; volition
development of modality 1, 2–3, 11, 13, 556, 557, 571, Cr 165, 166, 186–187, Es 315, 317, 326, 327–330, 331–336, 340–341, Fi 347, 354–355, 360–368, 368–373, Fr 194, 204, *205*–*206*, 207–208, 227, 228, 229–230, Ge 38–39, Gk 258, 259, 260, 297, 308–311, He 379, 389, 390, 391, 415–416, Li 79, 80, 81, 93–94, 95–96, 108, Ru 113, 124–125, 127, 131, 138, 151, 152, 153, Tu 463, 464, 466, 484–486
- agent-oriented Cr 160, *178*, **179**, 186–187, He 379, 380, 381, 387–389, 390, *391*, 392, 400–**401**, 402–407, 416
- deontic Cr 160, *178*, Ge 41, 42, 44, 45, *46*, *47*, *48*, *49*, *50*, *52*–*53*, *54*–*55*, 56–*57*, *59*–60, *64*–*71*, He 379, 389, 391, **392–393**, *402*, 403, 405, 416
- deontic vs. dynamic 559–564, Cr 180, 186–187, Fr 198, 200, 208, Ge 38, He *402*–403, 405, Ro 235, 237, 241–242, *247*, 248, 250–251
- deontic/dynamic vs. epistemic/ evidential 559, 568, 570, Cr 159, 163, 175, Ge 38, Gk 258, 260, 297, 306, 309,

310, **He** 380–381, 400–**401**, 407, 408, 416, **Ro** 235–236, 237–238, 241–242, 246, 248, 249, 250, 251, **Ru** 447–448, **Tu** 463, *467–468*, 471–*472*, 483
– dynamic **He** 380, 381, 387, *402*–403, 405, 406, 407, 409, 414, 416
– epistemic **Cr** 163, 187, **He** 379, 387fn, 389, 391, 407, 408–409, **Ru** 421, 426–428, 429–439, 447, 448, **Tu** 467–475
– epistemic/evidential **Ko** 491–492, 500–512, 514–515, 516, 519–522
– epistemic vs. evidential 564–568, **Ge** 39, **Ro** 237–238, **Tu** 463, 464, *466–467*, 484–486
– evidential **Tu** 475–481 *see also* emergence, order; epistemic gap; modal verbs
directives 8, 556–558, 560, 569, 570–571, 572, **Es** 315–317, 326, **Fi** 347, 348–349, 352–355, 356–359, 360–364, 364–367, 368–373, 374–376, **Fr** 191, 192–194, *195*, 196–197, 199, 200, 203, 212, 215, 217–218, 220, 222, 223, *226–227*, 228, 229, 230, 231, **Ge** 25–26, 33–34, 35, 49, *50*, *51*, 52–54, 61–62, *68*, *69*, **Gk** 256, 258, 273, 289, 290, **He** 381–382, 389, 392, 415, **Li** 79, 81, 82, 95, 108, **Ma** 534, **Ro** 238, 251, **Ru** 113, 114, 115–120, *121–122*, 122–125, 127, *128*, 129, *130*, *131*, 132, 134–135, *136*, 139–*141*, 142, *144*, *146*, 147–151, 152, 153, 447 *see also* command; requests; speech acts; verbless utterances
discourse 11, 568, 571–572, **Fr** 215, 216, 226, 229, **Ge** 62
– contextual (in)dependence/variation **Fr** 193, 200, 206, 214, 220, 229, 230, **Ge** 27fn, 30, **Gk** 268–270, 275–276, 309, **Ko** 501, 504, 508–509, 517, **Li** 84, **Ro** 235, 236, 238–241, 248, 250, **Ru** 118, 120, 127, 141, 142–143, 434, 435, **Tu** 459, 461, 468, 475, 481, 486
– discourse-pragmatic factors **He** 411, **Ko** 491, 492, 494, 496, 516, 519, 520, 522
– type **Fr** 215–216, 229, **Tu** 484 *see also* conversation; pragmatics
discourse marker, *see* interjection

dubitative **Ma** 529, 546, 547 *see also* information
Dutch 38
dynamic modality 1, 4, 5, 7, 9, 559–564, 565, 569, 570, **Cr** 159, 162, 163, 173, 175, 180, 183, 186–187, **Fi** 348, 353–354, **Fr** 191–192, 198, 200, 202, 208, **Gk** 257, 258, 260, 264, 270, 273, 279–281, 287, 288, 290, 291, 296–297, 302, 304, 308–309, **He** 379–380, 381, 387, 389, 391, 397, *402*, **403–404**, 405, 406, 407, 409–414, 416, **Ro** 235, 236, 237, 238, 239, 240–241, 243–246, *247*, 248, 249, 250–251, **Ru** 421, **Tu** 456, *458*, 459, 463, 464, *467*, 471–*472*, 483, 485 *see also* ability; desire; intention; modal verbs; need

emergence, order 556, 559, 562–563, 566–567, 568, 569, **Cr** 159–160, 165, *166*–173, 175, 177, *178*, 181, 186, 187, **Es** 315, 326, 328–329, 330–331, 333, 334, *335*, 338, 340, 341–342, **Fi** 347, 360–364, 368–370, 371, 375, **Fr** 193–194, 203, 204, 210, *226–227*, 228, 230, **Ge** 38, 39, 62, **Gk** 259, 297, 302, 308–309, 310–311, **He** 381, 387, 388, 400, 402, 407, 408, 409, 414, 416, **Li** 82, *99–100*, 101, 102, 106, **Ro** 237–238, 241, *247*, 248, 250, 251, **Ru** 114, 115, 126fn, 141, 151, 424, 426, 429–432, 433–434, 439, *441–442*, 443, 444, 447–448, **Tu** 453, 463, 464, 467, *472*, **482–483**, 484, 485–486 *see also* development of modality
English 9–10, 11, 38, 81, 82, 84, 148, 197, 227, 231, 236, 237–238, 250, 259, 267, 270fn, 310fn, 341, 355, 416, 424fn, 499fn
entrenchment 568–569, **Es** 326, **Fi** 375, **Gk** 256, 259, 260, **Ru** 440, 442, **Tu** 455, 486 *see also* input–output relation
epistemic gap **Gk** 310, **Ro** 235, 238, 251 *see also* development of modality
epistemic marker, *see* modal adverbials, epistemic

epistemic modality 1, 4, 6, 7, 9–10, 11, 564–568, 569–570, 571, **Cr** 159, 163, 175, 187, **Es** 315, **Ge** 38, **Gk** 257–258, 259, 260, 261, 267–270, 279–280, 297–298, 300–304, 306–307, 309–311, **He** 379, 380, 381, 387fn, 389, 391, 398, 400, 408–409, 416, **Ko** 491, 494, 504, 506, 519, 521, **Li** 84fn, 102, **Ro** 235–236, 237–238, 239–240, 241, 246–247, 248–250, 251, **Ru** 421–428, 429–439, 446, 447–448, **Tu** 453, 454, 455–456, 457–458, 459–460, 463, 464, *466*, 467–475, 477, 483, 484
– assumption/assumptive 9, 10, **Ru** 424, **Tu** 456, 459–460, *468*, 469, 470, *471*, 472–473, 474–475, 484
– deduction/deductive 9, 10, **Ru** 424, **Tu** 456, 459, 461, 463, *468*, 469, 470, *471*, 472, 473, 474–475, 484
– epistemic/evidential **Ko** 494, 498, 503, 506, 508, 519, 522
– epistemic vs. evidential 566–567, **He** 380, **Tu** 454, 455–*456*, *458*, 461, 463, 464, 465, *466*–467, 484–486
– evaluation/evaluative 571, **Ro** 236, 238, 251, **Ru** 421, 424–426, 427, 435, 436fn, 437, 439, 447, **Tu** 453, 455, 471, 473–474
– inflectional vs. lexical expression 564, 567, **Gk** 258, 261, 267, 297, 302–303, 309, 311, **He** 382, 397, 398–399, 400, 408, **Tu** 453, *458*, 467, *468*, 469, 470, 471, *472*, *479*, 480, 484, 485
– speculation/speculative 9, 10, **Tu** *456*, 459, 460, *468*, 469–470, *471*, *472*–473, 474–475, 484 *see also* certainty; judgment; modal adjectives; modal adverbials; modal expressions; modal verbs; possibility, epistemic; propositional modality
Estonian *2*, 13, 17, 84, 315–345, 427, 448, 558, 559, 561, *562*, 563, 569, 570–571
event modality 4fn, **Ru** 421, **Tu** 456 *see also* agent-oriented modality
evidentiality 565, 566, **Es** 315, **Ko** 491, 494, 506, 519, 521, **Ma** 525–526, 527–528, 550–551, **Ru** 421, **Tu** 453, 454, 455, 460, 461, 477, 481 *see also* evidential modality
evidential languages **Tu** 455
evidential modality 1, 4, 5–7, 10–11, 564, 565–568, 569, 571–572, **Gk** 258, 261fn, 270, 299, 304, 305, **He** 380, **Ma** 525–526, **Ro** 246, **Ru** 421, **Tu** 453, 454, 455–456, 457–458, 460–462, 463, 464, 465, 466–467, 475–481, 484–486
see also hearsay; inference; information source; quotative; reportative
evidentials **Ma** 525–526, 527–529, 531, 534, 537–538, 540, 546, 548–549, 550, **Tu** 455, 461fn *see also* clitics; modal expressions, inflectional

Fennic *2*
fine-tuning **Cr** 180, 187, **Fr** 219, **Gk** 259, **Li** 109, **Ru** 445–446, **Tu** 473
Finnish *2*, 8, 13, 18, 38, 84, 108, 310, 340, 347–378, 557, 558, 559, 560, 561, *562*, 563, 569
Finno-Ugric *2*, 558, 559
French *2*, 9, 11fn, 13, 16, 38, 84, 191–234, 237, 238, 310, 448, 471, 557, 558, 559, 560, 561–562, 563, 569
frequency 561, 568–570, 571, 572, **Cr** 160, 167–*168*, 169–*170*, 172, 173, *174*, 175, 176–*177*, 178, **179**–*180*, 182–*183*, **184**, 185–186, **Es** *325*, 332, **336**, **337**, *338*, *339*, 340, 341, 342, **Fi** 352, 358, 359, 361, 362, 363–364, 367, 368, 375, **Fr** 193, 202, *203*, 204, 209fn, 210fn, *216*, 222, 223, 228, 229, **Ge** 25–26, 30, 32, 33, 34, 35, 36, 39, 40, 42, *43*, 45, *46*–*60*, 61–63, *64*–*72*, **Gk** 256, 258, 259, 260, 263, 273, 274, 275, 277–278, 283, 285, 287, 288, 289, 291, 296, 305, 307–309, 310, **He** 379, 380, 381, 386, 388, 389, 390, 397, **401**, **402**, **403–404**, 405, 406, 409, *410*, 411, 412, *413*–*414*, 415, 416, **Ko** 491, 492, 493, 494–495, 496, *507*–*508*, *509*–*510*, 511, **512**, *513*–**514**, 515, 517–**518**, 520, 521–522, **Li** 80, 81, 82, 90–91, 92–93, *94*–*95*, 95–96, *97*, 98–99, 101–102, 104, 106–107, 108, 109, **Ro** 241, 247–249,

250, 251, **Ru** 113, 114, 115, 119, *121–122*, 123–**124**, 125, 126, *130–131*, 132, 133–135, *136*, 138, *140–141*, 142, 143, 144, *146*, 147, 149, 151, 421, 426, 432–433, 439–442, **443–444**, 447, 448, **Tu** 453, 454, 455, 463, 464, 467, *468*, 470–471, *472*, 474–475, 477–478, 479, *480–481*, **482–483**, 484, 485–486
  see also input–output relation
future imperative 558, 559, 560, **He** 386, 390, **392–393**, 395, **396–397**, 415–416
future tense 560, **Cr** 173, 186, **Fr** *195*, 197, *226–227*, **Gk** 259, 261, 262–263, 264, 265–267, 273, 276, 277, 278, 279–283, 284–285, 286, 287–288, 290, 297–298, 307–309, **He** 384, 385, 386, 388, 397, 400, **Li** 83, *85*, 86, 91, 92–93, *94–95*, 102–103, **Ro** 238, **Ru** 116–117, 118, 119, 120, 126, *128–129*, 137, 144–147, 152, **Tu** *458*, 459, 462, 465, 470, 474, 482–483
future II **Gk** 297, 299, 310

gender-related communication **Ge** 63, **He** 387, 388, 411, **Li** 79, 81, 82, 108–109, **Ru** 427
– boys' vs. girls' speech **Cr** 166–167, 174, **Ge** 29, 39, 63, **He** 387–388, **Li** 82, 90–91, 92–93, 95, 96–97, *99–100*, 101, 106–107, 108, **Ru** 430–431, 439, 441
– fathers' speech **Fr** 203, 223, 227, **Li** 81, 89fn, 94–95
– mother–boy vs. mother–girl dyad **Li** 90–91, 94–95, 101–102, 105, 107, 108–109
German *2*, 8, 9, 11, 12, 13, 14, 25–77, 197, 198, 227, 250, 267, 310, 355, 556, 558, 559fn, 560, 569, 572
Germanic *2*, 119
gesture **Cr** 160, **Ma** 530, 531, 536 *see also* pointing gestures
grammatical complexity 569, **Cr** 159, 161, 166, 175, 182, 187, **Es** 315, 316, 318, 320, 326, 330–331, 333, 335, 341, 342, **Fi** 355, 361, 375, 376, **Fr** 209, 211, 230 **Gk** 259, 269, **He** 416, **Ko** 493, 519, **Li** 96, 105, 109, **Ru** 153, 426–427, **Tu** 454, 465, 473, 486

grammaticalization/grammaticization 3, 6, 10, 11, 559, 564, 565, 568, **Ge** 35, 39, 52fn, **Gk** 310, 311, **Ko** 519, **Ru** 117fn, 118, **Tu** 454, 486
Greek 1, *2*, 3, 9, 11, 13, 17, 38, 108, 147, 186, 187, 237, 255–313, 317, 340, 341, 355, 375, 415, 485, 557, 558, 559–560, 561, *562*, 563, 564–565, *567*, 569, 571

hearsay 7, 10, 555, 566, **Ko** 494, 495, 496, 502–**504**, 508, *509*, 510, *513*, **514–515**, **Ma** 528, 529, 530–531, 540, 549, **Tu** 455, 461, 463 *see also* evidential modality; information source; narrative
Hebrew *2*, 13, 18, 38, 310, 379–419, 557–558, 559, 560, 561, *562*, 563, 564, 565, *567*, 569, 570, 571
hortative 8, 557, 558, 560, **Cr** 161, 164, 171, 177, 178, **179**–180, **184**, 185, 186, **Es** 316, *318*, 321, 331, 332, *335*, **336**, **337**, 338, 340, 341, 342, **Fi** 350, 352–353, 363–364, 369, 375, **Fr** *195*, 197, *226*, 227, **Ge** 27, 29fn, 31, 36, 37, 42, 43, 46–47, 49, 56–57, *58*, **Gk** 265, 281–282, 290, **Ko** 493, **Li** 79, *85*, 87, *99*, *100*, 101–102, 106, 107, 108, **Ru** 113, 114, 117, 118, 120, **123**, **124**, 127, 129, 134, 135–139, 145, 152, 153, 447 *see also* suggestion

iconicity **Fr** 214
ideophone **Ma** 531, 536
illocutionary force/strength **Fr** 191, 192, 193–194, 196, 197–198, 199, 210, 211–212, 213, 214, 215, 217, 220, 221, 223, 226, 229, **Gk** 285, **He** 386fn, **Ma** 545 *see also* modal strength
imitation **Fi** 361, **Fr** 207, **Ge** 39, 42, **Tu** 454 *see also* rote-learning
imperative 8, 556–558, 559–560, 563, 569, 570, 572, **Cr** 159, 160, 161, 163, 164, *165–166*, 167–171, 173, *178*, **179**, *180*, *181*–182, 183, **184**, 185–186, 187, **Es** 315, *318*–319, 320, 321–322, 328, 329, 330, 333fn, 335, 337, 340, 341, 342, **Fi** 347, 348–352, 355, 358–359, 360, 361–362,

363, 364, 368, *369*, 370, 373, 374–375, 376, **Fr** 191, 192, 193, 194–196, 197, 199–200, 202–208, 209–215, 218–219, 220–226, 227, 228–230, **Ge** 25, 27, 28–29, 30–31, 33, 35, 36–37, 38–39, 42, 43, 44–45, 46, 47, 48–49, 52fn, 56–*57*, *58*, 60fn, 61, 62, 63, *64–67*, *70–71*, **Gk** 258, 259, 261, 262, 263–264, 266–267, 273–275, 276, 277–278, 279, 284, 288, 289, 307, 308, 309, **He** 379, 381–382, 385–386, 388, 390, **392–393**, 394–395, **396–397**, 415–416, **Ko** 493, **Li** 79, 81, 82, 83, 84, *85*, 87, 91–92, *94–95*, 96, 101, 108, **Ma** 542, **Ro** 238, 251, **Ru** 113, 114, 115, 116–118, 120, **123**, **124**, 125–126, 127, 129, *130–131*, 132–135, 138–139, 147–148, 149, 151–152, 153, 447, **Tu** 465
– imperfective **Gk** 263, 264, 273–274, **Ru** 118, 133, 134, 138–139, 147–148, 149–150, 151
– negated/negative **Cr** 161, 171, **Es** *318*, 319–320, 328–329, 330, 333fn, *335*, 338, 341, **Fi** 351–352, 358, 362, 373, **Fr** 195, 209, *219*–220, **Li** *85*, 86, 93, **Ru** 118, 123, 149-**150**, 151
– non-canonical/colloquial **Cr** 177, **Fi** 349, *350*, 351, *352*, 360–361, **Li** 83, 87, **Ru** 117, 135
– perfective **Gk** 263, 264, 273–274, **Ru** 118, 133, 134, 139, 147–148, 149, 150
– third person **Fi** 349–352, 359, 362, **Ru** 117, 118, 145 *see also* command; hortative; jussive; prohibition
imperative paradigm **Fi** 349–352, **Li** 83, **Ru** 115–116, 117, 118 *see also* hortative; jussive; particles, passive
indicative 8, 9, **Cr** 186, **Fi** 352, 355, 362, **Fr** 193, 220–221, **Ge** 29, 39, **Gk** 261, 279, **Ko** 493–494, **Ro** 240, 243, **Ru** 118–119 *see also* non-past; present indicative
individual/intersubjective differences/variation 572, **Es** 340, **Ge** 42, **Gk** 275–276, 311, **Ko** 496, **Ru** 113, 115, 124–125, 134–135, 139, 152, 153, 432–*433*, 439
Indo-European *2*, 558, 559, 564

inference/inferential 7, 10, 566–567, **Gk** 299, 305, **Ko** 494, 495, 497–498, 509, *510*, 511-**512**, *513*, **514**, 521–522, **Ma** 527, 531–532, **Tu** 455, *456*, 459, 461–462, 463, *475*, 476, *477–478*, *479*, *480*, *481*, 484–485 *see also* evidential modality; information source
infinitive 9, 12, 556–557, 558, 559, 560, 569, 572, **Cr** 160, 161, 163, *165–167*, 171, *176–177*, 178, **179**, 180, **184**, 185, 186, 187, **Es** *318*, 320, 321, 331, 332, 333, 337, 341, **Fi** 353, 355, **Gk** 261, **He** 382, 383, 384, 408, **Li** 79, *85*, 86, 87, 91, 92, 93, *94–95*, 108, **Ru** 447
– 3rd infinitive illative 560, **Fi** 348–349, 352–353, 359, 360, 361, 363, 368, 369, 370, 373, 375, 376
– deontic vs. dynamic **Cr** 186, **Ge** 30
– modalized **Cr** 172–*173*, *178*, 179, 180, 186, 187, **Ge** 25, 27, 30–31, 36–37, 38, 39, 42, 43, 45–46, 47, 48–49, 56–*57*, *58*, 61, 62, 63, *64–66*, **He** 385, 386, 388, **392–393**, 394–398, **Ru** 113, 114, 118–119, 120, **123**, **124**, 125–126, 127–132, 133, 134–135, 139, 151, 152, 153
– modalized vs. non-modalized 556–557, 558, 559, 560, 572, **Cr** 172, **Fr** 208–209, 217, **Ge** 33fn, **Ru** 115
– root infinitive 557, **Fr** 191, 193, 194, *195*, 198, 201–204, 208–215, 218–219, 220, 222, 228–229, 230, **Ge** 30–31
information 10, 555, 558, 565, 566–567, 571–572, **Ge** 34, 40, 62, **Gk** 307, **Ru** 423
– assimilated/old 566, **Ko** 491, 494, 501, 503, **504**, 514, 520, 522, **Tu** 461
– conflicting/contrastive **Ko** 495, 496–497, 509, *510*, 511, *513*, 515, 518–519
– factual/nonfactual 4, 5–6, 7, 566–567, 571, **Gk** 257, **Ko** 495, **Ru** 423, 425, 429, **Tu** 453, 455, *456*, 459, 460, 461, 484
– general/generic 10, 555, **Ko** 495, 496, 502, 504, 506, 518, **Tu** 455, *456*, 459, 461fn, 463
– new/surprise 566, 571, **Ko** 491, 494, 495, 496–497, **504**, 520, 522, **Tu** 453, 461–462, 463, *475*–476, *477*–478, *479*, *480–481*, 484–485

Subject Index — 585

- reliable 555, 571, **Ru** 421
- shared **Ko** 491, 493–494, 495, 496–497, 498–499, 501–502, 503, **504**, *509*, 511, **512**, *513*–**514**, 515, 518–519, 520–521, 522 see also evidential modality; knowledge

information source 7, 10, 555, 565, 566–567, 571, **Ma** 525, 529, 531, 540, 543–544, 547–548, 549–550, **Tu** 453–454, 455, 461, 481, 484
- direct 566, **Ko** 494, 495, 496, 497, 503, *509*, 511, *513*, **514**, 515, 521, **Tu** *456*, 460, 461, 475–476, 480, 485
- indirect 566, **Ko** 494, 496, 510, 514–515, **Ma** 532, 549, **Tu** *456*, 460, 484–485
- non-specified **Ma** 525, 527–528
- perceptual/sensory 7, 10, 558, 566, **Ko** 495, 496, 497, 501, 504, 509, *510*, 511, *513*, **514**, 520, 521, **Ma** 525, 527, 531–532, **Ru** 423, **Tu** *456*, 461, 463, 475–476 see also evidential modality; hearsay; quotative; reportative

input **Es** 317, **Fi** 347–348, **Ge** 25, 26, 27, 39–40, 50–*51*, 56, 62, 64, **Gk** 256, 259, 290, **He** 379, 389, 390, 415, 416, **Li** 80, 95, **Ma** 526, 534–537, 540–542, **Ro** 235, 241, 248–249, **Ru** 123, 124, **Tu** 453, 454, 463, 464, 477, 482, 484, 485–486 see also child-directed speech; input–output relation

input–output relation/input models 568–570, 571–572, **Cr** 161, 163, 172, 173, 180–186, 187, **Es** 336–340, 341, 342, **Fi** 356, 367, 373–374, 375, 376, **Fr** 227, 230, **Ge** 25, 39–40, 51, **Gk** 297, 304, 311, **He** 382fn, 386, 387–388, **392**–400, 400–409, 409–414, 415, 416, **Ko** 491, 492, 499fn, *507*–*508*, 509, *513*–**514**, 517–**518**, 519, 520, 521, 522, **Li** 81, 82, 83, *85*, 86, *89*–*90*, 91–98, 101, *106*–*107*, 108–109, **Ma** 540, **Ro** 241, 242, 248, 250, 251, **Ru** 127, 128, 130–132, 133, *136*–137, 139, *140*–*142*, 144–145, *146*–147, 148, *150*–151, 152, 153, 439–446, 448, **Tu** 463, 482–483, 484, 485–486

- high vs. low socio-economic status **Ge** 39–40, 43–49, 49–61, 61–63, *64*–*72* see also child-directed speech; frequency; structural resonance

instruction **Es** 317, **Fr** 192, 198, 215–217, 221–222, 226, 229, **He** 385–386, 397, **Li** 83 see also directives

intention 5, 9, 560, 570, **Cr** 159, 172, 173, **Gk** 264, 265, 267, 273, 279, 280–281, 282, 285, 287–288, 290, 297–298, 308, **He** 381, 391, 397, 399, 411–412, 414, **Ru** 117fn, 129, 130, 152, 447 see also dynamic modality

interjection **Cr** 170, 185, **Es** 327, **Fr** 196, 207, **Ge** 35–36, 52fn

irrealis **Ge** 32, **He** 385 see also conditional; counterfactual; subjunctive II

Italian 38

Japanese 9, 11, 81

joint action/activity/attention 570–571, **Cr** 185, **Es** 315, 317, *318*, 321, 340, 341–342, **Fi** 369, **Ge** 35, 38, **Gk** 281–282, 290, **He** 405, **Ko** 505, **Ru** 130, 135, 438 see also communication partners, speaker and addressee; hortative

judgment/opinion 6, 7, 9, 10, **Gk** 258, **He** 380, 416, **Ru** 422–423, 425–427, 430–431, 432–*433*, 438, *441*, **443**, 447, **Tu** 453, 455, *456*, 461fn, 473, 481 see also information

jussive 8, **Cr** 164, **Es** 316, *318*, 321, 333, **Fi** 359, **Ru** 114, 117, 118, 120, *144*–147

knowledge **Gk** 270fn, 304, 305, **He** 387fn, **Ko** 491, 494, 495, 498–499, 501, 503–505, 514, 515, 516, 519–521, 522, **Ru** 423, 425, **Tu** 455, 456, 459, 460, 461, 463, 471, 475, 484–485 see also also information; information source

Korean *2*, 3, 4, 6, 9, 10, 11, 14, 19–20, 238, 310, 311, 380, 485, 491–524, 526, 549, 558, 564, 565, 566–*567*, 568, 569, 571

Lithuanian *2*, 13, 14–15, 79–112, 340, 355, 558fn, 559, 560, *562*, 563, 569, 572

Mam 548–549
Mayan 2, 6, 10, 13fn, 20, 525–553, 564, 565, 566, *567 see also* Tojolabal; Yukatek
mean length of utterance (MLU) **Cr** 164, *166*–167, **Es** 326, **He** *391*, **Ro** *242*, **Ru** 125, **Tu** *465*
metapragmatics **Ma** 525, 529, 540, 543–544, 545, 549, 550–551
Mexicano 548
miniparadigm 12, **Cr** 160, *165*–167, 173, 175, 187, **Es** 328fn, 329fn, **Fi** 348, 363–364, 370, **He** 387fn
mitigation/softening 572, **Fi** 347, 352, 356, 358, 359, 373, 376, **Fr** 196, 197, 211–212, 218–219, 229, **Ge** 27fn, **Gk** 273–274, 284–285, **He** 386, **Li** 81, 82, 84, 86, 87, 99, 102, 105, **Ru** 117, 118, 132 *see also* politeness
modal adjectives 8, 9, 564, 570, **Ge** 27fn, **Gk** 258, **He** 379, 382, 383–384, 389, 400–409, 415, 416, **Ro** 237–238, **Ru** 114, 115–116, 118, 119, 120, 123, 127–*128*, 129, 424, **Tu** 458
– agent-oriented **He** 403–404
– agent-oriented vs. epistemic **He** 400–**401**, 407, 408
– deontic **He** 384, 389, 390, *391*, *402*, 405, 406, 407, 416
– dynamic **He** 385, 402
– epistemic **He** 381, 382, 385, 390, *391*, **401**, 408–409
modal adverbials/adverbs 8, 9, 10, 557, 558, 559, **Cr** 161, **Fi** 348, 354, 364, 366, 367, 370, 371, 374, 375, **Ge** 27fn, **Gk** 258, 261, 267, 270, 297, 300–302, 309, 310, **He** 379, 382, 400–407, 408–409, 415, 416, **Li** 79, 86, 91, *94–95*, 108, **Ro** 238, **Ru** 113, 114, 115–116, 118, 119, 120, 123, 127–*128*, 129, 131, 139–142, 152, 424, **Tu** 458, 480, 483, 484, 485
– agent-oriented **He** 402–407
– agent-oriented vs. epistemic **He** **401**, 407
– deontic **He** 385, 390, *402*, **Ru** 119
– epistemic (markers) **He** 381, 382, 385, 390, *391*, 408–409, **Ro** 235, 237–238, 240, 241, 243, 246–247, 249, 250, 251, **Ru** 421, 422–428, **429**–439, 439–440, 440–446,
447, 448, **Tu** 453, 458, 459–460, 467, 469, 470, 471, 473–474, 477
– epistemic vs. evidential 564–565, 567, 569, 570, **Tu** 477
– evidential **Tu** 477, *479*, *480 see also* parenthetical modal words; particles, modal
modal auxiliaries, *see* modal verbs
modal cluster **He** 385, 388, **392**–400
modal continuum, *see* modal scale
modal expressions
– inflectional 3, 8, 555, 559, 560, 562–564, 565–568, 569, **Cr** 161, 164, 165, 167–173, *178*–**179**, 180–182, 186, **Fi** 347, 353, 375, **Fr** *205*, **Gk** 258, 261–267, 273–290, 308, 309, **He** 379, 381, 385, 388, 390–*391*, **392**–400, 415, 416, **Ro** 235, 238, **Ru** 118–119, 134–135, **Tu** 453, 457, 460, 461, 465, *467*, 468, 469, 470, 471, *472*, 473, *475*, 477, 482, 483, 484, 485, 486 *see also* case marking; imperative; modal/non-modal distinction; subjunctive; tense
– lexical 3, 6, 8, 10, 11, 555, 559, 560–565, 567, 568, **Cr** 161, 163, 164, 173–*178*, 179, 182–185, 186–187, **Fi** 347, 353, **Gk** 258, 261, 267–270, 291–297, 302–303, 308, 309, **He** 379, 381, 382, 390–*391*, 400–409, 409–414, 416, **Ru** 118–119, 134, 427, 440–441, **Tu** 453, 467, 468, 470, 471, 477, 483, 484, 485 *see also* modal adjectives; modal adverbials; modal verbs; verbs
modality 1, 4, 7, 13, 555, 559, 569, 572, **Es** 315–316, **Ge** 25, **He** 381, **Tu** 453–454
modal/non-modal distinction/split 1, 3, 556–558, **Cr** 186, **Es** 340fn, **Fi** 355, 374, **Gk** 259, 288–289, 307–308, 310, **He** 381, 388, 415, **Ru** 113–114, 115, 125, 137, **Tu** 455, 463, 465, *467*, 471, *472*, 477, 482–483
– modally neutral **Tu** 455, *458*, 459, 460, 462, 473, 485 *see also* infinitive
modal scale 6, 571, **Fr** 231, **Gk** 267–268, 270fn, 286–287
– epistemic **He** 408, **Ko** 491, **Ru** 422–424, 442, **Tu** 453, 469, 484

– necessity–possibility 571, **Tu** 453, 455, 459 see also certainty; modal strength
modal strength 571, **Fi** 353, **Gk** 266, 270, 275, 286–287, 300, 301–302, **Ko** 491, **Ru** 148, 421, 428, 433, 442, 448, **Tu** 459–460, 471, 473, 484 see also illocutionary force; modal scale
modal verbs 8, 9, 10, 11, 564, 570, **Cr** 159, 160, 161, 163, 164, 172, 173–*177*, *178*–**179**, 180, 182–185, 186–187, **Es** 315, **Fi** 348, 353–354, 356, *357*, 358, 359, 367, 371–373, 376, **Fr** 212–213, 215, **Ge** 27, 32–33, 39, 47–*48*, 49, 59–60, 61, 63, **Gk** 258, 260, 261, 264, 267, 268–270, 273, 291, 293–297, 300, 302–304, 306–307, 308–309, 310, **He** 379, 381, 382, 389, 390–*391*, 400, 415, 416, **Li** 84, 103, **Ro** 235, 236, 238, 251, **Ru** 113, 114, 118, 119, 128, 424, **Tu** 484, 485
– agent-oriented meaning/use **He** 382, 388, *391*, 402–407, 408
– agent-oriented vs. epistemic meaning/use **He** 380, 400–**401**, 407, 408, 416
– deontic meaning/use 8, 9, 561–562, 563, 564, 570, **Cr** 163, 175, 183–184, 186–187, **Es** *318*, 320, 322, 323, **Fi** 353–354, 359, 367, 372–373, **Fr** *195*, 197–198, 200–201, 210, 214, 217, 220, *226–227*, 228, 230, **Ge** 25, 32, 33, 37–38, 39, 43, **Gk** 264, 294–295, **He** 382, 389, **Ro** 237, 239, 240, 244–246
– deontic vs. dynamic meaning/use 562, 563, 570, **Cr** 186, **Ge** 38, 39, **Gk** 291, 296, **Ro** 235, 237, 241, 244, *247–248*, 250–251
– deontic/dynamic vs. epistemic meaning/use 564–565, **Cr** 175, **Gk** 267–269, 297, 306–307, 309, **Ro** 235, 237, 238, 239–241, 248, 249, 251
– dynamic meaning/use 5, 9, 560–561, 562–563, 564, 570, **Cr** 163, 173, 175, 183, 186–187, **Es** 331, 332, 340, **Fi** 353–354, **Ge** 33, 39, **Gk** 291, 293–294, 296, 302, 308, 309, **He** 387, 388, *391*, 402, **403**–**404**, 405, 406, 407, 409–414, 416, **Ro** 235, 236, 237, 239, 240–241, 243–244, 245, 246, *247*, 248, 249, 251
– epistemic meaning/use 6–7, 9, 11, 564–565, 567, 569, **Cr** 163, 175, 187, **Fr** 197, **Ge** 39, **Gk** 261, 267–269, 270, 297, 300, 302–304, 306–307, 309, 310, **He** 380, 408–409, **Ro** 235–236, 239–240, 241–242, 246, 248–249, 250–251
see also constructions, modal; quasi-modal verbs; verbs of desire

narrative/story-telling 10, 566, **Ko** 495, 496, 502–503, **504**, 508–*509*, 510, **512**, *513*, **514**–515, 521–522, **Ma** 525, 531, 533–534, 540, 544, 546–549, 550, **Ru** 142–143, 152, **Tu** 461, 462, 463, 467, *475*, 476, *477*, *478*, *479*, *480*, *481*, 484 see also evidential modality; hearsay
necessity 5, 6, 7, 566, 571, **Gk** 257–258, 267–268, 270, 276, 294, 300, 304, **Tu** 453
– deontic **Es** *318*, 322, 333–334, **Fi** 353, 359, **Fr** *226*, 227, **He** 380, *391*, 402, 405, 406, 407, **Ru** 113, 116, 119, 121, 127, 139–*142*, 144, 149, **150**, 151, 152, **Tu** 459
– dynamic **He** 379, **Ro** 236
– epistemic **Cr** 163, **Ro** 241fn, **Tu** 455, 459
see also dynamic modality; modal scale; modal verbs; need
need 5, 562, 564, **Cr** 163, 173, **174**, *183*, **Es** 316, 322, 341, **Fi** 358, **Ge** 34, 38, 62, 63, **He** 379, 381–382, *391*, 396, 407, 414, 415, **Li** 79, **85**, 86–87, 96, 97–99, **Ro** 236, 238–239, 240, 241, 245–246, *247*, 248, 251, **Tu** 486
negation/negative 9, 562, **Cr** 170, 171, 174, **Es** *318*, 319–320, 324, 328–329, 330, 332–333, **335**, 339, 341, **Fi** 351, 352, 353–354, 355, 358, 360, 362–363, 366, 372, 373, **Fr** *195*, 198, 209, *219*–220, *226*, 227, 228–229, **Gk** 262–263, 270, 277, 288, 295, 304, **He** 380, 381, 385, 405, 406, **Li** *85*, 93, **Ru** 118, 120, 123, 141, *142*, 143, 149, 151, 152, 153 see also imperative, negated; negator; prohibition

negator
- particle **Cr** 161, **Es** 319–320, 330, 333, 338, **Fi** 366–367, **Fr** 209, **Gk** 262, 264, 277, **He** 405
- prefix **Li** 86, 88, 93

non-past
- imperfective 557, **Gk** 259, 262, 263–264, 268–269, 273, 277–278, 279, 286–289, 291, 292, 293, 294, 296, 297, 304, 305, 306, 307, 309
- perfective **Gk** 263, 279–280 *see also* future; present indicative; subjunctive

noun, *see* case marking

obligation/obligative 4, 5, 7, 557, 570, **Cr** 159, **Es** *318*, 322, **336–337**, 338, 342, **Fi** 348, 353, 373, **Fr** 191, 192, 194–198, 199–202, 217–218, 226–227, 228, **Gk** 257, 291, 294, 296, 306, **He** 379, 380, 383–384, *402*, 406, 407, 416, **Ma** 528, 529, 531, **Tu** 463 *see also* necessity, deontic

one-word utterances/holophrases 557, **He** 390fn
- modal **Cr** 160, 172–*173*, 176, **179**, 186, 187, **Fi** 364–365, 367, **Ko** 506, 508, **Li** 79, 91–92, 93, *94–95*, 96, 105, 108, **Ru** 125, 127
- non-modal **Cr** 172 *see also* imperative; infinitive; requests, elliptic; verbless utterances

opinion/viewpoint, *see* judgment
optative 8, 558, **He** 381, **Tu** 465
order, *see* command
overgeneralization **Cr** 175–176, **Fi** 361 *see also* productivity

parenthetical modal words 564, **Ru** 424, 425, 447 *see also* modal adverbials, epistemic
parenting/conversation style 572, **Ge** 25, 26, 61, 63, **Li** 95, 107, 108, **Ma** 534, 535, **Ru** 142
- behavior-directing/controlling 572, **Ge** 25, 26–27, 35, 39, 45, 51, 61–62, **He** 389, 415–416
- conversation-eliciting/explanatory/responsive 572, **Ge** 25, 26, 35, 40, 61–62, **He** 389, 415–416 *see also* child-directed speech; gender-related communication

participle **Cr** 162, **He** 382fn
- past **Fr** 204fn, **Ro** 240, 243

particles **Fi** 358, 373, **Gk** 279, 298
- future **Gk** 262, 279, 280, 297–298, 300
- modal **Cr** 170–171, **Es** 319, 321–322, 324, 333, 336, 340, **Ge** 27fn, 39, **Gk** 262, 265, 277, 279, 280, 300, 303, **Li** 84, 88, 102, 105, **Ru** 113, 117–118, 132, 134, 135–139, 144–145, 152, 423, 424
- passive **Fi** 347, 348–350, 351–352, 354–355, 356, *357*, 358, 359, 360, 363, 368, 369, 373, 375, 376
- question **Li** 84, 88, 102 *see also* imperative paradigm; negator; sentence-ending modal particles

past/past tense 556–557, 557–558, **Fr** 204fn, **Gk** 259, 262, 269–270, 291–292, 307, **He** 381, 382fn, 383–384, 388, 390, 399, 400, 411–412, 414, 415, **Ko** 493fn, 501, 505, 521–522, **Ru** 120, **Tu** *458*, 461, 470, 480
- evidential **Tu** 460, 461, 484
- imperfective **Gk** 259, 262, 273, 288, 300, 303
- perfective 557, 558, **Gk** 259, 262, 290fn, **Ru** 118–119, 120, **Tu** *458*, 459, 460, 465, 480 *see also* subjunctive II

pattern recognition 568–569, **Es** 326, 336, **He** 390, **Tu** 454 *see also* input–output relation

permission 4, 5–6, 7, 8, 561–562, 563, 570, **Cr** 159, 183–184, 187, **Fi** 348, 353–354, 372, **Fr** 192, *195*, 217, *226*, 227, **Ge** 35, 38, *52*, *53*, *68*, *69*, **Gk** 257, 264, 281, 285, 290, 291, 296, 308, **He** 379, 380, 382, 385, 391, 402, 406, 407, **Li** 85, 87–88, 102, 103, **Ro** 236, 237, 244–245, **Tu** 459, 463

pointing gestures **Es** 316, **Fi** 375, **Li** 80–81
Polish 1, 11fn, 238, 310fn
politeness 572, **Cr** 159, 164, 177–*178*, **179**–180, 182, **184**, 185, 186, **Es** 316, 319, 320, 321, 323, 334, **Fi** 347, 352, **Fr** 197, 200, 201, 212, 221, 223, 229, 230,

Subject Index — 589

Ge 29, 30, 32, 36fn, 37, **Gk** 264–265, **He** 386, 403, **Ko** 492fn, **Li** 80, 81, 82, 84, 85, 87, *99–100*, 101, 103, 106, 109, **Ru** 117–118, 120–121, 147–148 *see also* mitigation; socialization; social norms
Portuguese 38
possibility/impossibility 5, 6, 7, 555, 565–566, 566–567, 571, **Gk** 257–258, 267–268, 270, **Tu** 453, 455, *458*, 459
– deontic **Fi** 353–354, **Fr** *226*, 227, **He** 380, 385, 406, 416, **Tu** *458*, 459
– dynamic **Cr** 159, 163, **He** 379, 381, 407, **Li** 86, **Tu** *458*, 459
– epistemic 6, 564–565, 565–566, **Cr** 161, 163, **Ge** 38, **Gk** 270fn, 297, 300, 301–302, 304, 307, **He** 380, 381, 385, *391*, 407, 408–409, **Ro** 240, 249, 250, **Tu** 455, *456*, *458*, 459, 468, 469–470, 473–474 *see also* ability; modal scale; root possibility
pragmatics 555–556, 563–564, 568–569, 571–572, **Es** 316–317, 318, **Fr** 192, 194, 196, 204, 207–208, 210, 213, 215, *216*, 217fn, 218, 221, 222–226, 228–231, **Ge** 33, 49–61, 62, **Gk** 310, **He** 381, 388, 411, **Li** 82fn, **Ma** 526, 530, 532, 536, **Ru** 119fn, 120–121, 147, 149, 422, 447–448, **Tu** 461, 486
– speech/communicative situation **Fr** 206, 207, 215fn, 230, **Li** 80, 81, 92, **Ru** 115, 135, 142, 147 *see also* communicative function; conversation; discourse; illocutionary force; metapragmatics; speech acts
prediction **Gk** 266, 297–298, 309, **He** 386, **Tu** 459, 475 *see also* epistemic modality; future
present indicative 556–558, 560, **Cr** 161, 162, *165–166*, 175, 176, 177–178, 186, **Es** *318*, 320–321, 323, 324, 331, 332–333, 334, 337, 338, 341, **Fi** 352, 358, 360, 368, 369, 374, **Fr** 191, 193, 195–196, 196–197, 204, 224, **Ge** 28, 29, 32, 38, **Gk** 261, 269, 278, **He** 398, 399, 410, 415, 416, **Li** 83, *85*, 87, 98, 101, **Ru** 117, 118–119, 120fn, **Tu** *458 see also* non-past, imperfective

pretend/pretense mode/role play 566, **Fi** 355, 376, **Gk** 259, 297, 300, 309, **Ko** 502–503, 505, **Ma** 533, 538, 539, **Ru** 137–138, 142, **Tu** 461, 467, 473, 476–477, 481, 484 *see also* evidential modality
probability/improbability 6, 555, 571, **Cr** 163, **Ge** 38, **Gk** 258, 270, 297, 300, 301–302, 306–307, 309, **He** 380, 381, *391*, 408–409, 416, **Ko** 521, **Ru** 421, 422–423, 424, 425, 430–431, 432–434, 435, 436–438, 441, 442, 443, 444fn, 445–446, 447, **Tu** 455, *456*, *458*, 459, 468, 473, 474–475 *see also* modal adverbials, epistemic
productivity **Cr** 175–176, **Es** 328, 329, **Gk** 256, **Ko** 505, 521, **Tu** 464–465 *see also* overgeneralization
prohibition/prohibitive 9, 557, 562, 570, 572, **Cr** 159, 161, 171, 173, 181, 185–186, 187, **Es** 315, 317, *318*, 320, 326, 330, **336–337**, 338, 340, 341, 342, **Fi** 351–352, 353–354, 358, 362–363, 366–367, 372–373, **Fr** 191, 192, *195*, 200–201, 202, 209, 218, 219, 220, 221, 226–227, 228–229, **Ge** 27, 34fn, 35, 52, **Gk** 264, 266, 277, 296, **He** 385, 386, 389, 392–395, 397–398, 415, **Li** *85*, 86, 88, 93, *99–100*, 105, 106, **Ru** 118, 121, 123–124, 141, *142*, 149–151 *see also* imperative, negated; requests
pronoun **Fr** 194, 195–197, 203, 211, 215–218, 222, 224, **Ge** 28, 29, 30, 31, **He** 411, **Ru** 117, 119, 424
propositional modality 3, 4, 5–6, 7, 8, 11, 559, 564–568, 569, 571, **Cr** 161, 162, **Ge** 39, **Gk** 257, 261, 267–268, 291, 297, 302–303, 307, 309–310, **He** 380, **Ru** 421, 424–425, 447, **Tu** 455–*458*, 464, 466–467, 484–485, 486 *see also* epistemic modality; evidential modality

Q'anjob'alan 527 *see also* Tojolabal
quasi-modal verbs 560, **Gk** 270, 273, 291, 292–293, 308
questions/interrogatives 1, 9, 556, 561, **Fi** 347, 356, 358, 359, 373, **Gk** 255, 278,

279–280, 286, 288, 290, 305, **Ko** 493–494, 504, **Li** 82, 84fn, *85*, 86, 87–88, 97–98, *99–100*, 102–103, 105, 106, 107, **Ma** 530, 531, **Ru** 446
- for information **Es** 316–317, **Fr** 201, **Ge** 25, 35, *52*, *53*–54, 55, 61, 62, *68*, *69*, *71*, *72*, **He** 388fn, 389, 399, 407, 411, 412, **Li** 93, **Ru** 130fn
- modalized **Cr** 184, 185, 186, **Es** 316–*317*, *318*, 319, 322–323, 340, **He** 382, **Ru** 114, 127–*128*, 131, 143, 144–147, 149, **150**, 434, 435
- modalized vs. non-modalized **Tu** 469
 see also requests, indirect
quotative/quoted speech 10, 565, 566, 567, 570, **Ma** 525, 526, 527, 529–531, 532, 534–538, 539–545, 547, 548, 549–551
 see also evidential modality; information source

reportative/reported speech 10, 566–567, **Ko** 496, 521–522, **Ma** 525, 526, 527, 528–529, 530–531, 532, 534, 536–537, 538–541, 542–543, 545, 548, 549–551, **Tu** 456, *458*, 461–462, 463, *475*, *476*–*477*, *478*, *479*, *480*, *481*, 484–485
 see also evidential modality; information source
requests 1, 8, 9, 555, 556, 558, 559, 561–562, 570, 572, **Cr** 160, 162, 164, 168, 172, 181, 186, **Es** 315–317, 318–324, *325*, 326, 327, *335*, **336–337**, 340, **Fi** 347, 354, 356, 358, 359, 360, 364, 365–367, 369, 370–371, 374, 375, 376, **Fr** 192, 197, 200, 201, 215, *226*, 231, **Ge** 25, 26, 27–33, 34–40, 42, 43–53, *54*–62, 68, *69*, *70*–72, **Gk** 255, 256, 258, 276, 277–278, 279, 284–285, 307–308, **He** 381–382, **392–393**, 415, **Li** 79, 80–83, 84, *85*, 86, 89–91, **Ru** 113–116, 118, 122–**123**, **124**, 125–126, 127, 148, 151–152, 153, 426
- direct 555, 557–558, 559–560, 572, **Cr** 160, 161, 167–171, 181–182, **Es** 315, 316, 317, *318*, 319, 327–330, *335*, 337, *338*–*339*, 340, 341, 342, **Fi** 349, **Fr** 230, **Ge** 25, 27, 36–37, 39, 42, *54*, 55, 56–*58*, 61, 62, *69*,

70–71, **Gk** 264, 273–274, 275, 278, 284, 289, **He** 386, 390, 392, 393–395, 396, 415–416, **Ko** 500, **Li** 79, 80, 81, 82, 84, *85*, 86, 91–96, 106–107, 108, **Ru** 117, 127–135, 147, 152, 153, 447
- elliptic **Cr** 172, **Ge** 36, 46, *54*–*55*, 56, *69*–*70*, **Ru** 127, *128*, 139, 152
- indirect 8–9, 555, 560, 562, 569, 570–571, 572, **Cr** 159, 162, 177–180, 182–183, **184**, 185, 186, 187, **Es** 315, 316–317, 319, 320–324, 330–336, *338*–*339*, 340, 341, 342, **Fi** 352, 354, 362, 368, 369, 373, 376, **Fr** 193, 212, *226*–*227*, 230, **Ge** 26, 36, 37, 39, 42, *54*–*55*, 56, *59*–61, 62, *69*–*70*, *71*–*72*, **Gk** 264–265, 266, 273, 274, 275, 278, 280, 282, 283, 286, 289, 290, 308, **He** 381–382, 383, 385, 386, 389, 390, 392, 396, 403, 407, 411–412, 413–414, 415, **Li** 79, 80, 81, 82, 84, *85*, 86–88, 96–105, 106–107, 108–109, **Ru** 113, 115–116, 119–120, 124, 125, 129, 135–147, 149, 152, 447
 see also command; desire; directives; prohibition
rhetoric skills/structure **Ma** 544, 546, 550
Romance 2
Romanian *2*, 13, 16, 235–254, 310, 484, 485, 558fn, 559fn, 561, *562*, 563, 564, *567*, 569, 571
root modality 4fn
root possibility 4fn, **He** 379
rote-learning **Es** 329fn, **Fi** 347, **He** 387fn
Russian 1, *2*, 3, 11, 12, 13, 14, 15, 18–19, 38, 84, 108, 113–157, 162, 260, 274fn, 310, 340, 355, 375, 421–452, 556–557, 558, 559, 560–561, *562*, 563, 564, *567*, 569, 570, 571, 572

schema/pivot scheme 13, **Cr** 160, **Gk** 256–257, **He** 390
- vs. grammatical rules **Gk** 256–257
second language acquisition **Gk** 260
Semitic *2*, 558, 559
sentence-ending modal particles/suffixes 3, 9, 10, 558, 566, **Ko** 491, 492–499, 500, 503, **504**, 505–512, 512–519, 519–522, **Ro** 238

shifters **Cr** 175, **Es** 332–333, **Fi** 354, 371–372, **Fr** 203
Slavic *2*, 149, 162
social/behavioral norms/rules **Cr** 162, **Es** 315, 317, *318*, 323, 334–336, **336–337**, 338, 340, 341, 342, **Fi** 367, **Fr** *195*, **Ge** 37, **Gk** 264, 278, 286, 288–289, **He** 380, 381, 398, 406, 407, 416, **Ko** 520, 522, **Li** 80, 81, 83, 88, 102, 105, 109, **Ru** 140, 149 *see also* requests, indirect; statements, modalized
social factors 570, 572, **Ge** 25, 26, 38, 63–64, **He** 380, 406, **Ru** 147 *see also* social norms; socio-economic status
socialization **Li** 79, 108, 109, **Ma** 534–535 *see also* gender-related communication; politeness
socio-economic status/background (SES) 572, **Ge** 40–41, 63–64, **He** 389, 416, **Ro** 242
– High SES vs. Low SES **Ge** 25–27, 39–40, 42, 61–63, **He** 389, 415 *see also* child-directed speech; input–output relation
solidarity markers **Ge** 35, 52fn
source of modality, participant-/speaker-/subject-external/internal 7, **Es** 315, 317, 320, 322, 342, **Fr** *195*, 197–198, 226–227, **Ge** 38, 39, **Gk** 264, 286–287, **He** 379–380, **Ru** 139
Spanish 11fn, 108, 238, 310fn, 340, 355, 375, 546
speech acts **Es** 316, 317, 326, **Fi** 347, **Fr** 192, 193, 196–197, 220, 222, *226–227*, 228, 229, 230, 231, **He** 381, 389
– assertion/assertive **Ge** 30fn, 33, 34, 39, 40, 49, *50*, *51*, 61, 62fn, 63, *67*, *68*, **He** 413–414, **Tu** 455, 460, 474–475
– commissive **Ge** 33, 34, 40, 49, *50*, *51*, *67*, *68*
– expressive **Ge** 33, 34, 40, 49, *50*, *51*, *67*, *68*, **Gk** 255, **He** 399, 416 *see also* directives; illocutionary force
stages/periods/phases of development **Es** 317, **Fr** 193, 208, 209, 212–213, 215, 220, 227, 228–229, **He** 390, **Ro** 237, 250, **Ru** 115, 125, 131, 153, **Tu** *465*, 466,
468, 470, *471*, *472*, 473–474, *475–477*, *478–480*, *481*, 482fn
– early **He** 406, 411, **Ko** 500–505, 516
– later **Ko** 505–**512**, *513*, **514**, 515, 516
– one-word phase/stage **Cr** 160, **He** 409, **Ko** 491, 500–501, 520, 522
– premorphological phase/stage 11–12, **Cr** 159, 167–*168*, *169*, 172–*173*, 178–179, *182–183*, 187, **He** 387, **Ru** 116, 126, 128, 129, 131, 147, 151
– protomorphological phase/stage 11–12, **Cr** 159, *165*, 169–*170*, 173–*174*, 178–179, *180–181*, *182–183*, 187, **He** 387, **Ru** 116, 127, 147 *see also* development of modality
statements 1, 9, **Gk** 286–287, **Ru** 113, 436
– modalized 565–566, **Cr** 162, 186, **Es** 315, 316, 317, *318*, 320, 321, 323, 324, 332, 333, 334, *335*, 336, 337, 338, 340, 341, 342, **Fr** 193, *195*, 197, **Ge** 36, 37–38, 42, *59–60*, *71*, *72*, **Gk** 264, 270, 278, 288, 290, 297–298, 311, **He** 381–382, 406, 414, **Ko** 496, 497, 500–501, 502, 504, 516, 518–519, **Li** 79, *85*, 86–87, 88, 96, *97*, 101, 104, 105, 106, 109, **Ru** 121, 423–424, 433–434, 436–437, 447, **Tu** 459, 484
– non-modalized 556, 557–558, **Cr** 162, 186, **Fr** 208, 217, 223, *226*, **Ge** 33, 61, 62, **Gk** 255, 279–280, 304, **He** 415, **Ru** 113, 423, 429, **Tu** 455 *see also* modal/non-modal distinction; requests, indirect; social norms; speech acts
structural resonance **Ko** 491, 499–500, 501–502, 516–519, 522 *see also* child-directed speech, repetition; input–output relation
subjunctive 8, 9, 557, 558, 559–560, **Ge** 27, 31, 33, 38, **Gk** 255, 258, 259, 261, 262–263, 264–267, 273–278, 279–286, 287–288, 289, 290, 298, 307, 308–309, **Li** 99, 103, **Ro** 238, 239, 240–241, 243, 247–248, 249–250, 251, **Ru** 118–119, 147
subjunctive II/past subjunctive **Ge** 27, 32–33, 39, 42, 43, 48–*49*, *64–66*

suggestion/offer/proposal 8, 569, **Cr** 164, 172, 177, 181, **Es** 315, 317, *318*, 322, 331, 333–334, *335*, **336–337**, 338, 339, 340, 341, **Fi** 347, 350, 352, 355, 356, 358, 359, 360–361, 369, 376, **Fr** 197, **Ge** 33, **Gk** 264, 265, 285–286, **Li** *85*, 87, 105, 106, 107, **Ru** 118, 120–121, 123, 129–130, 135, 137, 138, 145, 148, 152, 424, 447
supine **Ro** 240, 243

tense **Gk** 258, 259, 261–262, 269–270, **Ko** 492–493, **Ro** 238, **Tu** 456–457, *458*, 460, 463, 465 see also future tense; non-past, imperfective; past tense; present indicative
theoretical models
– competition model **Fr** 230
– construction grammar 13
– constructivist approach 11, 13, **Es** 317, **Fi** 347–348, **Gk** 256, **He** 389–390, **Li** 79–80
– conversational analysis **Ko** 454
– dialogic syntax **Ko** 499–500
– functional grammar **Ru** 422
– pre- and protomorphological approach 11–12, 13, **Cr** 159–160, 178–179, **Fi** 348, **He** 387fn, **Ru** 116
– theory of mind 571, **Ru** 427, 439, 447
– unitary meaning approach **Ro** 236
– usage-based approach 13, **Es** 317, **Fi** 347–348, **Gk** 256–257, **He** 379, 389–390, **Ko** 492, 499fn, 512, **Li** 79–80, **Ma** 534, **Ru** 448, **Tu** 454–455
Tibetan 455, 526, 550
Tojolabal *2*, 13fn, 14, 20, 525–553, 558fn, 564, 565, 566, *567*
Tseltalan 527
Turkish 2, 3, 4, 6, 8, 9, 10, 11, 14, 19, 38, 238, 310, 311, 355, 453–490, 521–522, 526, 549, 558, 564, 565–566, *567*, 568, 569, 570, 571
Tuyuca 10fn

variability/variation/diversity 568–569, **Cr** 187, **Fr** 194, 229, 230, **Gk** 260, **He** 379, 407, 416, **Ko** 509, 522, **Ru** 127, 426, 440, **Tu** 454, 470 see also child-directed speech
variation set **Fr** 220–221, 222–223, 229–230
verbal inflection, see modal expressions, inflectional
verbless utterances 12, 557, 558, 561, **Cr** 160, **Es** *318*, 319, 327–328, 329–330, *335*, 337, **Fi** 347, 348, 354, 364–367, 370–371, 374, 375, **He** 392fn, **Ko** 506, **Li** *85*, 86, 87, **Ru** 114, 127, 139, 152 see also one-word utterances; requests, elliptic
verbs
– abstract **Fr** 206
– change-of-state **Fr** 206, **Tu** 476, 479
– cognitive/mental/of belief 9, 11, 564–565, 567, **Gk** 258, 261, 270, 297, 304–305, 309–310, **He** 381, 398, **Li** 102, **Ru** 427, 447
– dynamic **Fr** 206, **Gk** 274
– motion **Fr** 206, **He** 393, 396, **Ru** 120, 128–129
– of desire/*want* 8, 560–561, 562, 563, **Cr** 163, 173–176, *183*–184, 186–187, **Es** 316, *318*, 323, 331–332, *335*, **336–337**, 338, 339–340, 341, **Fi** 354, 355, *357*, 368, 373–374, 376, **Fr** 212, 227, **Ge** 32, 38, 39, **Gk** 258, 261, 270, 273, 291–293, 296–207, 308, 309, **He** 381, 382–383, 387, 388, *402*, 407, 409–414, 416, **Li** 80–81, *85*, 86–87, 92, 96–99, 103–104, 107, **Ro** 236, 237, 238–239, 240–241, 244, *247*, 251, **Ru** 119, 128–129, 142–143, 144, 152–153, 427
– of exchange/giving/taking/transfer 570, **Cr** *168*, *169–170*, *181*, 182, **Fr** *195–196*, 203–204, *205–206*, 210–211, **He** 382, 393, 394–395, 396, 415, **Ru** 114, 115, 134, 151–152
– of perception **Cr** 166, 170, 181, **Ma** 531–532
– of saying 565, 570 see also aktionsart; modal verbs
volition 5, 7, 8, 9, **Cr** 159, 173, 186, **Ge** 30fn, **He** 379–380, 381, 382–383, *391*, 405, 406, **Ro** 237 see also desire; dynamic modality; verbs of desire

warning 9, 570, **Cr** 169, **Es** 317, 318, 324, **336–337**, 338, 339, 342, **Ge** 30, **Gk** 264, 266, 267, 298, **Li** *85*, 88, 105, **Ru** 118, 120–121, 149–151 *see also* requests, indirect
Wasco 548
wish, *see* desire

word order/sentence position **Ge** 29, 31, **Gk** 300, **Ko** 492, **Ru** 130–131, 434–**436**, 448, **Tu** 456

Yukatek *2*, 10, 14, 20, 525–553, 558fn, 564, 565, 566, *567*, 570

www.ingramcontent.com/pod-product-compliance
Lightning Source LLC
Chambersburg PA
CBHW031659230426
43668CB00006B/53